DICKENS STUDIES ANNUAL
Essays on Victorian Fiction

DICKENS STUDIES ANNUAL
Essays on Victorian Fiction

DICKENS STUDIES ANNUAL

Essays on Victorian Fiction

VOLUME
23

Edited by
Michael Timko, Fred Kaplan,
and Edward Guiliano

AMS PRESS
NEW YORK

DICKENS STUDIES ANNUAL
ISSN 0084-9812

International Standard Book Number
Series: 0-404-18520-7
Vol. 23:0-404-18543-6

Dickens Studies Annual: Essays on Victorian Fiction welcomes essay and monograph-length contributions on Dickens as well as on other Victorian novelists and on the history of aesthetics of Victorian fiction. All manuscripts should be double-spaced, including footnotes, which should be grouped at the end of the submission, and should be prepared according to the format used in this journal. An editorial decision can usually be reached more quickly if two copies are submitted. The preferred editions for citations from Dickens' works are the Clarendon and the Norton Critical when available, otherwise the Oxford Illustrated or the Penguin.

Please send submissions to the Editors, *Dickens Studies Annual*, Room 1522, Graduate School and University Center, City University of New York, 33 West 42nd Street, New York, N.Y. 10036: please send subscription inquiries to AMS Press, Inc., 56 East 13th Street, New York, N.Y. 10003.

Manufactured in the United States of America

Contents

List of Illustrations   vii
Preface   ix
Notes on Contributors   x

MURRAY ROSTON
Dickens and the Tyranny of Objects   1

BARRY THATCHER
Dickens' Bow to the Language Theory Debate   17

ROBERT NEWSOM
Pickwick in the Utilitarian Sense   49

SYLVIA MANNING
Nicholas Nickleby: On the Plains of Syria   73

KERRY MCSWEENEY
David Copperfield and the Music of Memory   93

CARROL CLARKSON
Alias and Alienation in *Bleak House*: Identity in Language   121

RAZAK DAHMANE
A Mere Question of Figures: Measures, Mystery and Metaphor
    in *Hard Times*   137

WENDY CARSE
Domestic Transformation in Dickens' "The Haunted Man"   163

KATHERINE RETAN
Lower Class Angels in the Middle Class House: The Domestic
    Woman's Progress in *Hard Times* and *Ruth*   183

ADRIENNE E. GAVIN
Language Among the Amazons: Conjuring and Creativity in
    Cranford   205

CHRISTINE S. WIESENTHAL
The Body Melancholy: Trollope's *He Knew He Was Right*   227

ALISON BYERLY
"The Masquerade of Existence": Thackeray's Theatricality   259

THOMAS MCKENDY
Sources of Parody in Thackeray's *Catherine*   287

PETER L. SHILLINGSBURG
Thackeray Studies: 1983–1992   303

STANLEY FRIEDMAN
Recent Dickens Studies: 1992   337

Index   403

List of Illustrations

Upholstered couches from the 1830s and the 1850s.   5, 6

"Day-dreamer" armchair by H. Fitz-Cook.   7

Armchair of Irish bog-wood by A. J. Jones of Dublin.   8

Silver inkstand by M. Odiot.   9

Monkey bell-push, Cardiff Castle.   14

10 illustrations by Thackeray for *Vanity Fair*   beginning on 275

Preface

We are grateful for the services of many people who enable us to bring out this annual volume. To the members of our editorial and advisory boards we continue, of course, to welcome their collegiality and appreciate their expertise and cooperation. Very special thanks go to the members of our profession who serve as readers. The principle of peer-evaluation is at the heart of maintaining standards of excellence in research and publication. Those scholars and critics who give freely and generously of their time and expertise render an important service for which we extend our gratitude on behalf of the academic community. We also thank those who wrote the comprehensive review essays, a formidable task in the service of all students of Victorian fiction.

Since volume 8, three of us have co-edited *DSA* amiably. In April 1994, however, Fred Kaplan relinquished with regret his role as an editor for a host of personal reasons, none having to do with the operation or professional demands of the annual. So, this volume will be the last to bear his name as co-editor as he has now joined our advisory board. As co-editors and students of Victorian fictorian we are in his debt for the talent and energy he has supplied to the annual and to Victorian literature over the years and look forward to the fruits of his continuing labors. He is an esteemed colleague we will miss at the annual.

We note and express our gratitude to those in administrative posts in different institutions who continue to provide supports of various kinds: Chancellor W. Ann Reynolds, CUNY; President Frances Degen Horowits; Provost Jeffrey Marshall; Executive Officer, Ph.D. Program in English, Joseph Wittreich, The Graduate School and University Center, CUNY; Vice President for Academic Affairs, King Cheek, The New York Institute of Technology; Dean Raymond Erickson; Provost John Thorpe; and Chair, English Department, Charles Molesworth, Queens College, CUNY; and Gabriel Hornstein, president, and our valued editor, Jack Hopper, AMS Press.

—MICHAEL TIMKO
—EDWARD GUILIANO

Notes on Contributors

ALISON BYERLY is Assistant Professor of English at Middlebury College. Her previous publications include "From Schoolroom to Stage: Reading Aloud and the Domestication of Victorian Theater," which appeared in *Culture and Education in Victorian England*, ed. Patrick Scott and Pauline Fletcher; and an essay on music in George Eliot that appeared in *Nineteenth-Century Literature*. She has also written on Thomas De Quincey, Branwell Brontë, and Wordsworth. She is currently completing a book manuscript entitled "Realism at Risk: Aesthetics and Representation in Nineteenth-Century Fiction."

WENDY CARSE, Assistant Professor at Indiana University of Pennsylvania, received her doctorate in nineteenth-century British literature from Tulane University. Her dissertation is a study of domestic ideology in Victorian Gothic short stories. Her previous publications include an article on Elizabeth Gaskell's *Cranford* in *Journal of Narrative Technique* and several collaborative pieces on issues of professionalism and graduate studies.

CARROL CLARKSON is a junior lecturer at the University of Witwatersrand, Johannesburg, South Africa. Her article in *DSA* 23 is her first publication and is based on aspects of her M.A. dissertation. She is at present continuing her work on the names in Dickens at the doctoral level.

RAZAK DAHMANE is an Assistant Professor of English at Sangamon State University, Springfield, Illinois. He received his M.A. in English from L'Université de Tunis and his Ph.D. from the University of Kentucky, where he studied Victorian Literature with Professor Joseph Gardner and Dickens with Professor Jerome Meckier. His research interests include Dickens' legacy to twentieth-century British novelists, a comparative approach to French and English literatures of the nineteenth century, theories of colonial literature, and the teaching of writing.

STANLEY FRIEDMAN, Associate Professor of English at Queen's College, CUNY, has published a number of articles and notes on Dickens in *Dickens Studies Annual, Dickens Quarterly, The Dickensian, Studies in the Novel, Nineteenth-Century Literature,* and other journals.

ADRIENNE E. GAVIN lives in Cambridge, England where she has written an M.Phil. thesis on depictions of female criminals in Victorian fiction. Recently she completed a Ph.D. dissertation at the University of British Columbia on the use of the body in Charles Dickens' novels. She has had work published in *The D. H. Lawrence Review.*

TOM MCKENDY teaches English and Humanities at Marianopolis College in Montreal. He wrote this essay while on leave to serve as Coordinator of the Writing Proficiency Programme at Bishop's University in Lennoxville, Quebec. The essay is based on the dissertation he wrote under the supervision of Bert Hornback at the University of Michigan. His essays on the teaching of poetry and the testing of writing have appeared in *College Composition and Communication, Research in the Teaching of English,* and *English in Education* (U.K.).

KERRY MCSWEENEY is Molson Professor of English at McGill University in Montreal. His publications include *Tennyson and Swinburne as Romantic Naturalists, Four Contemporary Novelists, Moby-Dick: Ishmael's Mighty Book, George Eliot (Marian Evans): A Literary Life,* monographs on *Middlemarch* and Ralph Ellison's *Invisible Man,* and editions of the critical writings of Angus Wilson, Thomas Carlyle's *Sartor Resartus,* and Elizabeth Barrett Browning's *Aurora Leigh.* He is currently working on a study of sensory acuity and symbolic perception in five nineteenth-century writers.

SYLVIA MANNING is Vice President for Academic Affairs and Professor of English at the University of Illinois at Urbana-Champaign and Chicago. Until recently as a member of the faculty at University of Southern California she has been a frequent participant in the Dickens Universe at the University of California, Santa Cruz.

ROBERT NEWSOM is Professor of English at the University of California, Irvine. He has written two books, *Dickens on the Romantic Side of Familiar Things: Bleak House and the Novel Tradition* and *A Likely Story: Probability and Play in Fiction,* as well as essays and reviews. His current project is a book on Dickens and Utilitarianism, with the working title "Just Pleasure."

KATHERINE RETAN received her Ph.D. in Language and Literature from the University of Minnesota in 1991. She is an editor at Bedford Books of St. Martin's Press, in Boston, where she is working on a forthcoming reprint series of eighteenth- and nineteenth-century British texts accompanied by contextualizing historical and cultural documents.

MURRAY ROSTON, Professor of English at Bar-Ilan University and Director of Humanities Programs for the Open University in Israel, has published numerous essays on Victorian, Classical, and Renaissance literature and culture. Many of these essays delineate connections between literature and the visual arts, as do four of his eight books. He is a contributor to *Homes and Homelessness in the Victorian Imagination* (AMS Press, 1995).

PETER SHILLINGSBURG, Professor of English at Mississippi State University, is author of *Pegasus in Harness: Victorian Publishing and W. M. Thackeray* and is general and textual editor of a scholarly edition of Thackeray's works, formerly with Garland Publishing, now with the University of Michigan Press. He edits the *Thackeray Newsletter* and is revising the Thackeray entry for the *Cambridge Bibliography of English Literature.*

CHRIS WIESENTHAL is Assistant Professor of Victorian Literature at the University of Alberta. She has published a number of articles on nineteenth- and twentieth-century ficiton, eighteenth-century drama, and psychoanalytic theory. "The Body Melancholy: Trollope's *He Knew He Was Right"* is part of a longer study, entitled *Figuring Madness in Nineteenth-Century Fiction,* forthcoming with Macmillan Press.

Dickens and the Tyranny of Objects

Murray Roston

Dorothy Van Ghent's essay on animism in Dickens' novels has become a staple ingredient of criticism. Her perception was that objects take on a life of their own, frequently usurping the prerogatives of their owners while people themselves become accordingly deanimated (125 38). In an era of growing materialism, the Victorians, she maintained, felt engulfed or overwhelmed by the plethora of articles encroaching on them. Hence, in *Great Expectations*, a four-poster bed in an inn where Pip spends a night appears to him to be straddling the room like some despotic monster, ". . . putting one of his arbitrary legs into the fireplace, and another into the doorway, and squeezing the wretched little washing-stand in quite a Divinely Righteous manner" (347). Human impulses become appropriated by the nonhuman, even parts of the body seeming to assume an existence of their own. Wemmick's mouth becomes a grinning slot or letter-box at his place of work, Jaggers' forefinger, thrusting itself menacingly at the accused, functions as an independent symbol of the law; and as animate and inanimate exchange places, Miss Havisham, exploiting Estella and Pip as mere "things" dedicated to her vengeful purpose, becomes in her turn a mere thing, dead in life, awaiting the final decay of her wedding-cake before it is laid out in its place, for her relatives to "feast on."

That insight was given a new lease on life when J. Hillis Miller translated it into the terminology of semiotics, making people in Dickens' novels signs to be deciphered, cryptograms represented by articles of clothing, gestures, or idiosyncrasies of speech needing to be "read" ("Sketches" 9). Stylistically, he perceived in this technique a masterly demonstration of what Roman Jakobson had called "the metonymical texture of realistic prose," in which items adjacent to an object, or single attributes of a person are, by a process of synecdoche, linguistically substituted for the whole (Jakobson 375, Stewart

1

xix). Mrs. Gamp's late husband is thus, in a sense, dislodged by his wooden leg; he has become absorbed metaphorically into the appendage, while the piece of timber itself is imaged as instinct with life: "And as to husbands, there's a wooden leg gone likeways home to its account, which in its constancy of walkin' into wine vaults, and never comin' out again 'till fetched by force, was quite as weak as flesh, if not weaker" (*Martin Chuzzlewit* 625).

I would suggest that such a reading, widely adopted by others (Kincaid 10–11, Carey 101–03), is based on a dubious assumption concerning the Victorians' attitude to the proliferation of material objects, by which it is alleged that they felt overwhelmed and intimidated. The success of the Great Exhibition of 1851 testified to the pride of the Victorian in the splendid variety, quality, and sheer quantity of the commodities produced by craftsmen and industry; the contemporary response, as evidenced by the collections of Hobhouse and Gibbs-Smith, expressed a predominant mood of self-congratulatory awe. "We have long boasted of our age as a most remarkable one," Robert Hunt declared. "[T]he number of useful applications which we have made within a comparatively limited period are no doubt more numerous than were ever before made within the same time . . ." (Hunt 1). The Art-Journal catalogue lovingly described and illustrated the wide range of items displayed, with sections devoted to ceramics, textiles, wallpaper, furniture, cut glass, musical instruments, lighting fixtures, carriages, statuary, clocks, beehives, and a host of other objects. If the range and variety of these exhibited commodities overwhelmed the visitor, they overwhelmed, it would seem, with a confident glow of achievement rather than a sense of menace.

The welcoming of the proliferation of goods was not fortuitous, being symptomatic of a contemporary change in taste. Domestic furniture, which occupied so prominent a place among the items displayed at the Exhibition, had been undergoing a radical transformation. On the Continent as well as in England, furniture design and production throughout the preceding centuries had been remarkably conservative; chests of drawers in the Baroque period were rectangular, in the Rococo serpentine, in the Neoclassical semicircular (Symonds and Whineray 20–25). The individual craftsman may have designed the specific form of ormolu or carving, and local tradition may have dictated certain minor differences, but these variations occurred within the parameters of conformity to the dominant mode, not least because of the traditionalism inevitable among artisans employed in small workshops, each specializing in a very limited type of furniture, with the processes and technicalities of the craft being transmitted from generation to generation. The doubling of the population during the earlier part of the century, from nine million in the year 1800 to eighteen million by 1850, created a demand for furniture which the traditional small workshops could not possibly meet, while the growing prosperity of the upper and middle classes, as British exports rose in that same period from £34 million per annum to £197 million, ensured a much broader clientele. As John Store Smith noted in his *Social Aspects* of 1851, ''. . . the middle-class family now possesses carpets and hangings which would have excited great wonderment even at so recent a period as the American War, and not a few of our London middle-class tradesmen possess a better stock of family plate and linen than many a country squire, even of the last generation.'' But the change was not merely in the quantity supplied (single workshops now employing as many as three hundred men), nor in the new mass-production methods introduced, such as steam-driven wood-carvers in place of the traditional turner's lathe; for these innovations could have resulted merely in standardization. The most striking change was rather the extraordinary variety of items produced, which indicated a changed customer demand, and retailers, who had now entered the profession as middlemen, were increasingly reliant on the range of models they were able to offer. As Richard Redgrave commented, ''. . . the hunger after novelty is quite insatiable; heaven and earth are racked for novel inventions . . .'' Personal taste, previously displayed through individual items commissioned from the cabinetmaker, now expressed itself by a different process—the same process as pertains in our own day—namely the *selecting*, from the wealth of variegated items available, of those specific objects suited to the purchaser's own preferences, whether in furniture, ornaments, carriages, or clothing.

It was that new quality of the age which Dickens grasped so shrewdly, and incorporated into his fiction as a distinctive literary mode, seeing within that proprietary choice of goods a method of differentiating character. The marks of inner singularity could now be manifested through externals. The working-class area of Coketown may seem, from the distance, drearily composed of hundreds of identical people living in identical houses and performing identical tasks, but Dickens' fictional genius makes his cities and urban dwellings come alive with people perceived, upon closer view, as sharply distinguished from each other by their eccentricities and personal prejudices, such individuality being expressed by their choice of dress, their furnishings, or their idiosyncratic possessions:

> . . . a queer sort of fresh painted vehicle drove up, out of which there jumped with great agility . . . a queer sort of gentleman who seemed made for the

vehicle, and the vehicle for him. The vehicle was not exactly a gig, neither
was it a stanhope. It was not what is currently denominated a dog-cart, neither
was it a taxed-cart, nor a chaise-cart, nor a guillotined cabriolet; and yet it had
something of the character of each and every of these machines. It was painted
a bright yellow . . .   (*Pickwick* 560)

The new materials introduced for the manufacture of furniture at this time
revolutionized their design in a manner that has not been sufficiently noted
by historians, producing stylistic changes no less far-reaching than the introduction of plastics in our own century. Where armrests had until this time
required the skilful joining of two pieces of wood expertly carved to preserve
the curve, the "bentwood" steam-heating process, which molded the wood
into a shape retained after cooling, opened up endless possibilities for flexibility of design, as did the improved method for producing papier-mâché. Pasted
in sheets over a mold and hardened by heat, the strengthened product could
now bear considerable weight, becoming available for forming into tables,
chairs, and sofas, the original mold producing an effect of carving without
the need for skilled workmanship; while the use of gutta-percha, carton-
pierre, bamboo, and iron helped further release furniture design from its
earlier limitations.

The resultant effect is evidenced by comparing two catalogue pages advertising upholstered couches (fig. 1). The first, dating from the 1830s, offers
standardized, front-facing, four-legged couches with only minor ornamental
variations. The second, depicting models from mid-century onwards, reveals
the astonishing plasticity in design that had entered the manufacturing process,
the cabinetmaker now being free to exploit his imaginative faculty at will,
duplicating, tripling, quadruplicating seats in circular, oval, or rectangular
forms, the components facing whichever direction suited his fancy or, more
important, would be likely to suit the preferences of his customers.

The more personal relationship between owner and item that had entered
the furnishing trade found expression in the attempt now being made by the
designer to tailor his goods to suit the mood or eccentricities of a particular
buyer. The armchair produced by *H. Fitz-Cook* in mid-century (fig. 2), the
so-called Day-dreamer, employed a papier-mâché frame overlaid with the
new buttoned upholstery. The imitation carving included two figures along
the top of the backrest, one endowed with the wings of a bird to represent
happy and joyous dreams (as a note in the catalogue informs us), the other
with leathern batlike wings representing unpleasant or troubled visions. It
was therefore intended not only to welcome its owner into its comfortable
and capacious interior but to establish a more intimate, whimsical relationship

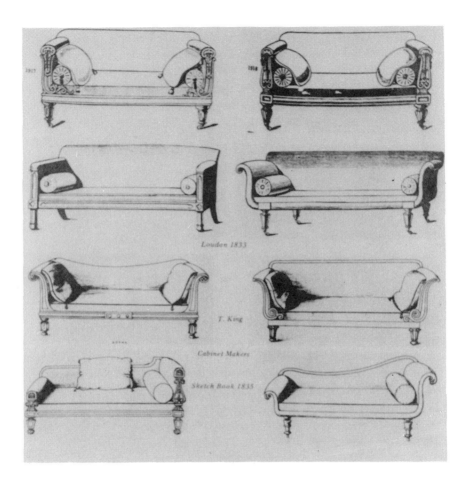

Figure 1A & 1B. Upholstered couches from the 1830s and from after 1850.

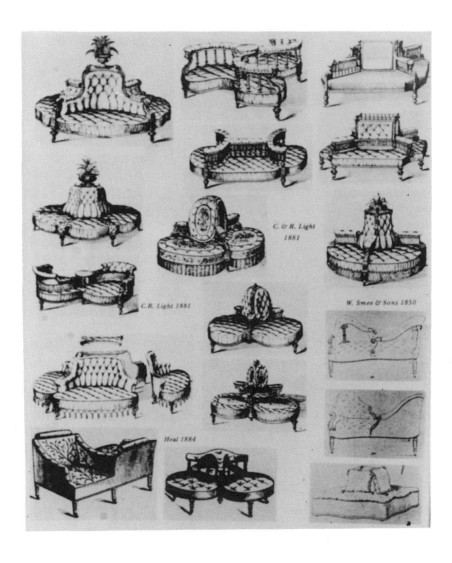

Figure 2. "Day-dreamer" armchair by H. Fitz-Cook.

with him, encouraging the daydreams that occupied so central a place in Victorian sensibility. Another armchair from the same period, made in Dublin from Irish bog-wood by A. J. Jones (fig. 3), displayed chivalric bustos of ancient Irish warriors and provided arm-rests in the form of two carved wolf-dogs, one recumbent bearing the motto "Gentle when stroked" and the other barking, with the motto "Fierce when provoked." The chair is not only designed to suit the moods and predispositions of a very specific purchaser—a dog-lover proud of his Irish ancestry—but seems itself to come alive as the wolf-dog on the left aggressively guards the recumbent owner. The symbiotic relationship that it establishes with the owner's moods deprives the object of its formal impersonality, making it almost animate—not as a replacement or *dislodgement* of the owner but as an extension of his personality. The new vitality imparted to Victorian furniture cannot be unconnected with such incidents in Dickens' writings as the story of the Bagman in his room at the inn, who gazes at a high-backed chair which had seemed human to him even before the dream-vision began—"carved in the most fantastic manner, with . . . the round knobs at the bottom of the legs carefully tied up in red cloth, as if it had got the gout in its toes." Then a further change came over it:

Figure 3. Armchair of Irish bog-wood by A. J. Jones of Dublin.

The carving of the back gradually assumed the lineaments and expression of an old shrivelled human face; the damask cushion became an antique, flapped waistcoat; the round knobs grew into a couple of feet, encased in red cloth slippers; and the old chair looked like a very ugly old man, of the previous century, with his arms a-kimbo . . . and what was more, he was winking at Tom Smart. *(Pickwick* 183–84)

This seems scarcely to represent, as Dorothy Van Ghent has argued for such objects in Dickens' fiction, the crushing despotism of a materialistic age. The armchair in the tale in fact offers some very friendly and helpful advice, leading to the Bagman's marrying the widowed innkeeper and living in enviable comfort ever after.

The notorious bric-à-brac, which to modern eyes seems merely to clutter the Victorian room, functioned in much the same way, as a means of personalizing the home, transforming it into an extension of self. The innumerable antimacassars lovingly embroidered by spinster aunts, the souvenirs of remembered visits, the samplers fashioned in girlhood, and the family albums displayed about the room may appear, as they have so often been described, the result merely of a *horror vacui*, since we ourselves see them impersonally, stripped of the sentimental associations that they bore for the owner; but clothed in those associations, their presence brought the room to life, each cherished object, by stimulating nostalgic reminiscence, creating a personal congeniality. Queen Victoria's writing desk at Osborne House, preserved today as it was at the time of her death, with its proliferation of photographs, carved paperweights, and other paraphernalia, may have left her little space for writing; but it provided her with a personal enclave, serving as a comforting barrier between her private world and the pressures of her public life. Henry Tallis commented in mid-century on his contemporaries' penchant for objects that told a story, their desire to ". . . have everything in a house touched by the divining rod of the poet. An inkstand, instead of being a literal glass bottle, or a fine piece of ormolu or bronze, significant of nothing but costliness, might be fashioned to represent a fountain, with a Muse inspiring its flow" (Briggs 61). Even more often it would, as in the silver inkstand

Figure 4. Silver inkstand by M. Odiot.

intended for the amateur angler (fig. 4), reflect the avocational interests of its owner, not suppressing his individuality but sustaining and extrapolating it.

The bond between the Victorian and his possessions also accounts in large part for the sentimental depiction of animals at this time, with especial prominence accorded to the faithful canine. Paintings of this type no longer serve as disinterested exercises in anatomical accuracy, as in the eighteenth-century work of George Stubbs. Instead they portray, often somewhat mawkishly, the enduring affection between man and beast, as in Landseer's enormously popular *The Old Shepherd's Chief Mourner* of 1837, depicting a sheepdog grieving beside the coffin of his master, or Briton Reviere's *Fidelity* of 1869, where the despair of a man cast into prison is shared by his canine companion.

There is in such sympathy a sense of muted dialogue, that dialogue extended even to inanimate objects. The famed Kenilworth sideboard aroused widespread interest at the time of its display largely because it had been carved from an oak tree standing for centuries within the grounds of the castle, and had therefore itself witnessed the historic scene depicted on its panels, the entertaining there of Queen Elizabeth by the Earl of Leicester. The silent eloquence of the piece, the stimulus it offered for dreamy thoughts, catered to this Victorian disposition to instill objects with life, in much the same way as Lizzie Hexam in *Our Mutual Friend* gazed each evening into the hearth to conjure up from its glowing coals shapes and figures evocative of past and future.

In that context, the celebrated description of the Veneerings' home in *Our Mutual Friend* should be seen not only as a powerful satire on the false pretensions of the *nouveau riche* but as a recognition of this peculiarly Victorian predilection for displaying oneself *through* one's possessions. The massive mirror—in a metaphorical as well as a literal sense—"[r]eflects the new Veneering crest, in gold and eke in silver . . . Reflects Veneering . . . Reflects Mrs. Veneering . . ." (10). And in the no less famous passage describing the Podsnaps' dinner, the items of heavy silver plate are portrayed as extensions of their owner, "speaking" in his own self-satisfied and pompous voice, while in the process, like Podsnap himself, unwittingly betraying his least attractive qualities:

> Everything said boastfully, "Here you have as much of me in my ugliness as if I were only lead; but I am so many ounces of precious metal worth so much an ounce . . ." Four silver wine-coolers, each furnished with four staring heads, each head obtrusively carrying a big silver ring in each of its ears, conveyed the sentiment up and down the table, and handed it on to the pot-bellied silver salt-cellars.   (131)

David Copperfield's first suspicion of the scatter-brained untidiness of his

child-bride Dora is aroused by that very quality in her most beloved possession, her dog Jip, who David wishes ". . . had never been encouraged to
walk about the table-cloth during dinner . . . putting his foot in the salt or
in the melted butter," a foretaste of the way his mistress spills ink over the
household accounts, forgetting in the process entirely what she is about (641).
Mr. Dick's kite in that same novel is, as David senses, far more than a
plaything. It is a surrogate for its owner's desire to escape from the perplexing
realities about him, soaring into the skies as a projection of self:

> I used to fancy, as I sat by him of an evening, on a green slope, and saw him
> watch the kite high in the quiet air, that it lifted his mind out of its confusion,
> and bore it (such was my boyish thought) into the skies . . . [and afterwards]
> I remember to have seen him take it up, and look about him in a lost way, as
> if they had both come down together. (216)

Characters in *Our Mutual Friend* are not "turned into objects by money,"
as J. Hillis Miller claims ("Afterword" 904). Instead the purchased objects
by that act of selection become projections of their owners, articulating their
hidden traits for good as well as ill. Wegg, we are told, with imagery that
cannot be missed, ". . . was a knotty man, and a close-grained, with a face
carved out of very hard material . . . he was so wooden a man that he seemed
to have taken his wooden leg naturally" (45–46). The appendage, indeed, is
seen with a touch of whimsy as complementing his character so perfectly
that its lack was somehow felt even when he possessed two legs. And in the
same novel appears the room designed by that affectionate couple the Boffins,
in which they sit amicably together each evening. Divided precisely down
the middle, it is by mutual consent furnished on the lady's side in conformity
with current Fashion (for which she has recently developed a fondness), with
flowered carpet, stuffed birds, and waxen fruits. But along the line where
Fashion ends, a region of Comfort commences, the habitation of Mr. Boffin
being characterized by sawdust floor, shelves displaying a large veal-and-
ham pie together with a cold-joint, and a table bearing a pipe ready for
smoking. Each regards these surroundings as congenial externalizations of
self, not to be sacrificed even in the interests of matrimony but to be enjoyed
with mutual tolerance, the dividing line liable to alteration in conformity with
any future changes in the tastes of their occupants:

> If I get by degrees to be a highflyer at Fashion, then Mrs. Boffin will by degrees
> come for'arder. If Mrs. Boffin should ever be less of a dab at Fashion than she
> is at the present time, then Mrs. Boffin's carpet would go back'arder. If we
> should both continny as we are, why then *here* we are, and give us a kiss, old

lady.   (56)

Although this is not the place for any detailed examination of the topic, it is relevant to cite the view that Victorian architecture is a sad story of pastiche, a potpourri of imitations without any style that could legitimately be called its own. For the very eclecticism prompting its hybrid combination of styles should be seen as representing not a lack of inventiveness but this same desire for personal selectivity, the wish to produce, by combining different stylistic elements, a product distinctively one's own. Georgian houses, with their standard rectilinear form and squared sash windows, had offered little opportunity for flexibility, for individualism, or for personal whim; but as Robert Kerr recorded in his architectural survey *The Gentlemen's House* of 1864, the Victorian owner was now offered by his builder an extraordinary variety of styles, which he was invited to tailor to his own tastes:

> Sir, you are a paymaster, and must therefore be pattern-master; you choose the style of your house just as you choose the build of your hat—you can have *Classical*, columnar or non-columnar, arcuated or trabeated, rural or civil, or indeed palatial; you can have *Elizabethan* in equal variety; *Renaissance* ditto; or, not to notice minor modes, *Mediaeval* in any one of many periods and many phases,—old English, French, German, Belgium, Italian, and more.
> (Dixon and Muthesius 33)

Dickens' novels partake of that same principle, the character of the fictional owner imposing itself upon the building and permeating it with his or her essential qualities, making even its minor ornamental details reliable clues to personality. "Whenever we visit a man for the first time," Dickens remarked in one of his early sketches, "we contemplate the features of his knocker with the greatest curiosity, for we well know, that between the man and his knocker, there will inevitably be a greater or less degree of resemblance and sympathy" (*Sketches by Boz* 40). And the houses in their entirety are no less imbued with their owners' traits, the residences of the haughty deriving their cold air of superiority and condescension from their socially pretentious inhabitants:

> Like unexceptionable Society, the opposing rows of houses in Harley Street were very grim with one another. Indeed, the mansions and their inhabitants were so much like in that respect, that the people were often to be found drawn up on opposite sides of dinner-tables, in the shade of their own loftiness, staring at the other side of the way with the dullness of the houses.
> (*Little Dorrit* 246)

Dickens is, indeed, the very last of novelists to be accused of dehumanizing his characters, which emerge from his fiction with such irresistible vitality—not drained of their humanity but vibrant with life, overflowing with the vigor of their own being. The mainstream of his fictional figures, whether virtuous, comic, or villainous—the Pumblechooks and Wopsles, the Wemmicks and Drummles whom he moves in and out of his novels with such exuberance—consistently infuse their environment with the spirit of their own amusing or deplorable traits. The charming home Wemmick has constructed possesses its own miniature drawbridge and moat, its flag hoisted regularly every Sunday, and its gun fired at precisely nine each evening to the joy of his Aged P. There is a similar playfulness and eccentricity in the rebuilt Cardiff Castle and its adjacent Castell Coch, designed by William Burges in close collaboration with their owner Lord Bute—both buildings in recent years admirably restored to their pristine splendour. Castell Coch he equipped with a fully functional drawbridge and portcullis, even providing apertures in the walls through which burning oil could be poured on supposed besiegers, while throughout the main building he inserted riddles, surprises, puns, and jokes reflecting his own delight, well known to his friends (Girouard 274), in lighthearted jests and facetiousness, the bell-push in the dining-room being disguised as an acorn held in a monkey's mouth (fig. 5). A similar love of ingenious gadgets and witticisms characterizes Wemmick's home, the arrival of its owner at the drawbridge outside being announced ". . . by a sudden click in the wall on one side of the chimney and the ghostly tumbling open of a little wooden flap with 'John' upon it" (*Great Expectations* 280). The amusing objects with which he surrounds himself constitute for him a refuge from the soul-destroying obsequiousness and bureaucratic anonymity required at his place of work, where he is indeed little more than a letter-box. This is a home of which he is the master, and to which he can impart the filial affection and prankishness so stifled outside. The privacy of that home he guards jealously from his employer for the very reason that it reveals so much of his true inner self. "No; the office is one thing, and private life is another," he explains to Pip. "When I go into the office, I leave the Castle behind me, and when I come into the Castle, I leave the office behind me. If it's not in any way disagreeable to you, you'll oblige me by doing the same" (197).

To interpret Dickens' characteristic use of metonymy as representing the usurpation by material goods of human prerogatives—a sense that people ". . . were being de-animated, robbed of their souls" (Van Ghent 130)—is, I think, to miss the richness that his technique lent to the characters he

Figure 5. Monkey bell-push, Cardiff Castle.

portrayed, the investing of belongings or appendages with the foibles, eccentricities, and spiritual aura of their owner, an intimacy delightfully projected by Dickens into his imaginary world. If that vital spirit is withdrawn, the objects collapse into anonymity, losing their independent life. The moment that Pecksniff's hypocrisy is exposed towards the end of *Martin Chuzzlewit* and his pomposity deflated, the author informs us, "Not only did his figure appear to have shrunk, but his discomfiture seemed to have extended itself even to his dress. His clothes seemed to have got shabbier, his linen to have turned yellow, his hair to have become lank and frowsy; his very boots looked villainous and dim, as if their gloss had departed with his own" (810). Even when objects do appear to overwhelm the human, as in the instance of the four-poster bed cited by Van Ghent, the situation needs to be interpreted in reverse. For the bed's suffocating encroachment upon Pip is in fact a projection upon the room of his own emotional condition at that moment, his sense of being utterly crushed by Estella's rejection of his love just before he entered the room itself.

James Carker, we are told in *Dombey and Son*, infused the objects about him with his own spirit: ". . . there issues forth some subtle portion of himself, which gives a vague expression of himself to everything about him" (472). The same holds true for the well-meaning but illiterate maidservant Charley in *Bleak House*, ". . . in whose hand every pen appeared to become perversely animated, and to go wrong and crooked, and to stop, and splash, and sidle into corners, like a saddle-donkey" (404). There is the chimneyed, superannuated boat house of Mr. Peggotty seen from afar "smoking very cosily" like its owner; and in contrast, the filthy, rat-infested wharf where Quigley feels most at home, or the clawing, snarling cat seated perpetually on Mr. Krook's shoulder. The gigs, kites, wooden legs, and other appurtenances appropriated by Dickens' characters served of course as a narrative device wonderfully appropriate for the newly serialized novel, helping readers at each issue to identify them afresh by their distinctive dress, accoutrements, or turns of phrase. But that device succeeded no less in expressing the Victorian's personal, often sentimental attachment to his possessions. If the armchairs and other furnishings began to be regarded as more animate at this time, it was still, as Dickens informs us in his *Sketches by Boz*, the human who initiated the process, who constituted the source of that animation by projecting his own moods upon them:

> . . . we should have gone dreaming on, until the pewter-pot on the table, or the little beer-chiller on the fire, had started into life, and addressed to us a long story of days gone by. But, by some means or other, we were not in a romantic humour; and although we tried very hard to invest the furniture with vitality, it remained perfectly unmoved, obstinate, and sullen.   (239)

Conversely, when he *was* in a "romantic" humor, such investing of furniture with vitality was to constitute a major ingredient of his art.

WORKS CITED

Briggs, Asa. *Victorian Things*. London: Batsford, 1988.

Carey, John. *The Violent Effigy: A Study of Dickens' Imagination*. London: Faber, 1973.

Crook, J. Mordaunt. *William Burges and the High Victorian Dream*. Chicago: U of Chicago P, 1981.

Dickens, Charles. *Works*. New Oxford Illustrated Ed. London: Oxford UP, 1948–58.

Dixon, Roger, and Stefan Muthesius. *Victorian Architecture*. London: Thames, 1985.

Gibbs-Smith, C. H. *The Great Exhibition of 1851*. London: 1964.

Girouard, Mark. *The Victorian Country House*. New Haven: Yale UP, 1985.

Hill, Nancy K. *A Reformer's Art: Dickens' Picturesque and Grotesque Imagery*. Athens: Ohio UP, 1981.

Hobhouse, Christopher. *1851 and the Crystal Palace*. New York: 1937.

Hunt, Robert. "The Science of the Exhibition." *The Crystal Palace Exhibition: The Art Journal Illustrated Catalogue*. 1851. New York: Dover, 1970.

Jakobson, Roman. "Linguistics and Poetics." *Style in Language*. Ed. Thomas A. Sebeok. Cambridge, Mass.: MIT P, 1966.

Kincaid, James R. *Dickens and the Rhetoric of Laughter*. Oxford: Oxford UP, 1971.

Miller, J. Hillis. "Sketches by Boz." *Charles Dickens and George Cruikshank: Papers Read at a Clark Library Seminar*. Ed. J. Hillis Miller and David Borowitz. Los Angeles: Clark Library, 1971.

———— Afterword. *Our Mutual Friend*. By Charles Dickens. New York: Signet-NAL, 1980.

Redgrave, Richard. *Supplementary Report on Design*. London, 1852.

Stewart, Garrett. *Dickens and the Trials of Imagination*. Cambridge, Mass.: Harvard UP, 1974.

Symonds, R. W., and B. B. Whineray. *Victorian Furniture*. London: 1962.

Van Ghent, Dorothy. *The English Novel: Form and Function*. New York: Holt, 1953.

Dickens' Bow to the Language Theory Debate

Barry Thatcher

The breadth and type of influence that the nineteenth-century language theory debates exerted on nineteenth-century culture and literature have been ignored by most literary scholars, including dickensian scholars. This fact is surprising given the persuasiveness and consequences of the debates during this time. The language theory debate was one of the major concerns of the nineteenth century because each conception of language constituted a foundation of ideology, culture, religion, education, and legal and political systems. The radical materialist philosophers used their language theories to back up the larger cultural implications of their rational thinking, while adherents of the new philological movement used their language theories to reject eighteenth-century reason and to champion their own conservative cultural and ideological agendum. As a result, the language theory debate "became the basic issue that divided conservative and radical opinion" (Aarsleff ix). Not surprisingly, political parties, philosophical factions, and religious intellectuals "made the philosophy of language the expression of its definition of man," and consequently, "each party took its stand on a theory of language" (Aarsleff ix).

Unfortunately, Dickens' *Hard Times* has never been seen as a reflection of the language theory debate, which perhaps explains why this novel remains divisive and puzzling. Although most critics agree that *Hard Times* "seems to be concerned with a radical criticism of the very structures of society" (Monod 444), many disagree about how well and to what extent the novel addresses these structures. For example, Michael Goldberg argues that the novel effectively portrays "the Utilitarian prospectus with its eighteenth-century rationalist heritage and the essentially transcendental Romantic view

17

with its roots in German idealism'' (79). Other critics such as Richard Arneson, Patrick Brantingler, James Brown, and Earle Davis discuss the novel's illustration of the social, religious, and political conflicts in which Utilitarianism played a part. But some critics, Ernest Baker for example, argue that the dogmatic portrayal of Utilitarianism in *Hard Times* smacks of political pamphleteering, making the novel ugly and unartistic. And for some critics, Dickens' portrayal of Utilitarian political economy and of the labor union movement is flawed and exaggerated (Hodgson, Knight). Certainly, *Hard Times* is Dickens' most overtly political novel, yet its politics do not adequately satisfy many of the political intellectuals of his time or of ours. In addition, it lacks the Victorian sentimentality seen in his other novels, and the narrator's highly intrusive participation is new to Dickens' readers. However, though these characteristics make *Hard Times* somewhat of an anomaly in the Dickens canon, they do not make the novel flawed or imbalanced. Rather they reflect the language theory debates that give structure and consistency to this novel, perfectly serving Dickens' purposes for condemning, and finding a corrective for, Utilitarianism.

Charles Dickens knew of this language theory debate and took part in it. In *Household Words* (1850–59), a periodical that he carefully controlled, Dickens published articles that address current linguistic issues. *Hard Times* (1854), a novel Dickens published serially in *Household Words*, is based on these linguistic issues, and the only way to understand the purpose and structure of the novel is to understand the nature of the language theory debate that occurs in it. Gradgrind and the narrator respectively reflect Bentham's and Richard Trench's language theories, and these theories structure the novel's depiction of ideological and cultural clashes. As a result, the novel's interrogation of these issues is consistently focused and ideologically coherent, not flawed, imbalanced, or exaggerated, as most critics contend. Previously thought to be a disparate mixture of political pamphleteering, allegory, and biting satire, *Hard Times* uses the language theory debate to create a schematic but unified portrayal of the ideological structures of Victorian society. Furthermore, Dickens may use the language theories to highlight the connection between language and ideology and to arm Victorian readers with the right type of language to combat the radical political values promoted by materialist language theories.

I

Hard Times appeared in 1854 at the height of a language theory debate in Victorian England. This debate centered on the materialist theories of Étienne

Condillac, Horne Tooke, and Jeremy Bentham and the new philological movement of William Jones, John Kemble, Benjamin Thorpe, and Richard Trench, who rejected the materialism of the previous movement.

Étienne Bonnot de Condillac developed a language theory based on two materialist foundations: universal grammar and Locke's origin of ideas in sensation. In his first language treatise, *Essai sur l'origine des connoissances humaines* (1746), Condillac argued that universal grammar was the simple connection between language and thought. He postulated that if discourse is the "image of thought, and if thought is subject to the laws of reason, then discourse itself must reveal and illustrate the laws of reason" (Aarsleff 14). As a result, Condillac tried to explain rationally all parts of speech as being based on the structures of the mind.

Condillac bases his theory on Locke's idea that all thought originates from sensations, arguing that language is the mechanism that derives reflection and eventually thoughts and ideas from the sensations. Since the processes of mind are based on, and perhaps are, the processes of language, language should directly reflect the human mind and therefore become the best insight into it. This idea is extremely important because philosophers began to study the human mind as they studied language, using concrete, scientific means. This philosophy also implies that the mind is basically a passive receptor of sensations: the mind does not create the meaning from the sensations; it just coordinates it. Perhaps Condillac himself did not believe or fully comprehend that his language theory denies the existence of God or the human spirit. However, other more radical materialists used this philosophy of language to defend their atheism, which bothered many Victorians who believed in innate thoughts or thoughts that originate outside the senses.

Condillac's theories became even more problematic because he tried to explain the infinite variety of linguistic expressions by hypothesizing related infinite operations of the mind. This problem inspired Horne Tooke into developing a new and influential philosophy of language. In *The Diversions of Purley* (1805), Tooke argues that all language originates from two groups of words: words that are signs for sensations and words that are either abbreviations of, or signs for, other signs of sensations. He labels this concept his theory of Abbreviation. The theory is an enhancement of Locke's doctrine that ideas originate from the senses and that language is supposed to communicate thoughts as quickly as possible so as to approximate the speed of thought. From his theory of abbreviation, Tooke outlines three important subdivisions. First, a sign ties together a mixture of ideas to form a single word. This theory closely resembles Locke's idea that words can knot together ideas into a single concept, a concept that is important because language and its subdivisions become the glue holding together the ideas that make communication possible. This ability to represent numerous ideas makes language a sort of abstract or abbreviation of ideas, enabling quick communication. Secondly, Tooke explains in *Diversions of Purley* that nouns and verbs are the only types of words that originate from sensations, and all other types of words are only abbreviations of these two. For Tooke, the mind receives only materialistic, and therefore, nominal sensations. As a result, the only signs that represent sensations, the original source of thought, are signs for nouns. And finally, according to Tooke, other words such as pronouns, adjectives, adverbs, and articles are merely abbreviations or linguistic subsets of the original nouns. Organized in this abbreviated way, language bypasses the cumbersome use of just nouns and therefore, can quickly and effectively communicate ideas.

The influence of Horne Tooke's linguistic philosophy was astounding, especially for the Utilitarians who delightedly embraced this materialist and rational analysis of language. And Tooke's prominence as a language theorist reveals one attitude prevalent in nineteenth-century England about science and the nature of man. For example, William Hazlitt said that because Tooke's theories treated words as chemists do substances, they were "a flash of light" to the scientific and rational minds of the Utilitarian radicals (*Historical Sketches* 114). In addition, James Mill placed one of Tooke's theories at the head of his chapter in *Analysis of the Phenomena of the Human Mind* (1829). Others such as Erasmus Darwin, Thomas Belsham, and Henry Brougham, adopted Tooke's premises on language, making Tooke the most prominent language theorist of the late eighteenth century and the early nineteenth (Aarsleff 73).

Jeremy Bentham not only praises Tooke's theories but uses them as a base for his own language theory. Agreeing with Tooke's idea of abbreviation as the base for universal grammar, Bentham similarly breaks language down into three parts:

> These are 1. The name of the subject of the discourse, of the communication made by it. 2. The name of some attribute, attributed or ascribed to the same subject. 3. The name of copula, the attributive copula by which the attribution is performed.   ("Chrestomathia" 186)

These three parts follow Tooke's principles of universal grammar, that a word is either a sign of the impression made on the mind, or a sign or abbreviation of another word that is a sign of an impression. Bentham's first part of speech is the sign of the sensation, or "the name of the subject." The second part is a sign or an abbreviation of the sign of sensation, and the third is the verb (copula) coordinating this sign.

After accepting Tooke's premise of abbreviation, Bentham further develops Tooke's second part of speech into his major language theory, this theory of fiction. After claiming that Tooke "half concealed or left unperfected" this discovery of the second part of language ("Chrestomathia" 120), Bentham claims that this second part is the base of linguistic difficulties. He calls this second part the fictitious entity, a sign that corresponds to something intangible such as another sign or to immaterial things such as feelings, passions, and imaginings. Bentham devotes most of his "Ontology," "Universal," and "Language" essays to rooting out and clarifying fictitious words.

For *Hard Times* scholars, it is interesting to note that Bentham argues for an education based on his principles of universal grammar:

> An acquaintance with universal grammar, as above-described, will naturally be among the acquisitions to be made in a Chrestomathic school. So far from adding to, it will subtract from, the quantity of labour necessary to the acquisition of a given degree of acquaintance with the particular languages therein proposed to be taught.   ("Chrestomathia" 188)

Later, Bentham hypothesizes that this rational system for learning languages could easily apply to all types of learning. This theory of fiction forms the base of Gradgrind's pedagogy, which Dickens satirizes in *Hard Times*.

Despite Tooke's and Bentham's popularity, historical, philosophical, religious, and literary language theorists began to react to, and reject these rational and materialist theories. At the start of the nineteenth century, the most decisive turn in language study occurred when the "philosophical, a priori method of the eighteenth century was abandoned in favor of the historical, a posteriori method of the nineteenth" (Aarsleff 127). Sir William Jones, Benjamin Thorpe, and John Kemble pioneered the work in the new philological movement that sought to undermine the materialist philosophies of Condillac, Tooke, and Bentham.

Religious figures also rejected the materialist roots and atheistic ramifications of Tooke's and Bentham's language theories. One who was important to Dickens' *Hard Times* was Bishop Richard Trench, the most prominent voice of the new philological movement. After publishing his enormously popular works *On the Study of Words* (1851) and *English Past and Present* (1855), Trench became a member of the Philological Society and exerted a great influence in the new philological movement. Trench did not believe in language study for its own sake; rather he wanted the study of words to elucidate a great many other fields such as religion, history, and sociology. Unlike Tooke and Bentham, whom he rejected as chaotic and atheistic, Trench saw language as a transcendental, religious tool given to man by God. Evading the polemics of the origin of language, Trench focused on the ways the meanings of words behaved in shifting contexts over time. He also studied how words contain information about the spiritual and moral life of speakers. In addition, Trench openly opposed Bentham's pedagogy based on his theory of fiction.

During this change from materialist to historical theories of language, Dickens published *Hard Times* (1854) in his *Household Words* (1850–59), both of which participate in this linguistic controversy. In his periodical, Dickens published more articles about the new linguistic theories than did "*Bentley's Miscellany* or *Chamber's Journal, Eliza Cook's Journal, Douglas Jerrold's Shilling Magazine*, or *Once a Week*, the roughly contemporary rival periodicals which made their appeal essentially to the same inclusive middle-class audience" (Deering 12). In particular, in several key articles published in *Household Words* Dickens armed his readers against the materialist theories by satirizing them and supporting the opposing theories of the new philological movement. The article "Saxon-English" (1858) traces some of the history of the English language, an important subject in the new philology. This article refers to Trench's "valuable work" *On The Study of Words* and is almost completely based on it ("Saxon-English" 91). The article "Our P's and Q's" (1857) satirizes Horne Tooke's and Lindley Murray's obsession with grammatical correctness. The article "Calling Bad Names" (1858) satirizes the Benthamite tradition of using fancy Greek and Latin words in the classroom. "Wisdom of Words," which appeared in *Household Words* in November 1851, just after the publication of Trench's *On the Study of Words*, follows Trench's thesis that words reveal the spiritual and moral condition of the people. The article does not directly acknowledge Trench as a source, so its clear adaptation of Trench's concepts establishes that *Household Words* and its audience had comprehensively appropriated Trench's ideas, as well as establishing the connection between language and politics, culture, and society.

II

Roderick McGillis argues that Dickens' *Hard Times* "is about language as much as anything else, and its theme is the confrontation of languages:

the scientific language of the Hard Fact school, the political language of Slackbridge . . . and poetic language . . ." (102). In this linguistic confrontation, Gradgrind's language "represents the sterility of life" because he believes "that words can capture an external reality . . . that they reflect something that exists in a permanent reality outside the mind" (McGillis 102). Also noting this confrontation of languages, Randolph Quirk maintains that Sleary and Gradgrind emerge "solely as a particular kind of linguistic behavior" (20). Though both these critics never cite Bentham's theory of fiction as a source for Dickens' Gradgrind, both correctly describe Gradgrind's language. Gradgrind's language represents external reality according to Bentham's materialist language theory, which makes it, as Quirk contends, a particular linguistic behavior. However, Dickens' creating Gradgrind to embody Bentham's theories of language is not important just because it reflects Benthamite Utilitarianism. Rather it is more important because by parodying Benthamite language theory it significantly clarifies the materialist orientations and implications of Bentham's cultural, political, and social philosophies.

Hard Times quickly sets the tone and stage for Gradgrind's embodiment of Bentham's theory of language, along with its cultural, social, and political implications. In chapter 2, following Bentham's theory, Bounderby and Gradgrind explain how to uncover immaterial or "fictitious" words. Bounderby asks Gradgrind's young students if they would paper a room with representations of horses. After half the students say yes and the other half no, the two Utilitarians explain that one should not use representations of horses on walls because one would never "see horses walking up and down the sides of a room in reality—in fact" (5). Using the same rationale, Bounderby explains that one should not print flowers on the carpet. Such representations of horses and of flowers are "fictitious" signs because they do not directly correspond to something tangible or real. Bounderby lauds this way of thinking as a "new principle, a discovery, a great discovery" (5), of which Gradgrind heartily approves. This new discovery exemplifies the process of clarifying Bentham's "fictitious" words, which is actually Bentham's new pedagogy.

Bentham develops his process of uncovering and cleansing "fictitious words" from the second part of Tooke's language theory. According to Tooke, the second part of language consists of words that "are merely abbreviations employed for dispatch, and are the signs of other words" (Aarsleff 46). Following this concept, Bentham argues that

[a] fictitious entity is an entity to which, though by the grammatical form of the discourse employed in speaking of it, existence be ascribed, yet in truth

and reality existence is not meant to be ascribed. . . . Every fictitious entity
bears some relation to some real entity, and can no otherwise be understood
than in so far as that relation is perceived.   ("Ontology" 197)

A fictitious word is the second part of language because it too corresponds
not to a tangible word, but to the sign itself, or the abbreviation, of a tangible
word. For example, the word "plant" is fictitious when it refers not to a
specific, concrete object, but to "every individual plant that grows; and not
only to those, but moreover to all those which ever grew in time past,
and . . . in time future. . . . The word plant is, therefore, a fictitious entity"
("Ontology" 121). Bentham later develops his theory of fictitious words to
include feelings, passions, imaginings, and other intangible realities. Bentham labels various degrees of fictitious words depending on how many times
removed, or figuratively how far away, the sign is from the thought or object
it represents. For Bentham, these words "may be classed in different ranks
or orders, distinguished by their respective degrees of vicinity to the real
one" (Ogden liv).

According to Bentham, we have to use fictitious words in order to converse,
but to use them clearly we must speak of them as if they corresponded directly
to material objects. First, Bentham argues that all fictitious or immaterial
words originate from a material word or are attached to one: "to every word
that has an immaterial import there belongs, or at least did belong, a material
one" ("Language" 329). Next, Bentham contends that the only way to avoid
linguistic difficulties with a fictitious word is to find the word's original
material beginning and to speak of the word as if it belonged to this material
origin:

> For producing in any other mind any conception whatsoever of an object of
> this class [fictitious word], a man has absolutely but one means, and that is to
> speak of it as if it belonged to the other class . . . the character of a sign of
> some material object.   ("Language" 328)

For Bentham, we must un-abbreviate the abbreviated word or materialize the
immaterial word. In other words, the speaker has to reconnect the original
sign with the original material object from which it originated, a process that
eliminates the indefinite and immaterial sign and its concept that figuratively
stand between the material sign and object.

Gradgrind's language exemplifies Bentham's perverse materializing of immaterial words and reveals its broader cultural and social implications. For
example, when Gradgrind discusses immaterial things such as emotions or

feelings, he tries to materialize or link these fictitious words to some remote
material origin, thus perverting the real meaning of the words. As he talks
to his daughter, Louisa, about her marriage to Bounderby, Gradgrind materializes the word "love" into a tangible fact:

> "Father," said Louisa, "do you think I love Mr. Bounderby." Mr. Gradgrind
> was extremely discomfited by this unexpected question. "Well, my child," he
> returned, "I—really—cannot take upon myself to say . . . because the reply
> depends so *materially*, Louisa, on the *sense* in which we *use* the expres-
> sion. . . . I would advise you (since you ask me) to consider this question, as
> you have been accustomed to consider every other question, simply as one of
> *tangible Fact*. The ignorant and the giddy may embarrass such subjects with
> irrelevant fancies, and other absurdities that have no existence properly
> viewed."   (91–92; emphasis added)

Closely following Bentham's principles and even words, Gradgrind asserts
that the only way to talk about love is to materialize it into a "tangible Fact,"
which is the age difference between the two prospective spouses. And, after
citing statistics asserting that age difference does not matter, Gradgrind suggests that Louisa marry Bounderby. Therefore, Louisa marries Bounderby
based on material "facts," not the fictitious and immaterial "irrelevant fancies and other absurdities" such as emotions, feelings, and desires that for
Louisa should be important to developing love and be a major part of it.
Gradgrind's trying to materialize these immaterial emotions and imaginings
forces him to distort their real meanings for Louisa. Here, perhaps Dickens
warns his readers about the disastrous effects of using Gradgrind's system,
a type of distorted moral arithmetic that Utilitarians were famous for using
to weigh not only marriage proposals, but also other important personal and
social decisions (Altick 118).

Following his theory of strict materialism, Bentham's theory of language
leaves little room for figurative and metaphoric language. Bentham agrees that
all language is based on signs and their objects represented; hence language is
figurative. So Bentham redefines "figurative" language as problematic if it
is more than what is absolutely necessary to convey meaning: "If all language
be thus figurative, how then (it may be asked), how then is it that the character, and, in so important a class of instances the reproach, of figurativeness,
is cast upon the uses made of it in particular instances? ("Language" 330).
Bentham answers that figurative words are "other images not necessary to,
and thence not universally employed in, the conveyance of the import in
question" (331). Besides superfluous words, "other images" include overt

metaphors, which are not necessary to convey meaning and are "fictitious" because they do not correspond directly to the material signs.

Gradgrind's language imitates Bentham's theory because it is tediously literal. For example, in the first chapter Gradgrind exemplifies deformed precision by literalizing the most remotely figurative word. He wants to call Sissy Jupe "Cecilia" or "Number 22" (3) rather than his nickname, "Sissy." In another example, when Gradgrind visits Sleary's circus, Gradgrind cannot comprehend the circus people's metaphoric words. Gradgrind becomes so perplexed and annoyed at their metaphoric words such as "cheeking," "stow," "tumbling," "missing his tip," and "goosed" (20–30) that finally, after Kiddermaster hits him with the metaphoric "tight-jeff," he collapses in desperation: " 'What does this unmannerly boy mean,' said Mr. Gradgrind, eyeing him in a sort of desperation, 'by Tight-Jeff' " (30). Sensing Gradgrind's inability to understand the metaphoric vernacular, Mr. Childers explains " 'There! Get out, get out . . . Tight-Jeff or Slack-Jeff, it don't much signify; it's only tight-rope and slack-rope' " (30). The word "Jeff" is a metaphor for "rope," something Childers understands but Gradgrind does not because it is a metaphor. Later, Gradgrind is forced to use the metaphoric word "goosed," but he does so with great difficulty: " 'Why has he been—so very much—goosed?' said Mr. Gradgrind, forcing the word out of himself, with great solemnity and reluctance" (30). Metaphors seem to baffle Gradgrind because he is incapable of materializing and therefore understanding them.

As well as literalness, Bentham's theory of language emphasizes nondescriptiveness. For Bentham, words that represent quantities, qualities, form, or figures are often very "fictitious" because they are one sign away from the material object they modify ("Logic" 262–64). For example, Bentham says it is hard to understand the sentence "The apple is "ripe" because "ripe" is a quality, which does not represent the apple itself but the immaterial concept of the apple's quality. It would be clearer, he asserts, to say "that in this apple is the quality of ripeness" because it materializes the adjective "ripe" into the more tangible, measurable noun "ripeness" ("Language" 329–31).

Gradgrind's language exemplifies Bentham's avoidance of descriptive words and phrases. For example, in chapter 1 Gradgrind uses only one adjective in ten lines of speech, whereas the narrator uses approximately twenty-four adjectives or adjectival phrases in twenty-seven lines, almost one adjective a line. Appropriately, Gradgrind uses the present participle "reasoning" (1) to describe the students. In chapter 6 the narrator uses about 180 adjectives or adjectival phrases in about 200 lines, again almost one adjective a line. In contrast, Gradgrind uses about six adjectives or adjectival phrases in about sixty lines of text, or about one adjective every ten lines.

Gradgrind's language not only represents this avoidance of descriptive words but also mimics Bentham's phraseology. When Sissy Jupe cannot define a horse, Gradgrind criticizes her because she is "possessed of no facts" (3). This odd syntax mimics Bentham's philosophy of changing immaterial descriptions—"ignorant" in Sissy's case—into measurable and tangible words. One should not say "Sissy is ignorant," just as one should not say "the apple is ripe." One should say "this fact does not reside in Sissy" just as "the quality of ripeness resides in the apple." It is not surprising, therefore, that in the narrator's words Gradgrind sees the children as "little pitchers before him" who are not to become "knowledgeable," but "who were to be filled so full of facts" (2).

In addition to having this tendency to nominalize words, Bentham's language avoids describing motions because they represent the immaterial concept of motion, not objects in motion themselves, and thus are one sign away from representing the actual material object. Bentham contends that

> [i]n the physical world, in the order of approach to real existence, next to matter comes motion. But motion itself is spoken of as if it were matter; and in truth, because, in no other way—such is the nature of language, and such is the nature of things—in no other way could it have been spoken of.
> ("Ontology" 263)

According to Bentham, the speaker has to materialize motion in order to speak of it. For example, Bentham materializes the motion of a ball. He says that "the *motion* of a ball is really a *receptacle*, i.e., a hollow substance; and that in this hollow substance, the ball is lodged" ("Logic" 263). In other words, instead of saying that the ball is moving "between two points," one has to think that "the ball resides in a hollow receptacle that exists between the two points." It is not surprising, therefore, that Bentham likes to nominalize verbs. In section 6 of his essay "Language," Bentham gives some rules for clarifying language, and rule 4 states: "Prefer verbal substantives to verbs" (315). Bentham wants to nominalize verbs because the "adjuncts" (tense and case) of verbs represent motion, "the time of the action, the number of the person or persons concerned in it, and the point of view" (315). Since motion, time, action, number, and, as is pointed out later, relation represent signs of tangible objects, they are fictitious words.

Gradgrind's inactive language is highly noticeable because Dickens juxtaposes it with the narrator's descriptions of the circus people. In about a hundred lines of chapter 6 that the narrator uses to describe Gradgrind, one of about twenty-five words produces images of action, and most of these words are past tense and concrete. Thus in at most one of four lines there is an image of action. In contrast, in lines from the same chapter the narrator describes the circus people with two images of action for every three lines of text. For example, the circus people

> are in the habit of balancing . . . dance . . . stand . . . catch knives and balls, twirl hand-basins, ride upon anything, jump over everything and stick at nothing. All the mothers could—and did—dance upon the slack-wire and the tightrope, and perform rapid acts on bareback steeds.   (33–34)

This contrast in verbal activeness highlights the distinction between Gradgrind's material world and the circus people's world of imagination. It also parallels the theme of oppositions in the novel.

Gradgrind is also associated with the Utilitarian world in which time, motion, and activity have stopped. For example, the narrator says that the people of Coketown, including Gradgrind, "had been walking against time towards the infinite world, twenty, thirty, forty, fifty years and more" (47). In another passage, the narrator says that for most people, "in some stages of his manufacture of human fabric, the processes of Time are very rapid. . . . Mr. Gradgrind himself seemed stationary in his course and underwent no alteration" (87). These images of Gradgrind's inert language and time being stopped perhaps reflect Dickens' contention that Utilitarianism stopped social, political, and cultural progress.

Bentham is as suspicious of "relation" as he is of the concept of motions, because it also exists between two objects at the same time:

> In so far as any two objects are regarded by the mind at the same time—the mind, for a greater or less length of time, passing from the one to the other—by this transition, a fictitious entity *Relation*, is considered as produced.
>   ("Ontology" 264)

In this definition, Bentham considers a "relation" as that which passes from one object to another during some length of time. Relation is even more suspect than motion, because unlike the material ball, relation is often based on immaterial things such as affection, trust, and friendship. There can be no "hollow receptacle" to lodge the relationship between two people because unlike the tangible ball this immaterial "relation" is "unlodgeable."

Much as Bentham's theory states, Gradgrind's discussion of relations is almost completely limited to the concrete material. In the beginning of the novel, the narrator first describes Gradgrind's factual calculation of human relations:

> A man of acts and calculations. . . . Thomas Gradgrind. With a rule and a pair of scales, and the multiplication table always in his pocket, sir, ready to weigh and measure a parcel of human nature, and tell you exactly what it comes to.
>
> (3)

The only way Gradgrind can measure a relation is with a multiplication table or a pair of scales. For example, Gradgrind marries Mrs. Gradgrind not because of love but because "she was most satisfactory as a question of figures; and, secondly, she had 'no nonsense' about her" (17). And as already noted, the only way Gradgrind measures the future relationship of Louisa and Bounderby is by materializing it into the most tangible facts possible. In both cases, Gradgrind completely misunderstands what makes up an important human relationship. Gradgrind's relation to his students is also based on facts because, in the narrator's words, he sees them as pitchers and himself as the pourer of tangible facts. However, Gradgrind has problems with his method because he knows that there is something in Sissy "which could hardly be set forth in a tabular form" (86). In other words, Gradgrind is unable to define his relationship with Sissy because he cannot measure her personality, as the narrator notes in the paragraph quoted earlier. This inability to really understand and deal with human relationships reflects Bentham's various cultural, educational, social, and political theories, all of which presumed that "every human being on earth prized nothing but material values" (Altick 118).

This prizing of material values results in figurative death for both the characters and the language itself. During her last moments of life, Mrs. Gradgrind realizes that " 'there is something—not an ology at all—that your father has missed, or forgotten' " (187). Mrs. Gradgrind asks for a pen to write what her husband has missed, but she is only able to write a little. The narrator comments that "it matters little what figures of wonderful no-meaning she began to trace upon her wrappers. The hand soon stopped in the midst of them" (187). Richard Fabrizio argues that this scene is a metaphor for the linguistic difficulties of the whole novel. He calls it the novel of "Wonderful No-Meaning," and he is correct because the whole novel is full of "No-meaning." When Louisa talks to her father about marriage, Gradgrind produces no meaning at all, completely thwarting communication. The narrator describes this scene in a verbless passage that further emphasizes the feeling of inertness as it symbolizes the complete lack of communication: "Silence between them. The deadly statistical clock very hollow. The distant smoke black and heavy" (91). Louisa becomes so frustrated because of their inability to communicate that she gives up, exclaiming, "What does it matter" (94), the phrase having metamorphosed from question, to statement of resignation, to defeated silence.

III

For Richard Watts, the narrator's "exuberant personality" persuades the reader to disagree with Gradgrind's principles, making him "a powerful antidote to Gradgrind's philosophy" (125). Watts's assertion is unique because most other literary scholars believe that the narrator is a critic of Utilitarian principles of education and politics, not an antidote to them. Because the narrator's language reflects Trench's theory of language, it becomes an antidote for Gradgrind's Benthamite language. Since both Trench and the narrator believe that the principles involved in the language debate are important religious, social, and economic questions, they both reject the material origin of thoughts, the theory that language operates the mind, and the notion that words are independent, unchanging, and impenetrable entities. Trench and the narrator similarly criticize education based on universal grammar, and both contend that language measures the speaker's moral, spiritual, and cultural condition.

Since language theories involve "the highest spiritual things" and "the serious questions" (*On the Study of Words* v, vi) such as the definition and origin of man, language, and knowledge, Trench sees them as deeply religious matters. Trench focuses most of his efforts on Tooke and Bentham, those "professing philosophers [who] have blundered grossly" (vi). In *On the Study of Words*, his first book, Trench refutes "Tooke's shortcomings, whether in occasional details of etymology, or in the philosophy of grammar or in matters more serious still" (v). And by the time Trench writes his second book, *English Past and Present*, he believes that the study of language is such an integral part of religion that he hopes his language theory "may yet in the providence of God have an important part to play for the reconciling of divided Christendom" (28–29).

Like Trench, the narrator of *Hard Times* regards linguistic issues as religious matters, a perspective that he reveals by using religious words and imagery to assail Utilitarianism. Robert Green believes that the narrator's language resembles a sermon, and "the use of such language only underlines the fact that *Hard Times* is a sermon in fiction, a withering and blistering attack . . . on utilitarians (1394–95). For Green, the repetition in phrases and "the periodic sentences" make the novel sound like Newman's *Tracts for the Times* (1395). Besides this evangelical style, as Green notes, the narrator explicitly uses religious words and imagery. For example, in chapter 2 the narrator ironically contends that the pompous Bounderby deifies himself so much that he could "bring about the great public-office Millennium, when Commissioners should reign upon earth" (5), a phrase that parodies Revelation 20:16. Here, the narrator denigrates Bounderby's and his colleagues' apotheosis, exemplifying, according to one critic, the "violent revulsion" of *Hard Times* to the self-made man and his social ambition (Gibbons 78).

Trench follows traditional religion and adopts Romantic values to reject Locke's theory of basing thoughts on sensations. For example, the real truths about language are received not as materialist sensations but as divine inspiration through the imagination:

> A meditative man cannot refrain from wonder, when he digs down to the deep thought lying at the root of many a metaphorical term, employed for the designation of spiritual things, even of those with regard to which professing philosophers have blundered; and often it would seem as though rays of truths, which were still below the intellectual horizon, had dawned upon the imagination as it was looking up to heaven.   (*Study* vi)

Here Trench "religionizes" the geological metaphor of the study of language to show that he believes not only in God and inspiration but also in the power of the mind. The mind does not passively receive materialist thoughts; rather it powerfully and imaginatively brings in inspired truths and connects them with language. This view of the mind reflects not only the religious view of divine inspiration and divine human origins, but also the romantic valorization of the individual powers of the mind. The Romantics were a powerful force for the rejection by the new philology of Locke's belief that ideas originate in the senses.[1] Throughout all his studies, Trench argues that language carries or creates intangible and immaterial things such as the imagination, emotions, and spirituality, all of which, as Bentham and Gradgrind show, are annihilated by the materialist language philosophy.

Similarly, the narrator satirizes the Lockean tradition of ideas based on sensations and argues for the imagination, emotions, and human impulses.

First, the narrator toys with the term "Fact." For Gradgrind and the Utilitarians, facts are either received through the sensations or based on them. The narrator plays with this materialism by turning Gradgrind's facts into rock-breaking entities. For example, he claims that the rocks in the Gradgrinds' mineralogical cabinet "looked as though they might have been broken from the parent substance by those tremendously hard instruments their own names" (10). And perhaps the narrator's most biting satire of this materialist tradition is his portrayal of Mrs. Gradgrind. The narrator claims that Mrs. Gradgrind is "invariably stunned by some weighty piece of fact tumbling on her" (14). Consequently, Mrs. Gradgrind avoids talking with Bounderby so as to "avoid a collision between herself and another fact" (17). In addition, the narrator might play with Gradgrind's word "tabular." Gradgrind tries to tabulate everything, including human relations, but his system breaks down with Sissy: "somehow or other, he had become possessed by an idea that there was something in this girl which could hardly be set forth in tabular form" (86). Here, the word "tabular" might refer to "tabula rasa," Locke's concept that our minds are a "blank slate" until a material sensation engraves its presence. For Gradgrind, Sissy offers something that is not material, something that cannot be physically written down, let alone engraved on a slate.

As a counter to this materialism, the narrator valorizes and exemplifies the power of the imagination. The narrator openly calls for the healing power of the imagination. He laments the fact that Louisa and Thomas have "a light with nothing to rest upon, a fire with nothing to burn, a starved imagination keeping life in itself somehow" (12). And unlike Gradgrind, the narrator has the imaginative power to understand human relations. He notes that Louisa and Sissy drift apart when Louisa decides to marry Bounderby: "from that moment she was impassive, proud and cold—held Sissy at a distance—changed to her altogether" (98). And certainly the narrator's linguistic abilities demonstrate his imaginative powers. The narrator's use of metaphors to articulate thoughts, his ability to manipulate the reader through subtle and not-so-subtle rhetorical images, and his artful linking of words with people to measure their morality reveal great imaginative ability. Just as much as Gradgrind lacks powers of imagination, the narrator possesses them.

According to Trench, language does not operate the processes of the mind; rather the mind composes language as it articulates thoughts (*Study* 22). As a result, rational principles of universal grammar do not structure the mind: "there are anomalies out of number now existing in our language, which the pure logic of grammar is quite incapable of explaining" (*English* 17). There-fore, man does not parrot but rather articulates:

> Yet this must not be taken to affirm that man started at the first furnished with a full-formed vocabulary of words, and as it were with his first dictionary and first grammar ready-made to his hands. He did not thus begin the world *with names* but *with the power of naming*: for man is not a mere speaking machine; God did not teach him words, as one of us teaches a parrot, from without; but gave him a capacity, and then evoked the capacity.   (*Study* 14–15)

This difference of "from within" or "from without" is extremely important. Condillac, Tooke, and Bentham argue that language is "from without," that it comes into the mind and operates its process; and as a result, the words going out reflect that rational processes of the words going in. On the other hand, Trench argues that a person's mind has the capacity to conceive of words within and articulate those thoughts. Therefore, language is the power to name or articulate a thought. Accordingly, Trench argues that thoughts are independent from words:

> [Words are] co-extensive with things . . . that a multitude of things exist which, though capable of being resumed in a word, are yet without one, unnamed and unregistered; of that, vast as is the world of name, the world of realities is even vaster still.   (75–76)

This concept is important because it rejects the arguments of Condillac, Tooke, and Bentham that thoughts are based on words.

The narrator's great power for coining words and using metaphors exempli-fies Trench's assertion that man is not a machine but an articulator of thoughts. Perhaps the best examples of this power occur in the first chapter. After Gradgrind emphasizes his bare-bone facts, the narrator articulates some pow-erful criticism of Gradgrind. Gradgrind's forehead is a "wall"; his eyes "found commodious cellarage in two dark caves"; his hair "bristled on the skirts of his bald head, a plantation of firs to keep the wind from its shining surface." Gradgrind's bald head "was all covered with knobs, like the crust of plum pie." Gradgrind's "square coat, square legs, square shoulders" grasped him "by the throat . . . like a stubborn fact" (1). In the first two chapters, the narrator uses over twenty overt metaphors, while Gradgrind, perhaps unwittingly, uses one. This huge difference in language abilities shows different assumptions about the functions and origins of language. For Gradgrind, metaphors are shunned because they are "fictitious." For the narrator, metaphors represent the power to articulate thoughts or ideas, even those that have not been articulated or named before. Throughout the novel, the narrator epitomizes what Trench calls the God-given power to name.

While Bentham and Gradgrind want to isolate the origins of words in order to understand them, Trench wants to see how words get their meaning. Trench argues that words get their meaning not from an individualized sensation, as Bentham asserts, but from language, which "is the amber in which a thousand precious and subtle thoughts have been safely embedded and preserved" (23). Consequently, Trench focuses his studies on the word and its relation to the language and culture. The significance of this theory of language is that the meanings of words are not based on some materialist origin, as Bentham would argue, but on usage, which encodes and builds human communities. Perhaps as a counter to Bentham's traditional contempt for the history of words, Trench devotes the latter half of *On the Study of Words* and the whole of *English Past and Present* to discussing how the meanings of many words changed according to context.

The narrator's sense of historical and cultural contexts of words reflects Trench's philosophy. For example, the narrator plays with the word "blue," referring to the Blue Books, those infamous collections of statistics that detail the local conditions of the slums and factories (Altick 39). The narrator says:

> Although Mr. Gradgrind did not take after Blue Beard, his room was quite a blue chamber in its abundance of blue books. Whatever they could prove (which is anything you like), they proved there, in an army constantly strengthened by the arrival of new recruits.   (89)

The narrator knows that the word "blue" has taken on charged meaning because the blue books often justified Utilitarian philosophy. The narrator does the same thing with other words that had taken on important meaning during the industrialization of England. The narrator describes Gradgrind as "a galvanizing apparatus, too charged with a grim mechanical substitute for the tender young imaginations" (2). In addition, in the narrator's words, Gradgrind, Bounderby, and McChoakumchild see the children as 'little vessels then and there arranged in order, ready to have imperial gallons of facts poured into them" (2). In the newly industrialized England, the terms "galvanizing" and "grim mechanical substitute" reflects the influence of this mechanical age. The words "little vessels" and "imperial" may reveal the influence of British imperialism. The narrator really understands and takes advantage of the historical significance of words, which adds to the irony of his rhetoric.

In contrast to Gradgrind's Hard Facts, Trench argues that words are interrelated, living, and changing things:

> [Words are] not, like the sands of the sea, innumerable disconnected atoms, but growing out of roots, clustering in families, connecting and intertwining themselves with all that men have been doing and thinking and feeling from the beginning of the world until now.   (23, 25)

This directly contradicts Bentham's argument that all words have a distinct material origin and that their relation depends on the relation of their material origins, a view that essentially ignores context. On the contrary, Trench devotes much of time discussing the history of derivations, adaptations, and usages.

Although the narrator does not give us etymologies of words, his adpting words from different contexts to form new meanings perhaps shows his understanding that the meanings of words depend not so much on their material origins as on their relationship to other words and to the language and culture in general. Thus for the narrator words connect and intertwine "themselves with all that men have been doing and thinking and feeling." For example, in chapter 3 of part 1, the narrator dryly describes Gradgrind's mathematical house and metallurgical cabinets. But a few paragraphs later, the narrator takes the words "mathematical" and "metallurgical" from their context of science and uses them to describe Louisa and Thomas, Jr. At this time, Gradgrind has just noticed children watching the circus, and suddenly, "what did he then behold but his own metallurgical Louisa . . . and his own mathematical Thomas" (11) peeping in at the show. The narrator's use of these two scientific terms shows that he knows how to form new relationships with words, and that these new relationships derive much of their meaning from the current trends in culture. The words "metallurgical" and "mathematical" are especially loaded with meaning because of their relation to Utilitarianism. The narrator has a wonderful ability to appropriate all types of words from many different contexts, a technique that shows the narrator's knowledge of the fluid yet contextual meaning of words.

Building on this concept that words are related to other words and their context, Trench discusses how materialist language greatly hinders communication and education. Trench asks a question that sounds like a direct influence on the metaphor used to describe Gradgrind:

> For what is 'education'? Is it a furnishing of a man from without with knowledge and fact and information? or is it a drawing forth from within and a training

of the spirit, of the true humanity which is latent with them? Is the process of
education the filling of the child's mind, as a cistern is filled with waters brought
in buckets from some other source, or the opening up of its own fountains?

(Study 172)

Trench answers that true education is not furnishing people with facts, but
drawing forth from that person his or her inward powers:

> Education must educe, being from 'educare,' which is but another form of
> 'educere' and that is to draw out, and not to put in. . . . He must first have
> powers awakened in him, measures of spiritual value given him; and then he
> will know how to deal with the facts of this outward world.   *(Study* 172)

As a result, education for Trench is first spiritual and then factual. It begins
with the preparation of the inside and ends with the finishing touches on the
outside. In essence, a student is much like a word: he is not an entity independent from his place in culture, history, and social context. Not surprisingly,
a better part of Trench's inside education is based on the discussion of words:

> There is a sense of reality about children which makes them rejoice to discover
> that there is also a reality about words, that they are not merely arbitrary
> signs, but living powers; that, to reverse the words of one of England's "false
> prophets," [Bentham] they may be the fool's counters, but are the wise man's
> money;   *(Study* 25)

Just as Bentham bases his education on universal grammar, so does Trench
base his on the study of words. However, the assumptions about education
and the application of language are completely opposite. Bentham formulated
his theory of language to "ensure that men's opinions were framed in words
cleansed of ambiguities" (Dowling 53), which he did by stripping away all
fictitious words until he would come to the original material sensation of that
word. Trench's study of words is based on the relationships of words, and
on how language enables discovery, power, and joy.

The narrator reflects Trench's criticism of Utilitarian pedagogy. Just as
Trench condemns "the filling of the child's mind, as a cistern is filled with
waters brought in buckets from some other source," the narrator soundly
refutes Gradgrind's view of the students as "vessels then and there arranged
in order, ready to have imperial gallons of fact poured into them until they
were full to the brim" (2). And if the reader sees the narrator as the teacher
and the text as the classroom, the narrator, like Trench, wants to work inside
his students, helping them to form their own identities, instead of working
on the outside to form collective "models" for Gradgrind's school. The

narrator accuses Gradgrind of trying to "kill outright the robber Fancy lurking within—or sometimes only maim him and distort him" (8). And the narrator laments that when each child's imagination or fancy is sufficiently subdued, Gradgrind's pedagogy becomes "a monster in a lecturing castle, with Heaven knows how many heads manipulated into one, taking childhood captive, and dragging it into gloomy statistical dens by the hair" (8). Here, the heads of the children "are manipulated into one," forming models for Gradgrind's school. Finally, the narrator wants to use imaginative language and literature as an important part of the children's education. The narrator discusses reading *Tom Thumb* (9), "Peter Piper" (10), *Mr. William Button, of Tooley Street*, an untraced short circus comedy (11). Like Trench, the narrator argues for an anti-Benthamite pedagogy based on an anti-Benthamite language.

Dickens further emphasizes the connection between ideology and language by explicitly linking Gradgrind's rejection of Utilitarianism to his remarkable change in language. Seeing his Utilitarian system fail with everyone whom it touched, Gradgrind repudiates this materialist ideology, and for the first time he begins to communicate with his daughter Louisa. Furthermore, Gradgrind begins to use descriptive language, metaphors, and adjectives; and later, he embraces religious and emotive language as he rejects Utilitarian education. By the end of the novel, Gradgrind's language becomes like that of the narrator, showing that the narrator is perhaps Dickens' answer to the complex religious, social, and political questions of *Hard Times*.

After absorbing some of Sissy's imaginative influence, Gradgrind begins to see the failure of Utilitarianism and to reject it, and his change in language begins. The first evidence of this change occurs when Louisa returns home after failing in her marriage with the Utilitarian Bounderby. For the second time, Gradgrind and Louisa discuss marriage, but this time Gradgrind's and Louisa's communication is not interrupted by a dead statistical clock; rather it is warm, passionate, understanding. Gradgrind "sat down at the side of the bed, tenderly asking how she was. . . . He took her outstretched hand, and retained it in his" (206–07).

With her hand in his, Gradgrind speaks with metaphoric, descriptive, and emotive language, something that to this point has been uncharacteristic of him:

> "It would be hopeless for me, Louisa, to endeavor to tell you how overwhelmed I have been, and still am, by what broke upon me last night. The ground on which I stand has ceased to be solid under my feet. The only support on which I leaned, and the strength of which it seemed, and still does seem, impossible to question, has given way in an instant. I am stunned by these discoveries. I

have no selfish meaning in what I say, but I find the shock of what broke upon
me last night to be very heavy indeed.''   (206)

The phrases "broke upon me," ground "ceasing to be "solid," and being
no longer able to "lean" against Utilitarianism are metaphoric. In addition,
Gradgrind uses seven modifiers in nine lines in this paragraph, a great increase
over his previous literalness. And most of these modifiers, such as "hope-
less," "overwhelmed," "impossible," and "selfish," describe feelings and
human emotions that are anti-Utilitarian. To close the passage of this touching
change, Gradgrind uses two significant metonyms:

> "Some persons hold," he pursued, still hesitating, "that there is wisdom of
> the Head, and that there is a wisdom of the Heart. I have not supposed so;
> But, as I have said, I mistrust myself now. I have supposed the head to be all-
> sufficient. It may not be all-sufficient. . . . Louisa, I have misgiving that some
> change may have been slowly working about me in this house, by mere love
> and gratitude, that what the Head had left undone and could not do, the Heart
> may have been doing silently."   (208)

The "Head" of course symbolizes rational thinking, and the "Heart" emotions, both of which are part of the human dimension. Therefore, while
realizing that he needs a Heart as well as a Head, Gradgrind has completely
reversed his language to be more figurative, descriptive, and emotive, a style
that goes against the principles of linguistic materialism outlined in Bentham's
theory of fiction. In fact, Bentham lays a very heavy charge specifically
against metonyms, labeling them as misleading "fictions or incomplete symbols" (Shaw 81).

In this same touching scene when Louisa confesses her marital problems,
Gradgrind also begins to understand and to use words that describe relations
between people:

> "My dear, I have remained all night at my table, pondering again and again
> on what has so painfully passed between us. When I consider your character;
> when I consider that what has been known to me for hours has been concealed
> by you for years; when I consider under what immediate pressure it has been
> forced from you at last; I come to the conclusion that I cannot but mistrust
> myself."   (207)

Unlike the first scene, when Gradgrind fails to understand his relationship
with his daughter, Gragrind now "ponders" the relationship between himself
and Louisa rather than trying to measure its material circumstances. Again,
Gradgrind's change in language reveals his rejection of Bentham's theory of

language, a sign that he had repudiated Bentham's materialist principles. Despite Bentham's criticism that "relations" are fictitious, Gradgrind is now trying to ponder the hitherto imponderable relations, those intangible but real attributes that cannot be put into Utilitarian tabular form.

As this change in Gradgrind's language suggests, Gradgrind's words as well as his view of people are no longer rock-breaking entities based on materialist sensations. Gradgrind has rejected Locke's theory of basing thoughts on materialist sensations and has opted for a "softer" approach to knowledge and identity. For example, when Gradgrind realizes that Bitzer is as hard as the facts of his school, he tries in vain to penetrate and soften this inhuman creature:

> "Bitzer," said Mr. Gradgrind, stretching out his hands as though he would have said, See how miserable I am! "Bitzer, I have but one chance left to soften you. You were many years at my school. If, in remembrance of the pains bestowed upon you there, you can persuade yourself in any degree to disregard your present interest and release my son, I entreat and pray you to give him the benefit of that remembrance." (267–68)

Realizing that the hard facts of his school have created hard-fact creatures, Gradgrind "entreats" and "prays" that Bitzer not turn in his son. But Bitzer is hard-headed, his Utilitarian education and his present interest having calcified the heart to which Gradgrind appeals. Similarly, the eternally hard Utilitarian, Bounderby, rejects Gradgrind's new softness; seeing "Gradgrind being much softened, Mr. Bounderby took particular pains to harden him" (223). But Bounderby's efforts at hardening Gradgrind are fruitless, for Gradgrind has rejected the theories that language is a product of materialist sensations and knowledge is a product of hard facts. His language and own identity have become much less material and much more soft.

Since Gradgrind now realizes that humans as well as words are more than just material entities, he starts to believe that pedagogy should be based not on Bentham's materialist theory of fictions, but on Trench's theory that words are dynamic, living powers in need of nurturing from the inside. For example, Gradgrind concedes that he has not developed the inner qualities of Louisa:

> "Bounderby, I see reason to doubt whether we have ever quite understood Louisa."
> "Who do you mean by We?"
> "Let me say I, then," he returned, in answer to the coarsely blurted question. "I doubt whether I have understood Louisa. I doubt whether I have been quite right in the manner of her education . . . whatever the merits of such a system may be, it would be difficult of general application to girls. . . . I think there

are qualities in Louisa which—which have been harshly neglected, and—and
a little perverted.''　　　　　　　　　　　　　　　　　　　　(223–24)

In part, this passage shows Gradgrind's capitulation to the prevailing Victorian ethos of sexual differences. It is Louisa's culturally defined femininity,
her "softness," that has been perverted. But later, Gradgrind's useless entreaties to Bitzer call his entire previous pedagogical approach into question.
Realizing that his approach of filling students with facts only produces obdurate creatures like Bitzer, Gradgrind starts to look for and develop the inner
qualities, the dynamic living and feeling qualities of his students. Like Trench
and the narrator, Gradgrind has rejected Bentham's purely rational pedagogy
of universal grammar, which builds generic models from the outside for the
Hard Facts school. Instead he wishes to develop the individuality of each
person's inner qualities. Again, Gradgrind's assumption that inner qualities
exist rejects the materialism of Bentham's Utilitarianism.

Like Trench and the narrator, Gradgrind starts to see from the perspective
of religion and to use its language. When Gradgrind finally finds his wayward
son Thomas at Sleary's Circus, he invites him to repent:

> Atone, by repentance and better conduct for the shocking action you have
> committed, and the dreadful consequences to which it has led. Give me your
> hand, my poor boy, and may God forgive you as I do!　　　　　　(265)

These are the first religious words Gradgrind has ever used, and most likely
they are the first religious thoughts.

This complete conversion seems counter to many criticisms of *Hard Times*.
For example, Roger Fowler argues that in *Hard Times* Dickens "attacks an
unmanageable large and miscellaneous range of evils . . . mostly oversimpli-
fies them; . . . [and] is unclear on what evil causes what other evil" (106).
As a result, Fowler argues, Dickens' *Hard Times* is never able to resolve its
ideological conflicts, becoming by default, rather than design, what Bakhtin
calls a heteroglossic novel. According to Bakhtin, a pure heteroglossic novel
displays an arena of interacting and conflicting voices and corresponding
ideologies that are liberated from the author's own intentions, purposes, language, and ideology.

In the most extensive discussion of *Hard Times* in Bakhtinian terms yet to
appear, Fowler argues that *Hard Times* portrays a multiplicity of languages
and ideologies that are meant to clash: Gradgrind versus Sissy Jupe, Bounderby versus Blackpool, and Slackbridge versus Harthouse. Furthermore,
Fowler claims that the author does not objectify his own purposes or motives

by injecting his own language and ideology into the voices of the character. As a result, Fowler concludes "that *Hard Times* makes a prima facie claim to be a polyphonic novel" (96).

Fowler's argument fails, however, to account for Gradgrind's conversion as well as the ending of the novel, both of which conform to the narrator's language and ideology. Gradgrind's change in language symbolizes his rejection of Benthamite materialism and his acceptance of Trenchian language and view of life. Therefore, the novel does not portray an arena of liberated languages; rather it shows how one language eventually conforms to another, a characteristic of a monologic, not a polyphonic, novel. Furthermore, at the end of the novel the narrator uses his language and his ideology to unify and centralize the entire verbal and ideological world. While addressing the reader, the narrator predicts the future of all the characters. He omnisciently states that Thomas, Jr., has no future and that Bounderby, the incorrigible Utilitarian, will die soon, and his benefactors will begin their "long career of quibble, plunder, false pretenses, vile example, little service, and much law" (275) over the rights to Bounderby's fortune. The narrator prophesies that Gradgrind, Mrs. Sparsit, and Louisa will probably survive, but he argues that Sissy Jupe's future will be the best by far. The narrator then judges each person according to his moral standards based on Trenchian language theory: recalcitrant Utilitarians will not live; those who reject Utilitarianism will survive but be scarred; and Sissy, the least marked by Utilitarian intellectual machinery, will fare the best. His life-and-death dispensations of fate become the ultimate seal of his monologic control. Therefore, the narrator's language and ideology have become what Bakhtin calls a centripetal force, those "forces that serve to unify and centralize and verbal-ideological world" (270). By the end of the novel, the characters either conform to the narrator's language and ideology or are seen in the light of it. The multiplicity of voices running rampant throughout the novel has been corralled into a pale of divinely sanctioned words.

The narrator, in fact, is perhaps the most important character in this novel. He not only tells the story, authoritatively checks the languages and ideologies of the characters, and acts as an antidote to the Utilitarian philosophy, but he also injects his own interpretations, making him an obtrusive character, tensely waiting to surface and participate in the novel. The narrator even calls attention to his open participation in framing our understanding of events, indeed to his function as our authoritative counter-voice to Utilitarian fact-speak, to Slackbridgian demagoguery, even to carnivalesque circus jargon.

IV

"In large measure," Robert Spencer writes, "the technique of *Hard Times* puzzled the Dickensians; even the intentions of the author were obscured" (xiii). This quotation encapsulates the usual response to the novel as well as the purpose for this article, which has been to show how Dickens' use of language theories answers the puzzling questions and resolves the divisive issues of *Hard Times*.

First, the theories form a consistent ideological and artistic structure for revealing Dickens' political purposes. By connecting language with ideology, the theories show that language is the fundamental battleground for larger cultural, political, and social issues. Dickens shows how Bentham's language theory underlies Gradgrind's materialist view of life, his hard-fact concept of education, his view of social relations, and his ideas about religion. Critics have of course noted these issues in the novel, but they have not noted their relation to Bentham's language theory nor their dependence on it. On the other hand, the narrator symbolizes how Trench's language theory rejects Gradgrind's strict materialism and supports religion, Christian principles and ethics, and humanistic education, and social relations modeled after the slippery, dynamic, and contextual nature of words. Critics have never seen the influence of Trench on the narrator, nor have they noted how his language theory serves as a corrective for Bentham's Utilitarian language theory, which is why they do not see the structure in the novel. Since the language debate is a vehicle for consistently and comprehensively addressing the larger social, political, and cultural issues of Victorian England, the novel does not fall apart, nor is it politically or ideologically skewed or weak, as many critics have argued. Furthermore, establishing the narrator's discourse as normative, ameliorative, and worthy of emulation gives the novel an authoritative center that holds together its disparate parts. Thus, the technique is quite clear.

Secondly, the presence of the language theory debate in the novel also proves that *Hard Times* is an ideological novel to the core, that in Bakhtin's words

> we are taking language not as a system of abstract grammatical categories, but rather language conceived as ideologically saturated, language as a world view, even as a concrete opinion, insuring a maximum of mutual understanding in all spheres of ideological life.   (271)

Since both Bentham's and Trench's language theories underlie, define, strengthen, and justify the ideology of the theorist, language becomes ideology. Therefore, for Dickens language is neither neutral ground nor opaque medium. Rather it is the world view of characters, authors, and readers; only through analyzing language can we truly obtain what Bakhtin calls "a maximum of mutual understanding in all spheres of ideological life." Through the opposition of Bentham and Trench, the linguistic conversion of Gradgrind, the dominance of the narrator, and the resulting structural closure of the novel, readers are urged to retheorize their relationship to language and to the world.

Since language is ideology, language represents the social, political, and cultural battles occurring in Victorian England, all of which can be seen as components of a heteroglossic struggle. In Bakhtin's theory, each voice of a language struggles for dominance against all the other voices and therefore suppresses them or is suppressed by them. As a result, speech diversity represents social diversity, and this struggle of voices symbolizes the social struggle. In *Hard Times*, each language theory not only constitutes the foundation of a larger cultural and historical perspective, but also symbolizes the struggle against other languages and the culture and history they represent. Thus, the language theories in *Hard Times* symbolize the ideological battlefield and *the exact battle* over the cultural, political, social, and historical conflicts of Victorian England.

Through *Hard Times*, Dickens arms his readers with the linguistic ammunition to fight Bentham's materialist view of language and of society. In this sense, *Hard Times* is a highly political novel, specially designed to help readers contend with the complex ideological issues of Utilitarianism and Bentham's language theory. Recognizing Dickens' intent helps explain the choice of Richard Trench as the pattern for linguistic resistance and reformation. In an epigraph to *On the Study of Words*, Trench writes: "Language is the armory of the human mind, and at once contains the trophies of its past, and the weapons of its future, conquests." This epigraph alludes to the highly political overtones of Trench's work, which the Victorians saw "as a powerful ally in the war against materialism and unbelief . . . welcomed in England initially because it seemed so obviously to provide an arsenal against the speculative etymologizing of Horne Tooke . . . and Jeremy Bentham" (Dowling, 47, 53). This epigraph similarly fits *Hard Times* and underscores the novel's militant, even bellicose, spirit. Gradgrind's original Utilitarian language becomes both a trophy of conquest and a model to avoid for all those who fight against Utilitarianism. Furthermore, the narrator's language becomes the model to assimilate in order to defeat Utilitarian language in all the broad cultural, social, and political fronts that it underlies. The narrator's language theory contains the main political thrust of the novel because it shows how to use language to identify, understand, confront, and overcome materialist philosophies. The clear victor in the novel's battleground, the narrator makes monologic order out of heteroglossic chaos and offers his language practice as a weapon for his reader's future struggles.

Dickens' use of Bentham's language theory as a base for Gradgrind obviously reflects, even parodies, the extremes of radical Utilitarianism, while his use of Trench's language theory as a base for his narrator is perhaps less dramatic, but still very fitting and important. First, Trench symbolizes for the Victorians "a radical identification between language and civilization" (Dowling 44), which underlies the assumption that language and language theories represent broad cultural, social, and ideological issues. Secondly, Trench was a popular and "powerful ally against materialism and unbelief" (Dowling 47). Thus, Victorian readers would recognize him as the natural, logical opposition to Utilitarianism. Indeed, the opposition of Bentham versus Trench may be the originating dichotomy that generated the many oppositions structuring the novel. What could be called Dickens' oppositional strategy is evident even in his list of possible titles, such as "Black and White," "Hard Heads and Soft Hearts," "Heads and Tales," and "Extremes Meet" (Collins 146). All these suggested titles show Dickens' intention of building the novel bipolarly, and the last one suggests that he wished to present an authoritative resolution to the philosophies and political schisms in *Hard Times*. Most modern critics of course identify the extremes of Utilitarianism and the circus people's imaginative freedom, but contemporary readers who were familiar with Trench would have recognized him as the proper corrective to Bentham's Utilitarianism.

And lastly, Trench's combination of philosophical and cultural conservatism with a modest but staunch rejection of Benthamite materialism forms a flexible but not too radical view of the structure of society. This modestly conservative view is the right corrective for Utilitarian thinking. Sissy's Jupe's life is not the antidote for Utilitarian thinking because it is too imbalanced. Trench, however, seems to be the right mixture. His theories of language as a transcendental ability given to man from God are fairly conservative, as is his refusal to speculate about the "origins of language or the nature of its changes" (Shaw 88–89), a stance that bothered many intellectuals but appealed to Dickens, who as a practicing writer never really delved into scientific linguistics and preferred to concentrate on usage and history. Like Trench,

Dickens was concerned with how language shapes and records human communities; consequently, social reform is congruent with language reform. Perhaps the conservative faith in language as a divine gift, as the Adamic power to name and thus confer meaning and order on the material and immaterial things of the world, explains why *Hard Times* is not ultimately a revolutionary novel, as Shaw, Ruskin, Macaulay, and many other scholars have argued. It sets up the condition of social revolution by showing the injustices of society's economic base and by exposing the oppression materialized by the cultural superstructure, yet it retreats from the apocalyptic solution posited by Dickens' contemporaries Marx and Engels. The narrator's Trenchian language and the ideology it represents can reharmonize discordant voices and restore social order as fictional characters and real-world readers turn his *lexis* into *praxis*.

NOTES

1. See Dowling, especially chapter 1, for a representation of the Romantic and religious coalition against materialism.

WORKS CITED

Aarsleff, Hans. *The Study of Language in England 1780–1860*. Minneapolis: U of Minnesota P, 1983.

Altick, Richard D. *Victorian People and Ideas*. New York: Norton, 1973.

Arneson, Richard J. "Benthamite Utilitarianism and *Hard Times*." *Philosophy and Literature* 2 (1978): 60–75.

Bakhtin, Mikhail. "Discourse in the Novel." *The Dialogic Imagination*. Trans. Caryl Emerson and Michael Holquist. Austin: U of Texas P, 1981.

Bentham, Jeremy. *The Works of Jeremy Bentham*. Vol. 8. Ed. John Bowring. New York: Russell, 1962.

Collins, Phillip. *Dickens and Education*. London: Macmillan, 1963.

"Composition of *Hard Times*." *Hard Times*. Norton Critical Ed. Ed. George Ford and Sylvère Monod. New York: Norton, 1966.

Deering, Dorothy. "Dickens's Armory for the Mind: The English Language Studies in *Household Words* and *All the Year Round*." *Dickens Studies Newsletter* 7–8 (1978): 11–17.

Dickens, Charles. *Hard Times*. New York: Bantam, 1964.

———, Ed. *Household Words: A Weekly Journal*. Vols. 1–19. London: Bradbury, 1850–59.

Dinwiddy, John. *Bentham*. Oxford: Oxford UP, 1989.

Dowling, Linda. *Language and Decadence in the Victorian Fin de Siècle*. Princeton: Princeton UP, 1986.

Fabrizio, Richard. "Wonderful No-Meaning: Language and the Psychopathology of Family in Dickens' *Hard Times*." *Dickens Study Annual* 16 (1987): 61–94.

Fowler, Roger. "Polyphony and Problematic in *Hard Times*." *The Changing World of Charles Dickens*. London: Methuen, 1977.

Gilmour, Robin. "Dickens and the Self-Help Idea." *The Victorians and Social Protest: A Symposium*. Ed. John Butt and I. F. Clarke. Hamden: Shoestring, 1973. 71–101.

———. "The Gradgrind School: Political Economy in the Classroom." *Victorian Studies* 11 (1967): 207–24.

Goldberg, Michael. *Carlyle and Dickens*. Athens: U of Georgia P, 1972.

Green, Robert. "*Hard Times*: The Style of Sermon." *Texas Studies in Language and Literature* 11 (1970): 1375–96.

Historical Sketches. 2nd ser. London, 1839. 114.

Lodge, David. "The Rhetoric of Hard Times." *Language of Fiction*. London: Routledge, 1966.

Manning, Sylvia. *Hard Times: An Annotated Bibliography*. New York: Garland, 1984.

McGillis, Roderick F. "Plum Pies and Factories: Cross Connections in *Hard Times*. *Dickens Studies Newsletter* 11 (1980): 102–07.

Monod, Sylvère. *Dickens the Novelist*. Norman: U of Oklahoma P, 1968. 440–71.

Ogden, C. K. *Bentham's Theory of Fictions*. New Jersey: Littlefield, 1959.

Quirk, Randolph. *Charles Dickens and Appropriate Language*. Durham: U of Durham P, 1959.

Shaw, David. *The Lucid Veil: Poetic Truth in the Victorian Age*. Madison: U of Wisconsin P, 1987.

Spencer, Robert Donald. Introduction. *Hard Times*. New York: Bantam, 1964.

Tooke, Horne. *The Divisions of Purley*. London, 1805.

Trench, Richard C. *English Past and Present*. New York: Redfield, 1855.

————. *On The Study of Words*. London: Parker, 1853.

Watts, Richard J. *The Pragmalinguistic Analysis of Narrative Texts: Narrative Cooperation in Charles Dickens's Hard Times*. Tübingen: Narr, 1981.

Whewell, William. *History of the Inductive Sciences*. London, 1847.

Pickwick in the Utilitarian Sense

Robert Newsom

"[T]hat obscurity in which the earlier history of the public career of the immortal Pickwick would appear to be involved" (to quote the novel's own announcement in its opening sentence of Mr. Pickwick's murky origins) is twofold, entailing both a fictional obscurity arising out of the claim of the Pickwickian "editor" to know little about Pickwick's earlier history, and a parallel, real-life obscurity arising out of the peculiar circumstances of Mr. Pickwick's invention and the subsequent controversy between Seymour's widow and Dickens about whether etcher or writer (or publisher, for that matter) in fact created the fictional figure.[1] And on both fronts that obscurity has generated lots of writing and lots of candidates—real and fictional—for "originals" of the immortal Pickwick. Long before the death of the "author" became a critical—and greatly exaggerated—commonplace, what we might call Mr. Pickwick's corporate and cultural construction had been well established—in addition to his multiple and over-determined creation within the mind of "Charles Dickens." Thus we have long known that the origins of Pickwick are to be found in an idea of Robert Seymour's (based upon the popular success of works by such writers as Robert Surtees, Richard Penn, and John Poole) for a series of sporting sketches, as well as in Seymour's own previous etchings of various fat, bald, and jolly elderly men; in Edward Chapman's recollection of "a fat old beau who would wear, in spite of the ladies' protests, drab tights and black gaiters" (Forster 1:59);[2] and in countless beings populating the Dickens imagination and recollection, including Moses Pickwick, the proprietor of a coach running between London and Bath mentioned in chapter 35, and such literary antecedents as Fielding's Parson Adams and Goldsmith's Vicar of Wakefield, whose second son, Moses Primrose, indirectly supplies Dickens with his pseudonym and thus reminds us, as Steven Marcus points out, that "Boz and Pickwick are of course one" ("Language into Structure" 199).[3]

It will seem perverse to propose seriously in such jolly company the figure of Jeremy Bentham as among the originals of Mr. Pickwick, and indeed it might well be wrong, if by "original" were meant a person whom a writer consciously draws upon in inventing a fictional character. But since writers' conscious intentions are thought to be among the least interesting and determining things that go into the production of texts, it may prove significant merely to demonstrate a remarkable likeness—in spite of Dickens' own likely inability to see it—thereby enriching our understanding of these three fascinating and paradoxical figures, each of whom played so large a role in the culture of Victorian England. The similarities between Pickwick (and Dickens) on the one hand and Bentham on the other turn out to be striking enough to deserve attention, and while there is reason to suspect strongly that Dickens did have Bentham in mind, consciously or not, at that famous moment when he "thought of Mr. Pickwick" (as he says in the "Preface to the Cheap Edition, 1847," rpt. in Patten's ed. 44), the founder of the utilitarian movement is in any case a large figure in the cultural moment of *Pickwick*. I shall argue, moreover, that beyond the similarities in the figures, there is more importantly an essential *identity* between utilitarian and Pickwickian ethics, especially utilitarian ethics as actually formulated by Bentham, rather than as widely understood even by readers perhaps better read than Dickens. My claim therefore has two interrelated aspects: one connects Pickwick with the image of Bentham; the other connects Pickwick (and Dickens) more deeply with the fundamental ideas of utilitarianism.

Of course this is to run against the prevailing winds of Dickens criticism.[4] I am hardly the first critic to connect Bentham's name with Dickens', however. As early as 1885 the legal historian Sir Henry Maine wrote in *Popular Government* (qtd. in House 36):

> It does not seem to me a fantastic assertion that the ideas of one of the great novelists of the last generation may be traced to Bentham. . . . Dickens, who spent his early manhood among the politicians of 1832 trained in Bentham's school, hardly ever wrote a novel without attacking an abuse.

Humphry House takes up Maine's lead and devotes several pages of his chapter on "Benevolence" in *The Dickens World* to illustrating Benthamite strains in Dickens, and subsequently Raymond Williams has seen deeper connections between Dickens and the utilitarians (77–97).[5] Marjorie Stone recently has given a very informative account of Dickens' consonance with Bentham's ideas about legal fictions.[6] But with the notable exception of

Williams, critics have noted similarities only on the relatively restricted ground of the reform of legal abuses. Even House (38) concludes:

> it is clear that Mr. Pickwick is not Bentham's idea of a moral man. For the Benthamite *spoudaios* [the good, earnest Benthamite] has to act from the conviction that it is his duty to promote happiness: Pickick promotes it in spite of himself, almost against his will.

I will argue that this judgment is wrong on both counts.

The figure we recognize as Bentham is for most of us deeply colored by John Stuart Mill's essay about him, which is justly famous but in turn deeply colored by the figure of the elder Mill, who almost always stood, imaginatively and in fact, between Bentham and his most important Victorian interpreter, and who, along with several others of the younger utilitarians, in his own person embodied the stereotype of the utilitarian as humorless and cold—a rational, calculating machine. Let me therefore ask my readers to put aside that image insofar as possible and indeed pretend to put aside "Bentham" altogether. We may begin by considering some of the less well-known facts concerning this figure whom I want to include among candidates for originals of Mr. Pickwick, and to whom I shall refer for the moment simply as B.

In one important respect, Mr. Pickwick's earlier history does differ from B.'s, at least if Mr. Pickwick is himself to be believed, for he tells us in the very last chapter that "[n]early the whole of . . . [his] previous life . . . [has] been devoted to business and the pursuit of wealth" (57:893), whereas B. embarked on a full-time philanthropic career in his mid-forties. He was able to follow pursuits of his own choosing because his father's death left him, as one writer has put it, wealthy enough "to be as childlike and whimsical as he chose" (Mack 7).[7] Like Mr. Pickwick he was a thoroughgoing Londoner, born and bred in the city, though his amateur scientific interests led him at least to plan expeditions even as far as the interior of South America (Mack 98)—rather more ambitious than Mr. Pickwick's forays among the sources of the Hampstead Ponds—but then he never got there. He was of course also the founder of a club (of sorts, even if it did not have a club button), which was devoted to his own ideas and favorite causes, including scientific and philosophical ones. However, philanthropy and social reform were his passion, and late in life he confessed his ambition "to make himself the wisest and most *effectively benevolent* man that ever lived" (Mack 8)—just as "general benevolence was one of the leading features of the Pickwickian theory" (2:85). This ambition was no doubt both grandiose and naïve; certainly it was quixotic, and indeed his career was full of tilting at windmills.

Like Mr. Pickwick, B. was, except in one instance, a confirmed bachelor;[8] he escaped marriage on at least seven occasions, three times only narrowly and "once by disappearing through a window" (Ogden, *Bentham Centenary Lecture* 15). In later life he was the very type of the eccentric and jolly old bachelor, always wearing black suits and a broad-brimmed yellow straw hat and carpet slippers. He was fond of giving possessions playful names: his walking stick was "Dapple," a favorite teapot became "Dick." Actually rather more poetical than Mr. Pickwick, he referred to his daily walks as "postprandial circumgyrations." Going to bed entailed an elaborate one-hour ceremony. After undressing and tying on his night-cap, he handed his watch over to his secretary, who then read aloud to him (Mack 7). Here is a contemporary description of a visit paid to B.'s house in London late in his life by the diplomat Richard Rush, American envoy from 1817 to 1825 (and here one may recall Mr. Pickwick's description of the house in London to which he plans to retire [57:892]):

> In a little while I reached the purlieus of Queen Square Place [not in Mr. Pickwick's Dulwich, but Westminster]. The farther I advanced, the more confined was the space. At length turning through a gateway, the passage was so narrow that I thought the wheels would have grazed. It was a kind of blind-alley, the end of which widened into a small, neat court-yard. There, by itself, stood . . . Mr. B.'s house. Shrubbery graced its area, and flowers its window-sills. It was like an oasis in the desert, Its name is the Hermitage.
>
> Entering, he received me with the simplicity of a philosopher. . . . Every thing inside of the house was orderly. The furniture seemed to have been unmoved since the days of his fathers. . . . A parlour, library, and dining-room, made up the suite of apartments. In each was a piano, the eccentric master of the whole being fond of music as the recreation of his literary hours. It was a unique, romantic little homestead. Walking with him into his garden, I found it dark with the shade of ancient trees. In one part was a high dead wall, the back of a neighbour's house. . . . In that house, he informed me, Milton had lived. Perceiving that I took an interest in hearing it, he soon afterwards obtained a relic, and sent it to me. . . .   The company was small, but choice. . . . Mr. B. did not talk much. He had a benevolence of manner, suited to the philanthropy of his mind. He seemed to be thinking only of the convenience and pleasure of his guests, not as a rule of artificial breeding, . . . but from innate feeling. . . .
>
> After we rose from table, . . . Mr. B. sought conversation with me about [government in] the United States. . . . "[W]hat is this," he inquired, "called a Board of Navy Commissioners that you have lately set up? I don't understand it." I explained it to him. "I can't say that I like it," he replied; "the simplicity of your public departments has heretofore been one of their recommendations, but *boards* make *screens*. If any thing goes wrong, you don't know where to

find the offender; it was the board that did it, not one of the members; always the *board*, the *board*!'' (Qtd. in Ogden, *Bentham Centenary Lecture* 88–90)

B. was himself frequently to be rebuffed by officialdom. A friend writes (Wilberforce, quoted by Stephen 1:206):

Never was any one worse used. I have seen the tears run down the cheeks of that strong-minded man through vexation . . . at the indolence of official underlings when day after day he was begging at the Treasury for what was indeed a mere matter of right.[9]

The Circumlocution Office was understandably a favorite target, but not his first. His greatest indignation and indeed the inspiration for his life of reform was his horror at the inefficiency and plain dishonesty and jobbery of the English legal system. When only eleven, and having already been fascinated by *Gil Blas, Gulliver's Travels, Clarissa,* and *Pamela* (Everett *17–18), he came upon perhaps the most influential book he ever read, the best-selling and sensational three-volume memoirs of a prostitute, An Apology for the Conduct of Mrs. T. C. Phillips.* Full of accounts of lurid dissipations among the high and low life of England, France, and America, the book also contained an extremely detailed account of the continuing ruin of Mrs. Phillips' life: not her career as a prostitute, but rather a series of lawsuits (in Doctors' Commons, the Court of Arches, the Court of Delegates, and eventually in the Court of Chancery) that grew out of her one moment of lapsing into conspicuous respectability: her marriage to a solid member of the middle class. Her good husband's family decided that the marriage should be annulled, though her husband had known during their courtship of his wife's prostitution; he won his first suit by bribing a witness and later he even more cannily married the daughter of a drinking companion of the Masters in Chancery. The lawsuits eventually cost Mrs. Phillips £20,000 in legal fees, and she undertook the writing of her memoirs in hopes of paying her very large debts—whether she succeeded or not I do not know; her Chancery suit was in any case still unresolved as she finished the last volume (Mack 36–39). Young Master B. was deeply affected by this woman's persecution at the hands of English law, and resolved to devote himself to reforming it. As he later wrote:

[W]hile reading and musing [over the memoirs], the Daemon of Chicane appeared in all his hideousness. What followed? I abjured his empire. I vowed war against him. (Mack 40)

But he elected at first to wage war from within, and when only fifteen he began his training for the law—at precisely the same age that Dickens began work as an office boy for Ellis and Blackmore, attorneys of Gray's Inn (Johnson 47). Master B. stayed with the law a little longer than Dickens. For three years he daily observed the workings of English justice in the Court of the King's Bench at Westminster Hall as a pupil of Lord Mansfield. In due course he was called to the bar and actually began to represent clients in a couple of suits, but quickly began to wish in most unlawyerlike fashion to "put them [the suits, not the clients] to death," and in fact he urged one client to drop his suit as not worth the expense (Stephen 174).

We come now to the public aspects and better-known part of B.'s life. Instead of the profession of the law, he devoted himself to promoting his ideas first on legal reform and then on a whole series of related ethical, philosophical, and proto-sociological topics. Among the recurrent objects of his reforming zeal (and here again we are reminded no doubt more of Dickens than Mr. Pickwick himself) were of course the poor laws, prisons, sanitation, the disposition of the dead, and, most broadly, the fundamental philosophical problems underlying these issues—problems in ethics and language—as well as the practical question of how to move public opinion and do real, tangible good in the world. Although he did a lot of publishing, the vast bulk of what he wrote has never been published except as edited by others from very unfinished manuscripts, and his influence has been felt rather more indirectly through the work of the members of his "club" than directly through his own words.[10] This is unfortunate, both because Mr. B. has never had as good a biographer as Mr. Pickwick has, and because his followers in many respects stand in relation to him rather as Messrs. Tupman, Winkle, and Snodgrass do in relation to the immortal Pickwick: they are—particularly when it comes not just to benevolence, but to real tenderness of disposition—only faint reflections of his shining example.

Now clearly my survey of these facts of B.'s life has been carefully edited. Bentham really did have a faith in logic and calculation quite beyond Mr. Pickwick's, and his thinking about the Poor Laws, for example, led to certainly the greatest quarrel that Dickens ever picked with the utilitarians. But the quarrel, it is important to note, is one about means, not ends, and in fact the satire of *Oliver Twist* against the New Poor Law of 1834 is waged by Dickens on strictly Benthamite grounds: what is wrong with the law in Dickens' view is precisely that it does *not* promote happiness. Thus it is Bentham's *ethical* theory, which underlies both his psychology and all the specific reforms he and his followers proposed, that I want to identify with Dickens and Pickwick.

Dickens' contemporaries, and quite possibly Dickens himself, thought of him as an anti-utilitarian because he so loudly and effectively satirized many utilitarian practices and proposals, most conspicuously of course in the *Christmas Books* and *Hard Times*. He may have thought he was showing up utilitarianism also in those many passages in which he satirizes a psychology of selfishness (such as the scene in which Fagin instructs Noah Claypole in the philosophy of "number one" [*Oliver Twist* 43:293]). But if that is what Dickens thought he was doing, he was wrong, and in that case too he got Bentham's psychology wrong.[11] Bentham's ethics famously—and correctly—reduce to the Greatest Happiness Principle, which most simply states that the single absolute ethical obligation is to aim at increasing the happiness of the greatest number, or "pleasure" of the greatest number or, in a single word, "utility," which word Bentham came to regret using, as not widely suggestive either of the happiness of the greatest number nor indeed pleasure at all (*Principles of Morals and Legislation* 1n).[12] The principle of utility is hardly original to Bentham; what is original is his consistently holding it up as the sole ethical obligation throughout a long philosophical career. Chief among the consequences Bentham understood to follow from accepting utility as the ultimate ethical obligation, and a large part of his point in reducing all ethics to this one test, is of course to deny all other absolute ethical obligations (and rights): to God and country, duty, ethical "intuitions," virtue, justice—indeed any and all abstract ethical notions (that is, one not couched in terms of pleasure), which Bentham regarded as merely dangerous fictions. The principle is in fact quite complicated in its assumptions and consequences—which is why for two hundred years it has retained in philosophical circles an extremely prominent as well as controversial position.[13]

One thing immediately deserving of notice is that on the one hand it privileges pleasure as the only good, but on the other it privileges no individual's pleasure over any other's. Pleasure necessarily is experienced only by individuals, but in valuing everyone's pleasure equally Bentham's ethics have as a permanent feature a tension between the individual and the community. Bentham and his followers—notably John Stuart Mill—regarded the rightness of the principle as "at once unnecessary and impossible" to prove (Bentham, *Principles* 4).[14] But if there is something almost self-evident about the goodness of pleasure, it does not seem foolish to ask why everybody's pleasure should be as good as everybody else's, or more particularly, why you should regard the pursuit of my pleasure as carrying the force of as much ethical obligation as the pursuit of your own. Ironically, it is just this radically egalitarian aspect of the principle that most people outside the utilitarian club (as well as some within it) have either never quite appreciated or badly misinterpreted. Thus the utilitarians were frequently and inconsistently both accused of promoting a doctrine of selfishness and ridiculed for promoting measurs directed against acts that assisted individuals merely.[15]

Of course a great deal of the hostility directed against the utilitarians derived from their own apparent and sometimes real hostility to religion. For while almost everyone will agree that pleasure is good and pain is bad, it would seem to require a thoroughly secular view to admit pleasure as the *only* good. This is not quite the case, for as both Bentham and John Stuart Mill recognized, utilitarianism has no necessary quarrel on the one hand with the supernatural nor on the other with a God who is entirely benevolent in the sense of wishing only the happiness of his creatures. Both Bentham and John Stuart Mill write sympathetically about Christian ethics,[16] and in fact the most widely read articulation of utilitarian ethics before Bentham (not much before: in 1785, just two years before the first edition of Bentham's *Principles of Morals and Legislation*) occurs in William Paley's theologically orthodox *The Principles of Moral and Political Philosophy*, which remained a standard textbook at Cambridge well into the nineteenth century and which posited a God characterized precisely by his desire for human happiness. But what utilitarianism consistently has to deny is any God who does not subscribe to—indeed, is not subservient to—the principle of utility and has not given mankind the power—namely, reason—to figure out that principle for itself, and any God must be denied whose power to produce pleasure and alleviate pain is not in any case severely limited. Utilitarianism must therefore reject any God who expects his will to be obeyed simply because it is his will. Utilitarianism's possible gods therefore not only have limited powers, but must be willing to follow utilitarian ethics.[17] There is consequently a deep quarrel between utilitarianism and any religion—like Christianity—that posits a god who is omnipotent and/or possessed of independent and supreme moral authority.

Pickwickian ethics are usually taken to be essentially Christian. I want to ask whether they do not reduce, rather directly, to utilitarian ethics.

A first obstacle may be apparent in Dickens' own authorial intention clearly announced in the "Preface to the Cheap Edition, 1847" (45), wherein he defends himself against critics who have in fact charged him with irreligiousness:

> Lest there should be any well-intentioned persons who do not perceive the difference . . . between religion and the cant of religion, piety and the pretence of piety, a humble reverence for the great truths of scripture and an audacious

and offensive obtrusion of its letter and not its spirit in the commonest dissensions and meanest affairs of life . . . , let them understand that it is always the latter, and never the former, which is satirized here.

This is disingenuous if strictly speaking true: *The Pickwick Papers* never satirizes religion, piety, or "the great truths of scripture" per se. But it does satirize a number of doctrines dear to Christian enthusiasts: the conviction of sin and corollary importance of the Atonement, the importance of a second spiritual rebirth, and the importance of missionary work; and it satirizes enthusiasm itself.[18] The Rev. Stiggins is undoubtedly satirized because he is a hypocrite, but we are given no counter-examples of what true piety might look like; there are not here—nor indeed anywhere in Dickens—any good Christian enthusiasts. This is not of course to deny that there are plenty of good Christians in Dickens' work; but their Christianity is, we might say, all in the closet.

Nor is the satire of Stiggins merely incidental. Though it begins late in the text (in ch. 22), it is one of the first things to greet the reader, for the "beautiful and exhilarating sight" of Tony Weller beating and "immersing Mr. Stiggins's head in a horse-trough full of water, and holding it there, until he was half suffocated" (52:836) forms the unexpected subject of Phiz's illustration for the title page and therefore in some sense stands for the novel as a whole.[19] The satire on Stiggins too is literally central in that we actually first meet Stiggins at the beginning of the tenth number and by way of preface to the novel's positive ethical vision (and positive religious vision, if it can be said to have one): the chapter celebrating Christmas at Dingley Dell. It therefore forms half of the frame for the celebration of Christmas, the other half being "The Story of the Goblins Who Stole a Sexton"—the story of Gabriel Grub, the minor religious official who is paired with Stiggins as an instance of How Not to Do It. These three chapters, constituting the whole of the tenth number, are pretty plainly the ethical as well as literal center of the novel.

Although the narrator makes fun of the Christian enthusiast's doctrines, his most pointed satire is directed of course against the reverend's hypocrisy—his abandoning himself to the very pleasures he pretends to despise. But in his thinness and red nose and the "fierce voracity" (27:450) with which he pursued them, there are suggestions not merely that they are unwholesome pleasures, but that they fail after all to satisfy. Indeed, it is a remarkable feature of the Pickwickian world that gluttony leads to malnutrition: it is the generous who tend to be fat.[20] Gabriel Grub provides another and clearer instance. As just about every critic has recognized, his misanthropy and subsequent conversion give us an early version of Scrooge's story. He is

> an ill-conditioned, cross-grained, surly fellow—a morose and lonely man, who consorted with nobody but himself, and an old wicker bottle which fitted into his large deep waistcoat pocket—and who eyed each merry face, as it passed him by, with such a deep scowl of malice and ill-humour, as it was difficult to meet, without feeling something the worse for.   (29:480)

His drinking alone—not one of Scrooge's problems—turns out to be very much to the point. As Mr. Wardle puts it, his

> story as at least one moral, if it teach no better one—and that is, that if a man turn sulky and drink by himself at Christmas time, he may make up his mind to be not a bit the better for it: let the spirits be never so good, or let them be even as many degrees beyond proof, as those which Gabriel Grub saw in the Goblin's cavern.   (29:491)

More seriously, the scenes that the goblins have shown him have taught Gabriel

> that men who worked hard and earned their scanty bread with lives of labour, were cheerful and happy; and that to the most ignorant, the sweet face of nature was a never-failing source of cheerfulness and joy. He saw those who had been delicately nurtured, and tenderly brought up, cheerful under privations, and superior to suffering, that would have crushed many of a rougher grain, because they bore within their own bosoms the materials of happiness. . . .   (29:489)

Pleasure is here not just good, but *the* good we are ethically obliged to pursue, especially under difficult circumstances, for the simple reason that if we do not actively pursue and even make it, we are not likely to get it.

There is so little remotely touching on religion in the chapter describing Christmas at Dingley Dell, that it is difficult to demonstrate, other than negatively, actual hostility on the novel's part to religion itself. Except for a joke about religion in the chapter title,[21] I find only two direct references to religion, and one of those is clearly a guilty afterthought: the narrator from 1847 on refers to "this saint Christmas" (small "s" at that, 28:458), whereas in the first edition he had been "quite a country gentleman of the old school" (28:944 n1)—not only no saint, but a Tory! Just before this, the narrator has extolled "the happiness and enjoyment" of Christmas:

> How many families, whose members have been dispersed and scattered far and wide, in the restless struggles of life, are then reunited, and meet once again

in that happy state of companionship and mutual good-will, which is a source of such pure and unalloyed delight, and one so incompatible with the cares and sorrows of the world, that the religious belief of the most civilized nations, and the rude traditions of the roughest savages, alike number it among the first joys of a future condition of existence, provided for the blest and happy!
(28:458)

There is a curious and unthinking assertion here of an association between companionship and the unworldly that leads to thoughts of heaven. But the heaven imagined here is the one *all humans* imagine; it is not merely nondenominational, but broad enough to admit "the roughest savages," and its "first joys" are the human ones of "companionship and mutual good-will," not the pleasure of finally seeing God nor even the reward of eternal life in itself. It is interesting too that such an afterlife, in which one goes to heaven to see friends and family, seems to be reserved for "the blest and happy," not for the lonely and miserable. The imperative again is to *be* happy *now*, and if you expect to go to heaven, you had better make some friends first. Thus the paramount goods of Dingley Dell are not creature comforts alone, but comforts enjoyed in company—and "company" is just the right word in this context, alluding as it does not only to being with others, but specifically to eating with others (companions being literally those with whom we take bread).[22] Pleasure is not just better when pursued in company, pleasure really *means* (in good utilitarian fashion) pleasure shared.

Another apparent obstacle to reducing Pickwickianism to utilitarianism arises in the material for so many of the interpolated tales, but also more widely in the text: the really quite insistent fascination with aggression, death, and mutilations of the body, all of which suggest something much more sinister than the wholesome promotion of happiness—and perhaps here one thinks too of Joe, the fat boy, who "wants to make your flesh creep" (8:180).[23] The first several episodes of the novel all threaten physical violence, and early in chapter 2 Jingle tells a story about a decapitation in his own violently chopped up style: "other day—five children—mother—tall lady, eating sandwiches—forgot the arch—crash—knock—children look round—mother's head off—sandwich in her hand—no mouth to put it in" (2:79). Even the paradise of Dingley Dell does not escape these interests. Mr. Pickwick spends *Christmas morning itself* meeting Bob Sawyer and Ben Allen, who are smoking cigars by the kitchen fire, drinking brandy and eating oysters and fowl, and conversing thus:

"Nothing like dissecting to give one an appetite," said Mr. Bob Sawyer, looking round the table. . . .

"By the bye, Bob," said Mr. Allen, "have you finished that leg yet?"
"Nearly," replied Sawyer, helping himself to half a fowl as he spoke. "It's a very muscular one for a child's."
"Is it?" inquired Mr. Allen carelessly.
"Very," said Bob Sawyer, with his mouth full.
'I've put my name down for an arm, at our place, said Mr. Allen. "We're clubbing for a subject, and the list is nearly full, only we can't get hold of any fellow that wants a head. I wish you'd take it." (30:494)

But the ghoulishness of so much of *Pickwick* does not in fact necessarily vitiate its utilitarianism, however much actual utilitarians dourly deplored it. Graveyard humor need not be perverse from a utilitarian standpoint if it gives relish to life, and I would argue that such is precisely the point of the fun that the narrator has with Bob Sawyer. More difficult to explain is the sadism that one senses in some of the interpolated tales and the fat boy, for sadism so complicates the distinction between pleasure and pain as to pose a serious threat to any ethics of pleasure. Indeed, it might seem that in a post-Freudian age utilitarianism itself has to be viewed as hopelessly naïve about the possibilities of pleasure, which helps explain too the current fashion for discussions of "desire"—by definition, pleasure not yet achieved.

Certainly the psychoanalytic appreciation of the repressions blocking the satisfaction of individuals' pleasures makes attaining the utilitarian ideal even more difficult, but there is no reason to suppose that it displaces that ideal. Freud was of course the translator of Mill when a young man, and his entire work is focused on the battle of pleasure against pain. Even the late turn to the repetition compulsion and death instinct—by no means widely accepted among psychoanalytical theorists today in any case—does not displace pleasure and life as the goods against the evils of pain and death, however much gloom it may cast upon the human prospect. The capacity to achieve and experience such pleasures as life may offer remains always for Freud the only imaginable therapeutic and ethical ideal, and a life without any prospect of pleasure was for him literally not worth living. Thus, far from moving us beyond pleasure, psychoanalysis like utilitarianism renders pleasure not a simple matter, but rather a great problem, and indeed the whole problem. While there is reason to charge individual utilitarians with naïveté about the prospects for calculating and achieving pleasure (ironic though it may be to charge supposedly so gloomy a lot with over-optimism), such charges no more displace pleasure as life's ideal any more than the inevitability and pervasiveness of psychopathology do. Moreover, Dickens' appreciation throughout his career of the realities of pain and sadism, and of the complex ways in which pleasure and pain commingle, scarcely compares unfavorably with Freud's and surely contributed to it.[24]

And as every reader must notice, if there is any ambiguity about the view of pain in *Pickwick*, it is cleared up once Mr. Pickwick—who has not seemed to learn anything from the interpolated tales himself; they just tend to put him to sleep—begins to do good empirical research within the confines of the Fleet. It is on the one hand the reality of suffering ("Good fellow," says Jingle, pressing Pickwick's hand in the Fleet, "Ungrateful dog—boyish to cry—can't help it—bad fever—weak—ill—hungry. Deserved it all—but suffered much—very" [42:690]) and on the other hand the endurance of the companionship between Jingle and Job in spite of their suffering (45:731) that override every other ethical consideration. And it is thus the lesson of pain learned in the Fleet that also and finally lays to rest any challenge to Pickwickian utilitarianism in the form of appeals to principles beyond those spelled out by the calculus of pleasure and pain.

For Pickwick apparently goes to jail precisely for anti-utilitarian "principle" (35:577)—which occasions a comic debate between him and Sam, and Sam's story of the man who killed himself on principle (44:707–09)—but it is finally Perker's thoroughly utilitarian argument, an argument for the happiness of the greatest number, that persuades him to get out. Perker advises him thus:

> You have now an opportunity, on easy terms, of placing yourself in a much higher position than you ever could, by remaining here; which would only be imputed, by people who didn't know you, to sheer, dogged, wrongheaded, brutal obstinacy: nothing else, my dear sir, believe me. Can you hesitate to avail yourself of it, when it restores you to your friends, your old pursuits, your health and amusements; when it liberates your faithful and attached servant, whom you otherwise doom to imprisonment for the whole of your life; and above all, when it enables you to take the very magnanimous revenge—which I know, my dear sir, is one after your own heart—of releasing this woman from a scene of misery and debauchery, to which no man should ever be consigned, if I had my will, but the infliction of which on any woman, is even more frightful and barbarous. Now I ask you, my dear sir, not only as your legal adviser, but as your very true friend, will you let slip the occasion of attaining all these objects, and doing all this good, for the paltry consideration of a few pounds finding their way into the pockets of a couple of rascals, to whom it makes no manner of difference, except that the more they gain, the more they'll seek, and so the sooner be led into some piece of knavery that must end in a crash? (47:754–55)

The lesson of the Fleet—the supremacy of the realities of pleasure and pain over abstract or religious morality—are paralleled and underscored by the serious turn which Tony Weller's story takes with the death of Susan and her deathbed recantation of a religion of ascetic "self-indulgence" (which has in fact killed her)[25] in favor of a doctrine of making those around her "more comfortabler," even though that doctrine is cast in the apparently anti-utilitarian form of "dooties" (52:829). But the crucial question from the utilitarian standpoint again is what takes precedence, an abstract duty or a pleasurable consequence? As in the case of religion, utilitarianism has no quarrel with traditional moral categories as long as they are subordinate to the utilitarian end. (Nor does utilitarianism deny that the end may *usually* best be served by adherence to some conventional rule, for the security and predictability afforded by the existence of rules is itself a necessary condition for the stability of any community.)

Much remains to be explored on the subject of *Pickwick* and pleasure. In particular, many readers will want to historicize and materialize the question in ways I have not done. The demonstration of an essential identity between Pickwickian and utilitarian ethics may not surprise or interest critics who see in Bentham "the arch-philistine, . . . the insipid pedantic leather-tongued oracle of the commonplace bourgeois intelligence of the nineteenth century. . . . A genius in the way of bourgeois stupidity." The description is Marx's in *Capital* (2:671).[26] There is certainly no doubt that the ethos of *Pickwick* is bourgeois, nor that the novel seems largely content with relations between masters and servants, husbands and wives, and men and women generally in ways that are offensive today and inconsistent with the radical egalitarianism of utilitarianism.[27] A more productive (because less predictable) project I suspect would be to throw the ethical question back at Marx and explore the relations between Bentham's ethics and Marx's, which are notoriously murky. That is, what ethical aims does Marx uphold if *not* pleasure and the greatest happiness of the greatest number? To what extent are Marxist ethics themselves derived from those of the middle class?[28] Moreover—to complicate the Marxist view further—we need to recognize that utilitarianism cannot consistently ally itself on principle with any economic system (and in fact both Bentham and the younger Mill were socialists for substantial periods). Do the ethics I have described as Pickwickianism necessarily uphold private property and *laissez-faire* capitalism? I suspect not. A second valuable project therefore would be to explore the ways in which the radical disinterestedness of utilitarianism grows out of the middle-class ethos yet subverts much of its economic ideology.

I have been trying in the course of this to be a better Benthamite than Bentham, and I have similarly been arguing in effect that Pickwick (and

Dickens) are better Benthamites than Bentham. When Humphry House concludes that "Pickwick is not Bentham's idea of a moral man" on the grounds that the good Benthamite "has to act from the conviction that it is his duty to promote happiness" (whereas "Pickwick promotes it in spite of himself, almost against his will'[House 38]), we may reply that while many good members of the Benthamite club may have believed themselves to have such a duty, the better Benthamite would have to ignore the question of motive and duty and look only to the consequences of actions. Although we need to be suspicious of moral intuitions, intuitions that actually produce pleasure (and do not actually produce pain) deserve approbation.[29] And we may add that while Pickwick may have benevolent instincts, there is a pretty constant war going on within him between indignation and sympathy; he on more than one occasion has to be argued with and finally, as we have seen, is led out of the Fleet not by instinct but by reasoned conviction.

In conclusion I want to return to the "figure" of Bentham and the question with which I began: was that figure in Dickens' mind when he first "thought of" Mr. Pickwick? For even if Bentham is for our purposes more important as a cultural presence and body of ideas in the world of *Pickwick* than as the imaginative figure of a person present to Dickens' mind, nevertheless some interest still I hope attaches to that mind, the "death of the author" notwithstanding.

As Humphry House notes, however, "[o]ne of the most irritating things about Dickens' biography is that we know so little about his work as a reporter for the House of Commons," during the time, that is, when he was absorbing his knowledge of utilitarianism (House 37). We do know that he counted many prominent utilitarians among his friends and colleagues from very early in his career as a writer: Southwood Smith, Edwin Chadwick, and John Black, to name just three. It was apparently in 1840 that Dickens had his first contact with Smith (to whom Bentham bequeathed his body with directions both for its public dissection and preservation as an "auto-icon," and who later kept the mummy in his consulting room before it went on display at University College [Johnson 313 and Pilgrim Letters 2:164]). The first reference in the correspondence to Chadwick, also a close friend of Bentham's old age, is April 1839 (Pilgrim Letters 1:545). But before this Dickens was well acquainted with men who had been close to Bentham and Bentham's inner circle. Less well known than John Black (the Benthamite editor of the *Morning Chronicle* and close friend of James Mill, as well as the man Dickens credited with being his "first hearty out-and-out appreciator" [Johnson, 181–82]) was James Harfield, a fellow Parliamentary reporter on the *Morning*

Chronicle, certainly known to Dickens as early as February 1834 (Pilgrim Letters 1:36), and who had previously been Bentham's secretary. I would love to know what personal lore of Bentham passed from Harfield and Black to Dickens. It is certainly easy to imagine the editor and his reporters, one of them the intimate of the great man who had died only a couple of years before, the other insatiably curious about everything, chatting and reminiscing in the office about the peculiarities of one of the age's greatest eccentrics. One thing that perhaps unexpectedly strengthens the supposition is the very ambivalence which Dickens evidently first had towards Pickwick. As G. K. Chesterton reminds us concerning Pickwick's origin, "Dickens went into the Pickwick Club to scoff, and Dickens remained to pray." (96). His first intention, that is, seems to have been to satirize a scientific and philosophical club, and its founder as the chief among the fools. Under these circumstances it seems not only not far-fetched, but perfectly natural, that Dickens should have turned to a figure famous for eccentric, quixotic theories that grandiosely embraced ethics, science, logic, epistemology, and politics and that to many seemed to fly in the face both of tradition and common sense. Indeed, the greater wonder may be that having discovered the goodness in Pickwick, Dickens apparently failed, at least consciously, to discover the goodness in Bentham.

NOTES

1. *The Pickwick Papers* (67). Subsequent parenthetical references are to page and chapter. I use the Penguin edition as one of the most widely read. The Clarendon edition, edited by James Kinsley, is of course definitive, and I have checked Patten's readings against Kinsley's.
2. See also the account of the origin of *Pickwick* in the introduction to the Clarendon edition of the novel (xxiii).
3. See also Dickens' Preface to the Cheap Edition of 1847 (rpt. in Patten's edition 45). It is curious that the paragraph in which Dickens explains the origin of his pseudonym "Boz"—from the nickname "Moses" given to a pet younger brother and borrowed from Goldsmith's novel (then facetiously pronounced nasally, then shortened)—occurs without transition at the end of his defense of his own origination of Pickwick and just before a paragraph defending Mr. Pickwick's coherence as a character. There is no manifest reason either for its place in the preface or for its very existence, that is. The implicit logic seems to run: "now that I've justified my claim to be the proprietor of Samuel-not-Moses Pickwick, I'll explain how I came to call myself Boz/Boses/Moses-not-Charles."
4. The most recent article on Dickens' anti-utilitarianism that I am aware of is K. J. Fielding's "Benthamite Utilitarianism and *Oliver Twist*: A Novel of Ideas." Fielding argues that *Oliver Twist* is "an open satire of Benthamite Utilitarianism"

as it was generally known at the time of writing, rather than utilitarianism as later "refined" by J. S. Mill and others (55), and certainly Fielding—arguing from Bentham's *Deontology* and Mill's second essay on Benthamism, written as an appendix to Bulwer's *England and the English*—is quite right that there are large differences both between utilitarianism as articulated by Bentham himself and as it was understood even by the relatively well-informed in the 1830s and between Bentham's and J. S. Mill's accounts. I perhaps see much more consistency between Bentham and Mill than Fielding does, but also would argue that where Bentham and Mill diverge, Dickens would often have sided with Bentham. These important questions require and deserve extended treatment. For a similar argument see also R. J. Arneson. Critics of *Hard Times* have sometimes seen through Dickens' apparent hostility to utilitarianism. See especially Edward Alexander and Sylvia Manning.

5. Williams accepts without demonstration the heart of my claim: "Dickens . . . would have accepted happiness or pleasure as an absolute criterion, as against the emphases of most other contemporary religious and philosophical systems" (88–89). It would be more accurate to distinguish between Dickens and his works, however, for there is plenty of evidence that Dickens was personally a Christian first and a utilitarian second and that while he believed in a utilitarian God who benevolently desired nothing but the happiness of his creation, if put to the choice he would have chosen obedience to God over pleasure "as an absolute criterion." The ethics of the works, I will argue, put utilitarianism first and religion second.

6. Stone does not take up the question of Bentham's or Dickens' underlying ethical theory, however, and thus mentions happiness or pleasure only once and in passing. The relation between Bentham and Dickens on the subject of fictions would be interesting to consider in the light of the more fundamental ethical theory, for it is remarkable that the two writers should be obsessed, even if in sometimes different ways or with different results, by a subject that does not fit neatly or logically into a theory based on pleasure versus pain. For if pleasure and pain are fundamental, the only sources of ethical obligation and the only psychological realities, then the very question of fiction versus truth would seem to vanish into insignificance. The truth, that is, is precisely the sort of moral category, like duty and virtue, that utilitarians might be expected to dismiss (as itself fictional?). And both Bentham and Dickens do appear quite un-utilitarian in their railings against various kinds of falsehood—they appear, that is, to uphold a standard of truthfulness without reference to its consequences for pleasure or pain. Of course it is easy to rescue truthfulness (like duty) as of utility and therefore as having at least a secondary value, but both Dickens and Bentham have much more immediate, stronger, more visceral feelings about truthfulness than we might expect. Perhaps not coincidentally, both Bentham and Dickens were strongly affected as children by the ghost stories told them by their nurses, and Bentham at least seems never to have outgrown the childish terror they inspired. Where Bentham looked under the bed, Dickens' characteristically just got out of it and went for a night-walk. On Bentham's experience of nurses' and others' ghost stories see C. K. Ogden, *Bentham's Theory of Fictions* x–xvi.

7. A theme of Mack's biography is the wrong done Bentham by the younger Mill's portrait, and she convincingly corrects it.

8. Reported by Leslie Stephen in *The English Utilitarians* (1:185–86): "Miss [Caroline] Fox [daughter of Stephen Fox, later Lord Holland] seems to have been the

only woman who inspired Bentham with a sentiment approaching to passion. He
wrote occasional letters to the ladies in the tone of elephantine pleasantry natural
to one who was all his life both a philosopher and a child. He made an offer of
marriage to Miss Fox in 1805, when he was nearer sixty than fifty, and when
they had not met for sixteen years. . . . She replied in a friendly letter, regretting
the pain which her refusal would inflict. In 1827 Bentham, then in his eightieth
year, wrote once more, speaking of the flower she had given him 'in the green
lane,' and asking for a kind answer. He was 'indescribably hurt and disappointed'
by a cold and distant reply. The tears would come into the old man's eyes as he
dwelt upon the cherished memories of Bowood [Lord Shelburne's estate, where
Bentham met Caroline Fox].''

9. It is interesting in this connection to note that B. had a younger brother whose
career quite precisely suggests that of another Dickens character, Daniel Doyce
in *Little Dorrit*. This younger brother (Samuel, familiarly called Sam), was an
inventor who submitted to the Navy Board a design for a bilge pump. The Board
agreed that the design was superior to any they had seen. But they rejected it on
the grounds that it was *so* good that captains of men of war would like it *so* well
that they would not put to sea without the improved pumps on board, which
would occasion all sorts of trouble and expense. Not satisfied with this patently
absurd reasoning, the brothers B. persisted in seeking explanations from the
Circumlocution Office and at last discovered the real reason for Sam's design's
rejection: the Board had at the same time before them an inferior design, but one
that happened to have been submitted by a navy captain who happened to be a
near relation of the duke of Portland. And so rather than hurt the good captain's
and good duke's feelings, the Board elected to accept neither design. After more
such frustrations, the disappointed Sam went off to Russia, much to the sorrow
of his elder brother, and there his talents were quickly recognized and rewarded,
and both he and the Russian navy thrived (Mack 351–67).

10. S. E. Finer shows in great detail how Bentham's ideas were actually promulgated
and put into legislative and administrative practice by his circle, no less effectively
after his death in 1832 than before it. It is an interesting feature of Finer's essay
that is scarcely mentions Bentham at all, however. In fact Bentham was always
engaged in an enormous correspondence with legislative leaders, many of whom
he counted among his circle, so that there was always plenty of direct communication between him and the people originating legislation. Nevertheless, Finer's
work gives the distinct impression that the real work of putting the Benthamite
stamp on legislative and administrative reform was done by followers far more
canny in their manipulations of the political process than their leader.

11. Mack (207) quotes from a late manuscript (1831) Bentham's account of an expanding circle of sympathy that leads the growing child beyond its original
selfishness: ''As age and experience advance . . . [the affection of sympathy]
receives additional force and efficiency. It extends its influence . . . beginning
with the small immediate relations where the ties of consanguinity, affinity,
domestic contract or friendly intercourse are strongest, and advancing with experience and mental culture into a widening field of action. Its links become multifarious, and capable of great extension.''

12. The edition cited reprints the revised edition of 1823. The note explains why the
Greatest Happiness Principle is a better name than the original ''principle of
utility.'' See also Mack 225.

13. Two very good and not overly technical introductions to contemporary debates
about utilitarianism today are Anthony Quinton's *Utilitarian Ethics*, which also

gives a good overview of the history of the surrounding controversies, and J. J. C. Smart's and Bernard Williams's *Utilitarianism: For and Against*. The indispensable history of utilitarian ethics for the early Victorian period is part 1 of J. B. Schneewind, *Sidgwick's Ethics and Victorian Moral Philosophy* (1–187), which covers the history of British ethics from the late seventeenth century until Sidgwick.

14. And see Bentham and Mill 275–76 and 307–14 for Mill's disclaimer that utilitarianism's first principles can be proven.

15. Unfortunately they counted among their own worst enemies in this regard some very regular members of the club, such as Francis Place, who dismissed philanthropy of Mr. Pickwick's type thus: "[The mindlessly benevolent] relieve themselves by the performance of what is vulgarly called charity; they give money, victuals, cloths, &c., and thus by encouraging idleness and extinguishing enterprise, increase the evils they would remove" (Qtd. by Marcus, "The Blest Dawn" 48–49). See also Alexander Welsh's more extended discussion of Victorian attitudes towards "Charity" in his chapter of that name in *The City of Dickens* (86–100).

16. Bentham wrote (and Francis Place edited for him pseudonymously) "Gamaliel Smith," *Not Paul, but Jesus*, which argues that "in the religion of Jesus may be found all the *good* that has ever been the result of the compound so incongruously and unhappily made [of the Gospel's and Paul's Epistles],—in the religion of Paul all the *mischief*, which in such disastrous abundance, has so indisputably flowed from it" (vii). See also Mill's statement in *Utilitarianism* that "In the golden rule of Jesus of Nazareth, we read the complete spirit of the ethics of utility. To do as one would be done by, and to love one's neighbour as oneself, constitute the ideal perfection of utilitarian morality" (Bentham and Mill 288).

17. Indeed, the only god imaginable by John Stuart Mill is one who could not help but will utilitarianism. Thus Mill's possible gods have not even the limited free will he imagines for humans (Bentham and Mill 293–94); and see also his essay "Utility of Religion" in *Three Essays on Religion* (69–122).

18. There is an indispensable account of Dickens' attitudes on these heads throughout his career in Norris Pope's *Dickens and Charity*. See esp. the introduction (1–12) and the chapters "Dickens and Evangelicalism" (13–41), "Defence of the Sabbath" (42–95), and "Missions and Missionaries" (96–151).

19. In the first bound edition, the title page stood opposite the frontispiece, which shows Sam and Mr. Pickwick sitting together around a small table. (These illustrations were of course done last and first appeared in the last number together with the two final illustrations, preface, table of contents, and directions to the binder about where to tip in plates that included no page number.) Mr. Pickwick looks smilingly on Sam, who has his finger on the page of an opened book and returns the benign smile. Perhaps Sam has been reading to Mr. Pickwick and they are pausing to share a joke or other pleasure of the text. There are decanters and two partially filled glasses on the table. There is no indication that we are looking at a master and his servant. The scene is elaborately and theatrically framed in a Gothic arch, decorated with whimsical gargoyle-like impish figures at the top and small medallions with the heads of Snodgrass, Tupman, and Winkle at the bottom. More prominent in the bottom foreground are five laughing goblins—real ones, not part of the architectural decoration—dressed in the style of the goblins of the interpolated tale of "The Story of the Goblins who stole a Sexton," two of whom open billowing curtains just behind the arch and thus disclose the

pleasant, private domestic scene of the two Sams within. The frontispiece thus forms an interesting contrast with the violent vignette of the title page. Sam Weller appears there too, cheering his father on, but standing in the background in the doorway of the Marquis of Granby, and thus framed again by a rather elaborate arch, this time a rococo one, embellished by fat and jolly Bacchus-like classical figures. Together these two illustrations provide an unusually rich field for interpretation. There is an important discussion of the frontispiece by Robert L. Patten.

20. It may be due to Phiz's inexperience, but all the skinny, hypocritical, and selfish men in the novel—Stiggins, Job Trotter, Gabriel Grubb—look in his etchings like one another. The fat boy is an interesting exception to what might seem the contrary of the general rule: he is fat *and* selfish. But he is also presented as pathological, and in fact has been cited as an example of Dickens' clinically precise observation—so precise that it turns out Dickens was the first to describe the syndrome now known since 1956 through a predictable semantic slippage as "Pickwickian syndrome." This is characterized, as one of the "Fellowship Notes" in the *Dickensian* (68 [1972]: 201) tells us, by "obesity, excessive sleepiness during the day, heart failure, and a breathing difficulty which exists only during sleep. . . ." The syndrome is alive and well. A recent search in the MEDLINE database retrieved more than a dozen articles in the last five years.

21. The joke bewails the fact that even the secular customs ("Sports") of Christmas are "not quite so religiously kept up, in these degenerate times" as the custom of marriage, of course also celebrated in the Christmas chapter, in the wedding of Bella Wardle and Mr. Trundle (28:457).

22. An obvious reverberation in Pickwick's name, though I do not recall having seen it mentioned in Pickwick criticism is "picnic" (sometimes spelt "picknick"). The echo was picked up, probably by Dickens himself (see the Pilgrim Edition of the Letters of Charles Dickens 1:425n), in the title of *The Pic Nic Papers*, the book he edited (1838 to 1841) to benefit the widow of the publisher of *Sketches by Boz*. In the early nineteenth century, a picnic was typically an entertainment (indoors or not) to which each guest brought contribution for the provisions (and hence its appropriateness for a miscellany by many hands), not exclusively the sort of alfresco meal the Pickwickians enjoy in ch. 19. But either sense is appropriate to the novel.

23. Although bizarre, the novel's brutality about the body is also characteristic of the period in which it was set, which was at once anxious about and fascinated by horrible deaths and the vicissitudes of the grave. This is of course the period of Burke and Hare and their less well-known legislative inheritance, the Benthamite Anatomy Act of 1829, which is the central subject of Ruth Richardson's *Death, Dissection and the Destitute*. George Ford shrewdly attributes the popularity of *Pickwick* in part to its ability to bridge Regency high spirits and brutality on the one hand and the emerging culture of Victorianism on the other (esp. 12–14).

24. The most provocative claims for the influence of Dickens on Freud are made by Ned Lukacher, who argues nothing less than that Dickens is Freud's original, that Freud really gets the theory out of Dickens' work.

25. She has caught a cold from "imprudently settin too long on the damp grass in the rain a hearin of a shepherd who warnt able to leave off till late at night owen to his havin wound his-self up vith brandy and vater . . ." (52:826).

26. For a Marxist account of the *Pickwick* period—it says next to nothing about the novel itself—see N. N. Feltes.

27. I believe that Dickens progressively realizes the egalitarianism of his ethics as his work grows, but Bentham realized it from the beginning and is justly credited for his feminism (recall his reading of Mrs. T. C. Phillips's memoirs), which the utilitarians largely forgot until Harriet Taylor went to work on John Stuart Mill. Less well-known are his writings on sexual freedom. See Ogden, *Bentham Centenary Lecture* (94–105) for a remarkable discussion of sex, prostitution, and homosexuality.
28. See Eugene Kamenka, *Marxism and Ethics*; Philip J. Kain, *Marx and Ethics* (esp. 72, 102); D. Allen, "The Utilitarianism of Marx and Engels"; G. G. Brenkert, "Marx and Utilitarianism"; Allen's "Reply to Brenkert's 'Marx and Utilitarianism'"; and Brenkert's "Marx's Critique of Utilitarianism."
29. For the Victorians, the question of the status of moral intuitions was central and divided the utilitarians from just about everyone else. See for example Henry Sidgwick, *Outlines of the History of Ethics* (xxv). So intent on denying the reality of innate ideas were the empiricist-utilitarians that they often failed to see the inconsistency (from the utilitarian standpoint) of opposing intuitions without attending to their actual consequences.

WORKS CITED

Alexander, Edward. "Disinterested Virtue: Dickens and Mill in Agreement." *Dickensian* 65 (1969): 163–70.

Allen, D. "The Utilitarianism of Marx and Engels." *American Philosophical Quarterly* 10 (1973): 189–99.

———. "Reply to Brenkert's 'Marx and Utilitarianism." *Canadian Journal of Philosophy* 6 (1976): 517–34.

Arneson, R. J. "Benthamite Utilitarianism and *Hard Times.*" *Philosophy and Literature* 2 (1978): 60–75.

Bentham, Jeremy. *Not Paul, but Jesus.* London: Hunt, 1823.

———. *The Principles of Morals and Legislation.* New York: Hafner, 1948.

———, and John Stuart Mill. *Utilitarianism and Other Essays.* Ed. Alan Ryan. Harmondsworth: Penguin, 1987.

Brenkert, G. G. "Marx and Utilitarianism." *Canadian Journal of Philosophy* 5 (1975) 421–34.

———. "Marx's Critique of Utilitarianism." *Marx and Morality*, ed. K. Nielsen and S. C. Patten. *Canadian Journal of Philosophy* supp. vol. 7 (1981): 193–220.

Chesterton, G. K. *Charles Dickens.* 1906. New York: Schocken, 1965.

Dickens, Charles. *The Letters of Charles Dickens.* Ed. Madeline House, Graham Storey, and Kathleen Tillotson. Pilgrim Ed. Oxford: Clarendon, 1965.

————. *Oliver Twist*. Ed. Kathleen Tillotson. Oxford: Clarendon, 1966.

————. *The Posthumous Papers of the Pickwick Club*. Ed. James Kinsley. Oxford: Clarendon, 1986.

————. *The Posthumous Papers of the Pickwick Club*. Ed. Robert L. Patten. Harmondsworth: Penguin, 1972.

Everett, Charles Warren. *The Education of Jeremy Bentham*. New York: Columbia UP, 1931. 17–18.

Feltes, N. N. "The Production of a Commodity-Text: The Moment of Pickwick." *Modes of Production of Victorian Novels*. Chicago: U of Chicago P, 1986. 1–17.

Fielding, K. J. "Benthamite Utilitarianism and *Oliver Twist*: A Novel of Ideas." *Dickens Quarterly* 4 (1987): 49–65.

Finer, S. E. "The Transmission of Benthamite Ideas 1820–50." *Studies in the Growth of Nineteenth-Century Government*. Ed. Gillian Sutherland. Totowa: Rowan, 1972. 11–32.

Ford, George. *Dickens and His Readers: Aspects of Novel-Criticism since 1836*. 1955. New York: Norton, 1965.

Forster, John. *The Life of Charles Dickens*, ed. A. J. Hoppé. 2 vols. London: Dent, 1966.

House, Humphry. *The Dickens World*. 2nd ed. Oxford: Oxford UP, 1942.

Johnson, Edgar. *Charles Dickens: His Tragedy and Triumph*. 2 vols. Boston: Little, 1952.

Kain, Philip J. *Marx and Ethics*. Oxford: Clarendon, 1988.

Kamenka, Eugene. *Marxism and Ethics*. London: Macmillan, 1969.

Lukacher, Ned. *Primal Scenes: Literature, Philosophy, Psychoanalysis*. Ithaca: Cornell UP, 1986.

Mack, M. P. *Jeremy Bentham: An Odyssey of Ideas*. New York: Columbia UP, 1963.

Manning, Sylvia. "*Hard Times* in the Classroom." *Dickens World* 4 (June 1989): 1–5.

Marcus, Steven. "The Blest Dawn." *Dickens: From Pickwick to Dombey*. New York: Basic, 1965. 13–53.

————. "Language into Structure: Pickwick Revisited." *Daedalus: Journal of the American Academy of Arts and Sciences* 101 (1972): 183–202.

Marx, Karl. *Capital*. Trans. Eden and Cedar Paul. 2 vols. New York: Dutton, 1962.

Mill, John Stuart. *Three Essays on Religion*. 1874. New York: Greenwood, 1969.

Ogden, C. K. *Bentham's Theory of Fictions*. Paterson: Littlefield, 1959.

————. *Jeremy Bentham: 1832–1932, Being the Bentham Centenary Lecture, Delivered in University College, London, on June 6th, 1932*. London: Kegan, 1932.

Patten, Robert L. "The Art of *Pickwick*'s Interpolated Tales." *ELH* 34 (1967): 349–66.

Pope, Norris. *Dickens and Charity*. New York: Columbia UP, 1978.

Quinton, Anthony. *Utilitarian Ethics*. London: Macmillan, 1973.

Richardson, Ruth. *Death, Dissection and the Destitute*. London: Routledge, 1987.

Schneewind, J. B. *Sidgwick's Ethics and Victorian Moral Philosophy*. Oxford: Clarendon, 1977.

Sidgwick, Henry. *Outlines of the History of Ethics*. 5th ed. London: Macmillan, 1902.

Smart, J. J. C., and Bernard Williams. *Utilitarianism: For and Against*. 1973. Cambridge: Cambridge UP, 1987.

Stephen, Sir Leslie. *The English Utilitarians*. 3 vols. London: Duckworth, 1900.

Stone, Marjorie. "Dickens, Bentham, and the Fictions of the Law: A Victorian Controversy and its Consequences." *Victorian Studies* 29 (1985): 215–54.

Welsh, Alexander. *The City of Dickens*. Oxford: Clarendon, 1971.

Williams, Raymond. "Dickens and Social Ideas." *Dickens 1970*. Ed. Michael Slater. London: Chapman, 1970. 77–97.

Nicholas Nickleby: Parody on the Plains of Syria

Sylvia Manning

> One of the many to whom, from straitened circumstances, a consequent inability to form the associations they would wish, and a disinclination to mix with the society they could obtain, London is as complete a solitude as the plains of Syria . . .[1]
>
> (description of Miss La Creevy; chapter 20)

Through nineteen months of composition, Dickens complained of difficulty in getting *Nicholas Nickleby* going, keeping it going, and bringing it to an end, from a letter that is probably the 17th of February, 1838, to Forster ("Being utterly unable from intense stupidity to write a line, I have gone out riding . . .")[2] and another on (probably) March 8th:

> Thank God, all continues to go on well [in regard to the birth of Mamie at 1:00 a.m. on March 6]—except Nickleby and he does *not* go on well, and therefore we do *not* dine together, but I stick to it, in thorough style until a late hour of the night, and hope I shall be able really to "report progress" tomorrow.

—to a diary entry in September, 1839: "Finished Nickleby this day at 2 o'clock . . . Thank God that I have lived to get through it happily." That this thankfulness is more than simple pietism is attested by his letter to Forster on September 18: "I shall not finish entirely, before Friday— . . . I have had pretty stiff work as you may suppose, and I have taken great pains."

The intervening comments of this sort are numerous.[3] The reviewers, of course, sensed the problem. *The Examiner* lavished praise on character and setting, but complained that Dickens:

> has yet to acquire the faculty of constructing a compact and effective story. . . . A want of plan is apparent in it from the first, an absence of design. The plot

73

seems to have grown as the book appeared by numbers, instead of having been mapped out beforehand. The attention is ever and anon diverted from the story by digressions, introduced for the apparent uses of mere contrast and effect, while abrupt and startling recurrences are thus of course rendered necessary to recal [*sic*] us to the main interest and action. Admirable and very plausible reasons might no doubt be urged for all this, yet should none be admitted that contravene the sounder claims and more enduring requisites of high and perfect Art.[4]

Fraser's was less sure about the praiseworthiness of the characters, finding Nicholas "but the walking thread-paper to convey the various threads of the story" and several others inconsistent, especially Ralph, for whom

> . . . it is quite as probable that he would have been foiled by Lord Verisopht or Smike, as by a couple of such unredeemed and irredeemable idiots as the Brothers Cheeryble. Mr. Dickens assures us in his preface that he has drawn these insufferable bores from actual life. It may be so; if it be, we recommend him to abstain from the life academies which furnish no better subjects.[5]

After lambasting several characters and detailing Boz's ignorance of the law, the review proceeds to his "only fault," in which "the necessity of filling a certain quantity of pages per month imposed upon the writer a great temptation to amplify trifling incidents, and to swell sentence after sentence with any sort of words that would occupy space." This "spirit of a penny-a-liner" mars both *Nickleby* and *Oliver Twist*, which are stuffed with " 'passages that lead to nothing,' merely to fill the necessary room." In consequence, the review ends by bidding Dickens "not good *speed*, but good moderation of pace. . . ."

Was it simply that Dickens was writing too fast, or was writing too many things at once, or was pressed to write up to a set length with a set deadline for each number? What made it so doubtful that Dickens could get a plot running and keep it going?

Digression is the obvious form of impediment. In the first two numbers, it is almost thematized. By the end of the tenth paragraph of the first chapter, the narrative has gotten itself too involved with Ralph, or at least so the narrator seems to think. He assures his readers that Ralph will not be the hero of the work: "To set this point at rest for once and for ever, we hasten to undeceive them, and stride to its commencement." But we don't stride very far. The remainder of the chapter covers the bankrupting of Nicholas's father and chapter 2 takes us right back to Ralph. A finely detailed description of his dress and powder in the fourth paragraph concludes that these details "had not the smallest effect, good or bad, upon anybody just then, and are consequently no business of ours right now." And so the narrative picks up again and strides directly to the United Metropolitan Improved Hot Muffin and Crumpet Baking and Punctual Delivery Company, a name albeit parodic of names typical of such scams,[6] equally emblematic of the novel itself, of which verbosity and by-ways are multiply characteristic.

The achievement of forward motion may then be represented in the coach that sets off from the Saracen's head to carry Nicholas into Yorkshire. It breaks down: the coach doesn't make it to Yorkshire and the narrative stops for the interpolated tales of the Five Sisters of York and the Baron of Grogzwig.

Not only the narrator, but the characters within the narrative are subject to this digressive tendency. Mrs. Nickleby exhibits it most acutely. Ralph comes to say that he has found a situation for Kate:

> "Well," replied Mrs. Nickleby. "Now, I will say that this is only just what I have expected of you. 'Depend upon it,' I said to Kate, only yesterday morning at breakfast, 'that after your uncle has provided, in that most ready manner, for Nicholas, he will not leave us until he has done at least the same for you.' These were my very words, as near as I remember. Kate, my dear, why don't you thank your— —"   (chapter 10)

This is not just wordy: it is a little narrative of her conversation yesterday at breakfast, an interpolated tale complete with characters and dialogue. Other characters too interpolate tales: Miss La Creevy, for instance (the story of her brother in chapter 31), and Tim Linkinwater (the sickly child, chapter 40).

Mrs. Nickleby is ludicrous because she cannot sense the appropriate scope of discourse. It is not clear that the novel proceeds differently, at least if one assumes that plot is a controlling purpose parallel to the purpose of a conversation. Writing after Peter Garrett, one might question that assumption, arguing instead that in this novel "the multiplication and division of both narrative perspectives and developments produce unresolvable tensions because they articulate an underlying dialogue between irreducibly different structural principles, between the centripetal impulse that organizes narrative around the development of a protagonist and the impulse that elaborates an inclusive pattern of simultaneous relationships."[7] But I do not believe that *Nicholas Nickleby* is a "Victorian multiplot novel" of the sort Garrett describes. What opposes the centripetal plot of the hero is not an elaborated spatial pattern of "adjacent, analogous actions," nor is it "assimilated into a larger system of causes and effects." Rather, it is an irruptive, implosive force, not plural, social, or general, but scattershot, atomistic, and eccentric.

The centripetal plot is foiled repeatedly by the powerful impulses that drove everything from the *Sketches* and *Pickwick* to Dickens's comic roulade on the marriage of Queen Victoria. We can recognize those impulses as parody, understood in its broadest sense. David Musselwhite sees *Nickleby* as a failure of nerve, the shift-point from the collective, rhizomic mode of Boz to the familial romance, tree-structure mode of Dickens, from "anarchic energy" to a "more authoritative and collected narrative control."[8] Musselwhite prefers the former and finds political significance in the difference. With a similar preference but a very different set of terms, Margaret Ganz identifies the same centripetal effort of the plot, and the resistance to it: "Clearly a profusion of humorous figures resisting diminution is bound to threaten the orderly progression of a narrative that at least purports to be realistic."[9] She thinks that Dickens often sacrifices those characters to efforts at plot and finds this choice unfortunate because "a sentimental and melodramatic plot" is not worth it. What threatens—and generally defeats—the orderly progression of the narrative, however, is more than a profusion of humorous figures: it is the very form of the narrative itself. Digression, in fact, is not so much an impediment to forward movement as the failure itself of such movement, not a cause but a symptom. What keeps the story from achieving shape, as narrative and also as ethos, is the pervasion of parody.

This is a novel of the excluded subject and the desire for inclusion, a novel with multiple settings all on the plains of Syria. Robin Gilmour sees it as focussed upon a near-universal aspiration to a higher gentility.[10] More broadly, I would suggest, the novel projects the sense of exclusion, differing from a later generation's alienation in the open and obsessive desire to gain entrance. In this regard Miss La Creevy has been an exception, but is no longer: the paragraph from which this essay takes its epigraph goes on to describe the renewal of friendly impulses when she met the Nickleby family. Exclusion is from the next social level up, as Gilmour demonstrates, but it is also from the comfort of personal intimacy, most frequently represented as marriage, and from the comfort of economic security. (Economic security, which the Cheerybles finally provide, is not the same as economic life, which, as commentators on Dickens have often remarked, appears in *Nickleby* and in most of Dickens only in demonic forms.) The image of exclusion at its most primitive is Smike cold, deprived of access to the fire at Dotheboys. At its most refined, it is Sir Mulberry Hawk refusing to give Nicholas his name, excluding him from the privilege of a gentleman's quarrel (chapter 32).

The effect of the parody is to cast doubt upon every possibility of inclusion as it arises, upon the rationality of the desire for it and upon the ontological status of inclusion itself. The narrative peppers a plot that requires identification with the desire for inclusion, with parody that undermines it. Not only passages, but the entire story threatens to "lead to nothing," until at the end Dickens forces a resolution. To that point—and in some degree, even through it—the persistent parody creates a narrative in which the typical move is to go somewhere and then find that it is nowhere, to achieve something and then discover it was not worth achieving, to want something and then learn that it is dross, until the very possibility of a resting-place is itself in question. The fire denied Smike is after all the Squeers hearth; the contest Nicholas seeks is not with a gentleman but with a dissipated parasite.

The forms of parody in this novel may best be understood by starting from the theory of parody developed by Linda Hutcheon for modern parody, which she defines as "repetition with critical distance," "a stylistic confrontation" that "establishes difference at the heart of similarity."[12] Most of the parodies in *Nickleby* are stylistic or narrative similarities that point to putative difference and cause that difference to teeter. An episode may be repeated in a different register, or a register may be repeated in different circumstances. Either way, the parody threatens to collapse the two terms into each other, to the eclipse of both. The repetition-with-distance of a text creates uncertainty about the moral or ethical valence of both terms. It need not be comic, but usually is.

This repetition, for the most part, takes place entirely within the text of *Nickleby*. A signal characteristic of its parody is that, with one major and one minor exception, the texts parodied are other portions of the novel; that is, most of the parody is self-parody. The two exceptions, the Crummles repertory and "The Lady Flabella," as we shall see, operate both internally and externally. As Hutcheon claims in her very brief attention to self-parody, self-parodic art "calls into question . . . its own identity" (Hutcheon, 10). *Nickleby*, riddled with parody, hints not only the delusory nature of the desire it represents but the factitiousness of itself as representation.

Repetition with distance marks the very first paragraphs of the novel. The story opens:

> There once lived, in a sequestered part of the county of Devonshire, one Mr. Godfrey Nickleby: a worthy gentleman, who, taking it into his head rather late in life that he must get married, and not being young enough or rich enough to aspire to the hand of a lady of fortune, had wedded an old flame out of mere attachment, who in her turn had taken him for the same reason. Thus two

people who cannot afford to play cards for money, sometimes sit down to a
quiet game for love. (chapter 1)

This paragraph appears to establish some norms: that the young and the rich
who marry for money deserve satire, that those who have neither youth nor
fortune may chance instead upon "a quiet game for love." The falling rhythm
of that last sentence lands us quite firmly on a central triad of Dickensian
values: old (the "old flame"), quiet, and love.

Then comes the next paragraph:

> Some ill-conditioned persons who sneer at the life-matrimonial, may perhaps
> suggest, in this place, that the good couple would be better likened to two
> principals in a sparring match, who, when fortune is low and backers scarce,
> will chivalrously set to, for the mere pleasure of the buffeting; and in one
> respect indeed this comparison would hold good; for, as the adventurous pair
> of the Fives' Court will afterwards send round a hat, and trust to the bounty
> of the lookers-on for the means of regaling themselves, so Mr. Godfrey Nick-
> leby and *his* partner, the honey-moon being over, looked wistfully out into the
> world, relying in no inconsiderable degree upon chance for the improvement
> of their means.

This paragraph repeats the explanation of the marriage, but in the name of
"ill-conditioned persons" substitutes a more cynical simile, with the advantage in credibility that cynicism always enjoys over sentiment. Then, as
Dickens develops the simile into syllogism, he shifts the middle term, from
boxing to handball, so that the like behavior of the Nicklebys and the Fives
players seems to endorse the likeness of their marriage to a sparring match.
As that likeness opposes the quiet game of cards, the final sentence opposes
the final sentence of the previous paragraph. In place of the periodic melody of
the other, we get absolute flatness in rhythm and substance: "Mr. Nickleby's
income, at the period of his marriage, fluctuated between sixty and eighty
pounds *per annum*." In place of old, quiet love, we are offered a game of
violence and cold calculation. We do not yet know which description is true
of this marriage, and although much in the rhetoric supports the values of
the first paragraph, the parody in the second has at least questioned our
confidence in their reality. The first doubt about marriage as a reprieve from
exclusion has been seeded; it will blossom in the novel's final chapters.

The narrative has begun by starting off in two opposing directions. The
uncertainty of satiric direction continues immediately in the presentation of
the young Ralph, Godfrey's elder son, and Nicholas, Godfrey's younger son
and our hero's father. For if Ralph, who has learned from his father's early
trials to value money above all else, is a precocious young shark and a

loveless adult, Nicholas, who learned to shun the great world and married and bore children and loved and cared for them, is a fool. He speculates foolishly, and dies. When the bubble burst, the narrative tells us, "four hundred nobodies were ruined, and among them Mr. Nickleby"; the "nobodies" is first a satire upon the indifference and irresponsibility of the stockbrokers who escaped to villas in Florence, but by the end of the chapter it is clearly also a just description of Mr. Nickleby.

I have belabored this doubleness of direction because it is characteristic of the entire narrative. Although it appears as a matter of ethos and not plot, it nonetheless effectively impedes forward movement of the story. Again, Mrs. Nickleby's narrative habits are representative. In chapter 10, Ralph assures her that dressmakers in London can make large fortunes and after some hesitation her imagination triumphs:

> "What your uncle says, is very true, Kate, my dear," said Mrs. Nickleby. "I recollect when your poor papa and I came to town after we were married, that a young lady brought me home a chip cottage-bonnet, with white and green trimming, and green persian lining, in her own carriage, which drove up to the door full gallop;—at least, I am not quite certain whether it was her own carriage or a hackney chariot, but I remember very well that the horse dropped down dead as he was turning around, and that your poor papa said he hadn't had any corn for a fortnight."

The difference between Mrs. Nickleby and the narrator is that she tends to get things wrong, whereas the narrator is always right, but the difference is dwarfed by the similarity. They both offer a wealth of detail—white and green trimming and green persian lining, a horse at full gallop—and they both create ironic or satiric thrusts that go against themselves. The little tale about the milliner is in two parts, divided after the full gallop, and the second part is a parody of the first: in one the horse and carriage are dashing, in the second the scene is replayed with a starving horse and a hackney coach. The relationship it enacts between middle-class desire and demotic reality will become the characteristic structure of Mrs. Nickleby's anecdotes. It will also be repeated remorselessly on the larger canvas of each station in the progress of Nicholas and Kate.

Towards the end of Nicholas's sojourn with the Crummles troupe, a supper takes place at which the company includes Nicholas, Miss Snevellicci, her father Mr. Snevellicci, Mr. Lillyvick (erst of the Kenwigs family) and Mrs. Lillyvick, formerly Henrietta Petowker. The secret agenda is the enamoration of Nicholas with Miss Snevellicci. Mr. Snevellicci makes himself free of the liquor and trouble ensues:

Thus Mr. Snevellicci had no sooner swallowed another glassful than he smiled upon all present . . . and proposed "The ladies! Bless their hearts!" in a most vivacious manner.

"I love 'em," said Mr. Snevellicci, looking round the table, "I love 'em, every one."

"Not every one," reasoned Mr. Lillyvick, mildly.

"Yes, every one," repeated Mr. Snevellicci.

"That would include the married ladies, you know," said Mr. Lillyvick.

"I love them too, sir," said Mr. Snevellicci.

The collector looked into the surrounding faces with an aspect of grave astonishment, seeming to say, "This is a nice man!" and appeared a little surprised that Mrs. Lillyvick's manner yielded no evidences of horror and indignation.

"One good turn deserves another," said Mr. Snevellicci. "I love them and they love me." And as if this avowal were not made in sufficient disregard and defiance of all moral obligations, what did Mr. Snevellicci do? He winked—winked, openly and undisguisedly; winked with his right eye—upon Henrietta Lillyvick!   (chapter 30)

When Mr. Snevellicci compounds the insult by blowing her a kiss, Mr. Lillyvick falls upon him. But the worst of it, of course, is that Mrs. Lillyvick is impervious to the insult and proposes that Lillyvick apologize to Snevellicci for the attack. As she asserts that she is the best judge of "what's proper and what's improper" and all the ladies back her up with the insistence that they would be "the first to speak, if there was anything that ought to be taken notice of," Mr. Lillyvick becomes melancholy and we know that the Kenwigs children are secure.

The episode has plenty of intrinsic humor and some of the humor is satiric, arising from the burlesque of middle-class manners. But there is also a stunning element of parody. We look back eleven chapters (four monthly numbers) to Kate's dinner at Ralph's. Ralph has brought her into the room and introduced her to Lord Frederick:

"Eh!" said the gentleman, "What—the—deyvle!"

With which broken ejaculations, he fixed his glass in his eye, and stared at Miss Nickleby in great suprise.   (chapter 19)

When they are seated, the narrator pauses to assure us that Kate will prevail:

for however fresh from the country a young lady (by nature) may be, and however unacquainted with conventional behaviour, the chances are, that she will have quite as strong an innate sense of the decencies and proprieties of life as if she had run the gauntlet of a dozen London seasons—possibly a stronger one, for such senses have been known to blunt in this improving process.

Then Ralph looks around to ascertain the effect Kate has made, and Lord Frederick chimes in again:

> "An unexpected playsure, Nickleby," said Lord Frederick Verisopht, taking his glass out of his right eye, where it had, until now, done duty on Kate, and fixing it in his left, to bring it to bear on Ralph.

They go down to dinner, and when the conversation has taken a turn away from Kate, Sir Mulberry begins her ultimate torture:

> "Here is Miss Nickleby," observed Sir Mulberry, "wondering why the deuce somebody doesn't make love to her."
> "No, indeed," said Kate, looking hastily up, "I————" and then she stopped, feeling it would have been better to have said nothing at all.
> "I'll hold any man fifty pounds," said Sir Mulberry, "that Miss Nickleby can't look me in my face, and tell me she wasn't thinking so."

Poor Kate in fact can't, and finally flees the room in tears.

Almost every element will be repeated in the Lillyvick/Snevellicci parody: the dinner designed to prepare a tryst and the supper in hopes of a consummation; Kate's natural virtue and Mr. Lillyvick's sadly mistaken assumption of Henrietta's natural virtue, which she and the other ladies nonetheless claim; the staring through the right eye and the wink with the right eye; the old roué after the young virgin, and the old lecher after the not-so-young not-so-virgin.

The exaltation of Kate's natural virtue is parodied elsewhere as well, as in the dialogue between Nicholas and Mr. Lenville on the play Nicholas has prepared. Mr. Lenville will portray a man who turns his wife and child out of doors and stabs his eldest son (in the library):

> "After which," said Nicholas, "you are troubled with remorse all the last act, and then you make up your mind to destroy yourself. But, just as you are raising the pistol to your head, a clock strikes—ten."
> "I see," cried Mr. Lenville. "Very good."
> "You pause," said Nicholas; "you recollect to have heard a clock strike ten in your infancy. The pistol falls from your hand—you are overcome—you burst into tears, and become a virtuous and exemplary character for ever afterwards."
> "Capital!' said Mr. Lenville: 'that's a sure card, a sure card. Get the curtain down with a touch of nature like that, and it'll be a triumphant success."
>
> (chapter 24)

The most memorable instance comes later, as Squeers descants upon the parental instinct that led Snawley to take his strong interest in Smike:

"It only shows what Natur is, sir," said Mr. Squeers. "She's a rum 'un, is Natur."

"She is a holy thing, sir," remarked Snawley.

"I believe you," added Mr. Squeers, with a moral sigh. "I should like to know how we should ever get on without her. Natur," said Mr. Squeers, solemnly, "is more easier conceived than described. Oh what a blessed thing, sir, to be in a state o' natur!"   (chapter 45)

S. J. Newman points out that Squeers here is "caricaturing with savage gusto the naive conceptions that Dickens has tried elsewhere to endorse."[12] Squeers is also parodying the narrator.

In chapter 5 Nicholas takes his leave of Miss La Creevy before starting for Yorkshire:

> It was very little that Nicholas knew of the world, but he guessed enough about its ways to think, that if he gave Miss La Creevy one little kiss, perhaps she might not be the less kindly disposed towards those he was leaving behind. So, he gave her three or four with a kind of jocose gallantry, and Miss La Creevy evinced no greater symptoms of displeasure than declaring, as she adjusted her yellow turban, that she had never heard of such a thing, and couldn't have believed it possible.

Compare Nicholas about four pages later when Ralph has introduced Kate to Squeers:

> "Very glad to make your acquaintance, miss," said Squeers, raising his hat an inch or two. "I wish Mrs. Squeers took gals, and we had you for a teacher. I don't know, though, whether she mightn't grow jealous if we had. Ha! ha! ha!"
>
> If the proprietor of Dotheboys Hall could have known what was passing in his assistant's breast at that moment, he would have discovered, with some surprise, that he was as near being soundly pummelled as he had ever been in his life.

Nicholas the jocose gallant is parodied by Squeers the jocose gallant. The parody is pointed by the moral inconsistency of Nicholas' behavior, who thus participates as an agent in the parody of a text in which he is the lead actor; one could even argue that whereas Squeers is at least genuinely lecherous, Nicholas is dishonestly manipulative, kissing Miss La Creevy for the future services she might render. While the friendship between the Nicklebys and Miss La Creevy grows through the book as an almost singular representation of human kindness and generosity, its instability is suggested by touches like this one, until at the end it is annihilated in Mrs. Nickleby's jealous vanity.

At one point, Smike offers to die for Nicholas:

"I could not part from you to go to any home on earth," replied Smike, pressing his hand; "except one, except one. I shall never be an old man; and if your hand placed me in the grave, and I could think, before I died, that you would come in the summer weather, when everything was alive—not dead like me—I could go on to that home, almost without a tear."   (chapter 35)

It follows directly (one chapter earlier, in the same number) on this:

"I am a demd villain!" cried Mr. Mantalini, smiting himself on the head. "I will fill my pockets with change for a sovereign in halfpence and drown myself in the Thames; but I will not be angry with her, even then, for I will put a note in the twopenny post as I go along, to tell her where the body is. She will be a lovely widow. I shall be a body . . . ."   (chapter 34)

What is curious, but not unusual in this novel, is that the deflationary term of the parody precedes the target. It is not that the repetition mocks the original, but that having read the original, we cannot hear in the repetition only the voice it presents, but must hear the absurd version in reprise. The two terms of a parodic pair of episodes may also come so close together as to be interwoven with each other. Chapter 49 is a braid of two strands: the recognition of mutual attraction between Kate and Frank, and the climax of Mrs. Nickleby's flirtation with the gentleman in small-clothes. Which one is absurd?

Kate, Nicholas and Smike need not be involved in either term of the parodic repetition. Compare this:

"A most invaluable woman, that, Nickleby . . . ."
"Indeed, sir!" observed Nicholas.
"I don't know her equal. . . . I do not know her equal. That woman, Nickleby, is always the same—always the same bustling, lively, active, saving creetur that you see her now."   (chapter 8)

with this:

"You don't quite know what Mrs. Crummles is yet."
Nicholas ventured to insinuate that he thought he did.
"No, no, you don't," said Mr. Crummles; "you don't, indeed. I don't, and that's a fact. I don't think her country will, till she is dead. Some new proof of talent bursts from that astonishing woman every year of her life. Look at her, mother of six children, three of 'em alive, and all upon the stage!"
(chapter 25)

The callousness toward the three dead children seems more appropriate to the Squeerses than the Crummleses. The uxoriousness is precisely parallel.

The repetition appears to undermine both occurrences equally, and by identifying as trope the praise of fine women, to glance as well at the novel's own solemn efforts with Madeline and Kate.

The major parodic congeries in the book, and one of the two instances of parody directed at a text outside it, is comprised in the acts and speech of the Crummles troupe. J. Hillis Miller may have been the first to identify the parodic nature of these episodes,[13] and I will assume that it is well enough recognized that I need not elaborate instances. Much of it, like the Smike/ Mantalini parody cited above, is anticipatory: Nicholas leaves the Crummles troupe to re-enact in all apparent seriousness the scenes of melodrama that the Crummleses have performed both on- and off-stage. His challenge of Hawk is one example, parodied in advance by Mr. Lenville's challenge to him to appear at the theatre to have his nose pulled. There are four terms, rather than two, to this parody: (1) the melodramatic actions and speech of Nicholas and Kate; (2) the melodramas enacted by the Crummles troupe; (3) the melodramas enacted by the Crummles troupe off-stage—the Crummles life, so to speak; and (4) the real melodramas of the English theatre that the Crummles productions reference. The first of these, the actions and speech of Nicholas and Kate, are a pastiche of the fourth, the theatrical melodramas. The second and third, the Crummles plays and the Crummles actions and speech, are a parody of those melodramas. The derisive effect is aimed first at the melodrama; it glances secondarily upon Nicholas and Kate in so far as they imitate the latter without criticism, and whether this effect is intentional or not is debatable. When Nicholas and Kate talk, gesticulate, and act melodramatically, they constitute a perhaps unintended parody of melodrama not at the expense of the melodrama but at their own. That melodrama is represented in the text through the repertory of the Crummles troupe and parodied by them.

This serial embedding of parody suggests a literariness both to the Nicholas plot and story and to whatever referents one might construe for them. Any possibility of an unmediated readerly relation with that plot is obviated once we encounter the Crummleses. The recession of mirrors constituted by the Crummles plays, the Crummles life, the Nickleby life, and the melodramas that the first three re-enact puts them all at the critical distance that defines parody. Because *Nickleby* parodies not only an external text—the generalized "melodrama" its audience recognizes from prior experience—but itself, that critical distance is internal, and it opens up within the text repeatedly, unexpectedly, and disconcertingly. "The Lady Flabella" operates similarly, with the silver-fork novel in the position of the English melodrama. The doubt that mockery turns upon the external text soon turns as well upon the novel itself, from Kate's grace equal to the London lady's to Nicholas's stance upon his gentility in the confrontation with Hawk.

As the parody works its caustic process, a question starts to nag: in a world of the excluded subject, is anyone really included, or is inclusion a fantasm? Inclusion, to meet the desire that defines exclusion, must seem true, both in the sense of not being factitious and in a simple moral sense. The matter of whether Dickens can get a plot running becomes the matter of whether he can get Nicholas and Kate into a genuine inclusion, not an inclusion that by virtue of its falsity turns out to be just another exclusion.[14] This is the Sisyphean stone of the joiner, the parvenu, the assimilator: to battle his way into the group only to find that it is not *the* group after all. It happens over and over to the Nicklebys, more seriously to Nicholas and Kate, in burlesque to Mrs. Nickleby. She gets to be the object of courtship again and the man turns out to be a lunatic. She gets into "society" and goes to the play, and the men turn out to be rakes, sharks, and dissolutes. These exposed delusions occur at the level of story. More profoundly, and more threateningly to the text, others occur through the relentless parodies.

As the parodies ricochet against each other, they cast doubt as well on the substantiality of any standard. Parody, Hutcheon points out, need not be at the expense of either agent or target (Hutcheon, 6), but in *Nicholas Nickleby* the extensive self-parody folds the text in upon itself. This enfolded character is antithetical to an ordered universe, be that order narrative or moral. When Lillyvick and Snevellicci parody Kate and Hawk and Verisopht, what is parodied ultimately is the moral standard that defines the falsity of Hawk and his companions. Kate's purity is burlesqued here, and furthermore it is interrogated by Nicholas's flirtations, especially with Miss La Creevy. That purity is the basis of her marriage, so that it too, the "true" inclusion of the finale, is debunked. The comic impulse realized in parody threatens not just to relieve the serious but to relieve it of its credibility and of our emotional and unironic engagement. So long as this goes on, the melodrama, the sentimental tale, cannot proceed, the tale cannot be told, any more than one can tell a serious story against the interruptions of a witty and persistent heckler.

To bring the story to an ending that will insert the hero and heroine into a true inclusion and to escape from the parody thus become the same. If the comedy can be quashed by sentiment, the story can move from parody to romance. The possibility for romance—in marriage and in economic well-being—rests entirely in the Cheerybles.

For both Kate and Nicholas, the true mate is a Cheeryble scion—a nephew and a protegée. The two pairings mirror each other as through their consummations Kate becomes a niece and Nicholas a protegé. Earlier, Kate and Madeline have reflected each other directly not only in their insipidity but in that both have been offered for sale by men who should have been their guardians, to men who are odious. But this too has been parodied—in Morleena Kenwigs's kissings of her uncle Lillyvick and in the dance of the Indian Savage and the maiden, before the peripeteia:

> . . . there bounded on to the stage from some mysterious inlet, a little girl in a dirty white frock with tucks up to the knees, short trousers, sandaled shoes, white spencer, pink gauze bonnet, green veil and curl-papers; who turned a pirouette, cut twice in the air, turned another pirouette, then, looking off at the opposite wing, shrieked, bounded forward to within six inches of the footlights, and fell into a beautiful attitude of terror, as a shabby gentleman in an old pair of buff slippers came in at one powerful slide, and chattering his teeth, fiercely brandished a walking-stick.
> . . . and the savage, becoming ferocious, made a slide towards the maiden; but the maiden avoided him in six twirls, and came down, at the end of the last one, upon the very points of her toes. This seemed to make some impression upon the savage; for, after a little more ferocity and chasing of the maiden into corners, he began to relent. . . .

—and so the peripety.

More strikingly, Nicholas's enamoration of Madeline is doubly parodied. First, the narrator treats him with irony stronger by far than any Nicholas has been subject to since his fantasies of young noblemen at Dotheboys:

> Still, though he loved and languished after the most orthodox models, and was only deterred from making a confidante of Kate by the slight considerations of having never, in all his life, spoken to the object of his passion, and having never set eyes upon her, except on two occasions, on both of which she had come and gone like a flash of lightning—or, as Nicholas himself said, in the numerous conversations he held with himself, like a vision of youth and beauty much too bright to last—his ardour and devotion remained without its reward. The young lady appeared no more; so there was a great deal of love wasted (enough indeed to have set up half-a-dozen young gentlemen, as times go, with the utmost decency) and nobody was a bit the wiser for it; not even Nicholas himself, who, on the contrary, became more dull, sentimental, and lackadaisical, every day.   (chapter 40)

The register is akin to the Mantalinis'. The passage may remind us of David Copperfield, but one difference is that David's love for Dora will be flawed, and thus it is appropriately formulated from the start in the language of sentiment. Nicholas's love is supposed, by the time it is realized, to become true. The route to its realization, however, is detoured through an episode remarkable for its irrelevance to anything but an almost carnivalesque parody of his ultimate meeting with Madeline: the loony tryst with Cecilia Bobster. Just like Madeline, Cecilia is an unhappy young woman kept under strict control by a father "of a violent and brutal temper" (chapter 40). She is sought and found by Newman Noggs, as Madeline will be protected by him.[15] The situation had all the right ingredients: secrecy, danger, the cover of night, a faithful go-between, blushes, the fateful return of the dreaded father—but the "wrong lady," as the name Bobster almost warned Nicholas.

When Nicholas finally finds the right lady, and Kate recognizes her feelings for Frank, they both renounce any hope of consummation, in the name of self-respect and the Cheerybles' entitlement to a good financial match for their heir and their protegée. Although this motive is confused and problematic, as it will be in Dickens through his career, its conclusion may nonetheless be truer to the real course of the novel than what the Cheeryble brothers finally engineer instead. From the first two paragraphs, the representation of marriage as inclusion has been subject to parody. The parodic impulse that has defined marriage as sparring-match has had free rein for more than fifty chapters. Against it, the sentimental plot must pull hard.

When the Nickleby family receives its invitation to the grand dinner in chapter 63, Mrs. Nickleby launches her characteristic fantasy and Nicholas and Kate take up their characteristic roles of trying to keep her in some degree sensible. As usual, she is intractable:

> "I wouldn't be absurd, my dear, if I were you," replied Mrs. Nickleby, in a lofty manner, "because it's not by any means becoming, and doesn't suit you at all. What I mean to say is, that the Mr. Cheerybles don't ask us to dinner with all this ceremony, for nothing. Never mind; wait and see. You won't believe anything *I* say, of course. It's much better to wait; a great deal better; it's satisfactory to all parties, and there can be no disputing. All I say is, remember what I say now, and when I say I said so, don't say I didn't."

Mrs. Nickleby's manner and imagination are no different from what they were with the Mantalinis, the Wititterlys, Dotheboys, Pyke and Pluck and Hawk and Verisopht, or the gentleman in small-clothes. The difference is that this time she is right, and we know it all along, and from the perspective of this knowledge Nicholas's and Kate's modesty and self-abnegation seem narcissistic and even ascetic. This configuration constitutes a complete reversal of the character-typography the book has established. It is not just inconsistent, it is an outrage. It is also an ironic signal.

We are allowing ourselves to be sucked into the illogical happy ending, the ending that the rhythm of the entire work has shown to be false. To end this way, the book must divide against itself. As it does so, one marker remains of the road taken hitherto, and that is Mrs. Nickleby. We, author and readers, are about to indulge in folly, in self-delusion, against all that parody has taught us. In so doing, we are being like Mrs. Nickleby. The narrative and we go along with her expectations: unlike Nicholas and Kate, who have learned otherwise from experience, we are fantasists, like Mrs. Nickleby. As we accept the narrative assertion that this is real, that this will be a true inclusion, Mrs. Nickleby wins.

Her triumph actually begins significantly earlier in the narrative. In chapter 55 we learn of her initial opposition to Nicholas's plan to rescue Madeline from marriage to Gride by any means necessary:

> "Bless my heart, Kate;" so the good lady argued; "if the Mr. Cheerybles don't want this young lady to be married, why don't they file a bill against the Lord Chancellor, make her a chancery ward, and shut her up in the Fleet prison for safety?—I have heard of such things in the newspapers a hundred times. Or, if they are so very fond of her as Nicholas says they are, why don't they marry her themselves—one of them I mean? And even supposing they don't want her to be married, and don't want to marry her themselves, why in the name of wonder should Nicholas go about the world, forbidding people's banns?"
> "I don't think you quite understand," said Kate, gently.

But she does seem to understand something rather important: not marriage, as she roundly asserts in rebuking Kate, but the inanity of this plot she is being required to live. Her counter-proposals constitute parody that functions by *reductio ad absurdum*—or is it so absurd? Why not, O Cheerybles, marry Madeline, or anonymously pay off her father's debt? At the least, are either of these resolutions more absurd than what has just happened?

Further on in the chapter, Mrs. Nickleby confides in Nicholas:

> . . . Mr. Frank Cheeryble had fallen desperately in love with Kate.
> "With whom?" cried Nicholas.
> Mrs. Nickleby repeated, with Kate.
> "What! *Our* Kate! My sister!"
> "Lord, Nicholas!" returned Mrs. Nickleby, "whose Kate should it be, if not ours; or what should I care about it, or take any interest in it for, if it was anybody but your sister?"
> "Dear mother," said Nicholas, "surely it can't be!"

In the paragraphs that follow, the narrator seems to excuse Nicholas's dullness as a consequence of his absorption in his own passions, but the ironic light upon Nicholas remains, and Mrs. Nickleby is right.

Nicholas Nickleby presents a society in which class borders have begun to open and in consequence exclusion and aspiration are dominant affects. It is easy to write Dickens the parvenu into this picture: the newly-risen star, the man of growing means, friends, and influence, pushing himself ahead, pushing his inglorious lineage of servants and bankrupts back behind him. But he has the gift of critical distance, and in this text that distance gives rise to ironic parody. Beneath its high comedy, the parody presses towards the spectre that haunts the excluded subject: the fear that there is only an infinite regress of exclusion, that inclusion is always factitious. This fear engages alike the worldly cynic like Ralph, who therefore chooses exclusion,[16] and the world-forgotten innocent like Miss La Creevy, who on the plains of Syria seeks company in fancified portraits of her own creation.

The story of Nicholas and Kate is launched from the start on a trajectory to reverse their exclusion in a happy ending. All along, however, that movement is deflected, distracted, or undermined by parody, parody that questions the tale from inside and outside, as fiction and as representation. At the close, when the parody gives way to the consummation in marriages and easy fortunes, the narrative nonetheless retains a sharp trace of that voice: the troubling realignment by which the narrator, the reader, and Mrs. Nickleby see the same way.

In the world of the excluded subject, there is no undeluded inclusion. Ralph Nickleby lives the opposed fantasy: his satirist's eye for delusion leaves him remarkably free of the cant and aspiration that beset the other characters; knowing that inclusion is fantasy, he seeks a superior isolation. His Hobbesian view of human nature, however, is first eroded by his recognition—for he is always as brutally honest about himself as about others—of feelings for Kate and a recollection of feelings for his brother, and then lethally undermined by the irruption of feeling for his dead child. With Ralph, parody and sentiment are in reversed roles: the sentiment offers the competing vision that undermines the ironic, misanthropic vision of the Ralph we love to hate. As the anti-type or opposing principle to the desire for inclusion, Ralph operates in the story as the most powerful force of exclusion. Ralph is killed by an onslaught of sentiment, committing suicide as though such self-contradiction must self-destruct. Unlike Gride, who simply has to be gotten out of the way so that Nicholas's marriage will be unobstructed, Ralph must be eradicated for the inclusionary fantasy to prevail. The sentiment must work its irruptive task to the end: it must destroy Ralph.

The second character in the way of the inclusionary fantasy is Smike, improbable as this alignment of father and son may seem. Insofar as Smike is the novel's purest figure of exclusion, the novel dispenses with him much as *King Lear* dispenses with the Fool when Lear begins to see. When the Cheerybles have manufactured the happiness required, Smike, the embodiment of exclusion, is no longer either needed or appropriate. The hopelessness of his exclusion culminates in his love for Kate; while it further sanctifies her, it also creates a situation in which either the novel and its heroine will have to cross a class-barrier quite beyond Dickens or the novel will remain with a permanent figuration of Nicholas's exclusion. Since the one is impossible and the other undesirable, the solution is for Smike to die, which, obliging creature that he is, he does without too much ado. The benevolent brother Charles affirms his unfitness for a story about to end happily in inclusion: " 'Every day that this poor lad had lived, he must have been less and less qualified for the world, and more and more unhappy in his own deficiencies. It is better as it is, my dear sir. Yes, yes, yes, it's better as it is' " (chapter 61). Nicholas hastens to assure him that he has already thought "of all that."

But Smike doesn't go away. His grave becomes the final cynosure of the novel. That grave is closely associated with Nicholas's boyhood and his father's grave. It is on the paternal property that Nicholas buys as soon as he is prosperous, the small farm near Dawlish in Devonshire bequeathed to Nicholas, Senior when Ralph got the £3000 that set him up in business. And thus the novel returns to its opening—and not just to the consecration of everything "with which there was any association of bygone times" (chapter 65), but to the parody of the opening paragraphs and the questions raised first in that parody and then in those that followed it through the novel, questions specifically in this instance of whether marriage is a happy ending, questions generally about the delusional nature of inclusion. If in one sense the fantasy of inclusion requires that Smike, the emblem of exclusion, be eliminated, in another it requires his presence, because inclusion is a fantasm that is generated by desire, by the perception of exclusion. As the fantasm of inclusion can only be sustained by the perception of exclusion, the happy ending of this story needs the persistent image of Smike. That need reveals the obsessional structure of the novel, of the affect that drives it and the parodic repetition that turns it back upon itself.

NOTES

1. Citations are from the New Oxford Illustrated Dickens edition (London: Oxford UP, 1950).

2. Madeline House, Graham Storey, Kathleen Tillotson, et al., eds., *The Letters of Charles Dickens* (Oxford: Clarendon, 1965).

3. I will cite only enough to support my point (a need perhaps impelled by Steven Marcus's opening argument, based upon three quotations from the letters, that the writing of *Nickleby* was effortless [92]). The morning after the March 8 letter to Forster, Dickens was able to report progress, but not completion: "I wrote 20 slips of Nickleby yesterday, and only left 4 to do this morning. Up at 8 oClock too!" The next number was apparently no easier:

> The cold, or the mulled wine, or the driving, made me as bad as you. I couldn't write a line 'till three oClock, and have yet 5 slips to finish, and don't know what to put in them, for I have reached the point I meant to leave off with.   (?15 April 1838)

Nor was the next, as Dickens wrote to Talfourd on May 20: "I am desperately hard up just now, having only written one chapter of Nickleby number three. I hope to make a great dash tomorrow, however, to proceed at rail-road pace." Struggling with the number for December, he apologized to Forster: "I have just begun my second chapter—cannot go out to-night—must get on—think there *will* be a Nickleby at the end of this month, now, (I doubted it before) and want to make a start towards it, if I possibly can" (20 November).

Writing again to Forster on March 15, 1839, he remarked, "I must be alone in my glory to-day and see what I can do. I perpetrated a great amount of work yesterday and have every day indeed since Monday, but I must buckle to again and endeavour to get the Steam up. If this were to go on long, I should 'bust' the boiler." The metaphor continues in a letter to Thomas Mitton on April 7: "I am doing the Snail at present—not the Railroad, and if I finish the next No. by next Saturday shall consider myself well off." On April 11, 1839, he reported to Macready that "Nicklebeian fetters bind me here to-night. I may not sup abroad" and on June 7 wrote to Forster about chapter 50, in which Hawk and Lord Frederick Verisopht go to Hampton: ". . . we are just starting (for the *third* time) to the Races, at which we have worked much harder than the running horses."

4. *The Examiner*, no. 1656 (October 27, 1839), 677–78.

5. "Charles Dickens and his Works," *Fraser's Magazine* 21 (no. 124) (April 1, 1840), 381–400.

6. See N. Russell, "*Nicholas Nickleby* and the Commercial Crisis of 1825," *Dickensian* 77 (1981), 144–50.

7. Peter K. Garrett, *The Victorian Multiplot Novel* (New Haven and London: Yale UP, 1980), 9–10.

8. David E. Musselwhite. *Partings Welded Together: Politics and Desire in the Nineteenth-Century English Novel* (New York: Methuen, 1987), 181–86.

9. Margaret Ganz, "*Nicholas Nickleby*: The Victories of Humor," *Mosaic* 9 (1976), 131–48.

10. Robin Gilmour, "Between two worlds: Aristocracy and Gentility in *Nicholas Nickleby*," *Dickens Quarterly* 5 (1988), 110–18.

11. Linda Hutcheon, *A Theory of Parody* (New York and London: Methuen, 1985), 6.

12. S. J. Newman, *Dickens at Play* (London: Macmillan, 1981), 61.

13. J. Hillis Miller, *Charles Dickens: The World of His Novels* (Cambridge: Harvard UP, 1958), 85–97.

14. These false inclusions may appear similar to Jerome Meckier's false circles in "The Faint Image of Eden: The Many Worlds of *Nicholas Nickleby*," *Dickens*

Studies Annual 1 (1970), 129–46. They are, but they are not the same. Meckier sees more pattern than I can believe and his reading brings the novel to a happy ending in the one true circle.

15. See Edwin M. Eigner, "The Absent CLown in Great Expectations," Dickens Studies Annual 11 (1983), 115–33.

16. See Myron Magnet, Dickens and the Social Order (Philadelphia: U of Pennsylvania P, 1985), 24 ff.

WORKS CITED

"Dickens and his Works." Fraser's Magazine 1 April 1840:381–400.

Dickens, Charles. Nicholas Nickleby. Ed. Michael Slater. New Oxford Illustrated Dickens. London: Oxford UP, 1950.

Eigner, Edwin M. "The Absent Clown in Great Expectations." Dickens Studies Annual 11 (1983): 115–33.

Examiner 27 Oct. 1839:677–78.

Ganz, Margaret Ganz. "Nicholas Nickleby: The Victories of Humor." Mosaic 9 (1976): 131–48.

Garrett, Peter K. The Victorian Multiplot Novel. New Haven: Yale UP, 1980.

Gilmour, Robin. "Between two worlds: Aristocracy and Gentility in Nicholas Nickleby." Dickens Quarterly 5 (1988): 110–18.

House, Madeline, Graham Storey, Kathleen Tillotson, et al., eds. The Letters of Charles Dickens. Oxford: Clarendon Press, 1965.

Hutcheon, Linda. A Theory of Parody. New York and London: Methuen, 1985.

Marcus, Steven. Dickens: from Pickwick to Dombey. New York: Simon and Schuster, 1965, 92.

Magnet, Myron. Dickens and the Social Order. Philadelphia: U of Pennsylvania, 1985.

Meckier, Jerome. "The Faint Image of Eden: The Many Worlds of Nicholas Nickleby." Dickens Studies Annual 1 (1970): 129–46.

Miller, J. Hillis. Charles Dickens: The World of His Novels. Cambridge: Harvard UP, 1958.

Musselwhite, David E. Partings Welded Together: Politics and Desire in the Nineteenth-Century English Novel. New York: Methuen, 1987.

Newman, S. J. Dickens at Play. London: Macmillan, 1981.

Russell, N. "Nicholas Nickleby and the Commercial Crisis of 1825." Dickensian 77 (1981): 144–50.

David Copperfield and the Music of Memory

Kerry McSweeney

I

Human memory is described by the philosopher Mary Warnock as essentially a continuum. At one end is learning memory or habit memory. This mode, common to both men and horses, is "that by the possession of which an animal learns from experience" (6). At the other end is event memory or conscious memory—memory in its reflective or recollective aspect—which is an essential part of "the mysterious phenomenon of consciousness" (14). This mode is essential to the concept of personal identity, which is "meaningless to common sense unless it means identity . . . over a period of time." In fact, "memory and personal identity are inextricably linked" (54). So are memory and imagination: "We could say that, in recalling something, we are employing imagination; and that in imagining something, exploring it imaginatively, we use memory. There can be no sharp distinction" (75–76). Memory and imagination collaborate to produce a narrative reconstruction of a life, in which individual episodes are seen to be parts of a continuum and the subject's continuity in time is shown. For a person to "understand his continuity, to grasp his own duration is to defeat time." Memory saves a person "from the otherwise inevitable destruction brought by death and time" (145, 141).

In her monograph on the subject, Warnock makes good use of Wordsworth's *Prelude* and Proust's *A la recherche du temps perdu*—the two most influential of the many creative works of the past two hundred years that have explored what St. Augustine called "the power of memory . . . the great force of life in living man" (224). Dickens' *David Copperfield*, unmentioned by Warner, is another such text. Its exploration is conducted more indirectly and less discursively than those of Wordsworth and Proust, and the beneficent effects of the conjunction of memory and imagination are much less spectacular. The differences, however, are ones of degree rather than of kind. This is why, in the fresh examination of the operation of memory in *David Copperfield* that I propose to make, Wordsworth and Proust can provide points of reference as helpful as the three antecedent texts of Dickens that must first be considered.

II

The genesis of *David Copperfield* was an autobiographical document that Dickens wrote in the late 1840s. All that survives of it are the portions that John Forster printed in his life of Dickens. Forster recalled that early in 1847 a chance meeting with a third party had led him to ask his thirty-four-year-old friend if he had had "some juvenile employment in a warehouse near the Strand." Dickens' silence persuaded Forster that he "had unintentionally touched a painful place in his memory" (1:19). Sometime later, when Dickens showed him what the question had prompted him to write, Forster learned just how traumatically painful the memory was. When Dickens was around twelve years old, his impecunious parents had agreed to the suggestion that the boy be kept from school and sent out to work in a blacking warehouse. His mother and father "were quite satisfied" with the arrangement, but the young Dickens was "miserably unhappy" in having become a "shabby child," working "from morning to night, with common men and boys," and desperately lonely (1:21, 26, 25). From Monday morning to Saturday night he had "no advice, no counsel, no encouragement, no consolation, no support, from anyone" (1:24):

> The deep remembrance of the sense I had of being utterly neglected and hopeless; of the shame I felt in my position . . . cannot be written. My whole nature was so penetrated with the grief and humiliation of such considerations, that even now, famous and caressed and happy, I often forget in my dreams that I have a dear wife and children; even that I am a man; and wander desolately back to that time of my life.   (1:22–23)

Dickens' employment ended fortuitously when his father quarreled with the warehouse manager and decided that the boy should return to school (despite the remonstrations of his mother, who as Dickens would never afterwards forget, "was warm for" his being sent back). In concluding his account of this episode, Dickens could not say "how long it lasted; whether for a year, or much more, or less."[1] He did know that he and his parents never afterwards alluded to the episode and that until he revealed his secret to Forster more than two decades later, he had never spoken of it to anyone, his "own wife not excepted" (1:32, 33).

According to Forster, Dickens had initially intended to continue work on his autobiographical narrative, but had abandoned the project "when the fancy of *David Copperfield*, itself suggested by what he had so written of his early troubles, began to take shape in his mind" (1:20). The autobiographical fragment became the basis of chapter 11 of the novel, which describes the ten-year-old David's employment in Murdstone and Grinby's warehouse. The novel was published in monthly installments from May 1849 to November 1850. But between the writing of the autobiographical fragment and the serial publication of the novel there is an intervening work, the novella *The Haunted Man*, Dickens' Christmas story for 1948. He had begun work on it only a month after the wrenching death of his sister Fanny, his elder by a year, who had been his "constant companion" in early childhood ("A Child's Dream" 2), and who, it has been reasonably conjectured, provided the young Dickens "with a succoring substitute for what he took to be the inadequate concern and inadequate love of his parents" (Stone 5).

The title character of *The Haunted Man* is a scientist named Redlaw, who lives in an ancient college in the middle of London, and whose manner is "taciturn, thoughtful, gloomy, shadowed by habitual reserve . . . with a distraught air of reverting to a byegone place and time, or of listening to some old echoes in his mind." As he sits brooding in his rooms one night in the dead of wintertime, there appears an apparition—"an awful likeness of himself" (246). From their ensuing conversation, the reader learns of the past afflictions that weigh so heavily on Redlaw; "with slight modifications," as Edgar Johnson has noted (657), they represent Dickens' feelings about his own early life. The primary wound is deprivation of parental love: "I was easily an alien from my mother's heart . . . No mother's self-denying love . . . no father's counsel, aided *me*." At the best, his parents "were of that sort whose care soon ends, and whose duty is soon done" (266). Such "glimpses of the light of home" as the young Redlaw did know had streamed from his beloved and loving sister, the "sweet companion" who had come "into the darkness" of his life, "and made it bright" (267). This sibling bond had sustained him after an adult disappointment in love; but then the sister had died. Her death was "a loss that nothing can replace" (268).

The remedy for these deprivations proffered by Redlaw's double is the erasure of affective memory. The scientist will retain all his knowledge, all that he knows as a result of study; but his memories of early sorrows and wrongs will disappear, as will the 'intertwisted chain of feelings and associations, each in its turn dependent on, and nourished by, the banished recollections'' that are so painful to him. He is in addition given the power to eradicate ''the memory of sorrow, wrong, and trouble'' from the consciousness of others. ''Go,'' says the phantom: be ''the benefactor'' of mankind (270–71).

In the story's next section, Redlaw leaves the College in order to bring the gift of forgetfulness to others. The reader is first shown three examples of the result of memory's obliteration. Redlaw crosses a churchyard, stops among the graves, but is ''utterly at a loss how to connect them with any tender, softening, or consolatory thought.'' He then looks up at the expanse of the heavens—the moon surrounded by a host of stars—but, like Coleridge in the Dejection Ode, feels ''nothing he had been wont to feel.'' Lastly, he hears a plaintive strain of music that seems only ''a tune, made manifest to him by the dry mechanism of the instruments and his own ears, with no address to any mystery within him, without a whisper in it of the past, or of the future'' (309–10).

Redlaw then comes upon a distraught woman whom he attempts to benefit with his gift. But when he asks her about past wrongs and miseries he is ''amazed, and much disquieted, to note that in her awakened recollection of [past] wrong, the first trace of her old humanity and frozen tenderness appeared to show itself'' (312). In the next scene, Redlaw observes a grieving father at the deathbed of his reprobate son, and is made to realize that although the recollection of the past may bring great sorrow, it is greatly beneficial for both father and son to remember the time when the son was an innocent child. By the end of this section, Redlaw has realized that ''good and evil, happiness and sorrow'' are inextricable ''in the memories of men.'' He cries out to the ''Shadow of myself! Spirit of my darker hours,'' hoping to have taken back the fatal gift of forgetfulness and to be deprived of ''the dreadful power of giving it to others'' (322).

In the third and last section of *The Haunted Man* everything comes right in a highly unsatisfactory way. There is too much foreshortening, too much coincidence, and too many gross psychological improbabilities—all of which culminate in the Christian haze of a Christmas feast in the college hall, on a wall of which hangs the picture whose caption, repeatedly mentioned during the course of the narrative, is cited once again in its closing lines: ''Lord, keep my memory green'' (353). The lowest point in the section occurs when a young woman called Milly—one of those Dickensian female embodiments of the good—asks if she may tell "why it seems to me a good thing for us, to remember wrong that has been done us." Her answer is "[t]hat we may forgive it" (347)—a pious bit of moralizing that dilutes the key thematic point, crudely but clearly driven home in the story's second section: that painful memories and happy memories are inextricable and equally important parts of present identity.

It is patent that the Christmas-book format did not give Dickens the creative opportunity to work through and explore pressing questions concerning memory and its operation, particularly the persistence of painful early memories in adult life. As he admitted, his chief purpose in the Christmas books was through "a whimsical kind of masque . . . to awaken some loving and forbearing thoughts, never out of season in a Christian land." Limitations of space "necessitated what is peculiar" in the machinery of the stories and precluded "elaboration of detail, in the working out of character" (*Christmas* 1, xxix). *The Haunted Man* can nonetheless be seen as a necessary step in the process through which Dickens' autobiographical fragment about the blacking warehouse evolved into *David Copperfield*, his great novel of memory. Kathleen Tillotson has observed that the most important contribution made by the Christmas books to the novels that followed lies "in their treatment of time": by invoking the supernatural, Dickens was able to play "tricks with time, breaking through the barriers of ordinary experience" (14) and thereby, as Michael Slater adds, "deepening . . . his presentation of character and its continuity" (*Christmas* 1, xxii).

Indeed, the depths reached by *David Copperfield* can be better appreciated when its treatment of these matters is compared to that of an earlier Dickens novel, *Oliver Twist* (1837), his first imaginative exploration of the central traumatic experience of his childhood[2] and of the mysteries of memory and the continuity of individual identity. Let us begin with the uncanny experience described in chapter 12. Oliver is recovering from an illness in the home of Mr. Brownlow, where he has found refuge. When he wakes from a fevered sleep, the boy remarks that he almost feels as if his unknown mother had sat by him during his sleep. Later, when he has begun to recover, Oliver notices on the wall before him the portrait of a young lady and begins to return the gaze of the eyes in the portrait that "seem fixed" upon him: "It makes my heart beat . . . as if it was alive, and wanted to speak to me, but couldn't." Upon entering the room, Mr. Brownlow realizes that the face of which Oliver's had been reminding him is that of the woman in the portrait: the boy's countenance seems a "living copy" of the portrait drawn with "startling accuracy'' (12:68, 71, 72). Later in the novel, when the mysteries surrounding Oliver's history have been solved, the resemblance is explained: the portrait is of Oliver's mother, who had died in the workhouse after giving birth to him. But how does one explain the connection Oliver makes between the gaze of the portrait and that of the mother he has never known? As Tatar has suggested (179), the answer would seem to be—as reported in chapter 1—that his mother before expiring had asked to see her newborn son, gazed on him, and passionately kissed his forehead, and that Oliver had ever after retained a memory trace of this single experience of maternal love.

The lasting power of early memories is also the subject of two extraordinary passages embedded in the text of *Oliver Twist*. I quote both in full:

> The memories which peaceful country scenes call up, are not of this world, nor its thoughts and hopes. Their gentle influence may teach us how to weave fresh garlands for the graves of those we loved: may purify our thoughts, and bear down before it old enmity and hatred; but beneath all this, there lingers, in the least reflective mind, a vague and half-formed consciousness of having held such feelings long before, in some remote and distant time; which calls up solemn thoughts of distant times to come, and bends down pride and worldliness beneath it. (32:210)

> ....

> The boy stirred, and smiled in his sleep, as though these marks of pity and compassion had awakened some pleasant dream of a love and affection he had never known; as a strain of gentle music, or the rippling of water in a silent place, or the odour of a flower, or even the mention of a familiar word, will sometimes call up sudden dim remembrances of scenes that never were, in this life; which vanish like a breath; and which some brief memory of a happier existence, long gone by, would seem to have awakened; for no voluntary exertion of the mind can ever recall them. (30:191)

If one encountered these passages out of context, Dickens would hardly be the first writer one would guess to be the author of either. A more likely guess would be that the first passage came from an early George Eliot novel—*The Mill on the Floss*, for example, which contains some memorable reflections on the lasting importance of childhood perceptions of the natural world, including their value as a stimulus to piety and morality. (But the closing reference to the consciousness of having held such feelings in some antecedent time, which simultaneously begets thoughts of the distant future, might make one opt for Wordsworth's ''Essays upon Epitaphs.'') The second passage might also bring early George Eliot to mind; for example, chapter 32 of *Adam Bede*, in which the narrator attempts to explain why someone like Adam could love someone like Hetty Sorrel. But a shrewder guess would be that the passage is a translation of something from Proust's *Jean Santeuil* (or a paraphrase of something in *A la recherche du temps perdu*) concerning the quintessential Proustian subject of involuntary memory.

But both passages are by the author of *Oliver Twist* and both are examples of what Graham Greene called "Dickens' secret prose, that sense of a mind speaking to itself with no one there to listen," with its "delicate and exact poetic cadences, the music of memory" (104, 102). In the novel, both passages stand out sharply from their contexts. Their music is very different from the noisy sounds made by the intrusive, heavily ironic narrative voice of the opening chapters and from the robust style used to render the London world of Fagin and Bill Sykes. Moreover, both passages, which nominally refer to the consciousness of young Oliver, are almost wholly gratuitous on the level of characterization and theme. For one thing, the narrator of *Oliver Twist* rarely chooses to get inside Oliver's head. An outside point of view is generally preferred, as when it is reported that during his punishment for having dared to ask for more to eat, Oliver cried bitterly all day long and at night "spread his little hands before his eyes to shut out the darkness, and crouching in the corner, tried to sleep" (3:12). The relation here of narrator to character is intimate, but the point of view remains an outside one—as to all intents it does at the end of chapter 5, when one is told *that* Oliver thought over what had happened to him as he walked back to Mr. Sowerberry's shop, but not told *what* he thought about it.

The other reason the two passages are gratuitous is that the novel tells one nothing at all about the first ten years of Oliver's life. In chapter 1 he is born in a parish workhouse and then sent to a home for infant paupers, where it is reported that he spends his first nine years. At the beginning of chapter 2 he is returned to the workhouse. All the years between his birth and the beginning of his second decade are represented in the text only by the white space between the first and second chapters. By contrast, in *David Copperfield* it takes ten chapters and well over 100 pages to cover the period between the title character's birth and his being sent out at the age of ten to work at Murdstone and Grinby's, the equivalent to which in *Oliver Twist* is the shop of Mr. Sowerberry, the parochial undertaker.

A close parallel between the two novels is found in Oliver's and David's escapes from their respective hells. Both set out alone on six-day walks to what they hope will be something better—Oliver to London and David from London to Dover where his great aunt lives. During their solitary journeys both boys live rough, sleep in the fields, and go hungry. But while David has more than one terrifying experience on the road, what is most memorable for Oliver about his journey are two moments of tenderness. Both are said to affect him deeply and to remain indelibly stamped on his memory. In one of them, a dying boy flings his little arm around Oliver's neck saying "Good-b'ye dear! God bless you!" This blessing, says the narrator, "was from a young child's lips, but it was the first that Oliver had ever heard invoked upon his head: and through all the struggles and sufferings, and troubles and changes, of his after life, he never once forgot it"(7:43–44). In the other, an old lady gives Oliver "what little she could afford—and more—with such kind and gentle words, and such tears of sympathy and compassion, that they sank deeper into Oliver's soul, than all the sufferings he had ever undergone" (8:46). In both these vignettes, the narrator's point of view is omniscient, but gratuitously so. In the first, temporal omniscience is employed for rhetorical purposes: duration is used as a metaphor for intensity in order to heighten the pathos of the moment. In the second, omniscient telling is again used sentimentally, only this time spatial depth rather than temporal breadth is the figure for intensity. But what, upon reflection, can the reader conceivably make of the assertions that the old lady's act of kindness sank more deeply into Oliver's soul than all the sufferings he had ever undergone, of which a number of examples are given in chapters 2 to 7, including one that is glossed with the comment that Oliver possessed so much feeling that he was "in a fair way of being reduced, for life, to a state of brutal stupidity and sullenness by the ill-usage he had received" (4:22–23)? Even given the exacerbated and therefore heightened state of mind of the lonely ten-year-old vagabond, is either moment of tenderness and the value ascribed to it any more psychologically credible than the suggestion that a newborn infant retains the memory trace of a loving face?

This question is part of the larger question of whether it is at all plausible that Oliver was totally unaffected by his brutal, loveless upbringing and remained a wholly intact vessel of good. Even Wordsworth would not have said so. In the 1850 *Prelude* (551) a haunting question is asked:

[If] we found evil fast as we find good
In our first years, or think that it is found,
How could the innocent heart bear up and live[?]

The answer, clearly, is that the innocent heart could not bear up under the weight of evil. What is believable in *Oliver Twist* is the account of what a debased childhood and a life "squandered in the streets, and among the most noisome of the stews and dens of London" have done to the prostitute Nancy (40:270). In contrast, Oliver, with his incorruptible goodness of heart, seems a fairy-tale figure programmed to show, as Dickens puts it in his preface to the novel, "the principle of Good surviving through every adverse circumstance, and triumphing at last" (lxii).

There is one other moment in *Oliver Twist* in which something else that happens to Oliver is said to remain deeply memorable. This time the emotion is not pathos but terror; care is taken to make the experience psychologically credible; and a striking figure of speech is used to convey a sense of its intensity. One evening during his restorative stay in the country, Oliver dozes off while reading. A long paragraph details his state of consciousness. Oliver's "kind of sleep" is one in which the mind is not set free "from a sense of things about it." A consciousness of all that is going on around us remains, and, if one dreams, "reality and imagination become so strangely blended that it is afterwards almost a matter of impossibility to separate the two." Even if our senses of sight and touch be for the time dead, the visionary scenes that pass before us will be materially influenced by "the *mere silent presence* of some external object," regardless of whether it were present "when we closed our eyes: and of whose vicinity we have had no waking consciousness" (34:227–28). While Oliver is in this state, Fagin and Monks, two sinister creatures from the boy's criminal past in London, appear at the window. When Oliver becomes aware of them it is with an intensity of apprehension similar to the visionary dreariness experienced by the child Wordsworth on the bare common in the first spot of time episode in book 11 of the *Prelude*:[3] "they had recognized him, and he them; and their look was as firmly impressed upon his memory, as if it had been deeply carved in stone, and set before him from his birth. He stood transfixed for a moment; and then, leaping from the window into the garden, called loudly for help" (34:228).

Because Oliver's story ends when he is still a boy, there is no way of knowing whether or how this or any other of his intense childhood experiences (tender or horrifying) would have affected him in later life. His story ends with his union with the lovely Rose, technically his aunt but spiritually his sister ("I'll never call her aunt—sister, my own dear sister, that something taught my heart to love so dearly from the first!" [51:355–56]). The story of David Copperfield will end just as Oliver's does, in union with his spiritual sister. But becasue it is a first-person autobiographical novel with a sustained inside point of view, and shows its central character's inner development from his earliest memories through to adult life, *David Copperfield* is able to make one more consistently aware of the music of memory and to show (not simply assert) the lasting power of early memories, whether touching or terrifying.

III

Oliver Twist is a rough-hewn piece of work. At first glance, perhaps even at first reading, *David Copperfield* seems a much more polished performance. On closer examination, however, the first-person retrospective point of view can be seen to be not so seamless a device as it appears. For one thing, in novels employing this mode of narration there is a distinction to be made between the "I" as narrator and the "I" as character, between the narrating self and the experiencing self. And in first-person autobiographical narratives there is the additional question of the stance that the narrator chooses to adopt in relation to his or her past life. William Spengemann explains that if the connection between the two "I"'s is fully understood, the narrating self can adopt the superior point of view taken, for example, by St. Augustine in the first nine books of his *Confessions* and explain the process by which his younger past self became the present narrating self. If the connection between the two selves is not fully understood, as in Wordsworth's *Prelude*, the narrator can choose to limit the point of view to his younger developing self and relive his past imaginatively in the hope of arriving at a deeper understanding of his present self. In Spengemann's view, Dickens elected to use Wordsworth's autobiographical strategy in *David Copperfield*. The truth of the matter is that Dickens used both strategies, and that it is necessary to distinguish between them (indeed, to disentangle them) if the role of memory in the novel is to be clearly seen and properly understood.

One must first distinguish between two aspects of the narrative "I," the representational and communicative flow on the one hand and the expressive nodes on the other. Responsibility for the former may be assigned to David Copperfield the hard-working and successful author writing for the middle-class reading public. This David insists that it is not his purpose "in this record . . . to pursue the history" of his "own fictions" (48:588–89). But the reader can nonetheless infer a good deal about them. In an earlier chapter, David had listed the qualities that have made him a success: "a patient and continuous energy" and "the determination to concentrate . . . on one object at a time" were two of them. But the sine qua non of his success, the quality that has enabled him to overcome the "many erratic and perverted feelings constantly at war within his breast," was that he has "always been thoroughly in earnest"; "some happy talent, and some fortunate opportunity, may form two sides of the ladder on which some men mount, but the rounds of that ladder must be made of stuff to stand wear and tear; and there is no substitute for thorough-going, ardent, and sincere earnestness" (42:517–18).

In drawing up this account, David Copperfield the successful author sounds like nothing so much as a socially concerned Victorian who has read and been influenced by Carlyle and who might well feel a public obligation to articulate a moral vision.[4] In addition, as Q. D. Leavis noted, David seems "imprinted with the age's 'best' ideals of love, marriage, conduct of life and what is desirable in a woman" (44). His novels would thus be likely to point up the dangers of an undisciplined heart and might well present an angel-in-the-house female as the counterpart and complement of the earnest male. As Agnes, his spiritual mentor and the domestic angel figure in the novel, says to David in urging him to remain in England: "Your growing reputation and success enlarge your power of doing good; and if *I* could spare [you], perhaps the time could not" (60:721–22). At the same time, in order to insure the commercial success of his productions, there would be an equal emphasis on the importance of keeping the audience entertained with lively representations and incidents and abundant circumstantial detail. The earnest Agnes is not the only character who praises David's books. Mr. Omer the undertaker also does; for him the crucial test is that he has read every word of one of David's books without feeling sleepy at all (51:627).

The other aspect of the narrating "I" (the introspective expressive aspect with which I am concerned) intermittently comes to the fore. This David Copperfield, who often speaks in what Greene called Dickens' secret prose, is concerned less with moral urgencies and lively representations than with contacting and charting the deepest currents of his being. His direction is not onward-and-upward but downward-and-inward; and while the sequential chronological flow of his life inevitably moves from the past towards the present and the future, in searching for the quick of his being and trying to understand himself, this side of David is drawn back repeatedly into the past.

The distinction between the two aspects of the narrator is instanced in the novel's first two chapters. The former is dominant in chapter 1, which opens with the announcement that the narrative's principal subject will be a moral testing (whether the narrator "shall turn out to be the hero" of his own life [1]), suspends the first-person retrospective convention in order to render in detail the broadly entertaining scene following Aunt Betsey's arrival at Blunderstone on the night of David's birth, and ends with some funereal gravitas about the graveyard "as the earthly bourne of all . . . travellers" and "the mound above the ashes and the dust that once was he, without whom I had never been" (11). (The last phrases are borrowed from a poem by Tennyson, who became Victoria's Laureate in the same year that *David Copperfield* was published in book form [Gilmour, "Dickens, Tennyson"

132]). The narrator's expressive side is dominant in the second chapter: in beginning to think about his "own experience" of himself, David speculates on the lasting influence of the chidhood "power of observation" and recalls, with wonderfully evocative specificity, his earliest memories—the cheeks and arms of his nurse Peggotty: "so hard and red that I wondered the birds didn't peck her in preference to apples . . . the touch of [her] forefinger as she used to hold it out to me, and . . . its being roughened by needlework, like a pocket nutmeg-grater" (11).

A similar distinction can be made between non-title characters. One reason why subsidiary characters abound in *David Copperfield* is that they entertain and instruct. But they are also the result of restricting the point of view of the retrospective first-person narrator, who is aware of no more than the title character was at any given time. Rosa Dartle, in her splendid scene with Steerforth in chapter 29, and Miss Mowcher, in her first scintillating appearance in chapter 22, for example, are both needed to suggest Steerforth's evil underside in the time before his seduction of Emily, because until then David the character has no notion of his friend's perverse depths. Other characters, however, seem principally deployed to suggest below-the-surface aspects of David Copperfield that cannot be representationally or discursively communicated. Mr. Dick is one such character. When he is considered in relation to three other characters who also have things to say or suggest about memory or writing, one finds a distinction similar to that already noted between two different levels of narratorial engagement with the novel's autobiographical materials.

Aunt Betsey, Micawber, and Julia Mills all epitomize above-the-surface aspects of David Copperfield, the successful Victorian fiction writer. Aunt Betsey's declaration concerning the value of memory is characteristically pithy and assured: "It's in vain," she tells David, "to recall the past, unless it works some influence upon the present" (23:296)—that is to say, if it is to benefit one, recollection must be a moral exercise with self-improvement as its goal. Micawber's views on the subject are as copious as Aunt Betsey's are terse, and as indulgent as hers are severe. Contemplation of "the scenes and events of the past, tinged by the prismatic hues of memory, has ever afforded me, as it ever must continue to afford, gratifying emotions of no common description" (49:598). That is to say, for Micawber as for the late eighteenth-century man of feeling whom he resembles, memory is a sentimental indulgence and looking backward to the past a source of pleasing *frissons*. Finally, there is Julia Mills, whose babble about "the slumbering echoes in the caverns of Memory" (33:414) drolly epitomizes her taste for extravagant emotions, as does the journal in which she keeps an excessively gushy record of the courtship of Dora and David that differs only in degree from the narrator's representation of it.

Mr. Dick is something else entirely. Consider the details of his past life as they are given by Aunt Betsey in chapter 14. Mr. Dick, whose real name is Mr. Richard Babley, had a favorite sister, "a good creature, and very kind to him" who married and was "made wretched" by her husband (175). This, combined with Mr. Dick's mistreatment by his brother, who sent him away to an asylum, has had a great effect upon his mind. Ten years previously he had come to live with Betsey, but the intervening years have not mitigated the oppressiveness of his recollection of these painful events (any more than twice ten years mitigated the oppressiveness of Dickens' memory of the blacking warehouse). Mr. Dick is compelled repeatedly to try bringing past events under control through the creative activity of the mind—by writing his own history, which he calls his Memorial. Whenever he attempts to do so, however, his painful memories overwhelm him. His "allegorical way" (14:175) of expressing his inability to control the past by expressing it is to say that he cannot keep King Charles the First (beheaded in 1649) out of his narrative. But the ever-abandoned opening pages of the Memorial do not go up in smoke; they go up into the air, like the material of the kites that Mr. Dick loves to fly and that seem to lift his mind out of its confusion.

Commentators have not failed to note the similarities between the name of Charles Dickens and those of Mr. Dick and King Charles, and to suggest that the comparable obstruction in Dickens' creative life was the experience of the blacking warehouse, which he was unable to write about until many years later, and which reached print only after being transmuted into an episode in the life of a character whose initials were the reverse of his own.[5] There is however no need to make in so roundabout a way the connection between Mr. Dick's obsession and the expressive side of the narrator of *David Copperfield*. In the opening paragraph of chapter 15, David speaks of the "deep impression" (185) made on him by Mr. Dick's creative struggles. One paragraph above, in the closing sentences of chapter 14 (in which David learns Mr. Dick's story), he speaks of the curtain that "had for ever fallen" on his life at Murdstone and Grinby's:

> I have lifted it for a moment, even in this narrative, with a reluctant hand, and dropped it gladly. The remembrance of that life is fraught with so much pain to me, with so much mental suffering and want of hope, that I have never had the courage even to examine how long I was doomed to lead it. Whether it lasted for a year, or more, or less, I do not know. I only know that it was, and

ceased to be; and that I have written, and there I leave it.   (184)

So close is the collocation that one can hardly fail to sense a connection between David's traumatic memory and Mr. Dick's King Charles. One cannot say whether David's successfully completed narrative of his experience mitigated the painfulness of the memory or was beneficial to his psychic life; there is nothing to be known about David Copperfield as he was subsequent to the writing of his life story. But one can ask whether the experience at Murdstone and Grinby, and the other key episodes of his childhood, continued to press on David's consciousness and influence his life after childhood. Early on, David the narrator makes some generalizations about early memories and their relation to later experience that are based on his "own experience" of himself: "the memory of most of us can go farther back into such times than many of us suppose; just as I believe the power of observation in numbers of very young children to be quite wonderful for its closeness and accuracy." Moreover,

> I think that most grown men who are remarkable in this respect, may with greater propriety be said not to have lost the faculty, than to have acquired it; the rather, as I generally observe such men to retain a certain freshness, and gentleness, and capacity of being pleased, which are also an inheritance they have preserved from their childhood.   (2:11)

These remarks refer only to the heightened perceptual experiences and their afterglow. Nowhere in *David Copperfield* does David have anything direct to *say* about the lasting effects of his warehouse experience or other unsettling early experiences. But this does not mean, of course, that the novel has nothing to *show* us in this regard.

This distinction necessitates making another: that between two kinds of memory, one of which relates to the representational aspect of the narration, the other to the expressive aspect. The distinction is crucial and the failure to make it has limited the usefulness of earlier discussions of the subject, including those of such fine critics as George Ford and Robin Gilmour, though the latter does recognize that "the deepest, most intimate communication of *David Copperfield* is somehow at odds with its more explicit recommendation of prudence," that its "centres of vitality . . . lie elsewhere," and that in the novel "the rhythm of memory . . . becomes something more than simple nostalgia: it is an imaginative process which . . . complicates and enriches the book's total perspective" ("Memory" 30–31).[6]

For David Copperfield the industrious professional writer with a blank page before him, recollection is one of the tools of the trade, a voluntary, willed activity that oils the machinery of the narrative and provides important rhetorical opportunities. For David Copperfield the explorer of past time, memory is less conscious recollection than a felt contact between past and present and a vital part of the life experience. Moreover—this point is crucial—many of the most important moments in the life of his younger self are those during which he is overcome with memories of still earlier experiences and emotions. There are many examples of the first kind of memory, which I shall call literary-rhetorical memory. They include much of what people are referring to when they say that *David Copperfield* is a novel of memory. There are throat-clearing gestures like "Let me remember how it used to be, and bring one morning back again" (4:46). There are the places where memory is used for the purposes of intensification: "that evening . . . will never pass out of my memory" (8:99); "Shall I ever forget how . . . Shall I ever recall . . . without . . ." (52:654). (In both these examples, as in two of the passages from *Oliver Twist* examined earlier, duration is used in a hackneyed way as a figure for intensity of impression.) Literary-rhetorical memory is also instanced in the four "Retrospective" chapters, which employ the device, commonly used in films, of indicating the passage of time by running through a series of stills. Finally, this kind of memory is used by the retrospective narrator as a way of italicizing certain moments in the narrative that turn out to be exemplary or premonitory. A good example is the description of Emily looking out to sea in an early chapter, in which the determining event of her life is shadowed forth:

> She started from my side, and ran along a jagged timber which protruded from the place we stood upon, and overhung the deep water at some height, without the least defence. The incident is so impressed on my remembrance, that if I were a draughtsman I could draw its form here, I dare say, accurately as it was that day, and little Em'ly springing forward to her destruction (as it appeared to me), with a look that I have never forgotten, directed far out to sea. (3:31)

In separating literary-rhetorical memory from what it is tempting to call the real thing, it is helpful to recall the Proustian distinction between habitual and spontaneous memory. Marcel, the narrator of *A la recherche du temps perdu*, remarks that the image of whatever is habitually (or consciously) remembered inevitably weakens and fades, and eventually loses its power to recover the past for us. Images that are spontaneously recalled, however, retain their power to evoke the past and to move us deeply. The trigger of the spontaneous recollective activity is found not in a conscious reflective act, but in the objects of sense perception, the concrete particulars of the external world. That is why "the better part of our memories exists outside us, in a blatter of rain, in the smell of an unaired room or of the first crackling brushwood fire in a cold grate." It is through particulars like these that "we can from time to time recover the person that we were, place ourselves in relation to things as he was placed, suffer anew because we are no longer ourselves but he" (1:692). I do not claim that one can find in *David Copperfield* a clear distinction between voluntary and involuntary memory, though Dickens was perfectly aware of this distinction, as we know from one of the interpolated passages on memory in *Oliver Twist*. I do suggest that if particular attention is paid not to rhetorical telling but to showing, to the vividly remembered perceptual particulars of the novel, one can begin to hear the music of memory that runs throughout and to realize the essential importance to David's inner life of both childhood memories and memories of childhood experience.

IV

The rendering of David's childhood experiences in the first 200 pages of the novel is for many readers the best part of the book. The key to the compelling quality of these chapters is the vividly specific, self-authenticating perceptual notations. David's very first memories, as we have seen, are haptic: Peggotty's hard red arms and cheeks and her roughened forefinger. Other memories are evoked through the notation of scents: the "breathless smell of warm black crape" in Mr. Omer's shop (9:107), for example, or the schoolroom at Salem House and its "strange unwholesome smell . . . like mildewed corduroys, sweet apples wanting air, and rotten books" (5:67). And taste sensations are found in the chapter describing David's time at Murdstone and Grinby. In recounting the experience David cannot remember how long he toiled there; but that is unimportant. What both authenticates the account and makes it memorable is not quantitative information but the emphasis on the taste experiences of the ten-year-old boy, who had to buy his own food and had no other pleasure to look forward to than the choice between a pudding made with currants, a less expensive "stout pale pudding, heavy and flabby, and with great flat raisins in it," "a saveloy and a penny-loaf," and "a plate of bread and cheese and a glass of beer" (11:137–38).

In addition to the warehouse experience, there are three other particularly important nodes in David's childhood. One of them concerns his first home and the father whom he never knew. In chapter 17, the adolescent David learns from a letter that the Rookery at Blunderstone is empty and has been shut up. His reaction shows that he has both a vivid memory of the place and an active imagination:

> it pained me to think of the dear old place as altogether abandoned; of the weeds growing tall in the garden, and the fallen leaves lying thick and wet upon the paths. I imagined how the winds of winter would howl round it, how the cold rain would beat upon the window-glass, how the moon would make ghosts on the walls of the empty rooms, watching their solitude all night. I thought afresh of the grave in the churchyard, underneath the tree: and it seemed as if the house were dead too, now, and all connected with my father and mother were faded away.   (212)

When he finally returns to the place in late adolescence, it is with "a singular jumble of sadness and pleasure" that he "haunt[s] the old spots" just as he had often "haunted them" in memory. His reflections at this period of his development, however, are more concerned with the future: "with the figure I was to make in life, and the distinguished things I was to do." But two concrete particulars draw his thoughts back to the past: the sound of the church-bell that seems "like a departed voice" to him, and the poor lunatic gentleman who is always sitting at the window of David's old bedroom and who prompts him to wonder "whether his rambling thoughts ever went upon any of the fancies" that used to occupy his, on the rosy mornings when he "peeped out of that little window" in his night-clothes, "and saw the sheep quietly feeding in the light of the rising sun" (22:272–73). The lunatic gentleman in David's old bedroom inevitably recalls Mr. Dick, whom David had seen looking from an upper window when he first arrived at his aunt's. The connection between the two figures is not explicitly made, but for the careful reader the twinge of recollection caused by the visual similarity might prompt reflection on the psychological connection between David's sweet early memories (here the sheep feeding in the rising sun) and his painful memories. At the least, one is reminded (to recall *The Haunted Man*) of "the intertwisted chain of feelings and associations" that make up a person's past.

Another link in the chain is the complex of emotions, images, and memories relating to David's beloved mother. The last time he sees her alive she is calling out to him and holding her new baby up for him to see. But from the moment of his learning of her death, the image of his mother as he has lately known her vanishes from his consciousness and is replaced by "the young mother" of his "earliest impressions, who had been used to wind her bright curls round and round her finger, and to dance" with him "at twilight in the parlor" (9:115). The image of his mother figures in the fourth key experience of David's childhood, his lonely and sometimes terrifying journey from London to Dover. During the journey he is sustained and led on by the remembered images of his "mother in her youth"; and because his route takes him through the ancient cathedral town, her image becomes ever after associated in his mind with Canterbury and "the sight of its old houses and gateways, and the stately, grey cathedral with the rooks sailing round the towers." When his ordeal is over and David goes to bed for the first time in his aunt's house, he imagines that he might see his mother coming from heaven along the "shining path" of the moonlight to look upon him "as she had looked" when he "last saw her sweet face." But his final thought before he sleeps is not of heaven but of the earth: "I thought of all the solitary places under the night sky where I had slept, and . . . I prayed that I never might be houseless any more, and never might forget the houseless" (13:170).

By chapter 19, David Copperfield is a young man with the future spread before him. So powerful are his "visionary considerations" of the future that the partings caused by his school-leaving make no impression on him. It is even reported that "at that time" his "juvenile experiences" seemed to count "for little or nothing": "life was more like a great fairy story, which I was just about to begin to read, than anything else" (19:233). Precisely the opposite turns out to be the case. What the reader discovers over and over again in the remaining two-thirds of the novel is that David is drawn back into the past whenever he touches the deepest and "most secret current" of his mind (58:699).

This current has a name: it is Agnes Wickfield. Before charting its course through David Copperfield's life, it is once again necessary to make a distinction. Agnes is the focal point of the prudential morality of *David Copperfield*, the exemplary figure in its treatment of the theme of the undisciplined heart, and the terminus of David's Carlylean progression from romantic love through sorrow and sad experience to a self "more self-denying, more resolved, more conscious" of himself and his "defects and errors" (58:701). This static, emblematic quality in Agnes is evident from her first appearance, when going upstairs in her father's house she turns to look down on David: in "the grave light of the old staircase," she reminds him of "a stained glass window in a church" that he had once seen during his childhood; and "ever afterwards" he associates her with something of the "tranquil brightness" of this icon (15:191). David reports that at the time he did not love Agnes but even then felt "that there are goodness, peace, and truth, wherever Agnes is; and that the soft light of the colored window in the church, seen long ago, falls on her always," and on him when he is near her, "and on everything around"

(16:198). The "spirit of Agnes" is always with David to sustain him and impel his life onward and upward: "Ever pointing upward, Agnes; ever leading me to something better; ever directing me to higher things" (60:722).

For many commentators, Agnes Wickfield the Victorian icon is a distinct embarrassment. It even led the normally canny John Carey to the bizarre expedient of claiming that her characteristic gesticulation reflects "perfectly normal instincts: [she] is pointing not upwards but towards the bedroom" (171). An alternative to the onward-and-upward Agnes becomes available only when attention is concentrated on the downward-and-inward current that flows through the text. At one point, David reminds the reader that his story is "his written memory." He goes on to say that he "has desired to keep the most secret current of my mind apart, and to the last." This current, the central "mystery of my own heart" (58:699), is his love for Agnes, which he has come to recognize as the source of that gnawing sense of "the old unhappy loss or want of something" (44:552) that he had felt in the past. The touchstone of this love is not upwardly pointing fingers or other hints of transcendence. Just as certainly it is not the bedroom. It is rather the music of memory.

From this point of view, Agnes is the epitome and embodiment of David's past: not his "good angel" but his good sister, his "adopted sister" (39:484). Agnes' role in the expressive narrative is to represent the complex of David's past experiences, both the good and the painful, union with which is necessary for self-completion and happiness. As such, she resembles other Victorian angel-in-the-house figures less than she does other sister figures in nineteenth-century literature that are intimately associated with childhood memories. One such figure is addressed at the end of Wordsworth's meditation in "Tintern Abbey": from the "wild eyes" of his sister Dorothy, the poet hopes to catch "gleams" of his own "past existence" and thus fill a prospective void within himself (165). For similar reasons, the image of Coleridge's beloved sister Nancy (who like Fanny Dickens died prematurely of consumption) rises to the surface of her brother's consciousness during his meditation in "Frost at Midnight." The sister is the mirror-image of his childhood self, "My play-mate when we both were clothed alike"; she is the "companionable form" or answering other through which Coleridge hopes to overcome the subject-object dualism and fill the emptiness within him (240–42).

But the sisters who throw the most immediate light on Agnes as a figure of memory are those in Dickens' canon whom we have already noticed: the lost sisters of Redlaw and Mr. Dick, who make their brothers' memories nearly insupportable burdens, the oppressiveness of which they seek to alleviate through willed forgetfulness in one case and flying kites in the other. And in *Oliver Twist*, union with Rose, his blood relative and spiritual sister, is the radiant culmination of Oliver's story and, in the novel's fairy-tale logic, retrospectively provides him with loving and tender memories of a childhood that he had never known in fact. This is signaled in the very moment when Rose first sets eyes on Oliver. Worn out with pain and exhaustion, the boy is in a deep sleep when she stoops over him and is moved to tears, which fall upon his forehead. It is these tears—in the extraordinary passage about involuntary memory quoted above—that cause Oliver to stir and smile in his sleep, "as though these marks of pity and compassion had awakened some pleasant dream of a love and affection he had never known" (30:191).

We are now in a position to identify those places in the text where the presence of the deepest current in David Copperfield's life is most strongly felt. As noted above, David's first sight of Canterbury is associated with the guiding image of his mother. It later comes to be associated with Agnes as well. "Strange to say," David observes in describing a return to the ancient town on an early winter morning,

> that quiet influence which was inseparable in my mind from Agnes, seemed to pervade even the city where she dwelt. The venerable cathedral towers, and the old jackdaws and rooks whose airy voices made them more retired than perfect silence would have done; the battered gateways, once stuck full with statues, long thrown down, and crumbled away, like the reverential pilgrims who had gazed upon them; the still nooks, where the ivied growth of centuries crept over gabled ends and ruined walls; the ancient houses, the pastoral landscape of field, orchard, and garden; everywhere—on everything—I felt the same serener air, the same calm, thoughtful, softening spirit.   (39:481)

What is true of Canterbury in general is also true of the ancient house in which Agnes lives. When he arrives at the Wickfield residence for the first time, however, the first person that David sees is not Agnes but Uriah Heep, who is almost as much a part of his Canterbury life as she is. Many readers have remarked the special affinity between David and Heep, "who had a sort of fascination" for him (16:200), and to whom he is attracted "in very repulsion" (25:328). The node of this attraction-repulsion is Agnes. A key moment between the two characters occurs when Heep reveals to David his aspirations concerning Miss Agnes, whose image, he says, has been in his breast for years. David's reaction is striking:

> the image of Agnes, outraged by so much as a thought of this red-headed animal's, remained in my mind when I looked at him, sitting all awry as if his

mean soul griped his body, and made me giddy. He seemed to swell and grow
before my eyes; the room seemed full of the echoes of his voice; and the strange
feeling (to which, perhaps, no one is quite a stranger,) that all this had occurred
before, at some indefinite time, and that I knew what he was going to say next,
took possession of me.   (25:326)

Part of the explanation of David's strange feeling is that its intensity is an
indication from a below-the-conscious-level of his love for Agnes. But his
uncanny feeling also expresses his instinctive sense that the collocation of
Heep and Agnes is a repetition of the pairing of Murdstone and his mother,
which was the precipitate of the traumatic experiences of his childhood: his
mother's death, the warehouse, the flight to Dover. We have already seen
the Canterbury connection between David's memory of his mother and his
present image of Agnes. The symbiosis of Heep and Murdstone links the two
figures more closely. It is a critical commonplace that in marrying Dora
Spenlow, David married a child-woman with a close resemblance to his lost
mother. But the connections between the mother and Agnes have been less
noticed and only come into focus when Agnes is seen not as an angel but as
a sister and, in Alexander Welsh's phrase, "a true daughter of memory"
(114).

   In chapter 39, there is another experience of paramnesia. David has come
to Canterbury to see Agnes. Just before their meeting he is conversing with
Mr. Micawber, who observes in parting that if David had not assured him
that D (for Dora) was his favorite letter, "I should unquestionably have
supposed that A had been so." The effect of his words on David is uncanny:

We have all some experience of a feeling, that comes over us occasionally, of
what we are saying and doing having been said and done before, in a remote
time—of our having been surrounded, dim ages ago, by the same faces, objects,
and circumstances—of our knowing perfectly well what will be said next, as
if we suddenly remembered it! I never had this mysterious impression more
strongly in my life, than before he uttered those words.   (39:483)

What David has suddenly sensed (or remembered) is not that he and Micawber
had exchanged the same words before, but that his identity in time, which
depends upon the continuity of past and present that only memory can provide,
is linked not to his child wife but to his "sister."

   During their meeting, David tells Agnes he has missed her much of late
because "in the happy old days" of their childhood in the old house he had
come to rely on her counsel and support. Whenever he returns to his "adopted
sister," he comes to "peace and happiness": "I come home, now, like a

tired traveller, and find such a blessed sense of rest.'' The tired-traveler simile is not a tired trope. It recalls the six-day journey of the child David, and suggests that in Agnes is found the present locus of David's traumatic early memories. The older David goes on to comment on the declaration by his younger self and in so doing intensifies one's sense that Agnes represents that intertwisted chain of feelings and associations that is David's past life:

> I felt so deeply what I said, it affected me so sincerely, that my voice failed, and I covered my face with my hand, and broke into tears. I write the truth. Whatever contradictions and inconsistencies there were within me, as there are within so many of us; whatever might have been so different, and so much better; whatever I had done, in which I had perversely wandered away from the voice of my own heart; I knew nothing of. I only knew that I was fervently in earnest, when I felt the rest and peace of having Agnes near me.
>
> (39:483–84)

Later, when David is beginning to assess his marriage to Dora with un-clouded eyes, he finds himself aware of something missing in himself that is not a recent loss, that he cannot name, and that he calls ''the old unhappy loss or want of something.'' He wonders whether its source is simply in the psychological sleight of hand by which past experiences become endowed with a ''softened glory'' that makes present-time experiences inevitably pale in comparison. And while he could have wished his wife Dora to have had the wherewithal ''to fill up the void which somewhere seemed to be about'' him, he reflects that this was an unrealistic expectation ''that never had been meant to be, and never could have been'' (44:552). In the next chapter, David describes a walk on an autumn evening: ''I remember how the leaves smelt like our garden at Blunderstone as we trod them under foot, and how the old, unhappy feeling, seemed to go by, on the sighing wind'' (45:559). He does not at that time, however, connect his memories of his childhood home with the source of his unhappiness. And so,

> The old unhappy feeling pervaded my life. It was deepened, if it were changed at all; but it was as undefined as ever, and addressed me like a strain of sorrowful music faintly heard in the night. I loved my wife dearly, and I was happy; but the happiness I had vaguely anticipated, once, was not the happiness I enjoyed, and there was always something wanting.
>
> In fulfilment of the compact I have made with myself, to reflect my mind on this paper, I again examine it, closely, and bring its secrets to the light. What I missed, I still regarded—I always regarded—as something that had been a dream of my youthful fancy; that was incapable of realisation; that I was now discovering to be so, with some natural pain, as all men did.
>
> (48:594–95)

In chapter 52 David returns to Canterbury and early in the morning strolls through its tranquil streets:

> The rooks were sailing about the cathedral towers; and the towers themselves, overlooking many a long-unaltered mile of the rich country and its pleasant streams, were cutting the bright morning air, as if there were no such thing as change on earth. Yet the bells, when they sounded, told me sorrowfully of change in everything; told me of their own age, and my pretty Dora's youth; and of the many, never old, who had lived and loved and died, while the reverberations of the bells had hummed through the rusty armour of the Black Prince hanging up within, and, motes upon the deep of Time, had lost themselves in air, as circles do in water.   (52:634–35)

When David had revisited his first home, the church bells that sounded "like a departed voice" had called his thoughts back from building his "castles in the air" (22:272). In the above-quoted passage, the cathedral bells recall David's thoughts from outward-and-upwardly expanding vistas that bring a momentary sense of transcendence and changelessness. The bells speak rather of change, sorrow, and death in the centuries-long temporal span during which they have sounded. Finally, in the climax of the passage, the visual-spatial expansion and the aural-temporal contraction are fused in the spatio-temporal image of the deep of Time and in the simile of the dying echoes of the bells losing themselves in the air as ripples on the expanse of water. At this point in the novel, then, David's inner self seems unattached to the earth—a mote-like void losing itself in the larger spatio-temporal void.

In his next visit to Canterbury David becomes reattached to the earth and its quotidian sights and sounds through becoming united with Agnes—that is, through the repossession of his past in memory, which fills the void within him and is the cure for the old unhappy feeling of loss. The moment of visionary recovery of the past—the bringing to the surface of the deepest current in David's life—is understated. It is not declared or described but rather quietly enacted in an extraordinarily evocative paragraph of particularized description. David has returned from the continent after a three-year absence and has come to Canterbury to see Agnes. While being announced, he waits in the drawing room:

> I stood in a window, and looked across the ancient street at the opposite houses, recalling how I had watched them on wet afternoons, when I first came there; and how I had used to speculate about the people who appeared at any of the windows, and had followed them with my eyes up and down stairs, while women went clicking along the pavement in pattens, and the dull rain fell in slanting lines, and poured out of the waterspout yonder, and flowed into

the road. The feeling with which I used to watch the tramps, as they came into town on those wet evenings, at dusk, and limped past, with their bundles drooping over their shoulders at the ends of sticks, came freshly back to me; fraught, as then, with the smell of damp earth, and wet leaves and briar, and the sensation of the very airs that blew upon me in my own toilsome journey.
(60:718)

There is nothing onward-and-upward here, and nothing tinged with the transcendent: no sheep quietly feeding in the light of the rising sun, no rich country and pleasant streams seen in the bright morning light. There are rather wet afternoons and evenings, dull rain falling in slanting lines, tramps limping, the smell of damp earth, wet leaves and briar. These are the quotidian particulars through which, as Proust's narrator says, "we can from time to time recover the person that we were, place ourselves in relation to things as he was placed, suffer anew because we are no longer ourselves but he" (1:692). At the end of his toilsome childhood journey, David had prayed that he "never might be houseless any more, and never might forget the houseless" (13:170). And now, in this special moment, he does remember the houseless at the same time that he re-experiences one of the most painful links in the intertwisted chain of feelings and associations that have made him what he is.

In the next paragraph, the little door in the paneled wall opens and Agnes enters the room. When she begins to speak to David of his recent sorrows (Emily's disgrace, Steerforth's and Dora's deaths), "she touched the chords" of his memory "so softly and harmoniously, that not one jarred within" him. He "could listen to the sorrowful, distant music, and desire to shrink from nothing it awoke" (60:718). But it is not only recent sorrows that no longer jar within David and from which he no longer shrinks. The sorrowful distant music recalls the figure of "a strain of sorrowful music faintly heard in the night" (48:594) used to describe that undefined but persistent old unhappy feeling that pervaded David's life, the sources of which, as we have seen, lay deep in his childhood past. It is this wound that is finally cured in chapter 60, in an exceptional moment of psychological integration in which past and present are fused.

V

In his meditation on the power of memory in book 10 of his *Confessions*, St. Augustine tried to come to an understanding of how it was that a person would remember past experiences of fear and sorrow without re-experiencing the same emotions in the present: how could one "recall past fears and yet not feel afraid" and "be glad to remember sorrow that is over and done with"? In grappling with this paradox, Augustine was forced to resort to a bizarre simile. Memory could be said to be "a sort of stomach for the mind," and "joy and sadness . . . like sweet or bitter food" (220). When these emotions entered the memory, they lost their distinctive taste, just as food did when it passed from the palate to the stomach.

In the *Prelude*, Wordsworth offered a psychological explanation of the same phenomenon. The poet was interested in certain intense experiences of his childhood, particularly those characterized by fear and apprehension, because he recognized that they were in some mysterious way the sources of his adult creative power, the operation of which was dependent upon his ability to retain a felt sense of them through memory. How did these experiences become nourishing? How could they lose their terror but retain their affective power? His answer was that they had permanently sensitized him and enhanced his affective capacities, thus enabling him in later life to experience intensely: "Remembering how she felt" but not what she felt, his "soul" retained "an obscure sense / Of possible sublimity" (506). It is a version of this process of conversion of the bitter into the nourishing, the traumatic into the enabling, that is enacted in the expressive part of *David Copperfield*. At the end of the novel, David's old unhappy feeling is not transcended; it is rather shown to have become incorporated into the fabric of his being and to be a source of the music of memory that enhances his life experience and is an essential part of his sense of identity and of continuity in time.

NOTES

1. Allen provides evidence that the twelve-year-old Dickens worked in the blacking warehouse for twelve or thirteen months (104).
2. In the autobiographical fragment, Dickens observed: "but for the mercy of God, I might easily have been, for any care that was taken of me, a little robber or a little vagabond" (1:25). During his narrative, the comparably aged Oliver Twist is forced by circumstances to become both a vagabond and a robber. And as Dickens points out in the fragment, the evil Fagin, who supervises Oliver's criminal activities, is named after Bob Fagin, a co-worker in the blacking warehouse (1:22).
3. I chapter 9 of *Oliver Twist*, there is another detailed description of a state of consciousness between sleeping and waking that has a remarkable resemblance to the spots of time and related experiences in the *Prelude*; this time the resemblance is to their sublime aspects and their giving evidence that the mind is lord and master:

There is a drowsy state, between sleeping and waking, when you dream more in five minutes with your eyes half open, and yourself half conscious of everything that is passing around you, than you would in five nights with your eyes fast closed, and your senses wrapt in perfect unconsciousness. At such times, a mortal knows just enough of what his mind is doing, to form some glimmering conception of its mighty powers: its bounding from earth and spurning time and space: when freed from the restraint of its corporeal associate. (9:51)

4. See Dunn on the Carlylean features of the novel.

5. See for example Spengemann (121–28) and Tick.

6. Other noteworthy discussions of memory in *David Copperfield* (in addition to those cited) include J. Hillis Miller, *Charles Dickens: The World of His Novels* (Cambridge, Mass.: Harvard UP, 1958), 150–59; Robert E. Lougy, "Remembrances of Death Past and Future: A Reading of *David Copperfield*," *Dickens Studies Annual* 6 (1977): 72–101; Barry Westburg, *The Confessional Fictions of Charles Dickens* (Dekalb: Northern Illinois UP, 1977), ch. 2; Rosemary Mundhenk, "*David Copperfield* and 'The Oppression of Remembrance,' " *Texas Studies in Literature and Language* 29 (1987): 323–41; and Malcolm J. Woodfield, "The Endless Memorial: Dickens and Memory/ Writing/History," *Dickens Studies Annual* 20 (1991). Also see James E. Marlow, "Memory, Romance, and the Expressive Symbol in Dickens," *Nineteenth-Century Fiction* 30 (1975): 20–32.

WORKS CITED

Allen, Michael. *Charles Dickens' Childhood*. London: Macmillan, 1988.

Augustine. *Confessions*. Trans. R. S. Pine-Coffin. Harmondsworth: Penguin, 1961.

Coleridge, Samuel Taylor. *Poems*. Ed. Ernest Hartley Coleridge. London: Oxford UP, 1960.

Carey, John. *The Violent Effigy: A Study of Dickens' Imagination*. London: Faber, 1973.

Dickens, Charles. "A Child's Dream of a Star." *Household Words: A Weekly Journal* 6 Apr. 1850:25–26.

———. "The Haunted Man," *The Christmas Books*. Ed. Michael Slater. Harmondsworth: Penguin, 1971. Vol. 2.

———. *David Copperfield*. Ed. Nina Burgis. Oxford: Clarendon, 1981.

———. *Oliver Twist*. Ed. Kathleen Tillotson, Oxford: Clarendon, 1966.

Dunn, Richard. "David Copperfield's Carlylean Revolution." *Dickens the Craftsman: Strategies of Presentation*. Ed. Robert B. Partlow, Jr. Carbondale: Southern Illinois UP, 1970.

Ford, George. "Dickens and the Voices of Time." *Nineteenth-Century Fiction* 24 (1970): 428–48.

Forster, John. *The Life of Charles Dickens.* Ed. A. J. Hoppé. 2 vols. London: Dent, 1966.

Gilmour, Robin. "Dickens, Tennyson and the Past." *Dickensian* 75 (1979): 131–42.

———. "Memory in *David Copperfield.*" *Dickensian* 71 (1975): 30–42.

Greene, Graham. "The Young Dickens." *Collected Essays.* London: Bodley Head, 1969.

Johnson, Edgar. *Charles Dickens: His Tragedy and Triumph.* 2 vols. New York: Simon, 1952.

Lankford, William T. " 'The Deep of Time': Narrative Order in *David Copperfield.*" *ELH* 46 (1979): 452–67.

Leavis, F. R., & Q. D. Leavis. *Dickens the Novelist.* London: Chatto, 1970.

Proust, Marcel. *Remembrance of Things Past.* Trans. C. K. Scott-Moncrieff and Terence Kilmartin. 3 vols. London: Chatto, 1981.

Spengemann, William. *The Forms of Autobiography: Episodes in the History of a Genre.* New Haven: Yale UP, 1980.

Stone, Harry. "The Love Pattern in Dickens' Novels." *Dickens the Craftsman: Strategies of Presentation.* Ed. Robert B. Partlow, Jr. Carbondale: Southern Illinois UP, 1970.

Tatar, Maria M. "The Houses of Fiction: Toward a Definition of the Uncanny." *Comparative Literature* 33 (1981): 167–82.

Tick, Stanley. "The Memorializing of Mr. Dick." *Nineteenth-Century Fiction* 24 (1969): 142–53.

Tillotson, Kathleen. "The Middle Years: From the *Carol* to *Copperfield.*" *Dickens Memorial Lectures.* London: Dickens Memorial Fellowship, 1970.

Warnock, Mary. *Memory.* London: Faber, 1987.

Welsh, Alexander. *From Copyright to Copperfield: The Identity of Dickens.* Cambridge, Mass.: Harvard UP, 1987.

Wordsworth, William. *Poetical Works.* Ed. Thomas Hutchinson and Ernest de Selincourt. London: Oxford UP, 1960.

Alias and Alienation in *Bleak House*
Identity in Language

Carrol Clarkson

In a novel where polyonymy is a distinctive feature of several of the characters, it is hardly surprising that the novel's title should have undergone several changes as well. *Tom-All-Alone's, The Ruined House, Bleak House Academy, The East Wind* and *The Solitary House where The Wind howled*, are some of the titles Dickens considered before finally choosing *Bleak House*[1]. Yet if "Bleak House" itself is a "dreary name" (79) as the Lord Chancellor observes, the intricate patterns in the novel of naming and renaming, of concealing family names and adopting pseudonyms, are by no means "dreary"[2]. Using Plato's *Cratylus* as a starting point, I would like to show how personal identity in *Bleak House* is constituted both *in* and *like* a language, and how Esther Summerson's relation to her parents can be read as a metaphoric expression of the subject's relation to language and to the law.

Plato's *Cratylus* is the earliest extant philosophical text on names and the origins of language and takes the form of a dialogue between Cratylus and Hermogenes with Socrates acting as arbitrator. Cratylus believes that "there is a kind of inherent correctness in names which is the same for all men, both Greeks and barbarians" (7). Hermogenes, on the other hand, claims that "no name belongs to any particular thing by nature, but only by the habit and custom of those who employ it and who establish the usage" (9, 11). Socrates supports Cratylus' position, but his enthusiasm is modified in his claim that "this attractive force of likeness [between the name and its referent] is, as Hermogenes says, a poor thing, and we are compelled to employ in addition, this commonplace expedient, convention" (175).

Socrates proposes investigating the earliest names as a means of ascertaining the correctness of the names in current usage. Yet who conferred the earliest names, and were these names necessarily "correct"? It is possible that the earliest names were simply "distributed at haphazard" (51). Socrates, aware of these problems, remarks that "tragic poets . . . when they are in a dilemma, have recourse to the introduction of gods on machines," and proposes that they too (at least provisionally) "may get out of trouble by saying that the gods gave the earliest names, and therefore they are right" (143). Even assuming that the gods gave the earliest names, however, Socrates is unable to say what these names were. He resorts to etymological guess-work, and admits that his speculations on the earliest names are "quite outrageous and ridiculous" (143). He confronts an aporia, since 'if anyone is . . . ignorant of the correctness of the earliest names, he cannot know about that of the later, since they can be explained only by means of the earliest, about which he is ignorant" (143).

A serious undermining of the Cratylean position has emerged: if names "inherently correct," if they simply "made plain" the "essence" of the thing, then the thing itself would be able to dictate its unique name and we would not have to have recourse to other *names*. If, as Socrates maintains, the correctness of current names can be described *only* by means of the earliest, then the whole question of the correctness of names becomes one of the concatenation of *language* (a linguistic system of signification) and not one of elusive essences which may or may not be successfully captured.

Socrates assumes a playful, mock-innocent air in the dialogue. He speaks "on the spur of the moment" (61) and on the basis of "a fine intuition which has just come to [him]" (97). While there is also a "serious . . . account" of names, Socrates proposes to give the "facetious account, for the gods also have a sense of humour" (81), and he states that he "would not positively affirm any of the things [he] ha[s] said" (149). Nevertheless, the questions Socrates asks of Cratylus and Hermogenes reveal shortcomings in each of their arguments. Critical comment which makes reference to the *Cratylus* to discuss the names in literature does not generally give due consideration to the implications of the issues raised by Socrates, issues which (I shall argue) are of particular interest for this paper. Hillis Miller speaks of "the belief, affirmed in Plato's *Cratylus*, that the right name gives the essence of the thing" (23), leaving the vague impression that only one view is endorsed. Even the most recent criticism tends to use the dialogue as a simple debate between Cratylus and Hermogenes, giving priority to Cratylus' view. Anne Barton, while acknowledging the complexity of Socrates' role, discusses comic drama as "the principal arena in which the debate between Cratylus and Hermogenes has been played out," and shows how the "fundamental

bias'' of comic drama ''has always been cratylic.'' Moreover, Barton believes
that ''the position of Cratylus has always been far more attractive and interesting than that of Hermogenes'' (14), and while ''Hermogenes may be triumphant in the field of linguistic philosophy[,] [t]he voice of Cratylus . . . cannot be silenced'' (13). Dickens is generally thought to encapsulate Cratylus'
view[3] and A. D. Nuttall is perhaps the most adamant proponent of this stance.
He speaks of ''the violently cratylic mind of Dickens'' (19) and claims that
Dickens, ''in so many ways the natural heir of Jonson—is similarly bound
by his own vigorous cratylism of quasi-onomastic catch-phrases'' (18).

Apart from the fact that Cratylus' view is not given unequivocal support
in Plato's dialogue, it is important to realize (in an application of the *Cratylus*
to fictional names), as Hillis Miller does, that there is an ontological difference
between the referents of the names under discussion in the *Cratylus* and the
referents of the names in Dickens. Plato's dialogue is a philosophical text
which deals with the names of ostensibly pre-existent people and things.
The names have a *retrospective* bearing on their referents. Dickens' names,
however, have *fictive* referents which are fundamentally constituted in the
language of the text. An overtly metaphorical name, such as Esther Summerson, may strike one as an example of ''vigorous cratylism,'' especially
when we are told that the character who bears this name brings with her
''sunshine and summer air'' (482). However, the fact that the metaphor is
so ostensively defamiliarized (so blatantly ''laid bare''), points to the name's
metafictional quality: Esther Summerson is a fictive construct whose being
depends on the language which constitutes her, and it is precisely for this
reason that her name can be so pertinent. As Roman Jakobson points out, it
is in *literature* that ''the internal form of a name, that is, the semantic load
of its constituents, regains its pertinence. The ''Cocktails'' may resume their
obliterated kinship with plumage'' (376). Dickens' ludic use of metaphor in
his naming foregrounds language in a metafictional gesture which pre-empts
a reading of the names purely in terms of Cratylus' argument. Dickens'
naming complicates the notion that there is a transcendent ''essence'' which
can have a separate existence from the name and language which actually
comprise it.

''Surely,'' Socrates observes, the question of names ''is no small matter''
(9), and ''it is not for every man . . . to give names, but for him who may
be called the name-maker; and he, it appears, is the lawgiver, who is of all
the artisans among men the rarest'' (25). The subtle conjunction of language
and the law in Plato's *Cratylus* becomes crucial in *Bleak House*, where

Captain Hawdon makes a new name for himself and adopts the role of law-writer. Nemo, as the *law-writer* and Esther's father, is at the nexus of language, the law and personal identity which are inextricably linked through the slippery pattern of regress which Socrates encounters in his quest for the earliest name.

The analogy between language and the law takes on an explicit dimension in John Jarndyce's explanation of the process of Chancery. He tells Esther how

> Equity sends questions to Law, Law sends questions back to Equity; Law finds it can't do this, Equity finds it can't do that; neither can so much as say it can't do anything, without this solicitor instructing and this counsel appearing for A, and that solicitor instructing and that counsel appearing for B; and so on through the whole alphabet, like the history of the Apple Pie. And thus, through years and years, and lives and lives, everything goes on, constantly beginning over and over again, and nothing ever ends. And we can't get out of the suit on any terms, for we are made parties to it, and *must* be parties to it, whether we like it or not.   (146)

The history of the Apple Pie to which John Jarndyce refers is an alphabet nursery rhyme: the process of Chancery is a linguistic jingle enacted in the game of substitutions played by the members of Representative Government, and indexed in their rhyming and alphabetically arranged names. My Lord Boodle

> perceives with astonishment, that supposing the present Government to be overthrown, the limited choice of the Crown . . . would lie between Lord Coodle and Sir Thomas Doodle—supposing it to be impossible for the Duke of Foodle to act with Goodle, which may be assumed to be the case in consequence of the breach arising out of that affair with Hoodle. . . .   (211)

As Jarndyce says, everything goes on, constantly beginning over and over again: the reader subsequently encounters the Right Honourable William Buffy, M.P., and *his* alphabetic retinue. Needless to say, the social evils sown by Tom-All-Alone's are more than "Lord Coodle and Sir Thomas Doodle, and the Duke of Foodle, and all the fine gentlemen in office, down to Zoodle, shall set right in five hundred years—though born expressly to do it'' (273).

Socrates, in searching for the earliest name, wonders whether he will "ever get hold of a word which is no longer composed of other words," a word which no longer requires that he "refer to other words for its derivation" (131). He never does get hold of this "elemental" word and finds himself caught in an infinite regress where one word leads to yet another *word* rather than straight to the "essence" of things. The process of Chancery, too, follows this pattern of infinite regress, where one legal document simply displaces a prior legal document, and leads to yet another one without bringing the case of Jarndyce and Jarndyce to a resolution. Chancery is typified by "all sorts of blank forms of legal process" (178) where characters are "made parties" to the level of the signifier, and "can't get out of it on any terms." An entry into the semic realm of the signified is thwarted: the members of the high Court of Chancery are

> mistily engaged in one of the ten thousand stages of an endless cause, tripping one another up on slippery precedents, groping knee-deep in technicalities, running their goat-hair and horsehair warded heads against walls of words.
> (50)

The "scarecrow of a suit has . . . become so complicated that no man alive knows what it means" (52), and one "might look in vain for Truth at the bottom of it" (50). The case of Jarndyce and Jarndyce leads Richard Carstone to lament, "it's a weary *word* this Chancery" (108, my emphasis).

The process and effects of Chancery emerge as an allegory of the Derridean "différance" of language where meaning is continually deferred. Différance (which means both "difference" and "deferment") is, according to Derrida, the systematic play of differences in language which subverts a plenitude, an absolute presence of meaning in any one "element" in the chain of signification. Each element bears traces of others, and resonates with residual meanings. These

> syntheses and referrals . . . forbid at any moment, or in any sense, that a simple element may be *present* in and of itself, referring only to itself . . . This interweaving results in each "element" . . . being constituted on the basis of the trace within it of the other elements of the chain or system. (*Positions* 26)

Esther might call it a "captivating looseness and putting-off of everything" (578)—a phrase she uses in speaking of Richard Carstone, who lives in continual hope of a favorable outcome of the case of Jarndyce and Jarndyce. Richard's very identity bears the traces of différance: his actions are guided by "his hankering after the vague things yet to come of those long deferred hopes" (286). Everything is "postponed to that imaginary time" (583). "What [he] would have been without that blight, [we] never shall know" (578), and Richard himself admits, "[t]here's no now for us suitors" (580).

If, as John Jarndyce observes, "nothing ever ends," the text constantly points to the fact that in matters of law and equity, nothing ever has an accessible origin either. The lawyers of *Bleak House* can be seen

> diving through law and equity, and through that kindred mystery, the street mud, which is made of nobody knows what, and collects about us nobody knows whence or how.   (186)

Just as the street mud has always been there, and is of unknown origin, the actual beginning and the "original merits" of the case, Jarndyce and Jarndyce, "have long disappeared from the face of the earth." The Great Will is no longer the cause of the furore: "it was, once. It's about nothing but Costs now," "it was about a Will when it was about anything" (145). But this will is another unintelligible document, a literal "dead letter" which in turn disseminates "cartloads of papers" and "copies, over and over again" (145). When John Jarndyce's great Uncle Tom first "began to think of [the case], it was the beginning of the end" (146), but that end is in a state of continual deferment. We think of Socrates, who, if he could only remember "the genealogy of Hesiod, and the still earlier ancestors of the gods he mentions," would then be able to make "a complete trial of this wisdom which has suddenly come to [him], [he] know[s] not whence" (49). Socrates does not know the name of the earliest ancestor, and this prevents him from bringing a satisfying closure to his discourse. Like the lawyers in *Bleak House*, Socrates is faced with a "kindred mystery" of "slippery precedents."

Michael Ragussis identifies the law-writer, Nemo, (which in Latin means "no one") as the "father or originator" of the law ("The Ghostly Signs of *Bleak House*," 261), drawing on the paronomasia implicit in the analogy between law and equity and the street mud which "collects about us *nobody* knows whence or how." But Nemo as the law-writer is not strictly the originator in that he is only copying what has already been written. Apart from this, the polyonymous Captain, variously known as the Law-Writer, Nemo, Nimrod and Our Dear Brother, oscillates uncannily through a series of nominal permutations, making it difficult to attribute to him any stable locus implicit in the notion of originator.

Like George Rouncewell (Trooper George), we cannot "hold to the saying, once a captain, always a captain" (354) and before it is known that Captain Hawdon has become a law-writer, the question of the Captain's existence, the space he occupies, is raised. Trooper George makes an erroneous deduction as to his whereabouts by ascertaining where he does not seem to be, as he explains in his conversation with Smallweed:

"If I had found him, I must have gone to the other world to look. He was there."

"How do you know he was there?"

"He wasn't here."   (355)

To Smallweed's insistent "How do you know he wasn't here?" Trooper George offers an evasive answer, unverified in its assertion that Captain Hawdon drowned. He hastily breaks off the conversation by whistling a funeral march by Handel, and says, "They bury soldiers to it; so it's the natural end of the subject" (355–56). However, this is *not* the "natural end of the subject"—Captain Hawdon assumes his alias and sets in motion the mystery of his identity.

It is significantly as a law-writer that Captain Hawdon takes on the alias "Nemo" in a desperate bid to conceal his identity. The semantic constituent of this name (which Dickens so meticulously foregrounds) uneasily contradicts what one expects from a proper name, that is, its primary signalling of identity. From the very outset of the novel it seems questionable whether this can be a proper name at all:

"Nemo!" repeats Mr Tulkinghorn. "Nemo is Latin for no one."

"It must be English for some one, sir, I think," Mr. Snagsby submits, with his deferential cough. "It is a person's name."   (185)

The alias relegates the law-writer to the periphery of existence: it is ironic that it is precisely when the semantic component of the name becomes pertinent that the character's identity is most in question, and it is finally in *death* that the law-writer "establishe[s] his pretensions to his name by becoming indeed No one" (190).

Our Dear Brother is presented to the reader quite literally as a "shade . . . of names" (762). Only one tantalizing glimpse of the law-writer is granted—as a corpse in an obnubilated chamber. Yet this "anonymous character, his name being unknown" (464) paradoxically has more names than most other characters in the novel, one of which is Esther's family name. In this sense he is a central character is what has quite literally become the novel's "kindred mystery", despite the fact that his death (a physical absence) has been established in the incipient stages of the novel. It is this tension between life and death, the tension of a character at once absent, yet indispensable in the solving of the novel's mystery, that leads Connor to observe that the spectral image of the law-writer "flickers between conditions, present, absent, Hawdon, Nemo, some one, no one" (78). A surrealistic quality is at the core of the character whose voice we only hear through hearsay, whose identity is established posthumously through a faded handwriting. Krook's circuitous information about his former tenant deepens the mystery of Nemo's (non)-being:

> Than that he was my lodger for a year and a half, and lived—*or didn't live*—by law-writing, I know no more of him.   (191, my emphasis).

It is this elusive character who bears Esther's family name, a name which would provide her with a sense of personal history. Like Oliver Twist, she has had only the half-baptism of an orphan, and as a child feels that she is no one: she is "sensible of filling a place in [Miss Barbary's] house which ought to have been empty" (66). Her doll, her sole confidante, sits "staring at [Esther]—or not so much at [her] . . . as at nothing" (62). As Esther falls asleep before the fire in the Jellyby household, with Caddy on her lap, Esther registers, "I vainly tried to lose myself . . . among the scenes of the day." Gradually, though, the scenes become "indistinct and mingled." Esther begins to "lose the identity of the sleeper resting on [her]" until "[l]astly, it was no one, and *I was no one*" (94, my emphasis). These sensations that Esther has of being no one affiliate her proleptically, if parodoxically, with her parents. Nemo is a professed Nobody, and in her last letter to Esther before she dies, Lady Dedlock claims to have "done all [she] could do to be lost" and writes that she has "nothing about [her] by which [she] can be recognized" (865).

Yet Esther practically equates existence with the possession of a proper name, so that when Lady Dedlock reveals herself to be Esther's mother, the daughter exclaims: "So strangely did I hold my place in this world, that . . . I had never, to my own mother's knowledge, breathed—had been buried—had never been endowed with life—had never borne a name" (569).

But why should the possession of a proper name, and especially a family name, be so important for a sense of personal identity? Identity, or *who* you are, is largely determined by the place you occupy in the family and in society. The relations you bear towards your parents and family constitute a sense of origin and continuity and hence a sense of personal identity in terms of history and of a place in time. Relations with others in the community determine your place at any given time in the social sphere. We are reminded of the "syntheses and referrals" between the elements in Derrida's chain of linguistic signification: personal identity, like meaning itself, is not simply a self-presence. It is "constituted on the basis of the trace within it of the other elements of the chain or system" (*Positions* 26), of the "*spacing* by means of which elements are related to each other" (27). Like the "elements" of language, personal identity "functions and signifies, takes on or conveys meaning" by referring to *other* elements "in an economy of traces" (29). A proper name is a crucial index of one's kindred ties, and indirectly of one's social standing.

Esther's point of origin, indexed in part in her father's name, Nemo, No one, presents itself as a blank space, an enigmatic void, allowing the vestige of her identity to follow the movement of the Derridean trace. The father's name, which asserts a nobody, seems to undermine its own status and function as a proper name (as Tulkinghorn and Snagsby have realized). It reverberates the effect of the trace: "[i]n presenting itself it becomes effaced; in being sounded it dies away" ("Différance" 154). "[E]ffacement belongs to the very structure" (156) of the name, and Esther's identity as a "past that has never been present" (152) finds dramatic expression in an emotively charged incident where Lady Dedlock reveals that she is Esther's mother. Lady Dedlock establishes a familial identity for her daughter, but far from coming into a positive sense of self through the affirmation of family ties, Esther must conceal these newly-disclosed relations to protect Lady Dedlock's secret. An identity, in the instant of its appearing, must be effaced, and Esther frenetically seeks to escape from an incriminating identity: she has an active "terror of [her]self" and she perceives herself as "the danger and possible disgrace of [her] own mother, and of a proud family name" (569).

Esther's relation to her parents—the unreadable and eminently effaceable origin—thus becomes a metaphoric expression of the subject's relation to language, where the original name cannot be easily pinpointed. Esther's father is Captain Hawdon, the Captain, Nimrod, Nemo, No one. He is already dead, appears virtually only as Our Dear Brother, so that for Esther, the quest for a tangible and accessible point of origin becomes almost as "outrageous and ridiculous" as Socrates' quest for the earliest name. "Captain Hawdon", like the "original merits" of Jarndyce and Jarndyce, has "long disappeared from the face of the earth" (145). The history of Esther's identity is to be traced in a "kindred mystery" of "slippery precedents."

Not inheriting a family name, an orphan is, as Ragussis points out, born into a "special linguistic vacuum" ("The Ghostly Signs of *Bleak House*" 260). The given name never seems "proper enough" (258) since it does not operate as an index of a familial, historical identity. Esther registers that she is "nothing" and "no one." Esther has had "a great deal of difficulty in beginning to write [her] portion" of the narrative (62), and part of the text,

Esther writes, 'even if [she] rub[s] it out again" (482). Esther's "space" indeed threatens to be a "linguistic vacuum," a tabula rasa highly vulnerable to nominal rearticulation. And several names *are* conferred upon her: Cobweb, Dame Durden, Dame Trot, Little Old Woman, Minerva, Mother Hubbard. . . . Yet, if this plethora of names has been occasioned by her not having a "proper enough" family name, Esther's polyonymy (like her sensation of being no one) paradoxically links her to her father and his many names.

It has been argued by several critics, most notably Hillis Miller and Michael Ragussis, that language and the law obscure or undermine the notion of personal identity in *Bleak House*. Miller argues that "[a]ll proper names . . . alienate the person named from his unspeakable individuality and assimilate him into a system of language. . . . To name someone is to alienate him from himself by making him part of a family" (22). The polyonymy of so many of the characters in the novel is seen by Miller as a miming "in the permutations of language that movement within the social system which prevents each person from being himself and puts him beside himself into some other role" (23)[4].

According to Ragussis, a child is a "victim of . . . a system, lost in any number of family or class names" (*Acts of Naming: The Family Plot in Fiction* 8) "[L]anguage masks identity;" ("The Ghostly Signs of *Bleak House*" 268) it "betrays me into an unknown world where I am, necessarily, friendless and unknown" and "where identity is withheld from me" (277). Similarly, "the law stands for that language which confounds all familial ties and sends . . . children . . . into the world unknown and nameless" (267).

The underlying assumption of both Miller and Ragussis is that there is some intangible "himself" from which a subject may be alienated by being named, or by adopting a familial or social role. Donald Davidson, in his influential philosophical paper "Mental Events", shows how even mental events (that is, propositional attitudes such as beliefs, hopes, desires, intentions, decisions etc.) are physical events. Davidson avoids a materialist reductionism in his assertion that there are no psychophysical laws "on the basis of which we can predict and explain mental phenomena" (117). Nevertheless, a mental event will always be in the position of a physical event, just as for Derrida, "every signified is also in the position of a signifier" (*Positions* 20): a concept cannot be signified in and of itself without reference to a signifier. Davidson himself draws the analogy between "the place of the mental amid the physical, and the place of the semantical in a world of syntax" (112). According to Davidson, "we make sense of particular beliefs only as they cohere with other beliefs, with preferences, with intentions, hopes, fears expectations, and the rest . . . the content of a propositional attitude derives from its place in the pattern" (116). We are reminded of the Derridean "*spacing* by means of which the elements are related to each other" (*Positions* 27). What Davidson's thesis amounts to is that (as Derrida might phrase it) the mental has no self-presence, and this renders the notion of an "unspeakable individuality", an intangible "himself", problematic at its root[5]. The very concept of the "himself" is a highly sophisticated social construct, and it is *through,* rather than *in spite of* language, names, and social and familiar roles (tangible signs of personal identity) that we are able to constitute a notion of "himself" in the first place.

The identity of fictional characters is purely dependent on the language of their constitution, and a study of Esther's concern about her status as an orphan reveals that the discourse of quotidian existence is also a constitutive, rather than a debilitating aspect of personal identity. Esther, as an orphan, is a member of a household rather than of a family (Wilt 291), but it is the family that is a " 'narrative institution,' the place where we tell the story of where we came from" (Sacks 55). "From whom, other than our parents," asks Jonathan Sacks, "will we learn who we uniquely are?" (57). Certainly not from Miss Barbary! Esther implores her for the discourse of her identity, and it is explicitly *silence* and not language that leaves a child friendless, nameless, and unknown through its refusal to iterate family ties:

> "O, dear godmother, tell me, pray do tell me . . . ."
> "No," she returned. "Ask me no more, child!"
> "O, do pray tell me something of her [ie. Lady Dedlock]. Do now, at last, dear godmother, if you please! . . . No, no, no, don't go away. O, speak to me!"   (64)

On her deathbed, Miss Barbary's final refusal to offer a discourse of recognition practically amounts to a denial of Esther's existence. Esther "entreat[s] her to give [her] the least sign that she knew or heard [her]. No, no, no. Her face was immovable" (67).

Language and the law in *Bleak House* are seen by Ragussis to "confound all familial ties" and to render children "unknown and nameless." Yet a proper name (as Ragussis also notes), passed on from parent to child, is the primary linguistic iteration of a blood relation, of a family tie. The text of *Bleak House* suggests that language and the law tenaciously seek to uncover identities and identifying relationships, which have been concealed, significantly, by *individuals.* Miss Barbary has "bred [Esther] in secrecy from her birth, ha[s] blotted out all trace of her existence''—and it is she, in an individual capacity, who is responsible, for Esther's growing up ''entirely friendless, nameless and unknown'' (290). It is because they have borne an illegitimate child, have operated *outside* the accepted social boundaries of the law, that Lady Dedlock and Captain Hawdon have deemed it expedient to conceal their identifying relationships to each other and to Esther.

Nemo's occupation as a law-writer is therefore of intriguing complexity. It is almost as if the Captain has wished to ''blot out all trace'' of his own existence: he names himself a nobody and paradoxically writes the law which would brand him an outlaw. The final testimony to his identity is his law-hand (Nemo's handwriting matches that of Lady Dedlock's lover, and also that of Captain Hawdon's written instructions to Trooper George). As an actual (law)-hand from the grave, Nemo's letters survive the fire of Krook's Spontaneous Combustion, and his law-hand, a graphic conflation of language and the law, finally bears witness to a shady identity ''moving on'' (320) through a series of dissembling names.

It is precisely the assumed names of so many of the characters in the novel that seem to point to the fact that language can, and does obscure personal identity. The aliases adopted by Captain Hawdon certainly lead to confusion about the identity of the referent, but it is not the alias, or language *per se* that achieves this, as I will show by drawing on Frege's essay, ''On Sense and Meaning.''

I may refer to Venus as ''the morning star'' and ''the evening star,'' but unless I know that these are different ways of referring to the *same* planet, ''the morning star'' and ''the evening star'' appear to be two different things. This is what happens with Captain Hawdon's polyonymy: we know that ''Captain Hawdon'' and ''the Captain'' have the same referent, and we know that ''Nemo'', ''Nimrod'', ''the Law-Writer'' and ''Our Dear Brother'' all have the same referent, but initially we do not know that the two sets of names refer to the same person, and it is this blank space, this lacuna *between* the two sets of names, which actually obscures identity, *and not the different names themselves*.

In taking the name, Nemo, ''nobody'' the Captain attempts to iterate this lacuna, and in so doing, makes use of language, which ultimately identifies by marking a place which the subject occupies in discourse[6]. Nemo's dilemma becomes a dramatic reminder of Wittgenstein's dictum: ''I cannot use language to get outside language'' (54).

Proper names *of themselves* cannot simply mask, or eradicate identity, nor do they capture some elusive and transcendent ''essence'' in a simple Craty-lean sense. What they do reveal is that the ''essence'' of the subject has always already been imbricated in the names and language which are constitutive aspects of it. Proper names do not alienate the person named from something "unspeakable", but, like the Derridean arche-writing (where differential relations permeate even that which is perceived to be unitary) they reveal simply "the loss of what has never taken place, of a self-presence that as never been given, but only dreamed of" (*Of Grammatology* 112). The only "violence of language" (112) is not to destroy something sacrosanct that floats free of discourse, but to reveal that what we have always assumed to transcend linguistic formulations is already inscribed within a similar system of relations, of differences: identity itself already bears the traces of the arche-writing.

Esther's nicknames have been used as an example of the "violence of language" which *does* destroy an identity. William Axton, for instance, argues that they "deprive Esther of a measure of identity and status as an individual and reduce her to the relative anonymity of a housekeeper" (161). Yet if personal identity is bound up in social and familial roles, then Esther's position as "mistress of Bleak House" (as she is also called), is *part* of her identity, and her nicknames are a subtle indication of the way others in the household perceive her and relate to her. Esther acknowledges how her "own name soon bec[omes] quite lost" among her nicknames (148) and this response has been read in two different ways. On the one hand, the response has been seen as a tacit privileging of Esther's "own name" which is being usurped by her false names. On the other hand (as Ragussis and Northcutt Malone have observed), Esther's own name does not hold its own: it is simply one name amongst others, and as Guppy has discovered, "the little girl's real name [is] not Esther Summerson, but Esther Hawdon" (464).

Matthew Bagnet examines Woolwich in the catechism on his birthday, "accomplishing with extreme accuracy the questions number one and two, What is your name? and Who gave you that name?" (722). Esther, for whom (according to Miss Barbary) "[i]t would have been better . . . that [she] had had no birthday" (64) might, like Socrates, find herself in a "dilemma" upon being asked those questions: "Esther Summerson," "Esther Hawdon," "Esther Woodcourt," not to mention a host of nicknames, are all plausible responses to question number one. "Miss Barbary" is probably the answer to question number two, although this is not made explicit in the text. It is questionable whether the invention of a name like "Esther Summerson" is perfectly congruous with the Draconian austerity of Miss Barbary, but if she did not bestow this name, who did? To the improvised third question asked by

Matthew Bagnet, "And how do you like that name?" Esther might possibly respond, "not proper enough."

And when we read of the Somebody who brings with her "sunshine and summer air" (482), the ostensively defamiliarized metaphor of Esther Summerson's name leads the reader to "have recourse to the introduction of gods on machines" and to answer question number two with extreme accuracy: "Charles Dickens". The reader is patently aware of being caught up in a "masterly fiction" (68), that of *Bleak House*, and we, too, like the lawyers of Cook's Court, may be banging our heads against "walls of words." Yet it is precisely these "walls of words" that have allowed us to constitute the notion of an identity for "Esther Summerson" in the first place.

NOTES

1. For the other titles Dickens considered for *Bleak House*, see *Dickens' Working Notes for His Novels*. Harry Stone, ed. (Chicago: U of Chicago P, 1987).
2. For most stimulating discussions of names and naming in *Bleak House*, see Hillis Miller's "Introduction" to *Bleak House*, and Michael Ragussis' *Acts of Naming: The Family Plot in Fiction*.
3. Hillis Miller, however, cogently argues that the explicitly metaphorical names in Dickens reveal the characters to be "linguistic fictions." This "overt fictionality" Miller reads as "Dickens's way of demystifying the belief, affirmed in Plato's *Cratylus*, that the right name gives the essence of the thing" (23).
4. These claims appear to me to be at odds with Miller's earlier statement (which is not extensively explored) in the same essay: "To find out how I am related to others will be to find out who I am, for I am defined by my connections, familial or legal" (18).
5. It is thanks to Stephen Clarkson that I have used Davidson's paper as a critique of the claims made by Ragussis and Miller.
6. I am indebted to Stephen Clarkson for his insight here.

ACKNOWLEDGEMENTS

Thanks to Professor Brian Cheadle and Stephen Clarkson for their critical readings of the draft of this paper.

WORKS CITED

Barton, Anne. *The Names of Comedy*. Oxford: Clarendon, 1990.

Connor, Steven. *Charles Dickens*. New York: Blackwell, 1985.

Davidson, Donald. "Mental Events." *Readings in Philosophy of Psychology*. vol. 1. Ned Block, ed. London: Methuen, 1980:107–119.

Derrida, Jacques. "Différance." *"Speech and Phenomena" and Other Essays on Husserl's Theory of Signs*. Trans. David B. Allison. Evantson, Illinois: Northwestern UP, 1973:129–160.

Derrida, Jacques. *Of Grammatology*. Trans. Gayatri Chakravorty Spivak. Baltimore: Johns Hopkins UP, 1976.

Derrida, Jacques. *Positions*. Trans. Alan Bass. London: Athlone P, 1981.

Dickens, Charles. *Bleak House*. Norman Page, ed. Harmondsworth: Penguin, 1971.

Frege, Gottlob. "On Sense and Meaning." Translations from the Philosophical Writings of Gottlob Frege. eds. P. Geach and M. Black. Trans. M. Black. Basil Blackwell: Oxford, 1952. 3rd edn. 1980: 56–78.

Jakobson, Roman. "Closing Statement: Linguistics and Poetics." *Style in Language*. T. A. Sebeok, ed. Cambridge, Massachusetts: M.I.T. P, 1960, 350–57.

Miller, J. Hillis. "Introduction" to Dickens, Charles. *Bleak House*. Norman Page, ed. Harmondsworth: Penguin Ltd., 1971.

Northcutt Malone, Cynthia. " 'Flight' and 'Pursuit': Fugitive Identity in *Bleak House*." *DSA* 19 (1990): 107–124.

Nuttall, A. D. "True Words." *London Review of Books* (April, 1990): 18–19.

Plato. "Cratylus." *Plato with an English Translation*. H. N. Fowler, ed. and trans. London: William Heinemann, 1926:1–192.

Ragussis, Michael. *Acts of Naming: The Family Plot in Fiction*. Oxford, Oxford UP, 1986.

Ragussis, Michael. "The Ghostly Signs of *Bleak House*." *Nineteenth Century Fiction* 34 (1979): 253–80.

Sacks, Jonathan. *The Persistence of Faith: Religion, Morality & Society in a Secular Age*. London: Weidenfeld and Nicolson, 1991.

Wilt, Judith. "Confusion and Consciousness in Dickens's Esther." *Nineteenth Century Fiction* 32 (1977): 285–309.

Wittgenstein, Ludwig. *Philosophical Remarks*. Rush Rhees, ed. Oxford: Basil Blackwell Publishers. New York: Barnes & Noble, 1975.

"A Mere Question of Figures":
Measures, Mystery, and Metaphor in
Hard Times

Razak Dahmane

When in book 2, Chapter 10, of *Hard Times* Mrs. Sparsit asks Bounderby, "Have you received intelligence respecting the robbery?, he replies by using a Roman metaphor:

> "Why, ma'am; not yet . . . Rome wasn't built in a day, ma'am."
> "Very true, Sir," said Mrs. Sparsit . . .
> "*Nor yet in a week*, ma'am."

(151; emphasis added)

We are struck with the appropriateness of the Roman metaphor, here a result of Dickens' insistence on the sometimes comic congruence in a character of language with physiognomy. It is fitting that Mrs. Sparsit, that "Roman Matron" (91) "with the Coriolanian style of nose" (37) should understand the tenor of the Roman metaphor: great accomplishments take time. The interest of the metaphor, however, lies as much in the appropriateness of Mrs. Sparsit's grasp of it as in the interlocutor's reply. The addition of "Nor yet in a week" serves of course the purpose of characterization; it illustrates Bounderby's blustering temperament with its tendency, in the heat of boastfulness, towards humorless exaggeration; "humorless" because Dickens has from the start portrayed Bounderby as a strident bully, so that there is no risk of detecting the faintest echo of humor or irony in that earnest, peremptory talking at people that he mistakes for conversation. There is, however, something else at work here beyond humorless hyperbole, something, I shall argue, central to a reassessment of Dickens' alternative to the Gradgrindians: Bounderby's addition of "nor yet in a week" betrays his literal apprehension

137

of the whole figure of speech; the culprit is a mentality that has been—like Louisa's and Thomas's—"trained to mathematical exactness" (16) and that cannot therefore conceive of "day" as meaning anything else beside twenty-four hours' duration. A strict adherence to the statistician's figures, at the expense of the poet's accounts for Bounderby's failure to grasp fully the metaphorical import of "day" in his Roman metaphor. Dickens has Bounderby unwittingly literalize "day," by making him—again unwittingly—reduce it to its precise factual astronomical meaning at the expense of its figurative tenor of brevity. As we shall see, Dickens in *Hard Times* invites us to consider metaphorical proficiency a linguistic badge of moral decency and imaginative health; and where he histrionically pins this badge on the narrator, he seems unwilling to grant it to Bounderby, not even in the guise of a metaphor that has been deadened by usage into a cliché.

Dickens' sabotage of Bounderby's figurative percipience is but a part of his effort to undermine the language of the Utilitarians in *Hard Times* by selectively aborting in their speech any instances, deliberate or inadvertent, of figurativeness, however hackneyed the figures. This attempt I call "literalization," a rhetorical process that draws attention to the literal-mindedness of the Utilitarians, or to their deafness to the metaphoric import of figures of speech that they unwittingly use or hear used, or to ironic circumstances that fetter their metaphors with a satiric application beyond their grasp. In his characteristic exploration of language at the intersections of the literal and the figurative, Dickens for the first and, I think, only time pushes literalization beyond the conventional purposes of characterization, humor, and satire to press it into the sustained service of an idea. Literalization, I shall argue, represents his most convincing though so far critically overlooked answer to the Gradgrind philosophy. Not in the lisping, inarticulate humaneness of Sleary's pleas for tolerance of popular amusements, but in the narrator's blaze of figurativeness and in the memorable literalizations of the language of the Gradgrindians as they intone their mystery-denying gospel of facts and figures, does Dickens articulate his alternative to the hard-fact faction.

I

Clearly the conflict between fact and fancy is the central theme of *Hard Times*, the one which subsumes and unifies its otherwise loosely related subjects: education, divorce, industrialism, trade unionism, and hippodrama. The deep sympathies of the imagination, so Dickens' argument runs, if granted a measure of tolerance and freedom in an inimical Utilitarian society, would bring about happier, more productive teachers, school inspectors, legislators, employers, manufacturers, mine owners, workers, and entertainers; and a richer quality of life animated by a fancy-fostered vitality that is sure to urge insurgency against industrial blight.

The prevalent criticism of *Hard Times* regards the Slearys as representing the claims of the imagination and providing the chief counterpart to the forces of fact, and then goes on to expose their weaknesses.[1] Admittedly, the circus immediately strikes one as a tawdry arena that seems to have fallen on hard times long before Bounderby and Gradgrind come along to make matters worse. The ostensible precariousness of the warm-hearted Slearys, however, should be seen as proof that they are meant to illustrate the severity of the Gradgrindian threat, not represent an answer to it. Jupe's debilitating aches that call for "nine oils" and eventuate in his desertion of his young daughter and in his death in exile; Sleary's lisp; his timorousness of character that reduces what should have been a vigorous assertion of artistic freedom into a pitiable plea for tolerance—these impediments heighten our sense that far from representing an enduring alternative, the Slearys stand in pressing need of help themselves, of—as Sleary pleads—a "bethpeak" (213). Dickens seems fully aware of this fact as he comes to the rescue in the guise of an articulate, narrator-novelist enviably at ease with figurative language. This is the real counterpart to Gradgrindism, a subtle and sustained one articulated in the provocatively demonstrative figurativeness of the narrator's language and in the restrictions he imposes on Utilitarian speech through literalization.

Indeed Dickens images forth his objection to the Gradgrindians in the narrator's deliberate and pointedly provocative image-making; in his imagery of smoke serpents and melancholy-mad elephants and horses and flowers and light and dark; in his pausing to quote the lines "in a flowing scroll" beneath "The Pegasus's Arms" (26); in his quoting from *Oliver Goldsmith's The Deserted Village* (38); in his allusions to fairy tales, nursery fables, and *The Arabian Nights*; in his reference to "The Fairies, Sir, and the Dwarf, and the Hunchback, and the Genies" (37); and, generally, in his demonstrative delight at fancying and wondering despite the Utilitarians' pointed injunction to—in the title words of book 1, chapter 7—"Never Wonder."

This delight in metaphor amounts to a satiric flaunting of the verbal privileges that will be denied the language of Gradgrindism. Dickens' most apparent strategy of metaphoric divestment lies in his treatment of literalization in terms of symbol, theme, and character. First, there is the symbolization of

the literal in the celebrated opening chapter of *Hard Times* through a factualiz-
ing and a concretizing of the speaker.[2] In it the rhetoric works to reduce the
speaker to concrete non-sentience. He becomes an extension of the "plain,
bare, monotonous vault of a schoolroom" as much as it becomes an extension
of his "square forefinger," his "square wall of a forehead, which had his
eyebrows for its base, while his eyes found commodious cellerage in two
dark caves, overshadowed by the wall"; and, finally, an extension of his
"warehouse of a head," and of "his obstinate coat, square legs, and square
shoulders" (7). The ideological correspondence between the speaker, Gradgrind, and his materialistic school, coupled with the consistent application of
architectural and geometric metaphors to Gradgrind's physiognomy and with
the grammatical and stylistic repetitions of word, syntax, and (passive) voice,
erects him into the very symbol of that hard, mechanistic pedagogy. The
opening chapter of *Hard Times* is a figurative rendition of the literal and of
a literalist.

Similarly, chapter 2 dramatizes literal-mindedness through the government
officer's comico-grotesque confusion of word with thing. Literality clearly
lies in his explanation of "why you wouldn't paper a room with representation
of horses"—"Do you ever see horses walking up and down the sides of a
room in reality—in fact? Do you?"—and in hs indignant objection to Cecilia
Jupe's willingness in carpeting a room to "use a carpet having a representation
of flowers upon it" because she is "very fond of flowers": "and is that why
you would put tables and chairs upon them and have people walking over
them with heavy boots?" (11). The import of this literalization scene is
much subtler than may suggest the comico-grotesqueness of the government
officer's explanation. By objecting to literature, the verbal repository of meaning, the hard-fact fellows balk at the implication that meaning lies in words,
not in things—not in the bricks and chimneys of Coketown; not, in other
words, in what Bouderby considers "real" (179); hence their exclusive emphasis on facts. They are, Dickens intimates, semantic-literalist-empiricists
whose blindness to or rejection of the intrinsic worth and connotative wealth
of language prompts them to reduce its function to one that is restrictive,
definitional, and solely denotative.

The government officer from the Department of Practical Arts makes but
a brief appearance and is replaced by a bolder, harsher version of himself—Bounderby. In this professedly self-made businessman we are dealing
with the epitome of literal-mindedness. His wedding speech establishes him
as a literalist par excellence, "a man who, when he sees a Post, says 'that's
a Post,' and when he sees a Pump, says "that's Pump,' and is not to be got

to call a Post a Pump, or a Pump a Post, or either of them a Toothpick" (84). He is also a strident version of his father-in-law, Thomas Gradgrind, an earnest literalist with an "unbending, utilitarian, matter-of-fact face" (77–78) who comes to realize the inadequacy of an education by facts and figures alone.

II

The literalists' exaltation of facts and figures is solidly anchored in an enmity to fancy and a scornful dismissal of its claims as idle and puerile amusement. To them, then, Dickens must have felt the need to deny figurative percipience. Dickens does not, however, undermine the metaphoric import of every single utterance by the enemies of fancy; he does so selectively. Systematic literalization in a novel is of course impossible. It would mean dramatic and narrative paralysis, for "language," as Emerson tells us, "is fossil poetry" (1:1084), dead metaphor whose most common and ordinary usage is seldom literal. In the rare cases where Dickens allows the Gradgrindians a conscious rise to figurativeness, he seems to do so chiefly because the figurativeness furthers his satiric intent. Hence it is, for example, that he allows Bounderby to use an agricultural metaphor in his attack on Stephen Blackpool as "one of those chaps who have always got a grievance. And you go about, sowing it and raising crops" (115). This is a figurative concession to Bounderby, but one partly allowed at least because of its congruence with the extended meteorological metaphor that the narrator establishes at Bounderby's expense throughout the chapter. In the first sentence of book 2, chapter 5, the narrator notes Bounderby's "windy manner" (110), then develops the remark into an extended analogy: "Bounderby, who was always more or less like a Wind, finding something in his way here, began to blow at it directly. . . . The wind began to get boisterous" and was "springing up very fast. . . . (Gushing weather with deceitful calms. One now prevailing)" (111); but not for long because soon Bounderby was "blowing a gale" (113) that intensifies into "a hurricane" (114), the full brunt of which is borne by Blackpool, who is dismissed from Bounderby's employment.

Dickens grants Bounderby figurative speech only when it furthers satiric intent, but this is rare since more often than not the satire lies in denying the word-cherishing privileges of the metaphor to a literalist mentality that posits the supremacy of things over words. One means to such denial lies in the creation of a literalizing context in instances of conscious or unwitting figurativeness on Utilitarian lips. This method might be called literalization by juxtaposition. We note at least three instances where Dickens specifies circumstances propitiating literalization through the physical presence of an object, a referent, whose meaning was used figuratively. First, Bounderby sees in Stephen's dissatisfaction with the Divorce Laws "traces of the turtle soup and venison, and gold spoon" (57). The culinary metaphor effectively expresses Bounderby's dismissal of the aspirations of the working class as illegitimate and self-indulgent. Dickens however hastens to literalize the metaphor by putting it in a mouth full of chop and sherry. In the course of the dialogue Bounderby takes sherry and stays Sparsit from her feinting to leave the room, to ensure the privacy of her employer and his employee, "by holding a mouthful of chop in suspension, before swallowing it, and putting out his left hand. Then, withdrawing his hand and swallowing his mouthful of chop" (57), he resumes his conversation with Stephen. In other contexts Dickens would have invited his readers to admire the food metaphor as a clever adaptation of speech to circumstance, but here on Utilitarian lips he undermines it by emphasizing Bounderby's consumption of food and thus dwelling on the obvious hypocrisy of a glutton with a mouthful of chop and sherry using food as a metaphor for greed-fed discontent. Having established a literalizing context for the turtle-soup-and-venison metaphor, Dickens will allow Bounderby to use it again at least twice more, once to acquaint the visiting Harthouse with the "one ultimate object in life" of every "Hand in this town." During this same interview Bounderby also uses a variation on this food metaphor: "First of all, you see our smoke. That's meat and drink to us" (96). The turtle soup metaphor is used again by Bounderby in reply this time to Gradgrind's admission of the harsh neglect of "qualities in Louisa" (178); Bounderby vehemently answers that he knows the bricks, the works, the chimneys, the smoke, and the Hands of Coketown. "They're real. When a man tells me anything about imaginative qualities . . . he means turtle soup and venison . . ." (179). Bounderby's figure of speech incisively establishes here, at his own expense, what Dickens has only alluded to elsewhere: that the singleminded allegiance to the factual breeds a literal-mindedness that often evidences not alert and wise realism but subjection to materialism and a coarse hedonism betrayed by food metaphors. Again, Dickens allows Bounderby the use of food metaphors because these are consistent with the attack on the materialistic Benthamite philosophy which advocates the pursuit of quantifiable and weighable pleasures. These pleasures Dickens calls "grovelling sensualities," "the ghost" of the sound imagination (101).

The supervisor of Bounderby's meals, Mrs. Sparsit, "implied that in her stately person she considered lunch a weakness"; but not sweetbread: "In yielding my trust here" [Bounderby's home], says Mrs. Sparsit, "I shall not be freed from the necessity of eating the bread of dependence." And the narrator adds, undermining the metaphor, "she may have said the sweetbread, for that delicate article in a savoury brown sauce was her favourite supper" (82). In this instance the sweetbread is not actually present in the scene, but the narrator insists on reminding us of the literal basis, the physical occasion, of the food metaphor. Finally, when Bounderby during a fireside chat with Mrs. Gradgrind, dwelling on his (fictitious) childhood ordeals, declares, "I was so ragged and dirty, that you wouldn't have touched me with a pair of tongs," Mrs. Gradgrind "faintly looked at the tongs" (17). Her action of course dramatizes Mrs. Gradgrind's literal-mindedness but it also divests of its metaphorical import Bounderby's hyperbole. Dickens uses her action to make plain that Bounderby's figure of speech, ordinarily evidence of a clever adaptation of figures of speech to matters of fact, is inspired by the actual material presence of tongs in the room: Bounderby cannot be expected to use "a pair of tongs" to express forcibly his childhood mendacity unless he sees one. There would have been no figurative speech had there been no putative referent. Dickens thus literalizes by noting the literal basis of the figurative so that literalization becomes his stylistic means of dramatizing the Utilitarians' servitude to the material.

Sometimes the literalizing context is not physical but mental. It does not consist in the actual physical presence of the material occasion for figurativeness, but results from a mentality whose exclusive emphasis on facts and figures and immediate utility blinds it to the metaphoric import of even dead metaphors. Three chief examples of this type of literalization are anatomical. First, Dickens draws attention to the dehumanization implicit in the literal generic reference to "the multitude of Coketown [as] 'the Hands'—a race who would have found more favour with some people, if Providence had seen fit to make them only hands, or, like the lower creatures of the seas, only hands and stomachs" (52).[3] Dickens allows the Utilitarians to use this synecdoche to reveal their exploitative view of humanity. By reducing human beings to the most practical of their members, the reference divests them of hearts and souls, and implies a definition of men and women as animals of immediate, empirical utility. Literalization in this case is a form of dismemberment.

The same Utilitarian literal-mindedness informs Bitzer's implied definition of the heart through its function.

"Bitzer," said Mr. Gradgrind . . . "have you a heart?"
"The circulation, Sir," returned Bitzer, smiling at the oddity of the question, "couldn't be carried on without one. No man, Sir, acquainted with the facts established by Harvey relating to the circulation of the blood, can doubt that I have a heart."   (210–11)

The obsession with utility, which Dickens implies is often conducive to a cynical assessment of human nature, blinds Bitzer to the figurative use of "heart" to connote compassion. Gradgrind's conversion from an inflexible literalist to a man who has come to perceive the inadequacy of his views of men and women in statistical terms is mirrored in his figurative use of "heart," a linguistic intimation of heightened sensibility. And it is this sensibility that will afford the new Gradgrind a glimpse of what transcends the bottom-line materialism of facts and figures and the shallow cynicism of the self-interest cult. For the figurative—associated with "all the inappreciable things that raise [life] from the state of conscious death," "the graces of the soul," and "the sentiments of the heart" (161)—becomes an appropriate vehicle for "the unfathomable mystery in the meanest of [Hands]" (56).

Bitzer's literal understanding of "heart" saps the spirit out of the word just as his celebrated definition of a horse (9) saps the vitality out of the horse. This Dickens achieves by having Bitzer define "horse" piecemeal in a heap of factual and grammatical fragments that rely on numbers and quantity and minimize the use of that lifeblood of the English sentence, the verb. Dickens' point is that we should be aware of experience in both its affective and effective dimensions just as we should be aware of "heart" in its physiological as well as its figurative meaning. Any emphasis on the letter at the expense of the spirit, on the quantifiable at the expense of fluid and intuitive experience, results in a loss of our wholeness of vision, a loss which—Dickens warns us—would soon degenerate into a myopic and fragmentary view. As Colin Manlove points out, there is *bit* in Bitzer (63).

Where he suffuses with pathos the literalizing of hand and heart, Dickens imbues with comedy Bounderby's literalization of "nose" during the scene following the public deflation of his myth of the self-made man, the unforeseen disastrous result of his lady housekeeper's overzealousness:

"What's the matter now, ma'am?" said Mr. Bounderby, in a very short way . . .
"Pray, Sir," returned Mrs. Sparsit, "do not bite my nose off."
"Bite your nose off, ma'am?" repeated Mr. Bounderby. "Your nose!" meaning, Mrs. Sparsit conceived, that it was too developed a nose for the purpose. After which offensive implication, he cut himself a crust of bread and

threw the knife down with a noise."   (216)

Bounderby's repetition of Mrs. Sparsit's sarcastic plea betrays the literality that blinds him to the tenor of her figurative meaning: her resentment of his brutal manner. Bounderby's literal-mindedness humorously compounds the noise-nose pun with one less evident. The cutting of a crust of bread with a knife suggests, through the grimly humorous equivalence between biting off and slicing, the literalization of "matter": the nose has become as much non-sentient matter as the crust of bread. "Matter" in this context is a dead metaphor, a word whose metaphoric energy has been lost, deadened, through common usage; but Dickens here denies Bounderby even a dead metaphor. To dramatize Bounderby's literal-mindedness, which seems at least partly responsible at once for the repetition of Mrs. Sparsit's sarcastic hyperbole and of the subsequent slicing of the bread, Dickens divests the word "matter" of the thick patina of its normal and unquestioned dead "metaphoricality," its "fossil poetry," (meaning "problem") to reveal it in its starkly literal initial sense of inert mass. Dickens deftly shows the unwitting restoration to its literal basis of the word "matter" in Bounderby's exasperated question, "What's the matter now?" Literalization has become materialization, a result of Bounderby's unwitting poetic defossilization.

The most pervasive instances of literalization have to do with Dickens' treatment of the concept of Time, "Old Time, that greatest and longest-established Spinner of all" (74), the eponymous hero of book 1, chapter 14, "The Great Manufacturer." In book 2, chapter 3, young Thomas Gradgrind insolently boasts to James Harthouse, "I am not going to begin to be polite now, about old Bounderby. It would be rather late in the day" (102). His use of "day" is of course figurative, and the figure of speech has hardened into the unquestioned rigidity of the dead metaphor. It is doubtful, however, whether "old Bounderby" would have grasped this figurative use of "day," for the most notorious instance of literalization of that word occurs in his use of the Roman metaphor mentioned earlier. There are other examples of time-related literalization. One is inherent in the literalization of a key word in the novel, "fire." The word is used metaphorically by Louisa who, as the novel's fire-gazer, has come to see in the flames an objective correlative to her inner "fire with nothing to burn" emitting "a light with nothing to rest upon" (15). She tells her mother that "the red sparks dropping out of the fire, and whitening and dying . . . made me think, after all, how short my life would be, and how little I could hope to do in it" (45). Mrs. Gradgrind however dismisses as "nonsense" her daughter's subjective reading of the ephemerality of life in the red sparks dying into ashes: "after the lectures you have attended and the experiments you have seen! After I heard you myself going on with your master about combustion and calcination and calorification" (45).

Where the wife rejects the figurative connotations of a literal fire, after Louisa explains them to her, the husband cannot even see them. The classic example of the hard-fact fellows' inability to understand metaphor occurs in the seminal chapter 15 of book 1, "Father and Daughter." Gradgrind imparts to Louisa Bounderby's marriage proposal and awaits her response, which is so long in coming that he says at length:

> "Are you consulting the chimneys of the Coketown works, Louisa?"
> "There seems to be nothing there but languid and monotonous smoke. Yet when the night comes, Fire bursts out, father!" She answered, turning quickly.
> "Of course I know that, Louisa. I do not see the application of the remark."
> To do him justice he did not, at all.   (78)

Gradgrind perceives only the literal meaning of Louisa's words; sees nothing in fire but what his wife, not his daughter, has reductively seen. He is also blind to Louisa's figurative use of "night." She will later use the word at once literally and figuratively when, appealing to her brother's better nature in the name of "all the night of my decay," she entreats him to tell her "the truth now" (142). Her use of "night" in this example is explicitly figurative. It is fitting that she uses the word first literally, when she speaks to Tom of his lying "alone, my dear, in the melancholy night," then figuratively, for she is linguistically a double center. Her Utilitarian education did not altogether obliterate her struggling disposition towards the figurative. Book 1, chapter 15, pits Louisa's symbolization of the literal against Gradgrind's failure to see anything beyond it.

The ability to perceive metaphorical language Dickens links with a capacity for compassion and sensitivity. This Gradgrind lacks: he fails to see the "one wavering moment in her, when she was impelled to . . . give him the pent-up confidences of her heart," blinded as he was by "the artificial barriers he had for many years been erecting between himself and all those subtle essences of humanity which will elude the utmost cunning of algebra" (77). The systematic envisaging of "everything from the strong dispassionate ground of reason and calculation, [and] [f]rom that ground alone" (75) leads to an unwitting imperviousness to the emotive and connotative depths of language. Gradgrind fails Louisa here not because he fails to listen, not because he is a bad father—on the contrary he is from the start a responsible one—but because he fails to discern the somber poetry of his daughter's despair.

Another instance of literalization more closely related to the theme of time occurs in Louisa's use and Gradgrind's misapprehesion of "short."

> "Father, I have often thought that life is very short. . . ."
> "It is short, no doubt, my dear. Still the average duration of human life is proved to have increased of late years. The calculations of various life assurance and annuity offices, among other figures which cannot go wrong, have established the fact."
> "I speak of my own life, father."
> "O indeed? Still," said Mr. Gradgrind, "I need not point out to you, Louisa, that it is governed by the laws which govern lives in the aggregate." (78)

Louisa uses "short" subjectively to express duration of inner time; Gradgrind understands it in its statistical sense to mean chronology or clock time. The father confuses fugacity with fewness, longevity with fulfillment, failing to understand that life can be chronologically long yet short in terms of human aspirations. The Bergsonian distinction between time as chronology and time as duration is inherent in the Utilitarians' and the narrator's respective uses of language. More specifically, Gradgrindian time is mechanical, external, factual: the time of the "deadly statistical clock" in Gradgrind's Observatory which "measured every second with a beat like a rap upon a coffin-lid" (75), a mode of measurement appropriate to a life in which "every day [was] the same as yesterday and tomorrow, and every year the counterpart of the last and the next" (22). The narrator's time, on the other hand, is organic, the time not of being but of becoming, the time of the seasonal rhythm of natural life; of "Sowing, Reaping," and "Garnering"; a time qualitatively assessed in terms of the novelist's central themes—"human nature, human passions, human hopes and fears . . ." (42), "the capacity for good and evil, for love or hatred, for patriotism or discontent, for the decomposition of virtue into vice, or the reverse" (56). Book 1, chapter 15, dramatizes a clash between a static and statistical definition of life as an accumulation of years and a dynamic and organic definition of life as a striving towards spiritual, emotional, and social plenitude. Both definitions are imaged forth in the paradoxical personification of Time as at once the father of machinery and the mother of seasons: "Time went on in Coketown like its own machinery . . . [but also] brought its varying seasons even into that wilderness of smoke and brick" (71). This trope translates the clash between the literal and the figurative into the dialectical tension between the multiple and heterogeneous times

expressed in the main title and the homogeneous and cyclical time expressed
in the three books' subtitles.

III

The Utilitarians' blindness to the figurative import of language, Dickens
suggests, traps them into a joyless view of life as the mechanical unwinding
of grimly monotonous chronology. The culprit, of course, is an exaltation of
facts and figures based on what Dickens suggests is a mistaken notion of
scientific exactitude and a subsequent hostility to the imagination. Indeed,
Dickens debunks this obsession with exactitude as consistently as he notes it
carefully. Thomas and Louisa "have been trained to mathematical exactness"
(16). Their father becomes a "Member of Parliament for Coketown; one of
the respected members for ounce weights and measures, one of the representatives of the multiplication tables" (73), with a room that was "quite a blue
chamber in its abundance of blue books" (75). When his daughter insists
that he repeat "word for word" her answer to Bounderby's marriage proposal
he again fails to see the sardonic despondence of her request: "it is quite
right, my dear, to be exact" (78). Gradgrind finally comes to realize the error
of his exclusive emphasis on facts and figures, and Dickens tries to do justice
to his good intentions in quantitative metaphors: "In gauging the fathomless
deeps with his little mean excise-rod, and in staggering over the universe
with his rusty stiff-legged compasses, he had meant to do great things" (165).
    Mrs. Sparsit and Bitzer are also models of meticulous accuracy. "Mrs.
Sparsit's talent for—in fact for anything requiring accuracy—is too habitually
developed to admit of any question." The words are those of Harthouse,
who praises the bank guardian for having drawn Miss Gradgrind's "portrait
perfectly. Presented her dead image" (145). Her confidant, Bitzer, is also a
stickler for accuracy. When Bounderby informs his close friends that "In the
little safe in young Tom's closet . . . there was a hundred and fifty-odd
pounds," the porter specifies: "A hundred and fifty-four, seven, one" (136).[4]
In Bounderby's reply Dickens derides the compulsion for misplaced accuracy.

> "Come! . . . It's enough to be robbed while you're snoring because you're
> too comfortable, without being put right with your four seven ones. Mrs.
> Sparsit, ma'am, you say you have heard him snore?"
>   "Sir," returned Mr. Sparsit, "I cannot say that I have heard him precisely
> snore, and therefore must not make that statement. But on winter evenings,
> when he has fallen asleep at his table, I have heard him, what I should prefer

to describe as partially choke. I have heard him on such occasions produce
sounds of a nature similar to what may be sometimes heard in Dutch clocks."
(137)

Dickens, of course, does not object to accuracy per se. In his private life he
has shown himself to be by all accounts a stickler for accuracy and punctual-
ity.[5] His satire, however, focuses as much on a concern with factual accuracy
as on the implied rejection of fiction behind it: for, to the utilitarians, fiction
can never be anything more than lies invented for idle amusement. Further,
Dickens suggests that such an obsessiveness turns discourse into a means of
persecution similar in intent to the placards about Blackpool with which
Bounderby had the walls of Coketown covered. Language ceases to be a
bridge between human beings and becomes a center of indifference where
the humane hardens into the intransigence of the legal. Mrs. Sparsit assumes
the "air of giving strict evidence" and of bearing "testimony" (137).

An overriding concern for factual and numerical accuracy, Dickens implies,
not only spawns callous calculators but also falsifies human reality. The
paradox of the literal-factual-statistical error that is a figurative-moral-psycho-
logical truth is clarified in Cissy's "mistakes" in answering M'choakumchild's questions. M'Choakumchild reports that the mistakes of Girl Number
Twenty, a girl who is "extremely deficient in [her] facts" and whose "acquaintance with figures is very limited" (72), come from her reluctance to
take "the smallest conceivable interest in [the globe's] exact measurements"
and her being "extremely slow in the acquisition of dates, unless some pitiful
incident happened to be connected therewith" (46). Gradgrind is disappointed
in her: "You have not acquired, under Mr. and Mrs. M'Choakumchild,
anything like that amount of exact knowledge which I looked for" (71–72).
Hers are statistical mistakes but profoundly humane verities intuitively
reached through the gift of selflessness; of envisaging human sorrow not
from the safe, cruel, and abstract distances of facts and figures but from an
imaginative, personal participation in that sorrow. "National Prosperity"
should be "Natural." And the percentage of the "five hundred persons
drowned or burnt to death [out of] "the hundred thousand persons who went
to sea on long voyages" is indeed "Nothing—to the relations and friends of
the people who were killed" (48). Cissy's statistically incorrect answer is
morally right. In the light of the individuating imagination, the depth of
whose sympathies enables it to see that what is accurate does not always
mirror what is right, suffering humanity cannot be reduced to—in the words
of one of the proposed titles—"A Mere Question of Figures."

IV

Indeed, in a letter of 20 January 1854 to John Forster Dickens enclosed fourteen titles, among them "Two and Two Are Four," "Simple Arithmetic," "A Matter of Calculation" and "A Mere Question of Figures."[6] All four are apt, but it is the double sense of "figures" in the last proposed title that reflects the magnitude of Dickens' effort in *Hard Times*. For the dynamic fluctuations of the literal and the figurative Dickens conflates into a campaign of defense and attack, rejection and advocacy. The figures of title are seldom either poetic or numerical, and Dickens' sense of the myopic reductiveness of the numerical invariably exacerbates his sense of the indispensability of the poetic:

> So many hundred Hands in this Mill; so many hundred horse Steam Power. It is known, to the force of a single pound weight, what the engine will do; but, not all the calculators of the National Debt can tell me the capacity for good or evil, for love or hatred, for patriotism or discontent, for the decomposition of virtue into vice, or the reverse, at any single moment in the soul of one of these its quiet servants, with the composed faces and the regulated actions. There is no mystery in it; there is an unfathomable mystery in the meanest of them, for ever. Supposing we were to reserve our arithmetic for material objects, and to govern these awful unknown quantities by other means!   (56)

This passage fulminates against the materialism of the numerical approach, its inadequacy to express the "mystery." Where he feels the rejection of figures of speech as a personal affront and a professional threat, Dickens perceives as a national threat the Victorian ethos of the numerical-quantitative approach to life. The repetition of intensifiers and superlatives—"so many," "single," "one," "meanest"; the repetition of "hundred"; the repetition of "Hands," a synecdochical designation that he has already denounced as economic commodification (52); the use of categorical absolutes, "not all," "for ever"; the use of negatives, "not all," "no mystery," "*un*fathomable"—these stylistic devices convey not only a rhetoric of rejection, but a high pitch of vehemence in that rejection.

To Dickens the phrase "A Mere Question of Figures" crystallizes the essence of a Victorian economic orthodoxy that he denounces on several grounds: it resonates for him with the dismissive oversimplification voiced by at least four overlapping types of Utilitarian adversaries. First, the Hartleyan-inspired Benthamite empiricists who trace knowledge to sense-impression and by so doing deny that emotion is an integral part of the intellectual process. Such empiricists deny the existence of an innate moral sense, the existence of the "awful unknown quantities" and a fortiori of the existence of the "other means" that would "govern" them; hence the hostility to cultivation of the affective life, the inward culture of the individual. Second, the political economists, especially those whose statistical accounts of the socioeconomic state of the citizenry are relied upon by Members of Parliament like Gradgrind. Dickens rejects their statistically based conclusions because he questions the validity of their means: to Dickens statistics are abstractions divorced from flesh-and-blood humanity; they dehumanize, deindividuate; they reduce Cecilia Jupe to Girl Number Twenty and the Coketown workers to Hands. "Whatever [blue books] could prove (which is usually anything you like), they proved there [in Gradgrind's room], in an army constantly strengthening by the arrival of new recruits. In that charmed apartment, the most complicated social questions were cast up, got into exact totals, and finally settled—if those concerned could only have been brought to know it" (75). Third, the mainstream Benthamites who reduce happiness to a pain-and-pleasure calculus. Fourth, the Victorian demographers—Gradgrind names one of his sons Malthus—whose "mere figures" are Malthusian figures that chart a nightmarish discrepancy between production and reproduction, between the arithmetic progression of food increase and the geometric progression of population. Here "A Mere Question of Figures" resonates with the ring of exoneration. Malthus, Dickens believes, conveniently furnishes the ruling classes with the opportunity to wash their hands of any civic responsibility, chalking human misery up to rampant overpopulation whose rise can be checked only positively through birth control and negatively through infanticide, wars, famine, and epidemics.

V

The insistence on empirical accuracy and a numerically objective approach to life goes hand in glove with the Utilitarian emphasis on the diffusion of useful knowledge. The implication that fiction serves no useful goal also stands behind Dickens' satire on those whose emphasis on tangible exact facts is an effort to reduce the rich figurative realm of the emotions to that of literal information. The reduction is in his eyes a contamination of art by immediate utility. Dickens has already made a similar point in his lead article "Frauds on the Fairies," published only three months before he was to write the first page of *Hard Times*.[7] In that article Dickens rehearses his message to the Utilitarians in *Hard Times*: "Supposing we were to reserve our arithmetic for material objects and to govern these awful quantities by other means!" (56). Besides religion, imagination is one of these means. Indeed, Dickens makes high claims for the imagination since its virtues, he insists, are both aesthetic and ethical. The imagination "adorns" and "graces" lives of monotonous toil in somber industrial citadels of melancholy mad-elephants and smoke-serpents. Further, like Wordsworth's Nature, it serves as a moral guide without which "the sturdiest physical manhood would be morally stark death" (219).

But not all imaginations are good. Central to the case for the imagination as a vital and enduring alternative making its own case through defiant metaphorical density and unmaking the Utilitarians' through literalization strategies is the distinction in *Hard Times* between sound and perverse or "wicked" imaginations. Tom's and Louisa's imaginations have been perverted by the systematic repression of the natural imaginative impulse especially strong at childhood, but in Louisa too strong to admit of utter eradication. Her fire gazing reveals at once "a jaded sullenness" and "a starved imagination keeping life in itself somehow, which brightened her expression. Not with the brightness natural to cheerful youth, but with uncertain, eager, doubtful flashes" (15). As the contrite Gradgrind hesitantly tells an obdurate Bounderby, "there are imaginative qualities in Louisa, which . . . have ben harshly neglected . . . and a little perverted" (178).

The perversion of Tom's imagination through starvation and repression is more pronounced. Dickens defines this damaged imagination as the "ghost" of a sound one that has been "strangled in [Tom's] cradle" and is now inconveniencing him "in the form of grovelling sensualities" (101). The starved imagination consequently seeks other outlets and finds them in quantitative Benthamite pleasures; Tom becomes "quite a gentleman of pleasure" (73). Sparsit's and Bounderby's imaginations are similarly perverse; in Mrs. Pegler's words, "wicked imaginations" (192). She is addressing Gradgrind, who has innocently repeated to her some of Bounderby's accusations of maternal desertion, but her phrase aptly applies to her son's autobiographical inventions and his lady housekeeper's "allegorical fancy." Indeed, Mrs. Sparsit's "Staircase" shows a pernicious inventiveness but not a sound imagination because it is grounded in the gratification of malice, if not in downright evil:

> Now, Mrs. Sparsit was not a poetical woman; but she took an idea in the nature of an allegorical fancy, into her head. Much watching of Louisa . . . must have given her as it were a lift, in the way of inspiration. She

erected in her mind a mighty Staircase, with a dark pit of shame and ruin at
the bottom; and down those stairs, from day to day and hour to hour, she saw
Louisa coming. (150–51)

Dickens' point is that the wicked imagination can only invent lies actuated
by all gradations of evil, where the sound imagination spawns tales informed
by the wish for the common good and celebrates the "unfathomable mystery"
even in the meanest of human beings (56).

The distinction between good and pernicious imaginations entails a distinction between two types of imaginative speech.[8] Dickens exalts figurative
speech in *Hard Times* because it provides a barometer of cultural, moral, and
even spiritual aplomb. Not all the users of figurative speech, however, are
moral and aesthetic positives. Slackbridge, Harthouse, Sparsit, Gradgrind,
and Bounderby are articulate, even eloquent. In the case of the first three,
especially, their eloquence rises at times to the narrator's figurativeness. But
the difference is significant. Harthouse's smoothness of speech, Mrs. Sparsit's
"allegorical fancy," Slackbridge's hyperboles, and Bounderby's lies have
lapsed into the transparent polemics of malicious and manipulative rhetoric.
Like Mrs. Sparsit's "allegorical fancy," Harthouse's eloquence is contami-
nated by bad intentions. The good speech that his elder brother claims Harthouse could make is a "devilish good speech" (96) and would have lacked
the novelist's compassionate commitment.[9] The point is that these polished
rhetors are resourceful, clever, and even arresting in their incisive articulate-
ness, but Dickens gives them words and actions that deny them the benevolence, the vitality, of the sound imagination. This divestment of the moral
energy of the figurative dimension of language on articulate Utilitarian lips
is also a form of literalization.

Inherent in the distinction between sound and "starved," "wicked" imaginations, and between Gradgrindian and narratorial eloquence is one between
the good lies of art and the damaging lies of the Utilitarians, each of whom
is shown to be either lying or belied. Where, for example, Bounderby's lies
are immoral, the narrator's are not. The rhetoric of his defiant figurativeness
invites us to regard his lies as moral constructs grounded in the truth of inner
reality. The presence of Mrs. Pegler and its culmination in the explosion of
Bounderby's lies (book 3, chapter 5), arising partly from the need to hammer
home such a distinction, make it even more difficult to see how the forces
of fancy could be considered "fettered" and "confused" and the forces of
fact articulate and more imaginative (Sonstroem 531).

VI

Not the least distinction of *Hard Times* is its introduction for the first time in the Dickens canon of a new type of literalist. To note the differences between the literalists in this novel and those in his other novels, let us take the example of that notorious literalist in *Our Mutual Friend*, Nicodemus Boffin. In book 4, chapter 3, Boffin hastens to Venus at Clerkenwell, where he receives the much-dreaded intelligence that "Wegg is likely to drop down upon [him] tonight."

> "Why, therefore, you suppose he'll turn to at the grindstone, eh, Venus?" said Mr. Boffin.
> "Just so, sir."
> Mr. Boffin took his nose in his hand as if it were already excoriated, and the sparks were beginning to fly out of that feature.   (718)

Beyond recalling the comico-grotesqueness of caricature, the gesture and the thought illustrate the graphic quality of Dickens' humor as well as the powers of visualization that words exert upon his characters' vivid imaginations. Paradoxically, Boffin's keen sensitivity to words, despite his literal-mindedness, is nothing short of a poet's by virtue of his visceral, almost hallucinatory, response to language.

Generally speaking, before and after *Hard Times* we meet mainly two kinds of literalists in the novels of Charles Dickens. First, there are those whose utter naiveté renders them childish ignoramuses, fodder for farce. Second, there are those whose literalism makes them semiliterate poets. Childlike in their literalism, they perceive words in a fresh relation to things and so respond to language with a spontaneity unmediated by formal education or stylistic sophistication. Through an uncanny feel for the literal basis of language these literalists defossilize its poetry. They are poets of a kind because, paradoxically enough, their intellectual guilelessness sometimes heightens their untutored etymological awareness. Boffin seems to belong to both categories at once. The Boffin who believes "a Secretary to be a piece of furniture, mostly of mahogany" (227) belongs to the first category of literalists; to the second belongs the Boffin who holds his nose as if sparks were flying from it upon overhearing Wegg's threat to put Boffin's nose to the grindstone.

Boffin-like literalists, whom Dickens' comic linguistic exuberance made easy—and delightful—for him to create, radicaly differ, however, from the literalists in *Hard Times*, who are articulate and educated. Boffin, though semiliterate, is literary in his aspirations. The Gradgrindians, on the other hand, are literate but not literary; in fact, they are dogmatically anti-literary. They represent a type of vehemently ideological literalists whom Dickens has not introduced before *Hard Times* and to whom he was not to return afterward. To Dickens Gradgrindian literalists pose a twofold threat. First, their literalism stems not from an etymological keenness or liguistic innocence but from a scathing and unrelenting rejection of metaphor that amounts to a sworn enmity. "I should as soon have expected to find my children reading poetry," says an indignant Gradgrind who has just caught Tom and Louisa "peeping at the circus" (19). Second, because they are articulate and socially powerful Dickens must have feared that their gospel of facts could take them a long way, as indeed it did, in giving mid-Victorian culture its tone, its temper, and its doctrine. In the stridency of his fulmination against their faction, especially in the early chapters, we measure Dickens' resentment, perhaps dread, of their assault on his profession, on his very livelihood. And the rhetoric in this novel is essentially defensive, even when Dickens seems—in his narrator's figurative flourishes—at his most militant and affirmative, for the affirmation is too shrill and there is something too theatrical in the defiant metaphoricality. For *Hard Times* is at once Dickens' most anti-Utilitarian novel and his most utilitarian one.

VII

From *Pickwick* to *Our Mutual Friend* Dickens' extraordinarily keen sensitivity to the interpenetrations of the literal and figurative levels of language has led him to explore in their light and at their intersections the elements of fiction. In book 4, chapter 3, of *Our Mutual Friend* Dickens shows how a character, Venus, uses the distinction between the literal and the figurative to avert an altercation. Silas Wegg accuses Noddy Boffin of spying on him:

> "You've placed in this yard a skulking, a sneaking, and a sniffing menial [Sloppy].
> "He hadn't a cold in his head when I sent him here," said Mr. Boffin.
> "Boffin!" retorted Wegg, "I warn you not to attempt a joke with me!"
> Here Mr. Venus interposed, and remarked that he conceived Mr. Boffin to have taken the description literally; the rather for as much as he, Mr. Venus, had himself supposed the menial to have contracted an affliction or a habit of the nose, involving a serious drawback on the pleasures of social intercourse, until he had discovered that Mr. Wegg's description of him was to be accepted as merely figurative." (720)

The inconsequentiality of the figurative and the literal interpretation of Sloppy's nasality must be stressed, for the literal would mean a head cold for Sloppy and trouble for Boffin, where the "merely figurative" would at once further underscore Boffin's lack of formal education and reassure Wegg of the dustman's good faith and innocuous literal-mindedness: a first step towards defusing a potentially nasty confrontation that would have forced Venus to disclose prematurely his disgust at Wegg's blackmailing scheme. The passage is comic. The reader emerges from it with a sharper sense of Mr. Wegg's intransigence, Sloppy's comico-grotesqueness, and Venus's mental promptitude.

In stark contrast, the figurative in *Hard Times* is all but "merely figurative." Through figurativeness Dickens insists on an extension of significance beyond the literal. *Hard Times* is unique in the Dickens canon in its sustained use of the figurative and the literal. There is reason to insist on a larger role for these two levels of language than that of their service to the conventional goals of characterization, comedy, and satire: this role is enacted in the novel's metaphoric density; in the rendering of literalization in terms of symbol in the opening scene; in the creation of three memorable literalists in Gradgrind, Bounderby, and Bitzer; in the numerous instances of textual and contextual literalizations; and in the defense of culture beneath the satire on facts, figures, multiplication tables, statistics, quantities, ounce and pound weights, and measures. Literalization is part and parcel of the idea of *Hard Times*, at once its method and its meaning. And indeed method and meaning coalesce as Dickens runs Utilitarian speech aground on the shoals of literalism in an effort to alert his contemporaries to the cultural skull beneath Utilitarian skin by protesting the attempted repression of poetic vocabulary and narrative impulse and by denouncing the obsession with the thing behind the word, the matter behind the metaphor, and the pound weight and measures behind the mystery.

It is with a few words about the nature of the mystery in *Hard Times* that I would like to conclude. Grahame Smith, commenting on Dickens' assertion of the existence of "an unfathomable mystery in the meanest of [the Coketown Hands]," rightly argues that "[t]he mystery of humanity is hardly separable, in Dickens, from the absolute and unconditional value he accords the individual," a value which accounts for Dickens' method, his "work[ing] by indirections, because he believes that there is finally a core of personality which can only be guessed at, interpreted, implied and not explained" (Smith 168). True, Dickens advocates the supremacy of the human being as a unique individual, and this stance certainly justifies the particular stridency in *Hard*

Times of his criticism of the inadequacy of statistics to penetrate the socioeconomic reality of human suffering in mid-Victorian England. One should add, however, that the mystery with which Dickens suffuses this elusive "core of personality" is not only immanent but also transcendent.

The notion of transcendent mystery is inherent in Dickens' use of astronomical imagery in *Hard Times*. In the opening paragraph of book 1, chapter 15, Dickens draws an analogy between the futility of political economy's efforts to fathom "the most complicated social questions" and a windowless astronomical observatory:

> As if an astronomical observatory should be made without any windows, and the astronomer within should arrange the starry universe solely by pen, ink, and paper, so Mr. Gradgrind, in his Observatory (and there are many like it), had no need to cast an eye upon the teeming myriads of human beings around him, but could settle all their destinies on a slate, and wipe out all their tears with one dirty little bit of sponge. (75)

The passage implies an attack on the astronomical basis of empiricism. Indeed, Copernicus with his description in 1530 of the sun as the center of the solar system was the first to shift the concept of the universe from the religious to the secular. The Copernican revolution marks the abolition of sacramental astronomy.[10] In his Observatory Gradgrind goes a step further: He ushers Copernican astronomy into the Victorian bleak house of political economy. Astronomy becomes not only secular but fundamentally economic. Dickens' rejection of the statistical approach of political economy in terms of an extended astronomical simile suggests that the numerical approach to life is celestial divestment, spiritual nullification, a denial of the mystery. His astronomical observatory represents a microcosmic version of the Copernican macrocosm: a purely materialistic, mechanistic universe both in its nature and in its operation; a triumph of rationalism, materialism, and that fundamental tenet of Utilitarianism ethics, one that constitutes a denial of ultimate sanctions, secularism. The extended astronomical analogy exposes the limitations of this Benthamite triad of rationalism, materialism, and secularism.[11]

For this reason, were Gradgrind able to look upward and see through "the languid monotonous smoke" (78) the star that Stephen Blackpool sees as he lies dying at the bottom of Old Hell Shaft, he would neither see, feel, nor imagine what Blackpool sees, feels, and imagines. Blackpool's star shines on him with a promise of transcendent reality and redemptive vision:

> "It ha' shined upon me . . . in my pain and trouble down below. It ha' shined into my mind. I ha' look'n at 't and thowt o'thee, Rachael, till the muddle in

my mind have cleared awa, above a bit, I hope. If soom ha' been wantin' in
unnerstan'in me better, I, too, have been wantin' in unnerstan'in' them better. . . . [I]n our judgments, like as in our doins, we mun bear and forbear. In
my pain an' trouble, lookin' up yonder,—wi' it shinin on me—I ha' seen more
clear, and ha' made it my dyin' prayer that aw th' world may on'y coom
toogether more, an' get a better unnerstan'in o' one another, than when I were
in 't my own weak seln. . . .
    "Often as I coom to myseln, and found it shinin on me down there in my
trouble, I thowt it were the star as guided to Our Saviour's home. I awmust
think it be the very star!''   (201–02)

Clearly the star functions for Stephen as an agent of spiritual vision, a celestial
light that appears to him when he is on the brink of writing off his life as a
complete "muddle." Here, then, is the nature of the mystery at the core of
the human personality in *Hard Times*: it is religious—Christian—as well as
secular, however orthodox the symbol Dickens uses to intimate spirituality.

    Stephen Blackpool is able to read the star symbolically because Dickens
endows him with a good heart and a "fancy," however "rugged," that
allows him to see Rachael as a starlight of love. Stephen watches Rachael,
who has just saved him from becoming a partner to his wife's death, walk
down the road and

    As the stars were to the heavy candle in the window, so was Rachael, in the
    rugged fancy of this man, to the common experience of his life.   (71)

The saving power of Rachael's radiance illuminates Blackpool's common
experience, enabling him to "see or think o' onnything that angered" him,
"wi' a better eye" (123). Blackpool, the victim of an unjust social system,
is able to perceive the star metaphorically as the symbol of spirital vision.
Through Stephen—and of course Cissy—Dickens reiterates in *Hard Times*
one of his enduring themes, the contingency of social reform on spiritual
vision. Herein, precisely, lies the vital question of figures: it is a question of
seeing the mystery, the wonder—Carlyle's "natural supernatural"—at the
living heart of human reality, and of seeing it "with a better eye," a question
of vision. To reform society, Dickens implies in his defense of the metaphor,
we must first re-form it. We must re-imagine it. Any successful attempt
at banishing the poet's mystery-intimating figures in favor of the political
economist's would doom us to the tragic futility of the astronomer trying to
plumb the revolution of "the great wheel of earth" (195) and the depths of
"the starry universe" (75) from an observatory "made without windows."
Hard Times was Dickens' warning to his contemporaries against reenacting
the Victorian version of the myth of Sisyphus.
Sangamon State University, Springfield, Illinois.

NOTES

1. The bulk of the adverse criticism of *Hard Times* centers on the tawdriness and superficiality of Dickens' alternative to the Gradgrind-Bounderby world of Utilitarianism. John Holloway is disturbed by the frivolity of the novelist's "counterpart to the world of the 'hard-fact men' which operated at a relatively shallow level of consciousness, one represented by the Slearies not as vital horsemen but as plain entertainers." John Holloway, "*Hard Times*: a History and a Criticism," *Dickens and the Twentieth Century*, ed. John Gross and Gabriel Pearson (London: Routledge, 1962), repr. in *Hard Times: A Norton Critical Edition*, ed. George Ford and Sylvère Monod [New York: Norton, 1991] 362). David M. Hirsch laments that "tears, idle tears, bitter orgies of tears are the only alternative that Dickens seems to have to offer to fact-grubbing Gradgrindianism." "*Hard Times* and Dr. Leavis," *Criticism VI* (Winter 1964), repr. in the Norton Critical Edition of *Hard Times* 372). David Lodge deplores that the fancy which Dickens pits against facts is "merely a temporary escape from what is accepted as inevitably unpleasant. It is 'relief,' 'a vent,' 'a holiday.' To be cruel, one might say that Dickens offers the oppressed workers of Coketown bread and circuses." The Rhetoric of *Hard Times*," *Language of Fiction: Essays in Criticism and Verbal Analysis of the English Novel* (London: Routledge, 1966) 159.

2. David Lodge argues that the rhetoric here differs from that in the opening chapters of *Bleak House* and *Little Dorrit*. In *Hard Times*, he writes, the rhetoric "works to establish a thematic Idea—the despotism of Fact," whereas with "the fog at the beginning of *Bleak House* or the sun and shadow in the first chapter of *Little Dorrit* . . . the rhetoric works to establish a symbolic atmosphere." Could it not be, however, that in this first chapter of *Hard Times*, too, the rhetoric works not only to invest "this abstraction—Fact—with remarkable solidity through the figurative dimension of the language," but to establish a symbolic character? The hardness of massive matter here is as pervasive a symbol as the fog in *Bleak House* or the sun and shadow in *Little Dorrit*. The basic difference is that in *Hard Times* the symbol has become harsher, starker, more accurate. We do not so much witness the concretization of an abstract idea—fact—as we witness the solidification, as it were, of the speaker. Lodge, "The Rhetoric of *Hard Times*" 151.

3. For a full treatment of the proletariat topic in *Hard Times*, see Stephen J. Spector's article "Monsters of Metonymy: *Hard Times* and the Working Class," *ELH* 51 (1984): 365–84.

4. By adding seven and one and switching two digits, the sum becomes the year of publication: 1854. This is no mere ingenuity on my part but an (I hope) educated guess inspired by the obliqueness and surreptitiousness with which Dickens likes, or feels compelled, to refer in his fiction to autobiographical or biographical elements. See for example Henry Fielding Dickens' account of "The Memory Game" in *Dickens: Interviews and Recollections*, ed. Philip Collins (New York: Barnes, 1981) 1:162.

5. Dickens' staggering duties as a writer, speaker, editor, and provider for a large family would have been impossible without a fastidiousness about dates and details and an overriding carefulness about facts. In a letter of 18 March 1853 to W. H. Wills he demands that the facts about a submitted article on India Rubber be "closely enquired into. . . . Nothing can be so damaging to *Household Words* as carelessness about facts. It is as hideous as dullness." *The Nonesuch*

Letters of Charles Dickens, ed. Walter Dexter, 454–55. The last sentence especially leaves no doubt about Dickens' insistence on factual truth.

6. Dickens enclosed fourteen titles in a letter of 20 January 1854 to John Forster which is reprinted in the Norton Critical Edition of *Hard Times*, p. 273. Titles of a tenor to similar "A Mere Question of Figures" include "Two and Two are Four," "Simple Arithmetic" and "A Matter of Calculation."

7. "Frauds on the Fairies" was published in the *Household Words* issue of 1 October 1853. The fraudulence lies in the sabotage of fairy tales by Utilitarianism. To dramatize this abuse Dickens proposes to "write the story of Cinderella, 'edited' by one of these gentlemen, doing a good stroke of business, and having a rather extensive mission." In the retelling the editor parodies the effort to coerce the fairy tale through the specificities of time, place, facts, and calculations into obeisance to a pseudo-scientific spirit of exactitude further made appealing by a healthy dose of useful knowledge. Examples abound. When Cinderella was nine her mother died, "and all the Juvenile Bands of Hope in her district—the Central district, number five hundred and twenty-seven—formed a procession of two and two, amounting to fifteen hundred, and followed her to the grave, singing chorus number forty-two, 'O come,' and & co." This grave was "under the direction of the Local Board of Health, which reported at certain stated intervals to the General Board of Health, Whitehall" (98). The King proposed to adjourn the meeting at exactly a quarter before twelve. The Prince "hands Cinderella to one of the reserved seats for pink tickets on the platform." He rose to address his audience "at precisely ten minutes before eight" and "held them enthralled for four hours and a quarter" (99). In this mock sacrifice of an immortal fairy tale to a misplaced emphasis on exactitude, a misunderstanding of the scientific spirit, and a crass obsessiveness with the materialistic, the useful, and the practical, language becomes no more than a form of courtroom discourse in which human beings are made to give fastidious evidence. The fairy tale now reads like a writ from Chancery.

8. There are two types of figurativeness in *Hard Times* but four distinct languages. Besides the antithetical languages of the narrator and the Gradgrindians there is the language or rather the slang of the Sleary circus, which Dickens took pains to get right, as well as the Yorkshire dialect of Stephen Blackpool. Dickens brings Cecilia and Rachel together, but perhaps cramped by difficulties of space, not Sleary and Blackpool; yet the tenor of both their languages is similar in its advocacy of reconciliation and compromise. "Make the betht of uth; not the wurtht!", Sleary urges Gradgrind (36). Similarly Stephen tells Bounderby that "Not drawing nigh to fok, with kindness and patience and cheery ways . . . Most o' aw, rating [the workers] as so much Power, and reg'lating 'em as if they was figures in a soom, or machines wi'out souls . . ." will not solve the "muddle" (114). The similar messages of both Sleary and Blackpool at once stand in stark contrast to the Gradgrindians' theme and represent a variation on the narrator's. Underlying these four distinct languages are two views on the function of language. One view clamors that language is the handmaiden of the pragmatic and the objective, and should not therefore be seen as anything more than a vehicle of information. The other decries this restrictive view, arguing that the word is also a vehicle for emotion, the voice of the affective life, the poet's medium. *Hard Times* recognizes the inevitability of the literal view of language and life but also argues the cultural merits and perhaps necessity of a figurative apprehension of reality. The somber industrial landscape of Coketown is spawned as

much—Dickens insists—by the prevalence of the literalist view of language as by the smoke from the factory stacks.

9. For the same reason, Dickens openly (and unconvincingly) debunks Slackbridge's diction. The oratory in Slackbridge's two addresses to the members of his union Dickens derides as "froth and fume" (105), a result of the speaker's getting caught in the rhythms of his own hyperbolic truculence at Blackpool's expense. What is debunked, however, is not figurative language itself but the bad faith in which it is used.

10. "The dethronement of the Earth from the centre of the universe caused profound shock. No longer could the Earth be considered the epitome of creation, for it was only a planet like the other planets. . . . And the belief in a correspondence between man, the microcosm, as a mirror of the surrounding universe, the macrocosm, was no longer valid." *The New Encyclopaedia Britannica*, 15th ed., 16:761.

11. As if to emphasize the limitations of the mystery-denying empiricist world, Dickens furnishes Gradgrind's Observatory with "a deadly statistical clock . . . which measured every second with a beat like a rap upon a coffin-lid" (75). Gradgrind's star is timebound, phenomenal, where Blackpool's is timeless, noumenal; it is an eradication of time leading into eternity. Dickens, who has dedicated *Hard Times* to his mentor Carlyle, seems to agree with Carlyle's explicit statement in *Sator Resartus* that time and space are garments of the noumenal world and that, more to the point, time as chronology is only a custom, a convention whose eradication we tend to overlook because of the linearity of language.

WORKS CITED

Campbell, Jane. " 'Competing Towers of Babel': Some Patterns of Language in *Hard Times*." *English Studies in Canada* 10 (1984): 416–35.

Caserio, Robert L. "The Name of the Horse: *Hard Times*, Semiotics, and the Supernatural." *Novel: A Forum On Fiction* 20 (Fall 1986): 5–23.

Collins, Philip, ed. *Dickens: Interviews and Recollections*. 2 vols. New York: Barnes, 1981.

Dexter, Walter, ed. *The Letters of Charles Dickens*. 3 vols. Bloomsbury: Nonesuch, 1938.

Dickens, Charles. "Frauds on the Fairies." *Household Words* 1 Oct. 1853:35–39.

———. *Hard Times: A Norton Critical Edition*. Ed. George Ford and Sylvère Monod. 2nd ed. New York: Norton, 1990.

———. *Our Mutual Friend*. Ed. Stephen Gill. Harmondsworth: Penguin, 1971.

Emerson, Ralph Waldo. "The Poet." *Anthology of American Literature*. Ed. George McMichael. 2 vols. New York: Macmillan, 1985. 1:1077–91.

Fabrizio, Richard. "Wonderful No-Meaning: Language and the Psychopathology of the Family in Dickens' *Hard Times.*" *Dickens Studies Annual: Essays on Victorian Fiction* 16 (1987): 61–94.

Hirsch, David M. "*Hard Times* and Dr. Leavis." *Criticism* 6 (Winter 1964): 1–16.

Holloway, John. "*Hard Times*: A History and a Criticism." *Dickens and the Twentieth Century.* Ed. John Cross and Gabriel Pearson. London: Routledge, 1962. 167–74.

Lodge, David. *Language of Fiction: Essays in Criticism and Verbal Analysis of the English Novel.* London: Routledge, 1966.

———. *The Novelist at the Crossroads and Other Essays on Fiction and Criticism.* Ithaca, New York: Cornell UP, 1971.

Manlove, Colin N. *Critical Thinking: A Guide to Interpreting Literary Texts.* London: Macmillan, 1989.

Smith, Grahame. " 'O Reason Not the Need': *King Lear, Hard Times* and Utilitarian Values." *Dickensian* 86 (1990): 164–70.

Sonstroem, David. "Fettered Fancy in *Hard Times.*" *PMLA* 84 (1969): 520–31.

Spector, Stephen J. "Monsters of Metonymy: *Hard Times* and Knowing the Working Class." *ELH* 51 (1984): 365–84.

Domestic Transformations in Dickens' "The Haunted Man"

Wendy K. Carse

Like two of Dickens' other Christmas books, "The Haunted Man" features a supernatural force effecting an errant man's change of heart.[1] Here the protagonist, a chemist, is beleaguered by painful memories until a phantom, "an awful likeness" of himself, offers him the "gift" of forgetfulness (436). As Redlaw diffuses his gift to others suffering various forms of deprivation, he comes to realize that forgetting pain strips recipients of their humanity, and his horror at the changes his gift has wrought finally causes him to cry out for their release from its influence. The Phantom reappears to suggest that the key to reversing the gift lies in Milly, the daughter-in-law of the building's caretaker. The mere presence of this domestic woman the next morning restores the memories of all those afflicted and finally moves Redlaw to understand the full purport of the story's motto: "Lord! keep my memory green!" (430). Surrounded by the objects of his profession, the glass vessels trembling in the firelight "like things that knew his power to uncombine them," the chemist thus learns the danger of "uncombining" pain and memory (418).

For all that Redlaw's desire to forget is a " 'growth of man's presumption,' " however, it is not the egotistical drive for power motivating Frankenstein, Dr. Moreau, and a host of other fictional scientists; rather, it stems from an intense yearning for a home, a yearning that leaves him little solace in the career for which he has struggled (499). Alone in his chambers "part library and part laboratory" but no part home (418), Redlaw broods silently over his cheerless hearth until the Phantom steps from the shadows to articulate the central place domesticity holds in Redlaw's memory of " 'all that was and might have been' ":

163

> "I am he, neglected in my youth, and miserably poor, who strove and suffered. . . . No mother's self-denying love . . . no father's counsel, aided *me*. . . . My parents, at the best, were of that sort whose care soon ends, and whose duty is soon done." (437)

Against this image of a dysfunctional home arises that of the household Redlaw later formed with his sister—from whom streamed " 'such glimpses of the light of home as I have ever known' "—and his dreams of marriage for them both:

> "Pictures of my own domestic life, in after-time, with her [the woman he loved] who was the inspiration of my toil. Pictures of my sister, made the wife of my dear friend. . . . pictures of our sobered age and mellowed happiness, and of the golden links . . . that should bind us, and our children, in a radiant garland." (439)

With his sister dead and the woman he loved marrying his "dear" friend instead, Redlaw is haunted, then, specifically by lost dreams of a home.

To rehabilitate those memories, Redlaw must learn what apparently only a domestic woman can teach him. All images of home, in fact, coalesce to form in Milly the very source of Redlaw's transformation. As such, however, she becomes the site where ideological tensions meet, surfacing inevitably from the story's representations of gender, class, and the supernatural. Far from proving resolvable, those tensions persist to the end where the narrator questions the origin of the forces at work in the story:

> Some people have said since, that [Redlaw] had only thought what has been herein, set down; others, that he read it in the fire, one winter night about the twilight time; others that the Ghost was but the representation of his own gloomy thoughts, and Milly the embodiment of his better wisdom. *I* say nothing.
> (524)

All three explanations fail to account for Redlaw's experience, as the narrator's tongue-in-cheek "*I* say nothing" coyly acknowledges, for all three assume Redlaw is capable of transforming himself.[2] Despite its foreboding presence, the Phantom does not merely replicate Redlaw's "gloomy thoughts" but offers the means of exorcising them; despite the chemist's scientific wisdom, he does not know what Milly knows. The Phantom and Milly thus represent not a conflict within Redlaw but an alliance of transforming powers from outside him. As such a power, however, Milly's domestic influence proves far more unsettling than the overtly supernatural force of the doppelganger. Although Milly's virtues as a domestic Angel guide Redlaw to his happy fate, the story's conclusion turns abruptly away from the implications of her power. In fact, the attempt to defuse that power attests to its potential threat, for no matter how beneficently it may be wielded, it unsettles the very relationships—between classes and genders—that domesticity is constructed to contain and solidify.

Redlaw's obsession with images of home necessarily involves two other male characters granted the domestic roles his past has denied him. Responsible for shattering Redlaw's dreams, the former friend proves unworthy of his role as head of the family that might have been the scientist's. When Milly brings the man to Redlaw to be forgiven, she implicitly associates his domestic failure with a decline in social status:

> "He has long been separated from his wife and son—has been a stranger to his home almost from this son's infancy, I learn from him—and has abandoned and deserted what he should have held most dear. In all that time he has been falling from the state of gentleman, more and more, until—"   (517–18)

She can only complete her sentence by presenting "the wreck" himself, guilty of committing the ultimate wrong against domesticity and thus against his class. With no hope for the present or future, the "fallen man" can seek only the banishment that will remove him as a source of shame for his family (519). That man's son, now a student in Redlaw's chemistry classes, functions not only as the child Redlaw might have had but also as an image of the scientist himself in his youth, struggling against poverty in his quest for scientific knowledge. Despite his father's desertion, the student, unlike Redlaw, has known domestic happiness, thanks to his mother, and still possesses the dream of a future home. Consequently, his room, in contrast to Redlaw's, displays "remembrances of other and less solitary scenes" than those of scholarly endeavors: "the little miniatures [of his mother and fiancee] upon the chimney-piece, and their drawing of home" (466).

Against the images from what were once Redlaw's "pictures of the future" that these two middle-class men offer, another male character from the extreme end of the social scale, a child of the streets, embodies the scientist's condition once he receives the gift of forgetfulness. In fact, the boy is, as the Phantom explains, " 'the perfect type of what it was [Redlaw's] choice to be[,] . . . utterly bereft of such remembrances' " as Redlaw has " 'yielded up' " (498). An enlargement of the figure Ignorance that the Ghost of Christmas Present reveals to Scrooge, the feral child aptly represents the evil of "uncombining," for deprivation has separated him from humanity and left

him a "mcrc beast" (443). What renders this "creature" particularly " 'unnatural' " is the fact that he has never known a home, can only respond,
when asked where he lives, " 'Live! What's that?' " (445). Immune to
Redlaw's gift of forgetfulness precisely because he has no domestic memories
to forget, the nameless boy nonetheless is persistently attracted to signs of a
home, his reiterated demand for " 'the woman' " associating the food and
warmth Milly provides him and the security he finds in her presence. Redlaw's
"terrible companionship" with this "baby-monster" thus signals both the
"unnaturalness" of the scientist's desire to forget and the "naturalness" of
an elemental yearning for a home.

Even those male characters not representing some part of Redlaw's past
or current state are defined in terms of domesticity, all working-class men
fully cognizant and appreciative of the values of home. In fact, one of them,
Mr. Tetterby, the news vendor in whose house the poor student lodges,
becomes identified *as* home when his wife explains the effects of the gift's
reversal on her attitude toward him: " 'I thought there was no air about you;
but there is and it's the air of home, and that's the purest and the best there
is' " (508). Similarly, William Swidger, the old caretaker's son, is introduced
in terms of the story's most explicit sign of domesticity—the hearth. In an
early scene, William bustles to feed both Redlaw and his fire,[3] the blaze of
which "so quickly chang[ed] the appearance of the room, that it seemed as
if the mere coming in of his fresh red face and active manner had made the
pleasant alteration" (423). However much such men become associated with
domesticity, though, they themselves most often credit women with creating
their images of home.[4] Old Philip, the caretaker, for instance, recalls the
mother who walked with him on the first Christmas that he can remember,
" 'though I don't know what her blessed face was like, for she took ill and
died that Christmas-time' " (429). Women—specifically dead women—are
intrinsic to Philip's concept of home (and Christmas), as the following anec-
dote about his wife and Redlaw's sister demonstrates:

> "my wife invited her to walk in, and sit by the fire that is always a-burning
> on Christmas Day. . . . She and my wife fell a-talking about [the motto, "Lord,
> keep my memory green!"]; . . . [saying] that it was a good prayer, and that it
> was one they would put up very earnestly, if they were called away young,
> with reference to those who were dearest to them. 'My brother,' says the young
> lady—'My husband,' says my poor wife." (515)

Unlike the tortured memory of Redlaw through which the image of his dead
sister can only take shape as a desolate shadow, images of dead women shine
steadily in Philip's green memory to comfort him.

In Milly, though, old Philip possesses more than memories of women as the essence of home. " 'My quiet Mouse' " to him, " 'Mrs. William' " to his son, Milly is introduced as if she were half of a matched pair: "Mrs. William, like Mr. William, was a simple, innocent-looking person, in whose smooth cheeks the cheerful red of her husband's official waistcoat was very pleasantly repeated" (426). The red linking them both with the cheerful fire, however, ends the comparison:

> Whereas Mr. William's light hair stood on end . . . in an excess of bustling readiness for anything, the dark brown hair of Mrs. William was carefully smoothed down, and waved away under a trim tidy cap, in the most exact and quiet manner imaginable. . . . Whereas his coat had something of a fly-away and half-off appearance . . . , her little bodice was so placid and neat, that there should have been protection for her, in it, had she needed any, with the roughest people.   (426)[5]

Not simply the superior of her husband, who is, after all, essentially a comic character, Milly possesses all the stability that such neatness suggests. At first, this tidiness seems to relegate her to the uncomplicated role of what Michael Slater calls Dickens's "Good Provider," the efficient housewife who, if not a young girl (usually a daughter or a sister[6]), is most often a "simple, uneducated working class woman" (313). Administered "without any show of hurry or noise, or any show of herself even, she was so calm and quiet" (427), however, Milly's housekeeping quickly assumes what Nancy Armstrong calls "the peculiar combination of invisibility and vigilance personified in the domestic woman" (81). As she tends the sick student, Milly moves "noiselessly about the room, set[ting] everything exactly in its place, and in the neatest order; even to the cushions on the couch, which she touched with so light a hand, that he hardly seemed to know it" (471–72). In fact, her care of the student signals the presumably inherent maternalism that constitutes the basis of women's moral influence over men.[7] According to William, Milly's attention to the poor student has not interfered with her duties in her own home:

> "All at home just the same as ever—my father made as snug and comfortable—not a crumb of litter to be found in the house . . . —Mrs. William apparently never out of the way—yet Mrs. William backwards and forwards, backwards and forwards, up and down, up and down, a mother to him!"
>   (434)

With a touch hardly felt, a movement barely seen, Milly's surveillance is more than a mere crusade against "litter"; it constitutes the basis of a domestic woman's power.

As such, that surveillance also necessitates the watchful eye for detecting emotions and thoughts, the power of observation that domestic women, as "interpreters and evaluators of emotional life," must possess (Armstrong 220). Milly tells the student:

> "I am very different from you, Mr. Edmund, for I have no learning, and don't know how to think properly. . . . [But] I have read in your face, as plain as if it was a book, that but for some trouble and sorrow we should never know half the good there is about us."   (473)

Denied by class and gender the ability to "think," Milly interprets by seeing, feeling and reading,[8] a process qualifying her for the role of "moral and spiritual mentor and exemplar in the home" which, Slater argues, Dickens' fiction usually reserves for middle-class women (313). " 'You are like an angel to father and me,' " exclaims Milly's husband (521), and surely the character of a superior being is evident in her response to the ingratitude of the poor student (now under the influence of Redlaw's gift), a response demonstrating indeed all the 'angelic refinement and exquisite sensitivity" of the middle-class "lady" (Slater 313):

> "You owe me nothing; but it is right that you should deal as justly by me as if I was a lady . . . and if you suspect me of meanly making much of the little I have tried to do to comfort your sick room, you do yourself more wrong than ever you can do to me." If she had been as passionate as she was quiet, as indignant as she was calm, as angry in her look as she was gentle, as loud of tone as she was low and clear, she might have left no sense of her departure in the room, compared with that which fell upon the lonely student when she went away.   (475)

Milly thus functions as the "high pattern of gentle purity," whose "objective mind," according to a reviewer of Coventry Patmore's *The Angel in the House*, "is a mirror to show man his uncomeliness, for his refinement. . . . helping man to a knowledge and feeling of the excellent in the true woman's mind" (qtd. Helsinger, et al. 80).[9]

For such a supra-human representation, an alliance with the supernatural seems an inevitable progression. Milly's relationship to the Phantom, however, illustrates the uneasy dynamics of such a partnership. When the Phantom reappears at Redlaw's plea that the recipients of his gift have their memories restored, "it was not alone, but in its shadowy hand it held another hand":

Was the form that stood beside it indeed Milly's, or but her shade and picture? . . . A radiant light fell on her face, but did not touch the Phantom; for,
though close beside her, it was dark and colourless as ever.   (495)

Although the linked hands signal, at the least, a power shared with the
Phantom, even with her form "but a shadow," the contrast between the light
falling on Milly's face and the darkness enveloping the Phantom keeps the
two separated, a distancing the text consistently maintains between Milly's
"reality" and the Phantom (496). Moreover, when Redlaw asks the Phantom
" 'has she, henceforth, the consciousness of any power to set right what I
have done?' " the Phantom's reply, " 'She has not,' " suggests that just as
Milly herself presumably must not be touched by the darkness, so too must she
remain ignorant of possessing power, an ignorance evident in her reiterated
" 'What have I done to be so loved?' " (509).[10] That unconsciousness, in
fact, is essential, for awareness would render her unfit for the role of True
Woman, which demands humility in her inherent—i.e., unconscious—capacity for influencing others.[11] More problematic is the Phantom's ambiguous
response to Redlaw's second question:

"Has she the power bestowed on her without the consciousness?"
The Phantom answered: "Seek her out." And her shadow slowly vanished.
                                                                     (497)

Such a reticence raises significant issues of agency: "bestowed on her,"
Milly's power must originate outside her; if not bestowed, however, that
power must be Milly's own. As the text oscillates between hints that Milly
is but a passive medium through which some supernatural power works and
suggestions that hers is a "natural" power, the supposed opposition between
the Phantom and Milly becomes increasingly unsettled, revealing the tensions
inherent in the domestic Angel's possession of power.

On the one hand, Redlaw must "seek her out" before her "reality" can
begin her mission (496). Powerless to prevent the memory loss in her own
husband and father-in-law, Milly may well be merely the instrument, as
Redlaw later assumes, through whose " 'teaching of pure love' " God " 'has
graciously restored me' " (522). On the other hand, though, evidence that
Milly may possess a power not created but only heightened by contact with
the supernatural surfaces long before her shade appears with the Phantom.
" 'I can see very well now,' " she says, ascending the Tetterbys' dark stairs
to the student's room, and in assuring one of the boys that his father and
mother, who have received Redlaw's gift, " 'will be comfortable again,

tomorrow, and home will be comfortable too,' " she seems to be confidently promising, not merely placating (470). Even Redlaw's belief that Milly is only the medium through which he reverses the gift implies that she may have always possessed the power to redeem. From the first moments of "diffusing" his gift, Redlaw avoids contact with Milly for fear, he maintains, of influencing her " 'steady quality of goodness' " (471). This explanation, however, only partly disguises the possibility that he is simply not yet ready to be affected by her.[12] Once he seeks her out, her goodness seems no less powerful than the magic presumably responsible for the other characters' instantaneous transformations.

> [N]ow he truly felt how much he had lost. . . . [A] meek, submissive sense of his calamity was bred, resembling that which sometimes obtains in age, when its mental powers are weakened. . . . [H]e felt that he was quite dependent on her, and that she was his staff in his affliction. . . . [H]e put his arm through hers, and walked beside her; not as if he were the wise and learned man to whom the wonders of nature were an open book, and hers were the uninstructed mind, but as if their two positions were reversed, and he knew nothing, and she all. (512–13)

Redlaw apparently needs something as drastic as a phantom's gift to realize the value of Milly's knowledge, but he must learn the lesson of humility before he can realize the full humanizing force of memory. He can do so only by becoming the pupil of the uneducated Milly, literally attaching himself to the woman who has all along known instinctively what he must learn.

A "natural" power, Milly's capacity to interpret—and to teach Redlaw to interpret—nonetheless loses none of its affinity with the supernatural. For if the Phantom initially replicates the chemist's thoughts and then points to what those thoughts lack, Milly the domestic Angel reflects Redlaw's "uncomeliness" to direct him to his "refinement." With both the Phantom and Milly therey acting as mirrors, eye contact with Redlaw becomes central to their influence. During the Phantom's first appearance, it leans over Redlaw's chair and looks "down into his face with searching eyes, that seemed instinct with fire" (438). During the second, this same gaze shifts only to look at the shade of Milly who in turn looks only at the wild boy sleeping at Redlaw's feet. Once Milly's shade disappears, Redlaw and the Phantom "were face to face again, and looking at each other as intently and awfully as at the time of the bestowal of the gift, across the boy who still lay on the ground between them" (497). Pointing at the sleeping boy, the Phantom forces Redlaw to look at the child until he finally "stooped upon the ground beside the boy, and, with the same kind of compassion for him that he now felt for himself, covered him as he slept" (499). Such a mutual gaze with similar results figures prominently in a later scene as Milly replaces the Phantom at the side of Redlaw's chair. Again, Redlaw touches the child at his feet, "looking on him with compassion and a fellow-feeling, . . . [and] put out his other hand to Milly. She stooped down on that side of him, so that she could look into his face" (516). Already having acknowledged the child's right to compassion, however, Redlaw here must confront his old friend, the now "fallen man":

> "See how low he is sunk, how lost he is!" [Milly] whispered, stretching out her arm toward him, without looking from the Chemist's face. . . . His eyes wandered to the figure standing near the door, but came back speedily to her, on whom he gazed intently, as if he strove to learn some lesson from every tone of her voice and every beam of her eyes.   (518)

The differences between these tableaus thus serve only to emphasize their basic similarities: both the child and the man to whom the Phantom and Milly respectively gesture are objects of the pity that, through the activity of doubling, moves Redlaw closer to his complete transformation. Moreover, the light falling *on* the face of Milly's shade appears here as "a ray of clearer light [that] appeared to [Redlaw] to shine into his mind, *from* her bright face," a light matching, at least in intensity, the "fire" with which the Phantom's eyes are "instinct" (519; emphasis added).[13]

In "The Situation of the Looker-On," Beth Newman argues that for Heathcliff in *Wuthering Heights* the "woman's gaze as an object of male perception" offers "the possibility of a lost wholeness" (1038), and certainly the same can be said for Redlaw who searches Milly's face "as if to find in it the clue to what" he has experienced (519). Newman also elucidates the significance of the mutual gaze between the second Catherine and Hareton:

> What Bronte imagines, then, is a diffusing of the gaze: not a simple inversion in which the woman is permitted to turn the tables with an appropriating look back but a destruction of the hierarchical positioning of male and female that the gendered gaze entails.   (1037)

This look, of course, draws Catherine and Hareton together, ultimately domesticating Wuthering Heights. The gaze Redlaw exchanges with Milly, however, actually strengthens hierarchical positioning, but not that which would accord the male any power. In fact, just as the Phantom's gaze implies its strength, the domestic Angel's confirms her superiority. Here, not the gaze itself but the woman's goodness is "diffused," penetrating Redlaw's mind with its clearer light.

Significantly, too, this exchange ends when Milly stoops to cover the boy and thus prompts her admiring husband to exclaim " 'there's a motherly feeling in Mrs. William's breast that must and will have went!' " (521). Far from merely reinforcing her domestic credentials, this reminder of the childless Milly's inherent maternalism initiates a remarkable explanation for her goodness. When William remarks, " 'our little dead child that you built such hopes upon has made you quiet-like,' " Milly replies,

> "[The dead child] speaks to me in so many ways. . . . For poor neglected children, my little child pleads as if it were alive, and had a voice I knew, with which to speak to me. . . . Children love me so, that sometimes I half fancy . . . they have some way I don't know of, of feeling for my little child, and me, and understanding why their love is precious to me. If I have been quiet since, I have been more happy. . . . Not least happy, dear, in this—that even when my little child was born and dead . . . the thought arose that if I tried to lead a good life, I should meet in Heaven a bright creature, who would call me, Mother!"   (521–22)

Not simply the sobering effect of grief nor even primarily the sign of her capacity for interpreting, Milly's quiet calm now assumes the expectant silence of the mother listening for the voice of her child. Her vigilance in domestic duties is thus accompanied by an alertness to a voice that directs not only Milly in her ministrations to the suffering but also living children (and adults) in their attraction to Milly. That voice itself offers up the dead child as an emblem of salvation for the living,[14] a "use" of the dead implicit in Redlaw's response to Milly's words:

> "O Thou, . . . who through the teaching of pure love, has graciously restored me to the memory which was the memory of Christ upon the cross, and all the good who perished in His cause, receive my thanks, and bless her!"   (522)

To accept Redlaw's prayer as an accurate gloss of his relationship with Milly, however, is to ignore the context of this orthodox moral.[15] Milly herself credits her child, not Christ, with the power to speak to her and motivate her in her "good life," and the dead infant becomes the primary—if not only—presence in her vision of Heaven, a Home conspicuously lacking a father figure. Unlike the living Christ child who dies as an adult to live eternally and save humankind, this baby dies at birth to speak to its mother and thus enact its message of love through her.

Even in such an uncanny icon of Madonna and Child, the dead child refuses to be contained in a single set of associations. For the baby's message of love only partly conceals the grotesqueness of its image, that of a child whose

" 'sweet eyes turned up to mine . . . never opened to the light' " (521). In its impersonation of a living child, the speaking stillborn—whose otherness is forever guaranteed by its status as an "it"—resembles the Phantom, another "it" and "animated image" who also speaks a message of salvation. Like the Phantom's role as the visual embodiment of Redlaw's gloomy thoughts, the infant's personification of innocence assumes all the aura of supernaturalism expected of the "angel" its mother calls it. Innocence in any child, of course, can signal a kind of power, as old Philip recognizes when he gazes down at the adult profligate who was his wife's favorite child and remembers the boy George at this mother's knee: " 'Sorrowful as it was to her, and to me, to think of this, when he went so wrong, . . . this gave him still a hold upon us' " (487). Had Milly's child lived, she knows, it too might have met George's fate: " 'When I hear of youth in suffering or shame, I think that my child might have come to that, perhaps, and that God took it from me in his mercy' " (522). Philip may pray that God take back his errant adult son—" 'not as he is but as he was then, let him cry to thee, as he had often seemed to cry to us!' " (481)—and the child George preserved in his father's memory may display its power through a timeless cry like that of Milly's dead child. The adult whom George must and does become, however, forever superimposes himself over the image of the child dwelling only in memory.

Dead, Milly's child thus becomes the perfect image of permanent innocence since what it "might have come to" is no part of what it is. Neither is it merely a memory, for nowhere in Milly's long speech about her dead child does she even mention memory. The image of the child resides, in fact, only in Milly. When first introducing Milly by way of her neat "little bodice," the narrator exclaims, "To whom would its repose and peace have not appealed against disturbance, like the innocent slumber of a child!' " (426). With the stillborn speaking to its mother "all through life," however, what should be the permanent slumber of death becomes not so much a state of repose as one of activity, the child's noncorporeal presence no more a sign of passivity than Milly's own quiet surveillance is. This mother-and-child bond may well represent, then, not an appeal *against* disturbance but a capacity *for* disturbance. Baby Angel and domestic Angel—one with an unnatural power to speak, the other with a supranatural power to influence others—unite to suggest a dynamic supernaturalism already implicit in Milly's alliance with the Phantom. Even as this unity provides the source of Milly's influence over Redlaw, her power thus threatens to overwhelm all within its compass. With the middle-class scientist already "quite dependent" on her, the working-class woman assumes an authority of seemingly limitless potential, a mastery likely to destabilize the very gender and class roles that define her.

Turning away from the unearthly alliances created by its own promulgation of domesticity, the text must grant Redlaw his own mastery, turning toward a paternalism that first surfaces at his thanksgiving to God for restoring his memory. Thus, the man reduced to humble passivity quickly becomes the confident father of an extended family: First, Redlaw's vow "to protect him, teach him, and reclaim him" transforms the "it" formerly applied to the wild boy; second, seeing in the poor student and his fiancee "the softened shadow of that chastening passage in his own life," Redlaw entreats them "to be his children" (523). Finally, he bids all, including the Tetterbys and assorted Swidgers, to gather for Christmas dinner under a portrait of an Elizabethan gentleman who, besides endowing the school still operating in the building, left money for annual holly decorations:

> There was one thing in the Hall, to which the eyes of Redlaw, and of Milly and her husband, and of the old man, and of the student, and his bride that was to be, were often turned which the shadows did not obscure or change. Deepened in its gravity by the firelight, and gazing from the darkness of the panelled wall like life, the sedate face in the portrait, . . . looked down at them from under its verdant wreath of holly, as they looked up at it; and clear and plain below, as if a voice had uttered them, were the words "Lord! Keep my memory green!"   (524)

Redlaw's transformation is complete: at the hearth not of a lonely room but of a communal Dinner Hall, he now possesses a Home warmed by the fire that spotlights the motto of the tale, the lesson Redlaw has presumably learned.

Although he owes his newfound knowledge to the alliance between domesticity and the supernatural, Redlaw can now credit the "plain" written message that requires no mediator for its interpretation. One-dimensional and static, the portrait offers Redlaw a reassuring image of the familiar. First, as a learned benefactor of the all-male school, the gentleman fills the role of mentor that Redlaw, himself a mentor to appreciative male students, can certainly better understand as a directing force in his life than an uneducated Angel or a doom-saying doppelganger. And, as an aristocrat, the Elizabethan gentleman replaces uneasy relations between the working and middle classes with a steady benevolence flowing unambiguously downward from the mounted portrait. In the course of the story, Redlaw learns his error in thinking that " 'unenlightened minds and ordinary spirits do not feel or reason on these things [i.e., spiritual and emotional suffering] like men of higher cultivation' " (440); as the head of the working-class families surrounding him, however, he is raised to a status mirroring the Elizabethan gentleman's position of authority as the "better" of the "ordinary spirits" gathered beneath his portrait. Finally, as a man, the gentleman can supervise a hearth free of associations with distinctly feminine goodness and maternal bonds from beyond the grave. The mutual gaze in which the "learned gentleman" engages the gathered celebrants thus displaces Milly's surveillance as the transforming power in the home and re-establishes a familiar hierarchy of both gender and class.

With the wild boy already humanized, cured of his unnaturalness by Redlaw's vow to reclaim him, the story's ending completes the scientist's exorcism by assimilating the original source of the haunting, the visions of domesticity featuring the dead sister who presumably will no longer be a source of pain. Other characters, however, prove more difficult to incorporate, and some must be outright banished. Noticeably missing from the gathering of characters is not only the outcast friend but also his wife, the woman Redlaw had loved. Like her husband, she has no place in that gathering, for, though a loving mother to the student who is now one of the scientist's "children," she nonetheless sealed her fate by jilting Redlaw. He may forgive her but cannot allow this still-married woman a place before his hearth precisely because of the sexual tensions inevitably surfacing in her presence. This exclusion points to another absence of a woman imbued with even more disturbing sexual associations, a prostitute whom Redlaw encounters on his mission to relieve the most wretched of their memories. Like the street child, the prostitute represents a form of unnaturalness and a type "of thousands" doomed by society's indifference (498). Interrogating her about her life and the "wrong" done her, Redlaw stands amazed "and much disquieted, to note that in her awakened recollection of this wrong, the first trace of her old humanity and frozen tenderness appeared to show itself" as she protests that the bruises on her arms are self-inflicted (483).

> In the white determination of her face, confronting his with this untruth, he saw enough of the last perversion and distortion of good surviving in that miserable breast, to be stricken with remorse that he had come near her. . . . Afraid to look at her again, afraid to touch her, afraid to think of having sundered the last thread by which she held upon the mercy of heaven, he gathered his cloak about him, and glided up the stairs.   (483–84)

Though presumably only the street child is immune to Redlaw's gift, the woman shows no sign of its influence, even though Redlaw touches her on the shoulder and they lock glances. His fear that she be influenced, however, may well be the fear that her returning gaze indicates, as Beth Newman says of Lockwood's discomfort at receiving a woman's gaze, the loss of his "position of mastery and control" (1032). Her "fallen" state solidifying the gulf that gender and class create between her and Redlaw, the prostitute does indeed represent a "type" whose alienness—proven not so much by her lost virtue as by the "perverted" humanity still dwelling beneath such an "unwomanly" appearance—horrifies the "gentleman" who should know, as she proclaims, that " 'all such things' " as fathers and homes are dead to her (483).[16] But this representation of a type is soon stripped of its resonance as an unearthly image. The next morning Milly, accompanied by Redlaw, begins her own mission and meets " 'a woman at the door . . . who caught me by the hand, and blessed me as I passed' " (509). Since the prostitute then disappears from the story, her blessing must act as an end in itself, for she herself must remain irrevocably banned from the home.[17]

The moral antithesis of the prostitute, Milly must, of course, form part of the domestic circle she has made possible, but that part clearly diminishes her. Once Redlaw reduces her communion with her dead child to a Christian maxim, he seems to free himself of the submissive dependency into which his relationship with her casts him. With the gathering of Redlaw's new family, Milly becomes immobilized as just one of the mere human beings gazing up at the portrait, a symbol of paternalism relegating her to a position of dependency. Speaking of another Dickensian Angel, Esther Summerson, the authors of *Corrupt Relations* maintain that the "moral impact she supposedly has on the characters of the household males" is totally the power of a dependent:

> the more idealized her role becomes, the more she is expected to enshrine the culture's beleaguered values, the more vulnerable her status becomes. . . . She becomes an icon, a symbolic creature of masculine desires. . . . [But] it makes little difference in terms of real autonomy that the system values her so highly.
> (85)

Milly, too, becomes an icon, denied real autonomy, doubly relegated by her social status to a literal dependency. As an already married woman, of course, Milly is denied an at least nominal position in the center of Redlaw's "family" as his wife; but such a conclusion as a marriage between Redlaw and Milly would have been highly unlikely anyway, given their respective class affiliations.[18] Thus, like the prostitute whose exclusion from the domestic circle implies that she must be kept in her place, Milly must be manipulated so that her power can be contained.

The Phantom shaped from shadows and gloom disappears once it accomplishes its mission, and, with Redlaw's reformation completed, the "forms and faces" from the past—conjured, too, from the shadows—have apparently been rehabilitated in his memory (522). Failing to "obscure or change" the portrait, shadows have not, however, been exorcised, for they "once more stole out of their hiding places," this time to dance about the Dinner Hall and show "the children marvelous shapes and faces" (524). "Marvelous," though, such entertaining shapes and faces are not necessarily powerless. Still capable of changing "what was real and familiar" in the room to "what was wild and magical," shadows act on the canny to produce the uncanny (524)[19]:

> [T]wilight everywhere released the shadows, prisoned up all day, that now closed in and gathered like mustering swarms of ghosts. . . . [T]hey fantastically mocked the shapes of household objects, making the nurse an ogress, the rocking horse a monster, the wondering child half-scared and half-amused, a stranger to itself.   (521–22)

Created by a combination of darkness and the hearth fire that in the final tableau signals the presence of Home, shadows thus target domestic "objects"—nurses, toys, and children—to possess and transform into ogresses, monsters, and strangers.

In contrast to such an alienating force, the "good" influence granted the domestic Angel makes better human beings. Also capable of transforming others, however, the domestic Angel's power necessarily becomes too unreal, too unfamiliar itself either to embrace wholeheartedly or to assimilate entirely. Turning away from Milly as the heart of the domestic circle, "The Haunted Man" thus obliquely recognizes the unsettling power that she—in league with her forever-baby Angel—can wield to work transformations. After his encounter with the wild and magical, Redlaw may well feel relieved to escape to such a tangible emblem of immutability as the shadow-resistant portrait. For that portrait assures him that he need no longer be a man haunted by what had been, what might have been, and, especially, what is: working-class, female, and spectral forming a strange alliance, a confederation of Others.

NOTES

1. I am, of course, referring to "A Christmas Carol" and "The Chimes," although both the context and precise nature of the transformation in "The Haunted Man"

are quite different from those in the other two. The fantasy element of a third book, "The Cricket on the Hearth," is limited to the cricket's passive chorus in the story's hymn to domesticity and thus hardly qualifies as the active supernatural force envisioned in the Phantom, the chimes, or three Christmas Ghosts. Although Robert L. Patten explores the means by which Dickens' hearth in these four Christmas books "domesticates Nature to man's purposes and comfort" (157), an in-depth study of what changes that hearth undergoes in each succeeding book would yield significant insight into the presentation by which Dickens' texts exhibit what Poovey calls the "double duty of voicing and silencing ideological contradictions" (124).

"The Haunted Man" has been variously criticized for what Michael Slater calls the "confusion" of a book "in which Dickens's personal preoccupations do not mesh easily with [its] combination of social purpose, celebration of domestic joys, and supernatural interventions" (18). Nearly every critic of the story mentions the autobiographical references, particularly Dickens' relationship with his sister Fanny, which he revised into "a sort of sexless marriage" (Slater 32). Many critics, too, view the fit between realism and fantasy as an uneasy one at best, often concluding, like Harry Stone, that the Christmas books in general were "dependent upon machinery that did violence to reality" (144).

Other critics explore particular motifs. George Levine, for example, discussing U. C. Knoephflmacher's work, examines the treatment of a scientist who must both learn the dangers of exercising what Dickens calls the power to "uncombine" and acknowledge his kinship with a double (or, in this case, multiple doubles). Deborah Thomas is primarily interested in the motif of reading, especially evident in the necessity for Redlaw to understand fully the story's motto, while Patten examines the parallels to the other supernatural Christmas books, particularly "A Christmas Carol." These studies, then, clearly deal with the role domesticity plays in the story, but none attempts to account for the slippages the predominance of that role creates. Regardless of their particular emphases, the consensus among critics seems to be that the story does indeed manifest, through the ministrations of the domestic woman, what Levine calls "the exorcism of private and social monstrosity" (23). But to read the story as settling all disturbances is, I believe, to overlook the implications of that exorcism's representation.

2. The Phantom acts here as Marley's ghost and the three Christmas Ghosts do in Scrooge's transformation: Scrooge is decidedly too unimaginative to create the means of his own reclamation.

3. Fire and food are two of the objects that Patten maintains Dickens consistently associates with the hearth; the third is the greenery, in this case, the holly with which William's wife and father soon appear.

4. Although he may exude the very air of home, Mr. Tetterby dotes upon his wife, persistently calling her his " 'little woman' " despite the fact that, "considered with reference to her husband, her dimensions became magnificent":

> Nor did they assume a less imposing proportion when studied with reference to the size of her seven sons, who were but diminutive. In the case of Sally [the baby], however, Mrs. Tetterby had asserted herself, at last; as nobody knew better than the victim Johnny [the son in charge of Sally's care], who weighed and measured that exacting idol every hour in the day.   (453)

Here exploited for comic effect, the "imposing" dimensions of the female members of a family mark women's spiritual superiority in the memory of old Philip.

5. Ruth Glancy's examination of the manuscript and Dickens' correspondence about the story reveals that Milly's tidy cap is no mere accessory of the housewife; in fact, Dickens asked the illustrator to give Milly a cap because " 'there is something coming in the last part, about her having a dead child, which makes it yet more desirable than the existing text does, that she should have that little matronly sign about her' " (qtd. 74).

6. Milly's relationship with Redlaw is suggestive of one between sister and brother, and her role as Philip's daughter-in-law is much more pronounced than her role as William's wife. This characterization supports Slater's claim that, for all Dickens' preoccupation with the domestic Angel, his fiction reveals a paucity of actual examples of women spiritually inspiring or redeeming husbands or sons. Slater credits this absence of sanctifying wives and mothers to Dickens's "extreme difficulty in reconciling the sexual with the domestic ideal" (311).

7. As Mary Poovey notes, "maternal instinct was credited not only with making women nurture their children, but also with conferring upon them extraordinary power over men" (7–8). Proof of women's essential virtue, maternal "instinct" thus provided the very basis of their domestic power.

8. Thomas' chapter on Dickens' Christmas books explores the significance of a capacity for reading correctly to Dickens' interest in the role of storybooks in the everyday world. The motif of reading could also be explored as a means of characterizing sex roles: although the men appreciating their homes are all "good readers" (Mr. Tetterby's propensity for reading newspaper clippings aloud for the edification of his sons offers the most explicit example), they all rely on the example of a woman for their ability; all the women are already (i.e., naturally) capable of reading.

9. Clearly, this "objective mind" does not refer to a faculty for thinking or reasoning; rather, it objectifies the woman's entire being into a mirror for reflecting what the man lacks. As Peter Gay comments, Patmore's Angel embodies the superiority of an intuitive knowledge: "what man must struggle to conquer, woman naturally possesses; what man must painfully learn, woman simply knows" (292). Painful learning appropriately describes Redlaw's experience.

10. Milly's repetition of this question also probably forces most modern readers to agree with Stone that Milly "is too angelic and too inanely self-congratulatory (a sort of Esther Summerson at her worst)." Stone clearly, however, does not grant the "too angelic" much power, for he argues that Milly is "a *mere* agency for removing the curse" (141, emphasis mine).

11. Here, for example, is a pronouncement from an 1859 *Saturday Review* article on the need for women to "know" only what will contribute directly to their domestic duties:

> No woman can or ought to know very much of the mass of meanness and wickedness and misery that is loose in the wide world. She could not learn about it without losing the bloom and freshness which it is her mission in life to preserve. (qtd. in Poovey 155)

Because Milly, in her charitable missions, must be quite familiar with both wickedness and misery, it is all the more important that, in order to remain pure, she be denied knowledge of her power to work transformations.

12. Stone believes that Milly is indeed "proof against" Redlaw's influence (133), but the text, I believe, is intentionally ambiguous; had it been explicit on this issue, Milly's power would be even more threatening in its comprehensiveness than it already is.

13. The imagery here echoes that in the description of the Christmas dawn: "some blind groping of the morning made its way down into the forgotten crypt so cold and earthy . . . and quickened the slow principle of life . . . with some faint knowledge that the sun was up" (449). Though nearly all the action of the story takes place indoors (almost to the point of feeling claustrophobic), the motif of the garden outside the building reflecting Redlaw's inner life correlates his awakening not only with a natural phenomenon but also with the greenery symbolism most pronounced in the holly with which Philip and Milly decorate the building.

14. Again, Glancy's study of the manuscript reveals the importance of Milly's neat little cap as a signal of her maternalism and thus the significance of the dead child, which is the source of Milly's compassion and thereby "an essential part of the plot" (73). Glancy emphasizes that this "turning of a tragedy into the source of compassion and moral strength" (74) was intended to move readers as much as Redlaw: "The manuscript is heavily blotted with tears at this point [Milly's speech], verifying Dickens's statement to William Bradbury on 1 December that he finished the book the previous night, 'having been crying my eyes out over it—not painfully but pleasantly as I hope my readers will' " (73).

15. Jerry Herron argues that such "explicit, Christian vocabulary" provides the key to "comprehend[ing] Dickens's plan for moving his protagonist from recollection to forgiveness" (48). In fact, he believes that modern critics with "deeper and more complex errands" have misread the simple content of "The Haunted Man," ignoring its "immediate, topical reference"—namely, its Christian symbology (45, 46). This attempt to historicize the text, however, works only if we overlook another historically significant symbology, what Nina Auerbach calls an "angelology" that 'the Victorian age feminized," with its distinctly non-Christian "emanations" (82).

16. Dickens' best known prostitute, Nancy of *Oliver Twist*, shares this perversion in her love for Bill Sykes—and has received a good deal of critical attention for it. Because of the context in which she appears, the prostitute of "The Haunted Man," however, also resembles two men: Redlaw and his former friend for whom past homes are "dead" as well.

17. The prostitute's disappearance can be likened to the banishment of both the "fallen" gentleman in this story and Emily in *David Copperfield*. It can also be seen, however, as a ghostly fading into the shadows of the doorway in which she lingers, an image redolent with implications for such an existence in the borderland between the house and the outside world.

18. As Elizabeth Langland argues, "the story of the working-class wife for the middle-class man became nonnarratable . . . because the mid-Victorian husband depended on his wife to perform the ideological work of managing the class question" (291). For all of her lady-like virtue, Milly, the caretaker's daughter-in-law, is unequivocally working class.

19. Freud's examination of the uncanny is clearly applicable here in that explicitly domestic objects are transformed into strange entities: "The German work *unheimlich* is obviously the opposite of *heimlich, heimisch*, meaning 'familiar'; 'natural', 'belonging to the home' "; *heimlich* is also, however, "that which is concealed and kept out of sight" (370, 375).

WORKS CITED

Armstrong, Nancy. *Desire and Domestic Fiction: A Political History of the Novel.* New York: Oxford UP, 1987.

Auerbach, Nina. *Woman and the Demon: The Life of a Victorian Myth*. Cambridge: Harvard UP, 1982.

Barickman, Richard, Susan MacDonald, and Myra Stark. *Corrupt Relations: Dickens, Thackeray, Trollope, Collins, and the Victorian Sexual System*. New York: Columbia UP, 1982.

Dickens, Charles. "The Haunted Man." *Christmas Books*. Vol. 18 of *The Works of Charles Dickens*. Intro. and notes by Andrew Lang. 34 vols. Rpt. 1867–69. New York: Scribners, 1907–08.

Freud, Sigmund. "The Uncanny." *Totem and Taboo*. Trans. A. A. Brill. New York: New Republic, 1927.

Gay, Peter. *The Bourgeois Experience: Victoria to Freud*. New York: Oxford UP, 1984.

Glancy, Ruth. "Dickens at Work on 'The Haunted Man.' " *Dickens Studies Annual: Essays on Victorian Fiction*. 15 (1986): 65–83.

Helsinger, Elizabeth, Robin Sheets, and William Veeder. *The Woman Question: Society and Literature in Britain and America*. 3 vols. Chicago: Chicago UP, 1989.

Herron, Jerry. " 'The Haunted Man' and the Two Scrooges." *Studies in Short Fiction* 19 (Winter 1982): 45–50.

Langland, Elizabeth. "Nobody's Angels: Domestic Ideology and Middle-Class Women in the Victorian Novel." *PMLA* 107 (March 1992): 290–304.

Levine, George, U. D. Knoepflmacher, eds. *The Endurance of Frankenstein: Essays on Mary Shelley's Novel*. Berkeley: U of California P, 1979.

Newman, Beth. " 'The Situation of the Looker-On': Gender, Narration, and Gaze in *Wuthering Heights*." *PMLA* 105 (October 1990): 1029–41.

Patten, Robert L. " 'A Surprising Transformation': Dickens and the Hearth." *Nature and the Victorian Imagination*. Ed. U. C. Knoepflmacher and G. B. Tennyson. Berkeley: U of California P, 1977.

Poovey, Mary. *Uneven Developments: The Ideological Work of Gender in Mid-Victorian England*. Chicago: U of Chicago P, 1988.

Slater, Michael. *Dickens and Women*. London: Dent, 1983.

Stone, Harry. *Dickens and the Invisible World: Fairy Tales, Fantasy, and Miracle-Making*. Bloomington: Indiana UP, 1979.

Thomas, Deborah. *Dickens and the Short Story*. Philadelphia: U of Pennsylvania P, 1982.

Lower-Class Angels in the Middle-Class House: The Domestic Woman's "Progress" in *Hard Times* and *Ruth*

Katherine A. Retan

I. GENDER, CLASS, AND THE "PROGRESS" OF THE DICKENS ANGEL

Dickens' portrayal of the meeting between the angelic Rose Maylie and the fallen Nancy in *Oliver Twist* provides an early example of the pairing of "pure" and "tainted" women which characterizes his fiction. However, the contact between middle-class daughter and prostitute in this novel is represented in somewhat different terms from the contact between Esther Summerson and Lady Dedlock in *Bleak House*, or Sissy Jupe and Louisa Gradgrind in *Hard Times*. Nancy is "burdened with a sense of her own deep shame" when she thinks of the contrast between herself and Rose Maylie (360). Rose manages to soften the pride which has prevented Nancy from betraying a "feeble gleam" of that "womanly feeling" which she thinks of as a weakness (361), and the lower-class prostitute falls to her knees before the middle-class angel, blessing her for her kind words. There are echoes of this scene in *Hard Times*, where the repentant Louisa, struggling against the pride which has led her to repulse her "better angel," falls to her knees before Sissy Jupe, who shines "like a beautiful light" upon her "darkness" (248). However, the class relationship between angel and fallen woman is reversed in *Hard Times*. It is the middle-class daughter who is tainted by desire and hardened by pride and resentment, and it is the daughter of a circus clown who plays the part of reforming angel.

The juxtaposition of Nancy and Rose in *Oliver Twist* works to underscore the process by which a friendless lower-class girl becomes a prostitute. Rose's own social and sexual identity, her status as a middle-class domestic woman, is never called into question, even when the shame attaching to her sister Agnes is revealed. Whereas in *Bleak House* Esther Summerson's encounter with female sexual guilt initially works to undermine her social identity, to lead her to feel that she is somehow tainted, in *Oliver Twist* the identity of the middle-class domestic woman is presented as a given.

In his middle novels, Dickens becomes increasingly preoccupied with representing a young woman's progress toward assuming the role of angel in her own middle-class household. As he becomes more critical of the values associated with the marketplace, of the failure of certain elements of the middle class to cultivate relationships beyond those of the cash-nexus with their social inferiors, he centers his novels on the process by which the middle-class woman's social and sexual identity is constructed, rather than representing this identity as a given. The angel's progress is portrayed as involving an encounter with transgressive sexuality which teaches her the necessity of maintaining a constant struggle against desire. Thus, in *Dombey and Son* and *Bleak House* it is the daughter's humble acceptance of shame which establishes her identity as the type of the middle-class domestic woman. As in *Oliver Twist*, it is women of the upper and lower classes who have actually transgressed in these novels. However, Florence Dombey and Esther Summerson, unlike Rose Maylie, come to feel that they themselves are somehow fallen as a result of their contact with women who are socially and sexually "other."

A number of feminist critics have commented on the connections drawn in mid-Victorian texts between the domestic angel and her "demonic" other. Nina Auerbach, in *Woman and the Demon*, argues that such links point to the power which writers such as Dickens attribute to women, a power which they attempt to suppress in their fiction, but which is constantly reasserted by the very myths of womanhood they construct. Laurie Langbauer writes that "Dickens tries to deny the homebody's 'unheimlich' double, to separate her from the streetwalker, but he can't really keep them apart." She argues that Dickens' angels are closer to his fallen women than he intends, and that his works ultimately "rebel against his conservative insistence" (425–26).

I will examine the connections which are drawn between "homebody" and "streetwalker" in Dickens' texts in order to argue that the "merging" of such pairs of women as Esther Summerson and Lady Dedlock performs a conservative function. It is by means of a ritualistic encounter with shame that the middle-class daughter learns humility; it is her "infection" by desire which teaches her the necessity of keeping up that constant refrain of "duty, my dear'' which Dickens attributes to Esther. Both gender and class "dis-ease'' are represented in terms of that transgressive desire which the domestic woman learns to manage as a result of her contact with degraded female sexuality.

The association of "angel" and "magdalen" in *Dombey* and *Bleak House* works to consolidate middle-class authority by reinforcing boundaries of both gender and class. The daughter's acceptance of shame establishes her identity as a middle-class angel and teaches her that regulatory capacity which, for Dickens and other domestic ideologists, ensures the quality of life associated with the middle-class home. Florence and Esther gain the power to foster those moral values which are seen as an antidote to the dis-ease associated with the public sphere through their encounters with that transgressive sexuality associated with class unrest, and their "reforming" power works to legitimize middle-class social authority.

In *Desire and Domestic Fiction*, Nancy Armstrong discusses the manner in which the figure of the "monstrous" woman in mid-Victorian fiction worked to gender and neutralize political resistance by transforming working-class unrest into aberrant sexual desire. I feel that it is important to examine the related, and equally political, process by which the figure of the sexually degraded woman worked to transform the middle-class daughter into the type of the domestic angel. Armstrong writes: "How these mad, bad, and em-bruted women represented political differences is, I think, a more interesting question than how the fictional norms of femininity kept women in line" (253). I would argue that it is impossible to separate these two questions, for the reason that gender issues are always, ultimately, political issues. That class conflict is, as Armstrong argues, gendered and contained in mid-Victorian domestic fiction does not mean that issues concerning gender were not themselves sources of political tension for middle-class Victorians. In contributing to the construction of the ideal type of the domestic woman, the deployment of the figure of the "monstrous" woman in domestic fiction worked to depoliticize both gender and class conflict.

Florence Dombey and Esther Summerson learn the importance of waging an unrelenting battle against desire by means of their encounters with the "sin and shame" that attach to the aristocratic Edith Granger and Lady Dedlock, women who stand in the relationship of mothers toward them but whose transgressive sexuality prevents them from fulfilling a mother's duties. Dickens suggests that Florence and Esther are "pattern" ladies because they are suitably impressed with a sense of the shame that attaches to them as women. Both daughters are troubled from childhood by the feeling that they have committed some crime. Florence feels that she must have done something to merit the aversion her father feels for her, and Esther is subjected to her godmother's refrain of ''Your mother, Esther, is your disgrace, and you were hers. The time will come—and soon enough—when you will understand this better, and will feel it too, as no one save a woman can'' (65). Florence's and Esther's ritualistic encounters with the sins of the mothers give concrete shape to feelings of guilt that have haunted them from childhood, and emphasize that humble acceptance of shame that distinguishes them from the fallen Edith Granger and Lady Dedlock.

In *Dombey and Son*, Edith Granger refers to herself in a manner which suggests that to be a woman is to be ''a little bit fallen.''[1] She accuses her mother of having robbed her of her childhood: ''I was a woman—artful, designing, mercenary, laying snares for men—before I knew myself, or you, or even understood the base and wretched aim of every new display I learnt. You gave birth to a woman. Look upon her. She is in her pride tonight'' (333). Womanhood is equated with shame and degradation, and Dickens suggests that Florence and Esther are able to assume the role of angel in their middle-class households only because they have learned humility and the art of self-effacement, only because they are able to regulate desire.

Dickens sets Florence's humility and innocence against Edith's pride and dangerous knowledge of sexuality, and yet the text continually draws our attention to the tenuous line between the pure and the degraded woman. Thus Mrs. Skewton remarks upon meeting Florence that she sees ''a decided resemblance'' to what Edith was in childhood ''in our extremely fascinating young friend'' (357), and the kindly but dissipated Couisin Feenix continually applies the same epithet to both Edith (''my lovely and accomplished relative'') and Florence (''the lovely and accomplished daughter of my friend Dombey''), doing so within the space of a single sentence after Edith has left Dombey and ''stained'' Florence's name (727).

In addition, the text establishes connections between Florence and the lower-class prostitute Alice Marwood, who is Edith's double. Good Mrs. Brown, Alice's mother, abducts Florence in childhood and steals her clothing, dressing her in what are presumably Alice's old things. Florence catches her hair in Alice's bonnet, drawing attention to her luxuriant curls, which Mrs. Brown is tempted to cut off and sell. The old woman accuses Florence of having excited her, and ''ruffling her curls with a furious pleasure,'' remarks that ''anybody but me would have had 'em off, first of all'' (60). In the end she spares Florence's hair because it reminds her of Alice's. Dickens, in drawing a connection between Florence and Alice, emphasizes the sexuality of the former, turning her into an object of desire as he removes her middle-class clothing. Florence's sexuality, like her luxuriant hair, threatens to assert itself and thus to obliterate the distinctions between middle-class daughter and fallen lower-class woman.

Florence's most dramatic encounter with the shame associated with female sexuality occurs when she unknowingly interrupts Edith's flight from the Dombey household. To her amazement, her stepmother recoils from her embrace and shrieks. The narrator tells us that

> As Florence stood transfixed before the haggard face and staring eyes, she noted, as in a dream, that Edith spread her hands over them, and shuddering through all her form, and crouching down against the wall, crawled by her like some lower animal, sprang up, and fled away.   (552)

The mere suggestion of sexual transgression (for we learn that Edith does not intend to become Carker's mistress), the decision to abandon one's duties in the home and thus one's struggle against desire, transforms a woman into "some lower animal."

Edith becomes the embodiment of a monstrous female sexuality in this scene, and Florence experiences a symbolic fall, dropping upon the floor "in a swoon" as Louisa Gradgrind will after her near-transgression with Harthouse. When Florence tries to console her father, he identifies her with her rebellious stepmother, striking her "with that heaviness, that she tottered on the marble floor; and as he dealt the blow, he told her what Edith was, and bade her follow her, since they had always been in league" (557). Presumably, Dombey uses language which the proper Victorian lady is not supposed to understand, and when Florence leaves her father's house after this highly indelicate encounter the narrator describes her flight in those terms which Dickens and his contemporaries characteristically use to describe the flight of the fallen woman:

> In the wildness of her sorrow, shame, and terror, the forlorn girl hurried through the sunshine of a bright morning, as if it were the darkness of a winter night. . . . Somewhere, anywhere to hide her head! somewhere, anywhere, for refuge, never more to look upon the place from which she fled! . . . She thought of the only other time she had been lost in the wide wilderness of London—though not lost as now—and went that way.   (557–58)

Florence, like Esther, is literally marked by her contact with female sexuality. Just as Esther is initially afraid to look in the mirror after her illness, afraid to see the scars on her face which are the visible sign of her connection with desire, Florence is troubled by the mark on her breast where her father has struck her:

> After cooling her aching head and burning face in the fresh water which the Captain had provided while she slept, Florence went to the little mirror to bind up her disordered hair. Then she knew—in a moment, for she shunned it instantly—that on her breast there was the darkening mark of an angry hand.
> Her tears burst forth afresh at the sight; she was ashamed and afraid of it; but it moved her to no anger against him [Dombey].   (569)

Florence is ashamed and afraid, and it is her humble acceptance of shame which establishes her as the type of the domestic angel. The mark on her breast becomes a sign of her purity, of that ability to regulate desire which characterizes the figure of the domestic woman in mid-Victorian texts. It establishes her social and sexual identity, much as Esther's scars work to distinguish her from the fallen Lady Dedlock. Christine van Boheemen-Saaf notes that the taboo on Esther's sexuality is lifted only after she has "owned her mother," after she "has looked the evil of her birth in the face and accepted it as her own" (248). Dickens is able to portray Florence and Esther as mothers at the centers of happy middle-class families only after he has demonstrated their acceptance of the fact that they are inevitably tainted by desire, and I would argue that this is because, for him, such an acceptance of shame signifies the daughter's ability to contain that desire and division which threaten to undermine middle-class domesticity.

On the first occasion of her being lost "in the wide wilderness of London," Florence finds herself transformed into the fallen Alice Marwood. She is rescued by Walter and returned to her father's household. When Florence is lost for the second time, she carries that mark on her breast which, paradoxically, identifies her as the type of the Victorian domestic angel. It is at this point in the text, when she is no longer in danger of unconsciously performing actions which will associate her with a lower-class prostitute, that she marries Walter. The mark on her breast, which is described as lying "between her and her lover when he pressed her to his heart" (660), signifies her ability to guard against those monstrous displays of female sexuality which characterize Edith, and the text connects this ability with her power to regulate those excesses of Dombey's which have resulted in class conflict and financial ruin.

Florence's and Esther's successful struggles with desire culminate in the establishment of middle-class homes which have been symbolically purged of the ills associated with the public sphere. However, as Dickens becomes less optimistic about the ability of a middle class which he has begun to see as morally bankrupt, as guided solely by the principles of political economy, to alleviate social distress and prevent working-class combination, his representation of the middle-class daughter's progress undergoes a number of significant changes. *Hard Times* is a novel which is more directly concerned than either *Dombey and Son* or *Bleak House* with the need for social and political reform, and Dickens connects Thomas Gradgrind's inability to effect such reform with his daughter's inability to perform the role of domestic angel, to regulate desire.

In *Hard Times*, the middle-class daughter is directly associated with gender and class unrest, and it is her sacrifice, rather than that of a woman from the upper or lower classes, which enables the reformation of the middle-class family. Louisa Gradgrind is more than "a little bit fallen," and Dickens connects her with the prostitute Nancy and the rebellious, aristocratic Edith Dombey and Lady Dedlock rather than with his middle-class angels. There are direct echoes of Nancy's speeches to Rose and of the "fallen" Edith Dombey's speeches to Florence in the speech which Louisa makes to Sissy after her near-elopement with Harthouse: "Sissy, do you know what I am? I am so proud and so hardened, so confused and troubled, so resentful and unjust to every one and to myself, that everything is stormy, dark and wicked to me" (248). Louisa's pride and resentment signify her kinship with Dickens's fallen women, and her close connection with both social and sexual unrest disqualifies her for the role of angel in the middle-class household.

Barbara Leah Harmon compares Gaskell's treatment of Margaret Hale's symbolic encounters with the "shame" of female sexuality in *North and South* with Dickens' treatment of Louisa's near-seduction. She argues that "Gaskell seems to be saying that the experience of being tainted is oddly beneficial, that it is in fact positive and educative" (372). It is Margaret's perception that she is "degraded and abased" in Thornton's sight which eradicates her snobbishness for "shoppy people" and causes her to acknowledge that she is in love with the mill-owner. Harmon writes that

> Gaskell's procedure looms all the more significantly if we compare her handling of Margaret's fate with, say, Dickens's handling of the fates of his female characters when they too are associated with, but do not actually commit, adultery. Louisa Gradgrind is rendered sterile merely for listening to Harthouse's advances.   (372–73)

As I have argued, Dickens, like Gaskell, suggests that the experience of being tainted is "oddly beneficial." Florence's and Esther's marriages, like

Margaret Hale's, are facilitated by their encounters with sexual shame, which teach them the necessity of waging a constant battle against that desire which Dickens and Gaskell associate with social unrest. However, Louisa's contact with shame is more direct than Margaret's, for she actually contemplates adultery. She questions the Victorian code of "feminine" behavior, reaching the point at which she can say "I do not know that I am ashamed, I do not know that I am degraded in my own esteem" (242). Unlike Margaret, she is openly rebellious.

While Gaskell represents the contact between Margaret and the working-class Nicholas Higgins as leading to a lasting friendship which reaffirms the existing social order, Dickens portrays the encounter between Louisa and Stephen Blackpool as having disastrous consequences for both woman and worker, which lead to their separation. The association between middle-class woman and mill-hand has more radical implications in *Hard Times* than in *North and South*, for the parallels which Dickens draws between Louisa's discontent over her position as Bounderby's wife and Stephen's discontent over his position as Bounderby's worker serve to underscore the connections between gender and class oppression. Woman and worker share a common "master," and thus, when Louisa visits Stephen and offers him financial assistance after her husband has fired him, her act of charity has potentially disturbing implications. The meeting between Stephen and Louisa raises the possibility that worker and woman might combine to oppose the system that oppresses them. The plot device of the bank robbery, which places Louisa's interests in direct opposition to Stephen's, works to manage the threat of gender and class combination. To use Harmon's terms, both worker and woman are rendered sterile in *Hard Times*.

Louisa, unlike Margaret Hale or Florence Dombey and Esther Summerson, is humbled not by her contact with "sin," which leaves her proud and defiant, but by her contact with Sissy. Because Louisa lacks the ability to contain social and sexual tension, because she signifies the failure of the Gradgrind system, she herself is an inadequate figure for effecting reform. It is Sissy Jupe, the poor stroller's daughter, who becomes the angel in the Gradgrind household, for in *Hard Times* Dickens attempts to resolve social and sexual unrest and symbolically reform a middle class which he sees as somewhat "fallen" through his portrayal of Sissy's reformation of the middle-class daughter.

Interestingly, Gaskell herself had set the example of portraying a woman of lower-class origins as the ideal type of the domestic angel. In her novel *Ruth*, which was published a year before the serialization of *Hard Times* and which Dickens had read and praised, it is a former dressmaker's apprentice who plays the role of angel in the middle-class household. The humble Ruth possesses the ability to "soften" Jemima Bradshaw, the sullen and rebellious middle-class daughter, and to reform the Bradshaw family. However, in Gaskell's novel it is the lower-class angel rather than the middle-class daughter who has come into direct contact with "sin." Ruth is seduced as a young, motherless girl, and it is the revelation of her former transgression which chastens Jemima, teaching her that humility which is an essential characteristic of the domestic angel. Jemima is able to perform the role of angel once she has learned the necessity of guarding against desire, and her marriage to her father's business partner, unlike Louisa's marriage to Bounderby, is represented as a successful one. Jemima is not rendered sterile as a result of her humbling encounter with female sexuality, and yet Ruth suffers as a result of the revelation which transforms Jemima, losing first her position in the Bradshaw family and, finally, her life.

In *Hard Times*, as opposed to *Ruth*, the abandoned girl of humble origins is permanently installed as angel in the middle-class household. Sissy is exalted as Louisa is lowered, and she literally re-forms the Gradgrind family, placing herself at its center. Dickens suggests that Sissy is ideally suited for the role of angel because of her ambiguous social position. She attains a certain degree of refinement as a result of her upbringing in the Gradgrind household, losing the trace of dialect which she exhibits at the beginning of the novel, so that Harthouse takes her for a relation of Louisa's (256). Sissy speaks the language of the middle classes, and yet Dickens represents her as being permanently humbled by the knowledge of her origins. She is untouched by that rebellious pride which "perverts" Louisa.

Dickens' portrayal of Sissy as belonging to both the lower and the middle classes works to obscure the class affiliations of the figure of the domestic angel. However, Sissy's story, even more than Florence's or Esther's, ultimately underscores the ways in which representations of the angel in the house legitimize middle-class authority at the expense of other social groups. Sissy gives up all allegiance to the lower orders when she is adopted into the Gradgrind family, and she uses all of her powers to protect their middle-class household. It is she who arranges young Tom Gradgrind's escape from the country after he robs Bounderby's bank and does his best to frame Stephen Blackpool. Sissy's "wisdom of the heart" works to reform the Gradgrind family, but the values associated with Sissy and the domestic sphere prove powerless to heal those social ills which produce gender and class unrest.

Thus, while Helena Bergmann feels that Dickens grants excessive powers to Sissy (110), I would argue that her power proves to be extremely limited. She cannot even completely heal the rifts in the Gradgrind family, for Tom dies alone in a foreign country and Louisa remains childless and unmarried. In spite of the narrator's frequent assertions that the cultivation of fancy and the affections, Sissy's attributes, will facilitate the reformation of both the family and society, the visions into futurity which conclude *Hard Times* are bleak. Thomas Gradgrind makes ''his facts and figures subservient to Faith, Hope, and Charity'' only to be ''much despised'' and taunted ''by his late political associates'' (312), and we are left with the troubling image of Louisa staring into the fire, rather than with a detailed description of bourgeois domesticity. Indeed, Dickens' narrator gives us the latter: ''Herself again a wife—a mother—lovingly watchful of her children,'' only to cancel it: ''Did Louisa see this? Such a thing was never to be'' (313).

Sissy is an inadequate figure for managing gender and class unrest and symbolically reforming a ''fallen'' middle class because she herself is not represented as experiencing that sense of shame which teaches such women as Esther and Florence the need to guard against desire. Her encounter with the ''fallen'' Louisa does not lead her to feel that she herself is somehow tainted. Rather, Dickens attributes Sissy's humility to her knowledge of her inferior social status and her inability to learn. Dickens portrays Sissy as being untouched by the shame associated with transgressive sexuality, and because her progress toward assuming the role of angel in the Gradgrind household involves no symbolic conflict, no struggle to contain that desire which he connects with both gender and class dis-ease, she loses some of the reforming power which he grants to Florence and Esther.[2]

In *Hard Times*, rather than focusing on the construction of the figure of the domestic woman, Dickens reverts to his earlier practice of portraying the angel's status as a given. This reversion is an indication of both his increasing concern over the failure of the middle classes to cultivate those values associated with the domestic sphere and his related fear of working-class revolt. The middle-class daughter's contact with desire is particularly subversive in *Hard Times* because her discontent is connected with that of the workers. Gender and class unrest are more directly linked than in *Dombey* or *Bleak House*, and because the implications of the daughter's contact with desire are thus potentially explosive, the role of angel passes to the impossibly pure Sissy.[3]

II. THE TAMING OF THE MIDDLE-CLASS DAUGHTER IN GASKELL'S
RUTH

Gaskell's Jemima Bradshaw possesses a degree of rebellious anger and obstinate pride which connects her to Louisa Gradgrind, rather than to Dickens' more humble middle-class daughters. Like Louisa, Jemima rebels against her father's narrow definitions of correct behavior, against the rigid principles of a system which takes no account of human emotions, and the resentment which consumes her is represented as disqualifying her for the role of domestic angel. As in *Hard Times*, the part of angel falls to a woman of lower-class origins who has gained a place in the middle-class family. Ruth, a former dressmaker's apprentice, is able to produce a degree of harmony in the Bradshaw household. Jemima Bradshaw, like the unrepentant Louisa, is secretly tormented by her own apparent lack of grace, and she begins to resent the unassuming Ruth. Much as Louisa, struggling with her anger at both Sissy and herself, feels that "In this strife I have almost repulsed and crushed my better angel into a demon" (240), Jemima's "better angel" leads her to ask herself "What was this terrible demon in her heart? . . . Was she, indeed, given up to possession?" (245).

A number of critics have pointed to similarities between Dickens' portrayal of the Gradgrind family and Gaskell's portrayal of the Bradshaws.[4] In each novel the middle-class family threatens to disintegrate as the result of the children's reactions against their father's rigid system. Louisa Gradgrind contemplates adultery as a result of her marriage to Bounderby, her father's friend, and Jemima Bradshaw stubbornly rebels against *her* father's plans for her marriage with Mr. Farquhar, his friend and business partner. Young Tom Gradgrind commits bank robbery and young Richard Bradshaw embezzles money from the family firm. However, the relationship between Gaskell's and Dickens' portrayals of the taming of a middle-class daughter by an angelic woman of humble origins has been virtually ignored.[5] Both Jemima and Louisa find it difficult to combat the "demonic" aspects of their natures, and both are humbled by those lower-class "sisters" whose sympathies they initially reject.

Louisa is humbled by her near-transgression and by the example Sissy sets for her of selfless behavior. Jemima learns humility from Ruth, but it is important to note that Ruth's angelic qualities have little to do with her reformation. Jemima is chastened by means of a symbolic encounter with the "demon" of desire, and her contact occurs through Ruth, for in Gaskell's novel it is the lower-class angel who has transgressed. Ruth, the orphaned child of a bankrupt farmer, ''too young when her mother died to have received any cautions or words of advice respecting *the* subject of a woman's life'' (44), is seduced and abandoned by the son of a wealthy family. She is then taken in by a dissenting minister and his sister, Thurstan and Faith Benson, who successfully pass her off as a widowed relation. Ruth's humility and gentleness, which stem from her sense that she is tainted, strike the stern Mr. Bradshaw, the most powerful member of Benson's congregation, as the very qualities he would like to see cultivated in his own daughters. He employs her as governess to his younger girls and encourages her to provide his eldest daughter, Jemima, with an example of correct feminine behavior.

Significantly, it is only after the story of Ruth's ''fall'' is disclosed that she is able to effect real change in both Jemima and the Bradshaw household.[6] Jemima is humbled by her discovery of Ruth's ''sin,'' for she begins to feel that she too might have fallen had the circumstances of her life been different. She recognizes the need to control desire. Like Louisa, she is reformed in part through an encounter with female sexual guilt. However, because it is Ruth who has actually transgressed, and because Jemima's rebellious behavior is not connected with working-class unrest, the suitably-chastened middle-class daughter is ultimately permitted to perform the role of domestic angel in Gaskell's novel.

Gaskell's overt purpose in *Ruth* is to convince her middle-class readers to exercise Christian forgiveness in the case of the fallen woman. She is writing in part to expose the hypocrisy of the double standard according to which fallen lower-class women were condemned while the actions of their upper or middle-class seducers were condoned. As Gaskell suggests, the double standard worked to protect middle-class daughters from seduction at the expense of their lower-class sisters.[7] Significantly, what happens in *Ruth* is that the story of Jemima's reformation and the reformation of the Bradshaw family takes precedence over Ruth's own story. The taming of the rebellious middle-class daughter, her transformation into domestic angel, becomes the novel's central project. Thus, Gaskell ends by inscribing the double standard in her own text, for the fallen Ruth, though portrayed as an angel, is ultimately sacrificed in favor of the middle-class Jemima.

Gaskell was prompted to write *Ruth* by what she had learned of the story of a young Irish girl named Pasley, whom she had visited in Manchester's New Bayley prison. Like Ruth, Pasley was orphaned at an early age, her father dying and her mother renouncing all responsibility for her. She was apprenticed to a dressmaker at fourteen, seduced by a surgeon who attended her during an illness, and lured into prostitution by a woman whom she met in the penitentiary.[8] Gaskell gives her heroine the second chance she desired for Pasley, on whose behalf she wrote to Dickens to enquire about Angela Burdett-Coutts's home for the rehabilitation and eventual emigration of "fallen" women, telling him "I want her to go out with as free and unbranded a character as she can, if possible, the very fact of having been in prison & c to be unknown on her landing" (*Letters* 99). Thurstan Benson and his sister Faith give Ruth the opportunity to begin a new life when they bring her from Wales, where she has been abandoned by Bellingham, to their home in Eccleston, passing her off as the widow of a distant relation so that she and the child she is carrying will not be branded as outcasts.

It is the process by which the Victorian angel, rather than the Victorian prostitute, is constructed which emerges as the focus of Gaskell's novel, and Ruth's own transformation into domestic angel, like Jemima's, is presented as a lengthy process. The sense of shame and knowledge of sin which follow from Ruth's growing awareness of her position as a fallen woman are represented as playing a large role in developing her domestic virtues and endowing her with a new kind of purity. Thus Thurstan Benson, justifying his decision to counsel Ruth to accept Bradshaw's offer of the position of governess, tells Faith: "I have watched Ruth, and I believe she is pure and truthful; and the very sorrow and penitence she has felt—the very suffering she has gone through—has given her a thoughtful conscientiousness beyond her age" (199). In addition, Ruth's sorrow, her maternal devotion and the influence of the Bensons combine to produce the following transformation: "whereas, six or seven years ago, you would have perceived that she [Ruth] was not altogether a lady by birth and education, yet now she might have been placed among the highest in the land, and would have been taken by the most critical judge for their equal . . ." (209). Rather than slipping further down the social scale as a result of her fall, as Pasley did, Ruth attains a degree of refinement which leads Bellingham, when he sees her again, to exclaim that "she might be a Percy or a Howard for the grandeur of her grace!" (278).

Gaskell represents Ruth's fall as both fitting her for the role of angel and ultimately disqualifying her for the part. Ruth is both impossibly pure and irrevocably stained. She can serve as an example of correct behavior to Jemima and scare her into submission by bringing her into contact with transgressive sexuality, a contact which teaches the middle-class daughter the need to "take heed lest she fell" (370). Jemima's own subversive desire is projected onto Ruth, who, unlike Sissy Jupe in *Hard Times*, has actually transgressed and therefore remains irrevocably "other."

Gaskell's overt political agenda in *Ruth* of exposing the double standard and advocating the rehabilitation of the fallen woman differs from Dickens' agenda in *Hard Times*. However, much as Dickens' concern over improving the condition of the working class and relations between masters and men gives way to his project of rehabilitating the middle-class family, the reformation of the Bradshaw family ultimately takes precedence over Ruth's plight in Gaskell's novel. Ruth's fate, like Stephen's and Louisa's, works to contain that desire which, for Dickens and Gaskell, threatens to undermine middle-class social authority.

The middle-class Jemima becomes openly rebellious when she learns of her father's scheme to marry her to his business partner, Mr. Farquhar, an arrangement which would benefit the family firm. She determines to thwart what she sees as a conspiracy between her father and Farquhar by behaving in a sullen manner which will convince the latter that she would be a bad bargain as a wife. She does so by enacting a grotesque parody of "correct" womanly behavior. Bradshaw has cautioned Jemima to avoid contradicting Farquhar and she responds by making her actions "so submissive that they were spiritless" (226), annoying her father without displaying any "positive fault" which he can object to. Disturbed by his daughter's "sullen, sulky" behavior, Bradshaw asks Ruth to speak to her about it, to teach her better manners.

Initially, Ruth's gentleness, her wisdom of the heart as opposed to Bradshaw's wisdom of the head, gives her the power to soften Jemima, who feels that it is "a relief to be near some one on whose true pure heart she relied" (228). However, Ruth loses her ability to influence Jemima when the latter learns of her conference with Bradshaw. Jemima is revolted by the idea that Ruth has lent her services to the enforcement of paternal law. "Management everywhere!" is her disgusted response (238). In addition, Ruth's apparent perfection begins to irritate the rebellious middle-class daughter as she witnesses its effect on Farquhar:

> Ruth was beautiful, gentle, good, and conscientious. The hot colour flushed up into Jemima's sallow face as she became aware that, even while she acknowledged these excellencies on Mrs Denbigh's part, she hated her. The recollection of her marble face wearied her even to sickness; the tones of her low voice were irritating from their very softness. (245)

Mr. Farquhar is attracted by Ruth's pale face and soft voice. He contrasts Jemima, "turbulent and stormy in look," with Ruth, "to all appearance, heavenly calm as the angels,'' and decides that the latter would make a more suitable wife (233). Farquhar associates those qualities he approves of in Mrs. Denbigh with the sorrow and care he believes she has known as a result of her husband's death (241). In fact, it is sorrow and shame which have produced Farquhar's ''type of what a woman should be'' (308).

Significantly, once Ruth comes to feel shame, once she comes to understand her position as a fallen woman and to recognize the necessity of guarding against desire, she is represented in sexual terms. The desire that Ruth suppresses in becoming the type of the domestic angel surfaces in images of nightmare and disease.[9] Thus, when she reencounters Bellingam, the sands heave and tremble beneath her feet and she feels ''the heavy press of pent-up passion'' (268–70). Her behavior when left alone in her room is described in terms which provide a marked contrast to the standard references to her ''shy reserve'' and ''heavenly calm'':

> She fastened her door, and threw open the window, cold and threatening as was the night. She tore off her gown; she put her hair back from her heated face. . . . She threw her body half out of the window into the cold night air. The wind was rising, and came in great gusts. The rain beat down on her. It did her good. A still, calm night would not have soothed her as this did.
> (272–74)

It is Ruth who has literally transgressed, and yet Jemima's ''perverseness,'' her rebellious behavior, is described in the same terms as Ruth's repressed desire. There is a direct echo of the passage in which Ruth leans out of the window in the following description of Jemima's behavior after being forced to witness an example of Farquhar's devotion to Ruth:

> She went into the schoolroom, where the shutters were not closed. . . . She opened the window, to let the cool night air blow in on her hot cheeks. The clouds were hurrying over the moon's face in a tempestuous and unstable manner, making all things seem unreal. . . . It was a waking nightmare, from the uneasy heaviness of which she was thankful to be roused by Dick's entrance.
> (333)

Jemima, like Ruth, is consumed by repressed desire, but Gaskell's narrative suggests that whereas Ruth cannot erase ''this mocking echo, this haunting phantom, this past that would not rest in its grave'' (313), the middle-class daughter can permanently control her unruly emotions through the socially sanctioned avenue of marriage to Farquhar.

Jemima has her first encounter with the demon of sexual desire when the new Eccleston dressmaker, the sister-in-law of Ruth's former employer, mentions Mrs. Denbigh's striking resemblance to a Ruth Hilton who distinguished herself by her "vicious conduct" with a young gentleman in Fordham. Jemima recognizes Ruth's maiden name, and is "stunned" by the shock she receives. Her contact with that which is repressed, that which cannot be spoken in the mid-Victorian middle-class family, fills her with terror and repugnance. Jemima's sensations are compared to those of the diver, who "down in an instant in the horrid depths of the sea, close to some strange, ghastly lidless-eyed monster, can hardly more feel his blood curdle at the near terror than did Jemima now" (323). The narrator informs us that up until this point in her life, Jemima "had never imagined that she should ever come in contact with anyone who had committed open sin." She had imagined "that all the respectable, all the family and religious circumstances of her life, would hedge her in, and guard her from ever encountering the great shock of coming face to face with vice" (323). Now she finds that one whom she had imagined to be the image of purity, one who occupies a position of trust in her father's house, one who has won the regard of the man she loves, is "stained with that evil most repugnant to her womanly modesty, that would fain have ignored its existence altogether" (324).

Jemima's contact with "vice" initially undermines her faith in the feminine ideal, in the standards according to which she has been raised, for if the middle-class family can be infiltrated by a fallen dressmaker's apprentice, if such a woman can appear to be the type of the domestic angel, then there are no longer any clear-cut boundaries between "good" and "evil," between the pure middle-class daughter and the degraded needlewoman.[10] "Who was true? Who was not? Who was good and pure? Who was not? The very foundations of Jemima's belief in her mind were shaken" (326).

Gaskell suggests that both Jemima's initial shock and repugnance and the sympathy which she later displays toward Ruth stem from the realization that there is only a thin line separating her situation from Ruth's. Significantly, Mrs. Pearson's exposure of Ruth's "sin" occurs during a scene in which she informs Jemima that the bonnet she has just persuaded her to try on is the same one she persuaded Mrs. Denbigh to wear on the previous day. It is after drawing this connection between middle-class daughter and governess, in much the same manner in which Good Mrs. Brown connects Florence Dombey and Alice Marwood, that the dressmaker reveals Ruth's identity.

While initially contributing to Jemima's horror, her sense that there is a connection between herself and Ruth finally teaches her to forgive her former friend and to reform her own conduct. "I have been thinking a great deal about poor Ruth's ———'' Jemima tells Benson, unable to give a name to the "lidless-eyed monster," unable to speak female sexual desire:

> and it made me think of myself, and what I am. . . . if you knew all I have been thinking and feeling this last year, you would see how I have yielded to every temptation that was able to come to me; and, seeing how I have no goodness or strength in me, and how I might just have been like Ruth, or rather, worse than she ever was, because I am more headstrong and passionate by nature, I do so thank you and love you for what you did for her!   (365)

Jemima 'forgives'' Ruth, and her forgiveness is contingent on her sense that she too might have "sinned" had she been outside the protection of the middle-class family.

Jemima openly defies her father when he dismisses Ruth from her position as governess. However, the very sympathy which enables Jemima to oppose her father's harsh judgment also works to transform her into the dutiful daughter he has long wished her to be. Bodenheimer writes that "Ruth's influence on Jemima . . . inverts the fearful Victorian idea of the tainted woman," teaching Jemima "to develop womanly sympathy and successful love" (163). I would argue that Gaskell in fact reproduces the very cultural myth she is attempting to subvert by suggesting that it is Ruth's "sin" which teaches Jemima the value of submission. Jemima, humbled by her encounter with unregulated sexuality, learns to control that pride which has made her rebel against Mr. Farquhar's "pattern idea" of a wife. She marries her father's business partner and becomes an angel in his house.

Ruth loses the place she has attained in the Bradshaw household and in the social hierarchy as Jemima assumes her "proper" position. The former dressmaker's apprentice carries the stain of sexuality for the middle-class daughter. Jemima's passionate nature, her confused feelings for Mr. Farquhar, are described in the same terms as Ruth's contradictory emotions on reencountering Bellingham. However, it is only Ruth, who has literally transgressed, who is perceived by the people of Eccleston as tainted. Indeed, where Jemima's sexuality does escape, at the margins of the text, it is associated with Ruth. Thus, the young Jemima "could have kissed her [Ruth's] hand and professed herself Ruth's slave" (183–84), and the older Jemima, "all flushed and panting," reacts against her father's abuse of Ruth by taking her hand "in her warm convulsive grasp, and holding it so tight, that it was blue and discoloured for days" (338).

As a result of her "sin's" disclosure, Ruth is forced to find her work in the world "very low" (357). She goes out as a nurse, a profession which, like that of the needlewoman, was associated at mid-century with women of doubtful reputation. She regains the respect of the townspeople as a result of her courageous behavior during a typhus epidemic, and is once more described as an angel. Benson reassures his household, who are concerned about Ruth's health, by telling them that "he had never seen her face so fair and gentle as it was now, when she was living in the midst of disease and woe" (428).

In spite of Benson's optimism, Ruth catches "that fever which is never utterly banished from the sad haunts of vice and misery, but lives in such darkness, like a wild beast in the recesses of his den" (424). She contracts it not from the poor, but from her former lover, whom she insists on going to nurse when she hears he is ill. Ruth has nursed Bellingham through an illness once before, in Wales, the scene of her original transgression. Desire and disease are connected in Gaskell's novel, as they are in *Bleak House*. The lidless monster which Jemima encounters is akin to the wild beast in the dark recesses of his den. At the moment at which Ruth succumbs to the fever, she is described in sexual terms:

> It so happened that the rays of the lamp fell bright and full upon Ruth's countenance, as she stood with her crimson lips parted with the hurrying breath, and the fever-flush brilliant on her cheeks. Her eyes were wide open, and their pupils distended.   (445)

Critics have frequently objected to Ruth's death, reading it as a concession to convention on Gaskell's part. Nina Auerbach writes that "Until the ending's abrupt reversal, Gaskell practices what liberal reformers preached: she defiantly reclaims this sweet soul for reintegration and respectability" (169). I have been arguing that *Ruth* is as much about the transformation of the rebellious middle-class daughter into the type of the angel in the house as it is about the plight of the fallen woman. The reformation of the middle-class family, rather than the rehabilitation of the fallen dressmaker's apprentice, becomes the novel's central project. That desire which threatens the stability of the Bradshaw family is managed by being projected onto Ruth, who remains socially and sexually "other," and her death is merely the culmination of this process, rather than an "abrupt reversal."

In a novel ostensibly written in defense of the working-class woman's right to the same protection as the middle-class daughter and the fallen woman's right to be given a second chance, Gaskell sacrifices Ruth for the good of the middle-class family. However, a message more radical than anything Gaskell is likely to have intended emerges at the margins of her text, for her portrayal of Jemima's "progress" suggests that the middle-class woman is more than "a little bit fallen." Jemima exhibits those signs of self-torment and stubborn pride which Dickens attributes to his fallen women. She is represented as a rebellious daughter who is badly in need of reform. Thus, in *Ruth*, desire is ultimately located within each woman, within both Ruth and Jemima, rather than being represented as the difference between middle-class woman and fallen upper or lower-class woman. The dichotomy between middle-class domestic angel and fallen working-class woman breaks down, and I would argue that it was this which caused so many contemporary readers, "women infinitely more than men" (*Letters* 153), to condemn *Ruth* as immoral. The novel might have offended less if Gaskell had made Ruth a prostitute, for the line between fallen needlewoman and middle-class daughter would then have been more distinct.

Elizabeth Gaskell became ill shortly after the publication of *Ruth*, and in the following passage from a letter to her friend Eliza Fox, she associates her illness with public condemnation of the novel:

> I *have* been *so* ill, I do believe it has been a "Ruth" fever. . . . I was so poorly! and cd not get over the hard things people said of Ruth. I mean I was just in that feverish way when I could not get them out of my head by thinking of anything else but dreamt about them and all that. I think I must be an improper woman without knowing it, I do so manage to shock people.
>
> (*Letters* 222–23)

The middle-class novelist, accused by her reviewers of having "lost her reputation" (*Letters* 223), begins to feel tainted as a result of her connection with *Ruth*. She has been infected by that desire which erupts in nightmare and disease, and which is, in *Ruth*, located within every woman.

NOTES

1. As Nancy Armstrong has argued, for a mid-Victorian readership "that understood the ideal woman as an imaginary construct. . . . Every woman was, like Louisa Gradgrind, a little bit fallen. What mattered was that she never gave into her own desire but waged an unrelenting battle against it" (252). While I agree with Armstrong's overall point, I will argue that Dickens represents Louisa Gradgrind as being more than "a little bit fallen," for Louisa's battle against desire is not an unrelenting one.
2. Sissy resembles Ada Clare, Jarndyce's ward, rather than Esther Summerson. Ada, as Alex Zwerdling has noted (430), is an idealized version of Esther.

Dickens represents her as being untouched by the stain of female sexuality, even when she goes against Jarndyce's wishes and marries her cousin Richard. However, he is unable to imagine Ada performing the role of angel in a home of her own. She lacks the power to reform Richard, who wastes away as a result of his obsessive interest in the Chancery suit, and she must finally take Esther's place in Jarndyce's Bleak House, when Esther becomes the mistress of her own middle-class Bleak House.

3. In the novels which follow *Hard Times*, Dickens continues to represent the status of the domestic angel as a given. Such heroines as Amy Dorrit and Lucie Manette do not experience transforming encounters with transgressive desire. It is not an acceptance of "sin and shame" which establishes their identity as domestic women. Even the impetuous Bella Wilfer, in *Our Mutual Friend*, is humbled by the lesson which John Harmon and the Boffins teach her, rather than by an encounter with that transgressive sexuality which Dickens associates with gender and class dis-ease. I would argue that the implications of the middle-class daughter's contact with desire become too explosive for Dickens as he becomes increasingly pessimistic about the possibility of alleviating social unrest.

4. See, for example, Page; Craik 72, 75–6; Lansbury; and Bodenheimer 162.

5. Bodenheimer notes that in both Gaskell's and Dickens' novels, the "turbulent careers of the children in a 'model' household" are set against "the simple domestic generosity of a young woman 'tainted' by her earlier experience" (162) but does not explore the connections between the relationship of middle-class daughter and lower-class angel in each novel.

6. George Watt argues that it is Ruth's "fall" rather than Ruth herself which is responsible for "the ultimate rejuvenation of society" in Gaskell's novel and Bodenheimer notes that it is only after Jemima learns Ruth has "fallen" that Ruth's life helps her to "develop womanly sympathy and successful love" (163).

7. Lansbury notes, in her discussion of *Ruth*, that "the occasional sexual use of working girls" by upper or middle-class men was regarded as "fair sport" by respectable families in Victorian England, largely because it helped prevent the seduction of their own marriageable daughters by young men who did not yet have the means to support a wife (53). For more detailed discussions of the "double standard" see Basch 195–209 and Walkowitz.

8. Gaskell recounts Pasley's story in her letter to Dickens of 8 January 1850 (*Letters* 98–100).

9. Patsy Stoneman notes that after Ruth has begun to understand her social position as a fallen woman her "consciousness is split between an ideological surface articulated in moral and social terms, and an inarticulate sub-text of metaphors and dreams" (106). In addition, Stoneman connects the fever Ruth catches from Bellingham with sexual desire and notes that sexuality generally appears as sickness in *Ruth*.

10. As Mary Poovey notes, the figure of the needlewoman was specifically linked by middle-class commentators such as Henry Mayhew with the dangers of unregulated female sexuality, for distressed needlewoman frequently turned to prostitution as a means of support (131). In *Ruth*, a fallen needlewoman assumes the position of governess in a middle-class household, thus blurring the lines of distinction between the distressed working-class woman and the distressed middle-class woman in search of "genteel" employment. Such an erosion of gender and class boundaries would have been particularly disturbing to middle-class Victorian readers.

WORKS CITED

Armstrong, Nancy. *Desire and Domestic Fiction: A Political History of the Novel.* New York: Oxford UP, 1987.

Auerbach, Nina. *Woman and the Demon: The Life of a Victorian Myth.* Cambridge: Harvard UP, 1982.

Basch, Francoise. *Relative Creatures: Victorian Women in Society and the Novel 1837–67.* New York: Schocken, 1974.

Bergmann, Helena. *Between Obedience and Freedom: Woman's Role in the Mid-Nineteenth Century Industrial Novel.* Gothenburg Studies in English 45. Gothenburg, 1979.

Bodenheimer, Rosemarie. *The Politics of Story in Victorian Fiction.* Ithaca: Cornell UP, 1988.

Boheemen-Saaf, Christine van. " 'The Universe Makes an Indifferent Parent': *Bleak House* and the Victorian Family Romance." *Interpreting Lacan.* Ed. Joseph H. Smith and William Kerrigan. New Haven: Yale UP, 1983. 225–57.

Craik, W. A. *Elizabeth Gaskell and the English Provincial Novel.* London: Methuen, 1975.

Dickens, Charles. *Bleak House.* 1853. Ed. Norman Page. New York: Penguin, 1971.

———. *Dombey and Son.* 1846–48. Ed. Alan Horsman. New York: Oxford UP, 1982.

———. *Hard Times.* 1854. Ed. David Craig. New York: Penguin, 1969.

———. *Oliver Twist.* 1836–39. Ed. Peter Fairclough. New York: Penguin, 1966.

Gaskell, Elizabeth. *The Letters of Mrs. Gaskell.* Ed. J. A. V. Chapple and Arthur Pollard. Cambridge: Harvard UP, 1967.

———. *North and South.* 1854–55. Ed. Dorothy Collin. New York: Penguin, 1970.

———. *Ruth.* 1853. Ed. Alan Shelston. New York: Oxford UP, 1985.

Harmon, Barbara Leah. "In Promiscuous Company: Female Public Appearance in Elizabeth Gaskell's *North and South.*" *Victorian Studies* 31 (1988): 351–74.

Lansbury, Coral. *Elizabeth Gaskell: The Novel of Social Crisis.* New York: Barnes, 1975.

Langbauer, Laurie. "Dickens's Streetwalkers: Women and the Form of Romance." *ELH* 53 (1986): 411–31.

Page, Norman. "*Ruth* and *Hard Times*: a Dickens Source." *Notes and Queries* ns 18 (1971): 413.

Poovey, Mary. *Uneven Developments: The Ideological Work of Gender in Mid-Victorian England*. Chicago: U of Chicago P, 1988.

Stoneman, Patsy. *Elizabeth Gaskell*. Bloomington: Indiana UP, 1987.

Walkowitz, Judith R. *Prostitution and Victorian Society: Women, Class, and the State*. Cambridge: Cambridge UP, 1980.

Watt, George. *The Fallen Woman in the Ninteenth-Century English Novel*. London: Helm, 1984.

Zwerdling, Alex. "Esther Summerson Rehabilitated." *PMLA* 88 (1973): 429–39.

Language Among the Amazons:
Conjuring and Creativity in *Cranford*

Adrienne E. Gavin

> My dear Mrs. Forrester, conjuring and witchcraft is a mere
> affair of the alphabet.
>
> *(Cranford* 84)

In the town of Cranford conjuring and witchcraft *are* affairs of the alphabet.
It is their arrangements of the alphabet, in speech and in writing, that enable
the women of Cranford to sustain and protect themselves and to experience
and create moments of magic in their lives. Miss Pole may not readily achieve
the sleight of hand that she believes she might in following written "receipts"
for conjuring tricks, but she is party to an understanding and use of language
that might seem pure blindfold trickery to an outside observer. With skilled
legerdemain she and her friends can turn "maccaroons sopped in brandy"
into "little Cupids" (67), the black parlor where one ties up preserves into
the "sanctuary of home" (113), and the straitened pecuniary circumstances
in which they live into "elegant economy" (3). Their lives are steeped in a
consciousness of the creative powers of language; it is with language that
these Amazons conjure.

Considering the pervasive concern in *Cranford* with language (style, sentences, words, and even letters of the alphabet), surprisingly little has been
written on the subject. Hilary M. Schor in her book on Gaskell (1992) does
examine the subject,[1] reading *Cranford* as "a woman writer's experiment
with narrative, an extended commentary on the ways women are taught to
read cultural signs, and a serious critique of the role of literature in shaping
female readers" (87). Schor examines language issues and acknowledges the
differences between female and male writing and the importance of "women's
languages" (84) within the novel, but like many critics commenting on the

division between male and female experience in the novel, she denies the older women of Cranford full credit for the integrity of their beliefs concerning language. Indeed criticism has often either ridiculed these women in their dealings with language, or taken it as virtually a given that they have had "male language" imposed upon them. In fact, as this paper will show through a close reading of the text, the women's beliefs about language and their use of it show a freedom from imposition, a self-reliance, and a creativity long ignored.

These older women perform magic with language. Out of the words they use in conversation and the tales they carry about the town they create intricate oral fictions; they conjure up a world for themselves, at times exciting, at times refined or rarefied. But if the women speak fiction, they write truth. It is in their unique styles of writing that they reveal truth and individuality (however ingenuously, circuitously, or fragmentarily). Written language, for the women, is almost sacred, and they will protect and defend the writings of those they hold important. Although the women's concerns with language are portrayed with generous irony in the novel, it is their belief in language and their facility in using it that are their creative achievement and victory over those who would change or "modernize" them. The ladies' lives are restricted in many ways, but they will not allow their language or their views on styles of language to be altered, attacked, or even criticized. They are creators with language and style, and not, as critics often assume, mere passive (or even societally restrained) receptacles for, or regurgitators of, anyone else's language. Their decisions about language and literature are very much their own, and language, unlike many other desirables for a comfortable life, is free for the using, something the women are not about to ignore.

The Cranfordians' use of language draws in Mary Smith, the narrator, who despite her youth and extra knowledge of the world includes herself as an apprentice Amazon through her use of "we" and "us". It is not, however, issues of narration or of the female creativity of either Mary or Elizabeth Gaskell that I wish to focus upon (issues examined by Schor among others), but rather the ways in which characters, specifically the older women, use and regard language within the town of Cranford. I will examine the oral fictions of the Cranford women and suggest differences between their spoken language and that of the men and the young women of the town. I will also show that truth and individuality are revealed in what and how the women write, and posit the view that their beliefs about literature and written language are firmly, instinctively, and aptly held. I will end by showing that the women of Cranford are creators with language, while their male counterparts are mere readers and quoters of the language set down by others.

I

Orally, the Amazons of Cranford weave their own fiction: protective, adaptable, and imaginatively creative. The "phraseology of Cranford," with its refined speech and elaborate rules and regulations, is distinctly of the women's creation. It is a language bred out of old-fashioned usage, idiosyncratic ideas of taste and elegance, a desire to spice their restricted existence, and a need to protect themselves from both the harshness of their economic situation and the speech of others. Vulnerable in many ways, words are something that they can control, and language is their most treasured possession, as Miss Pole indicates when, prevented from speaking by a coughing fit, she implores the others with her eyes, "[d]on't let Nature deprive me of the treasure which is mine, although for a time I can make no use of it" (116). She wants the right to divulge incredible news, to choose the words, to create the fiction.

Through speaking, the women create a world to suit themselves. It is not, moreover, a sort of continuous accident. Mary tells us of the Miss Barkers circulating cap patterns "among the *élite* of Cranford. I say the *élite*, for Miss Barkers [sic] had *caught the trick of the place*, and piqued themselves upon their 'aristocratic connection' " (60; third emphasis added). There is, in other words, a kind of knack or gift that characters must acquire in order to join in the Cranfordian fiction, and it is these tricks that add magical touches of elegance to the women's lives. Theirs is a world in which "[u]nderstanding" is "such a coarse word" (114) and the use of the term "hoaxing" is to be apologized for (50), and in which they are "not so old as the ladies used to be when" they were girls (50). Rowena Fowler, pointing to the "shared fictions" of the women, correctly suggests that "[o]ne of the most pervasive mutually-understood conventions of women's language in Cranford is the avoidance of blunt, hurtful, or demeaning truths" (723). To tell the absolute truth in speech would be, for these women, an ungenteel abomination, revealing as it would the hardships of their existence and the vulgarities of the world. Their language, like their dress, must reflect "chaste elegance and propriety" (74).

They do not blind themselves to the truth, for at heart they know the "reality" of their situation. Mrs. Forrester sits in state pretending not to know what cakes will be served at her party, "though she knew, and we knew, and she knew that we knew, and we knew that she knew that we knew, she had been busy all the morning making tea-bread and sponge-cakes'' (3). Yet the ladies simultaneously come to believe in many of their fictions, which become a kind of concomitant reality, a magic for which all the performers suspend their disbelief. Their economy becomes ''elegant'' because their language makes it so. They enjoy a ''refreshing'' stroll in the night air because their spoken language will not reveal that they have to walk home because they cannot afford any other means of transportation; nor will it reveal other hardships, lost loves, or grief. Above all none of them speak of money ''because that subject savour[s] of commerce and trade'' (3), and ''money-spending [is] always 'vulgar and ostentatious' '' (4).

The women have their own rules for elegant living: calls are to take place after twelve noon and are never to be ''longer than a quarter of an hour,'' and one must ''not allow [one]self to forget [the time] in conversation'' (2). The strictness of the rules is ironically undercut: ''[a]s everybody had this rule in their minds, whether they received or paid a call, of course no absorbing subject was ever spoken about. We kept ourselves to short sentences of small talk, and were punctual to our time'' (2–3). But we must take care as to how much significance we place on this irony. Are we to believe, as the schoolboy Peter did, that ''the old ladies in the town wanted something to talk about'' (51), or that there is now ''a dearth of subjects for conversation'' (10)? To do so would be to suggest that their rules for discourse actually eliminate discourse, when in fact these ''rules'' of speech are a part of their verbal fiction. Miss Matty certainly believes that Peter was mistaken about the earlier ladies: ''[t]hey had the St. James's Chronicle three times a-week, just as we have now, and we have plenty to say'' (51). As of course they do. The women talk over old anecdotes, but they also have more than sufficient new material to discuss, and not just from the *Chronicle*. As Nina Auerbach puts it, ''Cranford threads its monotonous life with what Charlotte Brontë called 'the strange, necromantic joys of fancy,' peopling its world with self-created magic burglars, ghosts, spies, Frenchmen, and witches'' (87). Through their oral language the Cranfordians create their own fictions, whether tightly structured into quarter-of-an-hour slots, extended over an evening's entertainment, or episodically updated over days, weeks, or months.

The best example of an ''episodic update'' is ''the panic,'' during which time reports ''spread like wildfire'' and are enlarged and elaborated upon with every telling. Miss Pole, who regularly ''collect[s] all the stray pieces of intelligence in the town'' (82) and relates these to the other women, becoming "the heroine of the evening" (83), is now "the principal person to collect and arrange" reports of the robberies "so as to make them assume their most fearful aspect" (89). She and Miss Matty brush up their most "horrid stories of robbery and murder" (92), and the women come to believe the ghastly fiction they have created: that Miss Pole's house has been attacked, and that there is a murderous gang roaming the town led by the "French spy" Signor Brunoni. When the fictional consistency of this plot becomes too difficult to sustain, it is relegated to the anecdotal archives of the Cranfordians. Besides, they are on to a new plot: the curing of the sick Mr. Brown, who is the very same, so suspected Signor Brunoni (a name which "sound[s] so much better" [102]).[2]

In Cranford stories are told and retold, elaborated on and altered, and fictions are rewritten or adapted to suit the circumstances. The ladies await Captain Brown's apologies for "carrying [a poor old woman's] baked mutton and potatoes safely home." When the Captain does not, in due course, appear in order to apologize, his part is rewritten, and more than once: "it was decided that he was ashamed, and was keeping out of sight," then, that he had in fact shown "great goodness of heart" and would be "comforted" on his next appearance. When the Captain does appear, "untouched by any sense of shame," they are "obliged to conclude he had forgotten all about Sunday" (10–11). Captain Brown, who answers the women's "small sarcastic compliments in good faith' (4–5), has his role in the town repeatedly rewritten by the women, and he is in time "called upon, in spite of all resolutions to the contrary," and orally "his opinions [became] quoted as authority" (4). This acceptance is possible provided his faux pas are ony oral, which the Cranford spoken fiction can tolerably incorporate; when he challenges their literary authority, however, the fictional world of the women can no longer incorporate him, and he is, as will later be seen, left to his fate.

"Because Cranford is a predominantly female world, women's language and values are the accepted currency" (Fowler 720), but it is not just speech and behaviour that the women are concerned with; their standards extend to names. They discuss whether Mrs. Fitz-Adam (at whose name the line is so often drawn) should be admitted to Cranford society: "[n]o one, who had not some good blood in their veins, would dare to be called Fitz; there was a deal in a name" (64). Fitz-Adam is however certainly better than her maiden name, which her brother, the doctor, retains for life—Hoggins: "we disliked the name, and considered it coarse; but, as Miss Jenkyns said, if he changed it to Piggins it would not be much better" (63). The women's acceptance of his name would be expedited if he would own up to a connection with the Marchioness of Exeter, one Molly Hoggins, but however much the women will fictionalize in speech, Mr. Hoggins will not, and denies any such relationship. Thomas Holbrook too refuses to be called Esquire and sends back mail that is not directed to "*Mr.* Thomas Holbrook, yeoman" (28). Pure dismay is expressed by the ladies on learning that Lady Glenmire has dropped her title to become "Mrs. Hoggins," and there is consternation whether this union should be sanctioned by the community. And then there is Mrs. Forrester's story of her cousin Mr. ffoulkes, who "looked down upon capital letters, and said they belonged to lately invented families," and who went on to marry a Mrs. ffaringdon "all owing to her two little ffs" (64). Their language concerns go right down to words and letters, and like Miss Pole's "throwing A's and B's at [their] heads like hail-stones" (85), their speech is an "affair of the alphabet."

Those who have not learnt the art of conjuring with the alphabet, men and younger women, often impinge upon the Cranfordian ladies' fiction because of their unwitting habit of *speaking* the truth. Captain Brown, Thomas Holbrook, Mr. Hoggins, and Peter Jenkyns all speak their minds openly; all call a spade a spade, and what is so much worse, call it so in loud voices. Captain Brown speaks "in a voice too large for the room" (4), sings in a "sonorous bass" (6), talks openly of his poverty, and is "blind to all the small slights and omissions of trivial ceremonies with which he had been received" (4). Mr. Holbrook, although he reads aloud beautifully, sees "no necessity for moderating his voice" if people are not ill, and constantly uses the dialect of the country in conversation (29). (Perhaps this is why Miss Pole fears earache as they walk up to his house.) As for Mr. Hoggins, however proud they are of him as a surgeon, the women observe that he says "Jack's up," and "a fig for his heels," and calls Preference "Pref"; they can "only shake [their] heads over his name and himself, and wish that he had read Lord Chesterfield's Letters in the days when his manners were susceptible of improvement" (103). Men customarily speak loudly and speak as they find. The women specifically speak the truth on one occasion, ironically because they are "desirous of proving [them]selves superior to men . . . in the article of candour" (98) following Mr. Hoggins' denial of one of their fictional verities (their belief that he has been robbed). What they are candid about on this occasion are their private fears and precautions, which naturally enough are not based on firm facts, but arise out of imagination and superstition.

Because the women are attuned to belief in their own oral fiction, the spoken jests of men are sometimes taken seriously (these are to be distinguished from the ladies' fiction in that the male speaker of a jest does not believe his jest, while on one level at least the women believe their fictions); we need only think of Miss Betty Barker following Captain Brown's advice to clothe her Alderney in a "flannel waistcoat and flannel drawers" (5), or Mrs. Jamieson's horror at Peter's "shooting a cherubim" (159). Yet on other occasions the women are astonished by the credulity of married women. They cannot believe that Lady Glenmire swallowed Mr. Hoggins's "poor vamped-up story about a neck of mutton and a pussy, with which he had tried to impose on Miss Pole" (106), and Miss Pole notices that marriage "always ma[kes] people credulous to the last degree" (105). Miss Matty, however, later tells Mary that "a little credulity helps one on through life very smoothly" (108), though she thinks Peter was wrong in thinking that "the old ladies in Cranford would believe anything" (50). Their fictions are not totally outrageous, but a little credulity on their part goes a long way.

Rowena Fowler suggests that "[u]nlike the Amazons of Herodotus, the women of Cranford are not bilingual, and their nervous attempts to acquiesce in male discourse are foiled by the contradiction between men's words and women's manner of speaking" (719). While the women might at times be befuddled by male discourse, they certainly never "nervously acquiesce" in any discourse that is not their own. Indeed, the ladies "had often rejoiced, in former days, that there was no gentleman . . . to *find* conversation for" (6; emphasis added), which clearly indicates a "bilingualism" rather than an acquiescence. The women can speak male language, but prefer not to. Men, insisting on oral accuracy, can be an irritant to the women, who do not expect the response to a "[d]ecidedly" on their part to be a questioning as to "[w]hat there was to decide" (141), or the rebuff to "[w]hat a pretty book!" to be "[p]retty! madam! it's beautiful! Pretty, indeed!" (35).

The women's methods of speech are similarly not shared by the younger women of the town; it is not just men who can speak distastefully. Jessie Brown not only states, but repeats, that her uncle is a shopkeeper. Hearing this, the women feel physically sullied: "[i]t was to take the taste of this out of our mouths, and the sound of this out of our ears, that Miss Jenkyns proposed music" (8). Martha is also "blunt and plain-spoken to a fault" (26). She speaks the truth, though we are told that she writes 'hieroglyphics.'' Lady Glenmire, although she is "not over young," is "younger than Mrs. Jamieson" (71), and "a bright little woman of middle age" (76); she calls for tea when she wishes it, and does the unthinkable by requesting more bread and butter when she feels they all desire it. It is also she who asks Miss Matty if she is "fond of astronomy." Miss Matty replies "[n]ot very," and is "rather confused . . . to remember which was astronomy, and which was astrology" (80).

Yet if the Amazons confuse "astronomy" with "astrology," "graminivorous" with "carnivorous," or 'horizontal' with "perpendicular," it is the words they confuse, not the concepts, and these words are hardly crucial to their daily lives. Miss Matty, in replying to Lady Glenmire, knows that her opinion and answer are the same "under either circumstance" (80). These are scientific concepts that are not based on the instinctive tastes and understandings of the women, and there is no reason why they should be "fond" of them. Mrs. Forrester tells us "that in her day the only use people made of four-syllabled words was to teach how they should be spelt" (112). Miss Matty knows that the "stars are so beautiful" (80), and does not need the concept defined; she knows instinctively that their beauty is "sufficient" for her. This is not to suggest ignorance in the women, but to respect their inherent ability to judge what knowledge they will retain. Miss Matty states that "she never could believe that the earth was moving constantly, and that she would not believe it if she could, it made her feel so tired and dizzy whenever she thought about it" (80). She obviously "knows" of the rotation of the earth, and her comment is not evidence of the lack of intellect that is often imputed to the women, but evidence of thought, and after such thought, an idea rejected. The fiction of her world is honest, if not factual—who would not become dizzy thinking of such a thing? Indeed, part of the delight the women take in their world is based on their very lack of insistence on "verbal accuracy." For example, that marvelous stimulation to tangential thinking, the comment that Peter has been "elected great Lama of Thibet" (112), begins a passage of wonderful free association of language, including a dispute over whether llamas are carnivorous animals or not; the women are open to all hints and permutations of language, for enjoyment, argument, and entertainment, as well as for protection.

Writing of Cranford's ability to produce men at need and obliterate them at will, Auerbach argues that Cranford "veers . . . between being a sanctuary of unreality . . . and a repository of sudden, quasi-magical power that destroys or appropriates the reality it excludes" (82). Both sanctuary and magical power reside for the Amazons of Cranford in the fictions of the spoken word. They speak elegant creative fictions according to their own code, while the men of the town speak loudly, and, like younger women, bluntly and factually. The women's written world is also creative, but reveals more of their individuality. Male characters have a less evident and a more formal personal written world, and are sustained far more by reading language than by creating it.

II

Although the women choose to clothe or mask distasteful or unwieldy reality in their more public oral fictions, in the private world of their writing (letters and notes) they are able, through their personal styles, to reveal more of their individuality. They create their own styles of writing on the basis of their own beliefs, unconfined by any external (Cranfordian or non-Cranfordian) epistolary practices, or by any of the forms of their own oral fiction. Moreover, they consider the written word sacred and are secure in the knowledge that these writings will not enter the public domain. Just as they guard the truth revealed in their own letters, they defend what they judge to be the best in writing. Their regard for the written word comes, indeed, from knowledge and practice of their collective spoken fiction, which although magical and marvelous is limited in geographical range and needs constant adjusting, a continuous observance of strict rules, and a body of adepts to maintain it. Written language on the other hand, even if relatively formless, and requiring little or no "trick," is more individual and can be sent beyond the bounds of Cranford.

Miss Deborah Jenkyns writes pretentious, grand, overly philosophical, and stately letters: "[e]pistolary writing, she and her friends considered as her *forte*" (9). In writing, however, she is an arbiter of *taste*, and not the model to be *followed* that she is in speech. She writes and corrects, and re-corrects, yet wishes her letters to be considered as if she has " 'seized the half-hour just previous to post time to assure' her friends of this or of that" (9). "Everything in them [is] stately and grand, like herself" (12), even when, as in her letter to Mary, she is revealing something as basic as her nosiness about Captain Brown's visitor. Deborah does not use what we might consider appropriate language for her subject matter, but she does use language appropriate to her, priding herself, as she does, on her use of Dr. Johnson as "her model in these compositions" (9). Schor rightly points out that "the text never hesitates to mock gently" this language use of Deborah's (90), and suggests that her letter to Mary "uses a prose so Johnsonian as to approach . . . literary parody" (90). But while it may perhaps *approach* parody (although it would be more accurate to say that it is somewhat over-elegant), this does not demonstrate, as Schor contends, that "the style of *her* favorite has betrayed Deborah Jenkyns" (90). She is not very successful, naturally, in *being* Johnson, but her written style reflects clearly what *she* is; her view of Johnson is distinctly her own. I would similarly disagree with Schor's statement that "[t]he language, though rich, suggests no pleasure; nor does it allow for specific emotion" (91). The letter (12–13) suggests great pleasure in the roll of the words, the choice and placement of literary quotations, the sweep of the exact number of "many-syllabled words" across the page, and the evident satisfaction of putting things as "Johnsonianly" as possible. There is no evidence that she is less than pleased with her creation, for the letter is very much (overstated or not) her own, and Deborah in any case would never be a woman to splash her emotions wildly across either a page or a drawing-room. In her reserved and carefully composed (and quite cutting) remarks about Captain Brown's "sad want of relish for 'the pure wells of English undefiled' " (13), we are well aware what emotion she is expressing. To strike a low note instead of a "high note" in commenting on Captain Brown would, for Deborah, be the betrayal (of her own rules and of her self); it is not her high tone that would somehow betray her.

Much is made by critics of the fact that Deborah's father, the Rector, recommends Johnson to her in her youth. Patsy Stoneman argues that "[t]hough apparently 'strong-minded' and 'superior' . . . [Deborah] has as-similated the conditions of her own subordination" (89). Fowler writes of the "patriarchal forces and conventions which once overtook and destroyed Deborah Jenkyns" (725), and Schor argues that "[l]iterary daughters are not given the language they need; rather they are given languages, often dead languages, that mediate their experience for them" (94). True, a man (Debo-rah's father) has recommended a male writer of a previous generation to a woman (Deborah), and true, Deborah did read and write for her father and spend much of her youth ministering to his needs, even giving up her hopes of "marry[ing] an archdeacon, and writ[ing] his charges" (107). At the time we see Cranford, however, the Rector has been dead for a number of years, but Deborah still reveres "her" Johnson. She accepts Johnson as a model out of respect and love for her father and the education he gave her, but keeps him as a model because she knows instinctively that he is "her sort" of writer (there are, after all, critics and readers today who still choose the "imposing" Johnson as their life's work). She is quite capable of writing a letter to the bishop for her father, but in her own letters she is creating for herself; she does not possess only "useless literary skills" (Schor 112). We see more of her style after her death, when Mary and Miss Matty burn her letters, and there is no indication that she wrote with anything but pleasure and confidence in her own stylistic abilities: "[h]er hand was admirably calculated, together with her use of many-syllabled words, to fill up a sheet"; "the words gathered size like snow-balls, and towards the end of her letter, Miss Jenkyns used to become quite sesquipedalian" (47). She has more than "the appearance of a strong-minded woman" (*Cranford* 12), she *is* a strong-minded woman, and one who would not blindly follow the style of a writer she did not herself admire and respect.

Miss Matty regards Deborah as a writer almost as highly as Deborah regards Dr. Johnson. But Matty, just as individually, creates her own style, writing "nice, kind, rambling letters; now and then venturing into an opinion of her own" (12), or notes that are "rather circuitous and very humble" (23). They are reflective of her reticent, easily confused, kindly nature. Matty's letters, "in spite of a little bad spelling" (like her mother's), do express her thoughts and opinions, even if she recants in postscripts after discussion with Deborah (13). When she is excited, her style reflects this: "[s]he began many sentences without ending them, running them one into another, in much the same confused sort of way in which written words run together on blotting-paper" (81), and "words that she would spell quite correctly in her letters to [Mary], bec[o]me perfect enigmas" when she writes to Mary's father" (131–32). Bad spelling, however, does not conceal truth: Mary writes the address of the Aga Jenkyns "spelt by sound; and very queer it looked," yet the letter, "gone from [her] like life," finds its mark (128). Similarly, disorganized written discourse does not conceal truth, for Mary tells us that Miss Matty's rambling style gives her the most information about goings on in Cranford.

Miss Pole is not one for divulging facts straightforwardly either. She sends a letter to Mary, in which, "at the end of every sentence of news, came a fresh direction as to some crochet commission" (12), and later on secretly delivers an "involved and oracular" missive (135) signed with her "initials, reversed, P. E." (136). This is characteristic of Miss Pole's love of mysteries, and her style of expression increasingly reflects the complexly structured patterns of crochet.

The Jenkyns sisters learn early the truth-revealing capacities of written language when their father makes them keep a diary in which they are to write on one side the expectations of what will happen during the day and on the other side what has happened during the day. Both are truth; the truth of expectation and the truth of experience, and the difference between these truths reveals the perhaps more brutal truth of things lost or missed in their lives (as perhaps the ladies of Cranford insert their oral fiction between what they expect of the world and what their world provides). But the truth of life in Cranford is not easy to put down in words. Mary's secret letter to the Aga Jenkyns is written with care so that it "should affect him, if he were Peter, and yet seem a mere statement of dry facts if he were a stranger" (127). A hard letter to compose, which is perhaps why we have no extract from it in the text, though Peter, reading the truth within it, is moved to race home immediately.

Great importance and secrecy are attached to the written word. Mrs. Forrester is willing to give bread jelly to an invalid, but will give the "receipt" for it to no one during her lifetime: "it [is] bequeathed, as her executors would find, to Miss Matty" (104). During Miss Matty's time of crisis the ladies each write down the amount they can afford to give her annually in mysteriously sealed papers "under pledge of secrecy" (138). Written language holds truth, and thus is valuable to the women, but public displays of written language are undesirable. For Miss Matty to begin her operation selling tea "[a] small genteel notification of her being licensed to sell tea, would . . . be necessary; but [Mary] hope[s] that it [can] be placed where no one [can] see it" (133). It is in fact placed under the lintel of the door, out of sight; the written truth of her current hardship must not be proclaimed publicly.

If truth and individuality are revealed by writing, they can also be hidden again by burning. Miss Matty is concerned with what will be revealed to others through written language, and regularly makes "candle-lighters of all the notes and letters of the week" (72). The truth contained in the old letters which she and Mary burn is not to become part of the selective fiction of Cranford society either, and is not to be revealed to those who did not care deeply for the writers (despite Miss Matty's opinion that "[a]ny one might profit by reading" Deborah's letters [46]).[3] The letters contain some earlier truths of Cranford, an old Cranford which is burned with the letters, and from which only Peter, like a sole letter which is his, is preserved.

Many of the old letters reveal the personal histories of the Jenkyns parents. The young Rector's letters are "full of eager, passionate ardour; short homely sentences, right fresh from the heart; (very different from the grand-Latinised, Johnsonian style of [his] printed sermon . . .)" (43), while as an older, married man "he could hardly write a letter to his wife without cropping out into Latin" (45). His letters deal less and less with reality, but even early on, his fiancée could not understand "what he meant by repeating the same thing over in so many different ways" (43). Later in life she demonstrates continued bewilderment at his style through her own unintentionally comic docketing of her husband's letters: "Hebrew verses sent me by my honoured

husband. I thowt to have had a letter about killing the pig, but must wait"
(45). Her own writing has always been far more direct and unformed. From
the outset each has a way of writing and exhorts the other to adopt it—she
wants facts about finery, he expressions of love. Yet as time passes they both
keep their differing styles; his letters become grandiloquent, sermonizing
collections of quotations, while hers remain direct, ungrammatical, but factual
descriptions of home life. She seeks the reality or truth that she writes in her
letters, but does not receive it: "[s]he asked for his directions about the cows
and pigs; and did not always obtain them" (46).

The distinction between men's and women's letters is not as clear-cut as
are their differences in speech. Older men tend to keep self-revelation concealed under grandiose language, as the Rector does, or under the "small
talk" of letters. Deborah, the most structured of all the female letter writers,
makes use of quotations (fairly appropriately) to enhance her letters, while
her father inappropriately stacks his letters with quotations and copied language. Mary comments on a letter from her father, by saying that it "was
just a man's letter; I mean it was very dull, and gave no information beyond
that he was well, that they had had a good deal of rain, that trade was very
stagnant, and there were many disagreeable rumours afloat" (119). His letter
reveals very little about himself, and this letter, together with Mr. Holbrook's
"formal, old-fashioned" (30) note of invitation, are the only examples we
are given of contemporary men writing in Cranford. What are clearly distinct
between men and women in Cranford are beliefs about literature and practices
of reading.

III

The women are sufficient "for deciding all questions of literature . . . without troubling themselves with unnecessary reasons or arguments" (1). They hold views on literature which they will not allow to be
imposed upon, and they do not like the written word to be taken lightly. Miss
Jenkyns "on the strength of a number of manuscript sermons, and a pretty
good library of divinity, considered herself literary, and looked upon any
conversation about books as a challenge to her" (8). Although "[i]n many
respects . . . an idiosyncratic personality rather than an archetypal figure
(Tarratt 154), Deborah is the arbiter of literary taste for the women even after
her death, and her views become representative of those of the women because
of her emphatic enunciation of them. We should not be surprised that although

old-fashioned in dress and manner, the literature of the previous century (nevertheless the century in which they were born) is held up by the women as a model of excellence.

Literary differences are nowhere more dramatically revealed than in the great debate between Captain Brown and Miss Jenkyns over the literary merits of Mr. Boz and Dr. Johnson.[4] In his biography of Charles Dickens, John Forster asks, "where will the blame lie if a [wo]man takes up *Pickwick* and is disappointed to find that [s]he is not reading *Rasselas*?" (2:376). In Cranford the blame lies with the loud interloper who strides in and forces his affection for *Pickwick* upon the assembled Amazons. Deborah Jenkyns takes an attack on her literary taste as a "personal affront," and her "disappointment" cannot therefore be considered unprovoked. She has read numbers of *The Pickwick Papers* and feels qualified to judge their claims as literature, and even though some of the ladies present laugh heartily at the portion of *Pickwick* read aloud by Captain Brown, she reads from *Rasselas* to prove Johnson's superiority over Mr. Boz as a writer of fiction. One of her arguments is that she considers it "vulgar, and below the dignity of literature, to publish in numbers" (9), a comment doubly ironic since both the *Rambler* (as Captain Brown points out, though tellingly for once in a "low voice") and *Cranford* itself were published in parts. When the Captain tries to tell Deborah that they are different types of literature, she cuts him down with "I am quite aware of that . . . [a]nd I make allowances, Captain Brown" (9). When he informs her that he "should be very sorry for [Boz] to exchange his style for any such pompous writing" as that of Johnson's (9), she clinches her argument by drawing herself up with dignity and "saying with marked emphasis on every syllable, "I prefer Dr. Johnson to Mr. Boz" (9).[5] It is an irrefutable argument, and she has, in the world of Cranford, successfully defended what she considers to be the best in literature and style. The Captain after an alleged "D——n Dr. Johnson!" is forever silenced on this issue, and has learned better than to have "sport[ed] a bit of literature" (8) again among women who are in deadly earnest about the written word.

Given prevalent assumptions among critics that Deborah Jenkyns has had, to her detriment, views about language and literature imposed upon her, that she is trapped into ludicrous and blind notions about the literary worth of Dr. Johnson, and that she lacks access to a language with which to express herself, it might be useful to examine her actual arguments about Johnson versus Dickens, in contradistinction to her methods of arguing. The text's gentle mocking of Deborah during her exchange with Captain Brown implies general support for his *attitude* to the two writers. But are Deborah's *ideas*, and the arguments she gives to support them, being mocked, or merely the *way* in which she argues? Deborah's arguments are certainly pompous, her attitude towards Captain Brown's views over-dismissive, and her decision to wage such a war of words at an evening party seemingly ill timed—but that is Deborah. She is pompous, she can be dismissive, and according to her rules of behaviour, it is the Captain (publicly challenging her beliefs at a function) whose comments are ill timed. Once we get past the unapologetically presented *character* of Deborah (and in effect stop finding reasons to apologize for her character), we find that her arguments are considered, and are supported by her own examination. She has taken *Pickwick* into account, and her comments about Dickens are generally apt, in that the Mr. Boz described here has yet to complete his first novel; at this stage he does, as most modern critics would agree, have much to learn. Although Miss Jenkyns overstates the case by advancing Johnson as a model of "light and agreeable fiction" (11), and also errs in her comments on serial publication, that is more a product of her pompousness than her argument. In fact, Dickens did have aesthetic problems with "vulgar" serial publication and did take serious thought about the structures of his later, more finely crafted novels; Dr. Johnson the critic would not have been the worst influence in this regard. Miss Jenkyns is in effect reserving judgment on a talented but basically unproven literary upstart, and stating a preference for the proven oeuvre of an admitted literary giant, as many critics no doubt would, had Dickens died before completing *The Pickwick Papers*. Hers is a considered, intelligent judgment, however intolerantly expressed, and while we would agree with Captain Brown in admiring Dickens' lively style and in seeing him as "different" from Johnson, the Captain is really just quoting the (very) popular opinion of Mr. Boz. Far from being the product of "imposed thought," Deborah's argument (and our reception of her argument) is the product of her being resolutely herself, and speaking that way. It must be remembered that for her Johnson the great lexicographer would be quite a liberating figure, suggesting the infinite possibilities of her language, but it is distinctly Deborah-like to insist from this that all things, including "light and agreeable fiction" (11), are to be found in "Dr. Johnson."

Despite her victory, however, Miss Jenkyns can never forgive Captain Brown for his "disparaging remarks upon Dr. Johnson" (11). Their disagreement over language is described in the most physical of terms: "[t]he literary dispute . . . was a 'raw,' the slightest touch on which made them wince. It was the only difference of opinion they had ever had; but that difference was enough" (14). Captain Brown's walking around the streets reading Mr. Boz, and all but bumping into Miss Jenkyns, merely adds injury to insult: "she had rather he had knocked her down, if he had only been reading a higher style of literature" (14). Deborah maintains her belief in Johnson till her death, and similarly sticks to her view that Captain Brown's championing of his "[c]apital thing" (8) has proven a "capital" offense. Although to the end her methods of promoting her literary tastes are ironically presented (near her death we see Flora Gordon reading the *Rambler* to her with much difficulty, little "improvement," and a glad escape to *A Christmas Carol*), we should not dismiss her "reasons and arguments" just because she avoids "troubling [herself] with unnecessary" ones (1).

Deborah, then, can reasonably be considered "literary" and an authoritative judge of what *she has read*. But how wide is her range of reading, and what are the other women's reading habits? The Jenkyns sisters have a book room comprising the deceased Rector's books, and Deborah has read with and for her father when younger and makes use of literary allusions. She has also on occasion "learnt some piece of poetry off by heart" (112), perused the dreaded *Pickwick*, read Johnson, and spread her view of him among her friends. But beyond her, reading activity seems to fall off sharply. Miss Pole has heard or read of the fictional heroes "Thaddeus of Warsaw and the Hungarian Brothers, and Santo Sebastiani" (83) and refers to encyclopaedias and to "Dr. Ferrier and Dr. Hibbert besides" (99). Mrs. Jamieson has "a japanned table devoted to literature, on which lay a Bible, a Peerage, and a Prayer-Book" (75). Certainly many of the women know ghost stories and have heard of *The Arabian Nights* (154) and "Lalla Rookh" (112). Mary (far more literary as a narrator) is at a card party "provided . . . with some literature, in the shape of three or four handsomely bound fashion-books ten or twelve years old" (67). There is, finally, the *St. James's Chronicle* to look forward to, but we hear little else of the women's reading of "literature," and surprisingly in a novel that Schor argues is "a novel about reading" (110), they are rarely shown reading in the text. Matty herself treasures the language held in a book far more for whom it belonged to than for its contents. She is always loyal to the merits of Johnson out of love for her sister and keeps beside her bed his dictionary (which, to judge from her spelling, she rarely investigates), along with the book of poems from Thomas Holbrook. She similarly presents Mary with "the handsomest bound and best edition of Dr. Johnson's works that could be procured" as a mark of deep favor (153).

The literary tastes of the women are "old-fashioned," while the literary tastes of the men are more contemporary; Captain Brown and Mary's father show familiarity with Dickens, Thomas Holbrook with Tennyson. There is more to this than a question of taste; it is the fundamental difference between the older women of Cranford and the men, between reading and creating. "[W]e did not read much" (10), says Mary near the beginning of the novel, and she later comments that she gets plenty of plain sewing done while staying at Miss Pole's, "as [they] did not read much" (24). This indicates that as far as the older women of Cranford are concerned, Schor is incorrect to argue that "[i]n this world, books have created their ability to express themselves or to move with changing times" (287). The truth is that these women cannot be greatly influenced by what they read because, quite simply, they do not read very much at all. The only sustained reading we see is Mary's and Miss Matty's reading of old letters, which is in a sense also part of the women's creative sphere (of inclusion and exclusion), in that these letters are written by Deborah or others of Matty's family, and are read for reasons of love and duty, not literary desire. In fact, far from being shapers of the Cranfordian women, on private grounds these letters are actively excluded by the women from their world. The language and creation of Cranford are firmly in the women's hands, and there is little limit but self-imposed propriety on what can be expressed. Through language, the women are controllers of their world and are under no obligation to move with what others define as "the changing times"; they can almost do what is so much harder: halt time.

Male characters who attempt to write their own roles in the women's fiction can survive only if they do not attempt to take authority for the written word out of the Amazons' control,[6] and as long as they read enough to sustain themselves. The Rector has published a sermon and an ode, but is a man of the past, not the present. It is Captain Brown and Thomas Holbrook who best illustrate the importance to male characters in Cranford of reading. Captain Brown is absorbed in *reading* Dickens, while Miss Jenkyns uses Johnson as an arbiter of written composition, a stimulant to her own creativity. However delightful we might find the Captain's reading, he only reads, while Miss Jenkyns, however self-consciously, creates. Although private reading is his prerogative, in speaking publicly of his preference for Dickens over Johnson, Captain Brown forces his opinion about *written* language into the midst of the women's oral fiction. This the women (particularly Deborah) cannot ignore, and the Captain, however unwittingly, has rung his own death knell.

Views on written language at odds with their own cannot be incorporated into the woman's world. The implication of their oral fiction is that Captain Brown dies for what he chooses to read, and, ironically, dies when he stops reading. His Dickensian (even Pickwickian) character cannot be sustained by the women because it is not made from their language. It might almost seem that Miss Jenkyns's compulsive, spell-like, Johnsonian clove-sticking (at a time when the Browns "were seldom absent from her thoughts" [15]) has fated the Captain, who has questioned her self by questioning her preferences in language and style. Her many "rolling three-piled sentence[s]" (15) (the "conjuring and witchcraft" of her alphabet) have perhaps used language in a way powerful beyond her imagination or intention (although Deborah herself seems to believe in the fatefulness of words; she insists that the little rolls of tallow forming around candles be spoken of not as "winding-sheets" but as "roly-poleys" [84]). Miss Jenkyns stands her ground and Captain Brown dies, proving (in the Amazon fiction) her belief stronger. Her comment on hearing that his grotesque death was (in her view) caused by perusing a number of *Pickwick* is "[p]oor, dear, infatuated man!" (17). To her he was blindly infatuated with Dickens, while she judged Johnson with a clear eye. He glances up from his book, stops reading, and like a noble Dickensian hero runs to his death to save a child.

Thomas Holbrook, perhaps the most "literary" character in the novel, has a house full of books chosen according to his own taste, which he reads: "somehow one can't help it" (32). He is described as "a great reader" (34), and will impulsively set off and walk the "seven miles to Missleton" to order Tennyson's poems after reading a review of them (34). He is a Don Quixote, absorbing much of his character from what he reads, and wandering about his farm "repeating apt and beautiful quotations from the poets," even though he pronounces Byron as Bȳrron and Goethe "strictly in accordance with the English sound of the letters" (32). He reads "Locksley Hall," a poem reminiscent of his and Matty's lost love, to his unlistening guests. He honestly admits that he does not know Dr. Johnson's poems as well as Matty appears to (for whom "[i]t is so like that beautiful poem of Dr. Johnson's" [35] is a term of general approbation), and admits that he has learned from a poem that ash-buds in March are black.

Holbrook has "six-and-twenty cows, named after the different letters of the alphabet" (32). He tends the constituent parts of language, has language under his control, but is unable to do what the women can with their A's and B's; he can expertly read and quote, but he cannot conjure, he cannot create. Soon after his return from Paris he becomes ill, "not reading or anything" (38), and dies (it suits Miss Pole to believe that Paris has killed him). If he does not read he cannot survive, and when he reads he is bound to follow language as it has been set down by others, just as he abides by his father's law of the dinner table: "[n]o broth, no ball; no ball, no beef" (33). Minor male characters show similar reading or speaking patterns: Mr. Mulliner is rude and does "not speak except in gruff monosyllables" (75), but is seen engrossed in reading the *St. James's Chronicle*, while even the "civil butcher" of Cranford, one Mr. Johnson, who almost seems to repay loyalty to his namesake by sending Miss Matty customers when she begins to sell tea, has "a little want of tact" (125).

Peter Jenkyns, from childhood on, is more of a "jester" than a genuine story-maker. He comes closest to the oral fictions of the women when, ironically, his father believes his jest that he is a woman who wants a copy of the Rector's Assize Sermon. Peter is then briefly bound up in his own fiction, as he is made to his dismay to copy out twelve sermons for "the lady," and curses his fictional counterpart: "[c]onfound the woman!" (51). But this early incident is the exception to the rule that men do not create fiction in Cranford, and indeed Peter's second 'hoax' in women's clothing precipitates his exile from the town. He returns at the end of the tale, drawn by Mary's truth-containing letter, with a past unconventional enough to give him much leeway in the women's world. He can still tell outrageous tales which are essentially jests, but is sensible enough to be selective in whom he tells them to, and does not do so in front of Matty. His comments to her about Thomas Holbrook show, however, that he still possesses the brutal bluntness of male speech. His incorporation into the world of Cranford is in the women's hands, and they will need to adapt their fiction to cover his verbal and behavioral blunders. He has nevertheless gained a lifetime's sustenance from his time in India, and thus does not require the constant reading that the other men do; he is himself a virtual living tale, an "Arabian night."

With so much criticism declaring that the women of Cranford are restricted, repressed, and imposed upon, it is important to notice that in the vital area of language the Amazons have minds and wills of their own, and use them. They conjure up grand and adaptable oral fictions, they reveal truth, and respect those truths revealed, through their individualities of written style; they "decid[e] all questions of literature" aptly and firmly for themselves. These women must be granted credit for their imagination and integrity, for their conjuring and creativity, where language is concerned.

An anonymous critic wrote in 1866 that *Cranford* will remain immortal "while the langauge lives" ("Editor's Table" 186). Cranford, the town of the Amazons, will surely endure as long as the women's language does, or as long, perhaps, as it is allowed that the women, with verbal dexterity, can magically transform the A's and B's of their alphabet into their world.

NOTES

1. Schor's chapter on *Cranford* is based on her earlier article "Affairs of the Alphabet: Reading, Writing and Narrating in *Cranford.*" *Novel* 22 (1989): 288–304.
2. And indeed, as Barbara Weiss points out, a man whose wife "[l]ike the other ladies of Cranford . . . uses storytelling to impose verbal control on a life in which she otherwise has little power" (283).
3. Gaskell saw to it that after her death many of her own letters would be burned by her daughter.
4. I am indebted to Mark Eade for tireless help and discussion during the writing of this paper, and am particularly grateful for the valuable insights and suggestions he has contributed to my discussion of Deborah's preference for Dr. Johnson over Mr. Boz.
5. In light of Deborah's views on *Rasselas* and Matty's later saying that Deborah "could have said the same things quite as well [as Mrs. Chapone]" (46), it is interesting to note Gaskell's letter in 1857 to a friend, in which she discusses having little time in which to write: "[i]f I had a library like yours, all undisturbed for hours, how I would write! Mrs. Chapone's letters should be nothing to mine! I would out-do Rasselas in fiction" (Chapple and Pollard 489).
6. Auerbach writes: "[i]n the verbal and commercial battle of nineteenth-century England, the cooperative female community defeats the warrior world that proclaims itself the real one" (87).

WORKS CITED

Auerbach, Nina. *Communities of Women: An Idea in Fiction.* Cambridge, Mass.: Harvard UP, 1978.

Chapple, J. A. V., and Arthur Pollard, eds. *The Letters of Mrs. Gaskell.* Manchester: Manchester UP, 1966.

"Editor's Table. One Book of the Late Mrs. Gaskell." *Godey's Lady's Book and Magazine* (Philadelphia) Feb. 1866:186. Cited in *Elizabeth Gaskell: A Reference Guide.* By Robert L. Selig. Boston: G. K. Hall, 1977. 34.

Forster, John. *The Life of Charles Dickens.* 2 vols. 1872–74. Ed A. J. Hoppé. London: Dent, 1966.

Fowler, Rowena. "*Cranford*: Cow in Grey Flannel or Lion *Couchant?*" *Studies in English Literature* 24 (1984): 717–29.

Gaskell, Elizabeth. *Cranford.* Ed. Elizabeth Porges Watson. The World's Classics Series. Oxford: Oxford UP, 1972.

Schor, Hilary M. *Scheherazade in the Marketplace: Elizabeth Gaskell and the Victorian Novel.* Oxford: Oxford UP, 1992.

Stoneman, Patsy. *Elizabeth Gaskell.* Brighton: Harvester, 1987.

Tarratt, Margaret. "*Cranford* and 'the Strict Code of Gentility.' " *Essays in Criticism*
    18 (1968): 152–63.

Weiss, Barbara. "Elizabeth Gaskell: The Telling of Feminine Tales." *Studies in the
    Novel* 16 (1984): 274–87.

The Body Melancholy: Trollope's *He Knew He Was Right*

C. S. Wiesenthal

> I live a living death, my flesh is wounded, bleeding, cadaverized, my rhythm slowed down or interrupted, time has been erased or bloated, absorbed into sorrow.
>
> —Julia Kristeva, *Black Sun*

> Only this I will add, that if it be considered aright, which causeth this jealous passion, be it just or unjust, whether with or without cause, true or false, it ought not so heinously to be taken; 'tis no such real or capital matter. 'Tis a blow that hurts not, an insensible smart, grounded many times upon false suspicion alone, and so fostered by a sinister conceit.
>
> —Robert Burton, *The Anatomy of Melancholy*

> Why should the most active characteristics of our nature be termed the Passions? The word seems properly employed in Passion Week, the period commemorative of Christ's suffering or Passion. But we are said to fly or fall into a passion . . . and most persons agree that passion, carried to excess, constitutes madness—we live in a world of metaphor.
>
> —John Haslam, *Observations on Madness and Melancholy*

1. THE MELANCHOLIC ROOTS OF MONOMANIA

"The psychopathology of *He Knew He Was Right*," declares John Sutherland, "is as mid-Victorian as its creator," and the model for the "anatomy of jealousy" that Trollope presents in his protagonist, Louis Trevelyan, "is taken quite evidently," he suggests, from the influential early nineteenth-century work of Jean Étienne Esquirol: more particularly, from the French theorist's concept of a new disease entity called monomania (xiv). "Monomaniacal," as Sutherland notes, is the diagnosis ultimately arrived at in

Trollope's novel of 1869 to describe the fixed obsession of Trevelyan (900):
a character who, according to the narrator, though lucid in other respects,
"was, in truth, mad on the subject of his wife's alleged infidelity" (361).
Certainly, Trollope's use of the term "monomania," a word which formed the
technical basis of the first medicalized insanity defenses in history, accurately
reflects his novel's wider thematic concerns with problematic new medico-
legal definitions of insanity and questions of responsibility in mental disease.
For "partial insanities" such as monomania raised for the Victorians the
perplexing possibility that a man like Trevelyan might be deemed "neither
mad nor sane;—not mad, so that all power over his actions need be taken
from him; nor sane, so that he must be held accountable for his words and
thoughts" (902). It is, in fact, the text's scrutiny of the social, legal, and
ethical implications of such a newly-recognized medical condition which
imparts a distinctively contemporary accent to an otherwise familiar main
plot: showing how, that is, Trollope's self-conscious use of the Othello story
in *He Knew He Was Right* "goes further than association or allusion" to
"examine the relevance of Shakespeare's play to mid-Victorian society"
(Gatrell 95).

It is my position that the contemporary medico-legal discourse of monomania, though obviously pertinent to certain aspects of the text, is to Trollope's
"anatomy of jealousy" as epidermis to innards. For subtending the "timebound" "vogue" or monomania, which flourished but fleetingly as a popular
diagnostic category between 1830 and 1870 (Goldstein 155), the altogether
more ancient and amorphous pathological entity of melancholy signals its
ubiquitous presence: its bilious vapours, eluding the precise syntax of a clinical syndrome, pervade body and brain as a lowering affect, a lugubrious
mood, and exude through the pores of the nineteenth-century monomaniac.
In his introduction to Trollope's text, Sutherland himself observes that "Esquirol's theory [of monomania] drew strongly on the traditional symptomatology of melancholy" (xiv). But the intimate, indeed familial, relationship
between the two is perhaps more accurately underscored by the fact that
monomania, or at least the presence of a monomania-like delusive obsession,
had itself long been cited as a symptom or standard feature of melancholic
disorders.[1]

In her study of nineteenth-century French psychiatry, Jan Goldstein thoroughly explores the "tactical considerations" that motivated Esquirol, around
1810, to renovate the classificatory system of mental diseases by in effect
pruning the symptom of the single predominating idea or delusion from its
parent genus, melancholy, and assigning it a separate nosological status.

According to Goldstein, the value of the concept of monomania never inhered in any intrinsic scientific substance, for as a clinical entity it remained riddled with holes and internal inconsistencies, especially in regard to the ambiguous status of the passions.[2] The concept's worth lay rather in its "external" efficiency: more scientific-sounding that the "black humour" of melancholy, with its long trail of poetic, popular, and otherwise heterogeneous connotations, the diagnostic category of monomania proved a pivotal element in the professional boundary dispute between the law and the nascent speciality of forensic psychiatry (Goldstein 177–78, 192). Esquirol's concept, duly promoted by his student Georget, was an efficacious means of "carving a larger professional niche for the medical alienist" in the nineteenth-century courtroom, but by mid-century, as Goldstein shows, its fortunes were already waning under attack from prominent members of the medical community (192, 189–90). Ironically, by the last third of the century some psychiatrists were actually attempting to purge the term "monomania" from the technical vocabulary as deliberately as Esquirol had earlier "jettison[ed]" the word "melancholy" in search of a more specialized medical lexicon (Goldstein 189–91, 156). It is noteworthy too that late-century writers who did retain Esquirol's classification nevertheless seem to have reverted to emphasizing monomania as a subsidiary manifestation of melancholia.[3]

The historical origins of monomania and the relative superficiality of its diagnostic trend in the nineteenth century therefore constitute a compelling basis for suggesting that the "anatomy of jealousy" in *He Knew He Was Right* also needs to be firmly situated in the context of an anatomy of melancholy. For in Trollope's novel, the melancholic roots of Louis Trevelyan's "mono-maniacal" disorder are everywhere apparent in the semiological and iconographic dimensions of his psychopathology. Embracing a medical and literary tradition far from strictly mid-Victorian in scope, melancholy informs the representation of insanity in Trollope's text in a way that uniquely illustrates how "various levels of historial consciousness [may be] present in a given model of disease" (Gilman 9).

2. THE BODY MELANCHOLY: FROM BURTON TO TROLLOPE AND BEYOND

In his *Anatomy of Melancholy*, Robert Burton draws on ancient Greek humoral theory to distinguish between three basic kinds of melancholy "by reason of their seat," or the anatomical region from which the black humor was believed to proceed. As opposed to "head melancholy" and "windy" or "hypochondriacal melancholy," disorders respectively engendered in brain and bowel, "body melancholy," the third type, appears a more comprehensive species of derangement. The author describes it as a complaint that "sympathetically proceeds from the *whole body*, when the whole temperature is melancholy" (153–54). Burton's notion of a "melancholy from the whole body" (324) is as suggestive in relation to Trollope's Louis Trevelyan as his subsequently advanced conception of a species of jealous melancholy, a "bastard branch, or kind of Love-Melancholy" (821).[4] For Trevelyan is presented as a man of "moody temperament" (787) whose peevish humor appears to proceed "sympathetically from the whole body" insofar as his jealous torments and woes eventually culminate in a case of complete organic exhaustion: his is a dark affliction that broods in brain and body both, "wasting" the whole man, intellectually and physically.

In this essay I am however less interested in 'diagnosing'' the figure of Trevelyan with any specific form of melancholy, than in exploring the forms and dimensions of the body that is melancholy. Trevelyan's own physical form, to begin with, incarnates quintessential characteristics of the melancholic anatomy: from his physiognomy and body type to his gestural mannerisms, and even the attitudes and postures he adopts within distinctive topological settings, the array of corporal symptomatology that Trollope presents in this character import a range of variously nuanced registers from the voluptuous historical legacy of melancholia. Importantly, though, in Trollope's novel as in much of the earlier literature on melancholy (including Burton's *Anatomy*), the melancholy body is not to be construed as pertaining exclusively to an individual, anatomical body. Indeed, mental symptoms of the disease, metaphorically embodied, also construct a "body" of rhetorical dimensions: the "figure" of a melancholy body that is essentially ordered within and intrinsic to the realm of symbolic representation. In *He Knew He Was Right* Trollope, for instance, typically renders mental states or symptoms of melancholy, such as Travelyan's jealous obsession, or affects of sorrow and grief, either directly or indirectly in terms of corporal metaphors: a physical burden or load, an organic tumor-like growth, a flesh wound or an injury. At least in this respect, it might be said that the body melancholy proves an entity which "proceeds" as profoundly from a "whole body" of language as from a whole physiological body.

Such a distinction between the physiological and figurative seems requisite, for although they coincide at crucial points, corporal and metaphorical figures of the melancholy body do not emerge from Trollope's text as entirely homologous equivalents: the sum of symptoms structuring the one does not amount to the anatomy of the other. More precisely, the anatomy of the metaphorical body, transindividual and supplemented by fictive or mythic signs, is not in the end reducible to its physiological counterpart in the anatomy of Louis Trevelyan.

Both the physiological and figurative symptoms of the body melancholy established by Trollope can be approached from a diachronic, historical perspective which seeks to recover the conceptual antecedents informing his text. As symbolic structures, however, these symptoms also invite one to incorporate the insights of later writers on melancholia, such as Freud and Kristeva. Far from constituting an inherently anachronistic exercise in "retrojecting Freudian . . . notions into [Trollope's] narrative" (Sutherland xiv), such an approach serves rather to illustrate how the literary imagination in fact tends to anticipate and to a certain extent shape advances in scientific or clinical knowledge. At the same time, it provides a theoretical framework for exploring the psychological and semiotic dynamics subtending Louis Trevelyan's melancholic symptoms.

In particular, it is illuminating to chart the development of the commonplace metaphorical symptom of the bodily wound beyond Trollope's text to its theoretical elaboration in Freud's "Mourning and Melancholia" (1917), where it figures as the representative analogy of a neurotic "melancholic complex" precipitated by object loss. By foregrounding the cycle of sadomasochism implicit in Trollope's depiction of the relationship between Trevelyan's mental sorrows and bodily sufferings, Freud's essay provides a context in which it is possible to make some sense of the fundamentally contradictory manifestations of the "jealous melancholy" of a wounded ego.

More broadly, the mutual implication of physiology and language in Trollope's representation of melancholic symptomatology prefigures a major preoccupation of Kristeva, in her recent thought on the semiotic parameters and processes of depressive disorders. For in tracing the interplay of language and body throughout the course of Trevelyan's malady, Trollope is like Kristeva in his evident fascination with the existence and importance of discrete yet dynamic gradations of signification. And importantly, unlike his literary representation of the melancholy body, which relies fundamentally on rhetorical figures to flesh itself out, Trollope's analysis of the "modification of signifying bonds" characteristic of melancholia (Kristeva, *Black Sun* 10) points conversely to the way in which Trevelyan's progressive illness actually entails a sort of "break" with language: in this case, a regression to nonverbal and preverbal levels of cognition and communication. Ultimately, it is Trevelyan's increasingly pronounced melancholic alienation and retreat from verbal modes of symbolization that raise intriguing questions about the theoretical implications of relying on metaphor in literary and psychoanalytic representations and anatomizations of melancholy in general.

3. ASPECTS OF THE PHYSIOLOGICAL BODY

For nearly the first two hundred pages of Trollope's novel, it is not immediately evident that Louis Trevelyan is a man of melancholy "temperature." "Fear & Sorrow are the true characters and inseparable companions . . . of most melancholy," as Burton informs us (149), but anger or wrath is the affect most in evidence in the early scenes of the great quarrel between Louis and Emily Trevelyan. In a nutshell, Trevelyan is a wealthy, accomplished, insufferably proud and domineering husband, who at the novel's outset feels that his wife's honor (and his own) is in danger of being compromised by the less than strictly proprietous attentions of an "ancient Lothario" by the name of Colonel Osborne (7). Emily Trevelyan, a match for her husband in spirit and pride if not social status, is keenly provoked by her husband's insulting (and, she believes, absurd) imputation against a man she regards as an old family friend. Trevelyan's struggle for "mastery" and wifely submission begins: he issues commands that Emily cease to see or correspond with Osborne, then vacillates, rescinds his orders, and is furious when his wife proves the more steadfast and has the temerity to remind him that "he must not blow hot and cold too" (51). The situation deteriorates apace, Trevelyan becoming more and more rash in his accusations, more and more irrational in his labile demands, while the exasperated Emily assiduously cultivates a sense of righteous indignation and only hardens her position with respect to the innocence of both her own conduct and the intentions of Colonel Osborne. Eventually, stymied by Emily's staunch refusal to show herself "sufficiently broken in spirit" by "own[ing] that she had been wrong" (175), the irate *pater familias* breaks up his household, banishing wife and child to a life of provincial seclusion.

But as the prospect of separation looms, it becomes increasingly apparent that the jealous husband's hot-tempered choler is but half of a passional admixture: a foul melan-choler that smacks of "great grief" and "absolute wretchedness" as well as anger (96, 98). Trevelyan is conscious of the price of his obstinacy: "All my hopes and prospects in life," he professes to Emily, "will be blighted by such a separation' (96). After the fact, the narrator confirms Trevelyan's estimate of the personal impact of the separation:

> He was very wretched at this time,—so wretched that life was a burden to him. He was a man who loved his wife;—to whom his child was very dear; and he was one too to whom the ordinary comforts of domestic life were attractive and necessary. . . . There was no delight to him in being able to dine at his club, and being free to go whither he pleased in the evenings; and his mornings were equally blank to him.   (174)

It is while Trevelyan "liv[es] on a wretched life in London," alone, talking obsessively to friends "of the grief with which his mind was laden" (175–76), that his behavior begins to evince a more acute note of paranoid desperation and fear. He hires a duplicitous ex-policeman to spy on Emily and her suspected paramour. "In these days of his madness," as the narrator phrases it, "he took Mr. Bozzle into his pay" (177). "From morning to night," we read later, Trevelyan "sang to himself melancholy, silent songs as to the cruelty of his own lot in life;—and, in the meantime, he employed Bozzle to find out how far that cruelty was carried" (318).

Over and above the increasingly frequent narrative references to Trevelyan's misery and anguish, however, his melancholy is a story vividly inscribed in the corporal symptoms he soon begins to manifest. Emily Trevelyan eventually adopts mourning garb to symbolize her forsaken status, but Trollope's husband does not merely wear his heart on his sleeve, so to speak. His melancholy is signaled by more than an alteration of dress (which becomes decidedly more shabby and eccentric as the novel progresses): it is a condition announced by a profound physical transformation of limb and lineament.

At the novel's opening, there is evidently nothing amiss with the twenty-four-year-old anatomy of Trevelyan, who is described as "such a handsome, manly fellow, with short brown hair, a nose divinely chiselled, an Apollo's mouth, six feet high, with shoulders and legs and arms in proportion,—a pearl of pearls!" (3). How strangely the "pearl of pearls" has altered is Emily's first thought upon seeing Trevelyan again, a few months after their parting: "She thought that she would have hardly known him, had she not been sure that it was he." Emily herself is also "changed" by "sorrow," the narrator comments, "[b]ut the effect on her was as nothing to that which grief, remorse, and desolation had made on him" (568). "[L]achrymose, heartbroken, and a sight pitiable to behold" (566), Trevelyan is also hardly recognizable to family friends, who in the second half of the novel continue to intercede in futile attempts to reconcile husband and wife, and to note in graphic detail the extent of his changed aspect:

His cheeks were thin and haggard, and his eyes were deep and very bright,—and
he moved them quickly from side to side, as though ever suspecting something.
He seemed to be smaller in stature,—withered as it were, as though he had
melted away.   (633)
He was as wretched a being to look at as it might have been possible to find.
His contracted cheeks and lips, always open, and eyes glowing in their sunken
caverns, told a tale which even Sir Marmaduke, who was not of nature quick
in deciphering such stories, could not fail to read.   (649–50)
His beard had been allowed to grow, and he had neither collar nor cravat. His
trousers were unbraced, and he shuffled in with a pair of slippers which would
hardly cling to his feet. He was paler and still thinner than when he had visited
at Willesden, and his eyes seemed to be larger, and shone almost with a brighter
brilliancy.   (734)
His hand was mere skin and bone. His hair and beard so covered his thin long
cheeks, that there was nothing left of his face but his bright, large, melancholy
eyes. His legs had become so frail and weak that they would hardly bear his
weight as he walked; and his clothes . . . hung so loose about him that they
seemed as though they would fall from him.   (854)

A "tale" told by the feverish "melancholy eyes" which become the focal
point of Trevelyan's shrinking physical being, Louis's illness includes such
typical symptoms of melancholy as anorexia, insomnia, and profuse perspira-
tion, and takes the form of a literal self-consumption, a "wasting" of flesh,
muscle, and vital fluids which ultimately leaves little more than skeletal
remains. Its perfectly proportioned physique now disfigured by a noticeably
"bent" back (640), Trevelyan's warped body mirrors his warped judgment:
his increasingly impaired sense of the magnitude of Emily's "transgression"
or "sin." "[L]ean, withered, [and] hollow-eyed," with the "dejected looks"
and "flaggy beard" Burton notes as "signs of melancholy in the body"
(326), Trollope's protagonist also physically resembles the mournful sailor-
king Pericles, in that once "his happiness [is] shipwrecked" (363, 253) he
allows his short hair to grow long and refuses to shave (741).

The melancholy distemper which can be "read" in Trevelyan's altered
physiognomy and stature is also apparent in his physical mannerisms. Con-
ventionally, melancholia and depression are perhaps most immediately associated with forms of neurophysiological slowdown—a mental and motor leth-
argy that the ancients attributed to constricted blood vessels and a turgid
blood flow. In Trollope's novel, however, Trevelyan's fiery jealousy often
causes his melancholy to assume a more manic aspect, as his suspicious,
darting eyes suggest. His symptomatology in this respect corresponds to
"those strange gestures of staring, frowning, grinning, rolling of eyes" and
"broken pace, interrupt, precipitate half-turns" recorded by Burton as manifestations of "jealous melancholy" (840–41). But in Trollope's own time,
Trevelyan's repertoire of teeth-gnashing and fist-clenching (260, 424), of

hair-tearing, arm-waving, and room-pacing (246, 590, 808), may well have been regarded as prominent symptoms of "acute melancholia." According to Henry Maudsley, this form of disorder was characterized by

> [r]estless pacing up and down the room or unquiet wanderings from room to room, . . . perpetual moanings and groanings, rockings of the body to and fro, wringing of hands, beating of head and face . . . , pulling out of hair, biting of nails to the quick,—these and like gestures and acts of unrest and grief betray the active misery which, agitation being its chief note, has sometimes received the name of *melancholia agitata*. Between it and the opposite state of melancholic stupor, . . . there are intermediate cases marked by varying states of torpor and agitation. (*Pathology of Mind* 205)

Although alternating with increasingly prolonged lapses into contemplative silence and gloomy meditation, Trevelyan's nervous tics and fits of agitation elicit almost as much commentary from other characters as his changed appearance does. The characters remark on "the twitching motion of the man's hands, and the restless shuffling of his feet" (650); at times, as Lady Rowley notes, "he was not for a moment still," but continually changing "the posture of his hands and arms, moving them quickly with little surreptitious jerks," and "shuffl[ing] his feet upon the floor, almost without altering his position" (633). When others attempt to expostulate with Trevelyan, his excitement becomes so great that he proceeds to "stalk up and down the room, waving his hand in the air, as though he were continuing his speech'—even after his auditors leave him (592). Through "these and like gestures and acts of unrest and grief," Trollope thus indicates the rather paradoxically hyperactive nature of his protagonist's melancholy body.

"Above all things," Burton avers in his *Anatomy*, any body that is melancholy "love[s] solitariness" (366). In Trollope's novel, Trevelyan's physical withdrawal from society to Casalunga, the remote seat of his Italian self-exile, is presented as a definitive, symptomatic gesture of melancholic alienation. As isolated behind the "huge . . . wooden gateway" of Casalunga (731) as Milton's "pensive nun" in her convent cloister, or Johnson's mad astronomer in his tower, Trevelyan plays out his private version of "Il Penseroso" in the context of a recognizably pre-scripted iconographic tradition of melancholy. At Casalunga he lives the "life of [a] wretched hermit" (883) in a setting which externalizes the mental topography of the melancholic man. Since marital woes have turned "[e]verything for him now . . . hot and dry and poor and bitter" (634), Trevelyan chooses a deserted winery atop a sun-scorched hill for is new abode. Here "the intensity of his solitude" (853) is matched only by the intensity of the sun's heat, which bakes the "brown, and arid'' earth (733) and parches the vegetation into ''a faded yellowish green'' (867). Even sickly foliage vividly colors forth the complexion of Trevelyan's distemper, suggesting ''a green and yellow melancholy'' akin to that of the lovelorn Viola in *Twelfth Night* (2.4).[5]

Like the melancholy sufferers Burton describes, who ''delight to walk alone in some solitary Grove'' or orchard (214), Trevelyan haunts the olive groves at Casalunga, as often and as far as his strength allows him:

> He went out from the house, and made his way down by the narrow path through the olives and vines to the bottom of the hill in front of the villa. It was evening now, but the evening was very hot, and though the olive trees stood in long rows, there was no shade. Quite at the bottom of the hill there was a sluggish muddy brook, along the sides of which the reeds grew thickly and the dragonflies were playing on the water. There was nothing attractive in the spot, but he was weary, and sat himself down on the hard dry bank. . . . He sat watching the dragonflies . . . and told himself that of all God's creatures there was not one to whom less power of disporting itself in God's sun was given than to him. Surely it would be better for him that he should die, than live as he was now living without any of the joys of life.   (789–90)

In his recurrent ''reverie[s]'' among the olive trees (809) and upon the bank, Trollope's ''philosopher'' (869) strikes the very air and attitude of that ''melancholizing'' philosopher that Burton's ''Democritus Junior'' himself emulates. ''One of the chiefest reasons'' Democritus was suspected ''to be melancholy and mad,'' we are told in the *Anatomy*, was precisely that ''he forsook the City, lived in groves and hollow trees, upon a green bank by a brook side, or confluence of waters, all day long, and all night'' (337). Through his subtle employment of similar scenic details, Trollope is able to evoke the same ambience of bittersweet pastoral nostalgia that infuses the aesthetic tradition of melancholy, even in the midst of Trevelyan's semi-arid Italian wasteland. And so from symptoms of the body to signs of the setting in which it is situated, the semiology of Trevelyan's psychopathology sketches the contours of an anatomy of melancholy.

4. FIGURES OF THE BODY MELANCHOLY

In some respects, the metaphorical dimension of melancholy in *He Knew He Was Right* corresponds with certain morbid features of the physiological body surveyed above and even imaginatively accounts for them. Trevelyan's crooked back, for instance, can be regarded as a corporal realization and expression of his acute mental perception of the staggering "weight" of his grievances and miseries, a prominent figurative motif which attends his gradual physical transformation. "The slightest rumour on a woman's name is a load of infamy on her husband's shoulders," Trevelyan thinks to himself early in the narrative (43). It is a conceit he subsequently articulates to others through a similar, recurrent allusion:

> People choose to say that I am to blame and they may say so for me. Nothing that any one may say can add anything to the weight that I have to bear.
> (358–59)

> [Emily] came here the other day, almost as a stranger, and I thought my heart would burst beneath its weight of woe. What can you do that can add an ounce to the burden that I bear? (649)

According to Stanley Jackson, the metaphor of the oppressive burden or weight, associated with a "dropping body posture," is one which "stand[s] out in the long history of melancholia" from Galenic times (396–97).[6] But Trollope's use of the trope bears a relevance more specific to his text as well. Through other characters such as Emily are not, like Louis Trevelyan, actually cast down physically by their "load of sorrows," they do occasionally speak of themselves in such terms (575), and to that extent the image of the burdened melancholy body begins to establish a figurative frame of reference which transcends the physical frame of Travelyan himself.

That the body melancholy, as a metaphorical construct, is not coextensive with the individual body of Trollope's text is also suggested by the figurative symptom of "the black frown" which settles on "the brow" and face (12): a trademark of Trevelyan's "jealous melancholy," to be sure, but one Trollope also employs in relation to other characters of choleric complexion such as Emily (570) and her father, Sir Marmaduke (845). "Black" looks are indeed most evidently associated by Trollope with the passion of anger: the black "cloud" that Emily and Lady Millborough witness darkening Trevelyan's face (51, 26) functions as an index of rising fury that both women learn to recognize; it is "the angry brow" (259), "the old look" that the man who would be master assumes when spewing "the bitterness of his wrath" (923). But blackness is, of course, an attribute also inextricably related to the mythopoesis of melancholic semiology, to the very matter of the hypothetical "humour" or "juice" once imagined to be the causal agent of the illness. As in Burton's work, so in Trollope's novel do "black" faces and brows evoke the mythic material essence of melancholy: that "sort of melaina (black) chole (choler), from black choler," or those "fuliginous and black spirits'' thought to ''arise from the other parts [of the body], and fume up into the head'' of the sufferer (Burton 148, 321, 320).

With an appropriately dark emphasis, the faces of black choler in Trollope's text better underscore the sorts of fundamental distinctions emerging between the figurative and physiological symptoms of the body melancholy. Metaphoric signs of melancholy, that is, are not simply monoreferential in terms of a specific character's body, they are also signs not necessarily answerable to any objective, physiological referent whatsoever. As Sander Gilman has suggested in his *Disease and Representation*, the symptom of black bile in this respect affords the clearest illustration of the ''mythmaking that usualy surrounds fictive signs or symptoms, . . . as a means of representing an invisible state—mental illness'' (19).

The human tendency described by Gilman, to concretize and thus securely ''locate'' invisible forces of mental pathology ''in'' identifiable, if fictive, signs such as black bile, is similarly manifest in nineteenth-century aproaches to intangible mental signs of melancholy, such as ''monomaniacal'' obsession or delusion. For example, Henry Maudsley in one of his works compares the monomaniacal fixation to ''a morbid growth in some organ of the body . . . which cannot be brought under the correcting influence of the surrounding healthy tissues'' (*Physiology and Pathology* 324). And in Trollope's novel, Trevelyan's jealous obsession has similarly struck critics as appearing to ''gro[w] with the inevitability of a natural growth'' (Gatrell 112), like some cancerous tumor. The way in which Trollope achieves such a figurative effect without directly rendering this aspect of Trevelyan's melancholy in metaphorical terms of tumorous growths deserves closer attention.

In essence, the strategy that Trollope relies on might be characterized as one of displaced metaphor, or more precisely, metaphor displaced in metonym. He conveys the effect of the organic tumor through the implicit comparison that he draws between his protagonist's ever-escalating delusion and an unsightly ''growth'' that functions as a prominent metonym in the novel's comic subplot: namely, Arabella French's outrageous chignon. Michael Riffaterre has observed that ''the chignon sub-text'' operates as ''a hermeneutic model that dictates the reader's interpretation of the main plot'' (285). As he shows, the ever-vascillating and reluctant bridegroom, the Reverend Gibson, develops an almost hysterical ''*idée fixe*'' about Arabella's prized hairpiece that eventually ''takes on epic proportions,'' thus creating a humorous parallel to Trevelyan's more tragic *idée fixe* in the high plot (287, 285).[7]

For my purposes, however, the essential similarity between Trevelyan's jealous delusion and the very ''thing'' that Arabella French ''carrie[s] on her head" as bait for a bridegroom is also worth elaborating (446). That the hairpiece serves as a tangible equivalent of Trevelyan's mental obsession is suggested by the "monstrous" and distinctly pathological attributes it eventually takes on in the eyes of the Reverend Gilman: "he thought that he never in his life had seen anything so unshapely as that huge wen at the back of [Arabella's] head. 'Monstrum horrendum, informe, ingens!'" (441). The Reverend's invocation of "an awful, hideous, huge monster" distantly echoes Colonel Osborne's earlier monitory allusion to Emily, regarding Trevelyan's inflamed suspicions: "the green-eyed monster is of all monsters, the most monstrous,—and the most unreasonable" (89). Like Arabella's "huge wen," Trevelyan's jealousy also increases in scope, growing "bigger and bigger, more shapeless, monstrous, absurd, and abominable" as the plot unfolds (443). Just as Arabella appears to Gibson to be "perishing beneath an incubus which a false idea of fashion had imposed on her" (445), so too does it become manifest to the reader that Trevelyan "perishes" beneath the green-eyed "incubus" of jealousy which false ideas of honor and pride impose on him.

Like the sign of black choler, Trollope's clever chignon metonym graphically embodies an ideational or psychological phenomenon in anatomical terms: in this instance, an inner deformity of the melancholic mind projected as an outer deformity of the person. For as an unnatural, grotesque appendage on the back of her head, "bigger than the place inside where her brains ought to be" (211),[8] Arabella's chignon brilliantly serves as an externalized proxy of that burgeoning, malignant delusion which only less comically overwhelms Trevelyan's brain cavity.

Perhaps the most pervasive metaphoric constituent of the body melancholy in Trollope's text is that of the flesh wound or sore, by which the mental affects of pain and anguish associated with melancholy are similarly rendered incarnate. The figure of the melancholic wound, another veritable cliché in historical representations of the disease, receives particular attention from Burton in his discussion of "Jealous Melancholy." Though Burton strenuously objects that such wounds are "incurable," he cites Ariosto on the matter at length:

This is that cruel wound, against whose smart
No liquor's force prevails, or any plaster,
No skill of stars, no depth of magick art,
Devised by that great clerk Zoroaster;
A wound that so infects the soul and heart,
As all our sense and reason it doth master:

A wound whose pang and torment is so durable,
As it may rightly called be incurable.   (848)

While Burton is concerned to emphasize of the melancholic wound that " 'tis no such real or capital matter," " 'tis a blow that hurts not, an insensible smart, grounded many times upon false suspicion alone" (849), John Haslam in 1809 focuses on the etymological roots of the word 'sorrow" to stress quite the opposite. Haslam notes that the term "sorrow," though denoting a mental state or feeling, originally carried the sense of bodily "sufferance": sore, sorry, and sorrow, he points out, are all cognates, initially grounded in the corporal experience of pain (9). The extent to which sorrow, sorriness, and bodily sufferance are profoundly interrelated elements in iconographic traditions associated with melancholia is perhaps nowhere more dramatically illustrated than in Christian representations of Christ's Passion and death, where the scourged, flogged, crucified "Man of Sorrows" suffers in the flesh as an act of supreme atonement.[9]

In *He Knew He Was Right*, the melancholy sorrows of both Emily and Louis Trevelyan are consistently prefigured as forms of bodily sufferance that tap into the related tradition of Christian martyrdom and sacrifice. Wounds symbolically sustained appear in the early chapters as angry sores, sores that arise from a sense of injured pride. When Louis, for example, first instructs his wife to forward to him unopened all correspondence from Colonel Osborne, and then promptly receives a note from the gentleman addressed to Emily and containing purely innocent information regarding the Rowley family, he knows that "he had created for himself a terrible trouble": "He must tell his wife what was in the letter, but the very telling of it would be a renewing of the soreness of his wound" (50). Any time afterward that Emily chances "even [to] imply that she need forget,—that she should forgive" rather than "accept forgiveness" from Louis (744), the husband's wound bleeds anew: "As it was, her words wounded him in that spot of his inner self which was most sensitive,—on that spot from whence had come all his fury. A black cloud came upon his brow" (634). Reciprocally, Louis's words wound Emily: she "undergo[es]" her husband's "wise words" about the wicked ways of the world as a form of "infliction" that leaves her feeling "injured and aggrieved" (89). With each believing himself or herself the party "more sinned against than sinning," "each was so sore that no approach to terms" is possible (105).

Yet gradually, the "sore and angry" (26) wounds of the combative couple temper into wounds of sorriness. For the jealous husband, Trollope hints, this subtle change may come with the sad realization that perhaps Ariosto was right:

> He had not considered, when his resolutions to this effect were first forming themselves, that a separation between a man and his wife once effected cannot be annulled, and as it were cured, so as to leave no cicatrice behind. Gradually, as he spent day after day thinking on this one subject, he came to feel that even were his wife to submit, to own her fault humbly, and to come back to him, this very coming back would in itself be a new wound.   (362)

Initial regret at the scars of separation is here apparently subsumed by Trevelyan's obsessive, bitter belief that even the very cure he calls on to heal his wound, Emily's contrition, would serve only to exacerbate the injury: this, it seems, is a jealous wound which "infects" and "masters" "sense and reason" indeed.

As the nature of Trevelyan's wound alters from a maddening smart to a more melancholy pang, perversely and sadly incurable, his attitude toward suffering alters as well. At the beginning of the novel, Trevelyan exclaims to himself: "I am sorry that [Emily] should suffer; but it is better that she should suffer a little now, than that we should both suffer much by-and-by" (28–29). Near the end of the text, however, the narrator notes that Louis "declared to himself over and over again that it was better that he should suffer than that others should be punished" (786–87). This seemingly dramatic reversal from one who wished to make others suffer to one who wishes to suffer in their stead is confirmed at other points in the narrative, especially in Trevelyan's increasingly marked tendency to submit himself willingly to fresh and gratuitous symbolic wounds from the odious Bozzle. "Bozzle said things, and made suggestions to him which were as bad as pins stuck into his flesh" (317). "Every word" of Bozzle's letters is like "a dagger to Trevelyan, and yet he felt himself to be under an obligation to the man" (421).

Burton often refers casually to melancholy as a "malady . . . that . . . crucifies body and mind" (102), but in Trollope's work Trevelyan's ready submission to a form of symbolic crucifixion at Bozzle's hands carefully prepares the ground for the ultimate apotheosis of melancholy sorrow and suffering as a form of Christian "Self-Sacrifice" (ch. 84). The immediate context of the scene is that of Trevelyan's decision at Casulunga to return to the custody of Emily the child he has surreptitiously snatched from her:

> It was impossible that he should yield;—but it was yet open to him to sacrifice himself. He could not go back to his wife and say that he was wrong; but he

could determine that the destruction should fall upon him and not upon her.
(788)

Offering up his *only son*, Louis, Jr., is the way Louis, Sr., has of offering up himself.[10] And it is in this tragically noble self-conception that Trevelyan's melancholy "wound" can be seen to find its metaphoric culmination in a sacrificial act distantly analogous to that of the impaled and bleeding "Man of Sorrows" on the cross.

Emily, meanwhile, is eventually moved from the soreness of wrath to that of sorrow by Trevelyan's more and more visible bodily suffering. En route to England after Casalunga, "Trevelyan," as the narrator notes, "allowed himself to be carried in and out of . . . carriages and up and down . . . hotel stairs almost as though he were a child" (882). It is this pathetic physical feebleness that ultimately prompts the wife in effect to "forgive" the husband by asking on her knees for forgiveness of him (884). Later, Emily explains to her sister Nora:

> He is so weak. . . . He can hardly speak. . . . I have told him just simply that it was all my doing,—that I have been in fault all through. . . . What does it matter? He had suffered so, that I would have said worse than that just to give him relief.   (894)

Even though Emily proceeds to compare her false confession to a form of violent martyrdom—"My nails have been dragged out, and I have been willing to confess anything," she exclaims, in a vivid passage (899)—her wounds no longer excite anger or indignation, but rather a profound sense of melancholy resignation and dejection. She is left, near the conclusion, "so sad a creature, so sombre, so dark": "There could be nothing left for her but garments dark with woe, eyes red with weeping, hours sad from solitude, thoughts weary with memory" (926). Although this bleak prognosis is slightly mitigated by Trevelyan's imminent death; Emily Trevelyan does assume an iconographic aspect akin to that of the "Mater Dolorosa" who weeps at the death of the "Man of Sorrows" in the literal sense that her final role is that of the grief-stricken mother.[11]

No simple, self-contained imagistic motif, the concatenation of sores and suffering, sorrow and sorriness in *He Knew He Was Right* provides the most intricate illustration of a corporal figure of melancholy that transcends the anatomical figure of Trevelyan himself. For in the case of the metaphor of the "wounded" melancholy body, it is the "one flesh" of a couple torn asunder that is finally at (the) stake in Trollope's novel.

5. THE MELANCHOLY COMPLEX: DYNAMICS OF SADOMASOCHISM

From his earliest attempts at explaining neurotic states of melancholia, in 1895, to his well-known essay of 1917 on the subject, Freud repeatedly employed the metaphor of an "open wound."[12] "The complex of melancholia," he states in the latter work, "behaves like an open wound, drawing to itself cathectic energies . . . from all directions, and emptying the ego until it is totally impoverished" (262). Extending the figure of the wound as it does, Freud's conception of melancholia as involving a form of ego conflict provides an apt theoretical framework through which to explore the perplexing and perverse relationship between mental and physical suffering manifest in the pathogenesis of Louis Trevelyan's melancholic disorder. What I am interested in pursuing here is the nature of the dynamic between the emotional suffering of the "inner self" that is prefigured by the metaphor of the "wound," and the form of bodily sufferance that "wastes" Trevelyan's physical self. For although the doctor who finally diagnoses Trevelyan as "mono-maniacal" declares that "in his case the weakness of mind has been consequent upon the weakness of the body" (924), Trollope's text suggests that the reverse is more likely: that it is the "sore heart" that "make[s] the face thin, as well as fever or ague" (569).[13] And in this case, it is possible to read the signs of Trevelyan's "totally impoverished" physiology as the outward emblems of a wounded ego, torn between dialectical sadomasochistic tendencies.

The classical psychoanalytic theory of melancholia, or depression in the modern term, is succinctly summarized by Kristeva in *Black Sun*. "Like mourning," melancholy "conceals an aggressiveness towards [a] lost object, thus revealing the ambivalence of the depressed person with respect to the object of mourning" (11). Freud elaborates on the preconditions and development of the disorder:

> In melancholia, the occasions which give rise to the illness extend for the most part beyond the clear case of a loss by death, and include all those situations of being slighted, neglected, or disappointed, which can import opposed feelings of love and hate into the relationship or reinforce an already existing ambivalence. . . . If the love for the object—a love which cannot be given up though the object itself is given up—takes refuge in narcissistic identification, then hate comes into the operation on this substitutive object, abusing it, debasing it, making it suffer and deriving sadistic satisfaction from its suffering.
>
> (260)

Trollope's novel presents us with a strikingly similar situation in that the "slighted" Trevelyan remains unwilling or unable to relinquish his attachment to Emily, despite the separation he initiates. His contending impulses to break from his wife and yet not break from her are clearly apparent, for example in his employment of Bozzle, who while ostensibly charged with the task of finding "proof" for grounds of divorce, meanwhile supplies Trevelyan with a continual flow of information regarding the object of his obsession. Perhaps most tellingly of all, as the narrator is careful to point out, for all his claims of scandal Trevelyan never alters his will to disinherit his suspect spouse (743).[14]

Like Freud, Trollope stresses the nature of such self-tormenting ambivalence as a native element of the human constitution. "They who do not understand that a man may be brought to hope that which of all things is most grievious to him," the narrator interjects at one point, "have not observed with sufficient closeness the perversity of the human mind" (364). In this novel, "the perversity of the human mind" is indeed observed "with sufficient closeness" in respect to many characters, including Colonel Osborne, the good-hearted dowager Lady Millborough, and Emily herself.[15] What distinguishes Trevelyan's "perversity" from that of the others, Trollope shows, is mainly a matter of degree, the extremism "of the insane man, who loves to feed his grievance, even though the grievance should be his death" (364).

But the compulsive extent of Trevelyan's seemingly masochistic need to "feed his grievance" presupposes in itself another way in which his perversity differs from that of the other characters in the novel: his unique knack for eroticizing and fetishizing his own mental and physical suffering. For Trevelyan is the preeminent practitioner of an aesthetics of suffering which, at least for modern readers, seems fully inscribed in his very name, Travail-yen. This dimension of his pathology of course includes his self-image as the wounded "Man of Sorrows,"[16] but it is also more pervasively developed within the text in relation to Trevelyan's distinctly "literary" orientation toward the genre of tragedy.[17] "The truth is that when one is absolutely unhappy one cannot revel in the imagination. I don't believe in the miseries of the poets," Trevelyan proclaims at one point (357). But "the truth is" that in consciously modeling himself on the Othello prototype, the unhappy Trevelyan *does* tend to "revel" in the imagination, "in the idea of the tragedy he would make" (423).

A remarkable scenic interlude at Casalunga, on the occasion of a visit by Mr. Glascock, best illustrates Trevelyan's rather poetic prowess in carefully staging the affects of his melancholy suffering for maximal stage effect:

> [Trevelyan] walked out of the [patio] window and went down among the olive trees. He did not go far, however, but stood with his arm round the stem of one them, playing with the shoots of a vine with his hand. Mr. Glascock followed him to the window and stood looking at him for a few minutes. But Trevelyan did not turn or move. He stood gazing at the pale, cloudless, heat-laden, motionless sky, thinking of his own sorrows, and remembering too, doubtless, with the vanity of a madman, that he was probably being watched in his reverie. (809)

Somehow adolescent in its knowing naivety, this picturesque pose of melancholy woe graphically underscores Trevelyan's selfconscious and sensual desire to heighten the pathos of his situation, and clearly bespeaks the melodramatic, if not strictly literary, sensibility that is gratified by his masochistic drives.

That Trevelyan's is likely no innocent pleasure in pain for art's sake alone, however, follows from Freud's basic contention in "Mourning and Melancholia":

> The self-tormenting in melancholia, which is without doubt enjoyable, signifies . . . a satisfaction of trends of sadism and hate which relate to an object, and which have been turned round upon the subject's own self. . . . In [melancholia] the patients usually still succeed, by the circuitous path of self-punishment, in taking revenge on the original object and in tormenting their loved one through their illness, having resorted to it in order to avoid the need to express their hostility openly. (260–61)

Within the text, Trollope most clearly affirms that Trevelyan's "masochistic" eroticization of suffering similarly masks a sadistic trend, which through the "circuitous path of self-punishment" serves as a means of wreaking vengeance on Emily, at the moment of his protagonist's great "self sacrifice." "If he gave up his child, and then died, died alone, without any friend near him, with no word of love in his ears, in [the] solitary and miserable abode" at Casalunga, so the train of Trevelyan's thought begins, then perhaps "the coals of fire would be hot upon [Emily's] head":

> He put out his thin wasted hands and looked at them, and touched the hollowness of his own cheeks, and coughed that he might hear the hacking sound of his own infirmity, and almost took glory in his weakness. It could not be long before the coals of fire would be heaped upon her head. (788)

Far from the magnanimous act of atonement that Trevelyan would have us believe it is, Trollope implies instead that his protagonist's "self-sacrifice" of Louis, Jr., is but the most searing form of self-laceration by which he is able to "feed his grievance" and simultaneously heap retribution on the wife he loves to hate, or hates to love. And appropriately, perhaps, Trevelyan's avenging vision of Emily carrying her burnt offerings on her head in penitence draws as much on the traditional semiology of melancholy as it does on scriptural iconography.[18]

Almost greedily anticipating his death for the woe it will "heap" on Emily, and now caressing not an olive branch but the contours of his own suffering body, Trevelyan, the narrator states, "pitied himself with a pity that was feminine" (787). The essence of the above scene's erotic appeal, the womanly tenderness with which Trevelyan stokes the flames of his own bodily sufferance, also points toward the sort of "narcissistic identification" with the "lost object" posited by Freud. The "feminine" attributes that the once-"manly" Trevelyan now takes on, that is, suggest how in the melancholy complex the "lost object" or other is internalized and reconstituted within the ego of the self, the self which is in turn punished as a "substitutive object" of that other. What Trevelyan's perversity seems to entail in this respect is "a whole complex dialectic of idealization and devalorization of self and other," a "seesawing between . ./. the projection on the self of hatred against the other, and vice versa, the turning against the other of self-depreciation" (Kristeva, *Black Sun* 11, 196).[19] Such is the nature of the psychical conflict which leaves the Freudian ego "totally impoverished," sapping its vitality like an "open wound." And such too, I am suggesting, best approximates the vissicitudes of inner turmoil that in the case of Trollope's protagonist are made outwardly manifest in a form of melancholic consumption of the whole body.

Inasmuch as he comes to perceive his death as the ultimate form of revenge, the suicidal implications of Trevelyan's sadomasochistic "glory in his weakness" also come to the fore. For while on the one hand it is true that his physical deterioration is portrayed as a genuinely organic affliction beyond his control, Trevelyan's voluptuous awareness that his "weakness" may constitute his most effective weapon also leads him to cultivate that "weakness" in a patently self-destructive manner, whether by drinking to excess, or by "half-mind[edly]" exacerbating his condition by overexerting himself and letting "the night air come upon him" (791). That Trevelyan has been "wasted by the kind of life which he had led" is the opinion voiced by Dr. Nevill near the end (900), but the narrator drops his own ominous hint somewhat earlier, when he describes Trevelyan's condition as such "that the happiness and welfare of no human being—not even his own—could safely be entrusted to his keeping" (786). And to the extent that it can be regarded as a form of slow suicide, the decline and death of Trevelyan entail a more subtle homicidal significance as well, through the same "circuitous path" of self-punishment as outlined above. In the case of the melancholic complex, as Kristeva writes, "putting oneself to death [is] but a tragic disguise for massacring an Other" (*Black Sun* 11).[20]

Finally, whether or not Trevelyan may accurately be said to "resort" to his illness, in Freud's term, it is clear his bodily suffering does indeed serve a functional communicatory purpose of the sort outlines by psychoanalytic theory. In effect, Trevelyan's manifest body melancholy is his most eloquent accusation. "I am ill;—very ill! *Look* at me. *See* what she has brought me to!" (736; emphasis added). To the degree that Trevelyan's suffering body succeeds in acting as a solvent on Emily's conscience, as we have seen, his illness serves effectively though indirectly to convey a "hostility" which he is unable to "express . . . openly," to recall Freud's words. For Trevelyan represses, to the very end, any direct verbalization of that debased suspicion which he "would . . . have rather cut his tongue out before he would have expressed to anyone" (364). That his wife is an adulterous "harlot" is a conviction he hints at through allusion and innuendo, but ultimately leaves for Emily herself to articulate (927). Against "words which seem to convey accusation" Emily can always find the strength to "protest" (921). But the mute rebuke of her husband's pathetically wasted body, by an appeal, presumably, to her "feminine" sense of pity, chastises Emily in spite of her knowledge of her essential innocence. It induces in the once-proud wife an unprecedented measure of humility and remorse, a self-abjection more painful, for the reader, than Trevelyan's own abject condition.

6. MELANCHOLY AND MODALITIES OF REPRESENTATION

That the weak, wizened body often prevails where words fail points up the interplay of distinct semiotic modalities in Trollope's anatomy of melancholy. The corporal symptoms of Trevelyan's malady are indeed shown to be inextricably related to linguistic phenomena through what appears, in Trollope's text, as a sort of sliding scale of signification: a representational continuum perhaps most helpfully approached in the context of Julia Kristeva's concept of *le sémiotique*. The basic distinction drawn by Kristeva is between a symbolic realm of signification, a realm of "grammar and the logic of discourse," and a semiotic order encompassing primary processes, "drives and their articulation" (*Black Sun* 264–65). "Her semiotic," Shuli

Barzilai explains, is a "drive-affected dimension of human experience" at "the borders of language" that "disrupts (even as it interfuses with) the symbolic"; "it involves dynamic, pre-linguistic operations rather than thetic or static modes of articulation" (297). At the outer limits of the Kristevan semiotic, and "irreducible to verbal or semiological expression," remains the enigmatic sphere of affects, those inexpressible experiences or moods of fear, joy, or (especially) sadness, whose precise status has not, as yet, been determined. Kristeva conceives of affect as an "archaic energy signal," the most "rudimentary" form of representation, and stresses in her definition of the term the "twofold aspect" of affect as both "energy flow and psychic inscription" (*Black Sun* 21, 178).[21] "Sadness (like all affect)," she writes, "is the psychic inscription of energy displacements caused by external or internal traumas" (*Black Sun* 21).

Trollope's interest in modalities of representation that approximate Kristeva's schema is generally apparent in his novel's concerns with the physiology of speech: a phenomenon seen to entail a symbolic realm of "Hard Words" (ch. 10) that recedes metaphorically to the pre-linguistic level of a bodily event, and beyond, to the least hypostatized trace of the sign in the physical energy traces of speech. For in *He Knew He Was Right*, the "grammar and the logic of discourse" is everywhere figuratively represented as a form of physical altercation linked to more primal, preverbal instincts of aggression. There is indeed a "dreadful substantiality" and "relentlessness" about the uttered word within the text (McMaster 201, 198), and nowhere is the capacity to wield words as weapons of bodily assault more marked than in the progress of the Trevelyans' quarrel. Just as it is Emily's condescending language that "wounds" Trevelyan to the "inner self" (634), so Trevelyan himself is depicted as "hurling" hard words (592), like rocks, on the retaliatory basis that "she had hit him hard, and should he not hit her again?" (261).

By choosing metaphors of the brute force of "hard words," whether as a 'broadside" shot "fired" (454) or a provoking jab "throw[n] in the teeth" (927), Trollope represents symbolic wounds as entities sustained and inflicted at the proprioceptive semiotic level of the body. But he also evinces thereby a sharp authorial awareness of the physics of speech as a form of energy displacement. As the narrator pointedly reminds us, speech "cannot be recalled" once unleashed from the tongue (7), and that it is endowed with a vital quantum force of its own is made ironically apparent from the moment when readers find Trevelyan in the midst of writing a "scientific article," "intent on raising a dispute with some learned pundit about the waves of sound" (12). Interrupted by the "waves of sound" raised in consequence of Trevelyan's first angry words, this article, presumably, remains unfinished. Trollope's early evocation of the image of sound waves thus carries a thematic relevance in relation to the repercussions of passional speech, but it is also intriguing from a representational perspective. For such undulating "waves" are like the representations Kristeva theorizes as "proper to affects" in that they appear as "fluctuating energy traces." At the same time that they obviously refer the reader to a symbolic realm of verbal signification, "waves of sound" also connote imperceptible vibrations, which like the inarticulate affects of our moods, are in themselves 'insufficiently stabilized to coagulate into signs" (Kristeva, "Melancholy Imaginary" 108). In calling attention to the latent nature of the speech act as a form of energy flow or displacement, in other words, Trollope's sound waves function as an apt metaphorical measure of a pre-symbolic modality of significance: they are physical energy traces which simultaneously suggest the psychical energy traces of an unrepresentable affect or semiotic rhythm.

The dynamics of various parameters of representation during the experience of melancholy are a subject pursued at length by Kristeva in *Black Sun*.[22] In depressive individuals, she argues, "the surge of affect and primary semiotic processes comes into conflict with the linguistic armor (which I have called alien or secondary), as well as with symbolic constructs (apprenticeships, ideologies, beliefs)" (64–65). Because Louis Trevelyan's malady never progresses to the point of complete asymbolia, it would be inaccurate to suggest that the manifestations of his melancholy signal precisely the sort of "spectacular collapse of meaning" or wholesale "neutralization of the signifier" that Kristeva identifies as characteristic of the "dead language" of the profoundly disturbed depressive (53, 20). Nonetheless, the pathogenesis of Trevelyan's melancholy in Trollope's text, as I hope to show, does appear to involve a conflict similar in nature, if not degree: a progressive disjunction between on the one hand Trevelyan's symbolic and linguistic constructs, and on the other a preverbal semiotic modality associable to his black mood.[23]

The disruption of the symbolic realm in *He Knew He Was Right* is evident through Trollope's careful portrayal of Trevelyan's growing alienation from his own speech. This facet of his disorder is initially marked as a slight perversity, as Trevelyan's ear becomes inured to the abrasive modulations of "hard words." Not only does he come to "hardly recogniz[e] the force of the language which he used," but "every harsh word" that his letters to Emily contain becomes "in some sort, pleasant to his ear" (257, 261).

Trevelyan's increasing inability to gauge the "force" of his language indicates a measure of symbolic dissociation which becomes more pronounced upon his withdrawal to Casalunga. There he assumes rhetorical positions or "attitudes" of verbal address as highly stylized and artificial as any that he adopts in bodily posture. But in contrast to those manifestly melancholic corporal "attitudes" he strikes, the verbal roles he adopts are recurrently presented as "attempt[s] at joviality" or "high-flown spirit," which, ironically, serve better to underscore the man's genuine despair (805, 871). Trevelyan's "affected air of ease and [his] would-be cynicism" (868) are "painful" to those who witness it, as the narrator notes:

> This attempt at satire, so fatous, so plain, so false, together with the would-be jaunty manner of the speaker, who, however, failed repeatedly in his utterances from sheer physical exhaustion, was excessively painful to Stanbury.   (870)

The dislocation between the intended style and import of Trevelyan's speech and its actual tormented delivery creates a "painful" effect similar to that of the speech of the depressive patients described by Kristeva, the meaning of whose words, she observes, typically "seems secondary, frozen, somewhat removed from the head and body of the person who is speaking": it is a sort of "artificial, unbelievable language, cut out of the painful background that is not accessible to any signifier and that intonation alone, intermittently, succeeds in inflecting" (*Black Sun*, 43, 44). Like the "gaudy" Italian style of dress he drapes over his feeble frame (873), the pseudo-stoical style of address Trevelyan assumes is glaringly foreign, ex-centric to himself. And in the schism thus opened between the speaking being and his speech, one perceives something akin to that "speech of the depressed" which is like "an alien skin": for "melancholy persons are foreigners in their maternal tongue" (Kristeva, *Black Sun* 53).

Not only do other characters remain unconvinced by the artificial language Trevelyan comes to speak, deeming him "not responsible for his expressions" (806), but the narrator also suggests a more serious symbolic breakdown when he intimates that Trevelyan himself fails to believe in the words he speaks. Drawn compulsively toward "elements of fiction and game-playing" in his discourse, Trollope's protagonist comes to "speak at a level of parareality at odds with [his] authentic beliefs and feelings," as Rowland McMaster suggests (197, 202). Indeed, the ever-escalating incongruity between Trevelyan's inner thoughts and his verbal expressions is an aspect of his mental pathology that the narrator does not fail to drive home. "In the sorrows which had come upon him in his unsuccessful struggle" with Emily, as he comments of Louis at one point, "his mind had wavered so frequently, that his spoken words were no true indicators of his thoughts; and in all his arguments, he failed to express either his convictions or his desires" (743). The precise nature of the "conviction" Trevelyan fails to express is later elaborated by the narrator. Though Trevelyan "considered himself to have been so injured by the world, to have been the victim of so cruel a conspiracy,"

> through it all, there was something approaching to a conviction that he had brought his misery upon himself by being unlike to other men. . . . When he was alone his reflections concerning his wife were much juster than were his words when he spoke either with her, or to others, of her conduct. (786–87)

In other words, at some deep level of his being, the husband of *He Knew He Was Right* knows he is wrong, and, as the narrator writes, "acknowledged to himself that [Emily's] conduct had been the result of his own moody temperament" (787).

Trevelyan may sense that he is, in the final analysis, at fault in his marital dispute, but as the narrator observes:

> He could not say that he had been wrong. He could not even think that he had been wrong as to the cause of the great quarrel. He was one so miserable and so unfortunate—so he thought—that even in doing right he had fallen into perdition. (787)

On the one hand, Trevelyan's inability to express or even to "think that he had been wrong" in the face of a simultaneous "conviction" that, nevertheless, he has somehow erred may be simply attributed to the force of insane obstinacy. But in another sense, if Trevelyan cannot verbalize, or even mentally represent to himself, the essence of his contradictory "conviction" of his wrongfulness, it is perhaps because that "conviction" is not something that he intellectually knows, but rather something that he simply feels, like a mood, at the more inexplicable semiotic level of drives and instincts, as a sort of bodily intuition within his gut. That is to say, the inexpressible contradiction Trevelyan senses within himself may be a knowledge of guilt experienced at the more archaic cognitive level of a "preverbal self-sensuality" (Kristeva, *Black Sun* 205): as a form of knowledge that "approaches" but does not quite attain the level of articulate signification, and more properly belongs to the semiotic sphere of the body.

At any rate, to the extent that at bottom Trevelyan is unbelieving in the worst calumny he speaks against Emily, his mental alienation reflects an element of the "empty speech" characteristic of melancholics. "Empty speech," in Kristeva's sense of the term, refers to signifiers which, "while they have a signification in themselves, . . . are experienced by the subject as *empty* . . . because they are not bound to semiotic imprints (drive-related representatives and affect representations)" (*Black Sun* 52). Trevelyan's "hard words" against Emily, conflicting with his "much juster" unstated estimates of her conduct, are likewise "empty" words which he speaks, but does not in truth believe, belying as they do the "semiotic imprint" of his innermost sense of Emily's essential innocence. Kristeva contends that when the "archaic psychic inscriptions" of the semiotic and affective realms are thus divorced from speech, "they give rise to acting out, which replaces language in depressive persons" (*Black Sun* 52).

The substantial degree to which representational modes of "acting out" come to supplement, if not entirely "replace," language for Trollope's melancholy man is manifest by his increasingly frequent recourse to "expressive" bodily postures, as well as by his progressively marked lapses into "motionless" and "speechless" states of "half-dreaming . . . vacancy" (786, 881). But Trollope reserves the most climactic instance of such body language for the penultimate scene of Trevelyan's "Acquitt[al]" of Emily (ch. 98). "Can you say one word for your wife, dear, dear, dearest husband?" Emily begins and the dying Trevelyan responds:

> "What word?"
> "I have not been a harlot to you;—have I?"
> "What name is that?"
> "But what a thing, Louis! Kiss my hand, Louis, if you believe me." And very gently she laid the tips of her fingers on his lips. For a moment or two she waited, and the kiss did not come. Would he spare her in this the last moment left to him either for justice or for mercy? For a moment or two the bitterness of her despair was almost unendurable. . . . But at length the lips moved, and with struggling ear she could hear the sound of the tongue within, and the verdict of the dying man had been given in her favour. He never spoke a word more either to annul it or enforce it.   (927)

What is the status of the "verdict" thus given? The narrator's comment that "[Trevelyan] never spoke a word more either to annul it or enforce it" suggests that Louis has summoned the strength to articulate a faintly audible verbal rejoinder. But the nature of Trevelyan's acquittal is inherently ambiguous. What Emily finally requests of Trevelyan is after all not a word, but the gesture of a kiss. And it is in the form of a kiss that the narrator subsequently characterizes Trevelyan's deathbed "reparation": "With that slight touch of his dry fevered lips he had made the assertion on which was to depend the future peace and comfort of the woman whom he had so cruelly misused" (928). Trollope thus unsettles our certainty whether "the sound" formed by "the tongue within" actually amounts to anything more than the inarticulate raspings of the "slight touch" of a kiss: whether any "real" word in fact escapes those 'dry fevered lips," never mind the ones Emily "almost" deludes herself into believing she has heard, after the fact (928).[24]

Left wavering equivocally somewhere between the sound of speech and that of the touch of lip and tongue to flesh, the gesture that constitutes Trevelyan's ultimate pledge of faith in Emily aptly consolidates the trend of symbolic alienation and impairment that attends his melancholy decline. For although it must also be understood in the context of an expiration of physical strength, Trevelyan's struggle to symbolize that "one word" which Emily initially requests presents a concrete narrative instance of a representation that is in itself "insufficiently stabilized to coagulate" into a sign (to re-echo Kristeva), rather like the "fluctuating energy traces" of melancholy affect. Suggesting as it does both a signal kiss and a linguistic signifier, the scene of acquittal "acts out" the final extent of a melancholic regression from the order of language to a "discursive strateg[y] working at the intersection of affective and linguistic inscriptions, at the intersection of the semiotic and the symbolic" (Kristeva, *Black Sun* 52–53).

Poised ultimately at the threshold of linguistic and corporal modalities of representation. Trevelyan's malady precludes the most extreme fate of the severe melancholic in life, the total asymbolia of a wholly blank and mute meaninglessness. And yet the clinical culmination of melancholia in complete asymbolia is nevertheless worth a final pause in comparison to the fictional body of melancholy which this essay has explored. "To transpose," Kristeva notes, "corresponds to the Greek *metaphorein*, to transport; language is, from the start, a translation" (*Black Sun* 41). In actual melancholy disorders, it is this native gift of translatability, this rhetorical capacity for metaphor, which is steadily diminished, and in the worst instances entirely abolished. "Melancholia then ends up in asymbolia, in loss of meaning," Kristeva emphasizes: "if I am no longer capable of translating or metaphorizing, I become silent and I die" (*Black Sun* 42). In other words, metaphor and metonymy, the two active principles of the substitution and replacement of terms, begin to falter with the death of desire and energy in melancholia, and end, in a state of signifying paralysis, where melancholy reigns absolute.

This semiotic phenomenon perhaps casts a new relevance on the rich meta-phoricity of the melancholy body in literary representations and psychoana-lytic discourse. For it may suggest that the creative forces giving rise to the literature of melancholy impart to it a certain therapeutic potential, a potential in fact perceived by writers from Burton to Kristeva herself. Burton, who compares himself to a physician bleeding melancholy readers of their ill humors, quite clearly conceives of his anatomical exercise as a form of antidote (104). More recently, Kristeva has referred to creative art as an "antidepressant" whose "triumph over melancholy" consists in its ability to transpose and "stag[e]" affects through the "construction of a symbolic object'("Melancholy Imaginary" 116). Psychoanalysis, figuratively pre-sented in *Black Sun* as helping to effect a sort of symbolic skin graft by which melancholics can reclaim the "alien skin" of their native tongue (52–53), is similarly upheld by her as a "counterdepressant" (1–32).

Even as it reproduces the melancholy body, the language of literature and psychoanalysis therefore attests in some sense to the power of translation—the power to generate or construct meanings—which precludes the silent hope-lessness of the subjective melancholic position in actuality. In this respect, to attempt the representation of melancholy is perhaps always implicitly to resist or counter "the symbolic abdication that is germane to depression" (Kristeva, *Black Sun* 40). Writing about melancholy, as Kristeva contends, "causes the affect to slip into the effect": "at the boundaries of emotion and action, writing comes into being only through the moment of the negation of the [melancholy] affect so that the effectiveness of signs might be born" (*Black Sun* 217). And to this extent, Trollope's literary creation too can be seen to constitute not only a "faithful semiological representation of the [melancholy] subject's battle with symbolic collapse," but also a kind of "therapeutic device" which "possesses a real and imaginary effective-ness"(*Black Sun* 24). In *He Knew He Was Right*, Trollope simultaneously writes about the melancholy body and against it. *Contra* the body of melan-choly stands the textual body: a body translated against the very grain of the silent black humor it so deftly anatomizes; against a pain so numbingly profound that it subsumes and exhausts even the smallest possibilities of metaphor.

NOTES

1. See for example Jackson 384.
2. These were aligned by Esquirol with the intellect but by followers such as Étienne Georget with the faculty of the will. See Goldstein 177.

3. Hence the British alienist Forbes Winslow: "Melancholics are often monomaniacs, that is to say, insane upon one subject. The mind is absorbed by one predominating idea to the exclusion of all else" (46).

4. Burton defines the overriding passion of such a species of melancholy "to be a certain suspicion which the Lover hath of the party he chiefly loveth, lest he or she should be enamoured of another: or any eager desire to enjoy some beauty alone, to have it proper to himself only: a fear or doubt, lest any foreigner should participate or share with him in his love" (821). Whereas species of head, body, and windy melancholy are organically defined, the forms of disorder described in the third part of Burton's book, Love-Melancholy, Jealous Melancholy, and Religious Melancholy, are based on emotional or psychological distinctions.

5. My thanks to Juliet McMaster for pointing out the connection between Trollope's landscape imagery and the colors of love melancholy, and for referring me to Shakespeare's play.

6. In iconographic terms, Dürer's *Melancholia* (1514), which depicts a pair of scales balanced directly above the head of a drooping cherub, is an example which comes to mind.

7. As his title "Trollope's Metonymies," indicates, Riffaterre's main concern is with the larger question of Trollope's use of metonymy in general, and particularly with its function and effect in the context of Trollopian realism.

8. Aunt Stanbury's words cited here actually refer to Camilla French's "bandbox," but since elder sister Arabella clearly sustains the larger "edifice" of the two, I feel justified in making the substitution.

9. See also Kristeva, *In the Beginning Was Love*: "Christ's passion brings into play . . . primitive layers of the psyche; it . . . reveals a fundamenal depression (a narcissistic wound or reversed hatred) that conditions access to human language" (43).

10. Incidentally, the arid hilltop of Casalunga furnishes an appropriate site for Trevelyan's supreme surrender of the son, his own Golgotha as it were. For as Georges Mounin observes of the Hebrew term: "Golgotha designates perhaps no more than a rounded hill, cleared of trees, of a sort commonly found on the shores of the Mediterranean and which are often called 'Bald Hill' " (130).

11. I allude in particular to Holbein's diptych "Christ as the Man of Sorrows" (1519) and "The Virgin as the Mater Dolorosa," briefly discussed by Kristeva in her chapter "Holbein's Dead Christ," in *Black Sun*, 106–38.

12. See the editor's note to *On Metapsychology* (262).

13. In *Mad Humanity* Forbes Winslow offers the following observation on mind-body influence in melancholy, a virtual textbook description of Trevelyan's case itself: "[The] whole symptoms [of melancholics are] depression, suspicion, suicidal tendencies, and a general mistrust of those near and dear to them, with frequent ideas of persecution. This is accompanied by one or more delusions. The bodily health of the patient frequently gives way in consequence of the continued anxiety and restlessness, and many sleepless and agitated nights" (46–47).

14. According to Maudsley, this was a preeminent sign of forms of masculine "insanity of jealousy." "An insanely jealous husband might plead excuse for doubting the fidelity of his wife," he states, but "[a] curious proof that the delusion is not the belief of his whole mind, but something which at bottom he believes but partly," is that he does not take legal steps "to discard his wife, as a sane husband might be expected to do." Instead, he "pesters her with reproaches for

her sin, lectures on its enormity, appeals to her conscience, and [makes] importunate entreaties to confess." "His keenest grievance seems to be," Maudsley concludes, "that she wil not make a clean breast of it; if only she would confess he would forgive her and say no more, he protests" (*Pathology of Mind* 326).

15. For passages pertaining to the respective "perversity" of these characters, see for example ch. 22, 186; ch. 13, 118; and ch. 20, 191.

16. "One should not forget," as Kristeva remarks, "that a whole ascetic, martyrizing, and sacrificial Christian tradition has magnified the victimized aspect of [Christ's] offering by eroticizing both pain and suffering, physical as well as mental, as much as possible" (*Black Sun* 131).

17. On the close connections between this genre and the tradition of melancholy, see Lyons 44.

18. According to Burton, Hippocrates "in his book of Melancholy" compared burning coal to the melancholy humor (152).

19. Kristeva paraphrases the dynamics of identification at stake in melancholy patients thus: " 'I love that object', is what that person seems to say about the lost object, 'but even more so I hate it; because I love it, and in order not to lose it, I imbed it in myself; but because I hate it, that other within myself is a bad self, I am bad, I am nonexistence, I shall kill myself' " (*Black Sun* 11).

20. It may well be that Trollope's gradual insights to the abidingly and inherently aggressive underside of Trevelyan's sorrow account for the apparent loss of narratorial sympathy—particularly the narrator's astonishingly "hard words" in the moment after Trevelyan's death (ch. 99, 928)—to which critics such as Simon Gatrell have called attention.

21. See also Kristeva, "Melancholy Imaginary" 107–08.

22. It should be noted here that in contrast to Freud's concept of a neurotic melancholy complex, Kristeva focuses on a potentially psychotic modality of sorrow that is "the most archaic expression of a narcissistic wound, unable to be symbolized or named" because it occurs at a stage of psychosexual development precisely prior to language acquisition ("Melancholy Imaginary" 106–07) and the emergence of a distinct and separate self (*Black Sun* 182–83). Overly simplified, Kristeva's melancholy "wound" consists of a form of "impossible mourning" for the "real object" or maternal "Thing" inevitably lost at the point of the child's induction into the paternal realm of symbolic substitutions. It arises, she speculates, as a result of a sort of pathologic double disavowal: a denial or suspension of the negation of (maternal) object loss necessary for "every 'normal' speaker" to take the artifice of signs seriously (*Black Sun* 43–44). While Kristeva stresses that both the neurotic melancholic and the psychotic "narcissistic depressive" have a "common experience of object loss and of a modification of signifying bonds" (*Black Sun* 10), the latter is distinguished by having a pathology originating at a point logically anterior to the establishment of libidinal object relations, and does not hide an aggression against the lost object: "For this type of narcissistic depressive, sorrow is in reality his only object; more exactly, it constitutes a substitute object to which he clings, cultivating it and cherishing it, for lack of any other" ("Melancholy Imaginary" 106–07).

23. In "The Curse of Words in *He Knew He Was Right*," Rowland McMaster has similarly examined "the rift between language and reality" in Trollope's novel (197). The characters' fascination with preformed linguistic and aesthetic constructs, he shows, works to supplant or "displace reality" and effectively bar the expression of inner convictions, "authentic beliefs and feelings" (198, 202).

However, where McMaster is concerned to demonstrate "a general linguistic malaise, extreme in the Trevelyans but evident in many other characters" as well (200–01), my focus falls more exclusively on Trevelyan's linguistic regression and its relation to melancholic disorders.

24. In this regard, the final scene of Trevelyan's acquittal of Emily comes as something of a dramatically intensified replay of a proleptic moment early in the quarrel, when "it was almost on [Trevelyan's] tongue to beg her pardon, to acknowledge that he had made a mistake"—"almost," but not quite (53).

WORKS CITED

Barzilai, Shuli. "Borders of Language: Kristeva's Critique of Lacan." *PMLA* 106 (1991): 297–305.

Burton, Robert. *The Anatomy of Melancholy*. Ed. Floyd Dell and Paul Jordan-Smith. New York: Tudor, 1955.

Freud, Sigmund. "Mourning and Melancholia." *On Metapsychology: The Theory of Psychoanalysis*. Trans. James Strachey. Ed. Angela Richards. Vol. 11 of the Pelican Freud Library. Harmondsworth: Pelican, 1984. 245–68.

Gatrell, Simon. "Jealousy, Mastery, Love, and Madness: A Brief Reading of *He Knew He Was Right*." *Anthony Trollope*. Ed. Tony Bareham. London: Vision, 1980. 95–115.

Gellert Lyons, Bridget. *Voices of Melancholy: Studies in Literary Treatments of Melancholy in Renaissance England*. London: Routledge, 1971.

Gilman, Sander. *Disease and Representation: Images of Illness from Madness to AIDS*. Ithaca: Cornell UP, 1988.

Goldstein, Jan. *Console and Classify: The French Psychiatric Profession in the Nineteenth Century*. Cambridge: Cambridge UP, 1987.

Haslam, John. *Observations on Madness and Melancholy, including Practical Remarks on Those Diseases*. London: Hayden, 1809.

Jackson, Stanley. *Melancholia and Depression: From Hippocratic Times to Modern Times*. New Haven: Yale UP, 1986.

Kristeva. Julia. *Black Sun: Depression and Melancholia*. Trans. Leon S. Roudiez. New York: Columbia UP, 1989.

———. "On the Melancholy Imaginary." Trans. Louise Burchill. *Discourse in Psychoanalysis and Literature*. Ed. Shlomith Rimmon-Kenan. New York: Methuen, 1987. 104–23.

———. *In the Beginning Was Love: Psychoanalysis and Faith*. Trans. Arthur Goldhammer. New York: Columbia UP, 1987.

Lyons, Bridget Gellert. *Voices of Melancholy: Studies in Literary Treatments of Melancholy in Renaissance England.* London: Routledge, 1971.

Maudsley, Henry. *The Physiology and Pathology of Mind.* London: Macmillan, 1867.

———. *The Pathology of Mind: A Study of Its Distempers, Deformities, and Disorders.* London: Macmillan, 1895.

McMaster, Rowland. "The Curse of Words in *He Knew He Was Right.*' *The Novel From Sterne to James: Essays on the Relation of Literature to Life.* By Juliet McMaster and Rowland McMaster. London: Macmillan, 1981. 195–212.

Mounin, Georges. "Iconography and Semiology: Representations of the Crucifixion." *Semiotic Praxis: Studies in the Pertinence and in the Means of Expression and Communication.* New York: Plenum, 1985. 127–34.

Riffaterre, Michael. "Trollope's Metonymies." *Nineteenth-Century Fiction* 37 (1982): 272–92.

Sutherland, John. Introduction. *He Knew He Was Right.* Oxford: Oxford UP, 1985. vii–xxiii.

Trollope, Anthony. *He Knew He Was Right.* Ed. John Sutherland. Oxford: Oxford UP, 1985.

———. *An Autobiography.* Ed. Michael Sadleir and Frederick Page. Introduction by P. D. Edwards. Oxford: Oxford UP, 1980.

Winslow, L. Forbes. *Mad Humanity: Its Forms, Apparent and Obscure.* London: Pearson, 1898.

"The Masquerade of Existence":
Thackeray's Theatricality

Alison Byerly

In a short essay written for *Fraser's Magazine* in 1840, William Thackeray described his reaction to the public execution of the murderer Courvoisier. While Thackeray begins the essay with the neutral intention of seeing "the effect on the public mind of an execution" (419), the structure of "Going to See a Man Hanged" reproduces Thackeray's own progression from detached interest to guilty horror as he watches the execution and, more importantly, watches the crowd watching the execution. Thackeray gradually distances himself from the reaction of the crowd, aligning himself instead with the murderer-victim. In the end he is less horrified by Courvoisier's crime than by its official reenactment: "I fully confess that I came away down Snow Hill that morning with a disgust for murder, but it was for *the murder I saw done*" (3:204). The sense of complicity evident in this "confession," I will argue, anticipates the complex attitude towards his own art that informs his fiction, particularly *Vanity Fair*.

The obsessive replication of arts associated with Becky Sharp—visual art, music, theater—underscores the false aestheticism of her self-presentation. And yet, Thackeray's uneasy recognition of his similar role as a paid public performer is reflected in the famous theatrical metaphor he used to describe his project in the novel's preface, "Before the Curtain." In a letter to G. H. Lewes, Thackeray defended the "dismal roguery" of *Vanity Fair* by claiming: "my object is to make every body engaged, engaged in the pursuit of Vanity."[1] Thackeray's fiction posits a reader who is not a mere spectator, but an accomplice to the vagaries of the world he describes. The effect of Thackeray's relentless emphasis on the theatricality of social life is in fact the opposite of "theatrical." Thackeray uses the idea of theatricality to generate a critique of art that, paradoxically, is central to his realism.

Critics have disagreed about the extent to which *Vanity Fair* can be considerd metafictional, and whether or not its aesthetic self-consciousness contributes to its "realism." Robert Alter sees self-conscious devices like the puppet-show metaphor as "discontinuous, incomplete," and "inconsistent," claiming that the "underlying conception of the novel is realist in the central nineteenth-century manner" (116, 136). Wolfgang Iser, on the other hand, sees not the subject but the mode of presentation as realist, suggesting that *Vanity Fair* does not present "social reality": instead, it presents "the way in which such reality can be experienced" (113). *Vanity Fair* seems to fit Patricia Waugh's definition of a metafictional novel as one "constructed on the principle of a fundamental and sustained opposition: the construction of a fictional illusion (as in traditional realism) and the laying bare of that illusion" (6). For Thackeray, however, laying bare the illusion does not produce a revelation that the novel is, after all, fiction, and not the real world. It constitutes an assertion that the real world is in many ways like fiction, and that the difference between *Vanity Fair* and the society it describes is one of material embodiment rather than ontological status.[2] Thackeray uses the idea of theatricality to dramatize the similarity between the cultural constructs that make up his novel and the cultural constructs that make up what we call "reality."

"Going to See a Man Hanged" begins in a tone of innocent curiosity. Thackeray's description, as he starts his excursion to Newgate, of the "white pure smoke" of his friend's cigar, the bright green trees, the fresh air, and the streets so "cool and clean" that "they would not soil a lady's white satin shoes," creates an atmosphere of freshness and purity (*Works* 26:420). But the implication of the spectator in the sight he witnesses is signalled early in the essay by the sudden breakdown of Thackeray's descriptive skills when faced with the gallows. He writes: "Before us lies Newgate Prison; but something a great deal more awful to look at, which seizes the eye at once, and makes the heart beat, is　　　　　" (3:192). The text is suddenly interrupted by a picture of the gallows—not an elaborate sketch, like those of Thackeray's novels and many other essays, but a dark, geometric blot that arrests the reader's eye just as its original had arrested Thackeray's. Thackeray's reproduction of his own visual shock brings us into the text with him. The gallows is indecipherable, unrepresentable, unnamable: it can be defined only by its anticipated function. "There it stands black and ready, jutting out from a little door in the prison." Thackeray cannot describe it, only describe "our" reaction to it. "As *you* see it, *you* feel a kind of dumb electric shock, which causes one to . . . gasp for breath. The shock is over in a second; and presently *you* examine the object before you with a certain feeling of complacent curiosity . . ." (3:192, italics added).

Thackeray soon recovers from this shock, however, and his description of the crowd's "festive" mood (3:196) makes explicit the theatricality of the spectacle: "We were all . . . in just such a frame of mind as men are in when they are squeezing at the pit-door of a play, or pushing for a review or a Lord Mayor's show" (3:199). At this moment, Thackeray's inclusive "we" acknowledges his own participation in the crowd's excitement. But he must distance himself from this attitude in order to evaluate the spectacle, and his evaluation is embodied in a series of novelistic questions: "How does an individual man feel under it? In what way does he observe it,—how does he view all the phenomena connected with it,—what induces him, in the first instance, to go and see it,—and how has he moved by it afterwards?" (3:201–02) Thackeray decides that the best answer is a personal one: "The writer has discarded the magazine 'We' altogether, and spoken face to face with the reader, recording every one of the impressions felt by him as honestly as he could" (3:202). He no longer takes refuge in the anonymity of the crowd, but speaks as an individual, "honestly" confessing his sense of complicity in this "murder":

> I must confess, then, . . . that the sight has left on my mind an extraordinary feeling of terror and shame. It seems to me that I have been abetting an act of frightful wickedness and violence, performed by a set of men against one of their fellows; and I pray God it may soon by out of the power of any man in England to witness such a hideous and degrading sight. (3:202)

Thackeray's horror here seems directed, not simply at the act itself, but at this "sight," the "witnessing" of which transforms the crowd from spectators into legal accessories. In fact, Thackeray himself did *not* see this sight. He is unable even to watch, let alone describe, the event that he is engaged in representing: "I am not ashamed to say that I could look no more, but shut my eyes as the last dreadful act was going on . . ." (3:201) Thackeray's refusal to be coerced by the seductive theatricality of the spectacle would become the foundation of his narrative style in *Vanity Fair*.

The guilt that Thackeray feels at his participation in this spectacle is intensified by his sympathetic identification with Courvoisier himself. The night before the execution, he tells us, he lay awake imagining Courvoisier's thoughts, and attempting to bring them into alignment with his own experience: "I could not help thinking, as each clock sounded, what is *he* doing now? has *he* heard it in his little room in Newgate yonder?'' Significantly, Thackeray's recreation of the murderer's final hours (retroactively derived from newspaper accounts) depicts him feverishly *writing*.

Thackeray uses Courvoisier's written account of his crimes as the most damning evidence against his accusers. The hypocrisy of the government's pretended interest in the sinner's repentence is exposed by the patent coercion involved in the production of the various confessional documents released to the public: ''Were ever letters more painful to read? . . . it is evidently the writing of a mad, distracted man. The horrid gallows is perpetually before him . . . Clergymen are with him ceaselessly; religious tracts are forced into his hands'' (3:203–04). Thackeray recognizes the inauthenticity of the voice that Courvoisier assumes: ''See the Scripture phrases brought in now and anon; the peculiar terms of tract-phraseology . . . one knows too well how such language is learned,—imitated from the priest at the bedside, eagerly seized and appropriated, and confounded by the poor prisoner'' (3:204). The government's interest in Courvoisier's repentance is merely a show; it provides church services and clergymen, but insists that his soul ''be ready by Monday morning'' (3:203). The prisoner's confession is solicited in order that it may be circulated to the public. Foucault points out, in reference to French criminal procedures, that ''through the confession, the accused himself took part in the ritual of producing penal truth'' (38). Courvoisier is not an author, but an actor, a puppet; his account is not really his own. His ''life'' has been taken away, figuratively as well as literally.

The objects of Thackeray's satire in this essay are not the callous spectators who ''partake of this hideous debauchery, which is more exciting than sleep, or than wine, or the last new ballet, or any other amusement they can have'' (3:202). Thackeray goes out of his way to praise the ''good sense'' and ''sound humour'' of the people who surround him (3:195), claiming that he has ''never yet . . . been in an English mob, without . . . wonder at the vigorous, orderly good sense and intelligence of the people'' (3:196). His anger is directed against the government that has turned this solemn occasion into a spectacle that is at once stimulating and stupefying.

John Bender has pointed out that the architecture of New Newgate added to the theatricality of executions, which were ''delimited into illusionistic drama by the visual imagery of the new setting . . . any view of a hanged criminal had to include the consideration of state authority present in this backdrop'' (246). The public staging of the execution relieves the spectator of responsibility by defining the hanging as entertainment rather than as a political act. The theatricality of this ''moral spectacle'' (3:205) transforms it from a real, physical action—the taking of a human life—into an edifying fiction. This fiction, authored by the state, serves to ratify the state's authority.

Thackeray seems to find his own account of the event as problematic as Courvoisier's: "If a public execution is beneficial—and beneficial it is, no doubt, or else the wise laws would not encourage forty thousand people to witness it—the next useful thing must be a full description of such a ceremony, and all its *entourages*, and to this end the above pages are offered to the reader" (3:201). But if, as Thackeray's irony suggest, a public execution is *not* beneficial, the reader must question the value of Thackeray's own representation of it.

The questions about the morality of representation evoked here can be extended to Thackeray's fiction. What is *Vanity Fair* itself but a "moral spectacle"? Like the government, the novelist performs an act of judgment founded on the assumption of omniscience, and creates a theatrical manifestation of power in order to maintain authority.[3] The narrative structure of *Vanity Fair*, like the social structure it criticizes, is constituted by a ritualized set of conventions. Why should the reader/spectator trust Thackeray's own dramatic representation, if such representations are inherently coercive?

The potential value of his own representations, Thackeray suggests, lies in their ability to restructure the relation between audience and spectacle. As we will see, his novels, essays, and illustrations consistently undermine the aesthetic distance that is the hallmark of the theatrical. We cannot watch Thackeray's puppet-show without feeling profoundly implicated in the world he creates. Although at the beginning of *Vanity Fair* he asks merely that we "step in for half an hour, and look at the performances" (2), by the end he has put us on stage. The sense of guilt Thackeray felt at watching a public execution is recreated in his readers, who are made to feel their own responsibility for the social conventions so relentlessly skewered in *Vanity Fair*.

While Thackeray had himself hoped at one time to be an artist, and produced many drawings to accompany his texts, his works form a sustained critique of the potential dangers of art. Critics have long recognized that Thackeray's works are full of "tensions pulling against his realist aesthetic" (Rawlins 59), and these are usually seen as forming a dichotomy in which "the aesthetic" is opposed to "the true." Juliet McMaster writes of the "incongruity between romance and reality, or between the pose and the truth" in *Vanity Fair* (32), while Jack Rawlins suggests that Thackeray was attracted both to "the delightful and aesthetically satisfying lie that is romance and the uncomfortable but unquestionably valuable truth that is fact" (59). The many forms of art that are represented in Thackeray's fiction seem to consist of aesthetically pleasing "poses" through which his characters attempt to obscure uncomfortable truths about themselves and their society.

In Thackeray's novels, essays, and illustrations, "art" often involves not faithful representation but deception. Different artistic media are all depicted as arenas in which people play out complex and dangerous games. Thackeray does not, however, suggest that art is by its nature false. On the contrary, it can stand as an expression of highest moral truth. But it can also embody the exploitative hypocrisy of the artist, falling into a false mode which can be characterized as "theatrical." Its facticity is signalled by a gap between the self's inner reality and its public representation. This gap is something that the novel of course, is uniquely qualified to depict: it can show both the "real" person and the face he or she presents to the world. According to Thackeray, that public face usually turns out to be a mask. *Vanity Fair* uses the idea of theatricality to create a multiplication of perspectives within the text that both exposes the inconsistencies of Thackeray's characters and destabilizes the position of his own audience.

The Victorian sense of theatricality as a form of deception was part of a long historical and philosophical tradition. While the nineteenth century saw a strong revival of interest in theatrical productions, it also produced an outpouring of criticism that warned against the theater's "immoral tendencies" (Cross 79). Jonas Barish points out that antitheatrical prejudice originates in the *Republic*, where Plato's argument against 'imitation" is marshalled with particular force against drama, "the mimetic art par excellence." In fact, Barish might be describing Victorian England when he outlines Plato's conflict: "a haunting acknowledgment of the potency of the theater [led] to an all the more stinging repudiation of it" (6).

Jean-Jacques Rousseau's restatement of Plato's ideas in his own antitheatrical writings gave them renewed vigor in the nineteenth century. Rousseau's critique of the theater, as David Marshall has pointed out, went beyond "standard warning about how plays arouse passions," offering "a more radical analysis of the pathos, subjectivity, and sympathy that take place in the playhouse" (Marshall 143). This acknowledgement of the role of *sympathy* in theatrical experience reminds us that theatricality can be seen as immoral even when a spectacle promotes proper moral feeling: the evil lies in the substitution of false sympathy directed at actors for active sympathy expressed towards real people. Rousseau suggested, in Lionel Trilling's words, that "theatrical art falsifies the self" and reduces its "autonomy" by promoting the impersonation of feeling (64–66).

The Victorian prejudice against acting is exemplified by the life of one of the century's greatest actresses. Fanny Kemble, raised in a family that included John Philip Kemble, Charles Kemble, and Sarah Siddons, abandoned her triumphant acting career to make a living by public readings of Shakespeare. She had always hated the theater, writing at the height of her fame: "How I do loathe the stage! these wretched, tawdry, glittering rags, flung over the breathing forms of ideal loveliness . . ." (*Journal* II: 16–17).[4] In an essay for *Cornhill Magazine* in 1863, Kemble distinguishes between "drama" and "theater," claiming that the "dramatic in human nature . . . has no relation . . . to that which imitates it, and is its theatrical reproduction; the dramatic is the *real*, of which the theatrical is the *false*" ("On the Stage" 733). The two are often confused, she admits, but while the "dramatic temperament" manifests itself in "a certain vivid simplicity of nature, which produces sincerity and vehemence of emotion and expression," the "theatrical element," she says, is characterized by "*consciousness*" (733). This distinction rests on the question of congruity between inner state and outer representation. Emotional behavior is "theatrical" only if it is an insincere representation of feeling that is deliberately directed at a spectator. In an essay on *Pendennis*, Edgar F. Harden suggests that theatricality can have a positive value: "to dramatize genuine feelings of sympathy and love, and thereby to bring a temporary end to human isolation" (93). But Thackeray seems to follow Kemble's distinction between the dramatic and the theatrical. In Thackeray's writings, "consciousness," that is, consciousness of being looked at, is the defining feature of "theatrical" art.

Thackeray depicts not just theater but all forms of art as potentially "theatrical" in their effects. Visual art seems to present a peculiar paradox in Thackeray's work. His novels are insistent warnings against the seductions of appearance; illustrations, as visual reproductions of aspect, would seem to belong to the realm of illusion. As we will see, Thackeray's illustrations depict his characters' entrapment in the theatrical shows of society. But the illustrations themselves reinforce the solidity of Thackeray's own illusion. As part of what Gerard Genette has called the "paratext" of a novel, they "surround and prolong" the text in order to "assure its presence in the world" (261). The paratext's "materialization" (263) of the text creates "a zone not just of transition, but of *transaction*" between author and public (261).

The type of "realism" that can be achieved by visual art is a constant theme of Thackeray's early art criticism, and the key characteristic of such realism is its antitheatricality. Thackeray's art criticism has generally been placed in the same class as his art, rather than ranked with his fiction and nonfiction prose.[5] Judith L. Fisher suggests that Thackeray subscribed to an "aesthetic of the mediocre," rejecting "high art," historical and neoclassical paintings, for mainstream, middle-class genre and landscape paintings.[6] Thackeray did prefer paintings on "realistic" subjects; as Robert A. Colby points out, his espousal of " 'pathetic and familiar' or 'bourgeois art' " was part of an effort to raise "not only the status of modern artists but also the prestige of the ordinary, the local, and the temporal as their proper subjects" (65). But realistic presentation was as important to Thackeray as realistic subject matter. Thackeray does not criticize all historical and neoclassical paintings, merely those that he describes, in "On the French School of Painting," as evincing "the bloated, unnatural, stilted, spouting, sham sublime, that our teachers have believed and tried to pass off as real, and which your humble servant and other anti-humbuggists should heartily . . . endeavour to pull down."[7] The "sham sublime" he attributes to certain French painters is typical of France, in which, he says elsewhere, everything seems to be "rant, tinsel, and stage-play. Sham liberty, sham monarchy, sham glory, sham justice" (42). However, English painters also indulge in this sort of dramatic posturing. Benjamin Haydon and John Martin, Thackeray says in "Picture Gossip" (1845), manifest what he calls the "theatrical heroic" (*Works* 25:321).

What Thackeray means by criticizing the "theatricality" of these paintings becomes clearer if we look at his description of a picture he admired. In an 1846 review of the Royal Academy Exhibition, Thackeray praises a Leslie painting depicting a scene from *Roderick Random*. Each of the people represented, Thackeray remarks,

> acts his part in the most admirable unconscious way—there is no attempt at a *pose* or a *tableau*, as in almost all pictures of figures where the actors are grouping themselves with an eye to the public, and, as it were, attitudinizing for our applause. In this picture everybody is busied, and perfectly naturally, with the scene, at which the spectator is admitted to look.[8]

The picture manifests a quality that art historian Michael Fried has called "absorption." According to Fried, eighteenth-century paintings depicting figures engrossed in activities like reading, listening, or sleeping sought to "neutralize the beholder's presence" (*Absorption and Theatricality* 68) by presenting an image of complete absorption. The "supreme fiction of the beholder's nonexistence" (108) allowed these absorptive paintings to create a more persuasive dramatic illusion than "theatrical" pictures. Fried points out that "the seeming obliviousness of one or more figures to everything but the objects of their absorption contributes to an overall impression of self-sufficiency and repleteness that functions as a decisive hallmark of the 'real' " (*Realism* 42–43). This sort of self-contained, unpretentious realism, the antithesis of the "theatrical heroic," defines Thackeray's ideal. Naturalistic depiction of individual details did not, in and of itself, satisfy him. He often made fun of such minute accuracy of execution, as in a supposed Academy review describing a picture by "Sandseer": "The bootjack is a miracle of art—had we not worn Bluchers, in good sooth we should have been tempted to try it; so marvellous is the illusion produced." (*Works* 8:468). The picture is all form, with no content. For Thackeray, realistic delineation of people and objects meant placing them in a realistic situation. Thackeray's art criticism recognizes that idealizing the world, making it seem heroic, is actually easier than reconciling unheroic reality with the demands of art.

The danger of idealization is that it can become an ingrained habit that renders the artist incapable of even perceiving, let alone depicting, the world as it really is. In spite of Thackeray's obvious affection for the artist's world, in *The Newcomes* he depicts Clive's artistic vision as a kind of practical blindness. One could argue that Clive's failure of vision is not an indictment of art because he is acknowledged to be a competent rather than a great artist. But even the artistic genius of the novel, J. J. Ridley, does not possess extraordinary insight into real life. J.J. is cut off from the real world, inhabiting instead the fictive realm depicted in Richard Doyle's frontispiece to the first volume, "J.J. in Dreamland."

The underlying cynicism of *The Newcomes*' portrayal of art is made explicit by Ethel's famous comparison of herself to a picture being sold at auction. When she attends a Water-Colour Exhibition with her dictatorial grandmother, Lady Kew, Ethel notices a green ticket in the corner of a painting and suggests to her grandmother that "young ladies in the world, when we are exhibiting, ought to have little green tickets pinned on our backs, with 'Sold' written on them; it would prevent trouble and any future haggling, you know" (I: 366).[9] Ethel ironically flaunts her own status as an item for sale by appearing at dinner with a green ticket pinned to her frock: "I am a *tableau-vivant*, Papa. I am No. 46 in the Exhibition of the Gallery of Painters in Watercolours" (I: 366). The theatrical image of the *tableau-vivant* shows Ethel's guilty recognition that while she is a commodity, she is also a self-created objet d'art; not a picture painted by another, but a living picture composed by herself.[10]

Becky Sharp is, like Ethel Newcome, a commodity, and she knows her own worth. Becky, however, is able to control her market value. Ethel's power is limited to creating herself as a picture; Becky is able to create pictures of others. Becky's drawings make her hypocrisy dramatically visible by satirizing the very people she pretends to value. She compliments Sir Pitt on his appearance in his diplomatic uniform, for example, then draws a caricature of him for Lord Steyne, who is "delighted with the accuracy of the resemblance" (377). Becky's caricatures render her malice utterly transparent, yet they alienate no one; in Vanity Fair, people are judged according to their entertainment value or financial worth, not their moral stature. Andrew Miller sees Becky as representing "the triumph of capitalist exchange; she expands and perfects the implicit principles of Vanity Fair" (1049). The products of her labor are emblematic of her own status as a commodity.

Becky's drawings link her with Thackeray, especially those drawings which are not merely described but reproduced in the text. Like Thackeray himself, she illustrates her letters, and the sketches which accompany her letter to Amelia are indistinguishable from the other illustrations in Vanity Fair. The first picture seems to proceed from the narrator's pen, and it is only when Becky announces her picture of the Miss Blackbrooks with a theatrical flourish—"Here they are. 'Tis the very image of them" (123)—that we are tempted retrospectively to credit Becky with the earlier drawing. The precise origin of the drawing that depicts Becky dancing with Rawdon Crawley, however remains ambiguous. Thackeray made no attempt to alter his style in order to distinguish "Becky" 's pictures from his own. The multiple perspectives created by this temporary diversion of authority reinforce Thackeray's emphasis on the reader/viewer's interpretive role. Becky's satiric drawings do present an accurate, if one-sided, depiction of her victims. Their deceptiveness resides not in the artworks themselves but in what they say about the artist. They are "true" as pictures of the pretensions of Sir Pitt and the Miss Blackbrooks, but "false" as signs of Becky's intimacy with her audience. Whatever fault they embody lies in the artist's use of them and her audience's interpretation of them. Thus our interpretation of them is rendered doubly difficult; our tendency to appreciate Becky's energy, wit, and irreverence is tempered by our desire to dissociate ourselves from the spectacle of her friends' ludicrous gullibility.

In Vanity Fair, art is the product of mercenary calculation rather than creative inspiration. Becky treats her artistic ability as an economic resource, using it to further her own interests. Amelia's pathetic attempts to do the same form one of the many points of contrast between the two women. Amelia would never think of merchandising her accomplishment covertly, as Becky does, yet her efforts to sell it openly meet with failure. At the height of her financial distress, Amelia buys a couple of Bristol boards, and "paints her very best upon them—a shepherd with a red waistcoat on one, and a pink face smiling in the midst of a pencil landscape—a shepherdess on the other, crossing a little bridge, with a little dog, nicely shaded." The shopkeeper to whom they are offered "can hardly hide the sneer with which he examines these feeble works of art" (622). While Thackeray's dismissive diminutives suggest that these picturesque scenes are artistically inferior to Becky's compositions, Amelia's main problem is that she is selling them in the wrong market. Becky's pictures probably wouldn't earn her a living, either—as an artist. But they contribute to her charms as a seductress, and help her to earn money at that vocation. Unlike Amelia, Becky understands which roles are open to women and which are not.

Musical talent, too, is a commodity, as Becky quickly perceives. When Miss Pinkerton wants her to teach the younger pupils music, Becky insists on being paid extra; later, she complains when Mrs. Bute Crawley tries to get free lessons out of her. The Romantic privileging of music as the purest expression of the authentic self is a subject for satire, as Thackeray shows the absurdity of believing that a song is anything but a theatrical performance. In Thackeray as in Jane Austen, music is an accomplishment whose chief utility lies in its value on the marriage mart. The mulatto heiress Miss Swartz's limited repertoire of three songs is one sign of her general unfitness to be the wife of George Osborne. Similarly, frequent references in *The Newcomes* to "Miss Rosey's five songs" shows how carefully Rosey Mackenzie has been coached for her attempt to capture Clive Newcome. A more accomplished performer, such as Blanche Amory, who sings like a siren (*Pendennis* II: 14), can not only charm but mesmerize her listeners.

Becky, of course, is frequently described and depicted as a siren, and she is able to lure both men and women with her songs. She wins the sympathy of Jos and Amelia Sedley by singing a touching ballad about an orphan. Thackeray not only describes the performance, he gives the text of the song (which he wrote for the purpose), inviting close attention to the disjunction between the heart-rending words and Becky's calculating performance (42). At Gaunt House, Becky is faced with an audience that includes the wife of Lord Steyne, her current admirer. She sings "religious songs of Mozart, which had been early favorites of Lady Steyne, and with such sweetness and tenderness that the lady lingering round the piano, sat down by its side, and listened until the tears rolled down her eyes.'' The songs remind Lady Steyne of the ''brief period of her happiness,'' her girlhood at the convent (619–20). Becky miraculously chooses songs which create a temporary female intimacy between herself and Lady Steyne. The songs stir deep and real emotions; Thackeray's description of Lady Steyne's momentary reverie, and her pathetic gratitude when her husband speaks a kind word to her, is one of the few genuinely moving moments in *Vanity Fair*. Again, the artistic performance itself is not at fault. Thackeray presents a spectacle that may be as appealing to the reader as to Becky's audience. But the contrast between Becky's singing and her actual capacity for sympathy is quickly undercut by the irony of Lord Steyne's repetition of his wife's comment that Becky sings ''like an angel'' (620). Certainly no one is as aware as he is of the inappropriateness of that simile. As Nina Auerbach has shown, Becky, like other Victorian heroines, is both angel and demon, possessing a transformative power that allows her to ''incarnate character itself'' (9). Like the novelist, she can assume many guises. Thackeray deftly separates Lady Steyne's response from our own, allowing us to resume our detached observation of Becky—after having been momentarily taken-in.

In the art of music as in drawing, Amelia is a feeble echo of Becky not simply because she lacks her skill but because she lacks her marketing savvy. She does not theatrically exploit her performances; in fact, they can hardly be considered performances at all, since they represent real, though shallow and sentimental, feelings. The sincerity of Amelia's feelings do not, however, win her Thackeray's approval. Her purely emotional response to music is as dangerous as Becky's utter lack of emotion. Dobbin persistently identifies Amelia with music, but the piano he buys for her is a symbol of their mutual delusion. She assumes that it comes from George Osborne, while Dobbin assumes that Amelia will recognize it as his own gift. In the ''Pumpernickel'' section of the novel, much is made of Amelia's enjoyment of opera. But, as Robert T. Bledsoe has pointed out, Amelia's reactions are based on her simplistic identification with various characters. Thus, she sees herself as the faithful Zerlina in *Don Giovanni*, and as Leonore, the constant wife of *Fidelio*. Thackeray suggests that the sincerity of Amelia's music masks a deeper self-deceit. While Becky's deliberate role-playing is part of a carefully crafted performance, Amelia's role-playing is unconscious.

As we have seen, visual art and music are both susceptible to ''theatrical'' presentation, though also capable of conveying truth. The potential for false-ness lies in the assumptions generated about the artist/performer's relation to his or her creation, rather than in the creation itself. The audience thus bears partial responsibility for the naivete about representation that allows them to be taken in by such performances. Theater itself poses more complex problems. Thackeray emphasizes the duplicity of theatrical representation in two ways: by showing the reality of theatrical life, and by showing the theatricality of real life. Thackeray's interest in the demystification of theater can be seen in his very first book, *Flore et Zephyr* (1836), a series of nine lithographic plates satirizing Didelot's ballet (*Works* 5: xlix–lvii). Many of the plates show the dancers backstage, engaged in such unromantic activities as flirting with admirers and taking pinches of snuff. These glimpses of theater life emphasize the distance between these ordinary people and the idealized characters they portray.

Becky Sharp's skill as an actress, as Martin Meisel has shown, is "a leading part of her character, associated with her vitality and power of fascination on the one hand, and with her moral dubiousness on the other" (Meisel 331–32). While we are seldom told what Becky is actually thinking and feeling, the theatrical metaphors that Thackeray uses to describe her behavior provide a model that allows us to interpret what we see: we know that her thoughts are likely to contravene her demeanor. Thus, when Amelia's and Becky's tearful parting is described as "a scene in which one person was in earnest and the other a perfect performer" (76), we read Becky's feelings as the precise opposite of her representation of them.

Becky's childhood gift for mimicry is used for entertainment rather than deception, but even then she directs her satire against conventional sentiment: the dolls given to her by Miss Pinkerton and Miss Jemmy become vehicles with which to ridicule them, as if Becky already understands that these material objects are symbols of the feminine role that Miss Pinkerton will attempt to impose on her. After her father abandons her to Miss Pinkerton, Becky perfects her acting skill: "she had not been much of a dissembler, until now her loneliness taught her to feign" (19). Her isolation engenders the imaginative construction of an alternative world that will allow her the freedom she desires.

Theatricality is such an accepted feature of society that Becky's open display of her talent for mimicry does not call her sincerity into question; "sincerity" is simply not an operative category of evaluation in Vanity Fair. Becky amuses Miss Crawley with her renditions of Old Sir Huddleston wheezing at dinner, and Sir Giles Wapshot drinking his soup (127). When Miss Crawley is ill, Becky provides a "perfect imitation" of Miss Briggs's grief: "Briggs's weeping snuffle, and her manner of using the handkerchief, were so completely rendered, that Miss Crawley became quite cheerful" (162).

After being subjected to Lady Southdown's ministrations, moral and medical, Becky adds her to the repertoire: "She put on a nightcap and gown. She preached a great sermon in the true serious manner: she lectured on the virtue of the medicine which she pretended to administer . . . 'Give us Lady Southdown and the black dose,' was a constant cry amongst the folks in Becky's little drawing-room in May Fair" (528). Becky's verbal caricatures, like her pictorial ones, do embody a kind of truth. They expose the hypocrisy of Miss Pinkerton's exploitative condescension, Briggs' servile grief, and Lady Southdown's manipulative piety. But they also provide direct evidence of her own hypocrisy to anyone who stops to consider that her knowledge of these people was obtained under a pretence of friendship that should call their own "friendship" with Becky into question. Thus, they are not false in and of themselves, as representations: they are *signs* of prior deception. The reader, too, is forced to confront the question of whether their value is invalidated by what might be called the inauthenticity of their production.

The difficulty of distinguishing between performance and reality is best exemplified by the complex chain of signification created by Becky's appearance in the role of Clytemnestra in the Gaunt House charades. The inhabitants of Vanity Fair are unable to recognize a performance when they see one: even when her friends know that Becky is acting, they still assume some congruence between her role and her self. Thus, the charade that Becky performs at Gaunt House does not disguise but in fact *reveals* a facet of her character that she would perhaps prefer to keep hidden. She plays the murderous queen Clytemnestra "so well, and with such ghastly truth, that the spectators were all dumb, until, with a burst, all of the lamps of the hall blazed out again, when everybody began to shout applause." The audience seems briefly to sense a similarity between performer and part. "By ————————, she'd do it too," Lord Steyne murmurs (646). Their reaction is in a sense a sign of aesthetic naivete in its presumption that Becky could not play the part so well unless it were somehow true to her character. And yet their instinctive reaction is truer than they know. Becky probably *would* do it.

Thackeray deliberately complicates matters by showing Becky, not "in character" as Clytemnestra, but in the moments after the charade, when she has resumed her former role, and is now the amateur actress Mrs. Rawdon Crawley, accepting applause for her performance. But this plate is labelled, not "Becky's triumph," but "The triumph of Clytemnestra"; Becky and Clytemnestra have become one. By thus blurring the distinction between them, Thackeray prepares us for a famously ambiguous later plate, "Becky's second appearance in the character of Clytemnestra,'' which shows her lurking behind a curtain, eavesdropping on the frightened Jos, apparently holding a vial of poison. We are never told whether Becky resembles Clytemnestra only in Jos Sedley's mind, or whether she really does transform the part into reality by murdering him.[11] The fitness of the role in which Becky has been cast remains ambiguous to us as well as to Jos' associates. By emblematizing society's perception of this assertive and opportunistic woman in the figure of Clytemnestra, Thackeray reminds us that we, too, participate in the distortions such categorization may create.

Becky's theatricality is at least in part a response to her uncertain social status. Her life itself is a sham, without substance; she has ''no ground to walk upon'' (601). As Lord Steyne points out, her life in high society is ultimately untenable because she lacks the material backing necessary to sustain the role she assumes. When Becky becomes bored, she trades her current part in for a new one; she cannot simply abandon acting. She says to herself, ''I wish I were out of it,'' but the only alternatives she can imagine are wildly different roles: ''I would rather be a parson's wife, and teach Sunday school than this; or a sargeant's lady and ride in the regimental wagon; or, oh, how much gayer it would be to wear spangles and trousers, and dance before a booth at a fair'' (638). In a sense, she longs for complete honesty: she would like to *play* a performer. The self she imagines is a free, androgynous, carnivalesque figure who would liberate her from the feminine roles to which she has been limited.

Thackeray forces the reader to recognize that theatricality is a particularly tempting mode of behavior for women, who are judged to an even greater extent than men by their compliance with social convention. The disjunction between an individual woman's desires and the role she must play in society teaches women that any relation between self and behavior is arbitrary. But she must be very skilled at dissimulation, because simplicity and sincerity are among the most highly prized female virtues: if she is caught in the act, and her theatricality is recognized, she will be punished for doing what she was trained to do.

In depicting feminine theatricality as the result of social conditioning, Thackeray countered a longstanding tradition of seeing theatricality as somehow natural to women. Theatricality represents a kind of false show that is historically associated with femininity.[12] While any form of theatricality was suspect, nothing was more dangerous than a woman who could act. In Thackeray's fiction, actresses are indeed very dangerous, but they do not act alone.

They are products of and participants in a social world where the accepted—indeed, the required—mode of behavior is theatrical.

Theatricality, it seems, both expresses and creates the performer's place in society. The social imperative underlying Becky's performances is emphasized by Thackeray's illustrations for *Vanity Fair*, which reveal not just Becky's theatricality but the theatricality of all social situations. Characters are shown in groups, performing to audiences within the picture. Although they depict theatricality, the illustrations themselves are in a sense "absorptive," to return to Fried's term; the characters are too busy posturing among themselves to show any awareness of us. By setting up a theatrical relation within each picture, Thackeray makes it clear that the staginess of certain poses reflects his characters' personalities, not simply the illustrator's style. He thus creates realistic sketches that catch their subjects as "spontaneous" moments (they do not know that we are watching them) while also showing how far removed from spontaneity their behavior is (they are conscious of being watched by others).

George Osborne is shown striking a pose in front of the other men, acting the role of a debonair, Don Juan officer (141, "Lieutenant Osborne and his ardent love-letters"); he himself, we are told, was "a great lover of the drama," and had performed in garrison theatricals (316). When Becky goes to the opera, she is acutely conscious of being looked at, and acts accordingly. Thackeray places her in a box that is framed by curtains, emphasizing the fact that she herself is on stage; meanwhile, one of her companions is busy with a glass, watching someone else (Fig. 1). The novel's final illustration shows Becky once again framed by curtains, as if in the booth of a puppet-show, an image that aligns the world of society with the world of Thackeray's novel by showing us Becky as an actress in Vanity Fair and Becky as a puppet in *Vanity Fair* (Fig. 2).

The performances that constitute social interaction in *Vanity Fair* are often defined by frames within the frames of the pictures as well as by the presence of internal spectators who watch the drama unfold. "Mr. Joseph entangled" (Fig. 3), for example, has George and Amelia peeking through a door at Becky and Jos. "A Family Party at Brighton" (Fig. 4) repeats the same scene, but with a different cast: Becky seduces George on a balcony, while Amelia and Rawdon watch anxiously from inside. These pictures recede in two directions, situating us as viewers in a strange space: we are like mirror images of the spectators we see. This double regression parallels Thackeray's narrative technique, which attempts to draw the reader into the text by "picturing" him, as the "lady correspondent" who doesn't care "a fig" for Amelia

Fig. 1

Fig. 2

Figure 3. Mr. Joseph entangled

Figure 4. A Family Party at Brighton

(131), or as "Jones, who reads this book at his Club," who is literally pictured (8). We are ourselves incorporated into the paratext of the novel.

The theatrical behavior that constitutes the texture of social intercourse in *Vanity Fair* is most obvious when it is associated with material gain as well as mere social ambition. Thackeray's depiction of "Miss Crawley's Affectionate Relatives" (Fig. 5) reveals that the "affection" of the rich old lady's relatives is all show. The perfect symmetricality of the arrangement, with the two girls extending their feet like dancers, suggests that this is a carefully choreographed performance. These illustrations reinforce the point that Thackeray makes again and again in *Vanity Fair*: that "social customs" are in fact theatrical gestures, utterly false in their relation to reality, and that they function as commodities in a society that values appearance over substance.

Thackeray's portrayal of the falseness of theatricality renders problematic his own status as *Vanity Fair*'s most prominent performer. In his preface to the finished novel he describes himself as "the Manager of the Performance," but the cover illustration for the monthly numbers of *Vanity Fair* shows the novelist taking a leading part: using a barrel as a stage, he lectures to the crowd. Thackeray says that "the moralist, who is holding forth on the cover" is "an accurate picture of your humble servant" (95); this "moralist," however, is dressed in the sort of jester costume Becky has in mind when she says that she would like to "wear spangles and trousers, and dance before a booth at a fair." Just as Thackeray found himself guiltily identifying with Courvoisier in his account of the execution, so the narrator aligns himself with his mercenary leading character. The narrator of *Vanity Fair* shares many points of resemblance with its unheroic heroine, including, as Barbara Hardy notes, the fact that he, too, performs for profit (72). Andrew Miller has suggested that "the cycle of deprivation and gain" resulting from Thackeray's loss of his patrimony led to social alienation and "characteristic self-objectification"; like the servants he depicts in his novels, Miller argues, Thackeray saw himself as a commodity (1045).

As we have seen, Thackeray and Becky are both artists skilled in the drawing of caricatures. They are both in a sense musicians; the apology which begins chapter VI, "I know that the tune I am piping is a mild one . . ." (60), is accompanied by a pictorial capital of the "piper" (Fig. 6) that anticipates Becky's appearance as a harp-playing siren a few chapters later (Fig. 7).[13] And, like Becky, who Lord Steyne calls "a splendid actress and manager" (663), the narrator combines performance with direction. His self-portrait as an unmasked harlequin (Fig. 8) reminds us that he, too, is an actor

Figure 5. Miss Crawley's affectionate relatives.

Fig. 6   Fig. 7

as well as a manager. Becky's appearance as a puppeteer (Fig. 9) prefigures
the narrator's depiction of his own "puppets" being shut up in their box
(Fig. 10), a simile Thackeray developed more fully in the added preface,
"Before the Curtain." Thackeray's sense of the narrator as performer seems
even more appropriate if we bear in mind the fact that Thackeray's novel,
especially in its original serialized version, was probably "performed"—read
aloud—in many homes.[14] How, then, does Thackeray's performance differ
from Becky's?

In spite of the profusion of theatrical metaphors Thackeray uses to describe
his project, Thackeray's relationship to his audience in *Vanity Fair* is not
"theatrical," according to the definition I have developed here. He does not
attempt to deceive his readers into substituting theatrical gestures for reality.
On the contrary, he tries to teach his readers how to look beyond the charade
to see what is real. Thackeray acknowledges that theatricality is an inevitable
part of social interaction. In "A Night's Pleasure—V.," part of his "Travels
in London" series, Thackeray uses the comic song of an amateur performer

Fig. 8

Fig. 9

Fig. 10

as an example of the many pretenses of human existence. Thackeray is impressed by the contrast between the young man's initially "rather sad countenance," and the "maniacal grin" he assumes during the performance of his piece, which he clearly does not enjoy (*Works* 9:431–33). This transformation is effected by the donning of a hat, which the young man uses as a prop to get himself into the proper spirit. Thackeray emphasizes the contrast in his before-and-after pictures of the young man, "Without his hat," and "In his comic hat." "O Grinsby," Thackeray moralizes, "what a number of people and things in this world so you represent!" (432) He goes on to ask:

> Who isn't like Grinsby in life? . . . When Bawler goes down to the House of Commons from a meeting with his creditors, and . . . becomes a patriot all of a sudden, and pours you out an intensely interesting speech upon the West Indies, or the Window Tax . . . When Tightrope, the celebrated literary genius, sits down to write . . . under the most miserable private circumstances, a brilliant funny article . . . when editors at their desks—forget their natural griefs, pleasures, opinions, to go through the business of life, the masquerade of existence, in what are they better than Grinsby yonder, who has similarly to perform his buffooning? (434)

Thackeray's list of "masqueraders" begins with deliberate hypocrites but ends with stoic sufferers who are in a sense "playing" themselves. Thackeray certainly knew what it was like to write "funny articles" under "miserable private circumstances." He acknowledges that sometimes the masquerade of existence is not a game undertaken for private pleasure but work required by the "business of life." His own masquerade was justified by his belief that he could teach an audience not to simply watch the show in detached amusement, but to understand their own complicity in the performance.

Thackeray's success in implicating the reader can be measured by the language of his early reviewers, who found themselves rather uncomfortable in the world of *Vanity Fair*. The novel has a "foul atmosphere," wrote Robert Bell in *Fraser's Magazine*; "we pant for a little clean air in this pestiferous region; we feel oppressed by the weight of these loaded vapours, this stifling malaria." John Forster had the same choking sensation: "we gasp for a more liberal alternation of refreshing breezes of unsophisticated honesty."[15] Like Thackeray at the execution of Courvoisier, it seems, his readers feel befouled by their sense of having participated in the spectacle they witnessed.

NOTES

1. *The Letters and Private Papers of William Makepeace Thackeray*, ed. Gordon Ray, II: 354. Hereafter cited as *Letters*.
2. This view is, I think, consistent with that proposed by Robert Siegle in *The Politics of Reflexivity*. He sees *Vanity Fair* as constituted by the same "networks of cultural conventions" as 'real' discourse. He notes that "even if one strives just to reflect reality, that reality is always assimilated to some form of verbal and conceptual stylization. Indeed, its 'realistic' force may well depend upon just how subtly it uses reigning stylization to make its material consistent with the larger context of assumptions to which they are related" (25).
3. I am indebted here to Catherine Gallagher's "The Duplicity of Doubling in *A Tale of Two Cities*." Gallagher suggests that three social phenomena—the English public execution, the French Revolution, and the crime of grave-robbing—function as analogues for narration in Dickens' novel, working to "suppress the fear that novelistic omniscience verges on the demonic" by providing alternative versions of "the will to omniscience" that make the novel seem restrained by contrast (127).
4. Joseph Litvak has recently compared Kemble's ambivalence about the theater to that of Charlotte Brontë. He suggests that Kemble's movement from acting to reading plays to writing about theater shows an effort to displace her anxiety about the medium. "In *Villette*, as in Kemble's *Records*, the theater and its metaphorical extension, theatricality, prove capable of arousing profoundly and intricately mixed feelings because of their own ideologically heterogeneous character, their availability to both authoritarian and subversive discourses" (80).

5. The most generous commentators suggest that "his contributions as a critic were distiguished by no extraordinary sensitivity or farsightedness" (Stetz 83), and that his "taste in art reflected Victorian sensibility . . . [which] helps to explain why his art criticism has suffered neglect" (Roberts 23).

6. Judith L. Fisher, "The Aesthetic of the Mediocre," 68–71. Of course, Thackeray's assertion, in "On the French School of Painting," that in his heart he is "fonder of pretty third-rate pictures than of your great thundering first-rates" has to be read in the context of his mock despair at being faced with nothing but pictures of murders and deluges, and his claim that such a concentration of sublimity constitutes too rich a diet (FS 63). Thackeray's suggestion that "ordinary men" like himself and his readers may be made uncomfortable by the sublime, and prefer "the pleasures of mediocrity" (FS 64), seems to show, in addition to some resentment at the excesses of the sublime, humorous resignation at the public taste which demands to be made happy and comfortable.

7. William Thackeray, *The Paris Sketch-Book*, Vol. 22 of the Centenary Biographical Edition of *The Words of William Makepeace Thackeray*, 26 vols. (London: 1910–11; rpt. 1962 AMS Press), 54. All subsequent references to Thackeray's works will refer to this edition unless otherwise noted, and will be cited by volume and page number in the text.

8. William Thackeray, "The Exhibition at the Royal Academy," *The Morning Chronicle*, 5 May 1846, rpt. in Ray, ed., *William Thackeray's Contributions to the Morning Chronicle* 145.

9. Robert A. Colby points out that this literalization of the idea of the "marriage mart" was a popular image. *Punch's Pocket Book for 1847* depicts "The Matrimonial Tattersall's," where prospective wives and husbands are sold. The cartoon includes a woman wearing a price tag marked £20,000 (372).

10. Judith Law Fisher makes this point in "Siren and Artist" (397). She argues further that both Clive Newcome and Arthur Pendennis resemble sirens like Becky Sharpe and Blanche Amory in their adaptation of their artistic aspirations to the demands of the marketplace. But in fact Clive's abandonment of grandiose historical paintings and Pendennis' substitution of journalism for epic poetry are ultimately seen not as false compromises made for economic gain, but as realistic acknowledgements of their own limitations. They are being true to themselves by modifying their aspirations.

11. For a detailed analysis of the Gaunt House charades, see Meisel, 333–38. Maria diBattista analyzes the way in whch they dramatize "classical and Freudian intuitions of cultural pathology" (diBattista 828).

12. In medieval literature, woman is, "by her secondary nature, automatically associated with artifice, decoration," and, by extension, with the deceptiveness of rhetorical ornamentation (Bloch 11–12), while, as Jacqueline Lichtenstein notes, ornamentation itself is easily transformed into "makeup, which conceals rather than elucidates truth" (78–79). The makeup of the actress seemed to ally her directly with the prostitute. Both were " 'public women' whose bodies and whose simulated emotions were the tools of their trade" (Auerbach, *Ellen Terry* 138–39). The female body itself was potentially deceptive, according to nineteenth-century medical theory; the "inherent duplicity of hysteria" made it especially difficult to treat, since it was "a disease whose symptoms could be feigned" (Poovey 153). It was impossible to tell an ill woman from an actress, hysteria from histrionics.

13. Some "illustrated" editions of *Vanity Fair* reproduce only selected full-page plates, or only the plates and the woodcuts, omitting the pictorial capitals. The

Oxford edition includes all illustrations, and, unlike many editions, locates the
woodcuts carefully in the text. Properly placed, the woodcuts leap off the page
to spontaneously reflect current action, as in the description of Becky's welcome
to George Osborne at Miss Crawley's. The sentence "Miss Sharp put out her
right forefinger— . . . and gave him a little nod, so cool and killing . . ." (172)
is broken in the middle by a picture of Becky extending her forefinger. The
illustration seems trivial and irrelevant when, as in some editions, it appears
several paragraphs before or after the event happens in the text.

14. For a discussion of the connection between reading aloud and theatricality, see
Alison Byerly, "From Schoolroom to Stage: Reading Aloud and the Domestica-
tion of Victorian Theater," *Culture and Education in Victorian England*, ed.
Patrick Scott and Pauline Fletcher (Lewisburg: Bucknell UP, 1990).

15. Robert Bell, from an anonymous review in *Fraser's Magazine*, September 1848,
reprinted in *The Critical Heritage* 65; John Forster, from a review in the *Examiner*, 22 July 1848, reprinted in *The Critical Heritage* 57. Such metaphors of
contagion may have sprung to mind because concern about pollution and disease
in London was at a peak at this time; 1848–49 saw one of the century's worst
cholera epidemics. See Luckin, *Pollution and Control*.

WORKS CITED

Auerbach, Nina. *Ellen Terry: Player in Her Time*. New York: W. W. Norton, 1987.

———. *Woman and the Demon: The Life of a Victorian Myth*. Cambridge: Harvard
UP, 1982.

Barish, Jonas. *The Antitheatrical Prejudice*. Berkeley: U of California P, 1981.

Bender, John. *Imagining the Penitentiary: Fiction and the Architecture of the Mind
in Eighteenth-Century England*. Chicago: U of Chicago P, 1987.

Bledsoe, Robert T. "*Vanity Fair* and Singing." *Studies in the Novel* 13 (1981):
51–63.

Bloch, R. Howard. "Medieval Misogyny." *Representations* 20 (1987): 1–24.

Canham, Stephen. "Art and the Illustration of *Vanity Fair* and *The Newcomes*."
Modern Language Quarterly 43 (1982): 43–66.

Colby, Robert. *Thackeray's Canvass of Humanity: An Author and His Public*. Columbus: Ohio UP, 1979.

Collins, Philip. *Thackeray: Interviews and Recollections*. 2 vols. New York: St.
Martin's, 1983.

Cross, Gilbert. *Next Week—'East Lynne': Domestic Drama in Performance
1820–1874*. Lewisburg: Bucknell UP, 1977.

DiBattista, Maria. "The Triumph of Clytemnestra: The Charades in *Vanity Fair*."
PMLA 95 (1980): 827–37.

Ferris, Ina. *William Makepeace Thackeray*. Boston: Twayne, 1983.

Fisher, Judith Law. "Siren and Artist: Contradiction in Thackeray's Aesthetic Ideal." *Nineteenth-Century Literature* 39 (1985): 392–419.

———. "The Aesthetic of the Mediocre: Thackeray and the Visual Arts." *Victorian Studies* 26 (1982): 65–82.

Fried, Michael. *Absorption and Theatricality: Painting and Beholder in the Age of Diderot*. Berkeley: U of California P, 1980.

———. *Realism, Writing, Disfiguration: On Thomas Eakins and Stephen Crane*. Chicago: U of Chicago P, 1987.

Gallagher, Catherine. "The Duplicity of Doubling in *A Tale of Two Cities*," *Dickens Studies Annual* 12 (1983): 125–45.

Harden, Edgar F. "Theatricality in *Pendennis*." *Ariel* 4:4 (1973): 74–94.

Hardy, Barbara. *The Exposure of Luxury: Radical Themes in Thackeray*. Pittsburgh: U of Pittsburgh P, 1972.

Kemble, Fanny. *Journal of Frances Anne Butler*. 2 vols. Philadelphia: Carey, Lea, and Blanchard, 1835.

———. "On the Stage." *Cornhill Magazine* Dec. 1863:733–37.

Levine, George. *The Realistic Imagination: English Fiction from Frankenstein to Lady Chatterley*. Chicago: U of Chicago P, 1981.

Lichtenstein, Jacqueline. "Making Up Representation: The Risks of Femininity." *Representations* 20 (1987): 77–87.

Litvak, Joseph. *Caught in the Act: Theatricality in the Nineteenth-Century English Novel*. Berkeley: U of California P, 1992.

Luckin, Bill. *Pollution and Control: A Social History of the Thames in the Nineteenth Century*. Briston and Boston: Adam Hilger, 1986.

Marsall, David. *The Surprising Effects of Sympathy: Marivaux, Diderot, Rousseau, and Mary Shelley*. Chicago: U of Chicago P, 1988.

Meisel, Martin. *Realizations: Narrative, Pictorial, and Theatrical Arts in Nineteenth-Century England*. Princeton: Princeton UP, 1983.

Nochlin, Linda. *Realism*. Harmondsworth: Penguin, 1971; rpt. 1987.

Poovey, Mary. " 'Scenes of an Indelicate Character': The Medical 'Treatment' of Victorian Women." *The Making of the Modern Body*. Ed. Catherine Gallagher and Thomas Laqueur. Berkeley: U of California P, 1987.

Ray, Gordon. *Thackeray: The Uses of Adversity*. 2 vols. New York: McGraw-Hill, 1955; rpt. 1972 Octagon.

Roberts, Helene. " 'The Sentiment of Reality': Thackeray's Art Criticism." *Studies in the Novel* 13 (1981): 21–39.

Rosen, Charles and Henri Zerner. *Romanticism and Realism: The Mythology of Nineteenth-Century Art.* New York: Norton, 1984.

Stetz, Margaret Diane. "Thackeray's *The Newcomes* and the Artist's World." *Journal of Pre-Raphaelite Studies* 3.2 (1983): 80–95.

Sutherland, J. A. *Thackeray at Work.* London: Athlone, 1974.

Thackeray, William Makepeace. *The Letters and Private Papers of William Makepeace Thackeray.* 4 vols. Cambridge: Harvard UP, 1945.

———. *Vanity Fair: A Novel Without a Hero.* 1848. Ed. John Sutherland. New York: Oxford UP, 1983.

———. *William Thackeray's Contributions to the "Morning Chronicle."* Ed. Gordon Ray. Urbana: U of Illinois P, 1955.

———. *The Works of William Makepeace Thackeray.* Centenary Biographical Edition. 26 vols. London: 1910–11; rpt. New York: AMS, 1968.

Tillotson, Geoffrey, and Donald Hawes, eds. *Thackeray: The Critical Heritage.* New York: Barnes and Noble, 1968.

Trilling, Lionel. *Sincerity and Authenticity.* Cambridge: Harvard UP, 1971.

Sources of Parody in Thackeray's
Catherine

Thomas McKendy

As long ago as 1964 Lionel Stevenson in *Victorian Fiction: A Guide to Research* noted a general neglect of Thackeray's early writings and called for "a more sustained and coherent investigation of [his] literary ancestry" (186). Thackeray's early parodies clearly acknowledge some of this literary ancestry, if only as a demonstration of the kind of fiction he was trying to avoid. Much of the material in these parodies is topical, and Juliet McMaster's recent essay on *Novels by Eminent Hands* (originally published as "Punch's Prize Novelists") is the first study to point specifically to the targets of that set of parodies. She concludes that Thackeray was not only defining, by negative example, his own commitment to realism, but also absorbing a repertoire of techniques from the fiction he mocked (310).

Of Thackeray's earlier parody *Catherine*, it has been generally assumed that the target of satire is Newgate fiction.[1] Certainly the narrator reminds us that he is retelling, "strictly in accordance with the present fashionable style and taste" (3),[2] an episode from the *Newgate Calendar*, namely the murder of John Hayes by his wife, Catherine. Keith Hollingsworth, in *The Newgate Novel*, provides an excellent background to Thackeray's parody of this genre, but as Robert Colby has pointed out in *Thackeray's Canvass of Humanity*, the parody in *Catherine* is "not confined to the Newgate novel" (154). He suggests that *Catherine* might well have been subtitled *Fraser's Prize Novelists* (156), but does not have space in his essay on the theme of moral responsibility in *Catherine* to trace in detail the sources of the parody.

Reading *Catherine* we find continual references, both directly on the page and between the lines, to remind us that this is a book about books. Yet aside from the general strategy of adapting a story from the *Newgate Calendar* to fictional ends, much of *Catherine* is only obliquely aimed at the Newgate novels. In fact, it is remarkable how few direct references it contains to any of them. The last paragraph of chapter 13, "Being a Preparation for the End," decries the "foul Newgate garbage" in recent literature and prepares the reader for the seventh and final installment, in which Thackeray returns to his direct attack on Newgate fiction. Up to this point, however, every direct reference in *Catherine* to the five standard Newgate novels is contained in the following four passages:

> . . . though to tread in the footsteps of the immortal FAGIN requires a genius of inordinate stride, and to go a-robbing after the late though deathless TURPIN, the renowed JACK SHEPPARD, or the embryo DUVAL, may be impossible. . . .   (4)

> They don't quote Plato, like Eugene Aram; or live like gentlemen, and sing the pleasantest ballads in the world, like jolly Dick Turpin; or prate eternally about *to kalon*, like that precious canting Maltravers, whom we all of us have read about and pitied; or die whitewashed saints like "Biss Dadsy" in "Oliver Twist."   (46)

> For about six months after their capture and release of Mr. Hayes, those noble gentlemen had followed, with much prudence and success, that trade which the celebrated and polite Duval, the ingenious Sheppard, the dauntless Turpin, and indeed many other heroes of our most popular novels, had pursued, or were pursuing, in their time.   (101)

> The mind loves to think that, perhaps, in Mr. Hayes's back-parlour the gallant Turpin might have hob-and-nobbed with Mrs. Catherine; that here, perhaps, the noble Sheppard might have cracked his joke, or quaffed his pint of rum. Who knows but that Macheath and Paul Clifford may have crossed their legs under Hayes's dinner-table: and whilst the former sang (so as to make Mrs. Hayes blush) the prettiest, wickedest songs in the world; the latter would make old Hayes yawn, by quotations from Plato, and passionate dissertations on the perfectibility of mankind. Here it was that that impoverished scholar, Eugene Aram, might have pawned his books, discounted or given those bills at three "moons" after date which Sir Edward has rendered immortal.   (115)

Surprisingly, these passages contain almost as many references to Ainsworth's projected novel about Claude Duval (which was never actually written) as they do to *Jack Sheppard*.

The necessary vagueness of the references to "the embryo DUVAL" does not, however, make these stand out from the other references to Newgate novels in *Catherine*, for none of these references, direct or allusive, is particularly specific until the last chapter. *Paul Clifford* (1830), *Eugene Aram* (1832), and *Rookwood* (1834) were, after all, at least five years old when *Catherine* began to appear in *Fraser's* and no longer topical in interest or fresh in Thackeray's memory.[3] *Oliver Twist*, although more recent, did not feature a criminal in the starring role. Ainsworth's most recent novel, *Jack Sheppard*, ought to have been Thackeray's logical target, but amazingly he had not even read it as late as 2 December 1839, when he wrote to his mother:

> I have not read this latter romance but one or two extracts are good: it is acted at *four* theatres, and they say at the Cobourg, people are waiting about in the lobbies selling *Sheppard-bags*.   (*Letters* 1:395)

Only two of the seven installments of *Catherine* appeared after this letter was written, but Thackeray's critics seem not to have noticed his negligence, perhaps because his parodic description of "the Thames at midnight" alludes in detail to Ainsworth's description of London Bridge and the storm on the river. This parodic passage, however, appeared in the final installment of *Catherine* in February 1840, by which time Thackeray may have read the book,[4] or he may simply have used as his source one of the extracts that he acknowledges having read; the *Spectator* of 26 October, for example, reprinted Ainsworth's description of London Bridge in its review of *Jack Sheppard*.[5] In any case Thackeray's letter to his mother resolves Hollingsworth's puzzlement about why Thackeray passed up the obvious opportunity to create parallels between *Catherine* and Jack Sheppard:

> *Fraser's* . . . carefully arranged the last two parts to coincide with the last two parts of *Sheppard*. (Although this serial form of attack suggests that part-by-part correspondences might have been intended, no such plan is observable.)
> (152)

Nor is any pattern of parallels observable between *Catherine* and the other so-called Newgate novels. Paul Clifford and Dick Turpin (in *Rookwood*) are highwaymen, entirely different sorts of criminals from Catherine and her cohorts. Eugene Aram is a murderer, but we do not meet him until years after his crime, when he has become a philosopher, a philanthropist, and a good citizen. Oliver Twist, an orphan who remains pure and innocent in spite of living in a den of thieves, may have an ironic counterpart in the altogether different orphan, Tom Billings, but Thackeray neither makes the connection directly nor extends it very far.

These facts tend to corroborate Saintsbury's intuition that *Catherine* did not sufficiently "get at" the Newgate novels:

> . . . if the object was what it holds itself out to be—the satire by parody of books like *Jack Sheppard*, with something more than a glance backward at

Eugene Aram, and something of a glance sideways at *Oliver Twist*, then one may question, . . . whether in any true sense it "gets at" any of the originals. It is neither melo-dramatic enough, nor romantic enough, nor sentimental enough to do this; nor does it caricature any of these features sufficiently.[6]

What, or rather whom, Thackeray does "get at" in *Catherine* is his old adversary, Bulwer. Sometimes he contents himself with quick jibes: "And so saying, or *soi disant*, as Bulwer says . . ." (106). Other times he elaborates:

> But away with egotism and talk of one's own sorrows: my Lord Byron, and my friend the member for Lincoln, have drained such subjects dry.   (102)

> As I have heard the author of *Richelieu, Natural Odes, Siamese Twins* &c., say, "Poeta nascitur non fit," which means, that though he had tried ever so much to be a poet, it was all moonshine.   (100)

> Sir Edward is a mighty man, but even he cannot prove black to be white; no, not if he were to write a hundred dozen of volumes on the point, instead of half a dozen.   (32)

This final passage goes on to make fun of Bulwer personally for his pride in his title and his crest, but Thackeray also criticizes his fiction, not only in the passages about his Newgate novels that we have already looked at, but also in reference to his other works. He criticizes *Devereux* (1829) by name for drafting into its pages celebrities out of the past (79), and later refers to the same practice at the end of his description of "the Thames at Midnight":

> After this follows another episode. Two masked ladies quarrel at the door of a tavern overlooking the Thames: they turn out to be Stella and Vanessa, who have followed Swift thither; who is in the act of reading "Gulliver's Travels" to Gay, Arbuthnot, Bolingbroke, and Pope. Two fellows are sitting shuddering in a doorway; to one of them Tom Billings flung a sixpence. He little knew that the names of those two young men were—*Samuel Johnson* and *Richard Savage*.[7]   (171)

At the end of the first installment (May 1839), Thackeray points to *Ernest Maltravers* as a novel telling a tale parallel to his own:

> The amusing novel of "Ernest Maltravers," for instance, opens with a seduction; but then it is performed by people of the strictest virtue on both sides: and there is so much religion and philosophy in the heart of the seducer, so much tender innocence in the soul of the seduced, that—bless the little dears!—their very peccadilloes make one interested in them; and their naughtiness becomes quite sacred, so deliciously is it described.   (31)

He returns to *Ernest Maltravers* in the first paragraph of his second installment, suggesting that he might have made "tender and eloquent apologies"
for Catherine and the Count, had Bulwer not already done the same sort of
thing in his book. Bulwer's *Alice*, who maintains her natural innocence in
spite of her upbringing, is an antithetical character to Catherine, exactly the
kind of improbable example of "original virtue" that would have clashed
most strongly with Thackeray's ideas of the roots of evil in *Catherine:*

> But somehow or other, in her original conformation there was the happy bias
> of the plants, towards the Pure and the Bright. For, despite Helvetius, a common
> experience teaches us that though education and circumstances may mould the
> mass, Nature herself sometimes forms the individual, and throws into the clay,
> or its spirit, so much of beauty or deformity that nothing can utterly subdue
> the original elements of character.   (176)[8]

Certainly Bulwer's *Ernest Maltravers* with its opening seduction, illegitimate
birth, and parting of the lovers (as well as their subsequent reunion in *Alice*)
is closer in outline to *Catherine* than any of the other novels Thackeray
mentions. Moreover, the presence of Varney, Alice's father, gives it a Newgate tone in places, and *Alice* closes with a denunciation of capital punishment
and other punishments, legal or social, disproportionate to the offense committed. Most important of all, Thackeray had read these novels recently. He
had reviewed *Ernest Maltravers* in January 1838 for *Fraser's*,[9] and for the
Times he had reviewed not only *Ernest Maltravers* but its sequel, *Alice*, as
well.[10] Here, as in *Catherine*, it is the morality of the first few chapters that
draws most of his attention:

> He is a young man of genius and generous dispositions; he is an excellent
> Christian, and instructs the ignorant Alice in the awful truths of his religion:
> moreover, he is deep in poetry, philosophy, and the German metaphysics. How
> should such a Christian instruct an innocent and beautiful child, his pupil?
> What should such a philosopher do? Why, *seduce* her, to be sure! After a deal
> of namby-pamby Platonism, the girl, as Mr. Bulwer says, "goes to the deuce."
> The expression is as charming as the morality, and appears amidst a quantity
> of the very finest writing about the good and the beautiful, youth, love, passion,
> nature, and so forth.[11]

What Thackeray calls Ernest's "namby-pamby Platonism" Bulwer calls "his
high-wrought Platonism" (86); what Thackeray calls "his eternal whine
about . . . the good and the beautiful" Bulwer calls "his old familiar aspirations for the Beautiful, the Virtuous, and the Great" (263).

Thackeray is as much distressed about Bulwer's "poetising" as his "mor-
alising" in his *Fraser's* review, and he has Solomons in *Catherine* produce

"six columns of the best writing to be found in this or any other book," complete with "the real Platonic smack" to describe Catherine's reunion with Galgenstein after seventeen years. Of course he has already told us the mundane truth about their meeting; but after tossing off a quotation in Greek (spurious, actually) just to prove he can do it, he presents a second, more fanciful version of the event:

> Or suppose, again, I had said, in a style still more popular: —The Count advanced towards the maiden. They both were mute for a while; and only the beating of her heart interrupted that thrilling and passionate silence. Ah, what years of buried joys and fears, hopes and disappointments, arose from their graves in the far past, and in those brief moments flitted before the united ones! How sad was that delicious retrospect, and oh, how sweet! The tears that rolled down the cheek of each were bubbles from the choked and moss-grown wells of youth; the sigh that heaved each bosom had some lurking odours in it—memories of the fragrance of boyhood, echoes of the hymns of the young heart! Thus is it ever—for these blessed recollections the soul always has a place; and while crime perishes, and sorrow is forgotten, the beautiful alone is eternal.
>
> (141)

At this point Solomons' fictional editor cuts him off to get on with the story, but Thackeray's parodic intent has already been fulfilled. Here is Bulwer's description of Alice's reunion with Ernest after eighteen years:

> Maltravers rose, and they stood before each other face to face. And how lovely still was Alice! lovelier he thought even than of old! And those eyes, so divinely blue, so dovelike and soft, yet with some spiritual and unfathomable mystery in their clear depth, were once more fixed upon him. Alice seemed turned to stone; she moved not, she spoke not, she scarcely breathed; she gazed spellbound, as if her senses—as if life itself—had deserted her.
>
> "Alice!" murmured Maltravers.—"Alice, we meet at last!"
>
> His voice restored memory, consciousness, youth, at once to her! She uttered a loud cry of unspeakable joy, of rapture! She sprang forward—reserve, fear, time, change, all forgotten; she threw herself into his arms, she clasped him to her heart again and again!—the faithful dog that has found his master expresses not his transport more uncontrollably, more wildly. It was something fearful—the excess of her ecstasy!   (Alice 394)

This melodramatic and undisciplined passage, like so much of Bulwer's work, invites parody, but although he adapted the situation and perhaps the tone to his own ends in Catherine, Thackeray chose not to parallel it exactly. Many of the novels of the day displayed the same type of excess and Thackeray's parodic passage, like many others in the book, is vaguely reminiscent of a number of novels, a school of fiction, rather than specifically pointed at any one book or author. Bulwer was one of the leading literary figures of the day, and he is commonly considered an "infallible reflector of changes in taste."[12] As such, Thackeray places him at the center of a satire which nonetheless retains a much broader scope.

Aside from his direct attacks on specific novelists and his adaptation of his story from the *Newgate Calendar*, Thackeray constantly reminds his readers in *Catherine* of a whole range of literary traditions, conventions, and habits, drawn from the fiction of the day. The title of chapter 2 promises to depict "The Pleasures of a Sentimental Attachment," and chapter 3 promises "A Great Deal of Genteel Society." These two chapters actually depict the licentiousness, brutality, and revenge of a bunch of scoundrels, however, and Thackeray keeps the irony before us by specifically contrasting their behavior with the more normal course of sentimental attachments among the gentility in popular fiction. When Brock overhears Galgenstein plotting to have him drummed out of the service, for example, Thackeray describes his reaction like this:

> We shall not say after the fashion of the story-books, that Brock listened with a flashing eye and a distended nostril; that his chest heaved tumultuously and that his hand fell down mechanically to his side, where it played with the brass handle of his sword. . . . [T]hat gentleman walked away without any gesture of any kind, and as gently as possible.   (42–43)

So too when Brock tells Catherine that she is to be overthrown for an heiress, she appropriately faints, but she does not behave like a heroine from the pages of a fashionable novel:

> Nor did the poor wench indulge herself in any subsequent shiverings and hysterics, such as usually follow the fainting-fits of persons of higher degree. . . . [N]or did any tears, sobs, sighs, or exclamations of sorrow or anger escape from her.   (44–45)

Instead she calmly plans revenge, and Thackeray reminds us that even in this she is different from heroines of fashionable fiction:

> Catherine had no friend, as is usual in tragedies and romances,—no mysterious sorceress of her acquaintance to whom she could apply for poison,—so she went simply to the apothecaries, pretending at each that she had a dreadful toothache, and procuring from them as much laudanum as she thought would suit her purpose.   (45)

Thackeray also keeps us in mind of the fiction he is reacting against by a kind of crude travesty. He mocks pretentious and affected quirks of language, for instance, simply by adopting them for his own ironic purposes. We have seen this technique already in his parody of Bulwer's references to "the Beautiful," "the Eternal," and so forth, and he also satirizes Bulwer's tendency towards excessive capitalization by referring repeatedly to "Fate" and occasionally introducing absurdly inflated phrases like "the Great Harvest of Beef" (22).[13] Equally pretentious in Thackeray's view was the custom of parading erudition through extensive use of classical allusion and quotation: after the passage of "fine writing" describing Catherine's reunion with Galgenstein, Solomons is proud to announce that "Galgenstein has quoted Euripides thrice, Plato once, Lycophron nine times, besides extracts from the Latin syntax and the minor Greek poets" (142). Accordingly, Solomons sprinkles his tale with classical commonplaces, assuring us that an "*atrior cura*" may keep people awake at night even "among the *pauperum tabernas*" (23), and sometimes even referring to whole phrases: "*flectere si nequeo*, &c.; but quotations are odious" (102).[14] Even Galgenstein, the epitome of pretentious absurdity, strains after classical allusion, ignorantly comparing his elopement with the way "Aeneas bore his wife away from the seige of Rome" (134).

The over-use of French by fashionable novelists and their characters to establish their *ton*, their membership in the *beau monde*, struck Thackeray as equally artificial. Fashionable fiction abounded in words like *cadeau* and *chef d'oeuvre* as well as Latin phrases like *in terrorem* or *ad infinitum*;[15] such words and phrases replaced their everyday English equivalents as part of a spurious attempt at elegance. In an 1840 article, "The Fashionable Authoress,"[16] Thackeray summed up his objections to the pretentious use of foreign words and quotations:

> For the style, she does not know her own language, but, in revenge, has a smattering of half a dozen others. She interlards her works with fearful quotations from the French, fiddle-faddle extracts from Italian operas, German phrases fiercely mutilated, and a scrap or two of bad Spanish: and upon the strength of these murders, she calls herself an authoress.

In *Catherine*, Solomons also chooses words like "*ménage*" (36) and "*nuit de noces*" (67) instead of their English equivalents to establish his credentials as a fashionable novelist. We need only recall Brock's efforts to explain *ventrebleu* to his new recruits to be convinced of the *ton* of the characters in *Catherine*: "for *bleu*, in the French language, means through; and *ventre*—why, you see, ventre means —————" (23–24). Count Galgenstein, in keeping with his aristocratic character, naturally uses French more frequently than any of the other characters; he tries to impress young Billings with words like "*en croupe*," "*manquer*," and "*calembourg*" (134), and even explains to him the meaning of "*Geht zum Teufel!*" (136).

Much of the satire that we find here, then, is not directed exclusively or even primarily at Bulwer or at the Newgate novel. It is rather directed at the fashionable fiction of the day, usually written by female novelists (preferably titled) and including as subgenres the sentimental romance and the "silver-fork" novel. Mrs. Gore and Lady Bury were among the foremost practitioners of these genres, and their novels were populated with people of title and high fashion, altogether different people from Thackeray's satiric counterpart, Galgenstein. In *Catherine* we read about silverware only when Thackeray's rogues sit down to eat at places set with the spoils of John Hayes's sideline as a fence, and almost every reference to aristocrats and noblemen presents them as vulgar or stupid or both. Galgenstein, as we have already begun to see, is very much a case in point.

Thackeray's satire against noblemen, and against their contemporary representation in fiction, begins with our first encounter with Galgenstein. As a younger son his claim to his title is spurious, but even the head of the family is less than illustrious,

> . . . at home at Schloss Galgenstein breeding horses, hunting wild boars, swindling tenants, living in a great house with small means; obliged to be sordid at home all the year, to be splendid for a month at the capital, as is the way with many other noblemen.   (6)

Still a title is a title, and with a flashy wardrobe it is enough to gain for Galgenstein the hand of a rich, bourgeois heiress:

> This was obtained—for Pa was a tradesman; and I suppose every one of my readers has remarked how great an effect a title has on the lower classes. Yes, thank Heaven! there is about a freeborn Briton a cringing baseness, and lickspittle awe of rank, which does not exist under any tyranny in Europe, and is only to be found here and in America.   (41)

When Galgenstein reappears at the end of the book, he tells stories about the Duke of Bavaria and the Duchess of Marlborough, and reassures Tom that he is "a nobleman of seventy-eight descents" (134). Still only Tom's "respect for the aristocracy" (137) keeps him from the obvious conclusion that his father is a fool.

If Tom has respect for the aristocracy, it is clear that Thackeray does not. Although most of the characters in the story agree that Tom was born to be hanged, Thackeray intensifies his satire by reminding us, through Catherine, that Tom too "has noble blood in veins" (121). Tom himself dreams that he may be a lord if Catherine legitimizes her liaison with Galgenstein (159), and he certainly looks like "a very proper young gentleman" when he decks himself out in fancy clothes to meet his father for the first time (125). The irony of it all is that Tom is an apprentice tailor, indentured to a man named Beinkleider (pant-maker) who, Thackeray assures us, is "skillful in his trade (after the manner of his nation, which in breeches and metaphysics—in inexpressibles and incomprehensibles—may instruct all of Europe)" (118). *Sartor Resartus* had of course originally appeared in *Fraser's*, and as Colby has pointed out, Thackeray draws on Carlyle's "clothes philosophy" here for an additional comment on the trappings of the aristocracy (156).

If clothes make the gentleman, in the case of Tom and his father, so too do they enable Brock to introduce himself into London society, after he robs Galgenstein in the third installment of the story. He gets "high red heels" for his shoes and "three suits of laced clothes" and soon he even has Lord Peterborough introducing him to the queen at court (68–70). Unlike Tom and Galgenstein, he overcomes his background and acts as if he were to the manor born:

> In truth, it was almost a pity that worthy Brock had not been a gentleman born; in which case, doubtless, he would have lived and died as became his station; for he spent money like a gentleman, he loved women like a gentleman, he would fight like a gentleman, he gambled and got drunk like a gentleman. What did he want else? Only a matter of six descents, a little money, and an estate, to render him the equal of St. John or Harley.   (69)

He reminds us of Paul Clifford and of Dick Turpin in *Rookwood* for his ease of mingling in a genteel society that cannot recognize a cutthroat and a highwayman in disguise. His social success is as damning and satiric towards the artistocracy as Galgenstein's vulgarity. It is no wonder that Carlyle, who had already blasted the "dandaical" school of fiction in *Sartor Resartus*, found *Catherine* "wonderful" (Letters 1:421).

Saintsbury finds Carlyle's influence on Thackeray also in the opening passages of the book:

> . . . it begins with one of the vivid, slightly garrulous, half-historical, half-picturesque settings which [Carlyle] had done more than anyone else to teach Thackeray, but which Thackeray had, almost before Carlyle taught him, struck out and adjusted to his own idiosyncrasy.[17]

Thackeray's introduction to *Catherine*, however, is at least as reminiscent of contemporary historical fiction as of Carlyle. G. P. R. James, for instance, had set the scene for *The Robber* in this way in 1838:

It was in the olden time of *merry England*— . . . when, notwithstanding wars and civil contentions not long past, our country still deserved the name of merry England, and received it constantly among a class peculiarly its own, . . . in the days of Walton and Cotton, . . . while the wits and the libertines, the fops and the soldiers, the poets and the philosophers, of the reigns of Charles, James, William, and Anne, formed a world in which debauchery, vice, strife, evil passion, rage, jealousy, and hatred, seemed the only occupations of genius, and the true sphere for talent; while Oxford and Cambridge had their contentions, and vied with the capital in nourishing feuds and follies of their own; . . .
(1:1–3)

Thackeray uses a similar tone and rhetoric in his opening paragraph:

At that famous period in history, . . . when there was a queen in England, with such rogues for ministers as have never been seen, no, not in our own day; and a general, of whom it may be severely argued, whether he was the meanest miser or the greatest hero in the world; when Mrs. Masham had not yet put Madame Marlborough's nose out of joint; when people had their ears cut off for writing very meek political pamphlets; and very large full-bottomed wigs were just beginning to be worn with powder.   (3)

James goes on to contrast the "feuds and follies" of city and court with rural tranquility, but Thackeray of course has no such aim. He continues to snap at the heels of the aristocracy throughout *Catherine* and he adapts the device of historical fiction, the macrocosmic overview of vice and folly at the highest levels of society, to his own ends. From the beginning of his tale he establishes vice as the norm in society and thereby creates a backdrop against which his relatively petty characters act out crimes of their own.

Since *Catherine* is set a hundred years in the past, it naturally exhibits some of the standard characteristics of contemporary historical fiction, which is sometimes an influence, sometimes a source of parody for Thackeray. We have already seen him mocking the introduction of illustrious historical figures into fiction. His creation of new characters like Macshane while simultaneously proclaiming that he is bound to stick to "THE TRUTH" (79) may be a further slash at Bulwer for the invention of characters like Aram's fictitious lover, Madeleine Lester. Thackeray also makes fun of the elaborate use of sources from the past "from which the observant genius might borrow passages, and construct pretty antiquarian figments" (138). He suggests back issues of the *Spectator*, the memoirs of Colley Cibber, and the archives of the British Museum as sources for the would-be antiquarian, but he seems to disparage attempts at historical accuracy or realism:

It is not our purpose to make a great and learned display here, otherwise the costumes of the company assembled at this *fete* might afford scope for at least half-a-dozen pages of fine writing; and we might give, if need were, specimens of the very songs and music sung on the occasion.   (138)

Such disparagement seems purposeless, even self-defeating, for an author whose richest material was and would continue to be the past; certainly Thackeray was to introduce accurate historical detail and characters from history into *Henry Esmond* a few years later.[18] What Thackeray disliked, apparently, was "description . . . in a fine historical style" (170), the kind of set-piece of historical description, to be found in Ainsworth and others, that he parodies in his "Thames at Midnight" passage. Thackeray, after all, would later ignore his opportunity in *Vanity Fair* to present an erudite or vivid description of the battlefield of Waterloo.

In describing "THE THAMES AT MIDNIGHT" (170–71), Thackeray parodies Ainsworth both for the erudition of his historical description and the melodrama of his action.[19] He does not actually present, as Ainsworth does, a detailed description of the Thames, London Bridge, and their surroundings, but he gives a parenthetical summary of such a description supposedly to be found in Solomons' manuscript. He lists a number of the buildings depicted there, and he mocks Ainsworth by echoing his observations that the houses and shops built on Old London Bridge gave it more the appearance of a street than a bridge and that the bridge was in those days supported by twenty arches (nineteen in Ainsworth's version). Ainsworth sets his elaborate scene in order to stage a melodramatic brawl between Rowland and Darrell, in the middle of the Thames during the worst hurricane ever to hit London. Darrell, "mortally wounded," nonetheless manages to save the infant who has been tossed into the water after him, before he sinks "to rise no more." Ainsworth's language in recounting the clash is pompous and riddled with the cliché of romantic adventure:

> Hurled over the sides of the skiff, the ruffian speedily found a watery grave.
>   (124)

> "Seize this oar," vociferated the waterman.   (125)

> All was darkness, horror, confusion, ruin. . . . The end of the world seemed at hand.   (126)

> The intense darkness added to the terror of the storm. The destroying angel hurried by, shrouded in his gloomiest apparel.   (127)

Thackeray parodies this language by imitation (". . . the bodies of the captains plunged down, down, down in the unfathomable waters"), and by comic inflation (". . . drawing his snickersnee, he plunged it seven times in the bailiff's chest"). Thackeray adds his own absurd melodrama by having the two combatants remain locked in their death grip, still standing although "*they were both dead!*" (170–71). This whole passage is set off parenthetically in *Catherine*, with no relation to what comes either before or after. Thackeray's awkward injection of this material apparently implies that Ainsworth's showy description of the skirmish and its setting is simply a set-piece, unnecessary and irrelevant to its context in *Jack Sheppard*.

Ainsworth was of course a real antiquarian, and he frequently stopped his narratives to rhapsodize over the scenes and persons of times past, and to disparage by contrast "these degenerate days."[20] If Thackeray found this practice pretentious at best, he found it reprehensible when it included romantic lament for convicted felons:

> The last of this race [highwaymen], . . . Turpin, like the setting sun, threw up some parting rays of glory, and tinged the far highways with a lustre that may yet be traced like a cloud of dust raised by his horses' retreating heels.
> (*Rookwood* 2:7)

Thackeray parodies this kind of perverted eulogy after listing a number of criminals who might have gathered at the home of Catherine and John Hayes:

> . . . why desert reality for fond imagination, or call up from their honoured graves the sacred dead? I know not: and yet, in sooth, I can never pass Cumberland Gate without a sigh, as I think of the gallant cavaliers who traversed that road in old time.   (115–16)

So too he recalls Ainsworth's comparison of Turpin to Nelson (*Rookwood* 2:3) by comparing Brock and his mischief, in extended military metaphor, to Marlborough in his campaigns (114).

Catherine, then, is a parodic novel based on the model of the Newgate novels of the 1830s, but stretched out to include in its satire a cross-section of the fiction of the day. In it Thackeray mocks what he sees as the excesses of historical novels, "silver-fork" novels, and fashionable novels generally, and, as these trends in fiction tend to converge in the works of Bulwer, Bulwer becomes the focus of Thackeray's concern. On one level Thackeray simply criticizes the abuse of language to prettify or romanticize everyday reality:

His ride from Worcester had been a long one. He had left that city at noon, but before his return thither the sun had gone down; and the landscape, which had been dressed like a prodigal, in purple and gold, now appeared like a Quaker, in dusky grey; and the trees by the road-side grew black as undertakers or physicians, and, bending their solemn heads to each other, whispered ominously among themselves; and the mists hung on the common; and the cottage lights went out one by one; and the earth and heaven grew black, but for some twinkling useless stars, which freckled the ebon countenance of the latter; and the air grew colder; and about two o'clock the moon appeared, a dismal pale-faced rake, walking solitary through the deserted sky; and about four, mayhap, the Dawn (wretched 'prentice boy!) opened in the east the shutters of the Day: —in other words, more than a dozen hours had passed.   (85)

The nature of a character's or a narrator's language inevitably reflects the quality of his mind and thought, however, and Thackeray connects his criticism of language to the larger considerations of literature and morality. These same considerations would be echoed seven years later in "Punch's Prize Novelists" and in the miniature parodies that open Chapter 6 of *Vanity Fair:* "We might have treated this subject in the genteel, or in the romantic, or in the facetious manner." *Catherine* was Thackeray's first book-length fiction and Thackeray himself considered it a "failure" (*Works* 10:590). Yet through its flaws we can see themes and attitudes, even at times a theory of fiction, that look back to his literary ancestors and forward to his mature work.

NOTES

1. See for example Rawlins (76), Thrall (72–73), Wheatley (42), and Grieg (41). Loofbourow, however, reads *Catherine* as a parody of fashionable and romantic fiction generally (19–22). The novels usually considered "Newgate novels" include *Oliver Twist*, Bulwer's *Paul Clifford* and *Eugene Aram*, and Ainsworth's *Rookwood* and *Jack Sheppard*.
2. My text for all quotations from Thackeray's works is *The Oxford Thackeray*, ed. George Saintsbury, 17 vols. (London: Oxford UP, 1908). Parenthetical references to *Catherine* come from volume 3 of this edition, which is otherwise cited as *Works*. Letters are cited from *The Letters and Private Papers of William Makepeace Thackeray*, ed. Gordon N. Ray, 4 vols. (Cambridge, Mass.: Harvard UP, 1946).
3. *Rookwood* had been re-issued in 1836 and *Paul Clifford* in 1835, however.
4. Actually the passage must have been written by 18 January, at the very latest, since Thackeray announces the completion of *Catherine* in a letter to his mother on that date (*Letters* 1:412).
5. *Spectator* 26 Oct. 1839:1020–21.
6. *Works* 3: xi. Also Saintsbury 52. Saintsbury's book reprints the introductions to his Oxford edition of Thackeray.
7. The poet Richard Savage was also a convicted murderer. In Crook's edition of the *Newgate Calendar* his story follows immediately after that of Catherine Hayes.

8. Parenthetical citations to *Ernest Maltravers* and its sequel *Alice, or The Mysteries* refer to the Illustrated Sterling Edition of Bulwer's novels (Boston: Aldine, n.d.). In this edition *Alice* is bound together with *Ernest Maltravers*, but paged separately.
9. *Fraser's* Jan. 1838:85–89.
10. *Times* 30 Sept. 1837 and 24 April 1838. Gulliver (97–103, 111) attributes these reviews to Thackeray, and gives long extracts from them in his appendices (201–04, 214–17).
11. *Fraser's* Jan. 1838:86.
12. Tillotson 141. Other critics make similar comments: Rosa speaks of "his uncanny sense of the literary market" (98); Young says, "his versatility is not more remarkable than his anticipatory intuition for changes in public taste" (417).
13. A few years later, Thackeray was correctly to identify Bulwer, despite his disclaimers, as the author of the *New Timon*, at least partly because of Bulwer's "defects" of excessive capitalization:
    > Adjectives, by the help of a capital are elevated to substantive rank—the Good, the Beautiful, the True, the Past, the Future, &c. By this easy typographic artifice nouns substantive are exalted to extra importance—. . . . Why not advance to capital rank, as the Germans do, all the substantives in the dictionary?
    > (*Contributions to the Morning Chronicle* 133–34)
14. The original source of this quotation is the *Aeneid* (7:312).
15. These examples are drawn from Catherine Gore's *Mothers and Daughters* 1:24, 55, 116, and 134.
16. *Works* 1:561–76.
17. Saintsbury 53–54. Also *Works* 3: xii. That Thackeray had recently reviewed Carlyle's *French Revolution* for the *Times* (3 Aug. 1837; rpt. in *Works* 1:67–79) makes plausible these claims for Carlyle's influence on *Catherine*. See also Colby 156n.
18. Even in writing *Catherine*, for example, Thackeray had evidently drawn on Farquhar's *The Recruiting Officer* for the background and some of the names in his first chapter.
19. The passages that Thackeray parodies here appeared in the second installment of *Jack Sheppard* (*Bentley's Miscellany* Feb. 1839, 5:113–33). I have cited specific page numbers in the text.
20. *Rookwood* 1:39. See *Rookwood* 2:122 for a further example. S. M. Ellis speaks of Ainsworth's "innate taste for history and romance" (21).

WORKS CITED

Ainsworth, William Harrison. *Jack Sheppard. Bentley's Miscellany* Jan. 1839–Feb. 1840.

———. *Rookwood*. 2 vols. Cabinet Edition of the Novels of William Ainsworth. New York: Taylor, 1903.

Bulwer, Edward Lytton. *The Illustrated Sterling Edition of Bulwer's Works*. 14 vols. Boston: Aldine, n.d.

Colby, Robert A. *Thackeray's Canvass of Humanity*. Columbus: Ohio State UP, 1979.

Crook, G. T., ed. *The Complete Newgate Calendar*. 6 vols. London: Privately printed for the Navarre Society Ltd., 1926.

Ellis, S. M. *William Harrison Ainsworth and His Friends*. 2 vols. New York: Lane, 1911.

Gore, Catherine. *Mothers and Daughters*. 2 vols. Philadelphia: Carey, 1834.

Greig, J. Y. T. *Thackeray: A Reconsideration*. London: Oxford UP, 1950.

Gulliver, Harold Strong. *Thackeray's Literary Apprenticeship*. Valdosta, Ga.: Southern, 1934.

Hollingsworth, Keith. *The Newgate Novel, 1830–1847: Bulwer, Ainsworth, Dickens, and Thackeray*. Detroit: Wayne State UP, 1963.

James, G. P. R. *The Robber*. 3 vols. London: Longman, 1838.

Loofbourow, John. *Thackeray and the Form of Fiction*. Princeton: Princeton UP, 1964.

McMaster, Juliet. "*Novels by Eminent Hands*: Sincerest Flattery from the Author of *Vanity Fair*." *Dickens Studies Annual* 18 (1989): 309–36.

Rawlins, Jack. *Thackeray's Novels: A Fiction That Is True*. Berkeley: U of California P, 1974.

Rosa, Matthew Whiting. *The Silver-Fork School: Novels of Fashion Preceding Vanity Fair*. New York: Columbia UP, 1936.

Saintsbury, George. *A Consideration of Thackeray*. 1931. New York: Russell, 1968.

Stevenson, Lionel. *Victorian Fiction: A Guide to Research*. Cambridge, Mass.: Harvard UP, 1964.

Thackeray, William Makepeace. *Contributions to the Morning Chronicle*, ed. Gordon N. Ray. Urbana: U of Illinois P, 1966.

———. *The Letters and Private Papers of William Makepeace Thackeray*. 4 vols. ed. Gordon N. Ray. Cambridge, Mass.: Harvard UP, 1946.

———. *The Oxford Thackeray*. 17 vols. ed. George Saintsbury. London: Oxford UP, 1908.

Thrall, Miriam M. H. *Rebellious Fraser's*. New York: Columbia UP, 1934.

Tillotson, Kathleen. *Novels of the Eighteen-Forties*. London: Oxford UP, 1961.

Wheatley, James H. *Patterns in Thackeray's Fiction*. Cambridge, Mass.: MIT, 1969.

Young, W. T. "Lesser Novelists." *The Cambridge History of English Literature*. Ed. A. W. Ward and A. R. Waller. Vol. 13. Cambridge: Cambridge UP, 1964. Chap. 13.

Thackeray Studies: 1983–1992

Peter L. Shillingsburg

In the ten years since Robert Colby last summed up Thackeray studies in these pages, there has been no occasion to alter his elegant lament about Thackeray's place in modern scholarship (*DSA*, 12 [1983], 341–56). Dickens, Eliot, Trollope, the Brontes, and Hardy regularly attract more attention. One can conclude only that Thackeray is too good for the run of critics and scholars and predict that, as their ranks swell, Thackeray's portion of attention will diminish. After all, as R. D. McMaster points out, the "full enjoyment of Thackeray's work places considerable demands on his readers" (*Thackeray's Cultural Frame of Reference* (Montreal & Kingston: McGill-Queen's UP, 1991, 1). For one thing "allusions crowd his text: allusions to literature and history—ancient and modern, major and minor—to mythology, fairy-tale, music and opera, popular songs, nursery rhymes, painting, sculpture, architecture, cities and places at home and abroad, spas, museums, restaurants, politics, imperial affairs, politicians, dancers, singers, pugilists"; and it is difficult to imagine the casual unassisted reader recognizing and enjoying many of them (1). In addition, that narrative voice, which over the years has accounted for more commentary than any other issue or aspect of Thackeray's work, demands that the reader assume responsibility for every judgment, since the narrator is not to be trusted. As an anonymous writer put it in "A Conversation Overheard," *TNL*, 37 (May 1993), Thackeray's narrator

> lies, tells truth, is serious, is playful, is ironic, is sarcastic (irony is ambiguous, sarcasm is not), is this and that, so that you cannot tell what the *author* thinks. That is, he deliberately undermines your skills in figuring out what you are being told. I think he does this as a way of saying to the reader, "Look, don't you know who you are? don't you know what you think? Here is a situation that involves love, or hate, or deception, or trust (betrayed), or insensitivity—if you are half the reader I take you for, you will KNOW yourself what to think and you will detect in my insincere way of relating it the kind of self-deceptions

and insensitivities that ordinary people indulge in in order to think they are just fine.'' So I think Thackeray is refusing to tell people what to think (when he does tell them, he is not to be trusted—he does not want to be trusted); but he demands a very high order of intelligence and morality and understanding of human nature and compassion in his readers. If you aren't that, you won't get it. Worse, you'll think *he* didn't get it.

These are challenges that attract a steady but small audience. The MLA bibliographical listing for Thackeray from 1982 to 1992 contains just over 200 items, about the number we have come to expect in a year for Dickens.

Bibliography, Texts and Editions

The first ever full-scale scholarly edition of Thackeray's works, the Garland Thackeray edition, began publication in 1989 with *Henry Esmond* (edited by Edgar F. Harden) and *Vanity Fair* (edited by Peter Shillingsburg with a historical introduction by Robert Colby and an essay on illustrations by Nicholas Pickwood). *Pendennis* and a volume containing *Flore et Zephyr, Major Gahagan*, and *Yellowplush* (both edited by Shillingsburg with an introduction to *Flore et Zephyr* by S. A. Muresianu and an essay on illustrations in both volumes by Pickwood) appeared in 1991. *The Newcomes* is scheduled for 1994. The texts restore Thackeray's rhetorical punctuation and numerous manuscript readings corrupted by the compositors of the first edition. Notable among these is the correction in the description of Rachel and Henry's ascent to his bedroom upon his first return from college, which the first edition of *Henry Esmond* reports as "hand in hand" where the manuscript has "hat in hand"—the episode comes far too early for "hand in hand" as an indication of the relation between these two. In *Vanity Fair* Becky Sharp is called a minx rather than a mimic. The editions contain all of Thackeray's illustrations and a full record of textual variation in authoritative editions. Important notices of the edition by John Sutherland (*TLS*, June 15, 1990) and S. W. Reid (JEGP, Oct. 1991) have appeared, and Joseph R. McElrath, Jr., subjected Harden's *Esmond* to close and appreciative pre-publication scrutiny in *TNL* nos. 27 and 28 (May and Nov. 1988), but the most comprehensive and appreciative review of the first four volumes is by Judith Law Fisher in *SNNTS*, 24 (1992), 309–22.

John Sutherland's Oxford Classics edition of *Vanity Fair* (1983) reprints the text of George Saintsbury's 1908 Oxford edition. While the text therefore reflects early twentieth century punctuation practice rather than Thackeray's, it includes all the original illustrations and is superbly introduced and annotated. The question of Thackeray's manuscript punctuation, as opposed to that imposed upon his work by the earliest compositors, is discussed in the Garland edition textual introductions and by Natalie Maynor in ''Punctuation and Style in *Vanity Fair*: Thackeray versus His Compositors,'' *ELN*, 22 (1984): 48–55. The Garland text of *Vanity Fair* with new annotations and a selection of reviews, contextual material, and criticism is in production for a Norton Critical Edition prepared by Peter Shillingsburg. *Barry Lyndon,* edited by Andrew Sanders (1984), and *Henry Esmond,* edited by Donald Hawes (1991) were added to the Oxford World Classics, both with excellent introductions and notes, but each reproducing the 1908 Oxford text. *A Shabby Genteel Story and Other Writings,* edited by D. J. Taylor (Everyman, 1993) adds nothing to our knowledge of the text; Taylor's introduction attempts feebly to generate regard for Thackeray's early writings by denigrating, wittily but unconvincingly, the major novels and later work. *Vanity Fair* was also issued by Everyman (1991) with an introduction by Catherine Peters (not seen) and by Wordsworth (1993) stripped of illustrations and Thackeray's preface but costing a mere British pound. Alan Sutton of Gloucester has issued *The Book of Snobs* (1989) and *Sketches and Travels in London* (1989), each with a brief introduction by Paul Webb, and *The Irish Sketchbook* (1990) with Thackeray's illustrations and a good introduction by Christopher Morash.

An important project paralleling the Garland scholarly edition is Edgar F. Harden's compilation of *Annotations for Selected Works of William Makepeace Thackeray: The Complete Novels, the Major Non-Fictional Prose, and Selected Shorter Pieces*, 2 vols. (New York: Garland, 1990). This massive work provides annotations in the order in which the references appear in the works being annotated and is extensively indexed. The bulk of annotations are by Harden, but the project includes as collaborators Richard Oram, R. D. McMaster, Juliet McMaster, Carol H. MacKay, S. A. Muresianu, Ina Ferris, Judith L. Fisher, Ian Heywood, and Gerald Sorensen. In a completely separate effort, Oscar Mandel and John Sutherland update Mandel's useful and handy *Annotations to Vanity Fair* (second edition 1988) in paperback. In spite of much overlap each offers unique material. Both of these works are reviewed in *TNL*, no. 31 (May 1990). In what can be seen as an extended work of annotation, R. D. McMaster's *Thackeray's Cultural Frame of Reference: Allusion in ''The Newcomes''* (Montreal & Kingston: McGill-Queen's UP, 1991) provides one of the most informed and general studies of Thackeray and his times, for though McMaster concentrates on *The Newcomes*, the range and density of allusion in that work is so extensive that he has had to cover, in a sense, Thackeray's universe, providing first of all a very well-informed essay on the uses of allusion and then exploring Thackeray's uses of literature, art, history (particularly European and Indian), France, and London. Careful attention to this book and ready access to Harden's *Annotations* volumes will enhance any reader's appreciation of Thackeray's keen eyes, extensive knowledge, and easy prose—elements essential to enjoyment of Thackeray's works. In what amounts to a specialized kind of annotation, Joe K. Law's "The Prima Donnas of *Vanity Fair*," *CLAJ*, 31 (1987), 87–110, analyzes the novel's references to singers, songs and operas, providing historical assessments and descriptions of the singers, following the parallels between Thackeray's story and the librettos, and mounting a convincing theory about the use of music and musicians to reinforce and extend the characterizations of Becky and Amelia.

The Thackeray Newsletter continues its semi-annual publication of notes, reviews, and list of recent and forthcoming publications. Published by the English Department at Mississippi State U., its notes include brief descriptions of exhibitions, sales of rare Thackeray items, conferences, sources and contexts, as well as historical and critical notes. The announcement of a sale of Thackeray drawings in 1983 prompted their identification as forgeries in the May 1984 issue.

A number of new or previously uncollected items have also been made available. Richard Oram, " 'Catalogues of War': Thackeray's 'Essay on Pumpernickel,' " *VIJ*, 15 (1987): 127–33, newly transcribes an unfinished manuscript essay published only once before (in 1913). Beginning with observations on museum relics once belonging to Napoleon, Thackeray suggests that war is conducted for the very worst of motives—not 'patriotic ardour,' not 'chivalrous desire.' Oram's useful introduction dates the MS in the early to mid 1840s and relates its style and ideas to passages of similar import in *Barry Lyndon*, "Little Travels and Roadside Sketches: Waterloo," and early *Fraser's* essays. Juliet McMaster's "Early Verse by 'Unfortunate W. Thackeray,' " *VN*, 62 (Fall 1982): 1–2, prints an uncollected poem, identifies its recipient, and adds a humorous note on the "chicken jokes" connected to the Pulleyn family at Chanticlere in *The Newcomes*. John Sutherland's "Thackeray and France, 1842," *N&Q*, 33 (1986): 166–67, prints for the first time a fragmentary diatribe on the French and opines that Thackeray abandoned the piece and its general style in favor of "good-natured scorn" which characterizes his published work on France. Gary Scharnborst's "An Uncollected Letter from Thackeray to James T. Fields," *N&Q*, 24 (1985): 44–45, rescues one sentence of a letter from a sale catalogue and speculates on its significance to understanding Thackeray's early return to England at the end of his first American tour.

Items of bibliographical interest include Richard Oram's "The Confederate Thackeray: Evans and Cogswell's *The Adventures of Philip*," *ABC*, 4 (1983): 27–30, which succinctly places Evans and Cogswell's 1863 book in its historical context: South Carolina during the Civil War, Thackeray's literary reputation in the American South, and the publishing difficulties and achievements that the book represents. John Sutherland's "John Macrone: Victorian Publisher," *DSA*, 13 (1984): 243–59, focuses on one of Thackeray's earliest publishers. Oram and Sutherland cover ground not repeated in Peter Shillingsburg's *Pegasus in Harness: Victorian Publishing and W. M. Thackeray* (Charlottesville: UP of Virginia, 1992), which provides a history of Thackeray's literary/financial career; demonstrates the production processes of serial, three-decker, and single volume publications; explores Thackeray's personal and professional relations with his publishers, Bradbury and Evans, Chapman and Hall, Smith, Elder and Co.; details the market and legal relations with American publishers and Baron Tauchnitz; debates the issues of individual authorial autonomy against determinism and attempts to show the implications of that debate to a variety of approaches to editing and interpreting *Henry Esmond*; and provides a checklist and census of imprints of Thackeray's separate publications through 1863, including editions and printings which may not have survived.

Micael Clarke's "A Mystery Solved: Ainsworth's Criminal Romances Censured in *Fraser's* by J. Hamilton Reynolds, not Thackeray," *VPR*, 23 (1990): 50–54, corrects the misreading of a manuscript letter from Thackeray to *Fraser's Magazine*, and thereby correctly attributes to Reynolds two *Fraser's* essays formerly tentatively ascribed to Thackeray. Clarke shows the divergences between the views of Ainsworth in those essays and Thackeray's known views expressed in undisputed essays. Peter Shillingsburg's "Thackeray in Australia: the Periodical Press," *VPR*, 18 (1985): 134–37, surveys the evidence for an Australian readership and market for Thackeray's work by identifying book advertisements, notices, reprints, reviews and obituaries in Australian newspapers and literary periodicals.

Edgar F. Harden's *Thackeray's "English Humourists" and "Four Georges"* (Newark: U of Delaware P, 1985) applies to Thackeray's two collections of lectures the same approach he made famous in *The Emergence of Thackeray's Serial Fiction* (1979), meticulously tracing their composition, delivery, and publication. Harden once again convincingly refutes the Trollopian view of Thackeray as a careless genius. Though not as methodical a writer as Trollope, Thackeray is clearly a careful as well as imaginative writer; the manuscript evidence laid out by Harden demonstrates it.

Philip Collins's compilation, *Thackeray: Interviews and Recollections*, 2 vols. (New York: St. Martin's, 1983), reprints nearly a hundred personal recollections and notices ranging from one or two sentences to fifteen pages, all from the nineteen century or very early twentieth. Collins's well-known partisanship for Dickens displays itself clearly in the bias of his editorial account of the 1858 Garrick Club dispute between Thackeray and Edmund Yeates, but the collection of notices is well-documented and essential to any collection of Thackerayana. It significantly supplements Dudley Flamm's *Thackeray's Nineteenth Century Critics* (1967). Harold Bloom's *William Makepeace Thackeray's Vanity Fair* (New York: Chelsea, 1987) is a handy compilation of previously published articles and excerpts from books from more recent times.

Perhaps the most important new work on the horizon is Edgar Harden's eagerly awaited 2 volume supplement to Thackeray's *Letters*, now in an advanced stage of preparation for publication by Garland.

BIOGRAPHY

One of the more practical contributions to biographical interests in Thackeray is *The Two Thackerays: Anne Thackeray Ritchie's Centenary Biographical Introductions to the Works of William Makepeace Thackeray* with an introduction by Carol Hanberry MacKay and bibliographical note by Julia Maxey and Peter Shillingsburg, 2 vols. (New York: AMS Press, 1988). Aside from the bibliographical importance of the first appearance in print of a few pieces and the collection for the first time of a few more in the 1910, 24 volume set, the only lingering importance of the Centenary Biographical Edition was Anne Thackeray Ritchie's biographical introductions. Their collection in two volumes, while overpriced, puts those introductions within the reach of many libraries that could not obtain copies of the collected works. MacKay's lengthy introduction breaks new ground in our understanding of the relation between Thackeray and his daughter and of Lady Ritchie's achievements in her own right. There is some inevitable overlapping between MacKay's essay on Ritchie's introduction and her essay on Ritchie herself in " 'Only Connect': The Multiple Roles of Anne Thackeray Ritchie," *LCUT*, 30 (1985): 83–112: both unveil Anne's role as daughter and "keeper of the flame," but the former keeps William Thackeray firmly in mind while the latter, based in part on manuscripts at UT's Humanities Research Center, ranges over Anne's whole career.

In what can only be a symptom of his generosity, Robert Colby credits Anthony Trollope, at least indirectly, for Anne Thackeray Ritchie's decision finally to write the biographical introductions. In "Trollope as Thackerayan," *DSA*, 11 (1983), 261–77, Colby analyzes Trollope's English Men of Letters *Thackeray* and finds it wanting in every category except unselfconsciousness and dutifulness. Trollope's inability to appreciate his friend's philosophical stance or the fine edge of his satirical wit is compounded by his inability to get his facts straight even when they were supplied to him accurately by Anne Thackeray. At best Trollope was unaware of the way his depiction of Thackeray as the idle apprentice and careless genius was designed to put a good face on his own lesser talents. Colby's devastating, but evenhanded, essay was already finished when J. Hillis Miller issued his bland, uncritical call for an examination of Trollope's memoir of Thackeray in "Trollope's Thackeray," *NCL*, 37 (1982): 350–57. Miller comments briefly on four ways to read the memoir and critique: for what it says of Thackeray, his work and his time; for what it says about Victorian notions of the novel; for what it reveals about Trollope; and for the way it resembles Trollope's other biographical and fictional works. Colby lays to rest any hope that good will come of the first, and he makes very good way toward fulfilling the other three.

Ina Ferris's *William Makepeace Thackeray* (Boston: Twayne, 1983), though constrained in space and scope by the Twayne format, provides one of the decade's more refreshing presentations of Thackeray. Her account of Thackeray's thinking about women, faith, certainty, and evil surpasses that of many fuller studies. Her especially good discussion of Ethel Newcome reveals Thackeray's unease with his world as well as anything else written on the subject. Catherine Peters's *Thackeray's Universe: Shifting Worlds of Imagination and Reality* (New York: Oxford UP, 1987) is the fourth book-length biography of Thackeray since Gordon Ray's *Thackeray, the Uses of Adversity* (1955) and *Thackeray, the Age of Wisdom* (1958). Margaret Foster's unconventional (auto)biography, *Memoirs of a Victorian Gentleman* (1978), and Ann Monsarrat's *An Uneasy Victorian* (1980), and Peters's book all provide much more "user-friendly" accounts of Thackeray than Ray's formidable work, but they add little new to our acquaintance with original sources or to our understanding of the man. But each of these appreciative and enthusiastic shorter efforts provides a basically sound introduction to Thackeray, and Catherine Peters's discussion of *Vanity Fair* offers a convincing and insightful account of Thackeray's philosophical dissonance with his age.

ILLUSTRATIONS

One hopes that the availability of Thackeray's works in illustrated editions will increase the level of commentary on this important aspect of his work. Judith Fisher's review of the Garland edition (*SNNTS*) is suggestive in this regard and Catherine Peters's biography, itself generously illustrated, reflects the sense that Thackeray must be acknowledged for his drawing talent as well. David Skilton's "The Relation between Illustration and Text in the Victorian Novel: A New Perspective," in Holtgen, Daly, and Lottes, eds., *Word and Visual Imagination: Studies in the Interaction of English Literature and the Visual Arts* (Erlangen: Univ. Bibliothek Erlangen-Nurnberg, 1988), analyzes a variety of functions in the dialectic of text and illustration and concludes that there is a threefold gain derived from this approach to illustrated novels in their entirety: "enhanced awareness of the literary marketplace of the time; the prospect of richer analyses of these novels . . . ; and the perception that certain novels—those of Thackeray foremost among them—speak more insistently about the literarity of the novel than we usually assume" (30). Skilton's best observations are derived for the most part from Joan Stevens's articles on the London skyline and on the pictorial capitals in the Thackeray special issue of *Costerus* (1974). Stephen Canham's "Art and the Illustrations of *Vanity Fair* and *The Newcomes*," *MLQ*, 43 (1982): 43–66, notes that Thackeray alone among major Victorian novelists illustrated his own work. He compares *The Newcomes*, illustrated by Richard Doyle, and *Vanity Fair*, illustrated by Thackeray, to try to determine how the illustrations are used. Canham's analysis, neither very technical nor penetrating, concludes that the two illustrators were similar in technique and vision and that each successfully produced integral and extended visual aspects of the text, rather than supplying mere decoration. Though it has been said before, there is some fresh commentary on individual illustrations that make this a useful article. Jim Cheff's " 'With Illustrations by the Author': Some Author-Artists of the Nineteenth Century," *ABC*, 8 (1987): 13–18 contains a very general and appreciative but not terribly accurate account of Thackeray's self-illustrated work. Nicholas Pickwood's introductions to the Garland editions remain the most technically and historically accurate accounts of Thackeray as illustrator.

ART AND AESTHETICS

In two provocative and important articles, Judith Law Fisher advances our understanding and appreciation for the complexity of Thackeray's knowledge of art and aesthetics and the intricacy of his concepts of literary and visual art. In "The Aesthetic of the Mediocre: Thackeray and the Visual Arts," *VS*, 26 (1982): 68–82, Fisher delineates Thackeray's objections to the sublime and explains his recommendations. But Thackeray's choice of word, "mediocre," interferes with her exposition, for with him it stood for "ordinary" not "shoddy" and the distinction is not clearly presented. Nevertheless, the article brilliantly traces the variety of aesthetic dictums made in Thackeray's art criticism along with references to his own practice as a literary artist, showing how the principles of one medium are carried out in the other. In a more ambitious and complex essay, "Siren and Artist: Contradiction in Thackeray's Aesthetic Ideal," *NCF*, 39 (1985), 392–419, Fisher pairs the dichotomy of Virtue and Vice with those of Ideal and Real, of Sublime and Ordinary, and of High Art and Vulgar Taste. The moral, emotional and aesthetic conflicts are set in the context of art in the marketplace and traced during approximately eighteen years of Thackeray's working life. The result is not always persuasive, but it is always thoughtful. One might object that the attractive analogy of art and woman—both capable of high genuineness and beauty and of corruption and artificiality—would tend to cast Rachel Esmond (who becomes more beautiful and youthful as she ages) and Laura Pendennis (who is always too wise and sedate and patient and righteous to be truly attractive) as the epitomes of sublimity, virtue, and one—hesitates to admit—good art. If that is the case, is it Thackeray's failing? Fisher suggests an answer in another complication that shimmers in the background of this article but is never faced squarely: the effect of Thackeray's narrators in hiding or revealing the author's stance with regard to the questions of value central to this article.

ON READING THACKERAY

Michael Lund's *Reading Thackeray* (Detroit: Wayne State UP, 1988) has the air of excitement and enthusiasm of a new discovery. It is a full-length exploration of the effect of applying the insights of reader-response interpretive practice onto Thackeray's novels within the context of an attempt to recreate the experience of original readers of serial fiction. Its combination of historical interest and literary theory produces a provocative inter-textual and contextual reading that is unavailable to readers of ordinary paperback editions of the works. Readers who first encountered the chapters of this book in periodicals will be disappointed, however, to find no additional material here.

ON SOCIAL ISSUES AND CONTEXTS

Several articles reflect a resurgent interest in contextual or new-historical approaches to interpretive criticism. Three essays by Micael M. Clarke explore Thackeray's interest in and awareness of women's issues. In "Thackeray's *Henry Esmond* and Eighteenth-Century Feminims: A Double Vision of Feminist Discourse and Literary Narrative," *WD*, 5 (1987): 85–107, she documents Thackeray's acquaintance with Eighteenth-Century feminist texts and mounts an impressive analysis of Henry Esmond's blindness to his chauvinist attitudes toward women. Clarke credits Thackeray with a careful, detailed, and deliberate delineation of the narrow choices available to intelligent women in the Eighteenth-Century, seeing Rachel succumbing to the trap of overvaluation by men and Beatrice refusing to conform and being cast out. Her sense of the complexity of Thackeray's narrative dexterity is a pleasant alternative to that of a number of commentators mentioned below. Clarke's "William Thackeray's Fiction and Caroline Norton's Biography: Narrative Matrix of Feminist Legal Reform," *DSA*, 18 (1989): 337–51, traces Thackeray's and Norton's acquaintance and friendship through the scanty surviving personal documentation and indicates the parallels between Norton's personal, though well-publicized, history and agitation for reform in marriage, divorce and child custody laws, on the one hand, and Thackeray's portraits of Lady Lyndon, Becky Sharp and Clara Newcome on the other. The parallels are striking, convincing and important; for Thackeray appears to use them to support the cause of reform in child custody, women's property rights, and divorce laws. Thackeray's support in his fiction for these "Norton causes" is unequivocal. Though published earlier, Clark's "Thackeray's *Barry Lyndon*: An Irony against Misogynists," *TSLL*, 29 (1987): 261–77, should be read after the more general piece on Norton, for though there is some overlapping of commentary, this analysis of Thackeray's exposure of bararity to women and its support in custom and legislation drives home in specific detail the general conclusions about Thackeray's stand made in the later article. Clark's brief catalogue of real and fictional sources and analogues for the character of Barry Lyndon is supplemented by Judith Fisher's "A Curious Coincidence . . ." *TNL*, no. 36 (Nov. 1992).

Barbara Weiss's "The Dilemma of Happily Ever After: Marriage and the Victorian Novel," in Hargrove and Magliocco, eds. *Portraits of Marriage in Literature* (Macomb, IL: Essays in Lit., 1984), 67–86, is about the ambivalence of Victorian authors who were basically "pro-marriage" in a marketplace that demanded happy endings—but who found themselves repeatedly exploring the debacles, shames and shams of marriage. Weiss writes briefly about *The Newcomes*, complaining that Thackeray's Fableland ending, projecting possible bliss for Clive and Ethel, denies the implications of the whole novel. She seems to forget a) that Thackeray is an ironist whose invitation to dream at the end can easily be resisted and b) that just because many marriages are sordid economic conveniences and prisons for the mismatched, not all of them are. Garrett Stewart's "Signing Off: Dickens and Thackeray, Woolf and Beckett," in Cain, ed. *Philosophical Approaches to Literature: New Essays on Nineteenth and Twentieth-Century Texts* (Lewisburg: Bucknell UP, 1984), 117–39, argues the opposite point of view. Beginning with a remark from Nabokov on the deathlessness of the narrator and one from Barthes on the death of the author, Stewart points to several deaths and separations in the ending of *The Newcomes*: the death of Col. Newcome, whose final absence is ironically declared by his final word, "Adsum" (I am present); the disappearance of the novel's narrator, Pendennis, beyond the barrier line separating author and reader from "Fableland"; and the author/storyteller's own disappearance through his farewell. Stewart credits Thackeray with greater intuitive awareness of the author's death than can be found in Barthes. Ina Ferris's "Realism and the Discord of Ending," discussed below, adds valuable perspective to this discussion of Thackeray's endings.

Carol H. MacKay's "Controlling Death and Sex: Magnification vs. The Rhetoric of Rules in Dickens and Thackeray," in Barreca, ed., *Sex and Death in Victorian Literature* (Bloomington: Indiana UP, 1990) canvasses the appropriate scenes to demonstrate the way each author magnifies, sublimates, hides and exposes the powerful emotions evoked by sex and death in a rhetorical and moral climate of indirection. Her analysis of Thackeray's rhetorical control is complex, subtle and appreciative. In the context of shifting awareness of potential homosexual implications in male friendships, Eve Kosofsky Sedgwick's "The Beast in the Closet: James and the Writing of Homosexual Panic," in Yeazell, ed., *Sex, Politics, and Science in the Ninteenth-Century Novel* (Baltimore: Johns Hopkins UP, 1986; reprinted in Showalter, ed., *Speaking of Gender* [New York: Routledge, 1989]), explores Thackeray's development of the bachelor character, particularly Mr. Batchelor in *Lovel*, but also Jos Sedley and Major Pendennis. This context of potential homosexuality, Sedgwick argues, produced a panic in which the bachelor cultivates a sexlessness which is garrulous about heterosexual near misses and early flings that might have but did not result in marriage. Sedgwick is more interested in developments later in the century but her discussion of Thackeray opens a new perspective. She continues exploring the sexual/

political/power relations in "*Adam Bede* and *Henry Esmond*: The Historicity of the Female," in her *Between Men: English Literature and Male Homosocial Desire* (New York: Columbia UP, 1985): 134–60. Admitting that Thackeray "was no more a feminist than David Ricardo was a communist" (147), Sedgwick finds a sophisticated and sensitive "analysis of gender roles as forms of power" in the novel. Her primary focus is on how homosocial desire plays itself out in a variety of positive and negative ways, usually involving a woman over whose sexually discredited body the exchange is made. Though the approach occasionally has a mechanical ring, Sedgwick's work is remarkably serious, incisive, and thought provoking.

In their first two chapters, Richard Barichman, Susan MacDonald, and Myra Stark, in *Corrupt Relations: Dickens, Thackeray, Trollope, Collins and the Victorian Sexual System* (New York: Columbia UP, 1982), provide a preliminary survey of the role of major Victorian novelists in the exploration of sexual behavior and mores, arguing that they were profoundly sensitive to, conscious of, and circumspect about, sexuality. Their treatment of Thackeray sets him apart from the other writers, who, though also treated with respect and admiration, are not, in the final analysis, as clear-eyed and subtle about the subject as Thackeray. Of his work, they find *Vanity Fair* the most interesting because the most aggressively honest about the tension between Victorian theory and practice of sexuality. But the chapter on Thackeray does not dwell on the later novels, nor does it argue convincingly that they are retreats. The authors offer a thorough, sensitive, provocative and basically fair treatment of sexuality in *Vanity Fair*, where everything (war, money, social standing, family, religion, and politics) hinges on sexual relations, sexual frustrations, sexual power, sexual manipulation, and sexual betrayal. While some readers will disagree thoroughly with their analysis of the theme and its treatment, that disapproval is likely to come from readers like Jack Rawlins, F. R. Leavis, and perhaps, Warhol, Meckier, Musselwhite, and Simon (cited below) who tend to see Thackeray's avoidance of positivist statements as an abdication of responsibility or seriousness rather than as a deliberate strength and challenge to the reader. Thackeray's refusal to allow his narrator to be pinned down by any reader can and as been seen as his way of exposing the self-delusions of everyone. No one, not Thackeray, not his narrator, nor his readers, can comfortably point the accusatory finger at any of his characters. Yet *Vanity Fair* exposes the power relations (which are by definition always inequitable) that his characters (and his readers) live by. Focusing on the sexuality of power, Barichman, MacDonald and Stark have revealed something important about the narrative technique and the themes of *Vanity Fair*—to their credit and to Thackeray's.

Gary R. Dyer's "The 'Vanity Fair' of Nineteenth-Century England: Commerce, Women, and the East in the Ladies Bazaar," *NCL*, 46 (Sept. 1991): 196–222, starts with the scene at the end of *Vanity Fair* in which Becky restores her reputation (or seeks to) by serving in a stall at a "fancy fair" or charity bazaar. Dyer explains the background of bazaars and commerce generally, providing a better understanding of the scene and of that larger commercial bazaar, Vanity Fair itself, in which all wares, including humans, are for sale. The historical details Dyer finds extend our notion of the ambiguity of bazaars as places of "alternative employment" for women who might otherwise resort to prostitution; but, in addition, they were "places of public recourse" where either prostitution or the exposure of "goods" for the marriage market could also take place. Commerce had a similar ambiguous position, providing the wherewithal for social ambition, but requiring repudiation in order for the successful to maintain or gain social standing. Our sense of the moral and social ambiguities and tensions of the novel is intensified by Dyer's information.

John Peck has selected an important and neglected topic in "Thackeray and Religion: The Evidence of *Henry Esmond*," *English*, 40 (1991): 217–35. Though he touches here and there on interesting, if sometimes trite, insights (*Esmond* is about individualism; Esmond's individualism, like that of most Protestants, and of Catholics who abandon the stable absolutism of the Church to operate as loose moral canons, is liable to excess, poor judgment, selfishness, and self-deception), Peck is diffuse, unfocused, and unconvincing in his arguments and methods. The major part of the article deals with the religions of the characters in *Esmond*—which would be fine if the article were about the use of religion by characters or by Thackeray in portraying characters—but Peck keeps dropping hints about Thackeray's own supposed beliefs or positions relative to general concepts such as Catholicism or Anglicanism (both of which we are told he criticizes and "can be argued" to defend) and Peck tries to draw conclusions about Thackeray's belief and unbelief from a base of research both narrow and flawed. The subject awaits its first satisfactory treatment.

What Kenneth L. Moler gives with his right hand he takes away with his left in " 'Leveling' Motifs in *Pendennis*: A Strategy that Does Not Always Work," *PQ*, 67 (1988): 93–102. Focusing primarily on the ways Thackeray parallels the motives and moral flaws of characters from every level of society, showing the same humanity despite financial or class differences, Moler faults

Thackeray for then resorting to the cliched counter argument that breeding will out. He finds Thackeray much more willing to condemn the peccadilloes of servants and the poor (Major Pendennis's valet Morgan and Fanny Bolton) than those of "better" background and social standing. He also sees, with J. Y. T. Greig and Joseph Baker, an increasing breakdown in "the consistency of [Thackeray's] moral and social vision" in his later fiction, and concludes that "in his heart of hearts Thackeray was *never* quite clear as to the extent to which 'brudders' of various kinds were his and Pen's brothers." The charge has been made before and the supporting evidence as always has been carefully culled from the whole picture.

RACE, IRISH, JEWS

Deborah A. Thomas's *Thackeray and Slavery* (Athens, OH: Ohio University Press, 1993) and S. S. Prawer's *Israel at Vanity Fair: Jews and Judaism in the Writings of W. M. Thackeray* (Leiden: E. J. Brill, 1992) each takes a loaded subject and traces it meticulously through Thackeray's works and letters, and each reaches a somewhat surprisingly similar conclusion: that when allowance is made for his time, Thackeray emerges as a remarkably evenhanded critic of individual human foibles and the mass prejudices of his society, rather than as a thoughtless participant in them. Thomas provides a useful introduction to the subjects of slavery (East Indian, African and New Eastern), of the abolitionist movement in England, and of the slave-like institution of employer-employee relations and husband-wife relations in nineteenth-century England. Her work explores Thackeray's personal ideas and feelings in so far as they are available to biographical investigation and his use of the slavery and slavery-like themes in his novels. She acknowledges his blind spots and hardening opinions in his later years, but his criticism of racial and sexual insensitivity is also clearly evident. Thomas, along with Charles Heglar and Judith Fisher, contributed to a discussion of Thackeray's references to the "Hottentot Venus" and their possible racist implications in *TNL*, nos. 35–36 (1992). Prawer's work lacks the theoretical dimension developed by Thomas, but he more methodically canvasses Thackeray's uses of and attacks on Jews and Judaism throughout the works. There can be but a very few stones left unturned in Prawer's massive (and very expensive) survey. But, like Thomas, Prawer concludes that Thackeray's attacks on Jews in his works is of the same caliber, frequency, and intention as his attacks on persons of Anglo and French origins. His attacks, Prawer concludes, are primarily on the selfish, the greedy, the insensitive, the proud, the snobs of England regardless of creed or color. If these conclusions run counter to readers' impressions, they have the evidence laid out in generous detail for review in these two important new books. J. Russell Perkin has already weighed in on the other side in "Thackeray and Orientalism: *Cornhill to Cairo* and *The Newcomes*," *ESC*, 16 (1990): 297–313, where he tries to show *Cornhill to Cairo* "is a pervasively anti-Semitic work" (393) in which Jews were part of the undifferentiated 'east,' " and *The Newcomes* "suffers from the same inconsistencies of voice and tone that characterize much of Thackeray's work" (304). Perkin marshals sufficient evidence to support these views, were it not systematically taken out of context and without reference to Thackeray's criticisms of the British and of himself. The major flaws of Perkin's approach are his mechanical logic and his insensitive ear for ironic and shifting narrative voice. Accepting a similar position as a given not needing much exposition, Robert Lougy, in "The Dynamics of Exile and Desire: Narrative Form and Meaning in Thackeray's *Notes of a Journey from Cornhill to Grand Cairo*," *MLQ*, 50 (1989): 227–47, pursues the "seams and gaps" in the book looking for what Thackeray reveals, in spite of himself, about his position as outsider looking in, using distancing techniques to protect himself "against fears of failure not only of will but of love and the imagination." It is a thoughtful and careful reading which will occasionally try the patience of readers accustomed to look primarily for what texts yield voluntarily. Joseph Sherman's "Race and Racism as Narrative Strategies in 'Vanity Fair,' " *English Studies in Africa*, 34 (1991): 76–102, takes up in some detail the narrator's use of Blacks and Jews in *Vanity Fair*, which he reads as a novel refusing to enter the standard Victorian convention to end "fictional events with a desired state of things in lived experience" (76). Instead, the novel "attempts a sustained criticism of Victorian social values, and a radical deconstruction of conventional Victorian literary constructs, by exploiting . . . contemporary racial prejudice." Sherman, a white South African, takes the novel to heart as relevant to current racial conditions in his own country and finds the experience uncomfortable, disturbing, and uncompromisingly devastating to racist views; for by rejecting the fictional conventions and insisting on a continuum between life and book, the narrator becomes as fallible and unreliable and narrow as his readers who repeatedly find themselves in complicity with ordinary but untenable positions regarding poverty, race, religion, and politics. The reading is serious but not irrefutable, and Sherman makes the common mistake of believing that "Before the Curtain" (which was the last thing written) represents Thackeray's beginning of the novel, so that the puppets in the box at the end of chapter 67 can be seen as a call "back to his beginning" where the Manager of the Performance hopes his puppets *"have given* satisfaction" (emphasis added).

Gunther Klotz, in "Thackeray's Ireland: Image and Attitude in Thackeray's *The Irish Sketch Book* and *Barry Lyndon"* in Wolfgang Zach, ed., *Literary Interrelations: Ireland, England and the World* vol. III, "National Images and Stereotypes," (Tubingen: Narr, 1987), 95–102, debunks the notion that Thackeray's portraits of Ireland and the Irish were "prejudiced" or stereotypical and suggests instead "an assessment more in accord with Thackeray's texts and with his methods of irony" (95). Klotz insists that "Thackeray's contempts never were dominated by racialism or nationalism" (97). Klotz thinks Charles Lever did far more than Thackeray to perpetuate Irish stereotypes, and he disagrees with Sutherland's view of Thackeray as a racialist whose attitudes toward the Irish, Jews, and colored peoples "hardened as he grew older." Instead he argues that the English and English pride and prejudice are the butts of Thackeray's criticism in *The Irish Sketch-Book*. That book and *Barry Lyndon* tell us "less about Thackeray's feelings towards Ireland and the Irish . . . than about his contribution to the new literary movement which came to be called the glorious school of realism" (102). Robin Gilmour, discussing Thackeray's travels in the Mediterranean, Ireland, France, Belgium, Italy, Germany, and America, in "Thackeray: From Europe to Empire" in Michael Costell, ed., *Creditable Warriors: 1830–1876* (London: Ashfield, 1990), 97–110, concludes similarly that Thackeray's portrait of Ireland is nearly free of contemporary stereotypes. It remains to be seen if Mary K. Fitzgerald's dissertation (U of Ct), "William Makepeace Thackeray's Writings about Ireland and the Irish: The Use of Stereotype," will result in publications contesting these views.

ON HISTORICAL FICTION, REALISM, AND NARRATIVE TECHNIQUE

Harry E. Shaw's "Uses of the Past in Eliot and Thackeray: A Question of Power," *VIJ*, 15 (1987): 17–24, raises questions too large to handle in seven pages: What is the past? what is our relationship to it? to what uses is the past put? how do distortions of the past, in memory and in rationales for present action, reveal personal agendas and weaknesses? And what is the responsibility between individual uses of the past and social realities (whatever that is). Important as these questions are, Shaw dispatches them briefly and unsatisfactorily. He thinks Esmond a distasteful person who wants and exercises power from a position of irresponsibility, declaring himself the slave of that which he masters. It is an interesting reading, put irritatingly by one who appears to have solved all the complexities of the novel and of the questions raised above. Stephen Bann, "Anti-History and Anti-hero: Thackeray, Reade, Browning, James," in *The Clothing of Clio* (Cambridge: Cambridge UP, 1984), approaches these questions more satisfactorily. Bann discusses Thackeray's reversals of the uses and perspectives of history established by Sir Walter Scott. He finds in *Esmond* a raw, risky use of "real" history in combination with fiction where "known" history undermines, rather than adds to, the sense of historicity. But Bann suggests this is deliberate on Thackeray's part, who appears to have been satirizing and attempting to make conscious the acts of writing history, of attempts at bibliographical verisimilitude, and of constructions of the heroic in history. In a postscript, Bann briefly analyzes Stanley Kubrick's failure to realize in film the ironic reversals of *Barry Lyndon*. Ian Ousby brings a slightly different perspective in "Carlyle, Thackeray, and Victorian Heroism," *YES*, 12 (1982), 152–168. Arguing that Mario Praz's contrast between Carlyle's support for Hero Worship and Thackeray's Anti-Hero is a somewhat misleading oversimplification, Ousby finds both writers starting with an observation of human beings caught in the bonds of hero-worship—all too often worshipping false heroes. He then traces Carlyle's retreat from unqualified hero worship from *On Heroes* to *Past and Present*, finding in the "Hero as Man of Letters" and in Abbot Samson models, rather than take-charge heroes. He follows with an analysis of Thackeray's *Lectures on the English Humourists*, which he sees as adopting Carlyle's qualified hero and qualifying him more — hence, "Victorian" heroism. Real heroism for both writers is found "amid the small unheroic acts of everyday life" (167).

A. R. Humphreys's "Thackeray: Novelist of Society" in Joanne Shattock, ed., *Dickens and other Victorians* (New York: St. Martin's, 1988), 185–201, does not ask the big questions Shaw proposed, but he takes much more room than Shaw did to describe the ways Thackeray evokes history, things, and the social web. His tone is admiring and appreciative, and he distinguishes familiarly between Thackeray's movement from the particular to the typical or emblematic, on the one hand, and Dickens's focus on the particular as eccentric or individual. This essay resembles in tone and purpose Juliet McMaster's richly evocative "Thackeray's Things: Time's Local Habitation" in Richard Levine's *The Victorian Experience* (1976). Andrew Miller's "*Vanity Fair* through Plate Glass," *PMLA*, 105 (1990): 1042–54, presents a far more sinister view of Thackeray's rich materialist presentation, dubbing Vanity Fair a "commodity world" in which "desire and frustration remain unsynthesized" and in which therefore, of course, frustration overwhelms desire. Hence the title of his article, which mistakenly suggests that the novel, *Vanity Fair*, rather than the place, Vanity Fair, is separated from us, as its goods are from its aspiring but perpetually distanced characters, by a barrier like plate glass. It is not the only error in this frequently insightful, Marxist interpretation. It is a mistake to judge "Thackeray" as "the narrator" who can "by the standard of his own [Thackeray's?] desires" be defeated in a supposed "attempt to construct a dialectical relation between profane and sacred . . ." (1048). The error is not in looking for such a dialectic, for the tension between sacred and profane permeates the novel, but in equating author and narrator and demanding that the narrator resolve the ambiguities and tensions in some satisfactory triumph over, or rejection of, commodity standards for individual and social fulfillment. Miller objects to Thackeray's description of, without prescription for, the social condition. The seed for this error is planted early in the essay when Thackeray's famous rejection of rhetorical inflation in fiction, where a poker should be a poker and not "a great red-hot instrument like the Pantomime weapon," is taken by Miller to be the rejection of the metaphoric or symbolic significance of objects: "In Thackeray's view objects have no extrinsic, transcendental meaning." Such misjudgments unfortunately mar Miller's ambitious and potentially important work.

Christina Crosby assesses Thackeray's portrayal of desire more satisfactorily in "Henry Esmond and the Subject of History," in *The Ends of History* (New York and London: Routledge, 1991), 44–68. Her book is an attempt to understand the uses, both conscious and unconscious, of history in the 19th Century from the fiction and historical narratives of Scott and Carlyle onward. She traces the development of historiography and the role of "realism" and "truth" in fiction and reviews. Her other focus is on "the woman question"—the identity of man and woman and the roles which "history" assigned to women. It is in this context that Crosby analyzes Thackeray's *Henry Esmond* and *The Four Georges*. Comparing *Esmond* with Macaulay's *History of England*, she finds History and Truth in Macaulay to be very masculine, imposing the order of English constitutional law on the progress of history. By contrast Thackeray "privatizes" history—showing "public" history to be a series of posturings. Thackeray continually questions the order, authority, and legitimacy of official reality and history. Crosby praises the feminine quality of Thackeray's work that raises more questions than it answers and that focuses on the history of desire rather than on the distancing and objectification of the pursuit of history as truth. Truth itself is questioned, for Henry is revealed in ways he does not recognize—his truth is shown to be a series of postures as well.

Ina Ferris provides valuable insight into the tension between desire and frustration in "Realism and the Discord of Ending: the Example of Thackeray," *NCL*, 38 (1983), 289–303. She finds an opposition between the aims of realistic fiction and the conventional happy ending in particular and all endings in general. The conventional ending requires a firm sense of exterior authority and an ordered world in which things can end right. It is no wonder that serious, realist novelists had trouble with it. In some realist novels, Ferris finds authors adjudicating this opposition by refusing to take the ending seriously—offering it as a necessary but not integral part of the novel. With Thackeray Ferris finds no such accommodation. From *Barry Lyndon* to *Philip*, Thackeray subverts by one ploy or another the conventionality of endings, objecting to the morality of "poetic justice," to the arbitrariness of any ending whatever, and to the power of the narrator or author to provide an ending at all. In these strategies, Ferris finds Thackeray continuing to use the techniques of his fiction which emphasize the fictionality of the fiction and put the responsibility for ethical judgment onto the reader. Michael Lund would seem to offer a corroborating view in "Literary Pieces and Whole Audiences: *Denis Duval, Edwin Druid*, and *The Land Leaguers*," *Criticism*, 28 (1986): 27–49. Continuing his interest in the reader's role in the "creation" of fiction, Lund finds in the unfinished serial novels an open-endedness and sense of potential that characterized the mid-stream "process" of serial fiction generally.

Terence McCarthy's "Chronological Inconsistencies in *Barry Lyndon*," *ELN*, 21 (1983): 29–37, is a meticulous catalogue of Barry's errors about historical facts and his errors of inconsistency in fictional "facts." It is, further, a catalogue of the errors in Thackeray's editorial notes—all of which lead McCarthy to conclude that Thackeray was careless and therefore we cannot credit him with deliberately undermining Barry's credibility of intentionally introducing errors in the narrative. According to McCarthy, we cannot be sure Thackeray knew they were errors. Crucial to McCarthy's argument is the highly questionable notion that since Barry Lyndon's claim to fame involves "public glory" and specific historical events, then both narrator and author are forced to commit themselves to a certain kind of historical truth" (30). McCarthy does not say what he has in mind, but it clearly is not the kind of truth either Lyndon or Thackeray achieve. Also crucial to McCarthy's conclusion is the idea that chronological consistency and historical accuracy are essential to what the novel is about. He asserts but does not demonstrate it to be so. One can only assume that McCarthy thinks Thackeray tried and failed to characterize Barry through his errors. As in *Henry Esmond*, the significance of errors of fact and consistency depends, in advance, on a critical judgment about what Thackeray was trying to do. McCarthy's assumptions are not the only ones available to critics—who nevertheless can be grateful for having the inconsistencies ferreted out for them.

Two articles on the historical elements of *The Virginians* treat the subject without questioning the desirability of historical accuracy in fiction. Mary G. De Jong, in "The Way it Really Was: America's Quarrel over Thackeray's *The Virginians*," *MissQ*, 1984–85): 59–72, focuses on the way historical errors and unpopular judgments about historical events in the novel affected American responses to it. Though an important survey of these errors and responses, De Jong does not offer a theoretical assessment of Thackeray's intentions or of the principles for using history in fiction. Gerald Sorensen concentrates on what is historically right in the novel in "Some Sources for Thackeray's *The Virginians*," *RES*, 35 (1984): 208–13. He identifies printed sources for historical details, which are interestingly presented. But Sorensen also avoids the more serious question of the importance, if any, of the "authenticity" and verifiability of "historical fact" in fiction raised by McCarthy. He merely suggests that "each fact . . . is part of the picture of everyday life . . . that was part of Thackeray's conception of history." Ulrike Horstamann-Guthrie is less concerned with the historicity than with the way Thackeray develops character in historical fiction in "The Theme of Loyalty in *Henry Esmond* and *Vor dem Sturm*," *JES*, 14 (1984): 173–86. After a brief comment on the tradition of serious historical fiction, asserting that it is concerned "with the complex subtle exploration of a theme of universal significance, namely, that of loyalty," the essay develops the notion that Esmond's personal and political loyalties are inter-related and undergo painful changes. While it traces the theme in some detail, its conclusions do not challenge received opinion of Esmond's character or the significance of the betrayals of loyalty at the end of the book.

A much more interesting examination of *Henry Esmond's* narrative technique, one that focuses on what Henry does and does not know, both as a young man and older narrator, is found in Marjorie Garson's " 'Knowledge of Good and Evil': Henry and Rachel in *The History of Henry Esmond*," *ESC*, 9 (1983), 418–34. Garson argues that Henry knows of Rachel's sexual attraction to him from the moment she over-reacts to his "contamination" with the Sievewrights and spends the rest of his life in an Oedipal trap, denying both his knowledge and his right to be the recipient of that kind of love. It is a complicated psychological reading, depending for its plausibility on the highly debatable proposition that "it is difficult to imagine so sensitive and acute an observer as the narrator ignorant of what we ourselves cannot fail to comprehend" and that therefore "Henry must on some level 'know' everything which we can deduce, since it is his recording of the significant details which provides the clues for our interpretation" (418). One wonders if Garson applies this dubious principle to her reading of all dramatic monologues, but the reading is given its best light by the concluding remark that "Henry is not a deliberate hypocrite. He is an individual caught in a psychological bind so intense that the only way out is not to know what he knows" (432). Is there much difference between one who does not know and one who does not know what he knows? Garson's reading of the smallpox episode is insightful and thought provoking, though it did not strike in me any forceful chord of recognition.

In "The Kindness of Consanguinity: Family History in *Henry Esmond, MLS* 16 (1986): 213–26, Karen Chase focuses primarily on Henry Esmond's, rather than Thackeray's, concern with history: "Henry Esmond seeks not many close relations but many distant relations. What most heartens him is the thought that his family stretches back to the remote past and will reach forward to the remote future. . . . The sorting of family relations is the consuming domestic activity in *The History of Henry Esmond*" (213). History, in Henry's case, turns out to be what happened to him, not what he makes happen, at least not consciously. His is a career of failed and abandoned efforts: "the involuntary agent who does not want what he causes and does not cause what he wants" (218) and whose life cycle consists of exhausting his energies and enthusiasms in lost causes until he can return to his original destiny in the peace of Rachel's arms. For Chase, Esmond, but not Thackeray, is unconscious of this view of his life: for Esmond, establishing the family connections and procreating (a living) and leaving (a written) genealogy brings the satisfactions of life; for Thackeray, Esmond is an illustration of the principle that history works on people rather than the other way round.

Originally published in *Unities: Studies in the English Novel* (Athens: U of Georgia P, 1985), H. M. Daleski's catalogue of "Strategies in *Vanity Fair*," was reprinted in the *Vanity Fair* volume of Harold Bloom's Modern Critical Interpretations series (New York: Chelsea House, 1987), 121–48. In part one, Daleski analyzes the narrative strategies, identifying (a) changes of focus from one character to another, (b) transformations of narrator from one role to another, (c) shifts of dimension between the fictional and real world, subdividing these shifts into five categories, and (d) shifts of narratorial position amongst three "worlds": "the real fictional world, the shadow fictional world, and the fictional real world" (136). Daleski concludes that Thackeray is complex and dexterous rather than confusing and inconsistent, rebutting such criticisms by J. Y. T. Greig, Dorothy Van Ghent, and Wolfgang Iser. In part two, Daleski rehearses with clarity and vitality the proposition that war, rather than the fair, is the dominent metaphor in the book. There is no real connection between the two parts, nor is there any overall conclusion to be drawn, though Daleski suggests that Thackeray's narrative strategies and recurrent imagery replace plot as the unifying elements in the novel.

ON IRONY

J. Hillis Miller, in *"Henry Esmond*: Repetition and Irony" in *Fiction and Repetition: Seven English Novels*, (1982), rpt. in *Modern Critical Views: William Makepeace Thackeray*, ed. by Harold Bloom (New York: Chelsea House, 1987), brilliantly reveals first the ironic stance of the aged narrator with respect to young Henry and then the self-destruction of the image the narrator has constructed. Miller sees Thackeray's presence behind the narrator undercutting memory's sovereignty and denying the basis upon which Esmond allows himself to become "king" of the Virginia Castlewood where he accepts the "worship" of Rachel and his daughter. Miller's view of Thackeray undercutting the narrator is only a temporary stop, for he then deconstructs this level of irony by arguing that Thackeray was trying to "Understand and control his life by taking ironic authority over that assumed role and by showing the imagined person to have made a false interpretation of himself." For Miller, Thackeray fails in this attempt, as by definition all such attempts must fail. His conclusion about the novel cannot stop with resolution, for it is the nature of deconstructive criticism to deconstruct the deconstruction. Resolution would put an end to the fun and games. However, Miller's point is not without seriousness. Resolution cannot be reached with any conviction if one is fully cognizant of the slippery ground such a resolution must take for its base. For Miller, Thackeray, like his narrator, has revealed himself rather than justified himself in the endless cycle of ironic undercuttings. This view makes *Henry Esmond* "one of the best texts in

English fiction by means of which to explore the workings of irony in narrative'' (206). But in order to get boxed up, as Miller wants the reader to be, one must agree that Thackeray was seeking "authority over his own life by way of a detour representing that life in ironically displaced form in a fiction" (206).

Though a sense of history and consciousness of the effects of time are central to J. M. Rignall's "Thackeray's *Henry Esmond* and the Struggle Against the Power of Time," in Jeremy Hawthorn, ed. *The Nineteenth Century British Novel* (Baltimore: Arnold, 1986), 81–93, the approach does not worry much about historical accuracy, concentrating instead on the way Esmond and Thackeray resist the ironic encroachments of time. Rignall considers Thackeray an inconsistent ironist, and he hasn't much time or admiration for the later fiction, seeing *The Virginians* as a nostalgic failure vitiating the triumph of *Henry Esmond*. But his exploration of *Esmond*'s systematic reduction of history from the heroic to the ordinary and its acknowledgment of the ironic ravages of time, where beauty and vitality and hopes are forever slipping into caricatures of themselves, provides an interesting qualification on J. Hillis Miller's essentially nihilistic reading of the novel, for Rignall credits both Esmond and Thackeray with some success in the "struggle against the power of time." Miller's position is dictated more by the theory of irony being elaborated in the book as a whole than by a sensible reading of *Esmond*.

Although most articles on Thackeray touch in one way or another on the ironic dimensions of his work, some focus on it specifically and others, because they miss or mistake the irony, sound as if their authors had just missed the point. One of the most incisive examinations of Thackeray's voices—or rather those of the narrator of *Vanity Fair*—is James Phelan, "*Vanity Fair*: Listening as a Rhetorician—and a Feminist," in Claridge and Langland, eds. *Out of Bounds: Male Writers and Gender(ed) Criticism* (Amherst: U Massachusetts P, 1990) 132–47. Phelan's ear is as good as that of anyone who has tried to distinguish the modulations of the narrative voice, and he is sensitive to the ideological implications of the various registers of tone in the novel. He does not stop short at identifying and admiring the complexity of tonal shifts; he also examines his sense of Thackeray's limitations in "that he does not follow consistently through on his insights into patriarchy's shaping of women's behavior and . . . he sometimes reveals his own complicity with the patriarchy, thus inviting the reader to join in that complicity" (144). The criticism reveals the two-fold nature of Phelan's approach: first, listening and distinguishing the voices and, second, judging the effect from a position that requires a consistent criticism of the patriarchy. Phelan catches himself out in duplicity when he admits that "we are making him occupy our ground" if we complain that Thackeray's exposure of Becky's (predatory) vanity and Amelia's (passive) vanity "is tantamount to blaming the victim" (145). And he admits that the argument could not be stopped there either. Phelan's is one of the most important essays of the decade. Also among the more perceptive explorations of irony, Robert P. Fletcher's "The Dandy and the Fogy: Thackeray and the Aesthetics/Ethics of the Literary Pragmatist," *ELH*, 58 (1991): 383–404, credits Thackeray with a prescient awareness of twentieth century philosophical notions of how language and convention construct truths about social order, behavior, values, and belief. Fletcher finds in Thackeray's uses of irony a deliberate ambiguity, a distrust of assertion, that lives quite comfortably with the idea that life consists of assertions, conventions, and constructedness. At the foundation of this insight into the "fiction of reality" is, for Thackeray and for Fletcher, the question of the ethical status of the aesthetics of fiction and of life itself. This article is provocative and important. It takes Thackeray seriously and "accounts" for the "sentimentality," not as an indication of nostalgia or of weakmindedness, but as a longing for the stability that is unattainable to those who have come to a full realization of what B. H. Smith has called the contingency of values.

An even broader appreciation for the range of Thackeray's voice is seen in Barbara Hardy's "Thackeray: Inconstant Passions," in *Forms of Feeling in Victorian Fiction*, (Athens, OH: Ohio UP, 1985), 78–96, which discusses the rhetoric of passages presenting a variety of feelings. Hardy begins by assuming that Thackeray's analyses of feeling are "comic and profoundly serious." Her readings, through the comedy to the seriousness, are intelligent and appreciative. They range from the totally unselfconscious but revealing commentary of Barry Lyndon through the ironic and mock heroic presentations of romantic love and "pathetic scenes" to the straight, unridiculed presentation of powerful feelings. Equally perceptive and appreciative, but focusing on a single passage, Elaine Scarry, in "Enemy and Father: Comic Equilibirium in Number Fourteen of *Vanity Fair*," *JNT*, 10 (1980): 145–55, demonstrates how Thackeray coordinates things that are not equivalent in order to draw attention first to their seeming inappropriate comparison and then to their fundamental sameness. It is a function of his ironic vision to see and to distrust what is seen—to judge and to distrust what is judged—to identify the flaw in the character and then see the same flaw in himself. The final meaning of the book emerges from these contradictions which are identities—these rejections and acceptances—this ultimate undercutting of the "honesty" of every criticism and every sympathy.

Of course, anyone not appreciating Thackeray's brand of ambiguity, irony, uncertainty, or radical complexity of viewpoint might take exception, with this view, using it against his seriousness, commitment or purpose. Thackeray readers have been doing that since John Forster missed the humor and objected to the unadorned honesty of Thackeray work, seeing, instead, frivolity and pandering to certain social groups. This inability to recognize and take seriously Thackeray's ironic vision does not seem about to go away. And the reason lies perhaps in how closely his prose skates the edge of confusion in this age of censorship and indirection. Valerie Purton illustrates the difficulty from the writer's point of view in "The Two Voices: The Divided Style in Dickens and his Contemporaries," *Prose Studies*, 7 (1984): 38–54, in a brief analysis of the preface to *Pendennis*. Her conclusion that Thackeray fears art and nature cannot be sustained by reference only to published texts, but he certainly "feared" to publish anything very direct either about sex or religion. The voice he chooses, however, can be read in more than one way. Jerome Meckier offers one of the more interesting theses from the hostile positions relative to the narrative voice. In *Hidden Rivalries in Victorian Fiction: Dickens, Realism and Revaluation* (Lexington: U Kentucky P, 1987), he develops the idea that Victorian novelists competed with one another for a more adequate representation of reality. He reads each novel for its responses to and advancements on ideas, portrayals, styles, and moralities in previous novels by other novelists. To sustain this approach, Meckier rejects the idea of "A Victorian Mind" or "A Victorian Realism"—finding instead multiple realisms and a sophisticated double vision in many novelists who did not have simplistic notions of reality. He also rejects the least effective forms of post-structuralism, deconstruction in particular, which he says reduces differences either to a sameness or to a confusion. As a particularly bad example, he cites Peter Garret's study whose "seeing double" Meckier calls an imperfection of sight very different from double vision. Having chosen Dickens as the central figure against whom other Victorians vied and measured themselves, Meckier finds Thackeray curiously unwilling to play that game. He explains this by saying Dickens and Thackeray's vaunted rivalry was basically restricted to making money and that their visions were remarkably similar: both satiric, both pessimistic about social progress—Dickens caught out society in its complacencies while Thackeray caught out individuals in theirs. It seems more likely to me that Thackeray's failure to "rival" Dickens in Meckier's terms stems not from a basic similarity of vision and purpose but from so fundamentally different a concept of reality and value that Thackeray simply did not choose Dickens as a writer to spar with, though of course Thackeray's relatively modest financial success caused people to see them as rivals "at the top of the tree."

Meckier's "Distortion Versus Revaluation: Three Twentieth Century Responses to Victorian Fiction," *VN*, 73 (1988): 3–8, carries the thesis of his book into more recent times. After dismissing Michael Noonan's *Magwitch* and Jean Rhys's *Wide Sargasso Sea* as distortions and unsuccessful fiction on any grounds, Meckier praises Arnold Bennett's *The Old Wives Tale* as a revaluation of *Vanity Fair* because it offers a multi-layered, multi-viewed corrective to Thackeray's single-minded, jaundiced sentimentality. One cannot tell from this article whether Meckier actually ever read *Vanity Fair*.

Richard Keller Simon takes Thackeray much more seriously in "*Vanity Fair*: The History of Comedy," in *The Labyrinth of the Comic: Theory and Practice from Fielding to Freud* (Tallahassee: Florida State UP, 1985), where he examines theories of the comic through English fiction, Danish and German philosophy, Anglo-American psychology, and Austrian psychoanalysis. Simon traces parallels between Kierkegaard and Thackeray, developing a theory of repetition in history, finally focusing on *Vanity Fair* as the serious repetition of Fielding's comedy—a mirror reversal in which Becky demonstrates the hollow corruption of the frivolous world of Congreve and Wycherley, but in which *Vanity Fair* as a whole manages to mediate between comedy and sentimentality. "If there is a middle position between these two excesses in the novel it must be supplied by the readers" (136). Although that sums up nicely the challenge of *Vanity Fair*, and though Simon has much of interest to say about the novel (the narrator of *Vanity Fair* develops a Shaftsburian genial humor while Becky develops a cruel Hobbsian satire), it is all calculated to reflect his developing theory of the comic—and in the end one cannot escape feeling that Thackeray is a much more complex and subtle humorist than Simon recognizes or articulates.

David Musselwhite's "Notes on a Journey to *Vanity Fair*," in *Partings Welded Together* (London and New York: Methuen, 1987), is at once the most thought-provoking, ambitious, irritating and disappointing discussion of the novel in recent years. One gets the impression, reading the introduction, that this combination of historical, textual, psychological criticism conducted within a Marxist frame of reference is undertaken because criticism matters, because what and how we read makes a difference in the way we live. So it is with disappointment that one reads the chapter on *Vanity Fair* which is riddled with factual errors, crippled by ignorance, vitiated by a meandering organization, and inflated by speculation couched in the rhetoric of authority. Musselwhite's trust in the definitiveness of the revised edition, 1853, is untroubled by the fact that its revisions were dictated primarily by its cheapness and that it was prepared for publication while Thackeray was in America. He seems to think the cuts at the beginning of chapter six took place before the 1853 edition, predating the elimination of the illustrations. Not so. Lady Eastlake was still just Elizabeth Rigby when she wrote the review of *Jane Eyre* and *Vanity Fair*. Thackeray had three, not two, daughters—Jane died at 8 months (a rather important fact considering Musselwhite's attempts to account for psychological stress in Thackeray's life at the time). And the subtitle of the novel is *A Novel without a Hero* not *The Novel.* . . . Any critic who seriously appeals to Jack Rawlins's book *A Fiction that is True* (1974) as a corrective to Ray's description of Thackeray's sense of responsibility as a novelist must be clutching at straws. Rawlins is a good observer of narrative technique and an abysmal judge of it. Having identified Thackeray's most subtle strategy—forcing the reader to rely on his or her own intellectual and moral engagement with the text—Rawlins refuses the challenge, concluding that Thackeray abdicated his responsibility to be unambiguous. Musselwhite is not that obtuse, but like Rawlins he sounds as if he made up his mind what to think of *Vanity Fair* before reading the book. Musselwhite marshals a few circumstantial evidences, asserts that they support his view, and sails on. In this brief pursuit of political history as an explanation for the "constructed hodge-podge" of the novel, Musselwhite draws comparisons between it and Marx's *Eighteenth Brumaire of Louis Bonaparte* (1852), which he introduces as a "brilliant account . . . of the series of revolutions . . . in France between February 1848 and December 1851''—brilliant for political analysis and "stylistic ebullience" (122). He concludes with the following obscure double negation: "The *Eighteenth Brumaire*, in other words, no more than *Vanity Fair*, offers us not so much a critical description of a historical moment as a enactment of that moment via its register of stylistic devices and convolutions which are themselves available for intepretation" (124). Indeed?

Musselwhite opines that the genesis of *Vanity Fair* lay in the *Notes on a Journey from Cornhill to Grand Cairo* (1846), and he finds interesting parallels between Lt. Bundy in that book and Capt. Dobbin in *Vanity Fair*. But the most important observation drawn from *Notes* is the sharp contrast between classical, western, dirty, logical, formal Greek Athens—responsible for all that was miserable in the education of English schoolboys—and the exciting, fanciful, free, imaginative, eastern Smyrna. This contrast is applied as a kind of psychic schizophrenia in Thackeray that repeats itself in Jos/Becky,

George/Dobbin, and many other dislocations between desire and reality, between representation and being, and other appearances and realities. Musselwhite is probably on to something important here, but his flights of fancy and distortion for effect are quite irritating. His discussion of a 6 June 1848 illustrated letter from Thackeray to a Miss Smith, degenerates into piffle, his points depending on a humorless and utter disregard for perspective. The concluding idea that in killing off George Osborne Thackeray effected a cathartic rejection of his own callow youth fails to convince or even find a resonant chord. Musselwhite has occasional moments of lucid insight and an overall concern for a reading that matters; he draws together materials and ideas not previously considered; but his conclusions are unsupported and unconvincing.

Robyn Warhol's analysis of Thackeray suffers from a similar humorlessness that prevents her from seeing the seriousness of Thackeray's work, though the reason lies, I think, in the seriousness of a different subject that is more important to her. In *Gendered Interventions: Narrative Discourse in the Victorian Novel* (New Brunswick and London: Rutgers UP, 1989), Warhol's primary concern is to make room in critical debate for a feminine narrative strategy that tends toward the intimate and earnest. Criticism has neglected and devalued earnest, intimate narration in favor of a masculine strategy of creating distance through irony. Warhol opposes previous critical appraisals of what she calls feminine techniques, wishing instead to analyze them on their own terms for what they assume about speakers and reader and for what they accomplish in nineteenth century fiction—most of it no longer read. She begins her discussion of Thackeray with the "problem" of understanding Charles Kingsley's remark that Thackeray was "our most earnest and genial novelist" (83). It is the word "earnest" which, in light of the theoretical distinctions of the first two chapters, seems inappropriate. Warhol rejects claims that *Vanity Fair* is a "realistic" novel, for all its appeals to realism are undercut by the author who won't let the narrator or reader forget that it is fiction. She rejects too the claims that *Vanity Fair* "preaches" a serious sermon of any sort, choosing to see the narrator's motley as in indication that he only plays at preaching. She is not convinced by Ina Ferris's (to me quite convincing) claims that beneath the surface play is a serious intent. She concludes that Kingsley and others have attributed to Thackeray that which is not there. Thackeray, whom Warhol seems to admire and appreciate, is really ultimately just playful. Warhol, though she does not say so, seems to confirm F. R. Leavis's unsympathetic remark that Thackeray's novels do no more than pass time.

Lisa Jadwin begins far more perceptively, in "The Seductiveness of Female Duplicity in *Vanity Fair*," *SEL*, 32 (1992): 663–87. She analyzes the "shape shifting" voice of the narrator and Becky, who both use the attractive duplicity of feminine indirection to defeat their "enemies" and attract or trap their providers—in Thackeray's case the purchasers of the next number. This is an acute, observant, thought-provoking reading which ends in some confusion over "Thackeray's personal and authorial ambivalence" which may have "reflected a submerged radicalism hidden beneath his bluff clubman demeanor, a radicalism based on his ability to see and appreciate the viewpoints of renegades" (683). Earlier Jadwin appeared to have accepted the narrator's challenge to take responsibility for response, and she seemed not to need the authorial confirmation demanded here. Nevertheless, this essay ends better than Robyn Warhol's; for Jadwin finds not only mimetic dexterity in Thackeray's narrative voices but compassion and understanding for women and the genderlect that reveals virtue and crime as equally manipulative.

In what begins to feel like a postscript to this debate, William R. Elkins, "Thackeray's *Vanity Fair*," *Explicator*, 44 (1986): 31–35 unsuccessfully attempts "to narrow the investigation" of Thackeray's narrative technique, finding in the charades a metaphor and epitome of the "dual narrator." Elkins's view is oversimplified, adding nothing to the debate, which he rightly identifies as central to an understanding of *Vanity Fair*.

ON PARODIES AND IMITATIONS

Juliet McMaster's "Novels by Eminent Hands: Sincerest Flattery from the Author of *Vanity Fair*" *DSA*, 18 (1989): 309–36, brings a special perspective to a subject that will be appreciated by anyone who has painstakingly provided explanatory and historical annotations for a novel. The intimacy with a work which such labor entails led McMaster to the conclusion that Thackeray's parodies resulted from a similar detailed awareness of the originals. She suggests Thackeray's studies taught him both what to do and what not to do as a novelist. Further, McMaster documents the ways the parodees with the exceptions of Cooper and Disraeli, altered their writing styles in response to Thackeray's parodies. Cooper ignored it; Disraeli resented and resisted more than the other writers. Among the many interesting forms of intertextuality McMaster explores are the allusions buried wordlessly in the illustrations. This is an important article on Thackeray's development of narrative technique.

Louis James's "The View from Brick Lane: Contrasting Perspectives in Working-Class and Middle-Class Fiction of the Early Victorian Period," *YES*, 11 (1981): 87–101, contrasts the pseudonymously published plagiarism, *Oliver Twiss*, and G. W. N. Reynolds's *The Mysteries of London* (as representative working-class fiction) with Dickens's *Oliver Twist* and Thackeray's *Vanity Fair* (as middle-class fiction) in an enlightening exploration of taste, audience, and marketing in the "two nations." *Oliver Twiss* is both more realistic and more melodramatic than *Oliver Twist* and *Mysteries of London* portrays in many ways the same London Thackeray does, only without suppressing the siren's tail from polite view.

ON THE DIGNITY OF LITERATURE

Craig Howes's "*Pendennis* and the Controversy on the 'Dignity of Literature,' " *NCL*, 41 (1986): 269–98, provides the most detailed analysis yet published of Thackeray's side of the argument with Dickens and Forster over the dignity of literature and the economic and romantic images of authorship it entailed. Howes argues that this controversy separating the pre-market and post-market notion of writing, rather than Thackeray's 1849 illness, caused the change Ray has called Thackeray's shift from a Juvenalian to Horacean mode of thinking, feeling and writing. Howes's survey begins with Thackeray's review of Bulwer's memoir of Lyman Blanchard, includes the periodical debate in *The Examiner* and *Morning Chronicle*, and provides an extensive analysis of Thackeray's portrait of the literary life in *Pendennis*. My minor differences of opinion with Howes about Thackeray's position are presented in *Pegasus in Harness*. The central documents in the controversy are reprinted as an appendix in the Garland edition of *Pendennis*.

ON DRAMATIZATIONS

Robert Colby supplemented his 1981 *DSA* article " 'Scenes of All Sorts': *Vanity Fair* on Stage and Screen," with "Becky in the Twentieth Century," *TNL*, no. 25 (1985) when he discovered he had omitted mention of the 1932 Allied Pictures movie starring Myrna Loy. Robert Giddings, Keith Selby, and Chris Wensley provide a brief history of debate over the viability and problems of screen adaptations of literary works in *Screening the Novel: The Theory and Practice of Literary Dramatization* (New York: St. Martin's

[1990]). They discuss the more general problem of "re-creation" and the way in which history is "used" as a tourist attraction or as entertainment. Underlying their discussion is a sense of the impossibility of rendering history in full detailed accuracy and the recognition of a tendency of filmmakers to focus on accuracy of details rather than on style, point of view, interpretation, irony and moral dilemma. A major part of this book concerns the production of the BBC1's 1988 sixteen-episode adaptation of *Vanity Fair*. The authors conducted interviews with scriptwriters, editors, directors, producers, designers, and actors. A chapter each on dramatization, production, and transmission explores the purposes, problems and methods employed for the series.

Soviet and American interests in dramatizations of *Vanity Fair* are the subject of Svetlana Orchinnikova's "The Satirist Who has not Dated, for the 175th Anniversary of William Thackeray's Birth" in *Soviet Literature*, 9 (1986): 168–71, and Paul Pickrel's "*Vanity Fair* in America: *The House of Mirth* and *Gone with the Wind*," *AL*, 59 (1987): 37–57. Orchinnikova gives an account of Igor Ilyinsky's Russian adaptation of *Vanity Fair* for the Maly Theatre in Moscow. Its long gestation and singular success is detailed along with the enthusiasm of the playwright and several of the actresses who played the parts of Becky and Amelia. Pickrel gives a brief rundown of the popular stage adaptations of *Vanity Fair* in America, and then shows that Edith Wharton and Margaret Mitchell each was familiar with Thackeray's work and had ample opportunity and probably did see stage versions. Pickrel traces parallels in plot, scenes, characters, themes, and relationships between *Vanity Fair* and Wharton's *House of Mirth* and Mitchell's *Gone with the Wind*. The article ends with some interesting observations on the oddity of discovering such an important formative source for two of America's outstanding female writers in a transatlantic male writer and a brief commentary on the excesses of certain "ideological critics."

MISCELLANEOUS NOTES

Miles Lambert points to the surface "meanings" of dress and fashion in "The Dandy in Thackeray's 'Vanity Fair' and 'Pendennis': An Early Victorian View of the Regency Dandy," *CJCS*, 22 (1988): 60–69, but this essay is basically a survey, description and contrast of dandy costumes from the age of Brummell and the age of D'Orsay. T. E. Kinsey's "Podasokus," *N&Q*, 34 (1987): 491, identifies the name of a horse in *Pendennis* as a transliterated word from Greek describing Achilles in the *Iliad* as "swift of foot." Stefan Hawlin's "A Note on 'A Toccata of Galuppi's' and Thackeray's 'King Canute,' " *VP*, 28 (1990): 147–50, extends analysis of similarities between the two poems first noted by J. C. Maxwell. Ian Heywood's "Thackeray, Mary Berry, and *The Four Georges*," *N&Q*, 30 (Aug. 1983): 299, identifies the old woman referred to in *The Four Georges* as one who was patted on the head by George I and proposed to by Horace Walpole. She is also described in "Some More Words about the Ladies," *Punch*, 14 April 1849. Sheldon Goldfarb, in "Repeated Discomposure: A *Vanity Fair* Textual Problem," *ELN*, 24 (1987): 34–36, describes the well-known textual conundrum in *Vanity Fair* ("the auctioneer repeated his discomposure") and suggests as an emendation, "the auctioneer repeated his discourse." The word has too modern a ring for my ear, but until someone finds the manuscript for that page we shall not know for sure. Saintsbury's "respected his discomposure" still seems the best, though probably wrong, solution. In "Thackeray, Tennyson, and Bulwer Lytton," *N&Q*, 36 (June 1989): 182–83, Donald Hawes opines that the original for Becky Sharp's famous description of George Osborne as "that selfish humbug, that low-bred Cockney dandy, that padded booby, who had neither wit, nor manners, nor heart . . ." lies in Tennyson's spoof of Bulwer Lytton, "The New Timon, and the Poets" by "Alcibiades." Nancy Jane Tyson's "Thackeray and Bulwer: Between the Lines in *Barry Lyndon*," *ELN*, 27 (1989): 53–56, argues that Thackeray's characterization of Barry Lyndon has significant parallels to Bulwer Lytton and is, therefore, another parody. William Harmon, in "Hawthorne and Thackeray: Two Notes on Eliot's Reading and Borrowing," *Yeats Eliot Review*, 8 (1986): 123–24, claims to find in several T. S. Eliot poems evidence of his having read and used phrases and words from Thackeray's essay on Swift and from *Vanity Fair*. Thomas E. Recchio, in "The Pinkerton and the Jenkyns Sisters: a Literary Source for *Cranford*," *GSJ*, 2 (1988): 76–80, provides a plausible but very thin attempt to infer, from parallels between Thackeray's Pinkerton sisters and Elizabeth Gaskell's Jenkyns sisters (and from the fact that Gaskell refers once to Thackeray in connection with Charlotte Brontë), that *Vanity Fair* should be counted among the possible sources. Gail D. Sorensen, in "Thackeray's 'The Rose and the Ring': A Novelist's Fairy Tale," *Mythlore*, 57 (1989): 37–38, 43, surveys the "literary qualities" of Thackeray's fairy tale, compares its technique to those of Thackeray's other fiction, and finds in the fairy tale moral and aesthetic sophistication and significance. Sheldon Goldfarb, in "Yawning in Spirit or Trembling at the Portals? *Cox's Diary* and the Boredom of Becky Sharp," *DUJ*, 83 (1991): 39–43, argues that Becky is not bored, as the narrator claims, by high society once achieved, but rather is frightened by the dangers of that life and escapes from it into Bohemia once again. He reads both Barber Cox, who is also frightened out of the aristocracy to which he does not really belong, and Becky as "projections of Thackeray" who, according to Goldfarb, was more frightened than bored by high society. Aside from the dubious technique of reading authorial biography from fiction, what little recourse there is in this article to Thackeray's letters takes literally what seems to be ironic; so that, while the article may illuminate the portrayal of Becky Sharp and the Barber Cox, it does not add to our sense of Thackeray or his position in society. Richard W. Oram's "George Orwell's 'A Hanging' and Thackeray," *AN&Q*, 21 (1983): 108–09, traces parallels between Orwell's work and Thackeray's "Going to See a Man Hanged" and concludes Thackeray's essay "deserves to be better known and more frequently anthologized."

ABBREVIATIONS

ABC–American Book Collector

AL–American Literature

AN&Q–American Notes and Queries

CLAJ–CLA Journal

DSA–Dickens Studies Annual

DUJ–Durham University Journal

ELN–English Language Notes

ESC–English Studies in Canada

GSJ–Gaskell Society Journal

JEGP–Journal of English and Germanic Philology

JES–Journal of European Studies

JNT–Journal of Narrative Technique

LCUT–Library Chronicle of the University of Texas

MissQ–Mississippi Quarterly

MLQ–Modern Language Quarterly

MLS–Modern Language Studies

N&Q–Notes and Queries

NCL–Nineteenth Century Literature (NCF-NC Fiction)

PQ–Philological Quarterly

RES–Review of English Studies

SEL–Studies in English Literature

SNNTS–Studies in the Novel (North Texas State U.)

TLS–Times Literary Supplement

TNL–Thackeray Newsletter

TSLL–Texas Studies in Literature and Language

VIJ–Victorian Institute Journal

VN–Victorian Newsletter

VP–Victorian Poetry

VS–Victorian Studies

VPR–Victorian Periodicals Review

WD–Works and Days

YES–Yearbook of English Studies

Recent Dickens Studies: 1992

Stanley Friedman

An invitation to survey a year's work in Dickens studies is intimidating because of the sheer number of books and articles to be examined and the great diversity of topics and approaches. Just as King Canute in the legend could not halt the tide, so none of us can stem the flow of publications. Although this survey excludes such items as dissertations or theses not published in book form, studies in languages other than English, nearly all adaptations, non-scholarly editions, collections of previously published secondary materials, most works giving only tangential attention to Dickens, and electronic publications, I consider sixteen books and over sixty articles. Of course, I regret any inadvertent omissions.

So that readers may readily determine which items they desire to consult, I have provided relatively detailed summations. While I see my role as primarily that of guide rather than judge, I frequently offer appreciations and quibbles. Since any system of organization must be arbitrary, with many works classifiable under more than one heading, I occasionally provide cross-references.

I start with twelve scholarly books, the first seven containing fairly broad examinations of Dickens' development or overall achievement, the second five presenting specialized discussions of, respectively, *Oliver Twist, The Mystery of Edwin Drood*, pastoralism in Dickens, the Gothic in Dickens and others, and travel writing by Dickens and others. Next, I survey twelve articles on Dickens, the first two biographical, the others more or less general, before moving to essays on the novels (these items being considered according to the novels' order of publication) and then to four articles on the short fiction. I include with the periodical essays on individual novels two other short discussions, each of which is the lone chapter or segment on Dickens in a book. After brief remarks on two books containing only peripheral reference to Dickens, I give attention to two additional books and one brief story that may be viewed as "entertainments." Finally, I offer a short assessment of current trends.

Richard Maxwell's *The Mysteries of Paris and London* is an extraordinarily ambitious attempt to indicate how the conventions of the novel of urban mysteries, a genre derived from Victor Hugo's *Notre-Dame* and particularly exemplified by Eugène Sue's *Les mystères de Paris* and G. W. M. Reynolds' *Mysteries of London*, are reflected in major novels by Hugo and Dickens. Maxwell demonstrates that an awareness of this influence allows us to see the latter texts as efforts to comprehend urban life.

Impressively erudite in both range and depth of scholarship, the author makes adroit use of not only literary history and textual analysis, but also such disciplines as sociology, art history, philosophy, and film studies in examining two preeminent novelists. His book requires slow, careful reading, and at times re-reading, since the thesis is highly complex and is supported by admirably detailed discussion. Employing a modified older style of documentation rather than the method currently endorsed by MLA, Maxwell provides fifty-eight pages of notes, and these should be perused, for most are expository and relevant, while many are fascinating. Unfortunately, the division of the twenty-six-page bibliography into seven sections, with "no item . . . listed twice, though some could have been" (381), tests a reader's patience, for the particular heading under which a title appears is not always obvious. But although this book is demanding, it is also extremely rewarding and seems likely to be influential, a brilliant stimulus to further studies.

Distinguishing between traditional medieval or Renaissance allegory and a new nineteenth-century kind, Maxwell sees the latter as challenging rather than supporting ideologies, but suggests that such questioning may call for qualification of systems, not complete rejection. Despite the belief of both Goethe and Ruskin that "allegory could never be adapted to an urbanized civilization" (14), Maxwell argues that the novel of urban mysteries, by accepting "a probable and provisional order rather than an eternal one" (15), succeeds in modernizing allegory, especially through the use of four figures: (a) labyrinths or mazes, (b) crowds or phantasmagorias (magic-lantern slide shows), (c) panoramas (artificial visual displays that simulate "a 360–degree vista by painting and other illusionistic means" [17]) or "bird's-eye" views from high vantage points like steeples or towers, and (d) paper or paperwork (written documents and books). For Maxwell, these figures reveal coherence and sometimes even show a "sequence": "the secretive labyrinth" leading to "the spectacular vision of panorama or crowd" (or both) and then being superseded by ''a concern for paper and paperwork,'' especially written secrets (20).

After this theoretical opening, Maxwell supports his position with detailed commentaries on various texts, including *Oliver Twist, The Old Curiosity Shop, Martin Chuzzlewit, Bleak House,* and *The Mystery of Edwin Drood,* the latter two being compared, respectively, with Hugo's *Les Misérables* and *Les Travailleurs de la mer.* I will limit my remarks to the consideration of the five Dickens novels.

Maxwell's chapter on *Oliver Twist* shows how the London depicted in this novel ''is organized around the socializing principle of the gallows'' (72), relates the imagery of the hangman's knot to labyrinths or mazes, and examines how we are affected by the narrator's movement from maze to crowd. The ensuing chapter on *The Old Curiosity Shop* emphasizes the second of the four allegorical figures, crowds, which Maxwell finds linked with ''the bursting life'' of this novel and also with ''occasions of mortality'' (96). The author reviews the iconographic tradition of a crowd of characters shown flowing from the head of a creator who has imagined them and traces the relationship between this motif and the theme of melancholy. Woven into this chapter, too, are segments on the idea of curiosity, on the link between Hugo's Quasimodo and Quilp (two physically strong, monstrous characters), and on the importance of the narrator, Humphrey. Moving to *Martin Chuzzlewit,* Maxwell stresses the third of the figures he finds vital to urban allegory—panoramas (such as the famous one from the roof of Todgers' boarding-house)—and also explores the concepts of singularity and repetition, especially as manifested by the odd couple Jonas Chuzzlewit and Sarah Gamp, ''an opposed pair'' (139) with intriguing likenesses.

In studying these early works by Dickens, Maxwell points out the insights each affords into city living. Having illustrated the first three of his allegorical figures, he next concentrates on the fourth while examining paper as a dominant motif in *Bleak House,* a novel in which ''London is perceived as a gigantic web of secrets'' (161), secrets hidden in public legal documents and in private letters. Subsequently, Maxwell discusses *The Mystery of Edwin Drood* as ''a tale of two cities, London and Cloisterham'' (304), a narrative in which Dickens, ''committed to the link between London and death and its corollary that death is the revealer of urban secrets'' (306), tries ''to discover a usable passage between city and nature'' (308).

Besides the aforementioned analyses, Maxwell offers brief but valuable comments on other Dickens texts, explores the affinities between Dickens and Hugo, and compares these giants to such lesser figures as Sue, Reynolds, and W. H. Ainsworth.

Obviously, in responding to so long and so complex a study, we are likely to be more accepting of some arguments than of others, but I believe that Maxwell is usually convincing, and my own objections seem very minor. For example, the description of the book Fagin gives Oliver to read in chapter 20 of *Oliver Twist*—"a history of the lives and trials of great criminals"—suggests *The Newgate Calendar* or some similar compendium rather than "a Newgate novel" (86).

Two typographical slips may cause problems: the transposition of "*Drood*" and "*Travailleurs*" (291, near the end of the second paragraph) and the appearance, in the bibliography, of an extended dash (under "Green, Martin") instead of the name "Humpherys, Anne," the actual author of *Travels into the Poor Man's Country: The Work of Henry Mayhew* (393). In addition, I find a few misstatements: "the mother of the dead child" in *Bleak House* is Jenny, a brickmaker's wife, not "the serving-maid of Lady Dedlock" (186); in the *Arabian Nights* the tale of the merchant and the genie includes "defensive telling of tales" not by the merchant (who should not be called a "date merchant"), but by the three elderly men he meets (240); and in an account of Dickens' death "Georgina" refers to his sister-in-law, not "his daughter" (319). These are, however, trivial slips in an ingenious, original, masterly study, itself a labyrinthine work offering a crowded, panoramic, and well-documented view of important areas in nineteenth-century urban fiction.

In another highly ambitious book, *Modern Romance and Transformations of the Novel: The Gothic, Scott, Dickens*, Ian Duncan demonstrates how Scott took some elements of the Gothic—especially the feminine, subjective strain found in the fiction of Ann Radcliffe—and, by modifying the balance between romance (which Duncan sees as tending to express the private and conveying a mood of optimism) and history (which he views as examining the public sphere and often involving defeat), developed a form of the novel that quickly gained popular as well as critical approval and was soon inherited and adapted by Great Britain's next major national author, Dickens.

After examining various complexities of the Gothic, Duncan proceeds to differentiate between Radcliffe's narratives and those of Horace Walpole and Matthew Lewis, offers insightful comments on her novels, and then shows how Scott develops a "new kind of novel, the historical romance" (56). Considering Scott's differing balances of history and romance in several novels, Duncan proposes that *The Heart of Mid-Lothian* achieves "the capacious form of the mid-Victorian apocalyptic social allegory of Dickens, Thackeray, Gaskell, Eliot and Trollope" (150).

The remaining chapters, a little under a third of the book, deal with Dickens' reactions to Scott's fiction and also to Scott's life—especially the literary achievement (the acquisition of popularity, respect, and wealth through writing), the sudden financial disaster, and the valiant but self-destructive effort to recover. Observing that Dickens took pride in the earlier close association between George Hogarth, the man who was to become his father-in-law, and the great Sir Walter, Duncan persuasively suggests that Scott became for the young writer "the ideal shadow or archetype of the father-in-law, a figure . . . more impressive than any actual, personal, mortal father, the type of ruinous weakness and improvidence" (189), and also a revered "representative of the profession of novelist" (190).

This interest in Scott as professional author continued through the writing of *David Copperfield*, in which, according to Duncan, Dickens "mythologized his vocation" in an "autobiographical romance" (193). Noting some illuminating parallels between the significance of early reading for David and for Waverley, Duncan also comments on the "principle of narrative doubling, present in Dickens's work from his first 'progress' romance, *Oliver Twist*, onwards," a device derived "through Scott and Gothic fiction" (201) and especially noteworthy in *David Copperfield*.

In this book's final chapter, Duncan concentrates on Dickens' first historical novel, *Barnaby Rudge*, composed "in competitive imitation of Scott" (211), and on *Dombey and Son*, "Dickens's first carefully organized novel" (237). In both of these narratives, history becomes subsumed by elements of romance, for while Scott fused history and romance in balancing private, domestic themes with the public, historical element, Dickens would "perfect his own version" of "complex" narrative by looking to "Scott's romance rather than his history" (220). For Duncan, *Barnaby Rudge* concentrates on an Oedipal struggle "waged covertly" (224) in various father-son conflicts and examines the "inescapable, thrilling, but damnable uprising against paternal authority and its institutions" (231). In *Dombey and Son*, Duncan observes, Dickens "associates" Florence's saving of her father with "the theme of romance, which for the first time in his novels represents a magic at once worldly, beneficent and true" (237). Accordingly, the narrative is, as Duncan remarks, replete with "romance allusions" (239).

Modern Romance and Transformations of the Novel clarifies our understanding of Dickens' inheritance from Scott, another writer adept at absorbing and synthesizing diverse literary traditions. As Duncan emphasizes, Shakespeare is a particularly pervasive influence for both Scott and Dickens. Furthermore, the latter's direct borrowing from Shakespeare, "the studied deployment of Shakespearian echoes, themes and characters," is itself seen as a "technique [that] forms part of Dickens's imitation" of Scott (229).

Duncan makes skillful use of recent secondary literature and presents a cogent, valuable discussion, but I cannot accept his enthusiastic comment about "Agnes's 'pointing upwards' ": "John Carey was right [in *The Violent Effigy* (171)] to remark that she [Agnes] is pointing the way upstairs to the bedroom" (206–07). Agnes' "pointing upwards," mentioned late in chapter 60 and repeated in the novel's closing words, is explicitly linked by David, in chapter 60, with an earlier time when, just after Dora's death, he saw Agnes' "solemn hand upraised towards Heaven" (ch. 53). The suggestion, therefore, that "pointing upwards" represents not a silent reference to eternal verities but a sexual invitation seems bizarre. Despite this quibble, I find Duncan's book a very impressive integrated study of three major literary subjects—the Gothic, Scott, and Dickens.

Morris Golden, in *Dickens Imagining Himself: Six Novel Encounters with a Changing World*, examines the extent to which characters in six of the novels reveal the author's projection of diverse facets of his own personality: "Dickens develops sides of himself in all the major figures in his moral and social spectrum, male and female, young and old" (4). For Golden, as the pun in his book's title suggests, each of the narratives considered shows new ways that Dickens found to react to changes not only in the world but in himself at various stages of his life. Despite the attention to Dickens' personal history, however, Golden insists that his "concern is primarily critical, not biographical" (20). Acknowledging uncertainty about the extent to which Dickens "was conscious of his involvement in the characters and events" in his books (2), this study goes on to select six works "written at points of life to which most of us pay special attention" (17): *Barnaby Rudge* and *Martin Chuzzlewit*, composed, respectively, just before and just after Dickens became thirty, *David Copperfield* and *Bleak House*, written when he was "around forty," and *Great Expectations* and *Our Mutual Friend*, appearing when he was "around fifty" (18).

In *Barnaby Rudge*, Golden maintains, "Dickens spread his sense of himself most obviously among the six young men" (24)—not only Joe Willett and Edward Chester, but Hugh and Simon Tappertit, and even Lord George Gordon (called "not yet thirty" in the story, as Golden reminds us [28]) and Barnaby. Other characters, too, including the murderer Rudge, the blindman

Stagg, Haredale, and Varden, are shown to reveal affinities with Dickens' own past and present traits and impulses. For Golden, in this novel Dickens "effectively projects himself into both generations" (49), as he probes "son-father situations" (48) and displays "the shock of youth assuming maturity, of sons replacing fathers" (52).

Golden finds that in *Martin Chuzzlewit* Dickens presents in those men about his own age—young Martin, Tom Pinch, Mark Tapley, and Jonas Chuzzlewit—"varieties of complex youthful selves," as he develops the theme of "great expectations mocked" (57). But, again, projections of still different facets of the novelist are also seen in other characters—for example, in figures as antithetical to each other as old Martin and Pecksniff.

Moving to *David Copperfield*, a "novel summing up a life approaching middle age" (89), Golden sees "all the achieved characters," including the "young women," as "to some extent projections of tendencies within Dickens," even though "his clearest alternative selves after David . . . were David's male contemporaries—Heep, Steerforth, and Traddles—and more distantly the older men like Micawber, Mr. Dick, Murdstone, and Mr. Peggotty" (102). Although Golden, like many other critics, is correct in pointing to this novel's emphasis on memory, the claim that David is writing his narrative to "solidify the memory" and "make its testimony public" (89) neglects the wish for privacy stated in the parenthetical clause in Dickens' full original title—"Which He [David] never meant to be Published on any Account"—and also seems to overlook David's remark that "this manuscript is intended for no eyes but mine" (ch. 42). In assessing this central novel, Golden observes that Copperfield, at "life's middle," surveys his past and "finds grounds for encouragement and reconciliation, but also for atonement" (124).

In *Bleak House* and the three novels following it, Golden notices a change as Dickens moves from "a general acceptance" of the past, "modified only by a sense of incompleteness" (125–26), to a concern with the ways "in which past wrong or sin breaks with scouring effect upon present corruption," an apprehension that focuses on his "sense of a terrible mistake in his own past," a feeling attributed to "his growing unhappiness with his marriage" (126) and reflected, according to Golden, in Esther's sense of guilt over her birth. *Bleak House* is also seen as revealing its author's "rebellious qualities" in Hortense (137), his youthful ambition in the aspiring Guppy, his vulnerable childhood in Jo, and his distress at being a marital victim in Snagsby. The novel, Golden states, depicts a "world in the eternal present" (148) and expresses Dickens' feeling of "the obligation to endure—to persevere" (162).

As Dickens proceeded to face new problems "on his way to fifty" (164), he created, this study affirms, in *Great Expectations* a new set of projections to interact with the central one, Pip. For Golden, the latter's relationship with Magwitch reflects stages in Dickens' interaction with his own father, a man he resented but then came to respect and love, while Estella's influence on him reveals "the old pain and the new joy" that Dickens was finding in his love for Ellen Ternan (192).

Our Mutual Friend, the last completed novel, features projections derived from the various roles in which Dickens found himself—the "father of two grown daughters," the "grateful patron" of Georgina Hogarth, the "social conscience" of the nation, "Ellen's lover and guardian" (195). For Golden, the Bella-John and Lizzie-Eugene matches—"parallel stories of obsessive love" (227)—may be regarded as versions of Dickens' affair with Ellen, and "the world of *Our Mutual Friend*," despite its grim elements, "anticipates a fresh, new future" (227).

Golden implicitly attributes to Dickens as writer a variant of the habit acknowledged by David Copperfield as a reader. While describing his response to the books left by his father, David tells of "impersonating" his "favorite characters" and "putting Mr. and Miss Murdstone into all the bad ones" (ch. 4). For Golden, nearly all of Dickens' notable characters—noble or wicked—are impersonations of the novelist himself, with features also drawn from Dickens' parents, Maria Beadnell, Mary Hogarth, Ellen Ternan, and many other relatives, friends, and acquaintances. Indeed, this view may remind us of Spenser's sonnet 54 in *Amoretti*, a poem in which the love-distressed speaker asserts, "My love like the spectator ydly sits / Beholding me that all the pageants [roles] play."

Initially, Golden's approach may evoke skepticism, since just one or two traits may be adduced to claim that any particular character is a past self, a potential self, a limited part of a present self, or even an anti-self of a writer whose "range of selves" was "extraordinarily wide" (4). But Golden's skill in using biographical details, in citing Dickens' letters and essays, and in providing precise references to the novels themselves makes this enthusiastic discussion illuminating and often cogent. (One typographic slip may cause confusion: in a comment on *Hard Times* the name "Rebecca" should be changed to "Rachael" [18].)

Patricia Ingham, in *Dickens, Women and Language*, an analysis that often contrasts with Golden's, seeks to demonstrate that the female characters in Dickens' fiction do not present facets of the author or of women he knew but, instead, reflect stereotypes conveyed by the "linguistic conventions" used in such mid-Victorian non-fictional works as Sarah Stickney Ellis' books describing English women (4). Ingham maintains that close textual analysis discloses "the contradictory fears and desires that underlie" Dickens' fictional women (2), for she believes that in these novels "issues of gender, sexuality and class" are "in cultural and linguistic flux" (4), as seen in the conventional categories of "the virtuous and sexless middle-class woman" and "the oppositional figure of her defining other, the sexual and outcast fallen woman or prostitute, representative of the working classes" (6).

In considering "all those groupings of women under linguistic signs . . . in Dickens' novels" (11), Ingham offers chapters on five types: "Nubile girls," "Fallen girls," "Excessive females," "Passionate women," and "True mothers." The first category includes "marriageable virgins" marked by a "lack of physicality" (18) and an "emphasis on 'slightness' " (19), an "apparent asexuality" confirmed by metaphoric comparison to angels (20), "generic flowers," or "household pets" (21). Ingham notes that these heroines, "often presumed to be idealised" (24), are described with a relative "paucity of facial detail" that permits subjective completion of an image of "feminine perfection" (25). Pointing to Dickens' inclination to describe these girls in terms of their physical attributes and clothing, Ingham asserts that this technique denies these women "sexuality, physicality and individuality" (24), while the novelist at the same time suggests their edibility, since these nubile girls are "equated" with food (31), an equation that makes evident a contradiction: "Appearances declare them [Dickens' nubile girls] sexless, the food analogy defines them *only* as sexual objects, consumable by the watching male" (33).

On the other hand, Dickens' "fallen girls," in becoming sexualized, reach, "surprisingly, . . . some degree of autonomy . . . such as the nubile girls, always the object of menace, never attain" (54), for the fallen woman, by atoning, gains a kind of "agency" (54). The next category, the "excessive" women, includes characters like Mrs. Nickleby, Mrs. Gamp, Flora Finching, and Mrs. Joe Gargery, all of whom "are unwomanly not because they are endowed with masculine qualities but because they have female qualities in unregulated and disruptive excess" (68). These women are satiric butts whose "subduing, silencing and destruction play what is offered as a necessary and enjoyable part in the usual restoration of order in Dickens' novels" (86).

Ingham proceeds to consider Edith Dombey, Louisa Bounderby, and Lady Dedlock as "passionate women"—wives involved in what "might be described as near-miss [rather than actual] adultery" (87). Each of them attracts "narratorial admiration not derision" (87), and expresses her self-image through "a single object" (97): Edith with the looking-glass, Lady Dedlock with her portrait, Louisa with her interest in fire. As Ingham remarks, "the force of reticence, the withholding of a secret core, makes these women, for the narrator, . . . unknowable and desirable" (103) and gives them a "higher value" than that assigned to nubile girls (110).

The final group, "true mothers," is seen, however, as the most paradoxical, for these characters—figures like Nell, Amy Dorrit, and Jenny Wren (the name assumed by Fanny Cleaver)—represent "the social ideal," yet "are more radically destructive than adulteresses" (112). Distinguished from biological mothers, these nurturing females, who include representatives from all of the other groups except "excessive" women, disturb and transform traditional family relationships. In "making true mothers the category into which all positively-valued women are subsumed" (124–25), Dickens reshapes stereotypes of class and gender.

Ingham concludes her study by reaffirming her belief that Dickens derives his female characters from stereotypes in mid-Victorian writing, not from the actual women in his life, and she proposes that Dickens' portrayals of the latter—for example, his descriptions of Mary Hogarth, Catherine Dickens, and Ellen Ternan—are themselves literary creations, fictionalized portraits. I believe, however, that we may largely assent to this view but still see a flow in the other direction, since actual persons may manifest traits that seemingly confirm attributes displayed in stereotypes. Because of the complexity of literary creativity, to accept Ingham as a guide does not—at least, from my perspective—require us to reject the conflicting suggestions of Morris Golden or those of Michael Slater, some of whose points are challenged by Ingham. Perhaps Freud's principle of overdetermination—the existence of multiple, complementary causes of an act—suggests a way of reconciling these diverse positions.

In Ingham's richly detailed discussion, one proposal seems to me questionable. The claim that Rosa Dartle "turns out to have been willingly seduced by James Steerforth and Miss Wade by Henry Gowan" (59) is followed by the assertion, "The accounts of their sexual sinning are so brief and unelaborate that it is possible for the reader to overlook them altogether" (61). But this view appears to push Dickens to give us more than he wishes to, only a hint that there *may* have been actual physical intimacy, for these two relationships, I believe, remain ambiguous, perhaps cases of "near-miss" affairs, if I may use Ingham's expression for instances in which misbehavior is approached but narrowly avoided. When Dickens wishes to be clear about illicit sexuality, he leaves no doubts, as the depictions of fallen women like Nancy, Alice Marwood, Martha Endell, and Emily show.

Despite this disagreement, I find that Ingham, through her skillful focusing on Dickens' recurrent imagery and on his repetition of narrative patterns, makes her overall argument cumulatively persuasive. Her feminist viewpoint is well served by her seeking not to judge or chastise Dickens and his contemporaries but to enhance our understanding of their work.

Although John Lucas' *Charles Dickens: The Major Novels* appears in a series intended "for use by students in universities, colleges and schools," I believe that the volume will also be found valuable by Dickens specialists, for the author's analyses go well beyond basic comments. After an introductory chapter, "Becoming a Novelist," which emphasizes the extent to which Dickens found his calling "quite by chance" (4), Lucas discusses in detail those novels he regards as major. To the five that would be found in nearly any Dickensian's list—*David Copperfield, Bleak House, Little Dorrit, Great Expectations*, and *Our Mutual Friend*—Lucas adds *Dombey and Son*, recognized as the first novel to be given especial care in its planning. Observing that this book "has as its focal points two houses" at opposite ends of the social scale (22)—Dombey's and the Wooden Midshipman—Lucas goes on to examine Florence's taking refuge with Captain Cuttle and her later restoration to her father, who in a way seems to be regarded by her as "her true husband" (42) and eventually "is freed into human relationship by her loving kindness" (43). For Lucas, *Dombey and Son* "engages with Dickens's deep fears about the emergent society of industrial commercial capitalism" but "also offers a vision of alternative possibilities, which are identified with community of feeling," an outlook differentiated from "masculine competitiveness": "in this novel it is always women or womanly men like Captain Cuttle and Mr Toots who *are* right" (45). In responding to *David Copperfield*, Lucas stresses the book's "insistence on David's being a gentleman which makes . . . for a failure of imaginative generosity towards others," "an insistence on class immutability that requires Dickens every bit as much as David to scorn those who try to raise themselves" (48). This attitude, according to Lucas, leads to inconsistencies: Murdstone's condescension to Clara Peggotty is meant to be seen as unfeeling and wrong, but David, when sent to the wine warehouse, shows a comparable "class snobbishness" (50). These confusions, which Lucas finds pervasive in this novel, are for him related to Dickens' own sense of "guilt at being on the side of the winners" (70). Similarly, *Bleak House* is viewed as "a novel full of contradictions" (77), for these are what we find in "England in the 1850s, that place of civilization and barbarism'' (78). As the two narrators—''a painfully shy, inhibited, illegitimate girl'' and ''a worldly wise, sardonic male'' (77)—record both conflicts and links within society, Dickens, in Lucas' opinion, expresses a ''sense of union between middle and working class'' (98), and Esther, whose ''unprivileged position is no bar to her truth-telling'' (83), significantly serves as ''the main embodiment of that vision of alliance'' (99).

In discussing *Little Dorrit*, Lucas maintains that this work ''shows'' that Dickens is ''among the great psychological novelists'' (104). Continuing to point out contradictions or complexities, Lucas notices that this narrative ''endorses the idea of destiny, of the inescapability of fate,'' even though Dickens also expresses ''anti-determinism'' (116)—the view, for example, that ''Clennam has to assume responsibility for his own life'' (107). For Lucas, Amy, who ''represents a [partial] rejection of middle-class values,'' ''offers Clennam a way out of his own alienation,'' and the novel's conclusion—the marriage of Clennam and Amy—provides ''a redemptive vision'' that is essentially ''a *social* vision'' (123). The next novel examined, *Great Expectations*, is seen as deeply concerned with ''such distortions of human enterprise and relationship as are connected with ideas of class and especially 'the gentleman' '' (131): ''Joe stands for what is passing,'' since ''new laws, urbanization, and the establishment of an increasingly complex set of class relations and hierarchies, combine to marginalize and essentially supersede what he stands for'' (132). In Pip's story, which probes questions of heredity, upbringing, and identity, ''Joe's weakness''—''his almost feminine sensitivity''—''is also his strength,'' and Pip's ''intimate knowledge of Joe'' is ''both the cause of his self-dissatisfactions and his salvation'' (139).

Our Mutual Friend, for Lucas, depicts ''a society so determined by class'' that ''people become unknowable to each other except as expressions of class'' (150). In such a society, the moral superiority of Gaffer Hexam to Riderhood ''will pass unnoticed'' by most people, Lucas states, as a result of ''the incuriosity, the blindness, of class judgement'' (151). Eugene is described as a ''crucial'' character (155), for Lucas believes that Wrayburn, despite his shortcomings, displays ''a more disinterested awareness'' of Lizzie ''than any other man with whom she comes in contact,'' and he eventually ''is enabled to discover with and through her a relationship whose worth is not dependent on his power but on their mutual accord'': ''In a society where friendship is . . . habitually false, Lizzie and Eugene are the novel's true mutual friends'' (158). Lucas' study, which offers many valuable insights concerning Dickens' complex and troubled perceptions of social class, concludes with the statement that ''the society with which *Our Mutual Friend* deals'' is ''our society''—''And that is why we need Dickens'' (159).

In *Secret Journeys: Theory and Practice in Reading Dickens*, Nicholas H. Morgan examines the perils that study of "Dickens's multifarious universe" (21) poses to diverse camps of literary criticism. Asserting that to comprehend Dickens in a non-reductive way we need a methodology that is "flexible" but "consistent," since eclecticism is "an a priori admission of philosophical failure" (21), the author proposes in his first chapter a tripartite approach that investigates "the relationship between reader and narrator," the "narrative dialectic between the power of the imagination and the restraint of authority or discipline," and a combination of "our archaeological pursuit of the buried secrets in the characters' memories . . . with our teleological exploration of the symbolic life of the narrative" (28). Morgan frequently acknowledges the subjectivity in any one reader's interpretations, but hopes his own responses will prove persuasive. Although his desire to fuse what he calls the archaeological and the teleological is commendable, I am made uneasy by the use of these terms and the implication that we may always readily distinguish between repressed secrets and symbols, for these elements often blend, as Morgan himself points out.

Despite my reservations about some aspects of the theoretical discussion—misgivings that may stem from my unrepentant eclecticism—the ensuing four "practical" chapters offer stimulating, valuable considerations of four novels that "span Dickens's literary career and fairly represent the major phases of his development" (27). The method is sufficiently "pluralistic" so that Morgan can employ it in an unobtrusive, unforced way. For him, *The Old Curiosity Shop* is best approached as an allegory emphasizing the extreme contrast between Nell, whom he calls "the 'Angel without a House' " (36), and Quilp, "a demon of evil, of eroticism, of excess, of energy" (46), two characters around whom others "group themselves" (49). After describing *David Copperfield* as a narrative about a character fighting "a dialectical battle within himself, pitting . . . the dreamer against . . . the self-disciplined worker" (62), Morgan effectively describes Dickens' complex use of the motif of dreams and concludes that Copperfield never wholly resolves his internal conflict. *Little Dorrit*, for Morgan, develops "the dialectic between imprisonment and personal expression" (85), a struggle in which fancies may torment or protect, and at the novel's close "two emotionally scarred characters"—Amy Dorrit and Arthur Clennam—"have achieved only a limited peace" (99). In examining *Great Expectations*, Morgan concentrates on secrets and disclosures, on the imagery involving hands, and on the theme of "the exercise of power in personal relationships" (119).

The dialectical approach used in this study leads to balanced readings, and although I find Copperfield, Clennam, and Pip more clearly triumphant than Morgan does, his concise, perceptive discussions illuminate the intricacies of Dickens' narratives.

In *The Reader in the Dickensian Mirrors: Some New Language* (first published in London by Macmillan in 1990), John Schad studies the ways in which Dickens' fiction reveals an "overall preoccupation with reading" by readers of the novels and also "by the characters within them" (3), characters who "may be found not just emulating but actually mirroring the reader" (2). For Schad, Dickens' choices of diction and figurative expressions, as well as those syntactic patterns that mimic the act of reading, lead to "a re-imagining of language" so that "the key linguistic relationship is not . . . between word and world but rather . . . between word and word" (8). This language, "by embracing a sense of not only fixedness but also unfixedness," manages "to reconstruct even as it deconstructs" (11), since it ultimately emphasizes resemblances rather than distinctions. Schad proceeds to devote five chapters to demonstrating how Dickens' references to reading stress analogies between that act and various facets of Victorian life.

First, a chapter on the linking of reading and political economy examines such topics as "the reader as monarch" (15), rival claims for the "sovereignty" of the law as presented in texts (16), the uses of literacy in commerce, the "Dickensian equation of money and language" (22), and the relationship of texts to revolution. In the following chapter, Schad studies imagery that relates to nature: reading seen as a journey "from city to country" (51), Dickens' "recourse to the country for a language to articulate the new experience of the city" (54), and the use of reading to explore the Victorian "belief in a close affinity between family and nature" (79). The third and fourth chapters discuss analogues relating reading, respectively, to mathematics, a discipline that often seems blended with reading in that both skills tend to multiply and divide meanings, and to history, a field in which time and rhetoric come together, since Dickens' novels integrate an "invariable reference to themselves as 'history' " with "habitual apostrophising" and "repeated gestures to the reader" (125), while offering narratives in which the present is "constantly sliding into past and future" (139). In the fifth chapter Schad investigates ties between reading and Christianity: reading as interpretation, connected to "the Protestant emphasis on the study and exposition of the Bible" (159), with exegesis being regarded as a kind of prayer.

Schad's erudition—his familiarity with the novels, current critical theory, and the Victorian era—and his skill in adducing examples are impressive, but this book about Dickensian references to reading makes extreme demands upon its own readers. The five central chapters consist largely of lists of images, and while many of these illustrations are fascinating—especially those in the chapter on analogies between reading and mathematics—the quantity of examples proves difficult to assimilate. Because Schad offers a great many items with relatively little subordination of one feature to others, we must often provide our own emphasis in considering numerous coordinate details, and in many cases we must also pause to try to recall the contexts of passages in particular novels.

In an "Epilogue," Schad refers to his two goals: demonstrating an "overall linguistic hypothesis" and directing attention to many "ideas and conceits," some not directly tied to his argument (186). Asserting that the number of conceits involving the act of reading keeps him from "cataloguing them all," Schad maintains that the ones he does notice "represent a significant contribution to our understanding of the almost encyclopaedic Dickensian imagination" (186). With this claim I agree, since for me the book has value in adding to our already great awareness of Dickens' skill in wordplay and in the use of recurrent imagery, a verbal brilliance in which he seems second only to Shakespeare. But Schad's linguistic theory—the occasionally abstruse argument that Dickens' language is "a system of resemblances rather than differences" (187) and therefore "represents" both deconstruction and reconstruction—leaves me puzzled and uncomfortable, for while Schad affirms that Dickens' language may enable us to find a "sequel to poststructuralism" (187), I cannot avoid wondering if this book's material could be seen more simply as evidence to challenge various aspects of deconstructionist theory.

In two places Schad refers to a letter from David Copperfield to Emily (ch. 55) and incorrectly calls it a letter "from Mr Peggotty penned by David" (116) and a "letter written by David at Mr Peggotty's dictation" (184). Moreover, since Emily's written reply, subsequently shown to David, is intended not for him but for Ham, whose message David had conveyed in his letter, the "you" in her response refers to Ham, and she is therefore commenting not, as Schad remarks, on "the respective merits of David and Mr Peggotty" (184), but on the virtues of her uncle and Ham. These complaints notwithstanding, Schad's book does succeed in illuminating the depths of Dickens' mirrors and in helping us comprehend the complexity of his imagery.

David Paroissien, in *The Companion to* Oliver Twist, the fifth volume to appear in The Dickens Companions series, displays impressive and useful erudition in commenting on a wide range of customs and conditions in Dickens' actual and fictive worlds. The entries, arranged according to chapter in the novel and placed under tag-lines indicating the expression annotated and the paragraph in which it appears, are remarkably inclusive and consider such topics as law (crime, penology, the legal system, the Poor Laws regulating assistance to the needy), health (sanitation, disease, medical practices, diet), housing, religion, dress, topography, funeral customs, mail delivery, types of public houses, popular entertainment (like Punch and Judy shows), servants' duties, the use of children by chimney-sweeps, and workhouse architecture. Although the intention of this series is to provide "factual rather than critical" annotations (vii), Paroissien seems wisely aware that this distinction cannot always be a guide, since overlapping between the two categories is inevitable. For example, a note for chapter 32 suggests that the changed interior of the criminals' house pointed out by Oliver to Mr. Losberne may be explained by assuming caution was shown "on the part of the thieves" (208), while comments on the depiction of Rose Maylie in chapter 29 notice the influence of the dead Mary Hogarth and propose that "religious duty and domestic competence" may be seen as "the twin sources" of Rose's "cultural appeal" (198).

Paroissien provides particularly valuable notes on time and place in *Oliver Twist*, a novel with a complicated chronology and an extensive number of topographical details. The geographic listings and maps make us recognize the density of the references to actual places and remind us how fully Dickens' imaginary world was grounded in localities familiar to many of his readers. In considering topography, Paroissien cogently supports the view that Oliver's native town—named Mudfog in the original publication in *Bentley's Miscellany*—was based on Chatham, the site where Dickens spent much of his childhood, even though the author attempted to conceal this derivation by introducing details placing the town north rather than southeast of London.

In addition, because of the contents of *Oliver Twist* this volume includes annotation on the social views promulgated by Jeremy Bentham, prostitution in the London of the 1830s, attitudes towards capital punishment, discriminatory legal and social restrictions that led Jews into disreputable activities, the ways in which Dickens' own opinions reflected contemporary anti-Semitism and then moved, partly in response to the prompting of Mrs. Eliza Davis, to a more enlightened and tolerant perspective, and the duties of police magistrates. Among many other interesting tidbits are the notes on the medicinal uses of laudanum (234), sugar plantations in the British West Indies (290), the different roles of such medical practitioners as surgeons, physicians, and apothecaries (36, 181), the Bow Street Runners (201–03), and workhouses (34–36), as well as such miscellaneous gems as the annotation to Dickens' lines, "In our station-houses, men and women are every night confined on the most trivial charges" (ch. 11), a note that gives striking instances of ridiculous accusations: "one young girl, who was found crying on her father's grave in Clerkenwell, was arrested for creating a disturbance. Equally absurd was the case of a young boy whose cry, 'Hot beef!', was mistaken for 'Stop thief!' by a policeman and the cause of his being detained for wasting the policeman's time" (116).

After reading through all the annotations, I am moved to offer a slight objection in only one case. A note on Brownlow's advertisement for the missing Oliver (ch. 17) maintains, "Mr Brownlow has evidently initiated an attempt to recover Oliver himself because prosecutions at this time lay in the hands of private individuals, acting in concert with police magistrates, rather than the police force established in London in 1829" (158). Since Brownlow later tells Rose Maylie that after Oliver's disappearance he at first believed that the boy "had imposed" on him (ch. 40), a wish to have Oliver held accountable for the books with which he was entrusted may have been a motive behind the advertisement. Nevertheless, a more benevolent intention is suggested, I think, by the text of the notice itself (describing Oliver as someone in whose "previous history . . . the advertiser is, for many reasons, warmly interested"), by Brownlow's later asking whether Bumble knows the whereabouts of " 'this poor boy,' " and by the old man's subsequent comment that he would gladly have trebled the monetary reward if Bumble's account " 'had been favourable to the boy' " (ch. 17).

Since Paroissien's annotations may at times enlighten us about points that we thought needed no elucidation, this volume may best be used by considering the notes after reading each chapter or two in the novel. Moreover, in consulting this guide, we can benefit from the relatively thorough index and the sensible, reliable cross-references. Paroissien shows fine judgment in determining what to annotate and in deciding the degree of detail to provide, his own prose is direct and lucid, and his felicitous use of quotations from nineteenth-century sources may lead some of us to look—possibly for the first time—at a work like *London Journal, 1840*, by Flora Tristan, described as "a French traveller who made several visits to London between 1826 and 1839" (185): the samplings from this account (translated and published in 1980) suggest that Tristan was an alert, perceptive observer of early Victorian life.

The Companion to Oliver Twist is a commendable scholarly presentation of materials that can help us recall some of our lost past, for the entries give a stimulating impression of Dickens' world and its social and economic history.

Ray Dubberke, in *Dickens, Drood, and the Detectives*, begins his attempt to solve the many mysteries in Dickens' unfinished book by arguing that Dick Datchery is not a previously introduced character in disguise, but a new figure, someone who would eventually have been revealed to be a detective police officer privately employed by Mr. Grewgious. Observing that in twelve of Dickens' fifteen novels relatively significant characters make first appearances late in the narrative, Dubberke proceeds to maintain that Datchery may have been modeled on Sergeant Stephen Thornton, a colleague of Inspector Charles Frederick Field, the prototype of Inspector Bucket in *Bleak House*. After asserting that ''the clues and hints'' in Dickens' text ''are not sufficient'' to resolve the question of whether Drood survives (67), Dubberke reviews the testimony of Dickens' son Charley, John Forster, and two of the illustrators for the novel—Charles Allston Collins and Luke Fildes—as well as the endorsement by Dickens' daughter Kate of the views advanced by her brother and Forster, all of this outside testimony asserting that Dickens' intention called for the attempt at the murder of Edwin to be successful. Dubberke, convinced by these witnesses, dismisses two of many projected titles—''The flight of Edwyn Drood'' and ''Edwin Drood in hiding''—as expressions considered ''as a means of concealing'' Dickens' ''real intentions'' (68), even though Edwin's actual demise would make either of these titles ''misleading,'' not ''concealing.'' In subsequent chapters, Dubberke discusses numerous other details and proposes a conclusion to the story he considers more plausible than others so far advanced, an ending that calls for Helena Landless to disguise herself as the ghost of her brother, after the latter has also fallen victim to John Jasper. For me, Dubberke's study, although it provides a lucid, interesting assessment of the novel's problems, offers its most convincing contribution in the remarks on Datchery as a new character.

Derek Johnson's *Pastoral in the Work of Charles Dickens*, while conceding that ''urban life'' is Dickens' main concern, nevertheless maintains that his ''treatment of this, his major theme, is dependent upon certain assumptions about the extra-urban world, about Nature and the natural order, assumptions . . . inherited largely from the Romantics'' (2) and especially from Wordsworth. This study traces Dickens' expression of a pastoral ideal in various early writings and the subsequent movement from ''conventional pastoral . . ., where his nature-cult coexisted with the cult of the child,'' to "the worship of heroic maidens" and then to "the full-blown cult of the divine woman" (28). Observing that Dickens, despite his later recognition of rural distress, still always retained an "unwavering belief in the divinity of nature and in the moral superiority of the country over the town," Johnson notices that this faith at times led to regression "into conventional pastoral, . . . even in the late novels" (31). According to Johnson, the pastoral ideal depicted in the pamphlet "Sunday Under Three Heads" (1836), published under the pseudonym "Timothy Sparks," the Dingley Dell episodes in *Pickwick Papers*, and the country scenes involving the Maylie household in *Oliver Twist* all present idealized views of rural life very contrary to the reality that Dickens must have seen in "his travels as a journalist" (106). Johnson asserts that Dickens wanted to believe in the contentment of country workers, since the "docility" he attributes to them provides reassurance against fears of "violent insurrection" (119).

In much of this discussion, Johnson stresses the important influence of Wordsworth in confirming various ideas that Dickens had developed about nature and death. In *The Old Curiosity Shop*, Johnson finds Dickens depicting Nell as an "angelic and heroic maiden" (178), while including in the narrative disquieting details about rural life. Indeed, for Johnson the death of Nell is in large measure attributable to Dickens' growing awareness that rural life did not offer his heroine a perfect haven, that this was to be found only in heaven.

Johnson points out that Dickens' increasing comprehension of rural hardship led to the "attack . . . on the aristocracy and the landed gentry" in *Barnaby Rudge* (229) and then to the strong expression of sympathy for both the rural and the urban poor in *The Chimes*. But Dickens, Johnson remarks, never again focused as he had in *The Chimes* on "the complaints of the rural poor" (242), for the novelist's "fear of the peasantry" (250) moved him "towards a strict authoritarianism" (252).

Johnson's analysis—lucid, carefully documented, and well-argued—seems both perceptive and sensible, particularly in its relatively full examination of the extent to which Dickens—disavowals notwithstanding—responded to Wordsworth.

In *Daughters of the House: Modes of the Gothic in Victorian Fiction*, Alison Milbank examines the ways in which four "conservative" writers (1) use Gothic elements (such as the confinement and escape of a heroine) in developing the theme of a woman's "association with the domestic house" (1) and in considering the relationship between "private and public activity" (5). Concentrating on texts by Wilkie Collins, Dickens, Charlotte Brontë, and Sheridan Le Fanu, Milbank tries to synthesize feminist, deconstructionist, and genre studies with Walter Benjamin's " 'redemptive' aesthetics" in order "to challenge some feminist critical assumptions" about Victorian views on women and domesticity (1): her contention is that in certain instances the domestic activity of a woman is shown as leading to public empowerment for her and for men with whom she is associated. The ambitious fusion of methods, the wide range of interests, and the number of details presented make Milbank's study interesting, but also intricate and—in my opinion—at times difficult to follow.

A little under a third of *Daughters of the House* is devoted to chapters on three Dickens novels: *Bleak House, Little Dorrit*, and *Great Expectations*. Milbank believes that Esther's "role of housekeeper, and thus key-holder, . . . expresses not only her status within . . . [John Jarndyce's] house, but the nature of her role as narrator: opening up a situation and its mysteries to the reader" (83). For Milbank, both Bleak House and Chesney Wold are "Gothic mansions" (87) in a novel that seeks "to envisage the possibility of action and change in a society seemingly locked into the past" (89). Esther, according to Milbank, extends her domestic role and achieves "public action" through both her "voluntary selflessness" and "its corresponding echo in the professional activity of her doctor husband" (91). Milbank goes on to state that in this novel "the only way Dickens can envisage guiltless and effective action by men in society" is through "doctoring," which is presented as similar to "nursing . . . rather than scientific medicine," so that "even male action" remains "domestic in character" (93). Some of Milbank's later claims however, about the apocalyptic elements in *Bleak House* seem strained. Although there are certainly references to Revelation, we may question points like the assertion that "the marks on Esther's face show the mark of the beast (the ink of Tulkinghorn)" and the identification of the second Bleak House as "a replica of the holy city" (98).

Little Dorrit is seen as revealing "close parallels" in "plot, setting and characters" with Ann Radcliffe's *The Mysteries of Udolpho* (102). Milbank considers Dickens' use of "the imprisonment theme" (105) and notes, too, that the "the Clennam house fulfils every one of a list of Gothic criteria" (108). Finding a "Gothic ruining perspective" in Amy, Milbank sees her as someone who "dissolves barriers of hypocrisy . . . but also confirms the very existence of those walls and surfaces of mystification" (116). Milbank argues, moreover, that in this novel Dickens' "interest is shifting away from the heroine to the imprisoned male" (120) and observes that Daniel Doyce, not Little Dorrit, is Clennam's rescuer. But some other points seem less cogent, and the suggestion that Amy is "a relation of the favoured woman" (Clennam's actual mother) is not accurate (103).

In discussing *Great Expectations*, Milbank observes that in this narrative the women, instead of acting "as mediators" who allow men to enter "the realm of social action," assume "tyrannical roles" in exercising "the real power in the house" (122). Milbank considers the despotic behavior of Mrs. Joe and Miss Havisham and observes both "the Gothic gloom of Satis House" and the introducing of Wemmick's Castle as a "parodic" alternative (134). For Milbank, "the person most liberated by the action is Pip himself," who has been involved in what "was really a Gothic plot by women against men" (136). When Milbank, however, considers Wemmick's wooing and refers to the "gradual softening of the rigid Miss Stiffkins," the name should be "Skiffins," even though the erroneous variation would better support the point being discussed (134).

While *Daughters in the House* is a complicated, demanding book, it does offer various valuable insights concerning the subtle, complex ways in which the Gothic tradition was adapted by Dickens and some of his contemporaries.

More than one-third of Helen K. Heineman's *Three Victorians in the New World: Intepretations of the New World in the Works of Frances Trollope, Charles Dickens, and Anthony Trollope* is allotted to the three chapters discussing, respectively, the first part of Dickens' *American Notes* (the chapters on the East), the second part of this work (the West), and the American material in *Martin Chuzzlewit*. Noticing the greater use of personal material in the *American Notes* chapters on the West, Heineman finds that in this section of his book Dickens made much more extensive use of the letters he had written from America to John Forster and other friends. Heineman observes, too, that in writing about the various cities visited in the East, Dickens seems especially eager to be tolerant and to avoid criticizing and therefore tends to provide a large amount of "information and uncontroversial material" (89). While these earlier chapters reveal some of Dickens' interests, such as the concern with prisons, and even though Dickens' abhorrence of slavery leads him in the Washington chapter to change his tone and severely attack this institution, Heineman still calls the first part of the book "very disappointing" (107) and regards the chapters on the West as superior because Dickens, while he "maintained his desire to be fair and sympathetic," also chose to make greater use of "his own personal experiences" and "began to employ novelistic techniques instead of more conventional modes of description" (117). Praising Dickens' "creation of atmosphere" and his "imaginative evocations of the spirit of place" (124), Heineman also observes that despite the increased reliance in this second half of *American Notes* on letters to friends, Dickens frequently softens the criticism found in this correspondence. On the other hand, he could not restrain his anger, Heineman points out, concerning "one subject—the eating habits of Americans—and one setting—the [unattractive, depressing] area around Cairo, Illinois," both of which became features in *Martin Chuzzlewit* (133). After concluding that in *American Notes* we encounter "two different books" (140), with the second half clearly superior, Heineman proceeds to maintain that Dickens' use of his travels is even more effective in the American chapters of *Martin Chuzzlewit*, chapters that are particularly significant in presenting events leading to young Martin's moral improvement. For Heineman, two pervasive ideas—the belief that Americans, "under the guise of freedom," showed selfish lack of consideration for others (159) and the opinion that the young nation, despite its praise of individualism, produced citizens "lacking diversity of character"—enabled Dickens to incorporate in his narrative "a palpable image of Americans in the 1840s" (162). Although Heineman's detailed comments on likenesses and contrasts among passages in Dickens' letters, *American Notes*, and *Martin Chuzzlewit* are interesting and useful, as are her analyses of the responses and literary techniques in the travel writing and fiction of Mrs. Trollope and her son Anthony, this study's value would have been enhanced had the author given further attention to recent scholarship. The extensive bibliography, except for four titles (two of these by Heineman herself) listed as "Additional Sources," includes no entry later than 1966.

Before proceeding to discuss articles on the individual novels and then on the short fiction, I wish to consider two biographical articles and ten miscellaneous essays.

Arthur Adrian, in "Georgina Hogarth to Percy Fitzgerald: some Unpublished Letters," reprints "excerpts of possible interest to Dickensians" (5) and provides commentary on the significance of these passages. Adrian's overall summation states that the letters in question (dated from 1865 through July 1896) from Dickens' adoring sister-in-law to his young friend and admirer (twenty-two years his junior) "add little new biographical information," but "do offer some intimate details of life at Gad's Hill" (18). In writing to Fitzgerald, Georgina is, I think, surprisingly candid, condemning her nephew Charley Dickens' second daughter—"She is the coarsest little creature I ever saw in my life" (7)—and presenting disparaging remarks about Dickens' friends Wilkie Collins, John Forster, and Longfellow.

Throughout the excerpts, however, she reveals extraordinary devotion to her "Charles."

Doris Alexander's "In Defense of John Dickens" speculates that the early indebtedness of the novelist's father may have been attributable to financial assistance that he generously gave his fugitive father-in-law, Charles Barrow, who had fled to the Isle of Man to avoid prosecution for embezzlement from the Navy Pay Office. Although Alexander argues skillfully that her views offer a "likely hypothesis" (5), the evidence seems inconclusive, and we may wonder whether John Dickens would have been strong enough to keep so benevolent a deed so well concealed, especially during periods when his own reputation was beclouded. Moreover, his later financial troubles may leave us doubtful that in earlier trials he was "a martyr to his own generosity and kindness" (6). But because the huge total of his early debts *is* puzzling, Alexander's call for further research can certainly be endorsed.

In " 'With My Name on Every Page': Dickens References in *Household Words*," Anne Lohrli, after noticing the desire of Dickens—at least in the early years of *Household Words*—to exclude from this weekly any mention of his writings that might seem inappropriate, goes on to present an entertaining survey of "some sixty" references (9), by Dickens himself as well as by his contributors, that were allowed to appear. Lohrli concedes that various references may have been subtle enough to remain undetected, but believes that in most cases readers probably recognized the sources.

Wesley Britton, in "Carlyle, Clemens, and Dickens: Mark Twain's Francophobia, the French Revolution, and Determinism," explains that "Twain's rereading of *The French Revolution* and *A Tale of Two Cities* in Paris in 1879 helped reinforce his anti-French sentiments" (198). These two books, "second-hand accounts told from an English point of view," served Clemens as "sources and mirrors for his philosophical musings not only on the French, but on the human race in general" (199). Britton goes on to conclude that Twain, after assimilating Carlyle's "strains of determinism" and Dickens' "strong theme of social discontent," moved "beyond his mentors into a determinism so deep it dominated his dreamlife" (203).

Edwin M. Eigner's "Shakespeare, Milton, Dickens and the Morality of the Pious Fraud" asserts that the "plot device" of a benevolent deception or pious fraud is "employed frequently" by Shakespeare and Dickens, "but imitated by virtually no one else" writing in English and that these preeminent authors are the only ones in English literature, "with the possible exception of Milton, [who] appear to have . . . [included] the readers or audience among those to be benevolently deceived" (6). In a stimulating, cogent discussion of the pious frauds perpetrated by Paulina in *The Winter's Tale* and by Noddy Boffin in *Our Mutual Friend*, and of deceptions in *David Copperfield*, Eigner affirms that the misleading of characters and of the audience or readers is intended to correct a "lack of faith in human nature" (17) and teach us the lesson that skepticism may be unwarranted and pernicious. This essay finds the effects of such tricking of the audience comparable to the results achieved by the strategy that Stanley Fish, in *Surprised by Sin: The Reader in* Paradise Lost, attributes to Milton's epic narrator: readers, after being induced to reach conclusions that are subsequently shown to be erroneous, recognize the need to re-examine their own values. For Eigner, the pious frauds perpetrated by Shakespeare, Milton, and Dickens are interesting didactic efforts to re-educate and assist us.

"The Game of Speculation: Economics and Representation," by Tatiana M. Holway, investigates ways in which the representation of life in nineteenth-century English fiction is related to attitudes toward financial speculation. Since the latter involves imagining wealth and may prove illusory, novelists not only "made it a subject for representation," but "also exposed the economic practice as a problem *of* representation" (104). Using Jane Austen's *Mansfield Park* and Dickens' *Nicholas Nickleby* as examples, Holway discusses how the former narrative "defines speculative activities as misrepresentations" (105) that destabilize society, and she proceeds to observe that in *Nicholas Nickleby*, written when "socioeconomic conditions that were only emergent in Austen's generation" had become established, Dickens "did not find fully coherent terms" for his criticism, for "the contingency he reveals penetrating society also permeates the very form" of his novel (107), and speculation is seen in conflicting ways: it is "a release, an opening" (108), a source of "promise" (107), but also a dependence on chance that is "socially and ethically dangerous" (107). For Holway, *Nicholas Nickleby* reveals in a complex fashion its author's "critical perception . . . of the contradictions of capitalism," particularly in the "similar" fates of two "antithetical" brothers—Nicholas' father and uncle (110).

In "Nobody's Angels: Domestic Ideology and Middle-Class Women in the Victorian Novel," an essay offering just brief comments on Dickens, Elizabeth Langland uses etiquette manuals to study the manner in which the Victorian ideology of the "Angel in the House" conceals the middle-class wife's role in managing the household and controlling the servants. Referring to *David Copperfield*, Langland points to the contrast between Dora and Agnes as household managers and asserts that the former's domestic incompetence shows that womanly character is less important in this area than the possession of "a precise set of organizational skills that would not be inappropriate in a factory" (298). Langland affirms that despite David's attempt, in his role as narrator, to attribute Agnes' creation of domestic happiness to her spiritual nature, we know that her managerial ability is essential to her success: "far more important than grace and sympathy are the household keys Agnes carries at her side: the symbol of her authority, the tool of her management, and the sign of her regulatory power and control" (299). Nevertheless, we might add that while angelic traits alone will not bring domestic order, the woman who has such qualities (or the appearance of possessing them) may find that they sometimes enhance her executive talents by making her acts as household overseer more acceptable to both the servants and outside observers. The need to maintain class dominance explains, according to Langland, why a "plot that shaped the rise of the novel in eighteenth-century England—a virtuous serving girl winning the love of a master vastly her social superior—disappeared in the nineteenth century" (290).

John R. Reed, in "Authorized Punishment in Dickens's Fiction," discusses "the role of implicit [moral] values—in Dickens' case relatively traditional Christian values—in the shaping of narratives" (113). Since Dickens, Reed observes, ordinarily wishes to keep his virtuous characters from taking direct punitive action against the wicked, he uses in his fiction "elaborateness of . . . plotting" that provides "the coincidental circumstances, the ironies of fate, the sudden revelations" leading wrongdoers to "punish one another and themselves" (113). In investigating "how and why" Dickens "*authorizes* punishment in his narratives" (115), Reed asserts that "the Implied Author [distinguished from the narrator] suggests [through "the very intricacy of his plotting"] a pattern of retribution that extends beyond the novel's text" (114), for even though justice through legal processes is rarely seen in the novels, villainy does not go unpunished. After citing examples from such works as *Oliver Twist*, *Bleak House*, and *A Tale of Two Cities*, as well as from the story "No Thoroughfare," Reed offers a much more detailed discussion of justice and forgiveness in *Our Mutual Friend*. Despite Dickens' belief in Christian mercy, "he also felt a strong need to see evil punished," but thought "good characters" should avoid direct retribution (128). Reed then qualifies this last point: "A few, like young Nicholas Nickleby when he beats Sir Mulberry Hawk or Jenny when she enhances Fledgeby's pain, may have the excuse of immaturity, impetuosity, or extreme provocation" (128). Of course, we may remark that these reasons—especially "extreme provocation"—are far-reaching enough to explain nearly any exceptions. Moreover, one early claim in this essay, the idea that "Fagin's true suffering is his own

terrified recognition of the fact that he *deserves* punishment'' (116), seems
to require further support, since in the penultimate chapter of *Oliver Twist*
the old culprit angrily demands, ''What right have they to butcher me?''
These reservations notwithstanding, I find Reed's study a clear and convincing
account of Dickens' usual tendencies in providing his readers with both implied and explicit moral lessons.

In ''Character and Contradiction in Dickens,'' Brian Rosenberg, after observing that recent literary critics have shown ''heightened sensitivity'' to
conflicts and ''unresolved oppositions,'' notes that Dickens has commanded
the interest of such commentators ''because his work is rife with the tensions
and contradictions they seek out'' (146). Examining Jeremiah Flintwinch in
Little Dorrit as a sample case, Rosenberg considers some of Dickens' methods
of character description—especially the use of qualifying remarks, hesitating
or conditional comments, evasive, indirect statements, and tropes—and suggests that such techniques present ''fragments'' rather than clearly defined
personalities (154). For Rosenberg, these tactics help Dickens to demonstrate
the elusiveness of actual human beings. Assessing the contrast between the
critical viewpoint that sees fictional characters as just parts of an overall
structure and the opposing idea that literary personages reveal an autonomy
extending beyond a text's thematic needs, Rosenberg maintains that in Dickens' characters we find a ''pervasive tension . . . between [structural] dependence and autonomy'' (162). Dickens, this essay argues, is interested in
producing not a ''lifelike image'' but a ''lifelike reaction'': ''his characters
do not so much re-create actual individuals as re-create our reactions to actual
individuals'' (162), responses that reflect the efforts of both the writer and
his public ''to make sense of conflicting, unreliable pieces of information''
(162). Rosenberg's discussion offers a thoughtful, temperate overview that
seems applicable to many characters in Dickens' vast assembly, but that
amazing collection, of course, is so varied as to include some figures who
do not appear to fit this pattern precisely, characters that seem relatively
coherent and easy to understand.

Stephen Rubenstein, in ''Visual Aids, Mental Impediments; or, The Problem with Phiz,'' concisely argues that since Dickens' descriptive writing often
employs rhetorical devices that are not reproducible in illustrations, the latter,
despite their appeal, may at times not be in accord with the novelist's main
purpose in the text. The one example studied in detail—Hablot K. Browne's
rendition of a scene described in chapter 49 of *Martin Chuzzlewit*—*''Mrs
Gamp propoges a Toast''*—is well-chosen, but, although Dickens' descriptions frequently do far more than present verbal pictures, we may question

the extent to which the published illustrations actually "mislead" us about the intent in given passages (24), since readers might first respond to the text and then peruse the etchings or else look first at the illustrations and then read Dickens' chapters: in either situation, we might regard the drawings as complementary (or supplementary) rather than as precisely parallel attempts to "translate" prose into a visual medium. Moreover, in cases where Dickens feared that illustrations would have the effect of distorting, he was not shy about requesting changes. On illustrations for Dickens, see, too, the comments below on J. Hillis Miller's discussion of *Pickwick Papers*, Frank McCombie's essay on *Dombey and Son*, and David Parker's article on *David Copperfield*.

Michael Slater provides a brief introduction to a reprinting of G. K. Chesterton's *Criticisms and Appreciations of the Works of Charles Dickens*, a collection of prefaces written from 1907 to 1911 for editions of Dickens' works in the Everyman's Library series. Observing that these essays "remain comparatively unknown even though . . . they contain far more in the way of commentary on particular books" than does Chesterton's general study, *Charles Dickens*, published in 1906 (vii), Slater maintains that the pieces form "a major landmark in Dickens studies" (xix), since they offer fine insights and striking anticipations of views expressed by later critics.

Ella Westland and Simon Trezise, in "Plotting Critical Positions," the first of eight essays to be published by *Dickens Quarterly* over the next three years, state that their project "places writing about Dickens in a wider critical context" (172). Two future articles will consider, respectively, the 1830s to 1930s and the period from 1940 to 1970, with four subsequent pieces to be devoted to "different critical movements since 1970" (172). A final essay will examine "the 'Dickens generation' . . . since 1970 and look forward to new directions" (172). In this initial article, intended to offer a "provisional narrative of the post-1970 period" (174), the authors find that although writers on Dickens were slow to respond to the changes in criticism inaugurated by deconstructionism and feminism, new methods have become noticeable, and recent work "reveals an enormous variety of critical approaches" (177). Westland and Trezise see in "the new partnership of historicist and feminist criticism . . . the more fertile future for the re-making of Dickens" (177), and they call for recognition of the "need to increase our comprehension of the complex, historically determined interdependence of society, personal identity and literature" (178).

In considering essays on individual novels, we find that one of the two discussions focusing on *Pickwick Papers* appears in J. Hillis Miller's book

Illustrations, a largely theoretical study that is divided not into chapters but into two "Parts," the second of which, "Word and Image," contains a sixteen-page section entitled "Dickens and Phiz." Noticing that Robert Patten and Michael Steig, two of the leading commentators on Browne's etchings for *Pickwick Papers*, "affirm the relative harmony of Phiz's plates and Dickens's text," Miller states, "There would seem relatively little possibility for exploring the notion of an irreconcilable doubleness of text and picture" (96). But he goes on, of course, to do exactly that. Miller finds that "a solar drama, involving a doubling of the sun, is, somewhat surprisingly, enacted" in this novel (97), for there is a "consistent identification of Pickwick with a second sun" (98). At the beginning of chapter 2, the protagonist awakens "like another sun," and throughout the narration, as Miller observes, "Pickwick, with his shining spectacles and beaming face, is a human sun inexhaustibly radiating benevolence, love and confidence in human goodness" (99). Asserting that Phiz's etchings introduce details "not in the text" (102), Miller remarks, "The illustration, therefore, to some degree interferes with the text" (102), a point similar to that in Rubenstein's article considered above. But Miller goes on to make additional claims. In the etchings, he proposes, the sun is duplicated not only by Pickwick's head, for "Phiz displaces that doubling once more from Pickwick's round head to his round stomach," which in many of the plates "commands the centre of the composition" and "functions as a secondary source of illumination" (104). For Miller, Phiz's doubling of Dickens' original doubling provides "another indication that each sign, whether graphic or verbal, not only illustrates in the end itself, but is also divided within itself" (109) and therefore "brings something of its own into the light rather than copying, commenting on, or elucidating some other sign" (110). In this way, Miller believes, Phiz contributes "a meaning that exceeds, and even to some degree subverts, Dickens's text" (111). Unfortunately, while each of the eight plates reproduced by Miller includes at its center a corpulent man's stomach, only in one case, that of the etching entitled *The Valentine*, in which Tony Weller's stomach, as Miller comments, "replaces Pickwick's" (107), does the stomach seem to me like a sun, and with regard to this particular illustration Miller's other suggestion, "Weller's belly is outlined almost like a globe with lines of latitude and longitude" (107), appears more apt. I feel reminded of the emphasis on subjectivity—or perhaps deconstructionism—in Hamlet's query to Polonius, "Do you see yonder cloud that's almost in shape of a camel?"

James R. Kincaid's playful article "Fattening Up on Pickwick," with its attention to corpulence, does not refer to Falstaff, but may lead us to think of this character and also of the reaction his claim to have killed Hotspur evokes from John of Lancaster: "This is the strangest tale"—or the strangest essay. If Miller regards Phiz's depiction of Pickwick's stomach as not only the center of many of the etchings, but a representation of still another sun, Kincaid considers that stomach—or virtually any well-filled stomach—the center of the entire novel. Describing *Pickwick Papers* as "a fat book for fat lovers"—meaning presumably both those who love fat or are fat—Kincaid affirms that this narrative encourages erotic fascination with the flesh, a regression to "childish fantasies that always, one way or another, take the form of The Fat Boy" (236). According to Kincaid, *Pickwick Papers* stresses the importance of Christmas because it is a time when "we forget to be adult," "a great carnival luring us back to full eros" (239). Kincaid locates an abundance of references to food and beverages, an invitation to endless eating and drinking, while he lists, too, a dazzling number of "big," "fleshy" characters, figures described as "fat," "portly," "stout," "corpulent," "thick-set," or "plump" (241–42). The Fat Boy, for Kincaid, serves as "the image of pure ego, pure limitlessness, pure carnival, pure lust—what we all would love to return to" (243). Emphasizing the ways in which The Fat Boy combines "eating and sexual pleasure" (244), Kincaid asserts that *Pickwick Papers* "assures us that there is no end to our childhood, to our play, to our desire" (244). After reading this essay, some of us may become increasingly cautious about calling any book *weighty* or *heavy* or *tasteful*. If *Pickwick Papers* is a celebration of id indulged, its protagonist often consults his superego, and we may find more to him than is dreamt of in this philosophy.

Although no individual articles concentrated on *Oliver Twist*, valuable discussions appear in Paroissien's book and in the chapter by Maxwell.

Holway's essay on speculation considers *Nicholas Nickleby*, and in another article, "How 'the Infant Phenomenon' Began the World: the Managing of Jean Margaret Davenport (182?–1903)," Robert Simpson McLean makes use of various theatrical records to support the claims of the actor William Pleater Davidge that Vincent Crummles' stage troupe in this novel was probably inspired by the acting company of Thomas Donald Davenport. The most noteworthy resemblance between the Davenport and Crummles groups is the presence in each of an "Infant Phenomenon," the manager's performing daughter, whose age is falsified so that she can continue to be publicized as a child prodigy. Pointing out parallels between the ways in which Davenport and Crummles gained attention for their struggling companies, McLean suggests that the former's "sense of showmanship" and his "grandiloquence" made him "stand out above his peers" (138). After stating, "it is highly improbable that Dickens did not know about this colourful group" (141), McLean notices other details that suggest an influence on the novelist in his creation of the Crummles company: the kinds of roles played by the young Jean Margaret Davenport and her parents, the physical appearance of Davenport, and the latter's exaggerative advertising. While emphasizing that the portraits are not precise and include features derived from other models, McLean cautiously demonstrates the likelihood that the Davenports did serve as "the originals" of the Crummles family (152).

In addition to the chapters by Maxwell and Morgan, three journal articles deal with *The Old Curiosity Shop*.

In "Charles Dickens's *The Old Curiosity Shop*: The Triumph of Compassion," Wilfred P. Dvorak impressively synthesizes previous scholars' suggestions with his own approaches. Referring to the contexts of Dickens' personal life and also to various historical circumstances, Dvorak emphasizes the novel's concern with offering a "reformulation of the essential moral-philosophical conflict between right and wrong" presented in both of the immediately preceding works, *Oliver Twist* and *Nicholas Nickleby* (54). For Dvorak, *The Old Curiosity Shop* is an attempt "to motivate human beings to make their lives a triumph of compassion over avariciousness" (55). This essay skillfully argues that Dickens' growing sense of the responsibilities of parenthood and his participation in a Coroner's Inquest concerning a "young domestic servant . . . accused of infanticide" (56) were probably more of an influence on this novel than the sudden death of Mary Hogarth, which Dickens was thinking of when he composed Nell's "final scenes" (55). Indeed, Nell's need to care for her grandfather, a reversal of "the appropriate nurturing roles" (56), shows great concern with the problem of parental care, while the child's "pilgrimage," which Dvorak calls "a search for compassion" (57), reflects Dickens' strong desire to have this quality dictate the verdict of the Coroner's Inquest. This essay also attributes some features in the novel to such historical events as the marriage of the young Queen Victoria, the Chartist movement, and, particularly, the "national anxiety" over "the whole issue of avarice, especially as seen in gambling" (58), a topic considered in the popular play *Money*, written by Dickens' friend Bulwer-Lytton. Nell's grandfather's overvaluation of money and his addiction to gambling change him into a creature that proves even more menacing to Nell than the greedy Quilp. In fact, Dvorak maintains that Nell's death is caused by "the strain of her efforts to keep her grandfather from succumbing once again to avariciousness" (66). But Dvorak also insists that Nell's story and the other major plot strand involving Kit's problems reveal the ultimate "triumph of compassion over avariciousness in early Victorian society" (64). Here, Dvorak demonstrates Dickens' attempts to stress Christian views regarding mortality in his presentation of Nell's death and its remarkably positive effect on "the world of the living" (69). Seeing *The Old Curiosity Shop* as an effort to convince a wider audience of the validity of a specific "moral-philosophical" outlook, Dvorak sums up the book's "warning to society": "live avariciously and die miserably and alone [like Quilp], or live compassionately and transcend death [like Nell] by entering forever into the memory of others" (70). Even though our affection for Nell may make her victory seem too costly, Dvorak offers an extremely valuable reading that succeeds, I believe, in bringing us closer to Dickens' times and intentions.

Rosemary Mundhenk, in "Creative Ambivalence in Dickens's *Master Humphrey's Clock*," reviews the reasons for Dickens' experimentation with this miscellany, explains the main reasons for its failure, and indicates the lessons its author evidently learned. Dickens, of course, deviated from his original plan of a weekly devoted to short, varied pieces and used the publication for installments of two novels—*The Old Curiosity Shop* and *Barnaby Rudge*—before abandoning the venture. The change led to "many inconsistencies and contradictions" in "*Master Humphrey's Clock* as a whole and *The Old Curiosity Shop* in particular" (646), problems that Mundhenk believes reveal Dickens' conflicting "inclinations to improvise freely and to impose narrative order and unity" (646). Carefully examining such matters as the use in *The Old Curiosity Shop* of Master Humphrey as a narrator and the shift to an anonymous third-person teller, as well as the "unbelievable identification" of the latter with the Single Gentleman (655), Mundhenk concludes that the problems Dickens experienced with the *Clock* led him to abandon weekly installments of fiction until economic factors caused him to return to this mode over a dozen years later. In addition, the *Clock* experiment, according to Mundhenk, induced Dickens to plan more carefully before undertaking a novel: to seek "more control of the design of the whole, by fuller integration of theme and plot through metaphor, analogy, and juxtaposition" (657), and to be more astute in determining point of view and narrators.

In "Little Nell, Catholicism, and Dickens's Investigation of Death," Michael Schiefelbein contends that despite Dickens' frequent disparagement of Roman Catholicism, *The Old Curiosity Shop* reveals an interest in a Catholic "vision of mortality" (115). Numerous details in this narrative refer to the atmosphere of medieval Catholicism, and the plates done by George Cattermole, which were based on scenes in the text and approved by Dickens himself, include many features that reflect "the somber spirit of the Roman religion" (117). According to Schiefelbein, Nell herself, in dying, seems like the Virgin Mary in being "finally elevated to the level of the legendary" (120), but since Dickens cannot "accept the Catholic understanding of suffering as the means to redemption" (122), his heroine differs from the Virgin in showing a reluctance to consider thoughts of death. Schiefelbein concludes that Dickens faces a conflict: "he wants to confront mortality, as Catholicism does, but not under the conditions" imposed by the Catholic attitude toward suffering (124).

Dickens' next novel, *Barnaby Rudge*, besides being given close attention in the books by Duncan and Golden, is the subject of two essays.

In " 'Quoth the Raven': The Role of Grip in *Barnaby Rudge*," Jerome H. Buckley, after commenting that critics have recently given this novel "a newly positive assessment," remarks that no commentator "has paid much heed to the presence or function of Grip the raven" (28). Buckley claims that Barnaby's pet, despite the traditional association of ravens with "mystery and ill omen" (29), is "neither truly diabolic nor effectively benevolent," but, instead, "remains . . . enigmatic and ambiguous, observant but detached" (30). Indeed, according to this discussion, Grip is "a vocal presence, a sort of chorus character commenting with ironic effect on the current mood, but always the passive observer" (31). Buckley mentions, however, that while this pet "can approach or simulate human responses, Barnaby seeks to realize the attributes of a bird," especially in his mode of dress (31), and that Barnaby and Grip together contribute to a sense of "eerie surrealism" (32).

Charles Hatten's "Disciplining the Family in *Barnaby Rudge*: Dickens's Professionalization of Fiction" maintains that *Barnaby Rudge* marks a significant change as Dickens moves from "the almost picaresque openness to public sites and to diverse social strata which characterized his early fiction" (17) and turns to much stronger interest in familial and domestic subjects. This shift, according to Hatten, was in part prompted by Dickens' desire to elevate his professional status, a goal that led him to be receptive to the influence of the prestigious Sir Walter Scott and to follow the latter's example in linking "familial dissensions with larger social ills" (18). Seeing Scott's *The Heart of Mid-Lothian* as a narrative "organized around parallel societal and familial transgressions" (22), Hatten suggests that this work and *Barnaby Rudge*, both of which describe historical rebellion, reveal the inadequacy of excessively harsh "familial and social discipline" (21) and that Dickens'

novel "implicitly promotes an alternative . . . pattern" of control, one relying upon "the isolation of the nuclear family from larger . . . spheres" (21)
and upon "fostering the internalization of values through love and moral
example" (32). For Hatten, Dickens emphasizes his criticism of oppressive
and inadequate "masculine authority" by the inclusion in *Barnaby Rudge* of
many "problematic father figures" (24), especially the elder Rudge and Sir
John Chester (at times incorrectly called Sir Chester [26, 27, 28]). This
familial ideology serves, according to Hatten, to strengthen Dickens' "status
as a writer for middle-class audiences in the new industrialized order" (33)
and also to develop a "historical myth of family life and of its complex
relation to social life" that makes possible the probing societal analysis of
the "later and more complex novels" (33). Although I believe that earlier
works like *Oliver Twist* and *Nicholas Nickleby* give more attention to familial
concerns than Hatten implies, this essay still seems successful in illuminating
ways in which *Barnaby Rudge* advances Dickens' development as a novelist.

In "Repressive and Expressive Forms: The Bodies of Comedy and Desire
in *Martin Chuzzlewit*," Robert E. Lougy refers to Dickens' interest in "de-
pressions and protuberances inscribed on the surface of the human body" by
such features as noses, pimples, and mouths, as well as the changes reflected
in these (37), and proceeds to suggest that such details in the novels are not
merely satiric touches but ways to "enable the repressed to find expression":
"secrets are betrayed by the body's various disfigurements, transformations,
and gestures" (40). After examining hidden implications in one of Mrs.
Gamp's speeches, Lougy analyzes the episode (in chapter 24) in which Jonas
Chuzzlewit is hurt by Tom Pinch, Charity Pecksniff, who has been rejected
by Jonas, smiles and then goes to Tom in his room to thank him, and Tom
thinks of Mary Graham. For Lougy, Jonas' reaction to his wound is linked
to his "parricidal desires" (50) and his wish for self-punishment, while covert
erotic desire is expressed by the responses of both Charity and Tom. Lougy
considers the sexual pun noticed by Michael Steig—the narrator's reference
to Tom's "organ" and its "elevation"—and also discusses such details as
the relationship between the attack on Jonas and Tom's suppressed feelings
of Oedipal aggression towards Jonas' friend Pecksniff, as well as the manner
in which Tom's interest in Mary "only partially screens even more forbidden
desires" for his sister, Ruth (55). Lougy skillfully and cogently argues that
careful attention to these points makes us more aware of the family "entangle-
ments" that "pervade *Martin Chuzzlewit*, a novel especially haunted by
Oedipal dynamics" (55).

For other analyses of *Martin Chuzzlewit*, see the chapters by Maxwell and Golden, as well as the essay on illustration by Rubenstein.

Five articles, as well as the chapters in the books by Duncan and Lucas, consider *Dombey and Son*.

Richard Currie's "Doubles, Self-Attack, and Murderous Rage in Florence Dombey" sees this character as "one of Dickens' most effective depictions of the power of repressed anger" (113). According to Currie, the repressed hostility of Florence is shown in different ways at various ages: first, through verbal outbursts by her maid, Susan Nipper, who serves as her double and states what her mistress holds back; next, in the narrator's reports of Florence's thoughts as she grows older and seeks to shield her father from her anger over his rejection by blaming herself "for inadequacy and insufficiency" (113); and, then, in the adult Florence's dream that Dombey and Edith have both died, an instance of wish-fulfillment attributable to the young woman's "murderous rage" (113). Such a view of Florence, Currie argues, indicates that she "can no longer be regarded as a sentimental figure who lacks psychological reality" (114). Using various psychoanalytic approaches to develop and support his case, Currie concludes that in the creation of this heroine Dickens "has captured the delicate psychological dynamics in which a person will hide rage in order to hope for love" (126).

In "How Popular was *Dombey and Son*?," Simon Dentith explores the complexities in Raymond Williams' statement that *Dombey and Son* reflects Dickens' use of popular culture to present radical views. Arguing that the expression "popular" refers not just to readership but also to "popular forms" (69), Dentith points to this novel's use of the Dick Whittington narrative and the related story of the Industrious Apprentice, the many references to the fairy tale tradition, the employment of "a series of popular types," including the "Jolly Jack Tar, the termagant, the hen-pecked husband, the aspiring spinster" (71), and the inclusion of features from melodrama. Dentith proceeds, however, to remind us that the word "popular" is "a relational term" and that the "opposition in which the popular is contrasted with 'high' or 'elite' culture" is "an unstable one" (76): melodrama, for example, "in England and in France . . . begins in the demotic and 'illegitimate' theatres, only to be assimilated by the high prestige 'legitimate' theatres" and then to be subsequently "relegated once again to the basement of popular culture" (76). Dickens, as Dentith observes, refers in a satirical, parodistic way to melodrama in the popular theatres, but "his attitude to melodrama in its more prestigious embodiments is wholly positive" (78). Because, Dentith concludes, Dickens, in writing *Dombey and Son*, conducted "a struggle to take the diverse meanings of different forms and renegotiate them in specific ways," critical understanding demands a repetition of this complex "process" (80), as well as an awareness of how our era shapes our responses.

Michael Greenstein, in "Measuring Time in *Dombey and Son*," begins by restating a generalization: while the Romantics' "propensity for infinite vistas and vanishing points finds its temporal counterpart in the quest for eternity, . . . the Victorians' sense of time is grounded in the specific quotidian" (151). He then proceeds to show how fully *Dombey and Son* supports the latter part of this assertion, for this novel contains a very large number of references to various kinds of time and to diverse ways of measuring these, an obsessive interest that begins with the opening chapter. To demonstrate the importance of this theme, Greenstein reviews in a clear, interesting manner the narrative's inclusion of many clocks and watches, especially the "chronometers [that] fill the shop of Solomon Gills," and comments, "Characters make time, time fashions character in the chronometry of *Dombey and Son*" (154). Among the many facets of this motif considered in this article are the relationship between time and habit, the ways in which characters "look nostalgically to the past . . . [and] project their fantasies onto the future" (154), and the measurement of time by the waves and, for Dombey, by "the rhythm of retributive footsteps" (156). As Greenstein observes, the novel's "timepieces . . . captivate Dickens, his characters, and his readers" (157).

Frank McCombie's "Sexual Repression in *Dombey and Son*" develops the idea that this novel "is quite startlingly modern in . . . its presentation of male sexual repression" (25). McCombie observes Dickens' many textual references to female "breasts and bosoms" (26) and explains how these details and also corresponding anatomical features in a number of Hablot Browne's illustrations emphasize sexuality, especially that of Edith and Florence. Dombey, this essay remarks, displays an "unexamined fear of female sexuality" and therefore is "a sexually repressed protagonist" who remains "impervious to the feminine side of Edith" (28), while Carker, in contrast, seems "sexually aroused by her mere presence" (29). McCombie regards Edith as a "sexually frustrated" woman, but believes that "the significance of all the breast/bosom imagery" associated with her "devolves upon Florence," whose "femininity" is given greater attention by both Dickens and his illustrator as she grows older (33) and "becomes . . . a sexual presence that her father cannot ignore" (34). McCombie notices that when Dombey eventually strikes Florence (ch. 47), he hits her, as is later made clear, on the bosom, "that part which has symbolized female sexuality throughout the novel" (36). After examining Florence's role in her father's "reclamation," McCombie concludes that Dickens anticipates Freud in showing perceptive awareness of "the dangers of repression" and of the fact "that one repression was likely to lead to another" (37).

Helene Moglen, in "Theorizing Fiction/Fictionalizing Theory: The Case of *Dombey and Son*," also considers sexuality in Dickens' seventh novel, but takes a much more wide-ranging perspective. Her intricately argued discussion sees in *Dombey and Son* "an integrated, gender-based analysis," one referring to "the domestic division of labor" and presenting a "system of hierarchically ordered binary oppositions," each with a "dominant term" that is male and an "excluded term [that] is female" (159). In this novel, therefore, we find a "fundamentally dualistic world . . . of the railroad and the sea, power and powerlessness, domination and submission, time and eternality" (159–60), but, "instead of mediating between these dualities, the family fragments and divides along the line of gender: males claimed . . . by the world of culture, females by the natural world": "The father encourages in his son attitudes of control and exploitation; nurturance and love are left to women" (160). *Dombey and Son* is further complicated, Moglen maintains, by being divided into "two distinct but interdependent narratives": Dombey's is one "of social realism," while Florence's is "a pastoral romance of Woman and of nature" (160). As Moglen also observes, "Dombey's masculine world of progress, imagistically represented by the railroad," is countered by "the feminized world of Florence, a world of the sea presided over by Captain Cuttle and his cheery friends, who look back nostalgically to a less complicated, pre-industrial age" (161). Of course, this "female order . . . is brought to dominance by the magic of the novel's resolution," a conclusion featuring Florence's redemption of her "ruined and repentant" father (173). For Moglen, although Dickens in various ways questions the dichotomies established early in *Dombey and Son*, he "finally rejects his deconstruction of the binary oppositions . . . in order to embrace an essentialist view derived from what is ultimately a simple reversal of the hierarchical ordering" (175). But Moglen objects that this final position neglects "the fundamental interrelation of male and female" and "disguises crucial differences among women" (176). Suggesting that the relationship of Dombey and his daughter may be seen as revealing "a submerged fantasy of incest" (178), Moglen explores the ramifications of the novel's "erotic displacements" (179) and concludes by effectively stressing the complexity of "fictions, both male- and female-authored'' (179) that provide "alternative readings of the realities they seek to represent'' (180).

David Copperfield receives close attention in three periodical essays and in chapters in the books by Duncan, Golden, Lucas, and Morgan.

Malcolm M. Marsden's "Dickens' Mr. Micawber and Mark Twain's Colonel Sellers: The Genesis of an American Comic,'' studies "the parallelism between Mr. Micawber (and to a lesser extent Mrs. Micawber) . . . and Colonel Beriah Sellers in . . . *The Gilded Age*'' (64). While acknowledging that *David Copperfield* is not the only source for Twain's comic character, Marsden observes that the Micawbers and Sellers, although they claim to have "respect for the laws of capitalism, . . . implicitly attack'' this system (68). In addition, these characters share an inclination to the histrionic, a skill with language, and an "ebullient resiliency'' (72). Despite the contrasts between Sellers and Micawber, Marsden emphasizes the ways in which both characters "survive . . . by creating in the world of words a sanctuary of love and joy'' (74), an achievement that makes them lovable despite their moral weaknesses.

In "Our Pew at Church,'' David Parker considers the first illustration in *David Copperfield*, a plate bearing the title used for this essay, and proposes that "the male figure in the foreground, slightly to the right of the centre, leaning on the back of the pew,'' and looking at Murdstone, "represents David Copperfield the narrator, contemplating his early life'' (41). Because of Copperfield's frequent claims that he is summoning up images before him as he writes, this idea is tempting, and Parker tries to support his hypothesis in a reasonable way. Nevertheless, I remain dubious, for although, as Parker points out, the figure in question seems similar in appearance to the mature David that we see in the novel's last plate, the narrator, when describing his early church attendance (ch. 2), is clearly following the perspective not of an adult but of the small boy David sitting beside his mother and Peggotty in the illustration. In other words, the narrator does not here take a viewpoint detached from that of this child, as is done very late in the novel: "I saw a ragged way-worn boy forsaken and neglected'' (ch. 62). Moreover, I know of no other Dickens etching by Hablot Browne that departs from realism in a way like that which Parker believes is intended in this plate. For those of us who remain skeptical, Parker concludes with a fair question: "Who is this striking figure in 'Our Pew at Church', and what is he doing there?'' (42). I can only meekly and tentatively propose the Copperfield family's meek, kindly friend, Mr. Chillip. We know that in the church he is visible "in his Sunday neckcloth'' (ch. 2)—although I cannot tell if the figure in Browne's

illustration wears such an item—and perhaps he is courteously waiting for a
pause in the reading so that he can re-enter the pew without disrupting the
service.

Irène Simon's "*David Copperfield*: A Künstlerroman?" offers a positive
reply to the query in its title and argues that this narrative, despite the complaints of various critics, does depict its protagonist's "development as a
novelist" (41). Simon affirms that David's emphasis on "his hard work as
a writer" (42) is to be taken as a sign of professionalism rather than lack of
imagination, and she effectively reviews a number of details, such as the
uses of "the chapters of Retrospect" (45), to demonstrate the narrator's
self-conscious care in shaping his materials and in conveying his emotional
responses. For Simon, the theme of discipline extends beyond the protagonist's perceived need to overcome the mistakes attributable to an "undisciplined heart" and includes the achievement of "aesthetic distance," which
she sees as "largely a matter of control of tone and viewpoint, that is, a
matter of discipline" (46). *David Copperfield*, Simon cogently insists, does
offer a portrait of the artist, but the portrait is more Wordsworthian than
Joycean and the artist is a lesser one than Dickens himself. Nevertheless, the
"image of the artist" presented in David's narrative, Simon asserts, "is no
less characteristic of the mid-Victorian novelist than Stephen Dedalus is of
the *fin de siècle* artist" (56).

Bleak House, equalled only by *Great Expectations* in the number of discussions evoked, is considered in chapters by Maxwell, Golden, Lucas, and
Milbank, in an article by Michal Peled Ginsburg that is examined later since
it also comments extensively on *Our Mutual Friend*, and in seven other
essays.

Richard T. Gaughan, in " 'Their Places are a Blank': The Two Narrators
in *Bleak House*," seeks to show how the third-person narrator and Esther,
who employ different systems of language, "represent and embody two points
of view that go into making up the novel's world" and "also . . . the twofold way in which the novel is a response to that world" (80). The third-
person narrator, "essentially critical," reveals society's "unacknowledged
conflicts that . . . constitute a . . . blank at the center of a social world that
seems to be totally dominated by institutionalized systems of order"—especially the languages of Chancery and the world of fashion—while Esther,
"the missing center of the third-person narrator's story," stands for "the
individualized imagination" (80). Employing some of the theories of M. M.
Bakhtin on language, Gaughan sees Esther as "personal" and her co-narrator
as "objective" (82), the latter engaged in detached disclosure of secrets, the

former seeking "self-creation" (85) and emerging as someone who has to "interpret the same story the third-person narrator is telling from the point of view of personal identity" (87). After proposing that Jo and Lady Dedlock—the former suffering from "exclusion from language [that of Chancery]" and the latter from "imprisonment in it [the language of fashion]" (85)—are "antitheses of how language is used as a way of ordering the world in the novel" (86), Gaughan examines the complicated relationships among the language used by Skimpole and Bucket (at times antithetical figures) and the third-person narrator, who seeks to synthesize "both the diversity of possible meanings and the need for order and stability" (85). Esther is allowed to "escape her entanglement in the languages of others" through the "alienation" caused by her illness and disfigurement (90). For Gaughan, both narrators are interdependent in "the novel's attempt to represent its world as the subject of many stories and not the closed domain of just one" (92). Although some readers may wonder if Dickens' approach was as schematic as this essay occasionally suggests, Gaughan's complex discussion offers a number of valuable, stimulating insights.

In "The Grotesque and Urban Chaos in *Bleak House*," Kay Hetherly Wright first discusses the grotesque in terms of the reactions it elicits—feelings of confusion and bafflement—and then proceeds to demonstrate how central this quality is in *Bleak House*. Chancery itself, she observes, is "an embodiment of the grotesque" and "an emblem representing the principle of chaos that Dickens associates with modern urban life" (98). In "the world of Chancery . . . normal divisions of time, space, and species seem to have collapsed into each other" (99–100). Krook, "a sinister figure" likened to the Lord Chancellor, is a victim of spontaneous combustion in "the most obviously grotesque incident" in the novel, an event that Wright regards as a "mixture of the comic with the horrible" (102). *Bleak House* also emphasizes the grotesque through development of the theme of "uncertainty about origins" (103) and the motif of "loss of identity in . . . many host/parasite relationships" (107). For Wright, Dickens offers in *Bleak House* no "cure" for "the profound sense of dislocation he associates with London" (108) and implies that "the only solution is to escape the urban labyrinth" (109). Despite the remark that this "retreat into pastoralism . . . is disappointing," Wright still finds the work "a powerful depiction of modern urban life as a grotesque landscape which lacks any kind of coherent center" (109).

Timothy Peltason, in "Esther's Will," uses the topic of will to develop a sympathetic study of Esther Summerson's personality and the ways in which it is shown to us in *Bleak House*. While her self-denial is noteworthy, Peltason seeks "to trace out the counter-drama of Esther's growing self-assertion" and "the presence in Dickens of an alternative current of argument that stresses the importance not of transcending, but of discovering, the personal will" (672). Maintaining that Esther tells "the story of her progress in [attaining] healthy self-love," Peltason asserts that "when her desires are imperfectly suppressed . . . Esther's language comes most excitingly to life" (673). In John Jarndyce's character, Peltason finds both similarities to Esther's and also important contrasts. For this essay sees Jarndyce's "inability to assign blame" as "a culpable evasion" and notices, too, his lack of any "profession save for a kind of free-lance philanthropy, sometimes admirable in its effects, sometimes not" (676). Esther seems superior in finding direction for her energies and in her ability "to acknowledge and to gratify her own desires" (678). For Peltason, the highly emotional reunion between Esther and Ada is particularly significant in emphasizing the former's "special needs as an unloved child" and in revealing her tendency to project onto Ada "anxieties and desires that Esther cannot acknowledge" (682). In discussing Esther's reaction to Jarndyce's proposal, Peltason observes that while she appears "ready to meet Jarndyce in a new and eager way" that does not exclude physical desire, he is frustratingly non-responsive to this wish "to alter the terms of their relationship" (686). Concluding that by the end of the novel we can see that "the distance" between "the burstingly vital Dickens" and Esther "is not so great as it first appears" (689), Peltason suggests, too, that the "characters in *Bleak House* who most closely resemble their creator are the strange pair of Bucket and Esther Summerson, two penetrating observers" (690). Although in recent decades Esther has had many able defenders, Peltason, I believe, further strengthens the case for seeing her as one of Dickens' triumphs.

Another essay, "*Bleak House*: The *flâneur*'s perspective and the discovery of the body," appears as a chapter in John Rignall's book *Realist Fiction and the Strolling Spectator*, a study of the relationship between "the figure of the disengaged onlooker" and "the privileged role ascribed to seeing in the practice of literary realism" (2). In the volume's nine other chapters, the author examines this character, similar to the *flâneur*—"the strolling habitué of the boulevards who observes the life around him with a lively but detached curiosity" (3)—in Walter Benjamin's essays and in fiction by such writers as Poe, Scott, Balzac, Flaubert, George Eliot, Henry James, Ford Madox Ford, and Conrad. In considering *Bleak House*, Rignall asserts that "Dickens's imagination" is intent on "pursuing the grotesque and eccentric" and on presenting work in which "a margin of mystery remains" (62). Observing that Dickens evidently found walking along city streets to be at times "inspiring" and on other occasions "soothing" (63), Rignall goes on to comment, "if, as Benjamin suggests, the *flâneur* combines the casual eye of the stroller with the purposeful gaze of the detective, then Dickens's mature novels can be seen to rely more heavily than the early writings on the latter, most obviously and literally in *Bleak House . . .* where the figure of Mr Bucket plays a crucial organizing role" (64). For Rignall, the anonymous co-narrator "renders the London world familiar and meaningful, and yet at the same time mysterious" (65), while Esther emerges as "a trustworthy witness" whose "seeing [is] largely unproblematic," for "it is only with respect to herself that her vision is restricted," and "her narrative is the story of how she overcomes this inability" (66). Esther, in Rignall's opinion, serves as a "foil" not only to the anonymous narrator but also to such *flâneur*-like characters as Richard, Skimpole, and Bucket (66), and her illness is seen as liberating in that it leads her to become "aware of the stranger whose existence she has never fully acknowledged—her own body" (69). Moreover, her climactic journey with Bucket, in which she sees the city streets as "nightmarishly phantasmagoric," while he appears "professionally familiar" with them, mirrors "the duality of the novel's narrative structure" (71). After reviewing other details, Rignall concludes, "In the case of Dickens the gaze of the *flâneur* embraces the mysterious and the transparent, the comic and the sinister, connectedness and fragmentation" (79). The particular approach followed in this discussion leads to some fresh insights on much-studied features.

Anny Sadrin, in "Charlotte Dickens: The Female Narrator in *Bleak House*," entertainingly and cogently offers still another defense of both Esther and Dickens by arguing that critics would be far more tolerant of the heroine's personality and literary style if "the author of *Bleak House* had been a woman—say Charlotte Dickens" (49). For Sadrin, there is a likelihood that the novel was "conceived in a spirit of experimentation and sympathy" (50), one marked by a desire "to create a female narrator who is a mistress of negation, understatement and equivocation" (51). Following this conjecture, Sadrin is led to suggest that when Esther displays great coyness in referring to Woodcourt at the ends of chapters 13 and 14, she is seeking "to capture her former confusion. Truthfulness, not hypocrisy, has prompted this narrative strategy of emphatic reticence" (52). Sadrin also affirms that Dickens, by allowing Esther to become disfigured and yet remain "love-inspiring, sexually lovable" (55), creates an emancipated heroine superior in some respects to Charlotte Brontë's Jane Eyre, a character who keeps her attractiveness but marries a man that has been physically diminished. This essay reveals a feminist viewpoint confident and assured enough to seek to be scrupulously fair to Dickens, "a notoriously patriarchal author" (48).

Observing the tendency of commentators on *Bleak House* to assume that the disease which afflicts Jo, Charley, and Esther is smallpox, Gilian West, in "*Bleak House*: Esther's Illness," lists eight "reasons to doubt" this conclusion (30), two of these being the need for an incubation period about three times as long as the four-day interval between Charley's exposure and her being stricken and the fact that by 1840 vaccination against smallpox was available for the middle and upper classes. West then uses quotations from mid-Victorian medical sources to argue that the disease that Dickens had in mind was probably "erysipelas of the face," a complication of typhus (31–32). For West, this is significant, for while smallpox could be blamed on failure to be vaccinated, typhus—which, West remarks, "in Greek . . . means 'fog' "—would be "entirely to be blamed on the squalor of Tom-all-Alone's," and Esther's plight "would be the responsibility of no one but the Lord Chancellor in whose care Tom-all-Alone's lies" (33). West's medical details make her case impressive, but we are left with perhaps an even more pressing question: why is Dickens so strangely unwilling to name the various ailments that threaten the lives of Tiny Tim and Esther and prove fatal to Dora?

My own note "*Bleak House* and Bulwer-Lytton's *Not So Bad As We Seem*" suggests that Dickens' deep involvement with an amateur production of this play, a comedy "now virtually forgotten," may "have contributed to the development" of various details in *Bleak House* (25). I propose that—"at the very least"—absorption in the play as stage manager and actor provided Dickens with "reminders of themes and situations that held great attraction for him" (28).

Anne Hiebert Alton, in "Education in Victorian Fact and Fiction: Kay-Shuttleworth and Dickens's *Hard Times*," first reviews Kay-Shuttleworth's contribution to primary education and teacher training in England and then maintains that *Hard Times* attacks not all of this reformer's views, but mainly those that tend to "neglect of Fancy and . . . elevation of the importance of Fact" (67). In addition, Alton points out that although Kay-Shuttleworth was progressive in disapproving of rote learning, "his condescending attitude towards the lower classes" led him to connect "ignorance to evil, and pauperism to immorality" (72). On the other hand, in *Hard Times* we see the virtue of the "poor and uneducated" circus people (74) and the villainy of the educated Tom and the wealthy Bounderby. While Dickens criticized the narrowing features in the teacher-training program proposed by Kay-Shut-tleworth, both men were eager to find "a higher caliber of teachers to direct education for the poor" (78).

In "Dickens the Novelist: The Preston Strike and *Hard Times*," R. D. Butterworth considers the inconsistency between the account of the Preston weavers' union in Dickens' *Household Words* article "On Strike" and the "hostile" depiction of the Coketown workers' union in *Hard Times* (91). Although the *Household Words* essay includes an unflattering portrait of the agitator Gruffshaw, based on Mortimer Grimshaw, "a clear source for much of the character of Slackbridge" (93), Dickens gives in this article a balanced account of the Preston workers' organization. Butterworth suggests, therefore, that the much more negative view of a union presented in *Hard Times* is attributable not to Dickens' being "naive or ill-informed," but to his desire to offer a didactic warning against "the fragmentation of British society" (101). According to Butterworth, Dickens advocates in *Hard Times* a wish for relations between workers and employers to reflect Christian principles of brotherhood rather than the factionalism that unions tend to encourage: "Dickens looks not to the short-term," but to "the fundamental reform of society" (101). This explanation seems highly plausible, but when Butterworth refers to Dickens' "presentation of Stephen Blackpool as adopting this position" (100)—that of rejecting factionalism in favor of the ideals of brotherhood—we might add that although this does seem to be Stephen's view at the end of the novel, his refusal to join the union is based not only on this philosophy, but on the unexplained promise to Rachael. In asking Stephen to bind himself to such a vow, Rachael may have been motivated by Christian principles, but the only tenuous evidence for this is her unsupported claim, in a cancelled passage (written for bk. 1, ch. 13), that "such things" (laborers' efforts to improve the safety of working conditions) will "only lead to hurt" (247)—an argument advocating passivity and submission.

In "Physiognomy in *Hard Times*," Michael Hollington is concerned not merely with "reading character through the observation of the human face," but with "the deciphering of the observable surfaces of a variety of distinguishable human features—physical, gestural, linguistic—as well as those of comparable attributes of non-human and inanimate beings" (58). He describes the ways in which such investigation helps us to understand the significance of minor details in *Hard Times*, and he particularly emphasizes the importance of "a language of gesture" (58) as a technique Dickens uses to guide the reader. Showing how movements and posture reflect personality, the author suggests that Dickens may have gained "his awareness of imperial gesture" from the acting styles then in use (60). After noticing the dependence of physiognomy "upon the very imaginative capacity that has been denied by Gradgrindian utilitarianism" (62–63), Hollington describes a "relation between physiognomy and allegory" (64) that supports the novel's polemical purpose.

Katherine Kearns's "A Tropology of Realism in *Hard Times*" studies the ways in which Dickens uses a "surreal tropology of madness and nihilism" to subvert the realism endorsed by Gradgrind and the Coketown setting (858). Claiming that *Hard Times*, a "novel about the hazards of productivity, . . . reflects in its tropes" Dickens' "anxiety about and his resistance to the realistic mode" (864), Kearns cites numerous passages in which metaphor and metonymy expose the madness underlying this industrial society and also question "an artistry committed to realism" (865). Particularly noteworthy are the examples involving Coketown, Bounderby, and Louisa. Although I find this essay at times weighed down by frequent inclusion of terms like "syntagmatic" (863), "deictic" (865), "metadiscourse" (866), "diegetical" (873), and "semiosis" (878), Kearns succeeds in demonstrating how Dickens' inexhaustible imagination insists on magnificently complex extravagance even within the relatively restricted space of *Hard Times*. In this novel, Kearns affirms, "the real and the surreal coexist because they are interdependent" (877).

Kristin Flieger Samuelian, in "Being Rid of Women: Middle-Class Ideology in *Hard Times*," observes that Stephen Blackpool and Bounderby endorse opposing middle-class ideals, Stephen seeking "a bourgeois domestic ideal" in which his disreputable wife would be replaced by "the virtuous working woman Rachael" (58) and Bounderby claiming to embody "the myth of the self-made man" (59). Although Samuelian maintains that Stephen's ideology, which seems linked to a belief in "passive paternalism" (58), is favored by Dickens over Bounderby's, she points out an interesting relationship between the two competing ideals: both call for "the absence of women who challenge them"—Stephen's "drunken wife" (59) and Bounderby's "respectable, self-sacrificing mother" (60). Reviewing interesting parallels between the fantasies of "the novel's hero and villain" (60), Samuelian concludes that these links "suggest an instability in both ideas that disrupts Dickens' political argument" in support of Stephen's ideology (61).

H. M. Daleski, in "Large Loose Baggy Monsters and *Little Dorrit*," recalls that writing about this novel "some twenty years ago," in his book *Dickens and the Art of Analogy*, he had great confidence in the unity of the work, for he "envisaged its structure as a series of concentric circles cohering in the Marshalsea prison at its center'' and also ''posited the idea of arrest, evoking stoppage as well as custody, as the link between the central symbol of the prison and the circular manifestations of metaphorical imprisonment'' (131–32). In this essay, Daleski proposes to examine ''challenges'' to the ''artistic coherence'' of *Little Dorrit*, for he concedes that some characters remain ''free,'' that other figures who are ''marginal'' are not included in studies emphasizing the narrative's unity (132), and that Clennam and Little Dorrit ''do not seem to be at the thematic center of interest'' (133). In the ensuing discussion, however, Daleski uses close textual analysis to reveal another organizing principle: ''It is the idea of debt—the payment or non-payment of what is owed—that mediates between the free and the imprisoned in *Little Dorrit*'' (133). Referring to different kinds of indebtedness and to literal and figurative imprisonment and freedom, Daleski shows how this idea pertains directly not only to Clennam and Amy, but also to such characters as Doyce, Plornish, Pancks, Flora, and Fanny. In looking more closely for possible looseness, bagginess, and monstrosity in *Little Dorrit*, Daleski discovers coherence and beauty even more impressive than that he previously perceived.

F. T. Flahiff's '' 'Mysteriously Come Together': Dickens, Chaucer, and *Little Dorrit*'' proposes that while Dickens was writing *Little Dorrit*, various texts by Chaucer stimulated him and revealed ''possibilities for his art'' (257). Besides examining evidence indicating Dickens' familiarity with Chaucer's works, Flahiff suggests that such features as the reference at the end of Book 1, Chapter 2, to the ways in which ''we restless travellers [move] through the pilgrimage of life'' reflect an interest in the pilgrims who assemble in the *General Prologue* to the *Canterbury Tales*, while such remarks as those on Rumour's concern with Mr. Merdle (bk. 2, ch. 24) echo lines in Chaucer's *The House of Fame*. After also stating that an obscure reference to ''Wades boot [boat]'' in the *Merchant's Tale* may have provided a name for Miss Wade, Flahiff proceeds to his fullest argument for Chaucer's influence, the suggestion that the *Franklin's Tale* gave Dickens hints for various details in his novel: although Flahiff readily concedes that ''Amy Dorrit is never so reckless as Dorigen'' (262), he finds John Chivery reminiscent of Chaucer's chivalrous love-stricken squire, Aurelius. Moreover, in the Preface to *Little Dorrit*, Dickens mentions that prior to visiting the site of the Marshalsea, he wondered if ''any portions'' of the prison were ''yet standing,'' a remark that Flahiff links to Clennam's statement, while telling William Dorrit of his new freedom, that the prison wall was ''Gone'' (bk. 1, ch. 35). This comment recalls for Flahiff the illusory disappearance of the dangerous rocks in the

Franklin's Tale. Although Dickensians may disagree about whether these and other parallels cited are distinctive enough to demonstrate indebtedness, Flahiff convinces me that there is a strong possibility of Chaucer's having influenced *Little Dorrit*.

Trey Philpotts, in "Dickens, Patent Reform, and the Inventor: Daniel Doyce and the Question of Topicality," makes very skillful use of detailed historical research to argue that the difficulties experienced in *Little Dorrit* by the inventor Daniel Doyce were not, as some commentators have suggested, anachronistic by 1855, the year in which Dickens began composing this novel. Referring to "a heretofore overlooked [*Household Words*] article by Henry Morley" (158), published in 1853, Philpotts explains that the Patent Law Amendment Act of 1852 had not solved all problems and that a minority of inventors, including the distinguished civil engineer Isambard Kingdom Brunel, with whom Dickens was friendly, actually desired to have patents abolished on the grounds that they inhibited progress. By publishing Morley's essay, which appears to endorse "the view of the patent abolitionists" (159), Dickens, in Philpotts' opinion, seems to be shifting his own position on this issue. Moreover, the enormous harm done to the British army by governmental bureaucratic inefficiency during the Crimean War made Doyce's frustrations extremely topical in 1855, for there was national "fear that technological advance had slowed in England, undone by aristocratic languor and ineptitude" (167). Citing articles in *Punch* and diverse other sources, Philpotts concludes, "Doyce's troubles were not only not 'out of date' in 1855, they constitute the very substance of the political and social dialogue" (168).

See, also, for consideration of *Little Dorrit*, the chapters by Lucas, Milbank, and Morgan, as well as Rosenberg's essay on character development.

In "Language, Love and Identity: *A Tale of Two Cities*," the lone essay in 1992 on this novel, Tom Lloyd refers to the presence in *A Tale of Two Cities* of a noticeable self-consciousness about language and suggests that this attention to words forces us to seek to interpret them and to see how they signify identity. Besides stressing the importance of words, Lloyd points out the concern in this narrative with two kinds of "non-verbal communication"—one "based on vengeance, and another based on love," exemplified, respectively, by Madame Defarge and by Lucie, "standing outside Darnay's Paris prison" (159), as well as by Carton in giving comfort to the young girl he meets in the tumbril just before their execution. Lloyd finds common to both Goethe's *Faust* and *A Tale of Two Cities* "the idea that one must constantly strive to redefine and affirm identity" (162). But identity, Lloyd asserts, is determined not only by communication, but also by "a principle of love that inspires belief and action,'' the love shown by Lucie (162). Referring to Schiller's views on sublimity in tragedy, this essay relates these ideas to Carlyle's "ecstatic dramatization of Madame Roland's death in *The French Revolution*,'' a scene that provided a model for Carton's martyrdom, for, as Lloyd observes, "Carton and Roland both discover a transcendental language" (164), one that seeks to consider the ineffable. Lloyd suggests, too, that Carton's final thoughts, described by the narrator in a strangely ambiguous manner that "underscores the tentativeness . . . by stressing the 'if' '' (166), are "an evocation of mystery" (166), for in this novel "the mystery at the core of the self always remains" (167). For Lloyd, *A Tale of Two Cities* is far more sophisticated and subtle than most earlier commentators believed.

In addition to the chapters by Golden, Lucas, Milbank, and Morgan, eight essays concentrated on *Great Expectations*.

Philip V. Allingham's "Patterns of Deception in *Huckleberry Finn* and *Great Expectations*'' observes that despite the centrality of deception in each of these novels, there are important basic contrasts. Focusing on three types of deception—"a deliberate misleading of the reader by the author through the narrator; a fraud perpetrated or a practical joke played by one character upon another; and a character's deceiving himself'' (449)—Allingham points out interesting parallels and some important distinctions between the narratives, but for him the most significant contrast is that "while Pip grows in understanding, Huck does not" (453), a difference partly related to the fact that Dickens "reveals . . . a faith in the capacity of his society for reform,'' but Twain affirms "that freedom and society can never be other than antithetical'' (449). Allingham's discussion is perceptive and lucid, but his assertion that Ellen Ternan as well as Bulwer-Lytton persuaded Dickens to revise the original conclusion of *Great Expectations* seems to call for support, and the claim that we approve of Huck's lies and condemn Compeyson's "because of the differences in their motivations''—"Huck's lies are altruistic, Compeyson's exploitative" (472)—calls, I believe, for qualification: Huck's motives are not always unselfish, and not only intent but consequences will shape our judgment.

In "Dickens, Hunt and the 'Dramatic Criticism' in *Great Expectations*: A Note,'' Rodney Stenning Edgecombe observes that the ridicule of Wopsle's thespian efforts uses techniques very similar to those in reviews of dramatic productions and ballets by Dickens' friend Leigh Hunt and by another contemporary reviewer, Henry Robertson. As Edgecombe explains, Hunt and Robertson attack performances for not equalling what is suggested by imagination and also—contrastingly—for not being true to daily life. In *Great Expectations* the humor in Pip's "deadpan" account (88) of the performance of *Hamlet* is similarly based on "judging theatrical reality by the imagined ideal, or dismissing it by rational examination" (86). Pip's descriptions of the later theatrical efforts by his old acquaintance again suggest to Edgecombe "the world of a Hunt review" (89). Noting that Wopsle's "career on the stage" reflects the novel's theme of "expectations misplaced and exposed," Edgecombe concludes that when Pip applies to the performances "expectations aroused by the experience of life itself, and by the imaginative (and therefore unconstrained) experience of play and stories," he is "following the precedent of Leigh Hunt" (89).

Gail Turley Houston, in " 'Pip' and 'Property': The (Re)Production of the Self in *Great Expectations*," sees this novel as deviating from Dickens' earlier fiction, which presented self-denying heroines who redeemed the "public sphere of the male [who was] dedicated to success and money" (13). For Houston, *Great Expectations* includes, until the ending, only one nurturing female, Biddy, and she becomes unavailable to Pip when she agrees to marry Joe. The other main female characters—Mrs. Joe, Miss Havisham, and Estella—lack maternal qualities desired by the protagonist. Adopting Mark Seltzer's idea that production, traditionally seen as the male's function, and reproduction, ordinarily assigned to the female, combine to determine the creation of a self, Houston asserts that Pip, who has been denied "maternal nurture," may be seen as "falling from the sphere of reproduction into that of production" and as therefore "destined to become associated with property"—"becoming property as [well as] inheriting it" (17). Accordingly, Houston regards Pip as "particularly vulnerable in the cannibalistic world of Victorian England" (18), and she finds his story disturbing, for in presenting it "Dickens comes to realize that the possibility of escaping the market and effecting a return to the mother is practically nil" (16–17). Houston maintains that neither ending written by Dickens achieves Pip's "permanent regeneration" and that the published conclusion gains only the protagonist's "momentary . . . rebirth . . . at the expense of the female," since Estella is pushed "back into the mold of . . . earlier ascetic heroines" (23), characters sacrificed for the sake of the male protagonists. Near the end of the essay, Houston's interest in the imagery of eating leads to a slip in a reference to "just desserts" (22). In addition, the Eastern branch of Clarriker and Co., Pip's place of voluntary exile (ch. 58), is evidently in Cairo (ch. 55), not "in India" (22). But Houston provides a stimulating study that uses perceptive observations in supporting an overall view that complements other readings of *Great Expectations*.

Jerome Meckier's "Dickens, *Great Expectations*, and the Dartmouth College Notes" is an extremely detailed, carefully balanced, and admirably lucid examination of the controversy over whether handwritten notes about *Great Expectations* found in a copy of Samuel Johnson's *Dictionary* owned by the Dartmouth College Library are by Dickens himself or a forger. If these notes are genuine, the date included would indicate that Dickens first began considering this novel in December 1856, not September-October 1860. After reporting the claims for the notes expressed by Dick Hoefnagel and the objections raised by Kathleen Tillotson, Meckier uses his own study of the handwriting, calligraphic evidence from laboratory tests conducted by Joe Nickell, a colleague at the University of Kentucky, and inferences based on close scrutiny of Dickens' entries in the Book of Memoranda and the number plans to reach the conclusion that the author of these notes "was almost certainly not Dickens" (117). Meckier, who is collaborating with Edgar Rosenberg on the long-awaited Norton Critical Edition of *Great Expectations*, persuasively argues that the notes were written by "an imitator not quite familiar enough with the novelist's note-taking and number-planning habits" (128).

In another, even more highly detailed essay, "Dating the Action in *Great Expectations*: A New Chronology," Meckier makes use of "an essential clue" neglected by previous commentators on this book's dating (157). When Pip, after hearing of his expectations on a Saturday evening, tells of going the next day to church and listening to a reading "about the rich man and the kingdom of heaven" (ch. 19), he refers to a story found in each gospel except that of John. Meckier observes that by following Edgar Rosenberg's suggestion and looking at the Lectionary then in use we can learn the days on which these particular passages were to be read. By then following other clues in the text we can limit the number of possible Sundays to two, of which the second—July 6, 1823—seems the more likely. If this hypothesis is correct, the novel's "London section . . . commences at a time when previous daters thought Pip's adventures were already over" (158). Maintaining that in *Great Expectations*, "more than in other Dickens novels, good plotting depends on accurate dating," Meckier asserts that in this narrative "it is generally possible . . . to specify not just the year and month for major developments, but also the day of the week and the time of the day" (165). This very lengthy discussion makes extremely impressive use of close reasoning and subtle textual clues to buttress its suggestions about the probable ages of the characters and likely dates of occurrences. The hints that Meckier adduces imply that Dickens himself was remarkably precise and careful in planning this narrative. Although this essay, because of its specificity, calls for slow reading, Meckier's prose is admirably lucid. I raise just one minor quibble: after indicating reasons for believing that Pip and Estella are the same age, Meckier states, "The convict may have spared Pip for the simple reason that the lad reminded the hardened criminal of his lost child, who would have been about Pip's age" (169)—but while Herbert Pocket tells of learning from Magwitch that the child Pip did remind him of his lost daughter, " 'who would have been about your [Pip's] age' " (ch. 50), Meckier's word "spared" implies that without the resemblance Magwitch might have murdered the little boy, a crime far more extreme than any the convict previously committed. But, to close on a very positive note, Meckier's essay is masterfully cogent.

In "Repetitions During Pip's Closure," Robert A. Stein calls attention to the "many repetitive notes" in Pip's "final three chapters," which he sees as "inextricable from the one event that enables Pip's eventually stopping, Magwitch's death" (143), described in the chapter just preceding these concluding three. Using a psychoanalytic approach, Stein offers distinctions among various kinds of repetition—for example, repetition as *content* (the event or situation that recurs) and repetition as *process* ("the very fact of repetition itself" [144])—and proceeds, too, to analyze specific instances of recurrence, such as Pip's plan, near the end of the book, of "asking Biddy to marry him" (151). This example, according to Stein, "illustrates how tentative distinctions among forms of repetition necessarily are," since it seems a case of repetition as *process*, but is also connected with repetition as *content* in being closely related to a prior instance of repetition, Pip's affirmation of love for Estella during the scene at Magwitch's deathbed, a statement in which Pip has evidently "reinvested . . . in the very myth his impossible bride has perpetually denied" (151). Going on to consider the relationship between "the confluence of repetitions during Pip's closure" and "the requirements of closure itself" (152), Stein maintains that "closure cannot occur without repetition" (153). He then concludes this particularly complex and demanding essay with the assertion that Pip "would be discomforted to realize" (153) that "the various repetitions he employs [to achieve closure] embody truths contrary to the changes he expects" (153–54). If I follow Stein correctly, his main point seems to be that in *Great Expectations* "repetitions in effect seal" some "gaps or ambiguities of meaning" noticed during closure but they may also reveal "the potential endlessness of repetitions" (152)—a disavowal of change—and therefore serve not to clarify but to complicate.

Guerric DeBona's "Doing Time; Undoing Time: Plot Mutation in David Lean's *Great Expectations*" studies this particular version as "perhaps the best [film adaptation] of any [work] in the Dickensian canon" (79). After discussing methods used by Lean to achieve "marriage of the auditory and the visual" (82), this essay investigates how, for Lean, "the Miss Havisham plot becomes a fairy tale," while "the Magwitch plot moves toward a social commentary": "the convict does time; Miss Havisham undoes time" (84). DeBona, moreover, finds a "significant mutation" in that "Lean has been unable to integrate the two plots" (84), and, therefore, "the social plot has been submerged for the sake of the mythical plot" (85). A lengthy appendix offers some indication of parallels between the film's 751 scenes and Dickens' novel.

Like DeBona, Brian McFarlane, in "David Lean's *Great Expectations*—Meeting Two Challenges," examines ways in which Lean's motion picture handles the problem of adapting a novel to the medium of film. Considering the reactions evoked by Dickens' use of a first-person narrator and by the inclusion of various rhetorical devices such as symbols and tropes, McFarlane discusses the techniques Lean adopts in trying to incorporate corresponding features into his film. Among the devices in the film that are intended to reproduce the effect of first-person narration are the employment of voice-over, the "near-continuous presence" of Pip (70), "a great deal of subjective camera work that allows us literally to share Pip's point of view" (71), and the organization of screen space "so as to ensure our sympathetic alignment with Pip" (72). Nevertheless, the first-person narration of the novel cannot be wholly duplicated, McFarlane concedes, since in our response to the film we find that what Pip "*sees* will always be clearer to us than what he *makes* of that knowledge" (73). In seeking to meet the second challenge—that posed by Dickens' language—Lean, in McFarlane's opinion, can emulate only some of the novelist's effects, and the film therefore "creates its own style . . . that is something more than a reverent straining for equivalences" (76). Although both DeBona and McFarlane are largely concerned with film techniques, each of these essays also, I believe, increases our understanding of distinctive and complex features in Dickens' text.

Our Mutual Friend is given extended study in chapters by Golden and by Lucas, in Reed's essay on retribution, and in just two other articles.

In "The Case Against Plot in *Bleak House* and *Our Mutual Friend*," Michal Peled Ginsburg begins by referring to Franco Moretti's claim that "premodern texts" value "classification" (or preservation) over "transformation" and that this preference is also typical of the English bildungsroman, in contrast to the continental tradition (175). Commenting on this effort to see literary form as historically and culturally determined, Ginsburg explains that the English novel's favoring of classification involves a "positive evaluation of innocence and of choices made in childhood over the choices and changes of youth—which are seen as mere errors" and that this viewpoint "entails a negative evaluation of narrative and plot" (176); for, unlike the continental bildungsroman, in which "the plot is generated by a conflict between the protagonist and the world around him," the English tradition regards plot as created by the villain and as "a mere aberration or nightmare" to be opposed so that "legitimate order is restored," often with "the discovery of a rightful inheritance and of the heroes' identity" (177). According to Ginsburg, this endorsement of "justice based on . . . legitimacy" (177) offers what Morettir regards as the ideology of the English bildungsroman. Ginsburg, however, questions the precision of this view and proceeds to provide "a contrastive analysis" of *Bleak House* and *Our Mutual Friend* (178). She finds in the former novel an emphasis on waste and on a "feeling of endlessness" (181), a story that culminates not in "something new," but in "a restitution" (182), while *Our Mutual Friend*, on the other hand, stresses recycling or "constant transformation" (179) and uses change as its "organizing principle" (183). But Ginsburg, having pointed out this distinction, moves on "to complicate" her reading (185) by proposing that Lizzie and Eugene, although they seem to be transformed, are actually "the passive objects of a change 'inflicted' upon them" in a plot largely "generated by a villain" (187). Moreover, Ginsburg next maintains that the hero of this novel's other main story, the active Harmon, "does not undergo a genuine transformation" (190), but instead "merely puts on and takes off a disguise" (192). For Ginsburg, then, the stories in *Our Mutual Friend* do not follow either of the opposing plot models she originally described, but instead reveal a much more complex "combination of . . . features" (194). Although I resist a few of Ginsburg's suggestions—for instance, her emphasis on Eugene's being "totally passive" (190), a claim that seems overstated—her essay nevertheless offers a number of valuable insights.

In "Dickens's Secret Sharer, Conrad's Mutual Friend," Wayne W. Westbrook suggests that various details in *Our Mutual Friend* influenced Conrad's famous story "The Secret Sharer." Although Westbrook sees a number of similarities, I remain unconvinced, since some of the proposed parallels appear questionable. For example, this essay states that Dickens' Night-Inspector may be a model for Conrad's Captain Archbold in being "dull, unimaginative, and suspicious," yet dedicated to "the letter of the law and . . . the standards of duty" (206), but I find the inspector to be depicted in an admiring way, while Archbold remains just a timid comic butt. Moreover, any resemblance between Leggatt and the treacherous George Radfoot seems tenuous, since the former's crime was impulsive, not furtive and cowardly, and the claim that Leggatt goes to a "metaphorical" death that is parallel to Radfoot's "physical death" (208) sharply clashes with the concluding words of Conrad's captain-narrator, who refers to Leggatt as "a free man, a proud swimmer striking out for a new destiny." Then, too, the assertion that Riderhood is the murderer of Radfoot appears to overrule Dickens' determination to leave the nature of Riderhood's guilt in this matter ambiguous. Although *Our Mutual Friend* may have helped inspire elements in Conrad's story, I believe that any influence was relatively general in nature.

The Mystery of Edwin Drood is considered in Dubberke's book, Maxwell's chapter, one of the volumes examined below with other "entertainments," and three articles.

Doris Alexander, in "Solving the Mysteries of the Mind in *Edwin Drood*," a short but impressive essay, concedes that much about the unfinished novel remains unclear, but argues that the main theme is apparent and is one that suggests possible solutions to the puzzles. For Alexander, this theme is the "mystery of the human mind with its aberrations into criminality, with its derangements of perception and lapses of consciousness" (130), and she persuasively cites various details in the text to propose that John Jasper intended to commit his crime "outdoors in the Cathedral Close" (128) and that he may have had "a sudden lapse of consciousness" while seeking to perform the murder (128), a lapse during which Drood could have escaped and Jasper might have mistakenly killed another victim, possibly one of the vagabonds mentioned in chapter 3. Alexander, after affirming that Dickens, because of his "strong sense of responsibility to his reader . . . would not have wiped out a young life like Drood's casually" (128), goes on to stress the narrator's avoidance of any clear effort to evoke sympathy for the supposed victim. Moreover, this essay also cites Dickens' strong interest in an actual case of an unexplained disappearance that led to unfounded suspicions like those directed against Neville Landless. Although Alexander properly concedes that some of her views are speculative, she lends strong support, I think, to the position reaffirmed several years ago by Gwen Watkins: "all the evidence that Edwin is dead comes from outside Dickens' own work [a reference primarily to the statements by John Forster, two of Dickens' illustrators, and his son Charley and daughter Kate]: the evidence of the novel, studied within the pattern of Dickens' later works, shows the extreme likelihood of his being alive'' (140). Although the external evidence obviously deserves consideration, the survivalist position ultimately rests on a simple test: if the hearsay comments asserted that Edwin was not to die but to escape (as two of the projected titles suggest), would any readers have expressed doubt?

Ray Dubberke, in "Dating *Edwin Drood*," seeks to defend Percy Carden's argument, proposed in 1920, that the Christmas morning on which Drood disappears was intended to be that of 1842. Although Dubberke succeeds in challenging some of the objections raised by T. W. Hill in 1944, the placing of the novel's events in 1842 and 1843 remains for me only a possibility, for, except in the two historical novels and, as Meckier's previously discussed essay reveals, in *Great Expectations*, Dickens' narrators do not seem to wish to be tied to any one year and appear to share the mood expressed in the opening sentence of *Our Mutual Friend*, the novel immediately preceding *Edwin Drood*: "concerning the exact year there is no need to be precise."

In "Drood Renominated," Robert F. Fleissner, after defending the view that the surname *Drood* is intended to remind us of the holy rood, suggests that both the names *Neville*—or "*Ne-ville* (no city or home town)," an explanation attributed to Jane Vogel—and *Landless* serve to emphasize the displacement of the character (120). Fleissner also expresses doubt that Rosa's nickname *Pussy* is meant to have sexual associations. I would agree that neither Edwin Drood nor Dickens intends any indecency when referring to Rosa, and *Landless* certainly does connote deprivation. On the other hand, while the remarks concerning *Drood* and *Neville* are interesting, whether these contentions can be proved seems questionable.

Donald R. Burleson's concise note, "Dickens's *A Christmas Carol*," looks at the contrast between Scrooge and his nephew, an opposition emphasized in their conversation regarding Fred's attempt to invite his uncle to Christmas dinner. Burleson points out, however, that in this exchange Scrooge makes one remark that "adopts Christmas as his very paradigm for structuring and measuring time," while his nephew apparently accepts the regular calendar year, "Scrooge's year" (212). For Burleson, therefore, the two characters are not as wholly antithetical as they first seem to be.

For another item on *A Christmas Carol*, see the comment below on John Mortimer's "entertainment."

Philip V. Allingham's "Dickens' Christmas Books: Names and Motifs" sees thematic relevance in many of the names Dickens uses in the Christmas Books following *A Christmas Carol: The Chimes, The Cricket on the Hearth, The Battle of Life,* and *The Haunted Man.* This article offers clever suggestions but also includes proposals that seem a little forced or far-fetched. For instance, Allingham comments that Sir Joseph Bowley in *The Chimes,* a landowner who pretends to be benevolent towards the poor, is "given the name of the Old Testament figure who led the Children of Israel into the land of their bondage" (61)—but to regard the Biblical Joseph as a negative character is contrary to traditional Jewish and Christian readings and seemingly ignores Jacob's fear of starvation in famine-stricken Canaan (Genesis 42:2) and overlooks the fact that the captivity in Egypt was the fulfillment of a prophecy made by the Lord to Abram (Genesis 15:13). In addition, when Allingham maintains that in *The Haunted Man* Redlaw "spreads his callous view that nature is red in tooth and claw" (67), we may be troubled by the implication that the name alludes to an expression later made famous in Tennyson's *In Memoriam,* published two years after *The Haunted Man,* and we may ask why *law* suggests *claw* rather than *flaw* or simply *law.* Despite these complaints, however, Allingham provides other remarks that I find stimulating and plausible.

In another article, "Dickens's Unreliable Narrator in 'Hunted Down,' " Allingham examines this short story, first published in three installments in 1859, and states that for "the modern reader" the narrative's "salient feature" is "its unreliable (even devious) narrator," Mr. Sampson (86). In presenting an account of a treacherous, subtle murderer and a determined, obsessed revenger, Sampson employs a "manner" that Allingham calls "rambling, disconnected, and erratic" (89): the storyteller is often evasive, "clearly holding something back" (91), teasing "the reader with unexplained details" (92). Allingham regards this tale as "an interesting experiment in undermining the confidence that readers habitually place in the authoritative voice of the first-person narrator who is also very much a participant in the action" (92), even though "Sampson's deviousness" as a narrator is for the purpose of "entertaining and surprising" us (92). Because Sampson eventually does offer enlightenment, I prefer to call him "mystifying" or "teasing" rather than "unreliable."

In "Class Consciousness and the Indian Mutiny in Dickens's 'The Perils of Certain English Prisoners,' " Lillian Nayder observes that while Dickens in *Bleak House* ridicules Mrs. Jellyby for allowing her concern about proselytizing in foreign countries to distract her from helping English sufferers, he deviates from this "critique of imperialism as a pretence for ignoring domestic ills" (691) in "The Perils of Certain English Prisoners," a story that he wrote with Wilkie Collins and published in 1857. For Nayder, "The Perils" retells the story of the Indian Mutiny as a story of proletarian revolt" (692) in order to suggest that admirable members of the lower classes will during times of crisis recognize the ties that bind all English subjects and also to link the pirates in the tale, who reflect "the potential criminality of a resentful working class" (699), with the mutinous Indian sepoys. Moreover, Nayder reveals how Dickens in depicting the pirates expresses the racist disdain and hostility evoked in him by the Indian Mutiny. In Nayder's view, "The Perils" is "socially as well as racially elitist," for it "justifies" both the English class system and British imperialism (701). This essay carefully demonstrates the "regressive social ideal" implicit in the story (702) and reminds us that at times the sympathies of even someone as generous and benevolent as Dickens were disappointingly limited. One typographical slip, however, incorrectly identifies the narrative's heroine, Miss Maryon, as the "sister of Captain Carton" (698), whom she eventually marries—she is, of course, the sister of Captain Maryon.

Two books that give tangential consideration to Dickens are Martin A. Kayman's *From Bow Street to Baker Street: Mystery, Detection and Narrative* and Hilary M. Schor's *Scheherezade in the Marketplace: Elizabeth Gaskell and the Victorian Novel*. Kayman's intention in his erudite, demanding book is to examine "mystery/detective fiction"—a broad range of "narratives, mainly of the nineteenth century, concerned with the reading of mysteries of various sorts (including monsters)"—and to ascertain "how, largely in the hands of Conan Doyle, one particular reading of mystery, a historically specific 'detective fiction', emerged as the master" (4). The only extended mention of Dickens, however, comes in a relatively brief discussion of the essays he and W. H. Wills prepared for *Household Words* in 1850 on the recently established Detective Department, articles that offer the "first literary application of the epithet 'detective' " (105) and include a "disavowal of the uniformed police" in favor of "the plainclothes force" (106), a group that succeeds as a "preventive presence" because of "the ubiquity that invisibility permits" (107). As Kayman notices, however, despite the emphasis on the detectives' intelligence and ubiquity, the anecdotes provided in these articles tell of results mainly attributable to "traditional police skills" (109). Although *From Bow Street to Baker Street* is especially stimulating in its remarks on Doyle and in its references to Freud as "an alternative to Sherlock Holmes" (10), Kayman does not give explicit attention to Dickens' fictional detectives like Nadgett in *Martin Chuzzlewit* and Bucket in *Bleak House*, even though the latter is, of course, based on Inspector Field, a prominent character (called Wield) in the aforementioned *Household Words* series. In Schor's study, a careful, thorough analysis of Mrs. Gaskell's achievement in overcoming difficulties facing "a woman novelist in a time of intense social change" (5), Dickens is seen as someone who provided encouragement, since as editor of *Household Words* he invited submissions, and also as an influence that Mrs. Gaskell at times wished to resist, for his "editorial involvement . . . often felt like interference" (92). Schor also offers interesting comments on Gaskell's *Cranford* as "a female version" of *Pickwick Papers* (113), with some significant contrasts.

Two books and one short story can serve as exceptions to my rule of excluding adaptations and similar works from this survey.

The D. Case: The Truth about the Mystery of Edwin Drood is a three-way collaboration in which we find the twenty-two chapters that Dickens completed presented with interpolated chapters of a narrative by Carlo Fruttero and Franco Lucentini that satirizes international academic and professional conferences, modern technology, detective fiction, and literary scholarship. At "An International Forum on the Completion of Unfinished or Fragmentary Works in Music and Literature," a group of the most famous fictional specialists in detection—including Sherlock Holmes, Auguste Dupin, Father Brown, Jules Maigret, Inspector Bucket, Dostoevsky's Porfiry Petrovich, Wilkie Collins' Sergeant Cuff, and Hercule Poirot, among others—have each of the chapters of Dickens' last work read aloud to them or mentally implanted by subliminal technology. In the intervening chapters presenting the deliberations of the participants at the forum, these worthies review many of the previously proposed answers and then offer their own speculations and deductions. While nearly two-thirds of *The D. Case* consists of Dickens' text, the contributions by Fruttero and Lucentini provide an enjoyable survey of Droodian possibilities, including original solutions to both the disappearance of Edwin Drood and a hitherto unsuspected crime perpetrated in Kent in 1870. The Drood group's chairman, supposedly the editor of *The Dickensian*, is named Fred Wilmot, but *The D. Case* does not indicate whether he is a descendant of the Lord Fred Wilmot whose part was acted by Dickens himself in amateur productions of Bulwer-Lytton's comedy *Not So Bad As We Seem*.

The Highwayman and Mr. Dickens, "A Secret Victorian Journal, Attributed to Wilkie Collins," the second newly "discovered" record by Collins that William J. Palmer has edited, describes the adventures of Dickens, Inspector Charles Frederick Field (the model for Inspector Bucket [not "William," as he is incorrectly called in a prefatory "Editor's Note" (ix)]), Tally Ho Thompson (described as an actor and a former highwayman), and Collins himself in investigating a series of strange murders in London in early 1852. The events depicted reveal a Dickens fascinated by criminality and the London underworld and obsessed with the excitement of assisting the amazingly resourceful Field. The story Collins recounts—replete with deception, traps, and pursuit—is unquestionably stirring and offers vivid views of Newgate Prison and other unsavory locales. In addition, the journal contains many perceptive insights into such matters as the relationship between the callings of detective and novelist, as well as disclosures of previously unreported encounters involving Dickens and two young men who later became extremely famous—Richard Francis Burton and Henry Jekyll. Moreover, events and characters in Collins' narrative perhaps inspired a major scene in *A Tale of Two Cities* and seem to have provided hints for George Rouncewell and Phil Squod, two figures in the novel Dickens was then working on, *Bleak House*, but neither Collins nor his editor directly speculates about these possible influences. In a concluding note, the editor disclaims any kinship with his "notorious namesake," Doctor William Palmer the famous poisoner (272), a coincidence in names that would have entertained Dickens, who assured Forster that coincidences were much more common than we usually realize. Indeed, many other coincidences involving names are to be found in both the preceding Collins journal published by Palmer in 1990—*The Detective and Mr. Dickens*—and this record: the earlier diary contains over twenty characters who share names with respected Dickens scholars of the twentieth century, while *The Highwayman and Mr. Dickens* presents at least nine figures with names identical or similar to those of distinguished modern academics. But since many of the aforementioned characters in these two Collins journals are not entirely reputable, the editor is to be commended for his discretion in not mentioning these strange parallels.

In "Whatever Became of Tiny Tim?," John Mortimer provides an extremely short but immensely intriguing account of Sir Timothy Cratchit, living in 1894 in "his new home in a North African town" (1). When this character, who reveals surprising attitudes towards his memorable childhood experiences of Christmas, is taken on a journey by the spirit of Ebenezer Scrooge and the Ghost of Christmas Yet to Come, he views scenes of human suffering in 1992 that "would remain" with him "for the rest of his life" (38). But the immediate ways in which "the man who had, long ago, been

Tiny Tim'' (38) responds to this vision raise profound questions about moral sensitivity and the possibility of human redemption.

For me, the numerous books and articles on Dickens published in 1992 create two main impressions. First, the inclusiveness and variety of Dickens' interests and fictional narratives, as well as the forcefulness of his personality, continue to attract proponents of nearly every kind of scholarship and criticism. Second, despite utterly diverse allegiances, virtually all of these commentators see ever-increasing intricacy and complexity in Dickens' art. Obviously, we must find subtlety and profundity in order to justify writing about a text, but other factors also seem present, since most academics appear now to accept for Dickens the dictum DeQuincey applies to Shakespeare in the concluding sentence of "On the Knocking at the Gate in *Macbeth*": "Thy works are . . . like the phenomena of nature, . . . which are to be studied . . . in the perfect faith that . . . the farther we press in our discoveries, the more we shall see proofs of design and self-supporting arrangement where the careless eye had seen nothing but accident!"

Perhaps there is significance in the fact that the two works given most attention in 1992—*Bleak House* and *Great Expectations*—both contain noteworthy complicating features. In considering the first, scholars seem fascinated by the interaction between two extraordinary narrators, for Esther has continued to win understanding and strong approval. In discussing *Great Expectations*, commentators have been drawn to the remarkably tight interweaving of influences upon the protagonist, a character shaped by heiress and criminal, as well as by his own guilt and aspiration.

The sheer quantity of secondary material on Dickens makes the task of selecting what to read—and what to recommend to students—exceedingly difficult, since many of us whose other obligations leave little leisure for scholarly work must reserve some time for re-reading the novels themselves and for re-examining older secondary essays and books.

My overall estimate of 1992's harvest of Dickens studies is—as I hope my specific evaluations have indicated—very favorable. In expressing desiderata for the future, I admit a partiality for "practical criticism"—exposition meant more to elucidate the text being studied than to support a particular theoretical position—and I especially appreciate discussions presented in a style readily comprehensible to adherents of diverse critical schools. While I acknowledge the importance of showing Dickens' pertinence to our own time, I enthusiastically support efforts to remind us of the values and customs of the original mid-Victorian audience. Finally, we must welcome fresh approaches, but we must also remember that our ultimate goal is to make Dickens more accessible, not more arcane.

Acknowledgments

I wish to thank the editors of *Dickens Studies Annual* and their assistants Ms. Alicia Carroll and Mr. Fred Kameny for help in obtaining review copies. In addition, I greatly appreciate the generosity of Professor David Paroissien, Editor of *Dickens Quarterly*, and Mr. William G. Wall, a former compiler of that journal's checklists, in providing me with advance copies of these extremely valuable guides. I am also grateful for editorial advice given by my wife, Lita, and for instruction in word-processing techniques offered by my sons, David and Jeremy.

WORKS CITED

Since many libraries delay binding journal issues, I include in citations of periodicals the issue number after the volume and also indicate the month or season of publication.

Adrian, Arthur. "Georgina Hogarth to Percy Fitzgerald: some Unpublished Letters." *Dickensian* 88. [Part 1] (Spring 1992): 5–18.

Alexander, Doris. "In Defense of John Dickens." *Dickens Quarterly* 9.1 (March 1992): 3–7.

———. "Solving the Mysteries of the Mind in *Edwin Drood*." *Dickens Quarterly* 9.3 (Sept. 1992): 125–31.

Allingham, Philip V. "Dickens's *Christmas Books*: Names and Motifs." *English Language Notes* 29.4 (June 1992): 59–70.

———. "Dickens's Unreliable Narrator in 'Hunted Down.' " *Studies in Short Fiction* 29.1 (Winter 1992): 85–93.

———. "Patterns of Deception in *Huckleberry Finn* and *Great Expectations*." *Nineteenth-Century Literature* 46.4 (March 1992): 447–72.

Alton, Anne Hiebert. "Education in Victorian Fact and Fiction: Kay-Shuttleworth and Dickens's *Hard Times*." *Dickens Quarterly* 9.2 (June 1992): 67–80.

Britton, Wesley. "Carlyle, Clemens, and Dickens: Mark Twain's Francophobia, the French Revolution, and Determinism." *Studies in American Fiction* 20.2 (Autumn 1992): 197–204.

Buckley, Jerome H. " 'Quoth the Raven': The Role of Grip in *Barnaby Rudge*." *Dickens Studies Annual: Essays on Victorian Fiction* 21 (1992): 27–35.

Burleson, Donald R. "Dickens's *A Christmas Carol*." *The Explicator* 50.4 (Summer 1992): 211–12.

Butterworth, R. D. "Dickens the Novelist: The Preston Strike and *Hard Times*." *Dickensian* 88. [Part 2] (Summer 1992): 91–102.

Carey, John. *The Violent Effigy: A Study of Dickens's Imagination*. London: Faber, 1973.

Currie, Richard. "Doubles, Self-Attack, and Murderous Rage in Florence Dombey." *Dickens Studies Annual: Essays on Victorian Fiction* 21 (1992): 113–29.

Daleski, H. M. *Dickens and the Art of Analogy*. New York: Schocken, 1970.

———. "Large Loose Baggy Monsters and *Little Dorrit*." *Dickens Studies Annual: Essays on Victorian Fiction* 21 (1992): 131–42.

DeBona, Guerric. "Doing Time; Undoing Time: Plot Mutation in David Lean's *Great Expectations*." *Literature/Film Quarterly* 20.1 (Jan. 1992): 77–100, 54.

Dentith, Simon. "How Popular was *Dombey and Son*?" *Dickensian* 88. [Part 2] (Summer 1992): 69–81.

Dickens, Charles, Carlo Fruttero, and Franco Lucentini. *The D. Case: The Truth About the Mystery of Edwin Drood*. Trans. Gregory Dowling. New York: Harcourt Brace Jovanovich, 1992.

Dickens, Charles. *Hard Times*. Ed. George Ford and Sylvère Monod. 2nd ed. New York: Norton, 1990.

Dubberke, Ray. "Dating *Edwin Drood*." *Dickensian* 88. [Part 1] (Spring 1992): 19–24.

———. *Dickens, Drood, and the Detectives*. New York: Vantage, 1992.

Duncan, Ian. *Modern Romance: The Gothic, Scott, and Dickens*. Cambridge, Eng.: Cambridge UP, 1992.

Dvorak, Wilfred P. "Charles Dickens's *The Old Curiosity Shop*: The Triumph of Compassion." *Papers on Language and Literature* 28.1 (Winter 1992): 52–71.

Edgecombe, Rodney Stenning. "Dickens, Hunt and the 'Dramatic Criticism' in *Great Expectations*: A Note." *Dickensian* 88. [Part 2] (Summer 1992): 82–90.

Eigner, Edwin M. "Shakespeare, Milton, Dickens and the Morality of the Pious Fraud." *Dickens Studies Annual: Essays on Victorian Fiction* 21 (1992): 1–25.

Fish, Stanley Eugene. *Surprised by Sin: The Reader in* Paradise Lost. New York: St. Martin's, 1967.

Flahiff, F. T. " 'Mysteriously Come Together': Dickens, Chaucer, and *Little Dorrit.*" *University of Toronto Quarterly* 61.2 (Winter 1991/2): 250–68.

Fleissner, Robert F. "Drood Renominated." *Names* 40.2 (June 1992): 117–22.

Friedman, Stanley. "*Bleak House* and Bulwer-Lytton's *Not So Bad As We Seem.*" *Dickens Quarterly* 9.1 (March 1992): 25–29.

Gaughan, Richard T. " 'Their Places are a Blank': The Two Narrators in *Bleak House.*" *Dickens Studies Annual: Essays on Victorian Fiction* 21 (1992): 79–96.

Ginsburg, Michal Peled. "The Case Against Plot in *Bleak House* and *Our Mutual Friend.*" *ELH* 59.1 (Spring 1992): 175–95.

Golden, Morris. *Dickens Imagining Himself: Six Novel Encounters with a Changing World.* Lanham, MD: UP of America, 1992.

Greenstein, Michael. "Measuring Time in *Dombey and Son.*" *Dickens Quarterly* 9.4 (December 1992): 151–57.

Hatten, Charles. "Disciplining the Family in *Barnaby Rudge*: Dickens's Professionalization of Fiction." *Mosaic: A Journal for the Interdisciplinary Study of Literature* 25.4 (Fall 1992): 17–34.

Heineman, Helen K. *Three Victorians in the New World: Interpretations of the New World in the Works of Frances Trollope, Charles Dickens, and Anthony Trollope.* New York: Peter Lang, 1992.

Hollington, Michael. "Physiognomy in *Hard Times.*" *Dickens Quarterly* 9.2 (June 1992): 58–66.

Holway, Tatiana M. "The Game of Speculation: Economics and Representation." *Dickens Quarterly* 9.3 (Sept. 1992): 103–14.

Houston, Gail Turley. " 'Pip' and 'Property': The (Re)Production of the Self in *Great Expectations.*" *Studies in the Novel* 24.1 (Spring 1992): 13–25.

Ingham, Patricia. *Dickens, Women and Language.* Toronto: U of Toronto P, 1992.

Johnson, Derek. *Pastoral in the Work of Charles Dickens.* New York: Peter Lang, 1992.

Kayman, Martin A. *From Bow Street to Baker Street: Mystery, Detection and Narrative.* New York: St. Martin's, 1992.

Kearns, Katherine. "A Tropology of Realism in *Hard Times.*" *ELH* 59.4 (Winter 1992): 857–81.

Kincaid, James. "Fattening Up on Pickwick." *Novel: A Forum on Fiction* 25.3 (Spring 1992): 235–44.

Langland, Elizabeth. "Nobody's Angels: Domestic Ideology and Middle-Class Women in the Victorian Novel." *PMLA* 107.2 (March 1992): 290–304.

Lloyd, Tom. "Language, Love and Identity: *A Tale of Two Cities.*" *Dickensian* 88. [Part 3] (Autumn 1992): 154–70.

Lohrli, Anne. " 'With My Name on Every Page': Dickens References in *Household Words.*" *Dickens Quarterly* 9.1 (March 1992): 7–19.

Lougy, Robert E. "Repressive and Expressive Forms: The Bodies of Comedy and Desire in *Martin Chuzzlewit.*" *Dickens Studies Annual: Essays on Victorian Fiction* 21 (1992): 37–61.

Lucas, John. *Charles Dickens: The Major Novels.* New York: Penguin, 1992.

Marsden, Malcolm M. "Dickens' Mr. Micawber and Mark Twain's Colonel Sellers: The Genesis of an American Comic." *Dickens Studies Annual: Essays on Victorian Fiction* 21 (1992): 63–77.

Maxwell, Richard. *The Mysteries of Paris and London.* Charlottesville: UP of Virginia, 1992.

McCombie, Frank. "Sexual Repression in *Dombey and Son.*" *Dickensian* 88. [Part 1] (Spring 1992): 25–38.

McFarlane, Brian. "David Lean's *Great Expectations*—Meeting Two Challenges." *Literature/Film Quarterly* 20.1 (Jan. 1992): 68–76.

McLean, Robert Simpson. "How 'the Infant Phenomenon' Began the World: The Managing of Jean Margaret Davenport (182?–1903)." *Dickensian* 88. [Part 3] (Autumn 1992): 133–53.

Meckier, Jerome. "Dating the Action in *Great Expectations*: A New Chronology." *Dickens Studies Annual: Essays on Victorian Fiction* 21 (1992): 157–94.

———. "Dickens, *Great Expectations*, and the Dartmouth College Notes." *Papers on Language and Literature* 28.2 (Spring 1992): 111–32.

Milbank, Alison. *Daughters in the House: Modes of the Gothic in Victorian Fiction.* New York: St. Martin's, 1992.

Miller, J. Hillis. "Dickens and Phiz." *Illustration.* Cambridge, MA: Harvard UP, 1992. 96–111.

Moglen, Helene. "Theorizing Fiction/Fictionalizing Theory: The Case of *Dombey and Son.*" *Victorian Studies* 35.2 (Winter 1992): 159–84.

Morgan, Nicholas H. *Secret Journeys: Theory and Practice in Reading Dickens.* Rutherford, NJ: Fairleigh Dickinson UP, 1992.

Mortimer, John. "Whatever Became of Tiny Tim?" *The New York Times Book Review* 6 Dec. 1992:1, 37–38.

Mundhenk, Rosemary. "Creative Ambivalence in Dickens's *Master Humphrey's Clock*." *Studies in English Literature* 32.4 (Autumn 1992): 645–61.

Nayder, Lillian. "Class Consciousness and the Indian Mutiny in Dickens's 'The Perils of Certain English Prisoners.' " *Studies in English Literature* 32.4 (Autumn 1992): 689–705.

Palmer, William J. *The Detective and Mr. Dickens*. New York: St. Martin's, 1990.

———. *The Highwayman and Mr. Dickens*. New York: St. Martin's, 1992.

Parker, David. "Our Pew at Church." *Dickensian* 88. [Part 1] (Spring 1992): 40–42.

Paroissien, David. *The Companion to* Oliver Twist. Edinburgh: Edinburgh UP, 1992.

Peltason, Timothy. "Esther's Will." *ELH* 59.3 (Fall 1992): 671–91.

Philpotts, Trey. "Dickens, Patent Reform, and the Inventor: Daniel Doyce and the Question of Topicality." *Dickens Quarterly* 9.4 (Dec. 1992): 158–69.

Reed, John R. "Authorized Punishment in Dickens's Fiction." *Studies in the Novel* 24.2 (Summer 1992): 112–30.

Rignall, John. "*Bleak House*: The *flâneur*'s perspective and the discovery of the body." *Realist Fiction and the Strolling Spectator*. New York: Routledge, 1992. 62–79.

Rosenberg, Brian. "Character and Contradiction in Dickens." *Nineteenth-Century Literature* 47.2 (Sept. 1992): 145–63.

Rubenstein, Steven. "Visual Aids, Mental Impediments; or, the Problem with Phiz." *Dickens Quarterly* 9.1 (March 1992): 19–25.

Sadrin, Anny. "Charlotte Dickens: The Female Narrator of *Bleak House*." *Dickens Quarterly* 9.2 (June 1992): 47–57.

Samuelian, Kristin Flieger. "Being Rid of Women: Middle-Class Ideology in *Hard Times*." *Victorian Newsletter* [No. 82] (Fall 1992): 58–61.

Schad, John. *The Reader in the Dickensian Mirrors: Some New Language*. New York: St. Martin's, 1992.

Schiefelbein, Michael. "Little Nell, Catholicism, and Dickens's Investigation of Death." *Dickens Quarterly* 9.3 (Sept. 1992): 115–25.

Schor, Hilary M. *Scheherezade in the Marketplace: Elizabeth Gaskell and the Victorian Novel*. New York: Oxford UP, 1992.

Simon, Irène. "*David Copperfield*: A Künstlerroman?" *Review of English Studies* ns 43. [No. 169] (Feb. 1992): 40–56.

Slater, Michael. *Dickens and Women*. Stanford, CA: Stanford UP, 1983.

————. Introduction. *Criticisms and Appreciations of the Works of Charles Dickens.* By Gilbert Keith Chesterton. London: J. M. Dent, 1992. vii–xix.

Stein, Robert A. "Repetitions During Pip's Closure." *Dickens Studies Annual: Essays on Victorian Fiction* 21 (1992): 143–56.

Tristan, Flora. *London Journal, 1840.* Trans. Dennis Palmer and Gisell Pincetl. Charlestown, MA: Charles River Books, 1980.

Watkins, Gwen. *Dickens in Search of Himself: Recurrent Themes and Characters in the Works of Charles Dickens.* Totowa, NJ: Barnes and Noble, 1987.

West, Gilian. "*Bleak House*: Esther's Illness." *English Studies* 73.1 (Feb. 1992): 30–34.

Westbrook, Wayne W. "Dickens's Secret Sharer, Conrad's Mutual Friend." *Studies in Short Fiction* 29.2 (Spring 1992): 205–14.

Westland, Ella, and Simon Trezise. "Plotting Critical Positions." *Dickens Quarterly* 9.4 (Dec. 1992): 172–80.

Wright, Kay Hetherly. "The Grotesque and Urban Chaos in *Bleak House*." *Dickens Studies Annual: Essays on Victorian Fiction* 21 (1992): 97–112.

Index

Aarsleff, Hans, 17, 19, 20, 21, 23
Adam Bede (Eliot), 98
Adrian, Arthur, 38
Ainsworth, William, 288, 289, 298–99; *Jack Sheppard*, 288–89; *Rookwood*, 288, 289, 296, 299
Alexander, Doris, 359, 389–90
Alexander, Edward, 65
Allingham, Philip V., 383, 391
Alter, Robert, 260
Altick, Richard D., 25, 29, 34
Alton, Anne Hiebert, 378–79
Anatomy of Melancholy, The (Burton), 227, 229–30, 232, 234, 235, 236, 237–38, 239, 240, 254, 255 n.4, 256 n.18
Apology for the Conduct of Mrs. T. C. Phillips (Phillips), 53
Arabian Nights, 139
Armstrong, Nancy, 167, 185, 201 n.1
Arneson, Richard, 18
Auerbach, Nina, 184, 200, 208, 212, 224 n.6, 270
Axton, William, 133

Baker, Ernest, 18
Bakhtin, Mikhail, 40, 41, 42, 43
Bann, Stephen, 318
Barichman, Richard, 314
Barish, Jonas, 264
Barton, Anne, 122, 123
Barzilai, Shuli, 247–48

Bender, John, 262
Benjamin, Walter, 356, 376
Bentham, Jeremy, 18, 19, 22, 23, 24, 38–39, 42, 43, 50, 54, 63, 64, 157; "Chrestomathia," 20–21; "Deontology," 65 n.4; "Language," 24, 25, 26, 27; "Logic," 26, 27; "Ontology," 23–24, 27, 28; "Principles of Morals and Legislation," 55, 56
——— and J. S. Mill, *Utilitarianism and Other Esays*, 67 n.16
Bergmann, Helena, 191
Bergson, Henri, 147
Black, John, 63
Bloom, Harold, 308, 323
Bledsoe, Robert T., 270
Boheemen-Saaf, Christine van, 188
Brantlinger, Patrick, 18
Briggs, Asa, 9
Britton, Wesley, 359
Brontë, Charlotte, 208
Brown, James, 18
Browne, Hablot K. ("Phiz"), 57, 362–63, 364, 365, 373–74
Buckley, Jerome H., 368
Bulwer-Lytton, Edward, 290, 292, 294, 295, 299, 332, 333–34, 366; *Alice*, 291, 292; *Devereux*, 290; *Ernest Maltravers*, 290–91; *Eugene Aram*, 288, 289, 297; *Paul Clifford*, 288
Burleson, Donald R., 390–91

Butterworth, R. D., 379
Byerly, Alison, " 'The Masquerade of Existence': Thackeray's Theatricality,'' 259–86

Canham, Stephen, 310
Carey, John, 1
Carlyle, Thomas, 103, 158, 161 n.11, 319, 320, 359; Sartor Resartus, 296
Carse, Wendy K. "Domestic Transformations in Dickens' 'The Haunted Man,' " 163–81
Chadwick, Edwin, 63
Chapman, Edward, 49
Chase, Karen, 322–23
Canterbury Tales (Chaucer), 381–82
Cheff, Jim, 310
Chesterton, C. K., 64, 363
Clarke, Micael, 307, 312
Clarkson, Carrol, "Alias and Alienation in Bleak House," 121–35
Clemens, Samuel L. ("Mark Twain"), 359, 373; Huckleberry Finn, 383
Colby, Robert A. 266, 283 n.9, 287, 303, 308, 309, 332
Collins, Philip, 44, 307
Collins, Wilkie, 394
Condillac, Etienne, 18–19; Essai sur l'origine des connoissances humaines, 19
Confessions (St. Augustine), 93, 102, 116–17
Connor, Steven, 127
Copernicus, Nicolaus, 157
Cornhill Magazine, 265
Crosby, Christina, 320
Currie, Richard, 370

Dahmane, Razak, " 'A Mere Question of Figures': Measures, Mystery, and Metaphor in Hard Times,'' 137-62
Daleski, H. M. 323, 381
Davidson, Donald, 130–31
Davis, Earle, 18
DeBona, Guerric, 387
Derrida, Jacques, 128–29, 130, 131, 133
Deering, Dorothy, 22
Dentith, Simon, 370–71
DiBasta, Maria, 283 n.11
Dickens, Charles: American Notes, 357–58; Barnaby Rudge, 341, 342, 343, 368–69; Bleak House, 15, 121–35, 183, 184, 185, 186, 189, 192, 339, 340, 343–44, 348, 354, 356, 374–78, 388, 392–93, 395; "Calling Bad Names," 22; "Child's Dream of a Star, A," 95; Chimes, The, 172 n.1, 355, 391; Christmas Books, 55, 163, 179 n.8, 391, Christmas Carol, A, 177 n.1, 390–91, 394–95; "Cricket on the Hearth, The," 178 n.1; David Copperfield, 10–11, 93–119; 180 n.17, 341, 342, 343, 347, 349, 360, 373–74; Dombey and Son, 15, 184, 185–86, 187, 188, 192, 341, 347, 370–73; "Frauds upon the Fairies," 151–52; Great Expectations, 1, 13, 342, 344, 348, 350, 357, 383–87, 395; Hard Times, 17, 18, 21, 22–23, 25, 26, 29–30, 31, 32, 33, 35, 37–38, 39–41, 42, 44, 45, 55, 137–62, 183–90, 378–88; "Haunted Man, The" 95, 96, 97, 109, 163–81; "Hunted Down," 391; Little Dorrit, 12, 66 n.9, 348, 349, 356–57, 362, 381–82; Martin Chuzzlewit, 2, 14, 339, 342, 343, 357–58, 363, 369–70, 393; Master Humphrey's Clock, 367, 382; Mystery of Edwin Drood, The, 337, 339, 354, 389–90, 393; Nicholas Nickleby, 73–92, 360; Oliver Twist, 54, 55, 64 n.4, 74, 97–98, 99–101, 112, 180 n.16, 183–84, 288–89, 337, 339, 340, 352–54, 355, 362, 365; Old Curiosity Shop, The, 339, 349, 355, 366–67, 368; Our Mutual Friend, 10, 11, 154, 155, 201 n.3, 342, 344, 348, 360, 361, 388–89; "Our P's and Q's," 22; "Perils of Certain English Prisoners, The," 392; Pickwick Papers, 4, 49–71, 218, 219, 222, 355, 364, 365, 393; "Saxon-English," 22; Sketches by Boz, 12, 15, 68 n.22; Tale of Two Cities, A, 359, 368–69
Dickens, Henry Fielding, 159 n.4
Dickens, John, 359
Disraeli, Benjamin, 331
Dixon, Roger, 12
Dowling, Linda, 36, 43, 44, 45
Doyle, Richard, 310
Dubberke, Ray, 354, 390
Dudley, Robert, Earl of Leicester, 10
Duncan, Ian, 340–42
Dvorak, Wilfred P., 366–67
Dyer, Gary R., 315

Edgecombe, Rodney Stenning, 383–84
Eigner, Edwin M., 359–60
Elizabeth I, Queen, 10
Elkins, William R., 330–31
Esquirol, Jean Etienne, 227, 228, 229
Examiner, The, 73

Fabrizio, Richard, 29

Feltes, N. N., 68 n.26
Ferris, Ina, 305, 309, 313, 320
Fielding, Joseph, 49
Fiending, K. J., 64 n.4
Finer, S. E., 66
Fish, Stanley, 360
Fisher, Judith Law, 266, 283 n.10, 304, 310–11, 312, 316
Fitz-Cook, H., 4, 7
Fitzgerald, Mary K., 318
Flahill, F. T., 381
Flamm, Dudley, 308
Fletcher, Robert P., 325
Ford, George, 68 n.23, 106, 159 n.1
Forster, John, 49, 73, 91 n.3, 94, 150, 282, 326, 354
Foster, Margaret, 309
Foucault, Michel, 262
Fowler, Roger, 40–41
Fowler, Rowena, 207, 211
Fraser's Magazine, 74, 259, 282, 288, 291, 296, 307
Freud, Sigmund, 60, 346; "Mourning and Melancholia," 231, 243, 244, 245, 246, 247
Fried, Michael, 266–67, 274
Friedman, Stanley, "Recent Dickens Studies: 1992," 377–401; 378

Gallagher, Catherine, 282 n.3
Ganz, Margaret, 76
Garrett, Peter, 75
Garson, Marjorie, 322
Gaskell, Elizabeth, *North and South*, 189, 190; *Ruth*, 190–201; *Cranford*, 205–25, 393
Gaughan, Richard T., 374–75
Gavin, Adrienne E., "Language Among the Amazons: Conjuring and Creativity in *Cranford*," 205–25
Gay, Peter, 179 n.9
Genette, Gerald, 265
Gentlemen's House (Kerr), 12
Gibbs-Smith, C. H., 1
Gilman, Sander, 229, 238
Gilmour, Robin, 76, 106, 318
Ginsberg, Michal Peled, 388
Girouard, Mark, 13
Glancy, Ruth, 179 n.5, 180 n.14
Goldberg, Michael, 17
Golden, Morris, 342–45, 346
Goldfarb, Sheldon, 333–34
Goldsmith, Oliver, 49; *The Deserted Village*, 139
Goldstein, Jan, 228–29
Greene, Graham, 99, 103

Greene, Robert, 31
Greenstein, Michael, 371
Greig, J. Y. T., 323

Harden, Edgar F., 265, 304, 307, 308
Hardy, Barbara, 326
Harfield, James, 63
Haslam, John, 227, 240
Hattan, Charles, 368–69
Hawes, Donald, 305, 333
Hawlin, Stefan, 333
Haydon, Benjamin, 266
Hazlitt, William, 20
Heglar, Charles, 316
Heineman, Helen K., 357–58
Herron, Jerry, 180 n.15
Heywood, Ian, 305, 333
Hobhouse, Christopher, 1
Hollingsworth, Keith, 287
Hollington, Michael, 379–80
Holloway, John, 159 n.1
Holway, Tatiana M. 360, 365
Horstamann-Guthrie, Ulrike, 322
House, Humphry, 50, 51, 63
Household Words, 18, 22, 160 n.5
Houston, Gail Turley, 384–85
Howes, Craig, 331–32
Humphreys, A. R., 319
Hunt, Leigh, 384
Hutcheon, Linda, 77, 85

Ilyinsky, Igor, 332
Ingham, Patricia, 345–47
Iser, Wolfgang, 260, 323

Jakobson, Roman, 1
James, Louis, 331
Johnson, Derek, 354–55
Johnson, Edgar, 54, 63
Johnson, Samuel, 213–14, 215, 218, 219, 220; *Rasselas*, 218, 224 n.5
Jones, A. J., 7, 8
Jones, Sir William, 21

Kayman, Martin A., 392–93
Kearns, Katherine, 380
Kemble, Charles, 165
Kemble, Fanny, 265, 232 n.4
Kemble, John, 21
Kemble, John Philip, 265
Kincaid, James, 1, 365
Kingsley, Charles, 330
Kinsey, T. E., 333
Klotz, Gunther, 317
Kristeva, Julia, 227, 231, 243, 244, 246, 247, 248, 249, 250, 251–52, 253, 254, 255n.9,

256 nn.16, 19, 22
Kubrick, Stanley, 318

Lambert, Miles, 333
Langbauer, Laurie, 184
Langland, Elizabeth, 180, n.18, 360–61
Lansbury, Coral, 202 n.7
Law, Joe K. 305
Leavis, F. R., 314
Leavis, Q. D., 103
Levine, Richard, 319
Lichtenstein, Jacqueline, 283 n.12
Litvak, Joseph, 282 n.4
Lloyd, Tom, 382–83
Locke, John, 19–20, 32, 39
Lodge, David, 159 n.1
Lohrli, Anne, 359
London Journal 1840 (Tristan), 353–54
Lougy, Robert, 317, 360–70
Lukacher, Ned, 68 n.24
Lucas, John, 347–49
Lund, Michael, 311, 320–21

Macaulay, Thomas Babington, 320
McCarthy, Terence, 321
McCombie, Frank, 371–72
MacDonald, Susan, 314
McFarlane, Brian, 387
McGillis, Robert, 22–23
Mack, M. P., 51, 52, 53, 66 nn.11, 12
McKay, Carol H., 305, 308, 313
McKendy, Thomas, "Sources of Parody in
    Thackeray's Catherine," 287–302
McLean, Robert Simpson, 365–66
McMaster, Juliet, 263, 282, 305, 319, 331
McMaster, Rowland, 248, 250, 256 n.23, 305
McSweeney, Kerry, "David Copperfield and
    the Music of Memory," 93–119
Mad Humanity (Winslow), 255 n.3, 13
Malthus, Thomas, 151
Mandel, Oscar, 305
Manlove, Colin, 144
Manning, Sylvia, 65 n.4; "Nicholas Nickleby:
    Parody in the Plains Syria," 73–92
Marcus, Steven, 49, 91 n.3
Marsden, Malcolm M., 373
Marshall, David, 264
Martin, John, 266
Marx, Karl, 62; Eighteenth Brumaire of Louis
    Bonaparte, 329
Maxwell, Richard, 338–40
Mayhew, Henry, 202 n.10
Maynor, Natalie, 305
Meckier, Jerome, 91 n.14, 326–27, 385–86
Meisel, Martin, 271
Milbank, Alison, 355–57

Mill, John Stuart, 51, 55, 56, 60, 65 n.4, 67
    n.16
Miller, Andrew, 277, 319–20
Miller, J. Hillis, 1, 11, 84, 122, 123, 130,
    134 nn.2, 3, 4, 309, 323–24, 364
Mill on the Floss, The (Eliot), 98
Moglen, Helene, 372–73
Moler, Kenneth L. 315–16
Monod, Sylvere, 17, 159 n.1
Monserrat, Ann, 309
Morgan, Nicholas H., 349
Mortimer, John, 394–95
Multhesius, Stefan, 12
Mundhenk, Rosemary, 367
Muresianu, S. A., 305
Musslewhite, David, 76, 328–29
Mystères de Paris, Les (Sue), 338
Mysteries of London (Reynolds), 331, 338

Nayder, Lillian, 392
Newgate Calendar, 287, 293
Newman, Beth, 171, 176
Newsom, Robert, "Pickwick in the Utilitarian
    Sense," 49–71
Northcutt Malone, Cynthia, 133
Nuttall, A. D., 123

Odiot, M. 9
Ogden, C. K., 24, 52, 53, 65 n.6, 69 n.27
Old Shepherd's Chief Mourner (Landseer), 10
Old Wives' Tale, The (Bennett), 327
Oram, Richard, W., 305, 306, 307, 334
Orchinnikova, Svetlana, 332
Orlando Fusioso (Ariosto), 239–40
Ousby, Ian, 318–19
Outlines of the History of Ethics (Sidgwick),
    69 n.29

Palmer, William J., 394
Paradise Lost (Milton), 360
Parker, David, 373
Paroissien, David, 352–54
Pathology of Mind (Mandsley), 235, 238, 255
    n.14
Patten, Robert L. 68 n.19, 178 nn.1, 3
Peck, John, 315
Peltason, Timothy, 376
Penn, Richard, 49
Perkin, J. Russell, 317
Peters, Catherine, 309, 310
Phelan, James, 325
Philpotts, Trey, 382
"Phiz," see Browne, Hablot K.
Pickrel, Paul, 332–33
Pickwood, Nicholas, 304
Plato, 264; Cratylus, 121–24

Poole, John, 49
Poovey, Mary, 179 nn.7, 11, 202 n.10
Pope, Norris, 67 n.18
Popular Government (Maine), 50
Prawer, S. S., 316–17
Praz, Mario, 318
Principles of Moral and Political Philosophy (Paley), 56
Proust, Marcel, *A la recherche du temps perdu*, 93–94, 98–99, 107, 116; *Jean Santeuil*, 98–99
Purton, Valerie, 326

Quinton, Anthony, 66 n.13
Quirk, Randolph, 23

Radcliffe, Ann, 340; *The Mysteries of Udolpho*, 356
Ragussis, Michael, 126, 129, 130, 131, 133
Rawlins, Jack, 263, 314, 328
Ray, Gordon, 309, 328
Redgrave, Richard, 3
Reed, John R. 361–62
Retan, Katherine A. "Lower-Class Angels in the Middle-Class House: The Domestic Woman's 'Progress' in *Hard Times* and *Ruth*," 183–203
Richardson, Ruth, 68 n.23
Rignall, J. M. 324, 376–77
Ritchie, Anne Thackeray, 308
Robber, The (James, G.P.R.), 296–97
Rosenberg, Brian, 362
Roston, Murray, "Dickens and the Tyranny of Objects," 1–16
Rousseau, Jean-Jacques, 264
Rubenstein, Stephen, 362–63

Sacks, Jonathan, 131
Sadrin, Anny, 377–78
Saintsbury, George, 304
Samuelian, Kristin Flieger, 380
Scary, Elaine, 326
Schad, John, 350–52
Scharnborst, Gary, 306
Schiefelbein, Michael, 367–68
Schneewind, J. B., 67
Schor, Hilary M., 205, 214, 220, 224 n.2, 392–98
Scott, Sir Walter, 320, 340–41, 342, 368–69
"Secret Sharer, The" (Conrad), 389
Sedgwick, Eve Kosofsky, 313–14
Seymour, Robert, 49
Shakespeare, William, 359–60; *Othello*, 228; *Twelfth Night*, 236; *Winter's Tale, The*, 360
Shaw, David, 38, 44

Shaw, Henry E., 318
Shillingsburg, Peter L., 303, 304, 305, 307, 308; "Thackeray Studies: 1983–1992," 303–34
Siddons, Sarah, 265
Siegle, Robert, 282 n.2
Simon, Irene, 374
Simon, Richard Kellr, 327
Skilton, David, 310
Slater, Michael, 167, 168, 178 n.1, 179 n.6, 346, 363
Smart, J. J. C., 67 n.13
Smith, Grahame, 156
Smith, Southwood, 63
Social Aspects (J. S. Smith), 3
Sonstroem, David, 153
Sorensen, Gail D., 334
Sorensen, Gerald, 305, 321–22
Spectator, The, 289
Spector, Stephen J., 159 n.3
Spengemann, William, 102
Spenser, Robert, 42
Stark, Myra, 314
Stein, Robert A., 386–87
Steven, Leslie, 54
Stevens, Joan, 310
Stevenson, Lionel, 287
Stewart, Garrett, 1, 313
Stone, Harry, 179 nn.10, 12
Stone, Marjorie, 50, 65 n.6
Stoneman, Patsy, 202 n.9, 214
Stubbs, George, 10
Surtees, Robert, 49
Sutherland, John, 227–28, 304, 305, 306, 307

Tallis, Henry, 9
Tarratt, Margaret, 217
Taylor, Harriet, 69 n.27
Tennyson, Alfred, 103; "Locksley Hall," 222
Ternan, Ellen, 383
Thackeray, William Makepeace: *Barry Lyndon*, 306, 312, 317, 318, 320, 321, 334; *Catherine*, 287–302; "Fashionable Authoress, The," 294; *Flore et Zephyr*, 271, 304; "Going to See a Man Hanged," 259, 260–62, 263; *Henry Esmond*, 298, 304, 307, 312, 315, 318, 320, 321, 322–25; *Irish Sketchbook*, 317; *Lectures on the English Humourists*, 319; *Major Gahagan*, 304; *Newcomes, The*, 267, 269, 304, 306, 310, 313, 317; *Notes of a Journey from Cornwall to Cairo*, 317, 329; "On the French School of Painting," 266, 282 n.6; *Pendennis*, 269, 304, 315; *Vanity Fair*, 259–60, 261,

263, 264, 268–70, 271–73, 274–82, 300, 304, 305, 310, 314–15, 319, 323, 325, 327–28, 329, 330, 332–33, 334; *The Virginians*, 321, 324; *Yellowplush Papers, The*, 304

Thackeray Newsletter, The, 306

Thomas, Deborah A., 179 n.8, 316

Thorpe, Benjamin, 21

Thatcher, Barry, "Dickens' Bow to the Language Theory Debate," 17–47

Tooke, John Horne, 19, 21, 23; *Diversions of Purley*, 19

Treizise, Simon, 363

Trench, Richard, 18, 44; *English Past and Present*, 21, 30, 33, 34, 35; *On the Study of Words*, 21, 22, 30, 31, 32, 33, 34, 35, 43

Trilling, Lionel, 264

Trollope, Anthony, 308; *He Knew What He Wanted*, 227–58

Van Ghent, Dorothy, 1, 8, 13, 14, 323

Victoria, Queen, 9, 76, 366

Warhol, Robyn, 329–30

Watt, George, 202 n.6

Watts, Richard, 30

Warnock, Mary, 93–94

Weiss, Barbara, 224 n.1, 312–13

Welsh, Alexandra, 67 n.15

Wesst, Gilian, 378

Westbrook, Wayne W., 389

Westland, Ella, 363

Wiesenthal, C. S., "The Body Melancholy: Trollope's *He Knew He Was Right*, 227–58

Williams, Bernard, 67 n.13

Williams, Raymond, 50, 51, 65 n.5

Wordsworth, William, 355; *Prelude, The*, 93–94, 100, 101–02, 117 n.3; "Tintern Abbey," 111

Wright, Kay Hetherley, 375

Wuthering Heights (E. Brontë), 171, 176

Yeates, Edmund, 308

Zwerdling, Alex, 201